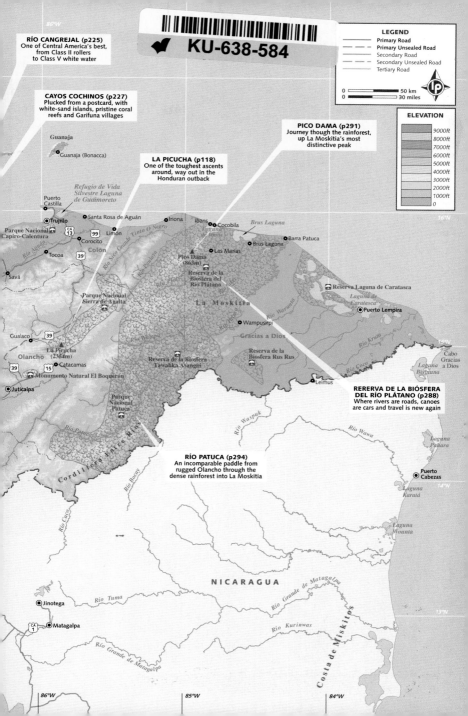

KU-638-584

LEGEND

Primary Road
Primary Unsealed Road
Secondary Road
Secondary Unsealed Road
Tertiary Road

0 — 50 km
0 — 30 miles

ELEVATION

9000ft
8000ft
7000ft
6000ft
5000ft
4000ft
3000ft
2000ft
1000ft
0

RÍO CANGREJAL (p225)
One of Central America's best,
from Class II rollers
to Class V white water

CAYOS COCHINOS (p227)
Plucked from a postcard, with
white-sand islands, pristine coral
reefs and Garífuna villages

LA PICUCHA (p118)
One of the toughest ascents
around, way out in the
Honduran outback

PICO DAMA (p291)
Journey though the rainforest,
up La Moskitia's most
distinctive peak

**RERERVA DE LA BIÓSFERA
DEL RÍO PLÁTANO (p288)**
Where rivers are roads, canoes
are cars and travel is new again

RÍO PATUCA (p294)
An incomparable paddle from
rugged Olancho through the
dense rainforest into La Moskitia

Guanaja
Guanaja (Bonacca)

Refugio de Vida
Silvestre Laguna
de Guaimoreto

Puerto
Castilla

Trujillo   Santa Rosa de Aguán   Iriona   Ibans   Cocobila
Parque Nacional   Laguna   Brus Laguna
Capiro-Calentura   Ibans
CA   99   Limón   Barra Patuca
13   Pico Dama   Brus Laguna
Corocito   (863m)   Las Marías
Colón   Tocoa   Reserva de la
39   Biósfera del
Río Aguán   Río Plátano   Reserva Laguna de Caratasca
Savá   Laguna de
                                        La Moskitia   Caratasca
Parque Nacional   Puerto Lempira
Sierra de Agalta
Gualaco   39   Wampusirpi
                                        Gracias a Dios   Río Kruta
Olancho   La Picucha   Reserva de la
           (2354m)   Biósfera Rus Rus   Cabo
39   Catacamas   Gracias
Monumento Natural El Boquerón   Reserva de la Biósfera   a Dios
Juticalpa   Tawahka-Asangni   Leimus   Laguna
                                                              Bisjtuna
                        Parque
                        Nacional
                        Patuca
                                        Río Waspuk   Río Wawa
Río Patuca   Laguna
Cordillera Entre Ríos   Pahara
                        Río Bocay   Puerto
                                                                 Cabezas
Río Coco   Laguna
                                                                 Karata

                        NICARAGUA   Laguna
                                                                 Wounta
Jinotega   Río Tuma   Río Grande de Matagalpa
CA
1   Matagalpa   Río Grande de Matagalpa

                        Río Kurinwas
Río Grande de Matagalpa

4

Honduras
& the Bay Islands

Gary Chandler & Liza Prado

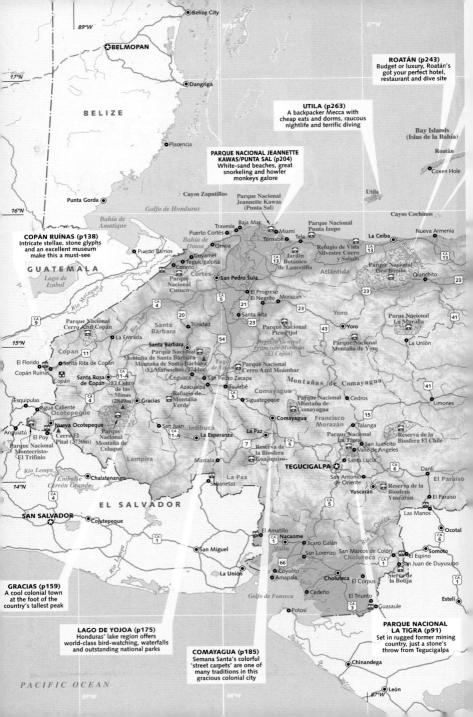

ROATÁN (p243)
Budget or luxury, Roatán's got your perfect hotel, restaurant and dive site

UTILA (p263)
A backpacker Mecca with cheap eats and dorms, raucous nightlife and terrific diving

PARQUE NACIONAL JEANNETTE KAWAS/PUNTA SAL (p204)
White-sand beaches, great snorkeling and howler monkeys galore

COPÁN RUÍNAS (p138)
Intricate stellae, stone glyphs and an excellent museum make this a must-see

GRACIAS (p159)
A cool colonial town at the foot of the country's tallest peak

LAGO DE YOJOA (p175)
Honduras' lake region offers world-class bird-watching, waterfalls and outstanding national parks

COMAYAGUA (p185)
Semana Santa's colorful 'street carpets' are one of many traditions in this gracious colonial city

PARQUE NACIONAL LA TIGRA (p91)
Set in rugged former mining country, just a stone's throw from Tegucigalpa

Destination Honduras & the Bay Islands

Honduras has long been a place of human migration, settlement, refuge, rampage and recreation. It has attracted everyone from South American Indians to North American banana barons, and from migrating Maya to sun worshipers of a different sort.

This is a country where the mountains literally reach the clouds and a vast living world lies just below the turquoise waters. There are cities bustling with all-night discotheques and small agricultural communities with wood-burning stoves. There are Hondurans with Hummers, and Hondurans with dugout canoes – on opposite ends of the economic and social spectra but still part of the same kaleidoscope of culture that is this big rich country.

It is possible – almost assured – that different travelers here will have wildly different experiences: one scuba diving, bar hopping and whale-shark spotting, the other forest hiking, mountain climbing and river rafting. You could easily spend an entire vacation exploring the expansive and impossibly lush rainforest that houses the indigenous communities of La Moskitia in the east, or tracing a series of other-era villages in the cool mountainous region of La Ruta Lenca in the west.

Honduras is often overlooked in the rush to experience Costa Rica's rain forests or Guatemala's indigenous cultures. Parts of Honduras are well known, of course; Copán is one of the most important Maya ruins in Mesoamerica, and the Bay Islands are famous for their affordable world-class diving. Yet much of Honduras retains (at least for now) an untouched quality that is increasingly hard to find. In a country whose name means 'depths' it should be no surprise to find so much hidden below the surface.

OPPOSITE: GARY CHANDLER   PHILIP COBLENTZ/BRAND X PICTURES/ALAMY

6

Parks, Preserves & Pretty Places

Get a bird's-eye view of an ancient Maya ball court (p152) at Copán

ALFREDO MAIQUEZ

JONATHAN SELIG

Sink your teeth into a serpent's head at Copán (p146)

Stare back at the sun god (Kinichi Ahau) at Copán (p146)

JANE SWEE

LIZA PRADO

Reflect on things as you float along the Mirror Trail in the Refugio de Vida Silvestre Cuero y Salado (p222)

LIZA PRADO

Unleash your inner Indiana Jones at Pulhapanzak Falls (p177)

Paddle past mangroves on the Río Plátano near Brus Laguna (p292)

TOM LEVY

Time stands still at the iconic 17th-century Las Mercedes church (p160) in Gracias

Shoot the breeze at Fortaleza de Santa
Bárbara de Trujillo (p230)

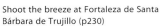

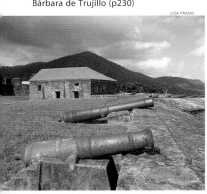

Admire the intricate architecture of Los Dolores
church (p76) in Tegucigalpa

Live the Garífuna life on Chachauate (p227), off the north coast of Honduras

Cruise on over to Anthony's Key Resort (p257) on Roatán

Into the Wild

Watch the birdie: observe keel-billed toucans at Parque Nacional Pico Bonito (p224)

STUART WESTMORLAND/THE IMAGE BANK/GETTY

M. TIMOTHY O'KEEFE/ALAMY

Focus on nature's exquisite filigrees at the butterfly enclosure (p146), near Copán

There's never a dull moment when raucous macaws (p52), sacred birds to the Maya, are around

DANNY LEHMAN/CORBIS

CRAIG TUTTLE/CORBIS

Bottle-nosed dolphins (p257) porpoisely mug for the camera off Roatán

Hang out with moray eels off Roatán (p247)

STEPHEN FRINK/CORBIS

M. TIMOTHY O'KEEFE/ALAMY

Spot whale sharks (p239) off the Bay Islands

Aquatic Adventure

White-water rafters (p214) rush down the roiling waters of the Río Cangrejal

M. TIMOTHY O'KEEFE/ALAMY

STEPHEN FRINK/STEPHEN FRINK COLLECTION/ALAMY

Dive in and inspect the wreck of the Jado Trader (p274), off Guanaja

Head lazily up the creek with a paddle under the towering Pico Bonito (p224)

M. TIMOTHY O'KEEFE/ALAMY

MICHAEL LAWRENCE

Resisting the temptation: a diver does the right thing by not touching the coral (p254)

Scuba divers (p240) drop in for a sun-speckled splash off Roatán

STEPHEN FRINK/PHOTOGRAPHER'S CHOICE/GETTY

Snorkeling in the serene waters off Utila (p266)

WOLFGANG KAEHLER/ALAMY

A Resplendent Tapestry
The People and Culture of Honduras

Go beyond the doorstep and experience the world of the Garífuna (p207)

NEIL COOPER/ALAMY

Traditional folk dancers, part of the rich cultural fabric of Honduras

PICTOR INTERNATIONAL/IMAGESTATE/ALAM

GARY CHANDLER

Don Eliseo creates pottery (p48) in his open-air studio in El Pino, near La Ceiba

LIZA PRADO

A Garífuna woman trims the edges of *casabe* (p62) in her kitchen in Plaplaya, La Moskitia

Overleaf:
Get some rhythm drummed into you at the Garífuna Festival (p195)
JIM WEST

A Miskito family heads for home near Laguna de Ibans in the Reserva de la Biósfera del Río Plátano (p288)

LIZA PRADO

Contents

The Authors   20

Getting Started   21

Itineraries   25

Snapshot   30

History   31

The Culture   41

Environment   51

Adventure Travel   58

Food & Drink   62

Tegucigalpa & Southern Honduras   68

TEGUCIGALPA   70
History   70
Orientation   70
Information   70
Dangers & Annoyances   74
Sights   74
Activities   76
Tegucigalpa for Children   77
Festivals & Events   78
Sleeping   78
Eating   83
Drinking   85
Entertainment   85
Shopping   86
Getting There & Away   87
Getting Around   87
AROUND TEGUCIGALPA   89
Santa Lucía   89
Valle de Ángeles   90
Parque Nacional la Tigra   91
Ojojona   94
Las Cuevas Pintadas   95

EL PARAÍSO DEPARTMENT   95
Yuscarán   96
Danlí   97
THE FAR SOUTH   100
Choluteca   100
El Corpus   102
Cedeño   103
San Marcos de Colón   103
Refugio de Vida Silvestre
Ojochal   104
Amapala & Isla del Tigre   104

Central Honduras   107

**CENTRAL HIGHLANDS &
BEYOND**   109
Reserva Biológico el Chile   109
Reserva Biológica Misoco   109
Cedros   109
Yoro   110
OLANCHO   112
Juticalpa   112
Monumento Natural el
Boquerón   113
Catacamas   114
Parque Nacional Sierra de
Agalta   117
Gualaco   119
La Unión   121
Parque Nacional la Muralla   121
Olanchito   122

Western Honduras   124

SAN PEDRO SULA   125
History   126
Orientation   127
Information   127
Dangers & Annoyances   128
Sights & Activities   129
Festivals & Events   130
Sleeping   130
Eating   132
Drinking   133
Entertainment   134
Shopping   134
Getting There & Away   135
Getting Around   136
VALLE DE COPÁN   137
La Entrada   137
El Puente   138
Copán Ruínas   138

Around Copán Ruínas 145
Copán Archaeological Site 146
LA RUTA LENCA **154**
Santa Rosa de Copán 154
Nueva Ocotepeque 158
Around Nueva Ocotepeque 159
Gracias 159
Parque Nacional Montaña
de Celaque 163
La Campa 165
San Marcos de Caiquín 166
San Manuel de Colohete 166
San Sebastián 167
Belén Gualcho 168
San Juan 168
Erandique 170
La Esperanza 170
Around La Esperanza 172
Marcala 173
THE WESTERN CORRIDOR **175**
Lago de Yojoa 175
Parque Nacional Cerro Azul
Meámbar 179
Parque Nacional Montaña
de Santa Bárbara 180
Trinidad 181
Santa Bárbara 182
Siguatepeque 183
Comayagua 185
Parque Nacional Montaña
de Comayagua 189
Yarumela 189
Tenampua 190
La Paz 190

The North Coast 192
Dangers & Annoyances 193
PUERTO CORTÉS &
AROUND **193**
Puerto Cortés 193
Travesía & Baja Mar 195
Omoa 196
TELA & AROUND **198**
Tela 198
Jardín Botánico Lancetilla 204
Parque Nacional Jeannette
Kawas (Punta Sal) 204
Refugio de Vida Silvestre
Punta Izopo 206
Tornabé 206
Miami 206
La Ensenada 208
Triunfo de la Cruz 209
LA CEIBA & AROUND **209**

La Ceiba 210
Refugio de Vida Silvestre
Cuero y Salado 222
Parque Nacional Pico
Bonito 224
Sambo Creek 226
Cayos Cochinos 227
TRUJILLO & AROUND **228**
Trujillo 229
Around Trujillo 233
Savá 235

The Bay Islands 237
History 239
People 239
Costs 240
Dangers & Annoyances 240
Diving 240
Getting There & Away 242
Getting Around 242
ROATÁN **243**
West End 244
West Bay 254
Sandy Bay 256
Coxen Hole 258
French Harbour 259
Around French Harbor 260
Eastern Roatán 261
UTILA **263**
East Harbour (Utila Town) 263
Outside East Harbour 269
Utila Cays 272
GUANAJA **273**
Guanaja Town (Bonacca) 274

La Moskitia 277
History 278
People 279
Dangers & Annoyances 280
Tours 280
Getting There & Away 281
Getting Around 282
WESTERN MOSKITIA **282**
Iriona 282
Palacios 283
AROUND LAGUNA DE
IBANS **284**
Rais Ta 284
Belén 285
Cocobila 286
Plaplaya 287
RESERVA DE LA BIÓSFERA
DEL RÍO PLÁTANO **288**

Las Marías 289
BRUS LAGUNA &
AROUND **292**
Brus Laguna Town 292
Outside Brus Laguna 294
RÍO PATUCA **294**
Ahuas 294
Wampusirpi 295
Tawahka Region 296
LAGUNA DE CARATASCA **297**
Puerto Lempira 297
Mistruk 299
Kaukira 300

Directory 301
Accommodations 301
Activities 303
Business Hours 304
Children 304
Climate Charts 304
Courses 305
Customs 305
Dangers & Annoyances 305
Disabled Travelers 306
Embassies & Consulates 306
Festivals & Events 307
Food 308
Gay & Lesbian Travelers 308
Holidays 308
Insurance 308
Internet Access 308
Legal Matters 309
Maps 309
Money 309
Photography & Video 310
Post 310
Shopping 310
Solo Travelers 310
Sustainable Travel 311
Telephone & Fax 311
Time 311
Toilets 312
Tourist Information 312
Visas 312
Volunteering 312
Women Travelers 312
Work 312

Transportation 313
GETTING THERE & AWAY **313**
Entering the Country 313
Air 313
Land 315

Sea   316
GETTING AROUND   **317**
Air   317
Bicycle   317
Boat   317
Bus   317
Car & Motorcycle   318
Hitchhiking   319
Local Transportation   319

Health   320

BEFORE YOU GO   **320**
Insurance   320
Recommended
Immunizations   320

Medical Checklist   321
Internet Resources   321
Further Reading   321
IN TRANSIT   **321**
Deep Vein Thrombosis
(DVT)   321
Jet Lag & Motion Sickness   322
IN HONDURAS   **322**
Availability & Cost of
Health Care   322
Infectious Diseases   322
Travelers' Diarrhea   325
Environmental Hazards &
Treatment   325
Children & Pregnant
Women   326

Language   327

Glossary   335

Behind the Scenes 337

Index   344

World Time Zones   350

Map Legend   352

Regional Map Contents

THE BAY ISLANDS p238

THE NORTH COAST p194-5

LA MOSKITIA p278

CENTRAL HONDURAS p108

WESTERN HONDURAS p125

TEGUCIGALPA &
SOUTHERN
HONDURAS p69

The Authors

GARY CHANDLER

Gary Chandler went to Honduras on his first assignment with Lonely Planet: *Central America on a Shoestring* in 2003. He returned to Honduras to find the same big, beautiful, fascinating, varied place he remembered. He and co-writer Liza Prado criss-crossed the country, from Puerto Cortes to Puerto Lempira, from Isla del Tigre to Parque La Tigra, from Plaplaya to *la playa*. A graduate of UC Berkeley and Columbia graduate school of journalism, Gary has worked on titles in North, Central and South America – from Rio to Reno. This is his sixth assignment with Lonely Planet. When not doing guidebooks, Gary works as a newspaper and radio journalist. He lives in Oakland, CA.

Authors' Favorite Trip

We like to start at the Bay Islands – if the diving is especially great, we may extend our stay a few days. **Roatán** (p243) is our favorite, but Utila and Guanaja are terrific too. We take a ferry to the mainland and get another day or two diving and beach-going at **Cayos Cochinos** (p227). Our coastal cravings satiated, we head inland to **Lago de Yojoa** (p175) for a couple days of hiking and birdwatching, maybe climbing **Montaña de Santa Bárbara** (p180) with a machete-wielding guide. We've seen Copán and the Ruta Lenca several times – if you haven't, don't miss them – so from Lago de

Yojoa we head to Olancho, the wild west of Honduras. There, we organize a three-day hike up La Picucha in **Parque Nacional Sierra de Agalta** (p117). If the planning fairies have been kind, we'll be just coming off the mountain in time to meet up with a tour headed toward **Dulce Nombre de Culmí** to start a hiking/rafting trip into **La Moskitia** and the **Reserva de la Biósfera del Río Plátano** (p288). An amazing week later, we reach **Belén** (p285) and we're back where we began, digging our toes into the warm Caribbean sand.

LIZA PRADO

Liza Prado was traveling through Yucatán when, on a whim, she decided to bus it to Honduras to learn to dive. Three years, a couple of return trips and over fifty dives later, Liza was thrilled to head back, this time as a Lonely Planet author. It was a fun and fast-paced assignment, one that saw Liza and co-writer Gary Chandler diving, hiking, croc-spotting and checking out a hotel or two. A graduate of Brown University and Stanford Law School, Liza has worked as a travel writer and photographer for guides to the Dominican Republic, El Salvador, Mexico and California; this is her fourth assignment with Lonely Planet. She currently lives in Oakland, CA.

LONELY PLANET AUTHORS

Why is our travel information the best in the world? It's simple: our authors are independent, dedicated travellers. They don't research using just the Internet or phone, and they don't take freebies in exchange for positive coverage. They travel widely, to all the popular spots and off the beaten track. They personally visit thousands of hotels, restaurants, cafés, bars, galleries, palaces, museums and more – and they take pride in getting all the details right, and telling it how it is. For more, see the authors section on www.lonelyplanet.com.

Getting Started

WHEN TO GO

Like most tropical countries, Honduras experiences a rainy season and a dry season, known locally as *invierno* (winter) and *verano* (summer), respectively. In the interior, especially the west and south, the rainy season runs roughly from May to November. Rains usually come in the afternoon and last an hour or so. On the north coast and Bay Islands, the rainy season is later, around September to December, with *nortes* ('northerners', cool storms from the north) possible into February. Hurricanes are most likely from September to October, though they rarely hit Honduras directly. However, even a far-off hurricane can send heavy rain Honduras' way and can cause flooding or minor mudslides. See climate charts (p304) for more information.

Travel is easier during the dry season, especially for scuba diving and trips to La Moskitia. Then again, the forests and countryside are more lush during the rainy season. February and March are good months to visit because the weather is fairly stable across the country; the trails and roads are drying out but the trees and underbrush are still full and green.

COSTS & MONEY

Honduras is an inexpensive country overall, but a trip here can be pricey simply because of the activities you're likely to do, namely diving.

Besides diving, lodging will likely be your biggest expense. Hotel prices run the gamut in Honduras, the majority being high-budget or low-midrange, around US$15 to US$25 per night. Budget travelers can manage lodging for under US$12 per day in popular destinations and under US$8 in remote areas, though the cheapest hotels can be pretty grim.

For most travelers, eating out will cost around US$6 to US$8 per person per meal, once drinks, taxes, and tip are added in. But you can save money by eating at street food vendors and no-name eateries, and

---

DON'T LEAVE HOME WITHOUT...

- Passport and US cash – universal travel essentials
- Sunscreen – very expensive in Honduras
- Bug repellent – expensive and can be hard to find
- Toiletries – you'll appreciate having your preferred brands of tampons, pads, condoms, deodorant, etc
- Travel alarm clock – it's rare to find alarm clocks in hotels, even high-end ones
- Copies of important documents – having a copy of your passport and plane tickets will make replacing them, if necessary, much easier
- Toilet paper – an extra roll has saved many a traveler in a pinch
- Diver certification card and logbook – bring them if you've got them. You don't want to repeat the Open Water course, do you?
- Extra eyeglasses or contacts – expensive and difficult to replace
- Large heavy-duty plastic bags – handy for travel in the rainy season, or anytime in La Moskitia

by getting lunch or breakfast items at a grocery store instead of a restaurant. Being careful, budget travelers can bring food costs down to US$5 per meal or less.

The big-ticket item for most travelers here is diving, plus the higher cost of hotels and restaurants on the Bay Islands. Figure an Open Water course will cost US$200 to US$240. with a half-dozen fun dives at around US$20 to US$35 per tank. Lodging and food tend to be more expensive on Roatán than Utila. Most shops on Utila have basic dorms, and offer their students either two to four free nights or two free fun dives (most people choose the latter). A trip to La Moskitia can also be pricey, whether by tour or on your own.

Buses are a bargain, especially considering how big the country is. There are three classes of service: *ordinario* or *parando* (literally, stopping) is the classic 'chicken bus' that stops frequently to pick up and drop off passengers. *Directos* make fewer stops and cost only slightly more – for most travelers this is the way to go. Some popular routes are covered by the luxury or deluxe lines Hedman Alas, King Quality or Saenz Clase Primera. Prices are double or triple, but it can be a worthwhile splurge.

Taxis are safe and affordable, with fares typically charged per person. Expect US$0.60 to US$1 per person within town, US$1.50 and up for destinations out of town or at night.

Other costs to consider are rental cars (midsize US$30 to US$60 per day including taxes and insurance), Internet (US$0.75 to US$1 per hour) and laundry (US$1 per pound).

HOW MUCH?

Moto-taxi ride US$1

Average hotel room US$15 to US$25

Open water dive certification US$200 to US$240

Plato típico US$2

Five-minute call to US US$0.50, to Australia US$2 to US$10

TRAVEL LITERATURE

Topics like Copán archaeological site, the banana industry and the Contra war have been well studied, while others, like non-Maya indigenous communities and environmental issues, have not. Gangs are a hot topic and have received extensive newspaper and magazine coverage; full-length books are still rare, though several are in the works.

Honduras: A Country Guide by Tom Barry and Kent Norsworthy (1991) and *Honduras: A Country Study* (1990) by the US Federal Research Division are oldish but have concise historical information.

The United States, Honduras, and the Crisis in Central America by Donald E Schultz and Deborah Sundloff Schulz (1994) discusses the role of the US in Central America during the region's tumultuous civil wars.

Don't be Afraid, Gringo (1987) is the intriguing first-hand story of peasant Elvia Alvarado's reluctant rise as a labor leader, and of the Honduran labor movement, flaws and all.

Bitter Fruit by Stephen C Schlesinger is mostly about the United Fruit Company in Guatemala, but provides insight on the banana giant's impact on Honduras as well. *The Banana Men: American Mercenaries and Entrepreneurs in Central America, 1880–1930* (1995) and *The Banana Wars: United States Intervention in the Caribbean, 1898–1934* (2002), both by Lester D Langley, are incisive accounts of the banana companies' political and economic influence in Central America and the Caribbean.

Alison Acker's *Honduras: The Making of a Banana Republic* (1989), lacks the detail and analysis of more recent studies, but is a very worthy read.

Copán is one of the most extensively studied archaeological sites in the Maya world; many studies are highly technical but several have been written with a more general readership in mind. *Copán: The History of*

TOP TENS

Small Towns

Small towns are one of the joys of Honduras, where a bit of Spanish and a friendly manner can earn you plenty of lunchtime conversations and interesting insights.

- Las Marías (p289) A Miskito-Pech village in the heart of the Reserva de la Biósfera del Río Plátano, and a perfect base for excursions in the area.
- Gracias (p159) A colonial town set at the foot of the lush Parque Nacional Montaña de Celaque.
- Jewel and Pigeon Cay (p272) Off the western tip of Utila, these sun-bleached islets are even smaller and mellower than Utila itself, and no less picturesque.
- Santa Lucía (p89) A quaint colonial village in the mountains, minutes from Tegucigalpa.
- Chachauate (p228) A traditional Garífuna village on a picture-perfect Caribbean cay.
- Rais Ta (p284) A quiet Miskito village on a thin strip of sand and trees between the Caribbean and a huge island lagoon.
- Yuscarán (p96) On the way to Honduras' cigar country, this colonial town has winding cobblestone streets and several *aguardiente* breweries.
- Miami (p206) A cluster of thatched-roof homes on a rustic beach at the end of a long sandy road near Jeannette Kawas National Park.
- San Marcos de Colón (p103) A cool colonial refuge in the otherwise sweltering southern region, with a seldom-visited wildlife refuge nearby.
- Travesía (p195) A Garífuna village with an excellent beach and good lodging options.

Festivals & Parties

Whether a local celebration or a national holiday, festivals are a unique window on Honduran culture, a chance to see how locals mark important events and also to have a little fun.

- Garífuna Festival in Baja Mar (p195) – July 9–24.
- Gran Carnival/Feria de San Isidro, La Ceiba (p216) – third weekend in May.
- Semana Santa, Comayagua (p187) – week before Easter.
- Sun Jam, Utila (p272)
- San Pedro Sula (p134) – any Saturday night.
- Guancasco, La Ruta Lenca (p161) – mostly December and Januray. Dates vary by town.
- Feria de la Virgen de Suyapa (p78) – February 2–8.
- Festival Nacional de Maíz, Danlí (p98) – last week of August.
- Noche de Fumadores, Santa Rosa de Copán (p156) – third Friday of August.
- Semana Santa, Tela (p200) – week before Easter.

Things to Buy

Remember that Hondurans don't engage in the same hardcore bargaining common elsewhere; a little back and forth is okay, but lay off the big guns.

- Lenca 'negativo' pottery
- T-shirt from Copán Ruínas
- Clay or stone Maya replica
- Cuadro de tunu – Moskitia tree bark art
- Garífuna rayador – Garífuna rasp used to grind yucca, comes in souvenir size
- Rosary at the Basilica de Suyapa
- Garífuna coconut bread
- *Baleadas* (Honduran national snack food)
- Fried chicken – hardening your arteries has never tasted better
- Aralen – cheap and easy to get antimalarial

PUTTING DOWN THE GUIDE *Matthew Firestone*

No, we're not talking about insulting the local guy who is leading you through the rainforest. We're talking about closing this book that you have in your hands and leaving it behind. We're talking about following your own trail and paddling up your own stream. It is bound to be an adventure more memorable than the one you'll find along the Gringo Trail.

We at Lonely Planet are dedicated to providing comprehensive coverage of every country and region that we cover, but we recognize the sometimes detrimental effect of places being 'discovered'. Even more than that, we are dedicated to creating a sustainable global traveler culture, and we recognize the universal benefit of 'discovery'.

So put your guidebook down for a day or – even better – a week. Explore the parts of Honduras that are not covered in the pages of this guidebook. And discover your own lonely planet.

an Ancient Kingdom, by William L Fash and E Wyllys Andrews (2005) is an excellent overview, while *Written in Stone: Guide to the Copán Ruínas Archaeological Park* (1998), also by Fash, is a fine on-site companion and is often sold at the Copán ruins' bookstore.

Los Barcos (The Ships; 1992), and *El Humano y La Diosa* (The Human and the Goddess; 1996) and *The Big Banana* (1999) are all by Roberto Quesada, one of Honduras' best-known living novelists. *Gringos in Honduras: The Good, the Bad, and the Ugly* (1995) and *Velasquez: The Man and His Art,* are two of many books by Guillermo Yuscarán, aka William Lewis, an American writer and painter living in Honduras. *Around the Edge* by English journalist Peter Ford (1991) relates Ford's journey along the Caribbean coast from Belize to Panama, especially in La Moskitia.

INTERNET RESOURCES

A growing number of sites provide reliable up-to-date information on Honduras. Many are maintained by expatriates, and are in English.

www.aboututila.com General info and news about Utila.
www.hondurastips.honduras.com The website of the free tourist magazine *Honduras Tips*.
http://lanic.utexas.edu/la/ca/honduras/ Extensive list of links to article and websites on everything from politics to sports to tourism.
www.letsgohonduras.com Honduras' ministry of tourism website.
www.lonelyplanet.com/worldguide/ The source of updated LP coverage.
www.marrder.com/htw The official site of *Honduras This Week,* Honduras' only English-language newspaper.
www.roatanonline.com A charmless but comprehensive guide to all things Roatán.
www.sidewalkmystic.com Private website with practical info on travel in Honduras.
www.travel-to-honduras.com Links to various services, including volunteer organizations.

Itineraries

CLASSIC ROUTES

THE WHOLE COUNTRY (ALMOST) — Three Weeks

From **Tegucigalpa** (p70), head to **Parque Nacional La Tigra** (p91) for hiking, or make a day trip to **Valle de Ángeles** (p90). Head north to **Lago de Yojoa** (p175) for bird-watching in the AM and **Pulhapanzak Falls** (p177) in the PM. Zip up to **San Pedro Sula** (p125) before flying to **Roatán** (p243) or **Utila** (p263). Spend at least three full days diving, snorkeling and wearing flip-flops. Don't dive? Take an Open Water course – one starts every day. Take the ferry back to **La Ceiba** (p210), where there's something for everyone: hiking, biking, rafting, horseback riding, canoeing, even canopy-rides. Next, hop over to **Tela** (p198) for a day at the beach, the **Jardín Botánico Lancetilla** (p204), or beautiful **Punta Sal** (p204). Afterwards, head to **Copán Ruínas** (p138). Visit the ruins, but hike or horseback ride as well. If you like colonial towns, make your next stop **Santa Rosa de Copán** (p154); otherwise head straight to **Gracias** (p159), gateway to **Parque Nacional Montaña de Celaque**. Continue down through the southern half of the **Ruta Lenca** (p154) to **Comayagua** (p185) and back to Tegucigalpa. So what's missing? **La Moskitia** (p277) for starters: budget a week. You could also add hiking in **Parque Nacional Sierra de Agalta** (p117). In the south, beat the heat in colonial towns like **San Marcos de Colón** (p103) and **El Corpus** (p102).

Here's Honduras from top to bottom: from the highest peak to a hundred feet underwater. It includes national parks, Maya ruins, and colonial plazas, which you can complete in three busy weeks. Add another week to visit La Moskitia and write the guidebook yourself.

INTO THE WILD   Two Weeks

Fly into **Tegucigalpa** (p70) where appropriately enough, your tour begins
with Honduras' first national park, **Parque Nacional La Tigra** (p91). Plan to
stay the night at one of the two entrances and make an all-day loop hike.
From La Tigra, head north to **Parque Nacional Cerro Azul Meámbar** (p179) with
its well-marked trails, easy-to-follow signs, and excellent campgrounds.
Continue north to **Tela** (p198) and the beautiful **Parque Nacional Jeannette
Kawas** (p204). Take it easy on a guided daytrip, or rough it by hiking in
from the tiny village of **Miami** and camping on the beach. Next head east
of **La Ceiba** to the tiny Garífuna village of **Sambo Creek** (p226), a jumping
off point for **Parque Nacional Marino Cayos Cochinos** (p227). Crystalline water
and pristine coral reefs make this a divers' and snorkelers' paradise, not
to mention one of the most photographed spots in Honduras. Back on
the mainland, take a bus from San Pedro Sula to Gracias, where **Parque
Nacional Montaña de Celaque,** (p163) with Honduras' highest peak, awaits.
If your time and energy permit, head straight to **Parque Nacional Sierra de
Agalta** (p117) to climb La Picucha mountain, one of Honduras' most challenging ascents, doable from either **Gualaco** (p119) or **Catacamas** (p114).
Otherwise, return to Tegucigalpa for your flight home.

**This itinerary takes
you to Honduras'
best national
parks, from the
rugged Sierra de
Agalta to coral-
fringed Cayos
Cochinos. Some
parks have
well-marked
hiking trails,
others require a
guide who's handy
with a machete.
You can complete
it in two to three
weeks.**

ROAD LESS TRAVELED

A WORLD APART: THE MOSQUITO COAST

Depending on your time, budget and tolerance for long land journeys, fly into La Moskitia or go overland – either way, make your way to **Belén** (p285) or **Rais Ta** (p284), neighboring towns on Laguna de Ibans. Take a day to get your bearings straight and check out the peaceful towns of **Plaplaya** (p287) and **Cocobila** (p286). Early the next morning, settle in for the five to six hour canoe ride to **Las Marías** (p289). There, arrange a mellow daytrip to the petroglyphs or a more challenging three-day rainforest hike to **Pico Dama** (p291). Back in Belén and Rais Ta, arrange a morning boat ride or flight to **Brus Laguna** (p292) for a night or two in the savannah cabañas there. Afterwards, head back to Brus Laguna town, stock up on supplies and fly to **Wampusirpi** (p295) where – knock on wood – you'll be able to hitch or hire a boat ride into the **Reserva de la Bíosfera Tawahka Asangni** (p296). Boat back to Wampusirpi and fly to **Puerto Lempira** (p297). Time permitting, bike to **Mistruk** (p299) or **Kaukira** (p300) for the day; otherwise fly from Puerto Lempira back to **La Ceiba** (p210).

An organized tour can be a very good option, visiting many of the same places but saving you the time and hassle of arranging transport and other details. In fact, one of the best ways to see La Moskitia is on a seven- to ten-day rafting trip (see p280 for more info), starting in Olancho. The trip takes you down the lush Río Patuka and through the Tawahka region – an incredible journey.

This tour includes the Río Plátano and Tawahka Biosphere Reserves and small Miskito and Garífuna villages along the coast. A full tour takes two weeks, but you can hit the highlights in seven to ten days. A five day visit will feel pretty rushed.

COBBLESTONES & CATHEDRALS

From **Tegucigalpa** (p70), head straight to **Santa Lucía** (p89), a pretty little village that is often overlooked for better-known Valle de Ángeles.
Loop around to **Yuscarán** (p96), a charming colonial town on the way to
nowhere. Back in Tegucigalpa, head north to **Comayagua** (p185) with its
soaring cathedral, broad Parque Central, and traditional religious festivals. Next, go up and around to **Copán Ruínas** (p138), which in addition to
its archaeological riches, is a picturesque and lively town, popular with
backpackers. From there it's a short drive or bus ride to **Santa Rosa de
Copán** (p154) and its recently restored city center and a boho bar scene.
Continue south to **Gracias** (p159) a cool mountain redoubt with clay tile-
roofed houses, cobblestone streets, and great hiking nearby. This is part
of the **Ruta Lenca** (Lenca Route), a string of small indigenous villages that
eventually leads back to the main highway, and to Tegucigalpa. Time
permitting, zip out to **San Marcos de Colón** (p103), an underappreciated
colonial gem near the Nicaraguan border and gateway to a nature reserve
brimming with monkeys.

A tour of the places many travelers skip en route to bigger, better-known destinations. You'll appreciate having a car for part of this itinerary – buses to some of these towns are few and far between. Budget two to three weeks.

TAILORED TRIPS

BENEATH THE SURFACE

From the US, Delta and Continental have non-stop flights to **Roatán** (p243), thus avoiding San Pedro Sula and La Ceiba. In Roatán, look for a hotel and independent dive shop in West End, or stay at a resort with its own dive shop in **Sandy Bay** (p256) or **West Bay** (p254). For more isolation, look for resorts further afield, at **Palmetto Bay** (p260) or **Paya Bay** (p262). Some of Roatán's most memorable dive spots include Hole in the Wall, West End Wall, Spooky Channel and Mary's Place. For snorkeling, West Bay is good (though showing increasing damage).

From Roatán, take the morning ferry to **La Ceiba** (p210) and get on the one going to **Utila** (p263). Utila caters mostly to backpackers and independent travelers, with just a few upscale resorts on the western end. Utila's best diving is on the north shore – don't miss Pinnacle, Black Hill, and Blackish Point – though the sea mounds on the south side are gorgeous. For snorkeling, try Airport Reef and Blue Bayou beach.

Take the ferry back to La Ceiba and get directly onto a plane for **Guanaja** (p273). Instead of staying in Bonacca, the main town, head to one of the resorts around the island, all of which offer diving and snorkeling. The Pinnacle, Lee's Pleasure, Jim's Silver Lode and the Jado Trader are all Guanaja favorite spots.

Fly back to La Ceiba for one last stop – **Cayos Cochinos** (p227). You can arrange a one-day snorkel or dive trip through Palma Real hotel or arrange an independent trip – snorkeling only – from one of the boatmen in Sambo Creek (p226). Plantation Beach Resort is the only hotel in Cayos Cochinos offering daily and weekly dive-and-lodging packages.

HONDURAS FOR KIDS

Honduras can be a fun and rewarding place to travel with children. Fly into **San Pedro Sula** (p125) and start your trip at **Copán Ruínas** (p138). Visit the ruins and the museums – the children's museum in the center of town is terrific. Don't miss the butterfly farm and tropical bird park, and consider taking a hike or horseback ride in the surrounding hills and coffee fields. Make your way to **Tela** (p198), which has a nice beach and interesting daytrips, including Jardín Botánico Lancetilla and Punta Sal. Continue east to **La Ceiba** (p210) for river rafting or canopy tours. Take the ferry to **Roatán** (p243) where resorts like Anthony's Key cater to families, or you can explore on your own – there are several canopy tours, an iguana farm, and terrific diving and snorkeling, including certification classes for all levels. Middle-schoolers and older should have no trouble in **La Moskitia** (p277); you're probably best off arranging a five- to seven-day tour, flying from La Ceiba to **Brus Laguna** (p292).

Snapshot

Like its neighbors, Honduras is experiencing tremendous changes: an expanding tourist economy (cruise ships in Roatán?!), a maturing political scene, and the whole globalization thing, including maquilas, free trade agreements – heck, even implementing Daylight Savings Time for the *second* time. Honduras remains deeply entrenched in a two-front war against gangs and HIV/AIDS. Illegal logging is emerging as another major concern (do you know where that new mahogany chest came from?) and a key issue among Honduras' growing environmental community.

In fact, logging was a factor in the 2005 presidential elections, in which both candidates were from Olancho, ground-zero for illegal logging. Both candidates had less-than-savory connections to timber interests – it's hard to climb the political ranks in Olancho without them – but Liberal Party candidate Manuel 'Mel' Zelaya was less besmirched than his National Party rival, and eked out a narrow victory. Though hard-fought, it was a mostly clean and fair election, no small feat for a country with a history of electoral fraud and military coups. One of President Zelaya's first major deeds was the implementation of the Central America and Dominican Republic Free Trade Agreement (CAFTA-DR), which was met with predictable applause from the business community and condemnation from anti-globalization activists. Everyday Hondurans were characteristically unfazed by the event, reserving judgment until the real effects begin to appear in the form of job growth or job loss.

Interestingly, most Hondurans you'll meet are very laid back and, while not disinterested, certainly disinclined to make much to-do over politics and world affairs. They do get animated when conversation turns, as it inevitably does, to crime and violence, especially related to gangs. And not without reason: in 2004, there were 45.9 murders per 100,000 residents, one of the highest murder rates in the world. (By comparison, the United States' rate is 5.7 per 100,000.) Still, it remains quite unlikely that any given person, local or traveler, will experience crime, violent or otherwise. But fear runs high thanks to the sobering numbers and the not-so-sober media coverage of the most sensational incidents.

The ongoing immigration debate in the United States is also of keen interest to many Hondurans. Around 400,000 Hondurans live in the United States, a third of whom do not have legal status. Hopes are high that an amnesty is in the offing, though that doesn't seem likely given the political climate in the United States. The debate is met with a mixture of hope and confusion by ordinary Hondurans, who rely mightily on money sent home from abroad, but are resigned to the Byzantine machinations of US immigration policy.

Honduras today is a place of change, too fast for those who'd like the country to remain 'undiscovered', too slow for those frustrated by persistent remnants of the 'Banana Republic' days, whether in undue foreign influence or lax enforcement of environmental laws. Hondurans themselves take it all in their stride, and travelers with an open mind and a bit of Spanish will find many fascinating conversations in store.

FAST FACTS

Population: 7.3 million

Life expectancy: women 71 years, men 68 years

People living with HIV/AIDS: 63,000 (1.8%)

Unemployment: 28%

Minimum wage: US$3.15 per day

Remittances in 2004: US$1 billion

Metric tons of bananas and plantains produced annually: 1.7 million

Size of Honduras: 112,090 sq km

Length of coastline: 820km

Number of tourists visiting Honduras each year: 1 million

History

PRE-COLUMBIAN HISTORY

The oldest known evidence of human presence in present-day Honduras are stone knives, scrapers and other tools thought to be 6000 to 8000 years old, and uncovered by archaeologists in 1962 near La Esperanza, Intibucá. Central America's earliest occupants almost certainly were Paleo-Indians from the north, but linguistic and other evidence suggests that many indigenous people present in Honduras today (Pech, Tawahka and probably Lenca) are descended from later migrations of people from rainforest regions of South America, especially present-day Colombia.

The Maya arrived in Honduras by way of Guatemala and Mexico, and settled in the fertile Sula, Copán and Comayagua valleys. Over centuries, they came to dominate the area, as they did much of Mesoamerica. Copán was a heavily settled, agriculturally rich trading zone and eventually became one of the great Maya city-states of the Classic Period (AD 300–900). The Classic Period ends with the rapid and mysterious collapse of most Maya centers, including Copán, where the last dated hieroglyph is from AD 800.

The Maya population declined precipitously, but did not disappear, of course. They were just one of many indigenous groups that made up Honduras' native population when European explorers began their conquest of the American mainland. Copán has since returned to prominence as an archaeological mother lode, having more hieroglyphic inscriptions and stone monuments than any other Maya ruin. Copán was the first site visited by John Lloyd Stephens and Frederick Catherwood on their groundbreaking exploration of Mesoamerica in 1839. It was also the first site to be studied by Alfred Mausley (in 1885), whose compendium of Maya stone monuments remains a classic in the field, and whose work prompted the preeminent Harvard Peabody Museum to enter into Maya investigation (and which in turn selected Copán as its inaugural excavation). And it was the first stop for Sylvanus Morley and the Carnegie Institute in the 1920s. More recently, research has focused on Copán's outlying areas; the site has provided important insight into the lives of ordinary Classic-era Mayas. For more on Maya history see p149.

See www.mostlymaya.com for a list of over 100 Maya-related websites, including Maya calendar translators, virtual ruins tours (including Copán), and scientific and general interest websites.

CONQUEST & COLONIZATION

On his fourth and final voyage, Admiral Christopher Columbus made landfall near present-day Trujillo. The date was August 14, 1502, and was the first time European explorers set foot on the American mainland. Columbus named the area Honduras, or 'depths,' for the deep waters there. Before the historic landing, Columbus also had had his (and Europe's) first encounter with mainland indigenous people: a crew of a large canoe he spotted near the Bay Islands. Columbus commandeered the canoe, which was laden with trade goods, and forced its captain (probably a Mayan merchant) to serve as his guide. The expedition continued east

Approximately 95% of the indigenous population in western and central Honduras died within 50 years of Columbus' landing in Trujillo.

TIMELINE

500 AD	822
First Maya immigrate to western Honduras	Collapse of Copán kingdom

LEMPIRA: MAN OF THE MOUNTAIN

The Spanish conquest was never kind to indigenous people, and the early 1500s saw native Hondurans enslaved and forced to perform difficult and dangerous work in colonial gold and silver mines. In 1537 a young Lenca chieftain named Lempira ('Man of the Mountain' in Lenca) gathered a large and disparate band of indigenous fighters – some reports say his army had 30,000 men from dozens of tribes – to oppose Spanish repression. Lempira directed a series of surprise attacks on Spanish stations, which in turn inspired indigenous revolts in other regions, including Comayagua and Trujillo. A Spanish force tracked Lempira to a fortified mountain redoubt called Peñol de Cerquín, near present-day Erandique. There, Lempira repelled all attacks, holding off better-armed and better-equipped Spanish soldiers for more than six months. In 1538 the Spanish finally resorted to treachery. Though there is disagreement about the exact circumstances, what is known is that Lempira was lured to peace talks and then murdered; resistance collapsed after his death. Lempira is now seen as a hero – the national currency is named after him, as are numerous towns and the state where he led his famous revolt.

around Cabo Gracias a Díos (another of Columbus' placenames) all the way to present-day Panama, where the admiral dropped his unlucky captive before returning to Spain.

Having been the site of such a historic landing, the Honduran Caribbean coast was all but ignored by explorers for the next twenty years, who focused instead on Mexico, Panama and the Caribbean islands. Hernán Cortés' expedition into the Aztec heartland, however, revived interest in Central America. Exploration of the region was marked by feuding among would-be conquistadores: Gil González Davila 'discovered' the Golfo de Fonseca and tried claiming it as his own, only to be captured by rival Spaniard Cristóbal de Olid, who had similar designs. González Davila turned the tables, however, by luring Olid's men to his side, then capturing and beheading Olid. Hernán Cortéz and others tried to quell the feuding, but to no avail.

The discovery of gold and silver in the 1530s drew even more Spanish settlers and, more importantly, increased the demand for indigenous slave labor. Native Hondurans had long resisted Spanish invasion and enslavement, and in 1537, a young Lenca chief named Lempira led an indigenous uprising against the Spanish. Inspired by Lempira's example, revolt swept the western region, and the Spanish were very nearly expelled. But Lempira was assassinated at peace talks arranged with the Spanish in 1538, and the native resistance was soon quelled. A cycle of smaller revolts and brutal repression followed, decimating the native population. African slaves were introduced in the 1540s to fill the growing labor shortage.

Mining sustained the colony for the remainder of the century, but a collapse of silver prices (and the constant challenges of excavating such rugged terrain) devastated the Honduran economy. Cattle and tobacco enterprises gained some traction, and a change in the Spanish throne in the early 1700s reduced corruption and helped revive the mining industry. However, another upheaval in Spanish rule in 1808 – when Napoleon installed one of his own on the Spanish throne – sparked revolts on both sides of the Atlantic, which irreparably damaged Spanish colonial rule.

Scribes, Warriors and Kings (2001) by William L Fash and Barbara W Fash, is a detailed and sometimes technical account of ongoing research and excavation at Copán by the authors, leading experts on the site.

1502	1537
Columbus lands near Trujillo, the first European contact with mainland America	Lenca chieftain Lempira leads indigenous uprising across western Honduras; lured into peace negotiations, he is assassinated in 1538

BIRTH OF A NATION

On September 15, 1821, Honduras, Guatemala, El Salvador, Costa Rica and Nicaragua declared independence from Spain, and shortly thereafter joined the newly formed Mexican Empire. The relationship didn't last long, and in 1823, the same countries declared independence from Mexico and formed the Federal Republic of Central America. Though Honduras was the poorest and least-populated of the countries, it produced some of the federation's most important leaders. Chief among them was the liberal hero General Francisco Morazán, commonly dubbed the 'George Washington of Central America', who led the federation from 1830 to 1838. But bitter conflicts between liberals and conservatives proved too divisive for the nascent union, and in May 1838 the Central American Congress freed its members to form independent states – Honduras did so on November 15th of that year.

Around 5000 pirates lived on the Bay Islands in the early 1600s.

The liberal and conservative factions continued to wrestle for power in Honduras after independence. Conservatives favored a pro-church,

---

BRITISH INFLUENCE IN HONDURAS

British influence in Central America is often thought to extend no further than Belize, which was a colony of the UK until 1981 and where English is still the official language. However, British merchants – and pirates – played an important role in colonial Honduras, and their influence is still very evident today.

Spain colonized and exploited Central America with little competition for almost a century. However, all those New World riches eventually caught the attention of rival countries. By the turn of the 17th century, British pirates (and some Dutch and French) frequently attacked Spanish fleets; in 1643, they destroyed the city of Trujillo, then Honduras' main shipping port. British merchants also began to establish timber operations along the coast, extending from Cabo Gracias a Díos to present-day Belize. For labor, the British brought Black slaves from their colonies in Jamaica and elsewhere. The British also armed indigenous groups to help contest Spanish rule; in fact, the Miskito people of the so-called Mosquito Coast actually derive their name not from 'mosquito,' but from 'musket,' a weapon they were given by British pirates and settlers, and used with notorious effect against the Spanish. Spain slowly regained the upper hand through the 18th century, and in 1786, Britain recognized Spanish sovereignty over the Honduran Caribbean coast. But just over a half-century later, Britain retook the Bay Islands during the chaotic years of the Central American federation, remaining there until 1859. Even as the UK ceded military control, British bankers hatched a sham railroad deal in the 1860s that left Honduras with less than a hundred kilometers of usable track and some £6 million in debt, which ballooned to US$125 million over the next half-century. In 1925 Honduras managed to negotiate a substantial forbearance, but many point to British loans as the beginning of Honduras' long struggle with foreign debt. Finally, the British also played an important role in the creation of the Garífuna ethnic group, one of Honduras' most well known. In 1797, following a deadly uprising on the island of Saint Vincent, British colonizers loaded several thousand slaves onto ships and shipped them to the island of Roatán. Over a thousand died en-route, but those who survived prospered and multiplied, mixing with indigenous people. Today Garífuna villages dot the Caribbean Coast as far as Guatemala and Belize.

British influence in Honduras is still quite evident today. English is the principle language on the Bay Islands, and almost 30% of the Miskito vocabulary is English, including the days of the week, and words like 'landing' (for pier). Many Hondurans from those areas feel a sentimental kinship with the UK; for some, it even exceeds their affinity for Spain or Honduras itself.

1540–45	1643
Two thousand enslaved Africans brought to Honduras to work in gold and silver mines	British pirates destroy Trujillo, Honduras's main shipping port

aristocratic-style government, while liberals supported free market development of the kind taking place in the US and parts of Western Europe. Power alternated between the two factions, and Honduras was ruled by a succession of civilian governments and military regimes. (The country's constitution would be rewritten 17 times between 1821 and 1982.) Government has officially been by popular election, but Honduras has experienced hundreds of coups, rebellions, power seizures, electoral 'irregularities,' foreign invasion and meddling since achieving independence from Spain.

Fighting between liberals and conservatives was briefly suspended in the 1880s when an American adventurer named William Walker launched a bizarre and ill-fated attempt to conquer Central America. He succeeded in gaining control of Nicaragua in 1856, but a joint Central American military effort forced Walker back to the US within a year. He returned in 1860, landing near Trujillo. He was captured by British agents and turned over to Honduran authorities, who promptly executed him. He is buried in Trujillo.

THE BANANA YEARS

Where William Walker failed, US free enterprise succeeded. In the 1880s the New York and Honduras Rosario Mining Company (NYHRMC) revived Honduras' promising but underdeveloped mining industry. The company enjoyed almost unfettered (and untaxed) access to the ore-rich mountains near the town of El Rosario, east of Tegucigalpa. In 74 years of operation – the area was turned into a national park in 1954 – the NYHRMC extracted an estimated US$100 million of gold, silver, copper and zinc; little of that money or product remained in Honduras, however.

But it was the banana that would most entangle Honduras with foreign interests and governments. In 1899 the Boston Fruit Company merged with the Snyder Fruit Company to form United Fruit Company. The new company imported most of its fruit from Panama and Costa Rica, but soon acquired seven small banana operations in Honduras. That same year, three Italian brothers named Luca, Felix, and Joseph Vaccaro founded Vaccaro Brothers & Co – the predecessor of Standard Fruit Company – and began exporting bananas from the La Ceiba region to their base in New Orleans. In 1902 Russian émigré Samuel Zemurray established the Hubbard-Zemurray company, which would eventually become the Cuyamel Fruit Company. United purchased Cuyamel in 1929 and made Zemurray company president in 1933. United and Standard – which are today known as Chiquita and Dole fruit companies – have been battling for control of the Honduran (and world) banana market ever since.

Bananas accounted for 11% of Honduras' exports in 1892, 42% in 1903, 66% in 1913, and 80% in 1929. The spectacular economic success of the banana industry made the banana companies extremely powerful within Honduras, with the rival companies allying themselves with competing political parties. Political, environmental, labor and bribery scandals have marred the industry throughout its existence, including Zemurray's support of a 1908 coup attempt against a Vaccaro-friendly

Gringos in Honduras (2nd ed 2000) by Guillermo Yuscarán is a very informative book, despite the flippant title, containing short biographies of seven Americans who have impacted Honduras, from William Walker to naturalist/humorist Archie Carr.

www.unitedfruit.org, operated by the nonprofit United Fruit Company Historical Society, offers detailed and independent information on the United Fruit Company's role in Central America.

The term 'Banana Republic' was coined by American writer O Henry in reference to Honduras.

1821	1822
Central America secedes from Spain on September 15; Honduran José Cecilio del Valle writes the Declaration of Independence	Central America joins the Mexican Empire

president, Chiquita's 1975 and 1976 bribery of the Honduran minister of economy, and in 1998, allegations of repressive labor practices and use of toxic pesticides in Honduras and Colombia. A two-month strike in 1954 – in which as many as 25,000 banana workers and thousands of sympathizers in textile, mining and other trades participated – remains a seminal moment in Honduran labor history. For more on the banana companies, see p235.

RISE OF THE STRONGMEN

The Spanish-American war in 1898 laid the groundwork for increased US involvement in the region. The US averted and mediated a number of conflicts in Central America, including Nicaragua's 1907 invasion of Honduras and a border dispute between Guatemala and Honduras in 1917. Of course, American involvement in those and other disputes had everything to do with protecting American business interests, especially its banana companies, by force if necessary. When workers struck against Standard Fruit Company in 1920, the US sent advisors – and a warship.

In 1932 General Tiburcio Carías Andino was elected president amid a deep worldwide depression. Carías strengthened the armed forces, thus gaining favor with banana companies by opposing strikes, and with foreign governments by strictly adhering to debt payments. He also consolidated his own power, outlawing the Honduran communist party and restricting the press. The Honduran constitution did not allow reelection

Elvia: The Fight for Land and Liberty (1988) is a half-hour PBS documentary about Elvia Alvarado and her path from rural girlhood to national peasant organizer.

Between 1920 and 1923, Honduras had 17 uprisings or coup attempts.

THE SOCCER WAR

There's little love lost between most Hondurans and Salvadorans, who seem to despise each other with equal vigor. Much of the enmity can be traced to a brief but embittered war the two countries fought in 1969, known commonly as the Guerra de Fútbol – the Soccer War.

During the '50s and '60s, El Salvador's flagging economy and severe overpopulation had led as many as 300,000 Salvadorans to cross illegally into Honduras in search of work and arable land. The Honduran economy declined in the same period, and Hondurans began to blame Salvadoran immigrants for stealing jobs and depressing wages. In June 1969 Honduras announced it would begin expelling illegal Salvadoran immigrants; hundreds were deported, and many thousands left on their own accord. Honduran media continued the blame-game, while Salvadoran reports alleged abuse by Honduran police and immigration officers.

That same month, by chance, the two countries were competing against each other in a World Cup soccer qualifying match. At the game, which was played in San Salvador, Salvadoran fans attacked Hondurans, and destroyed and ridiculed the Honduran flag and anthem. Back in Honduras, angry Hondurans assaulted Salvadorans on the streets.

Tensions soared and on July 14, El Salvador invaded its neighbor. Its troops penetrated several kilometers into Honduran territory and captured the western town of Nueva Ocotepeque. Honduras responded with air strikes, destroying military installations and oil and gas storage tanks.

The Soccer War lasted just four days; around 2000 people died, mostly Honduran civilians, and as many as 100,000 Salvadorans fled or were expelled. Relations between the countries took years to mend, and in many ways never have. (The official peace treaty wasn't ratified until 1980.) Relations between the two countries were tested again not long thereafter, when El Salvador erupted into civil war, bringing fresh waves of refugees across the border into Honduras.

1823	1838
Mexican emperor Agustine Inturbide overthrown; Central American states form independent Central American Federation	Central American Federation collapses; Honduras declares independence on November 15

so Carías had it amended, extending the presidential term from four to six years. He served as a virtual dictator, and did not step down until 1949, and only under pressure from the US.

And the Sea Shall Hide Them (2005) by William Jackson is the true story of the murder of ten crew members and passengers aboard the *Olympia* as it sailed from Utila to Roatán in 1905.

In 1956 a power grab by the country's vice president prompted a military coup, the first (but not the last) in Honduran history. The military soon stepped aside for civilian elections, but a new constitution ratified in 1957 made the head of the armed forces – not the president – the country's top military authority. In 1963, ten days before the next presidential election, the military again seized power. Colonel López Arellano suspended elections for two years, then ran himself (and won). He served the full six-year term, notable for his authoritarian excess and disregard for bureaucratic process. He stepped aside for civilian elections in 1971, only to be reinstalled a year later following another military coup.

In 1939 American explorer John Lloyd Stephens purchased Copán ruins for US$50 from the landowner who considered the land useless – too rocky, it seems.

A succession of military leaders, each as corrupt and ineffective as the last, ruled the country from 1972 to 1981. Arellano was removed following allegations he had accepted a US$1.25 million bribe from United Brands Company (formerly United Fruit Company); for his part, United Brands chief Eli Black committed suicide by jumping from his New York City office window when the accusations surfaced. Arellano was succeeded by General Juan Alberto Melgar Castro, who succumbed to a scandal implicating members of the military with murder and drug trafficking and was replaced by General Policarpo Paz García. Paz García was the only one to follow through with a long-standing promise to return Honduras to civilian rule. In 1980, voters elected a congress, and in 1981, a president. Honduras' era of military rule was over.

LATE 20TH CENTURY
The 1980s

During the 1980s, Honduras found itself surrounded on all sides by political upheaval and popular uprisings. In Nicaragua, the Somoza dictatorship was overthrown by Sandinista rebels in 1979, its guardsmen fleeing across the border into Honduras. The following year, full-scale war broke out in El Salvador as the government cranked up its repression of opposition leaders (Archbishop Oscar Romero was assassinated in March 1980) and the new Nicaraguan government provided insurgents with a fresh supply of weapons. Meanwhile, the civil war in Guatemala continued unabated.

In the 1980s the exchange rate was two lempiras for one US dollar.

Although Honduras experienced some unrest, the country never broke into out-and-out civil war, a fact that is puzzling to many observers. Certainly the conditions for civil unrest were there: military rule, a repressed (but organized) working class, a history of foreign meddling and exploitation, especially by the US, not to mention the example set by its neighbors.

Historians and political scientists point to a variety of factors to explain Honduras' emergence from the 1980s revolution-free. The long-standing domination of the banana companies seems to have prevented the development of a native-born economic and political elite. Honduras did not have the Somozas, whose excesses of wealth and power in Nicaragua

1856	1899
William Walker invades Nicaragua; he is expelled a year later; then returns and is captured and executed in 1860	Vaccaro brothers found a banana export company that would eventually become Standard Fruit Company

were legendary, or the 'fourteen families' of El Salvador whose control of the coffee industry and connections with the military turned the country into an agricultural oligarchy.

This in turn opened political space for genuine agrarian reform, the lack of which had heightened working-class frustration and militancy in other countries. Honduras has long had one of Central America's most effective and organized labor movements. Despite the overwhelming power of banana interests, Honduran campesinos and other workers have consistently managed to wrest concessions (and accept compromises) without resorting to violence. Notably, labor disputes in Honduras have rarely included a call for upending the government, rather the enforcement of existing laws. The Honduran military, more democratic and less beholden to the nation's elite than in other countries, played a more stabilizing, not repressive, role.

Of course, the US had a powerful interest in keeping Honduras stable. With Marxist revolutions erupting on all sides (and Cuban and Soviet influence plain to see) the US viewed Honduras as a crucial battleground in its effort to halt the so-called 'domino effect' and the spread of communism in the Americas. Economic aid poured into Honduras, quickly making it one of the top-ten recipients of US military and economic aid. In return, the US used Honduras as a staging ground for counterinsurgency efforts throughout the region. Nicaraguan refugee camps in Honduras were used as bases for a US-sponsored undeclared covert war against the Sandinista government, which became known as the Contra war. At the same time the US was training the Salvadoran military at Salvadoran refugee camps inside Honduras.

Economic aid slowed local opposition, but it wasn't long before Hondurans began agitating against US militarization in their country. Demonstrations drew 60,000 demonstrators in Tegucigalpa and 40,000 in San Pedro Sula, and a few nascent revolutionary groups appeared. In reply, military commanders ordered the kidnapping and killing of hundreds of opposition and student leaders – a first for Honduras. The tactic backfired, swelling the ranks of demonstrators and alienating many in the military establishment, who were themselves growing uneasy about the army's complicity with increasingly brutal US-sponsored conflicts in the region. In March 1984 the military's pro-American commander was toppled in a bloodless coup by his fellow officers. General Walter López Reyes was appointed the successor, and the Honduran government promptly announced it would reexamine US military presence in the country. In August 1984 it suspended US training of Salvadoran military within its borders.

In 1986 Washington was rocked with revelations that the Reagan Administration had secretly and illegally used money from the sale of arms to Iran to support anti-Sandinista Contras operating out of Honduras. The scandal rekindled demonstrations in Honduras; in November 1988, the Honduran government refused to sign a new military agreement with the US, and then-president José Azcona Hoyo said the Contras would have to leave Honduras. With the election of Violeta Chamorro as president of Nicaragua in 1990, the Contra war ended and the Contras were finally out of Honduras.

US military aid to Honduras jumped from US$3.3 million in 1980 to US$31.3 million in 1982.

http://nsarchive .chadwyck.com, the Digital National Security Archive, contains every officially released document related to the Iran-Contra affair and subsequent congressional investigation; registration required for access.

1908–25	1932–49
Honduras endures period of severe instability, with numerous attempted coups	Although elected fairly, Tiburcio Carías Andino rules as a virtual dictator, repeatedly revising the Constitution to extend his term

The 1990s

Elections in 1989 ushered in Rafael Leonardo Callejas Romero of the National Party, who had lost in 1985, to the presidency in Honduras; he won 51% of the votes and assumed office in January 1990. Early that year, the new administration instituted a severe economic-austerity

HURRICANE MITCH

Before Hurricane Wilma in 2005, Hurricane Mitch was the most powerful Atlantic hurricane ever recorded, with peak sustained winds of 290km/hour (180 mph). It was the most deadly since the Great Hurricane of 1750, with over 9000 confirmed deaths and an equal number still missing and presumed dead. Every country in Central America was affected, plus Mexico and the United States; only Belize escaped with no confirmed casualties. Honduras took the heaviest blow, with around 6000 confirmed dead and several thousand missing. Nicaragua was the next worst hit; more then 3000 people died, including 2000 who were buried when the crater of a volcano filled with water and collapsed, unleashing a catastrophic, 5-mile-wide mudslide.

The slow-moving storm made landfall east of La Ceiba on October 29, 1998 and then simply sat there – for four days. Honduran officials had had time to evacuate some 100,000 people from the coastal areas, including 45,000 from the Bay Islands. But the storm smashed through the heart of Honduras – in fact, the heaviest rainfall was in Choluteca, the country's southernmost major city, where 18in of rain fell in a single day. Up to 3ft of rain fell in most areas, twice that amount in the mountains. Most of the deaths came from flooding and landslides. As usual, the poor were the hardest hit, from rural campesinos to whole families swept from squatter camps alongside the Río Choluteca in Tegucigalpa. One woman, Laura Arriola de Guity, was rescued 80km out to sea, having been swept from her home by the storm surge. She survived for six days on a makeshift raft, eating coconuts and pineapples she found floating in the water. Spotted by a search plane, Arriola was returned home only to find her husband and three children had been killed in the storm.

The property damage was equally staggering. In Honduras, the destruction included the decimation of 70% of roads and virtually every bridge in the country. Thirty-three thousand homes were destroyed and another 55,000 damaged, leaving 20% of the population without shelter. At least 25 villages were wiped from the map. Fifty thousand cows and 70% of the nation's crops were lost. In all, Honduras suffered an estimated US$2.5 billion in damages.

The international community responded with a massive relief effort, but as in so many other natural disasters, funds dried up as the initial emergency subsided. Some US$9 billion was pledged; most never materialized and what did was often in the form of loans. Europe did not deliver on its US$250 million dollar pledge until three years after the storm. The US was the largest donor, giving around US$640 million in various relief and reconstruction projects. But that fell short of its initial $900 million pledge, and the US Congress placed a two-year deadline on all projects. Much of the work was done haphazardly or left unfinished, and news reports told of new houses without water or electrical wiring. Three years after the storm, as many as 20,000 Hondurans displaced by the storm still lived in temporary housing.

The recovery effort did have its successes; many of the houses, roads and bridges were built to exceed pre-Mitch standards. Farmers were encouraged to use relief money to plant a variety of crops, which lessened the blow when prices for coffee and other commodities plummeted in the early 2000s.

The storm's physical effects are slowly disappearing, but it dealt a social and emotional blow that has yet to heal. A decade on, many Hondurans still point to El Mitch as the root of the country's current woes, and their own.

1954	1969
Thirty thousand banana workers strike for better working conditions	Contentious soccer game between Honduras and El Salvador provokes a six-day battle known as the 'Soccer War'

program, which provoked widespread alarm, unrest and protest. Callejas had promised to keep the lempira stable; instead during his tenure the lempira's value jumped from around two lempiras to eight against the US dollar. Prices rose dramatically to keep pace with the US dollar, but salaries lagged behind. Hondurans grew poorer and poorer, a trend that continues today.

In the elections of November 1993, Callejas was convincingly beaten by Carlos Roberto Reina Idiaquez of the center-left Liberal Party, who campaigned on a platform of moral reform, promising to attack government corruption and reform state institutions, including the judicial system and the military. Reina had inherited an economically depressed country and a currency that seemed to be in an unstoppable slide. By 1996 it had fallen past 12 lempiras to the US dollar and was heading for 13; today it is at nearly 20.

The two-lempira bank note features the town of Amapala on Isla del Tigre.

On January 27, 1998, Carlos Roberto Flores Facusse took office as Honduras' fifth democratically elected president. A member of the Liberal Party, like his predecessors, he was elected with a 10% margin over his nearest rival – National Party nominee Nora de Melgar – in elections that were considered fair and clean. He instigated a program of reform and modernization of the economy. The arrival of Hurricane Mitch (see boxed text opposite) on October 1998, at that time the strongest Atlantic hurricane on record, dashed those plans. In fact, President Flores would later say the storm had erased 50 years of progress in Honduras.

The five stars on the flag represent the members of the former Federal Republic of Central America (ie Costa Rica, El Salvador, Guatemala, Honduras, and Nicaragua).

THE 21ST CENTURY

Honduras' tourist industry was just recovering from Hurricane Mitch, when the September 11, 2001 terror attacks slashed the number of travelers once more, especially the all-important American diver market. Later that year Hondurans elected Ricardo Maduro as their president, on promises to promote tourism and, more importantly, to reduce crime.

Gang violence was then – and still is today – the prevailing preoccupation of average Hondurans. Rival gangs (*maras*) have spread to Honduras from El Salvador, where gang members deported from the US, especially Los Angeles, had taken root. (Central American countries have long called on the US to stop deporting known gang members but to no avail – some 20,000 felons were sent to Central America between 2000 and 2004.) Maduro's own son was kidnapped and murdered in 1997, and he promised a get-tough approach to gangs. Maduro proposed legislation called 'Mano Dura' (Hard Hand), which dramatically increased penalties for gang-related crimes, and broadened the definition of 'illicit association'. The gang violence has been curbed and convictions have risen but with these changes come disturbing allegations of government-sponsored 'death squads' and prisoner abuse. (See boxed text p40 for more info.)

www.mayispeakfreely .org is a left-leaning website with detailed information of human rights issues in Honduras and other countries, including up-to-date 'News in Brief' section.

Maduro was succeeded in November 2005 elections by Manuel Zelaya, a cowboy hat-wearing rancher from Olancho. On April 1 2006, Honduras became the second Central American country, after El Salvador, to implement the Central America and Dominican Republic Free Trade Agreement, or CAFTA-DR. The trade deal, signed into law in 2005 by US President George W Bush after a bitter congressional fight, will end tariffs on as much as US$33 billion in goods and services when in full

1980–89	1998
United States uses Honduras as a base for Contra war against the new Sandinistas government in Nicaragua	Hurricane Mitch causes more than 6000 deaths and US$2.5 billion in damage in Honduras alone

GANGS IN HONDURAS

Mara Salvatrucha, or MS-13, is considered by some to be the most dangerous criminal gang in the Americas. It emerged in the 1980s from the poor, tough streets of Los Angeles, and its earliest members were Salvadoran children of refugees fleeing a US-sponsored civil war. M-18, a rival *mara* (gang), formed at the same time.

The gangs jumped to Central America in the 1990s, as new immigration laws had alien criminals deported rather than tried in US courts. The gangs quickly took root, with easier access to weapons, less-effective policing, and a virtually bottomless pool of poor, disaffected youth. Today, MS-13 and M-18 have around 100,000 members between them, mostly in El Salvador, Honduras, Guatemala, Nicaragua, Mexico and the US. In Honduras around 30,000 young people are thought to be gang members.

Mara members are known for their extensive tattooing and the gruesomeness of their attacks (machetes are popular weapons). Most attacks are on opposing gang members, but a few incidents – like a 2004 assault on a public bus outside San Pedro Sula that killed 28 people, including four children – gained international attention.

Honduras' former president Ricardo Maduro was the first Central American leader to adopt harsh antigang policies known as Mano Dura ('Hard Hand'). The policies made tattoos, hand signals and writing graffiti crimes of 'illicit association,' punishable by long jail terms. Mano Dura slowed gang recruitment and activity, but prisons quickly swelled beyond capacity and abuse allegations mounted. In 2003 a fire at a Honduran prison killed 68 suspected gang members, but an investigation found at least 59 had in fact been shot by the guards. A year later, another prison fire killed 104 suspected gang members as guards stood by doing nothing.

Off-duty officers and private security guards have also allegedly formed vigilante groups, reminiscent of military 'death squads' of the not-so-distant past. More than 2000 children and young adults have been killed in Honduras between 1998 and 2004; researchers say 15% to 20% of the killings were conducted by the police or with tacit police approval. In 2002 President Maduro took the unusual step of acknowledging extrajudicial killings but said a government study had found police involvement in only 23 cases in the previous five years. For now most Hondurans, unnerved by images of gang brutality, seem willing to overlook human-rights issues if they continue to stem the violence.

Enrique's Journey (2006) by Sonia Nazario is the book version of a Pulitzer-winning *Los Angeles Times* series about a Honduran boy who travels from Tegucigalpa to North Carolina, in search of his mother.

effect. The pact covers the US, El Salvador, Honduras, Guatemala, Nicaragua, Costa Rica and the Dominican Republic. All but Costa Rica have ratified the pact, but were required to make legal and regulatory changes before implementing it. Advocates say it will open markets to US businesses, especially farmers and ranchers, while providing manufacturing jobs to Central Americans that would otherwise go to Asia. American labor unions fought the plan, saying it will take jobs from Americans and did not provide enough protections for Central American workers. In Central America opposition came from the left which predicted the plan, like NAFTA before it, would lead to increased disenfranchisement of small farmers and business owners.

2004	2006
Gang members kill 28 people on a public bus in San Pedro Sula, epitomizing growing gang violence in Central America	Manuel 'Mel' Zelaya becomes president and implements the Central America and Dominican Republic Free Trade Agreement (CAFTA-DR)

The Culture

THE NATIONAL PSYCHE

Honduras is a very diverse society, so any attempt to define a national psyche is necessarily flawed. The experience and perspective of a ladino business owner in San Pedro Sula and a Tawahka farmer in the Moskitia could hardly be more different. And yet moving around the country (in a way few Honduras themselves ever do) it is possible to discern certain commonalities among Hondurans, a way of seeing things and reacting to them. From those common tendencies emerge what might be called a common consciousness.

It's safe to say that the attitude of most Hondurans is subdued compared to that of their neighbors. Guatemala, El Salvador and Nicaragua all fought fierce civil wars in the 1980s – how is it possible that Honduras, which had many of the same economic and social conditions, did not also erupt into class warfare? There are many answers to that question, starting with a very simple one: the United States didn't let it happen. But there is also a prevailing go-with-the-flow attitude among Hondurans that surely played a role. It is unlike most Hondurans to raise their voices or complain too vociferously, whether for having to wait in another seemingly endless line, or for having been born poor with little means of changing one's circumstances.

Which is not to say that Hondurans are accepting of injustice, or will turn a blind eye toward poor or unfair treatment, at least within a person's own sphere. Honduras has long been a deeply unionized country, and Hondurans have used collective action with great success to exact land reforms or force changes in pay or working conditions. There is a rich tradition of organizing, especially among the poor and the landless. Demands tend to be modest, but are pursued with unwavering convictions.

Understanding the nexus of those two tendencies – mellow and accepting on one hand, committed to justice and collective action on the other – is the key to understanding the Honduran national psyche. In one sense, Hondurans simply have a higher level of tolerance. Whereas Salvadorans and Guatemalans are quick to decry a perceived wrong, Hondurans are more likely to take a wait-and-see approach. You might compare Hondurans to, say, an especially large stone. It takes much more pushing to get it moving, but once moving, its momentum is almost impossible to oppose.

LIFESTYLE

Honduras is a deeply stratified country, where the rich are super rich and the poor are desperately poor, and lifestyle is largely determined by the accident of one's birth. For the very wealthy, Honduras offers virtually all the luxuries that wealth commands in more developed countries, whether it's import cars – SUVs are extremely popular, even with US$4 per gallon gasoline – or regular trips to beachside resorts in Roatán, New Orleans or Miami. The country's elite is divided between Tegucigalpa, where government and Honduras' nascent entertainment industry are based, and San Pedro Sula, where private business executives tend to live.

For the destitute, life can be very difficult. The official minimum daily wage is US$3.15, though people working on the fringes of the economy earn even less. The urban poor are crowded into decaying neighborhoods – often rife with gang violence – and shantytowns built on unused hillsides

More than half the population – around four million – is registered to vote.

Approximately 10% of the population – 700,000 Hondurans – live and work abroad.

www.honduras.com /catracho-forum is a Honduran chat room with forums on politics, religion, food, current events, sports, and women's issues.

and river banks, vulnerable to flooding and mudslides. The rural and coastal poor seem somehow less desperate, since, in the end, the land and the ocean provide at least minimal sustenance. But life in those areas poses its own set of challenges: Garífuna communities are in the fight of their lives to hang onto their traditional lands, which developers have long eyed for beach resorts. Likewise, farmers struggle to hold onto their modest plots, against the expansion of logging and commercial farming.

Family life in Honduras is similar to that of much of Central America, where strong Catholic and other religious traditions butt up against the practical concerns of life in a developing country. Family is deeply important, and ideally children grow up, marry, start a family and settle down near their parents (and their grandparents before them). However, the reality is that may families, especially rural and small town ones, are scattered by the need to find work; countless families have husbands, mother, brothers, sisters working in San Pedro Sula, Tegucigalpa, the Bay Islands (where there's a major construction boom) or else in El Salvador or the United States.

The same goes for sex and marriage: traditional beliefs run deep, but frequently bend under the pressure of young people living without one or both or their parents, or spouses separated for long periods of time. Divorce, sex before marriage, children out of wedlock: though frowned upon, they are a relatively common and tolerated aspect of modern Honduran life. Only abortion and homosexuality (especially in the age of AIDS) remain deeply taboo.

El Espíritu de Mi Mamá (My Mother's Spirit; 2003) is a film directed by Alí Allié which focuses on a Garífuna house-keeper in Los Angeles, who returns to Honduras to lay her mother's spirit to rest.

ECONOMY

Honduras is one of the poorest countries in the Western Hemisphere, along with Haiti, Nicaragua, Guyana, and Bolivia. Nearly two-thirds of Hondurans live in poverty – and 45% in extreme poverty – and the unemployment rate hovers at 28%. Honduras' GDP is US$7.5 billion; with a population of seven million, its per capita GDP is just over US$1000.

Like many developing countries, Honduras is saddled with enormous foreign debt, around US$5.6 billion. It was one of only seven countries outside of sub-Saharan Africa to qualify for the Heavily Indebted Poor Countries (HIPC) Initiative, which went into effect for Honduras in July 2006. Yet the HIPC relief amounts to only US$1.3 billion and Honduras will continue to face some US$370 million in annual debt servicing.

There are almost three times as many cellular phones (1,114,400) as landlines (400,000) in Honduras.

The Honduran economy was for many years almost entirely dependent on coffee and banana exports, and controlled by Standard and United Fruit Companies. Those companies – now Dole and Chiquita, respectively – still exert powerful economic and political leverage, but the economy as a whole has significantly diversified in the last two decades. Honduras has also expanded its nontraditional exports, such as shrimp and melons, and promoted tourism. *Maquilas,* which import US yarn and fabric and turn them into clothing for export, now employ 130,000 Hondurans, mostly around San Pedro Sula and Puerto Cortes. Remittances from abroad total some US$1.4 billion per year, or 15% of the country's foreign exchange.

The controversial Central America and Dominican Republic Free Trade Agreement (CAFTA-DR) went into effect in Honduras in April 2006. The agreement will lower tariffs and trade barriers for scores of goods, services, agricultural products and investments; supporters say it will stimulate the economies of Central American countries while critics say multinational corporations will squeeze out small businesses. CAFTA also includes safeguards for labor rights and environmental protection – it remains to be seen if it will help to end illegal pine and mahogany logging in Honduras (see p56) or accelerate it, as some predict.

POPULATION

Honduras is experiencing the most rapid urbanization in Central America: the urban population was 44% in 1990, but the percentage of the population in cities is expected to hit 59% in 2010. Around 85% to 90% of Hondurans are ladino, a mixture of Spanish and *indígena* (indigenous people). The rest are part of ten different ethnic minorities: some indigenous, some immigrants, others a mixture of the two.

The Tolupanes (also called Jicaque or Xicaque) live in small villages dotting the departments of Yoro and Francisco Morazán (see p112). They are thought to be one of the oldest indigenous communities in Honduras, having retained certain ancient traditions like making clothing from pounded tree bark (though this is fast disappearing). Reclusive and widely scattered, there were seven Tolupán communities that were not identified as such until the late 1980s.

The Maya-Chortí people live near the Guatemalan border, in the department of Copán. They are embroiled in a bitter land dispute with the government, which has promised to redistribute traditional lands but has found a thousand reasons to delay the process.

The Lenca live in southwestern Honduras in several colonial towns along the namesake Ruta Lenca (see p154). More than other groups, the Lenca have preserved their traditional clothing, easily spotted for their brilliant colors and designs, similar to those seen in Guatemala. The Maya-Chortí live near the Guatemalan border, in the department of Copán (see p137).

The Miskito (see p283) live in La Moskitia, on the northeastern coast and along the Río Coco, which forms the border between Honduras and Nicaragua. Miskitos are more involved with tourism than other groups, serving as guides and boatmen for the growing influx of visitors to the Mosquito Coast.

The Pech live in the interior river regions of La Moskitia. Though generally less outgoing than the Miskitos, the Pech are also involved in tourism to the Moskitia, mainly up the Río Plátano is Las Marías and beyond.

The Tawahka (see p296) also live in the interior of La Moskitia in the area around the Río Patuca designated as the Tawahka Asangni Biosphere Reserve. The Tawahka number less than a thousand, though their language has been preserved.

The Garífuna live on Honduras' north coast, from La Moskitia all the way across to Belize. Other Black people – descendants of immigrants from the Cayman Islands and other Caribbean islands, who came to work on the banana plantations – live on the north coast as well as the Bay Islands (see p207).

SPORTS

As in most Latin American countries, *fútbol* (soccer) is the number one spectator sport in Honduras. The country's soccer league, **La Liga Mayor de Fútbol Francisco Morazán** (Francisco Morazán Major League Soccer; www.hondurasfutbol .com), is made up of 10 teams from around the country. The league has two seasons – one from February to June, the other August to October; games

www.stanford.edu/group /arts/honduras/Teaching tool produced by the Latin American Studies Department at Stanford University, with extensive information on Garífuna history, culture and current issues.

Daylight Savings Time was adopted for the first time in 1994 but abandoned the same year.

Honduras' national soccer team qualified to play in the World Cup only once, in 1982.

Outfielder Gerald Young is the only Honduran to have played in Major League Baseball. He played for the Astros (1987–92), Rockies (1993) and Cardinals (1994).

are played around the country, although there are only three stadiums – in Tegucigalpa, San Pedro Sula, and La Ceiba.

Baseball is a distant second in popularity with a semiprofessional league, La Liga Mayor de Beísbol Francisco Morazán (Francisco Morazán Major League Baseball). It is made up of five teams from around the country, and is particularly popular on the Bay Islands and the north coast, where people keep track of the US major leagues.

Cockfighting is seen to a much lesser extent than even baseball, mostly in small villages and during the town saint's day festival.

MULTICULTURALISM

Honduras is surely one of Central America's most diverse nations, with 10 distinctive ethnic groups – five indigenous, and five that emerged from post-Conquest mixing and immigration. The groups vary in history, size, language and appearance, but together form part of Honduras' fascinating ethnic milieu.

The largest group are ladinos (or mestizos), who make up what can be called 'mainstream' Honduras. Spanish-speaking, they are descended from intermixing among European explorers and the indigenous people they encountered. Today ladinos, who range from very fair skinned to fairly dark, dominate most aspects of Honduran politics and economy.

Honduras' largest indigenous group are the Lenca, concentrated in southwestern Honduras (hence La Ruta Lenca, or Lenca Route). The Lenca are believed to have descended from Chibcha-speaking Amerindians of present-day Colombia and Venezuela who immigrated to Honduras around 3000 years ago. The Lenca were a large enough group to develop regional subgroups, mostly lowland vs highland, and internecine rivalries and even warfare were common. To minimize fighting, the Lenca developed peace treaties that were reaffirmed every year in elaborate ceremonies known as *guancascos*, which are still practiced in many communities today. The Lenca language has been lost, and what few non-Spanish words remain in the common vernacular are mostly Nahuatl, evidence of the strong Aztec and Central Mexican influence on Lenca society that took place before and just after the conquest. For more details on the Lenca, see p161.

You'll find links to schools, Spanish language programs, and cultural centers in Honduras at www.world wide.edu/ci/honduras.

The Maya-Chortí are the next largest of Honduras' indigenous groups. Concentrated in the Copán Valley, the Chortí are descended from the builders of the great Copán temples. Today Chortí communities are desperately poor, riven by drugs and alcohol, land loss and unemployment. Their circumstances are accentuated by the thriving tourism industry in Copán village. But if Chortí were once resigned to their circumstances, they are no longer; since the early '90s, indigenous activists have led a bitter fight to recover their traditional farmland, much of it acquired by private landowners during government-sanctioned land-grabs in the 1950s. Chortí protesters have occupied the Copán archaeological site several times to draw attention to their fight, and have paid dearly for their newfound outspokenness: dozens have been murdered or jailed for their political work (p153).

The Pech and Tawahka indigenous groups are both found deep in the interior of La Moskitia, and though ethnically distinct, share a common history. Both groups are descended from the Chibcha-speaking migration from South America around 1000 BC, which also gave rise to the Lenca. Both groups lived over a large area in pre-Conquest times, but receded into the rainforest in the face of Spanish incursion (and Miskito collusion; see opposite). Today both groups live mostly by subsistence

HOMOSEXUALS IN HONDURAS

With the emergence of AIDS in the mid-1980s, homosexuals in Honduras suddenly faced a dual challenge. The disease raged through the gay community, quickly making Honduras the 'AIDS capital of Central America' (a distinction it still holds). But almost of equal import was the change in attitudes toward gays by the general population. Though homosexuality was never widely accepted, it was generally tolerated. With AIDS came a dramatic increase in antihomosexual rhetoric and fear-mongering, and before long, physical assaults. In fact, the government began a campaign of harassment and marginalization that continues today.

In 2000 Amnesty International issued a scathing report of government-sponsored human rights abuses. The group pointed to more than 200 murders of gay and transsexual sex workers in the previous 10 years that had received only perfunctory police investigation, or none at all. Amnesty International also accused the government of hampering gay organizations by blocking their registration as nonprofits. In May 2002, then-President Ricardo Maduro signed the 'Social and Co-Existence Law,' which ostensibly targeted gangs and organized crime but in effect gave police the authority to wantonly arrest gays and lesbians (usually for the purpose of preventing 'amoral behavior'). In 2004 the mayor of San Pedro Sula – which has Honduras' most visible and outspoken gay population – ordered the raiding of a gay club, resulting in multiple arrests. And in early 2005, a constitutional amendment was unanimously ratified, prohibiting gay marriage and adoption by same-sex couples.

The gay community has responded to antigay sentiment with activism of their own. Several advocacy organizations have been founded to help homosexuals to protect their civil rights. As early as 1988, an organization called Las Hijas del Maíz (Daughters of the Corn) was active in supporting gays and lesbians, and promoting tolerance. At least three organizations are presently active in Tegucigalpa and San Pedro Sula; see p308 for contact information.

farming; the Pech are increasingly involved with ecotourism (mostly as guides in Las Marías; see p289). In 1999 the Tawahka (the smallest of the Honduran indigenous groups) won the establishment of the Tawahka Asangni Biosphere Reserve, protecting their ancestral lands; for more see p296.

The Tolupanes are the fifth and last indigenous group of Honduras. While some ethnologists believe they, like the other groups, emerged from the Chibcha migration around 3000 years ago, others believe the Tolupanes arrived from the north at least 5000 years ago. It is known that the Tolupanes once ranged over virtually all of present-day Honduras, but retreated into the mountains around today's Yoro rather than face the enslavement and disease brought by the Spanish. A deeply reclusive group, only a few pockets still speak the Tolupan tongue. For more info see p112.

Two of Honduras' best known ethnic groups are not truly indigenous, though they are often portrayed that way. Like mainstream ladinos, the Miskito and Garífuna people are the result of interracial mixing. In the case of the Miskito, it was between an unknown indigenous group in La Moskitia and African slaves, who most likely escaped slave ships and swam ashore. The Miskito also have English blood, from English pirates who used lagoons in La Moskitia as a hideaway. In fact British pirates befriended and armed the Miskito as a way to undermine Spanish control and to ward off other native groups. Today the Miskito are the dominant ethnic group in La Moskitia, and make up the majority of guides, boatmen, and guesthouse operators that travelers are likely to encounter.

The Garífuna are also a people of mixed race; in their case, freed African slaves with Caribe and Arawak native people who had migrated to the Caribbean islands, including St Vincent, many millennia prior. After

The term 'catracho' (a nickname Hondurans commonly use for themselves), is derived from the last name of General Florencio Xatruch, who successfully led the army against William Walker's 1857 invasion.

being literally dumped by British ships on the island of Roatán in 1787, the Garífuna have since spread all along the north coast and into Guatemala and Belize. Unemployment, especially among men, is a longtime issue for the Garífuna; many men have left Honduras to seek jobs in the United States. In fact, as many Garífuna live outside Honduras – around 100,000 – as inside it.

Other ethnic groups in Honduras include white islanders and non-Garífuna black islanders. The former are descended from British pirates, the latter from slaves or free Blacks from British-controlled Cayman Islands. Both primarily speak English, with a familiar Jamaican lilt. Finally, Chinese immigrants number relatively few, but are very visible in many communities, typically running Chinese restaurants.

MEDIA

Almas de Media Noche (Souls at Midnight; 2002) Honduras' first commercial feature film, written and directed by Juan Carlos Franconi, is a mystery-fantasy about six journalism students investigating a Lenca legend near Lago de Yojoa.

Honduras Tips (www.hondurastips.honduras.com) is a bilingual (English and Spanish) and biannual magazine-directory that makes a handy supplement to any guidebook. Most useful is the bus information in the front, with a guide to which lines go where, and select departure and contact information. It also has information on things to see and do, and places to stay and eat, with maps and photos of most tourist destinations. Theoretically the info is no more than six-months old, but do take some listings with a grain of salt.

Honduras This Week (www.marrder.com/htw) is a weekly English-language newspaper published in Tegucigalpa. The paper makes for interesting reading, covering serious issues of the day – immigration, the economy, environment, crime – along with a fair amount of fluff. It comes out every Saturday and can be found in major hotels and English-language bookshops in Tegucigalpa, San Pedro Sula, La Ceiba, Roatán and Utila.

The **Bay Islands Voice** (www.bayislandsvoice.com) is published twice monthly and includes a wide range of articles about issues facing the Bay Islands, both locals and expats. Mostly in English, and it has a searchable archive online. **Utila East Wind** (www.aboututila.com) is a monthly newspaper focused on Utila. On the **Travel-to-Honduras** (www.travel-to-honduras.com) website, follow the 'articles & news' link for a number of useful pieces, including 'miniguides' to Tegucigalpa, San Pedro Sula and Santa Rosa de Copán.

LOST LANGUAGES

Ethnic minorities make up nearly 15% of the Honduran population, yet only 1% speak an indigenous or minority language. Two of Honduras' major ethnic groups – the Lenca and Maya-Chortí – have lost their ancestral language altogether (though related languages are spoken by Lenca and Maya groups in Guatemala and El Salvador). The Tolupanes, Pech and Tawahka communities are so small – in the case of the Tawahka, less than a thousand members – their language is in danger of disappearing as well.

Bilingual education has been proposed to reclaim and reinforce these languages. But that is much easier said than done: all of Honduras' indigenous languages are fundamentally oral, and a full-scale 'language rescue' program would require establishing a standardized orthography, writing and producing grammar books and dictionaries, and recruiting and training teachers who can teach in both languages. The Honduran government, for one, seems unwilling to make the investment. International efforts have focused more on post-Conquest language groups, especially Miskito and Garífuna, which pose most of the same challenges but have many more active speakers. Those groups also have a more established and active leadership, who are able to mobilize community support and garner international attention.

Honduras has five daily Spanish-language newspapers. **El Heraldo** (www
.elheraldo.hn) and **La Tribuna** (www.latribunahon.com) are published in Tegucigalpa,
La Prensa (www.laprensahn.com), **El Tiempo** (www.tiempo.hn), and **El Nuevo Día** in
San Pedro Sula. Like many media outlets in Latin America, Honduran
newspapers are prone to sensationalism, often running large photos of
auto accidents or gang killings on the front page. Fortunately, coverage
of other subjects, whether politics, the economy or world affairs, is often
much more sober than the bloody front page might otherwise suggest.

www.spanishcourses.info
/OnlineRadioTV/AAA
OnlineRadioStations.htm
includes links to online
radio stations in
Honduras.

RELIGION

The Roman Catholic church has been a powerful institution in Honduras since the colonial era, and a vast majority of Hondurans consider
themselves Catholic. The Constitution calls for the separation of church
and state (and guarantees religious freedom) but the archdiocese receives government subsidies and Catholic instruction is part of the public
school curriculum.

In the 1960s and 1970s, the concept of 'liberation theology' was
adopted by many Honduran priests (and foreign priests working there)
who took up vocal positions against abuse by the Honduran military
and the exploitation of the poor. As in El Salvador and elsewhere, priests
became targets for right-wing attacks, including a notorious incident in
1975 when ten peasants, two students and two priests were murdered by
landowners in Olancho. Around that time, the government also began
arresting and deporting foreign priests who were seen as rabble-rousers,
and community groups that had been linked to the church were shut
down.

Honduran Cardinal Óscar
Andrés Rodríguez was a
candidate for pope in the
papal conclave of 2005.

Although the Moravians had been present since the 1930s in La Moskitia (p299), the 1980s saw a major growth in mainstream evangelical
Protestant denominations around the country. Methodists, Church of
God, Seventh-Day Adventists and the Assemblies of God began promoting their religions, primarily through much-needed social services, and
membership in poor communities rocketed. Today it is estimated that
over 100,000 Hondurans are Protestants.

WOMEN IN HONDURAS

Honduran women enjoy the same legal rights and status as men – they
can vote, own property, and are represented in government. But the majority are afforded a distinctly lower social and economic status, mainly
because of institutional barriers and age-old prejudice. Professional and
wage-earning women receive less pay for performing the same jobs as
men, if they are allowed equal access to those occupations in the first
place. In rural Honduras, women are the driving economic force, producing an estimated 60% to 80% of agricultural products consumed in
Honduras, not to mention their contribution in the form of domestic
work and artesanía production. And yet, Honduran women in general
live in greater poverty than men and have a higher mortality rate. Breast,
ovarian and cervical cancers are leading killers, and nearly 22% of wom-
en's deaths between ages 18 and 44 are associated with childbirth, mostly
due to poor access to healthcare.

There are a few good signs; in 2005, more women were elected to
congress than ever before – 32 of the 128 seats were occupied by women –
and there are nine female justices on the 17-member Supreme Court,
including the chief justice. Many hope that with the growing numbers
of women in positions of legislative power, circumstances for all women
in Honduras will change for the better.

1000 WOMEN FOR PEACE

One Thousand Women for the Nobel Peace Prize 2005 was a project, conceived by a member of the Swiss parliament, to identify 1000 women around the world doing peace-promoting work and nominate them collectively for the 2005 Nobel Peace Prize. Only 12 women have won the prize since its inception in 1901, compared to 80 men and 20 organizations.

Of the 1000 women from 150 countries selected for the group, six were from Honduras. They came from a variety of fields, reflecting the organizers' purposefully broad definition of peace work. The nominees included: Reina Isabel Cálix, peasant organizer and educator with National Peasants Union; Albertina García Argueta, of the National Organization of Native Lencas of Honduras; Bertha Oliva, coordinator of the Committee of Families of the Disappeared in Honduras; Itsmania Pineda, president of gang-alternatives group Xibalbá; Leticia Oyela, a lawyer and historian at the UNAH (the Independant National University of Honduras); and María Esther Ruiz Ortega, a rural education and development activist with New Hope Women's Association.

The idea was to nominate the thousand women en masse, but Nobel rules restrict the prize to no more than three recipients. So the project drew three names from the list to make up the official nomination, and to determine who would accept the prize on behalf of the group. The rules also prohibit lobbying for the award. In fact, Nobel nominees are never officially announced (only the winners) and nominators are discouraged from releasing the names of their nominees. In this case, even the name '1000 Women for the Nobel Peace Prize 2005' stretches both those rules, and organizers had to get special permission to use it.

In the end, the prize went to the International Atomic Energy Agency and its director general Mohamed El Baradei, for efforts to curtail nuclear proliferation. But the '1000 Women' project proved uncommonly compelling; the group published a book with pictures and biographies of the women, and has since changed its name to **1000 PeaceWomen Across the Globe** (www.1000peacewomen .org) and continues to draw attention to women peaceworkers worldwide.

ARTS

Honduras is not as renowned for its arts as nearby Guatemala and El Salvador, but it does have some interesting art forms, both artesanía and fine art.

Cabbage and Kings (1904), O Henry's first book, is a collection of humorous interconnected vignettes based in 'Coralio', a fictional village fashioned after Trujillo, where the famous author spent a year avoiding embezzlement charges in Texas.

Artesanía

Travelers are most likely to encounter – and are inclined to buy – folk art produced in the country's rural or ethnic-minority areas. Lenca 'negativo' pottery is recognizable for its black-and-white design, usually buffed to a high shine. Excellent replicas of Maya masks and glyphs can be bought fairly cheaply in Copán Ruínas. Miskito children in Las Marías are sure to find newly arrived travelers and break out a large collection of balsa-wood animals and miniature *pipantes*. Also produced in the Moskitia, though easier to find in artesanía shops elsewhere, are *cuadros de tunu*, designs made from tree bark pounded into a thick paper. Shops specializing in Garífuna folk art often carry 'naïf' style paintings, as well as handmade *tambores*, and souvenir-size *rayadores*, wood planks embedded with hundreds of tiny sharp stones and used for grating yucca. Other popular arts include basketry, embroidery, and leather goods.

Literature

Lucila Gamero de Medina (1873–1964) was born in Danlí and is considered one of the first Central American female writers, publishing stories as early as 1894. Her novel *Blanco Olmeda* was published in 1903 and was the first novel published by a Honduran writer, male or female. That, and other favorites like *Amalia Montiel* and *Adriana y Margarita*, are still widely read today.

José Trinidad Reyes (1797–1855) was a poet and playwright who founded the National University of Honduras and introduced the printing press to Honduras. José Cecilio del Valle, known as *El Sabio* (the Wise) was another important writer and philosopher, born in the southern Honduran city of Choluteca (for more on del Valle, see p100).

In modern times, important writers include Ramón Amaya-Amador (1916–1966), a one-time banana fieldworker turned prolific journalist who fled Honduras because of political persecution in 1944. He wrote over 30 books, among them *Prisión Verde* (1945), *Los Brujos de Ilamatepeque* (1958) and *Operación Gorila* (1965).

Roberto Quesada, one of Honduras' top living authors, has written *Los Barcos* (The Ships; 1992), *El Humano y La Diosa* (The Human and the Goddess; 1996) and *The Big Banana* (1999).

Visual Arts

Honduras' most characteristic style of painting is known as 'naïf' and was popularized by José Antonio Velásquez (1906–83), one of Honduras' most enduring visual artists. His paintings depict scenes of typical mountain villages, especially his adopted hometown of San Antonio de Oriente, with cobblestone lanes winding among houses with white adobe walls and red tile roofs. Velásquez reached an international audience thanks in large part to the patronage of Wilson Popenoe, the American agronomist who founded the Jardín Botánico Lancetilla and later the Zamorano agricultural school. The Zamorano school has a large collection of Velasquez's work.

Arturo López Rodezno (1906–75) was another influential early painter. A muralist, López Rodezno founded the National School of Arts and Crafts in Comayagüela, where a number of pieces can be viewed.

Other important Honduran painters include Miguel Ángel Ruíz Matute, Arturo Luna and Roque Zalaya, among many others. A 'virtual museum' can be viewed at www.honduras.com/museum/museo.html.

Music & Dance

Most of the music heard in Honduras is a combination of outside influences: Mexican ballads and *rancheras*, Caribbean merengue and salsa, Latin and English-language rock, as well as hip hop and reggueton (hip hop with a blend of Jamaican and Latin American influences).

Music created within Honduras is limited but still interesting: Aurelio Martínez has taken off as one of the stars of the new punta-rock rage, a

Walker (1987) directed by Alex Cox and starring Ed Harris, is a somewhat hallucinogenic portrayal of William Walker and his misadventures in 1850s Central America; it includes a mute lover and anachronisms like helicopters and Zippo lighters.

The Mosquito Coast (1982) by Paul Theroux is a gripping novel about a brilliant inventor who, fed up with American society, takes his family to a remote Honduran village and goes mad in the process.

PUNTA DANCE

Sometimes called *bangidy*, *punta* is one of the most recognizable Garífuna dances in Honduras. It is typically performed by a pair of dancers, swinging their hips and moving their arms to a throbbing, haunting sound made by two large drums, maracas, a conch and a turtle-shell xylophone. As they move, the dancers chant words like a litany, to which the audience responds. Although the meaning of the dance is debated, most agree that it was originally performed to mourn the death of a relative; a means to usher the deceased to a restful place so that they could be in peace.

Today, a new sound – punta-rock – has been created using the same beats mixed with an electric guitar. Although this new music is all the rage, traditional *punta* dance is still very much alive. Travelers can see it performed in any number of Garífuna festivals held on the north coast. The most famous of them is the Baja Mar Garífuna Festival (p195), during which an all-night dance competition is held among the 36 Garífuna communities that come together for the event.

Los Barcos (1992), written by Roberto Quesada, is a roundabout love story about a young man in La Ceiba, who aspires to be a writer but must work as a fruit picker to support himself.

fusion of traditional Garífuna *punta* with an electric sound. He has produced albums *Songs of the Garífuna, Garífuna Soul* and *Inocencia.*

Karla Lara, a folksy singer-songwriter, produced a popular album in 2004, *Dónde Andar,* and collaborated on the album *Mujer Canción, Canción Mujer* with Guillermo Anderson.

Finally, in the early 1980s, the hard-rock band Khaos was the first Honduran group to make a splash in the emerging *rock en español* scene. The band produced only one album – *Forjado en Rocka* – before breaking up in 1985, but songs like 'Roleando' and 'En las Garras del Diablo' are still popular in Honduras and throughout Central America.

Dance is another popular art form, as most indigenous and ethnic groups have traditional dances. Most notable are the Garífunas of the north coast, known for their distinctive music and dance, including *punta* (see p49) and *wanaragua* (masked warrior dancing) see p262. It's worth checking out a performance by the Ballet Nacional Folklórico Garífuna if you're lucky enough to be in the country when they are.

Environment

THE LAND

Honduras is the second-largest country in Central America, with an area of 112,090 sq km. Over three quarters of Honduras is made up of rugged mountains, a geologic jumble caused by the collision of three tectonic plates. Among the jumble are several discernable mountain ranges, including the massive Sierra Nombre de Dios along the north coast, the eastern Sierra de Agalta and Sierra del Río Tinto, which divide La Moskitia from the rest of the country, and the Sierra del Celaque and Sierra del Merendón in the west along the Salvadoran and Guatemalan borders. The western ranges are home to the country's highest peak – Cerro de las Minas (2849m) in Parque Nacional Montaña de Celaque.

Throughout the mountains there are a number of high valleys, which make ranching and agriculture somewhat more viable, especially in the interior. Many towns and cities, including Tegucigalpa, grew up in such highland valleys. Despite its rugged terrain, Honduras has no volcanoes and relatively little seismic activity, in stark contrast to neighboring Nicaragua, El Salvador and Guatemala.

Honduras has 644km of Caribbean coast, and 124km of Pacific coast, along the Golfo de Fonseca. Both coastal areas are low-lying alluvial plains. Along the Golfo de Fonseca, the lowlands form a strip just 25km wide; it is flat, hot and swampy near the shore – not exactly a welcoming environment for people, but ideal for mangroves and numerous wetland and shallow-water creatures, especially shrimp, shellfish and abundant birdlife.

The north coastal plain has long been the most intensely developed and exploited region in Honduras, enriched by several major rivers and by soils washed down from the Nombre de Dios mountain range. In the northwestern corner of Honduras, the Ulúa and Chamelcón rivers form the huge Valle de Sula, which contains Puerto de Cortés and San Pedro Sula and extends nearly to Lago de Yojoa and Copán Ruínas. This fertile region has supported human settlement for millennia. The central portion of the Caribbean coast has been utilized primarily for large-scale plantations, especially bananas, African palm, and (most recently) pineapples.

La Moskitia is, geologically speaking, part of the northern coastal plain. However the Río Aguán and Río Tinto (aka Río Sico and Río Negro) form natural barriers, as do the Sierra Río Tinto and Sierra de Agalta mountain ranges. La Moskitia is Central America's largest intact rain forest and the largest north of the Amazon; it contains two of the country's longest rivers, the Río Coco and Río Patuca.

WILDLIFE

Some of Honduras' most interesting animals are becoming endangered, primarily due to loss of habitat. The national bird, the *guara roja* or scarlet macaw, is on the endangered species' list, as are some species of *loros* (parrots), manatees, jaguars among others. Nevertheless, there's still plenty of wildlife to see in Honduras, especially in the national parks, wildlife reserves and other protected areas. As more areas become protected, populations of depleted species might be saved from early extinction.

Calling itself the 'global journal of practical ecotourism', www.planeta .com has a number of links and articles about Honduras in the Central America section.

The Bay Islands sit on the Meso-American Barrier Reef, the second longest in the world after the Great Barrier Reef in Australia.

Approximately 81% of Honduras is made up of mountains.

THE BIRDS OF PARADISE

Honduras is a birder's paradise; its variety of eco-systems – cloud forests, pine forests, savannahs, lagoons, mangroves, freshwater lakes and oceans – attracts and hosts an impressive number of birds; 725 species to be exact, in over 58 families, and birders are still counting.

Some favorite places to spot birds include Lago de Yojoa (p175), where it is often related that a birder spotted 37 species in one tree without leaving the front porch of his hotel room; Parque Nacional La Tigra (p91) and Parque Nacional Montaña de Celaque (p163), both cloud forests that are home to brilliantly marked and elusive quetzals (the best time to see them is during the mating season – March to May); Parque Nacional Pico Bonito (p224), where hawks, parrots and swallows can be spotted alongside keel-billed toucans, blue-crowned motmot and white-collared manakins; Reserva De La Biósfera Del Río Plátano (p288), located within the largest rain forest north of the Amazon, which has finds like scarlet macaws, yellow-eared toucanets and jabirus; and the coastal Parque Nacional Jeannette Kawas (p204) as well as the Refugio de Vida Silvestre Cuero y Salado (p222), where the wetlands boast ibis, egrets, roseate spoonbills and other water fowl.

For a wealth of information on birds and birding in Honduras, check out www.birding honduras.com.

Animals

Of the 225 mammal species found in Honduras, almost half are bats.

Honduras is home to over 200 species of mammals, nearly 300 species of reptiles and amphibians, and over 700 species of birds. While an exhaustive review is impractical, a few creatures are of special interest to many travelers.

Monkeys are plentiful in Honduras, and always a crowd favorite. Honduras has three species – *mono cara blanca* (white-faced monkey), *mono araña* (spider monkey) and *mono aullador* (howler monkey) – which are easiest to spot in La Moskitia, Parque Nacional Cuero y Salado, Parque Nacional Jeannette Kawas, Parque Nacional Sierra de Agalta and in the Refugio de Vida Silvestre Ojochal (Ojochal Wildlife Reserve). Even if you don't see howler monkeys, you may hear them; they get their name from their otherworldly howl, often heard at dawn or dusk.

In 2005 two new species of poisonous snakes were discovered in Olancho.

Everyone wants to see a jaguar, though very few actually do. La Moskitia is the best place to spot one, though they are known to exist in the Pico Bonito and Sierra de Agalta regions. Honduras has four other species of wild cats, all smaller than the jaguar: puma, jaguarondi, ocelot and tigrillo.

Divers and snorkelers see the most wildlife of any visitors to Honduras, and few animals evoke a more enthusiastic reaction than sea turtles. Hawksbill and olive ridley turtles are most common, but huge leatherbacks and loggerheads are known to be in the area, as they land on beaches in La Moskitia during turtle nesting season (see p287).

Whale sharks, which are seen year-round off Utila, can live to be 150 years old.

Whale sharks are another marine creature prevalent in Honduras, particularly around Utila. Seeing one is a true thrill and not a little intimidating – they measure up to 16m and can weigh 15,000kg. See the Utila section for more details, including the best time to spot these huge-but-harmless animals.

ENDANGERED SPECIES

The West Indian manatee, also known as the American manatee, was once plentiful in many parts of Honduras and the Caribbean. But a combination of overhunting, and encroachment by people and motorboats (which can maim or kill manatees grazing on the surface) has reduced manatee numbers severely. They are known to exist in the

Refugio de Vida Silvestre Cuero y Salado, and in less trafficked lagoons in La Moskitia.

On Utila, the spiny-tailed iguana is endemic to the island but endangered from overhunting – for both their meat and eggs – and habitat loss due to development. Also known as a 'swamper' or 'wishiwilli' the iguana has been the focus of a concerted conservation effort since 1994, when it was first identified as being in danger. See p265 for more information.

Other threatened animals in Honduras include the Central American tapir, the giant anteater, the Roatán Agouti and two species of bats.

Plants

Despite rampant deforestation, Honduras' forests still cover a larger total area and represents a larger percentage of its total land mass than any other country in Central America. Honduran forest falls into four general categories: pine forest, cloud forest, rain forest and mangrove.

It is a testament to Honduras' mountainous terrain that the pine is the national tree. In fact, Honduras has seven different species of pines, primarily the Caribbean pine and the ocote pine. They tend to occur at higher elevations, but the former extends well down the hillsides to the northern coastal plains.

Honduras has more than 36 distinct protected cloud-forest areas, containing a plethora of plant species including orchids, bromeliads, ferns as well as mosses and aggressive vines. Honduras has well over 600 species of orchids, though the number of orchids in bloom and within sight of the trail you happen to be hiking on is a craps shoot at best. The butterfly and orchid enclosures in Copán Ruínas (p146) and on Roatán (p246) are a good place to admire these fascinating flowers up close and personal, without having to risk wandering off the trail.

Mangroves are no less impressive, though their preference for a hot, humid climate and brackish water certainly makes them less accessible to human exploration. That said, gliding through tangled mangrove forests in a kayak in the early morning is surely one of the more sublime natural experience available in Honduras. Mangroves come in three general varieties – red, black and white – and provide a habitat for innumerable species, including shrimp, fish and birds, all of which can hide from predators in the mangroves' tangled root system (see boxed text p223).

Other notable members of Honduras' rich range of flora are the ceiba tree, a massive solitary tree found in the rain forests and coastal regions.

Amphibians of Honduras (2002) by James R McCranie and Larry David Wilson is an extremely detailed account of the 116 amphibian species in Honduras, with an insightful discussion of the country's environmental crisis as well.

Approximately 96% of all marine life found in the Caribbean has been spotted in the waters around Roatán.

TRAVELING RESPONSIBLY

A few simple guidelines will make any wilderness foray better and safer for you and for the plants and animals you encounter on the way.

Ask permission Always ask permission when passing through farm land, especially in indigenous areas, or if you want to camp nearby. Same goes for taking photos of people.

Buying souvenirs Do not buy souvenirs or other gifts that are made from protected or endangered animals, whether black coral, sea turtles, animal pelts or feathers.

Do not approach animals An animal that feels cornered or threatened can be very dangerous.

Going to the toilet Dig a hole at least 40m from the nearest water and cover well when finished.

Pack out what you pack in Never leave trash in the wilderness, even organic products.

Speak quietly You're more likely to see animals if they don't hear you from a kilometer off.

Stay on the trail You're less likely to get lost, and will do less damage to the environment.

NATIONAL PARKS & PROTECTED AREAS

Honduras has over 80 ecological protected areas, including 20 national parks, two biosphere reserves, plus another dozen or so semi-protected regions. For travelers, certain national parks, wildlife reserves and protected areas are especially important:

Jardín Botánico Lancetilla (p204) This botanical garden has more than 700 plant species and 365 species of bird. It's the second-largest botanical garden in the world, and has the largest collection of Asiatic fruit trees in the western hemisphere.

Parque Nacional Cusuco (p130) A cloud forest with a large population of quetzals, this national park has interpretive trails and a visitors center. The highest peak is Cerro Jilinco, at 2242m. The park can be reached all year round with a 4WD; the visitors center is 20km west of San Pedro Sula.

Parque Nacional Jeannette Kawas (Punta Sal) (p204) This has various habitats, including mangrove forests and swamps, a small tropical forest, offshore reefs and several coves. The park has a large number of migratory and coastal birds. The easiest access is on a tour from Tela.

Parque Nacional La Tigra (p91) This is Honduras' first national park, established in 1980. Located just 22km from Tegucigalpa, this cloud forest is set in former mining country and has interpretive trails and visitors centers at two entrances. Dormitories and camping are available.

Parque Nacional Marino Cayos Cochinos (p227) Known also as the Hog Islands, Cayos Cochinos form a national marine park. Thirteen cays – two of them large – with beautiful coral reefs, well-preserved forests and fishing villages make up the reserve. Access is by motorized boat from Sambo Creek or Nueva Armenia, just east of La Ceiba.

Parque Nacional Monataña de Celaque (p163) A cloud forest with four peaks over 2800m above sea level, including the highest peak in Honduras at 2849m. There are hundreds of different animal and plant species, many of which are visible through the park's four main trails. Access to the park is easy: there's a ranger station 6.5km southwest of Gracias and another entrance near Belén Gualcho.

Parque Nacional Pico Bonito (p224) The diversity of this park ranges from pine-oak forest to cloud forest, and includes numerous rivers and waterfalls. Most of the park is closed to development of any kind, including building and maintaining trails. Two short hikes on opposite ends of the park are about all you can do in the park proper. A number of outings, however, include hikes in the park's buffer zone.

Refugio de Vida Silvestre Cuero y Salado (p222) This is the largest manatee refuge in Central America, although that doesn't mean you'll necessarily spot one! Fortunately, it's also teeming with birds and monkeys. The park is 30km west of La Ceiba. Access is easy, either by tour or on your own.

Refugio de Vida Silvestre Laguna de Guaimoreto (p234) Just 5km east of Trujillo, this mangrove forest has an incredible coastal biodiversity, which visitors can explore by boat.

Refugio de Vida Silvestre Punta Izopo (p206) One of the most recently established national parks, Punta Izopo is made up of tropical wet forest, mangrove forest and wetlands. It has many migratory and coastal birds, a beautiful rocky point and attractive white sand beaches. It's accessible by boat.

Reserva de la Biósfera del Río Plátano (p288) A World Heritage site and the first biosphere reserve in Central America, the Río Plátano is 5251 sq km of lowland tropical rain forest with remarkable natural, archaeological and cultural resources. Access is through Las Marías, or by a multi-day raft-ride down the river from Dulce Nombre de Culmí.

Reserva de la Biosfera Tawahka Asangni (p296) A tropical rain forest on the ancestral lands of the Tawahka people, one of the most threatened indigenous groups in Honduras. Access is by plane to Ahuas or Wampusirpi then by boat upstream to Krausirpe and Krautara, or by a multiday rafting trip down the Río Patuca from Juticalpa.

Reserva Marina Turtle Harbour (p266) On the northwestern side of Utila in the Bay Islands, Turtle Harbour is a marine reserve and proposed national marine park visited frequently by divers.

Sandy Bay & West End Marine Park (p246) On the western end of Roatán, this area is still awaiting official reserve status. It has coral reefs that are easily accessible by divers.

NATIONAL PARKS & PROTECTED AREAS

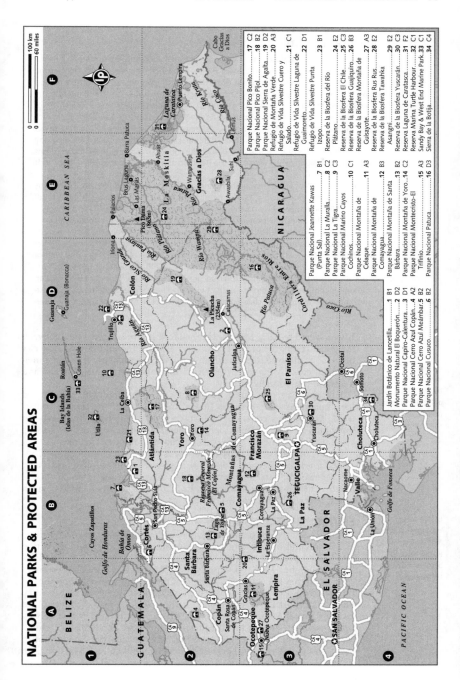

Jardín Botánico de Lancetilla........	1 B1
Monumento Natural El Boquerón....	2 D2
Parque Nacional Capiro-Calentura...	3 D1
Parque Nacional Cerro Azul Copán..	4 A2
Parque Nacional Cerro Azul Meámbar..5 B2
Parque Nacional Cusuco..............	6 B2
Parque Nacional Jeannette Kawas (Punta Sal)............................7 B1
Parque Nacional La Muralla...........	8 C2
Parque Nacional La Tigra.............	9 C3
Parque Nacional Marino Cayos Cochinos...........................10 C1
Parque Nacional Montaña de Celaque.........................11 A3
Parque Nacional Montaña de Comayagua......................12 B3
Parque Nacional Montaña de Santa Bárbara..........................13 B2
Parque Nacional Montaña de Yoro...14 C2
Parque Nacional Montecristo-El Trifinio..........................15 A3
Parque Nacional Patuca..............16 D3
Parque Nacional Pico Bonito.........17 C2
Parque Nacional Pico Pijol..........18 B2
Parque Nacional Sierra de Agalta....19 D2
Refugio de Montaña Verde...........20 A3
Refugio de Vida Silvestre Cuero y Salado...........................21 C1
Refugio de Vida Silvestre Laguna de Guaimoreto......................22 D1
Refugio de Vida Silvestre Punta Izopo............................23 B1
Reserva de la Biosfera del Río Plátano..........................24 E2
Reserva de la Biosfera El Chile......25 C3
Reserva de la Biosfera Guajiquiro...26 B3
Reserva de la Biosfera Montaña de Guisayote........................27 A3
Reserva de la Biosfera Rus Rus.....28 E2
Reserva de la Biosfera Tawahka Asangni.........................29 E2
Reserva de la Biosfera Yuscarán....30 C3
Reserva Laguna de Caratasca........31 F2
Reserva Marina Turtle Harbour......32 C1
Sandy Bay & West End Marine Park.33 C1
Sierra de la Botija...................34 C4

100 km
60 miles

CUTTING DOWN THE FORESTS

Honduras is facing a full-blown deforestation crisis; in October 2005 the Environmental Investigation Agency and the Center for International Policy published *The Illegal Logging Crisis in Honduras,* a 50-page exposé of environmental destruction and government corruption related to illegal logging in Honduras. The numbers alone are staggering: in 2004, the Honduran Ministry of Agriculture estimated the country was losing 1000 sq km of forest every year – nearly 2% of the country's total forest cover, or four times the combined landmass of the Bay Islands. According to the report, deforestation contributes to soil erosion, reduced water retention and a greater incidence of forest fires. There were 500 forest fires in the first four months of 2005, including one in April that blanketed the county in smoke and forced all four major airports to be closed. Most observers say deforestation significantly worsened the flooding and mudslides that killed thousands during Hurricane Mitch.

Pine trees account for 96% of Honduras' timber harvest; half are extracted illegally. Mahogany accounts for a fraction of the total harvest, but is one of the most valuable and sought-after hardwoods, fetching US$1300 per cubic meter on the world market. As much as 80% of the mahogany harvest is illegal; in 2003–04, an estimated two million board feet (one board foot equals a board one foot long, one foot wide and one inch thick) were illegally extracted from the Reserva de la Biósfera del Río Plátano, representing a tax loss of US$3 million, not to mention the much higher value of the wood itself and untold costs associated with environmental degradation. One auditor estimated Honduras' total losses due to illegal logging between 1998 and 2003 at US$6.5 *billion*.

To produce the 2005 report, undercover investigators posed as timber investors and used hidden cameras to document incompetence and corruption at virtually every stage of the timber-harvesting process, from improper permits, to clear-cutting in national park core zones, to the under-

It was sacred to early Mayas, who believed it represented a link between the godly realm, the present realm and Xibalba, the underworld. The city of La Ceiba derived its name from this tree, a particularly large specimen of which grew by the pier where fishermen and merchants gathered, and a township eventually formed.

Honduras' national flower was originally the rose, but was changed to the orchid in 1969 because roses are not actually native to Honduras.

Hiking in the rain forest, you're sure to spot a tree with smooth red bark known as *indio desnudo* (naked Indian) or *palo de turista* (tourist tree). The bark is constantly peeling – like a sunburned traveler – an ingenious defense against the innumerable bromeliads and strangling vines, which can never quite gain purchase on the tree's trunk.

Mahogany, known locally as *caoba*, is one reason so much of Honduras' forest has been cut down; it is prized for its durable and richly colored wood. This slow-growing tree takes decades to reach its full height. Other valuable hardwoods in Honduras' forests include Spanish cedar, rosewood and ironwood.

In 1980 Unesco recognized the Reserva de la Biósfera del Río Plátano as the first biosphere reserve in Central America.

ENVIRONMENTAL ISSUES

Deforestation (see boxed text above) is without question the number one environmental issue facing Honduras. But other issues of conservation and habitat protection remain critical.

In September 1999, oil experts hired by the Honduran government confirmed that the country is sitting on top of four to five billion tons of untapped oil reserves. However, the bulk of these lies along La Moskitia, one of the most environmentally sensitive regions in the country, and indeed Central America. The oil field stretches as far west as Tela, raising the prospect of oil rigs just off the coast of places like Parque Nacional Jeannette Kawas and Refugio de Vida Silvestre Cuero y Salado, not to mention the Bay Islands. Large-scale drilling would take US$250 million in initial outlay, which Honduras does not have. A call for international

reporting of lumber exports to the US and Europe. The report describes COHDEFOR, the agency that is supposed to oversee forest regulation, as ineffectual and corrupt, and calls for its abolition. On one hand, the agency is woefully understaffed; at one point only six people were dedicated to monitoring logging activity in the all-important Reserva de la Biósfera del Río Plátano, which spans 8000 sq km. On the other hand, COHDEFOR is itself deeply corrupt; in February 2005, the agency's regional director in Olancho was fired after it was proved he had allowed illegal logging for years. The director was related to congressional leader and then-presidential candidate Porfirio Lobo Sosa, who was himself linked to one of the major timber barons, Guillermo Noriega. The resulting scandal contributed to Lobo's loss in the 2005 presidential race.

Popular opposition to logging companies has been strong, rallied by groups like Movimiento Ambiental de Olancho (MAO; Environmental Movement of Olancho). MAO is led by Father José Andrés Tamayo, a fearless Catholic priest who received the 2005 Goldman Environmental Award – as well as numerous death threats – for his efforts. The group has organized marches and negotiations, and members even lay in front of logging machinery to prevent its advance. Three activists have been killed since 1996, and numerous others have been jailed under, of all things, new anti-gang laws that give judges broad powers in jailing people for 'illicit association'.

Of course, much stronger leverage could be applied by the US, which receives 38% of Honduran wood exports, far more than any other country. The US has pledged under CAFTA and other agreements to help halt illegal logging – steps which could include closing verification loopholes, advocating the addition of more species to the protected trees list, and link the US$1.3 billion in planned debt forgiveness to more rigorous enforcement of logging laws.

bids went out in 2000 but there have been no reports of progress since. With post-9/11 concerns about Middle Eastern oil, the plan will almost certainly re-emerge, and attract powerful backing.

Overfishing is another longstanding environmental concern in Honduras. Large fishing boats are not permitted to drop their nets within 5km of the low-tide mark, but the rule is often ignored, even in heavily trafficked areas near Tela and La Ceiba. For small-time fishermen, especially Garífuna, illegal net fishing means fewer fish can be caught from shore or canoes, and those that are, tend be smaller. The shallows are also a breeding ground for fish, shrimp, lobster, even dolphins and manatees, and overfishing can skew the delicate ecological balance found there.

Finally, the approach of the tenth anniversary of Hurricane Mitch (see boxed text p38) is an opportunity to reflect on the devastation, both human and environmental. The hurricane destroyed vital mangrove forests on Guanaja, Roatán and the mainland, devastating the North Coast's shrimp industry. The recovery has heightened awareness of the vital role mangroves play in any coastal environment, as habitat for juvenile creatures, as a natural filter for waste and contaminants in the estuary, and as a source of both above-water and below-water biomass that feeds the ecosystem's food chain.

The Bay Islands of Honduras (2003) by Honduran-born journalist Jacqueline Laffite Bloch is a beautiful coffee-table book with photos and text (Spanish and English). Proceeds go to a Garífuna clinic in Roatán.

Adventure Travel

Honduras is a big beautiful country, known for its underwater riches, but bursting with all sorts of outdoor opportunities. It has a well-deserved reputation as one of the best (and cheapest) places to learn to dive or complete your divemaster training. It's got the perfect combination of warm water, spectacular reefs and lively island communities. Just as travelers go to Guatemala for the culture and Costa Rica for the wildlife, they go to Honduras for the diving.

But what most people don't realize is how much more Honduras has to offer adventure-minded travelers, beyond snorkeling and diving. Did you know, for example, that it is home to the largest tropical rainforest north of the Amazon? La Moskitia (aka the Mosquito Coast) is one of the few truly pristine ecosystems left in Central America, and can be visited by plane, canoe, or on an unforgettable week-long rafting trip that starts deep in the Honduran heartland.

Other sporting opportunities in Honduras include hiking in its many national parks, mountain biking along the north coast, bird-watching around its largest freshwater lake, kayaking through mangrove forests and world-class sport-fishing. Enjoy!

CANOPY TOURS

Canopy tours – in which you don a harness, helmet and leather gloves, and slide from treetop to treetop on fixed cables – are the latest craze in Honduras. Jungle River Tours in La Ceiba (p214) had the first one, starting with a cable extended over the rushing Río Cangrejal. There are at least three more now, one east of La Ceiba (see p214), and two on Roatán. The new ones cater mostly to cruise-ship passengers and tourists at all-inclusive resorts.

HIKING & TREKKING

Honduras has excellent hiking, particularly on the country's many mountains. Well-marked and maintained trail systems are rare, however, and in most cases hikers will need to hire a guide. Foreign travelers tend to be averse to hiring guides, but it's worth remembering that this is one way local residents reap direct benefit from the national parks (and therefore have an incentive to preserve them). It's absolutely vital that travelers leave money in the local economy – that's the promise eco-tourism advocates have made in exchange for protecting natural areas.

The three highest peaks in Honduras are Montaña de Celaque/Cerro de las Minas (2849m), Montaña de Santa Bárbara (2744m) and Pico Bonito (2436m).

Parque Nacional La Tigra (p91) has the country's best trail system, with easy to follow trails of various lengths and difficulties. The park can be visited as a day trip from Tegucigalpa, but has camping and rustic lodging, plus a highly recommended guesthouse at the El Rosario entrance. Parque Nacional Montaña de Celaque (p163) is another great do-it-yourself spot, with a challenging day-climb (taking between one and three days) through cloud forest to the top of Honduras' highest mountain. Other areas with good do-it-yourself hiking include Parque Nacional Cerro Azul Meámbar (p179), Monumento Natural El Boquerón (p113), and on the beach from Miami to Parque Nacional Jeannette Kawas/Punta Sal near Tela (p204).

A number of other terrific hikes require guides, mainly for safety (see also p305 for information on hiking hazards). Most trails receive little or no regular maintenance and are criss-crossed by paths used by hunters and farmers, making it very easy to get off-track. In Olancho, climbing La Picucha (p118) in the Sierra de Agalta National Park is certainly one of the more adventuresome and rewarding hikes in the country, doable from either Catacamas or, more commonly, Gualaco. Parque Nacional de Santa Bárbara (p180) has the second-highest mountain in the country and tremendous views from the summit. There are several routes to the top, all involving lots of bushwhacking.

And of course La Moskitia offers unforgettable hiking as well. See p291 for more info. From Las Marías, two- and three-day hikes up Pico Dama and Cerro Baltimore take you through pristine rainforest, teeming with monkeys, birds and other wildlife.

MOUNTAIN BIKING

Honduras has the potential to be a great mountain-biking destination, with myriad dirt roads winding through stunning mountain terrain. Travelers with their own bikes could certainly grab a map and starting exploring, while those without gear have fewer options. Definitely plan to ride in the dry season – mud forms fast and thick even after a short rain.

The best guided mountain-bike trips are in La Ceiba (p214). At least two different tour outfits offer day trips or multi-day excursions for riders of all levels. Most rides are in the Río Cangrejal area, on the edges of Pico Bonito National Park, where the same tour operators also have jungle lodges – a free night's stay is included in all trips. You can also rent bicycles by the hour or the day, for exploring on you own.

In Tela, Jardín Botánico Lancetilla (p204) is a popular biking destination, and there are a couple places in town to rent bikes.

Experienced riders with their own bikes have many more options, of course. Western Honduras, especially the Ruta Lenca, has relatively little traffic and challenging, topsy-turvy terrain. For those looking for some serious up-and-down, the 50km road between Gracias and San Sebastian will have you sucking air in no time. The road is well-maintained and goes through several picturesque villages.

La Esperanza (p172) also has excellent riding nearby in the Valle de Azacualpa, a broad rolling valley circled by a well-maintained dirt road and dotted with small villages, churches and other sights along the way. The vast central interior has even better biking possibilities, but is quite remote and known for roadside hold-ups, especially in Olancho department.

Finally, Isla El Tigre (p104) is hardly a top destination but a visit there would be much nicer if you had a bike. An 18km paved road circles the island, with no major climbs, very little traffic and plenty of places to stop to enjoy the view or go down to the water.

Website of the official PADI Society magazine, www.sportdiver.com has frequent articles on the Bay Islands.

RAFTING & KAYAKING

Honduras has some of the best rafting and kayaking in Central America, dealing up solid Class II to Class IV whitewater (even Class V during high water) while paddling through beautiful gorges and river valleys. If there's a drawback to the rafting here, it is that trips are either half-day or week-plus, and not much middle ground.

Honduras' best rafting outfits are in La Ceiba (see p214 for details) offering half-day trips on the Río Cangrejal, east of town. The river tumbles down the coastal mountains toward the bottom, which form the border of the massive Pico Bonito National Park. Rafting trips generally include short excursions into the national park, like hiking to nearby waterfalls. Two of the outfits that do most of the Río Cangrejal business, Jungle River Tours (p215) and Omega Tours (p215) also have jungle lodges near the take-out, and all trips include a free night's stay.

For an experience of a whole different category, the same rafting companies offer multi-day expeditions down the Río Plátano or Río Patuca into La Moskitia (see p120 for more info). Trips start in Olancho – Dulce Nombre de Culmí for the Río Plátano and Juticalpa for the Río Patuca – and last a week to ten days. Both trips go through the heart of Honduras' most pristine natural habitat, the largest rainforest north of the Amazon. It includes stretches of four or five days during which you'll see no sign of human settlement, but plenty of wildlife. The Río Plátano trip also includes Class III rapids, and passes through Las Marías, a popular destination in La Moskitia where a number of additional trips are possible. The Río Patuca winds through the Tawahka Asangni Biosphere Reserve, home to the reclusive Tawahka indigenous group, and emerges at the town of Ahuas, where you can catch a flight back to La Ceiba or elsewhere in La Moskitia. Trips include camping on the beach and short excursions into the rainforest to see caves and waterfalls.

Kayakers can descend the Río Cangrejal along the same route as rafters. One of the tour operators, Omega Tours (p215), has kayak tours, and even offers kayak instruction and rental. For flat water excursions, try boating at Cuero y Salado Wildlife Refuge (see p223 for details) near La Ceiba or Punta Izopo National Park near Tela. Both are good places to spot birds and other wildlife.

External pressure on a diver's body doubles in the first ten meters of a dive.

Honduras & Belize: White Star Guides Diving (2005) by Roberto Rinaldi describes some of the top dive sites in Honduras.

SNORKELING & DIVING ADVENTURES

If you're in Honduras, or are thinking of going, snorkeling or scuba diving are probably high on your list of things to do. And with good reason: Honduras boasts world-class diving at famously affordable prices. Shops are almost uniformly top-rate, with experienced instructors and solid safety records. All this set on idyllic Caribbean islands – what more could you ask?

Honduras is rightly known as a great place to learn to dive. Shops focus heavily on the basic Open Water courses – Utila Dive Centre (p267) is regularly among the top shops *in the world* in terms of the number of PADI Open Water certificates it issues annually. But plenty of experienced divers come here too. Shops also offer all the advanced-level courses, from Advanced Open Water to Instructor. It is an especially popular place to come for multi-week divemaster courses, partly because life on the islands is as enjoyable as the diving is. Even for just fun diving, the Bay Islands do not disappoint.

Roatán and Utila attract the vast majority of divers, and everyone faces the same decision: which island to go to? The diving is comparable on both islands. Utila has incredible walls and sea mounds, while Roatán has somewhat healthier reefs and more dives to go to (ergo less crowding). Different people have favorites, but for novice divers especially, the difference is negligible. Utila has many more whale-shark sightings, especially in season. Utila's dive day starts at 7am, while on Roatán it's at 9am – with surface interval back on shore – which is no small consideration if you're not a morning person!

More often the decision comes to budget and style. Utila is known to be more geared toward backpackers and budget travelers, and tends to attract a younger crowd. Utila has a wider selection of budget accommodations and restaurants, though Roatán does have some of both. Roatán has more hotels with kitchen access, which can be nice if you plan to stay for a while. Dive prices are about the same, though Roatán has a one-time reef tax of just US$10, as opposed to US$3 per day on Utila.

UNDER THE STARS

And the nominees for the Oscar for the best place to camp in Honduras are:

- the lush cloud forest of **Parque Nacional Montaña de Celaque** (p163)
- the dwarf forest on the summit of **La Picucha** (p117) in the Sierra de Agalta National Park
- the **Reserva de la Biósfera del Río Plátano** (p288), on a hike up Pico Dama or Cerro Baltimore from Las Marías
- a riverbank on the Río Plátano or Río Patuca, halfway into a ten-day rafting trip from Olancho to **La Moskitia** (p120)
- the **Parque Nacional Santa Bárbara** (p180), on the way up Honduras' second-highest peak, Santa Bárbara.

SPORT FISHING

Honduras has terrific sport fishing, both deep-sea and flat-water. The bay Islands are a logical place for ocean fishing, of course. Roatán has several outfits, most at West End. Trips can be arranged through most of the larger hotels, for slightly higher prices. Fishing is not cheap, typically costing upwards of US$600 for an all-day trip for up to eight people. You may be able to save some money by hiring a local fisherman, but of course you are less certain your guide will know what he's doing.

Anglers can choose the type of fishing – and fish – they're interested in. Trolling is popular for snagging trophy fish, including dorado, barracuda, tuna, wahoo and even marlin in season. Deep-sea fishing produces grouper and snapper, which are the most common fish served at restaurants and are sometimes called 'dinner fish'. Flat fishing targets bone fish that live in shallow flat water of lagoons and estuaries, and are typically catch-and-release.

But for truly spectacular flat-water fishing, head straight to Brus Laguna in La Moskitia. The huge shallow lagoon teems with snook, grouper, snapper and – get this – tarpon weighing two hundred pounds or more. Now that's a wild ride! Anglers tell tales of four-, five- and six-hour battles to land one of those monsters.

Finally, Lago de Yojoa (p175) is famous for its fine lake-fishing, especially for bass. Ask at your hotel for a guide.

One of the largest tarpon caught in Brus Laguna weighed 210 pounds and took six hours to land.

The Coral Free Alliance (www.coral reefalliance.org) is dedicated to preserving coral reefs through local conservation, education and sustainable tourism programs worldwide, including on Roatán.

Food & Drink

An online bilingual cookbook of Honduran dishes can be found at www .honduras.net/foods

Honduran food is remarkably uniform: the menu at a *comedor* (basic eatery) or midrange restaurant in Choluteca would be virtually identical to one in Trujillo. Both would include some combination of fried and baked fish, fried and baked chicken, grilled steak, pork chops, and maybe sandwiches and pasta dishes, usually served with a small side salad (iceberg lettuce, sliced cucumber, tomato), rice and beans; which doesn't make the food bad, but travelers spending an extended period here (especially those who've come from Guatemala or Mexico) may tire of the sameness of it.

STAPLES & SPECIALITIES

Somehow, despite its ethnic diversity and many cultural influences, Honduras never developed a varied and distinctive local cuisine. The best variety is on the north coast, where the seafood is fresh and varied, especially fish, shrimp, conch and lobster.

For breakfast, the *plato típico* reigns supreme. From deep in La Moskitia to the heart of San Pedro Sula, the 'typical plate' means eggs, beans, fried plantains, cheese, cream, a piece of sausage or bacon, served with tortillas or bread, and coffee.

Reviviendo la Cocina Hondureña (Reviving Honduran Cuisine; 1987) by Dolores Prats de Avila is a Spanish-language cookbook with step-by-step instruction on preparing a variety of Honduran dishes.

A lunchtime *plato típico* includes a piece of meat – *bistec* (beef), *chuleta* (pork chop) or *pollo* (chicken) – served with beans, rice and a side salad and tortillas or bread. This is not much different from a standard dinner plate, though that would rarely be called a *plato típico*. And whereas lunch meats are usually just grilled or fried, dinner dishes might also include a somewhat more involved preparation, like *encebollada* (covered in grilled onions) or *entomatada* (covered in tomato sauce). If fish is one of the options, it can usually be prepared *frito* (fried) or *al ajillo* (with garlic).

With dinner or drinks, you may be served *anafre,* runny refried beans served with tortilla chips in a clay pot with a small chamber in the bottom for hot coals, which keeps the beans bubbly. A sort of Honduran fondue.

On the north coast, it's hard to go wrong by ordering fish – for the freshest piece, ask the server which of the dishes is prepared with fish caught that same day. Also be sure to try *ceviche de pescado* (fish ceviche) or *sopa de caracol* (conch soup); the soup, made with coconut milk and potatoes, is especially tasty.

Garífuna communities on the north coast are famous for *pan de coco,* a dense sweet bread made with fresh coconut. It's often sold on the street by women and children, and is good for long bus rides. A staple of the Garífuna diet is *casabe,* a crispy waferlike bread made from yucca roots in a long and time-consuming process. Eaten alone, *casabe* is rather bland, at least to most Western palates. More appealing is *tapado de casabe* (casabe stew) in which the wafers are boiled until soft, and mixed with broth, cabbage, salted pork, vinegar, salt and pepper.

Traditional Honduran healing utilizes 'hot' or 'cold' foods as remedies. 'Hot' medicines may include oranges and beef, 'cold' ones salt and seafood.

On the Bay Islands, another traditional – and delicious – food is *bando,* a seafood stew made from pretty much whatever is handy (including fish, crab, mussels, potatoes, yucca and coconut milk) boiled over a fire.

DRINKS
Nonalcoholic Drinks

One of Honduras' most popular drinks, among locals and foreigners alike, are *licuados* (smoothies), which are made of fruit, ice, and several tablespoons of sugar blended with either water or milk. Though

---

STAYING HEALTHY

- Never drink unpurified water, even in mountain areas where locals do. Bottled water is cheap and easy to find, and canned and bottled drinks are a safe alternative. Fortunately, virtually all eateries and restaurants use purified water in their drinks and ice.

- Avoid uncooked, precut fruit and vegetables. You have no way of knowing the cleanliness of the fruit, the cutting board, or the hands of the person who prepared it. Stick to fruits and vegetables that you can peel or wash in purified water yourself. Oranges, bananas, avocados and mangoes are all good. Remember to wipe the fruit down before peeling it so you don't end up with all the bad stuff on your hands.

- Skip the salad. Most *platos típicos* come with an enticing side salad, but grooves and ripples on their leaves are notorious for retaining drops of water, which is unlikely to be purified.

- Travel with and use hand sanitizer. Public restrooms often do not have soap, and the water is unsafe.

- Stay hydrated by drinking lots of water or, on especially sweaty days, Gatorade. Dehydration and heat exhaustion will knock you out as quickly as a bad *baleada*.

---

they can be made of just about any fruit, popular varieties include *piña* (pineapple), *guineo* (banana), *sandia* (watermelon), *fresa* (strawberry) and papaya. Granola, oatmeal and corn flakes are typical extras that can be added to turn a simple *licuado* into a hearty drink.

Jugos (juices) are typically made fresh right in front of you and are a great pick-me-up on a hot day. Popular flavors include *naranja* (orange), *piña*, and *zanahoria* (carrot). Very similar are a*guas*, fruit drinks made with water and a fruit or grain – the equivalent of an '-ade' in English. Favorites are *melón* (cantaloupe), *sandía* (watermelon), *mora* (blueberry), *tamarindo* (tamarind), *horchata* (sweet rice milk), and of course *limonada* (lime-ade).

Coffee also is popular in Honduras, and often perfectly good, even in modest eateries. It is served *negro* (black) or *con leche* (with milk), the latter usually costing a bit more.

Pupusas, which are sold throughout Honduras, originated in long-time rival El Salvador.

In 2006 there were over 90 million coffee bushes in cultivation in Honduras.

Alcoholic Drinks

Honduras has two well-known beers – Port Royal and Salva Vida; neither will impress serious beer drinkers, but they're decent enough (or cheap enough) to be popular here and in several neighboring countries. Rum, mostly Bacardi and Flor de Caña, are popular as well. *Aguardiente* is a cheap generic liquor that happens to be a national favorite, especially Yuscarán, which is made in the town of the same name. *Chicha* is a traditional drink made from fermented pineapple skins.

WHERE TO EAT & DRINK

Yucca, the base of Garífuna *casabe* bread, is a poisonous root containing cyanide.

Restaurante generally refers to restaurants on the slightly fancier side, often with tablecloths and a set menu. Informal eateries are usually called *comedores*; and are typically less expensive, with daily specials and a basic menu. Both are usually open daily from 7am to 9pm. Reservations are rarely needed (or taken, for that matter) even in upscale places. There are very few places in the country where only tourists go, though certainly some cater more to foreigners and their prices prove it. Most of the restaurants in this book are popular with locals and tourists alike or even just locals.

A coffee-lovers forum, www.ineedcoffee.com includes information on Honduran bean varieties.

Cooking the Central American Way (2005) by Alison Behnkeet et al is a cookbook containing a general overview of Central American recipes including Honduran favorites, vegetarian fare, and low fat options.

Da Núbebe: Un Compendio de Comidas Garífunas (Da Núbebe: A Collection of Garifuna Dishes; 1997) by Salvador Suazo is a cookbook containing traditional Garífuna recipes.

Quick Eats

No matter where you travel, eating on the street can be a great way to feel like you're connecting with local people and experiences; it's also a good way to get sick if you're not careful. *Baleadas* are the ultimate Honduran quick-eat: a flour tortilla smeared with beans and melted butter. Look for a stand where they're made and sold fresh; the pre-prepared ones sold from baskets are usually okay, too, but may be past their prime. *Pinchos* – kabobs cooked on small streetside grills – are tasty and fairly reliable, especially if you can see they've been cooked thoroughly, and haven't been sitting around. Corn on the cob, either grilled or boiled, is also popular and you may see tamales and *atole* (a thick drink made of corn or wheat) as well. With all street eating, pick a place that is relatively busy – locals aren't immune to spoiled food and will patronize stands they trust.

VEGETARIANS & VEGANS

Vegetarianism is not widely practiced in Honduras, and beyond the major cities and well-touristed towns like Copán Ruínas and Utila, vegetarians don't have many options. Rice, beans and tortillas are staples and can be ordered just about anywhere. Beans, however, are often made with lard – better ask first to be sure. Fast food restaurants, which are ubiquitous in Honduras, often have pizza or fries – not the healthiest of options but at least it gives you a couple more choices. Of course, for those vegetarians who make an exception for seafood, there are many more options, making traveling in Honduras much more interesting and enjoyable from a culinary perspective. There is at least one vegetarian restaurant in Honduras – a place called Fuente de Salud y Juventud in San Pedro Sula – but virtually all the restaurants listed in this book have at least some nonmeat alternatives.

EATING WITH KIDS

Children are very welcome in Honduran restaurants, where dining is traditionally a family affair. In fact, like in many Latin American countries, children are simultaneously *more* welcome at restaurants (and weddings, gatherings etc) than they are in other countries, but *less* likely to be the center of all the adults' attention. Children learn early to play amongst themselves when grown-ups are talking, and parents spend considerably less time responding to their children's every need.

Honduran food has very few hidden surprises – no extra-spicy sauces or unusual flavors. Most foods will be familiar to Western travelers, and should satisfy even picky eaters. Juices figure prominently, including

---

TOP FIVE BEST EATS

- Oregano's (p113) – the *morir soñando*, a Caribbean shrimp flambé, is to die for.

- Baleada Express (p132) – the best *baleadas* west of the Río Plátano.

- Chabelita (p219) – filled to the brim with mussels, clams, fish and shrimp, the seafood soup here is tops.

- Restaurante El Faro de Victoria (p106) – a rare find, the *pescado sudando* (fish baked in tin foil) is a taste delight.

- D&D Bed & Breakfast and Microbrewery (p178) – yep, it's a brewery, but the blueberry pancakes can't be beat.

TRAVEL YOUR TASTEBUDS

During Semana Santa, the traditional dish is *sopa de pescado* (fish soup) made with fish and egg patties, dunked in a broth made from garlic and fish heads. It is tradition that the father of the house and one of the sons beat the eggs used to make the fish patties and, later, traditional desserts like *pan de yema* (egg yolk bread) and *torrijas de piñol* (a type of cornbread French toast).

'regular' ones like orange, lime, apple and pineapple. Large grocery stores in Honduras carry a variety of baby foods and formulas, many of the same brands as found in the US and Canada.

HABITS & CUSTOMS

Dining habits and customs in Honduras are similar to those elsewhere in the region, and in the home countries of most Western travelers. As in many Latin American countries, the waiter won't bring you the bill until you ask for it.

EAT YOUR WORDS

Although hand signals can get you a long way when it comes to food, knowing a few key words and phrases will definitely enhance your dining experience, even if it's at a street cart. For pronunciation guidelines see p327.

Useful Phrases

I'd like to see a menu.
Quisiera ver la carta.   kee·*sye*·ra ver la *kar*·ta
Do you have a menu in English?
¿Tienen una carta en inglés?   tye·nen·oon·a *kar*·ta en·een·*gles*
What is today's special?
¿Cuál es el plato del día?   kwal es el *pla*·to del *dee*·a
What do you recommend?
¿Qué me recomienda?   ke me re·ko·*myen*·da
What's in that dish?
¿De qué es ese plato?   de ke es *es*·e *pla*·to
Can I have a (beer) please?
¿Una (cerveza) por favor?   *oo*·na (ser·*ve*·sa) por fa·*vor*
Is service included in the bill?
¿La cuenta incluye el servicio?   la *kwen*·ta een·*kloo*·ye el ser·*vee*·syo
Thank you, that was delicious.
Muchas gracias, fue delicioso.   *moo*·chas *gras*·yas *foo*·eh de·lee·*syo*·so
The bill, please.
La cuenta, por favor.   la *kwen*·ta por fa·*vor*
I'm a vegetarian.
Soy vegetariano/a. (m/f)   soy ve·khe·ta·*rya*·no/a
Do you have any vegetarian dishes?
¿Tienen algún plato vegetariano?   tye·nen al·*goon pla*·to ve·khe·ta·*rya*·no
Are you open?
¿Está abierto?   e·*sta* a·*byer*·to
When are you open?
¿Cuando está abierto?   kwan·do e·*sta* a·*byer*·to
Are you now serving breakfast/lunch/dinner?
¿Ahora, está sirviendo desayuno/   a·o·ra e·*sta* ser·*vyen*·do de·sa·*yoo*·no/
la comida/la cena?   la ko·*mee*·da/la *se*·na

I'd like mineral water/natural bottled water.

Quiero agua mineral/agua.
purificada

kee·ye·ro a·gwa mee·ne·ral/a·gwa
poo·ree·fee·ka·da

Is it (chili) hot?

¿Es picoso?

es pee·ko·so

Food Glossary

arroz	a·ros	rice
azucar	a·soo·car	sugar
caldo	kal·do	broth, often meat-based
coco	ko·ko	coconut
frijoles	free·kho·les	black beans
huevos fritos/revueltos	we·vos free·tos/re·vwel·tos	fried/scrambled eggs
miel	myel	honey
milanesa	mee·la·ne·sa	crumbed, breaded
pan	pan	bread
picante	pi·kan·te	any hot/spicy sauce
plato típico	pla·to tee·pee·ko	standard breakfast or lunch dish
postre	pos·tre	dessert
tapado	ta·pa·do	any kind of stew (beef, seafood etc)

SNACKS

anafre	a·na·fre	refried beans served fondue style
baleada	ba·le·a·da	flour tortilla with beans or other filling
golosinas	go·lo·see·nas	snacks (many varieties)
hamburguesa	am·boor·gwe·sa	hamburger
helado	e·la·do	ice cream
pastel	pas·tel	cake
pupusa	pu·pu·sa	stuffed cornmeal patty; Salvadoran
quesadilla	ke·sa·dee·ya	flour tortilla with melted cheese
tajadas	ta·ha·do	fried banana chips
tamal	ta·mal	stuffed, steamed corn-dough patty
tostada	tos·ta·da	flat crisp tortilla

MEAT

bistec	bees·tek	beefsteak
camarones	ka·ma·ro·nes	shrimp
caracol	ca·ra·col	conch
carne	kar·ne	meat
carne asada	kar·ne a·sa·da	tough but tasty grilled beef
ceviche	se·vee·che	raw fish/conch marinated in lime juice
chicharrón	chee·cha·con	pork crackling
chuletas (de puerco)	choo·le·tas (de pwer·ko)	(pork) chops
churrasco	choo·ras·ko	slab of grilled meat
filete de pescado	fee·le·te de pes·ka·do	fish fillet
langosta	lan·go·sta	lobster
mariscos	ma·rees·kos	seafood
mondongo	mon·don·go	tripe stew
nacatamales	na·ka·ta·ma·les	boiled pork tamales
pescado (al ajillo)	pes·ka·do (al a·hee·yo)	fish (fried in butter and garlic)
pincho	peen·cho	shish kebob
pollo (asado/frito)	po·lyo (a·sa·do/free·to)	(grilled/fried) chicken
puerco	pwer·ko	pork
puyaso	poo·ya·so	a choice cut of steak
salchicha	sal·chee·cha	sausage

FRUIT & VEGETABLES

aguacate	a·gwa·*ka*·te	avocado
ajo	*a*·kho	garlic
banano	ba·*na*·no	banana
cebolla	se·*boy*·ya	onion
fresas	*fre*·sas	strawberries
frutas	*froo*·tas	fruit
lechuga	le·*choo*·ga	lettuce
limón	lee·*mon*	lime or lemon
naranja	na·*ran*·kha	orange
papa	*pa*·pa	potato
papaya	pa·*pa*·ya	pawpaw
piña	*pee*·nya	pineapple
plátano	*pla*·ta·no	plantain, usually served fried
tomate	to·*ma*·te	tomato
verduras	ver·*doo*·ras	green vegetables
zanahoria	sa·na·*o*·rya	carrot

DRINKS

agua	*a*·gwa	water
café (negro/con leche)	*ka*·fe (*ne*·gro/kon *le*·che)	coffee (black/with milk)
cerveza	ser·*ve*·sa	beer
leche	*le*·che	milk
licuado	lee·*kwa*·do	fruit smoothie made with milk or water
limonada (natural/ con gas)	lee·mo·*na*·da (na·tur·*al*/ con gas)	lemonade (natural/ carbonated water)
naranjada	na·ran·*kha*·da	a fizzy drink made from orange juice

Tegucigalpa & Southern Honduras

It's true that Tegucigalpa and Southern Honduras don't have the pizzazz that other areas do – the region is mostly hot and flat with relatively few headline sights. But for travelers with time to spare, there are some genuine highlights to be logged, and many places that self-starters may find quite rewarding.

Take Tegucigalpa: it's not the most beautiful city in the world, but it has a way of growing on you nonetheless. The downtown area has some excellent colonial churches, a handful of worthwhile museums and, above all, a hustle and bustle that committed city-goers will appreciate. There are hotels and restaurants for all budgets, and a lively bar and club scene to boot.

Not far from Tegucigalpa are the sister cities of Valle de Ángeles and Santa Lucía, classic colonial towns with sturdy churches, stone-paved streets and brightly painted stucco buildings. In the same vicinity is Parque Nacional La Tigra, Honduras' first national park and its best equipped, with well-marked trails and decent overnight facilities.

Further afield, Southern Honduras ranges from the sweltering Pacific lowlands along the Golfo de Fonseca to the cool highlands of the Sierra de la Botija near the Nicaraguan border. If you love cigars, you can learn about their production in any number of cigar factories in the Jamastrán valley, Honduras' tobacco-growing heartland. This area sees very few travelers, especially foreigners; exploring here requires a bit more initiative, but is uniquely rewarding for the same reason.

HIGHLIGHTS

- Explore **Tegucigalpa** (p70), with its museums, lively nightlife and historic locales, like the restaurant men's room where the country's patron saint once turned up after disappearing from the cathedral

- Bask in birdlife at **Parque Nacional La Tigra** (p91), Honduras' first national park and still one of its best

- Score some stogies on a factory tour in **Danlí** (p97), Honduras' cigar-rolling capital

- Get up to your ears in howler monkeys hiking through **Refugio de Vida Silvestre Ojochal** (p104), outside pleasant San Marcos de Colón

- Seek out **Santa Lucía** (p89), which has all the colonial charm of nearby and better-known Valle de Ángeles but with only a fraction of the tourist traffic

TEGUCIGALPA & SOUTHERN HONDURAS

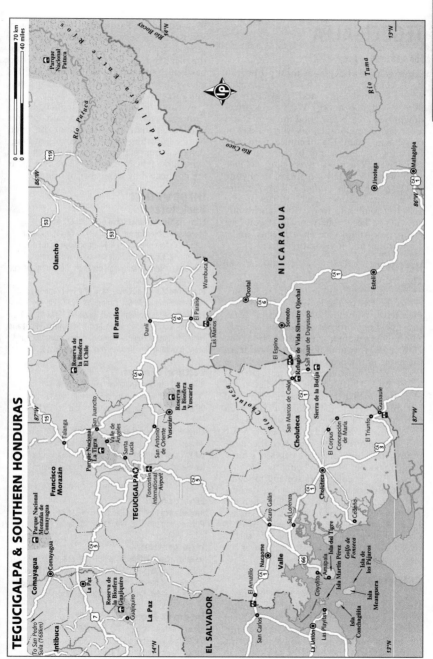

TEGUCIGALPA

pop 1,682,725

Tegucigalpa – or Tegus, as most people call it – is a bustling city in a bowl-shaped valley with a colonial center and sprawling residential neighborhoods. With a historical downtown area, a few good museums, and a variety of restaurants, it's worth a day or two. It's no Shangri-la, of course, with traffic, smog and crime, not to mention crazy taxi drivers. The press covers gang violence with obsessive detail – mention to anyone you're going to *la capital* and you're sure to be warned against it, with stories of robbery to assault and worse. But as with any city, if you keep your wits about you (see Dangers & Annoyances, p74), Tegus can be a rewarding and invigorating place.

HISTORY

The name Tegucigalpa (Teh-goos-ee-*gal*-pa) is a mouthful, and not just for newcomers to the city or the language. Hondurans themselves commonly shorten it to Tegus (*teh*-goos) or simply *la capital* (the capital). The modern name, which dates from the 16th century, is undoubtedly derived from the name of the original indigenous village here, and is most commonly translated as 'silver hill'. The problem with that story, of course, is that the original residents did not mine silver and probably didn't even have a word for the material before Spanish colonizers appeared on the scene. More recently, linguists have suggested the name means, roughly, 'place of painted stones' (which you can imagine being twisted into 'Silver Hill' by colonizers seeking to legitimize their presence). Tegucigalpa became the capital of Honduras in 1880, when the government seat was moved from Comayagua, 82km to the northwest. In 1938 Comayagüela, on the opposite side of the river from Tegucigalpa, became part of the city.

ORIENTATION

The city is divided by the Río Choluteca. On the east side of the river is Tegucigalpa, with the city center and the more affluent districts. Plaza Morazán, also known simply as Parque Central, with its imposing cathedral, is at the heart of the city. On the west side of Parque Central, Av Miguel Paz Barahona serves as a pedestrian shopping district, extending four blocks from the plaza to Calle El Telégrafo; this section has been renamed Calle Peatonal, and it's a busy thoroughfare with many shops, restaurants and banks.

Across the river from Tegucigalpa is Comayagüela, which is generally poorer and dirtier than the east side of the river, with a sprawling market area, lots of long-distance bus stations, cheap hotels and *comedores* (cheap eateries). The two areas are connected by a number of bridges.

INFORMATION
Bookstores

Librería Guaymuras (Map p79; ☎ 222 4140; libreguay@cablecolor.hn; Av Miguel de Cervantes, near Calle Salvador Corleto; ☜ 8:30am-6:30pm Mon-Fri, 8:30am-12:30pm Sat) A little bookshop with a great selection of Spanish-language books on the history, people and culture of Honduras.

Metromedia Av San Carlos (Map p81; metromedia2@ mulitvisionhn.net; Av San Carlos; ☎ 221 0770; ☜ 10am-8pm Mon-Sat, noon-6pm Sun); Multiplaza Mall (☎ 231 2410; Av Juan Pablo; ☜ 8am-8pm). Sells an excellent and wide selection of English-language books, magazines and more, including day-old *New York Times* for US$5.

Cultural Centers

Alianza Francesa (Alliance Française; Map p79; ☎ 239 6163; www.afhonduras.com; Parque Central) Offers cultural events, French classes and weekly French films.

Mujeres En Las Artes (Map p79; ☎ 222 3015; www .muaartes.org.hn; Av Miguel de Cervantes, near bridge to Col Palmira) Hosts art exhibits and performances by female artists. Workshops and lecture series offered occasionally.

Emergency

Ambulance (☎ 195; Red Cross; ☜ 24hr)
Police (Map p79; ☎ 199, 222 8736; 5a Av; ☜ 24hr)

Immigration

Immigration Office (Map p81; ☎ 238 5613; Av La Paz btwn 3a & 4a Avs; ☜ 8:30am-4:30pm Mon-Fri) Extend your visa and handle other immigration matters. Same day service (usually) if you come in the morning.

Internet Access

Cíber Karina (Map pp72-3; ☎ 208 0689; 6a Av btwn Calles 8a & 9a; per hr US$0.75; ☜ 8:30am-8:30pm) Local, national and international phone calls too.

Cíber Planet (Map p79; ☎ 237 0200; Cnr Av Máximo Jérez & Calle Finlay; per hr US$0.65; ✆ 8:30am-10pm Mon-Sat, 10am-10pm Sun) Also offers cheap international calling.

Downtown Hondutel office (Map p79; ☎ 222 1120; Av Cristóbal Colón at Calle El Telégrafo; per hr US$0.80; ✆ 7:30am-9pm Mon-Sat) Air-conditioning and sleek black Dells with flat screens.

El Ch@t C@ribeño (Map p81; ☎ 239 3287; Av República de Chile at Av República de Panama; per hr US$1.10, 20% off with student ID; ✆ 8:30am-8:30pm) Cheap international calls to USA, Canada and Europe.

Laundry
Lavandería Maya (Map p81; 4a Calle; per 10lb US$3; ✆ 7am-6pm Mon-Fri, 8am-4pm Sat)

Superc Jet (Map pp72-3; Av Juan Gutemberg; per pound US$0.50; ✆ 8am-6pm Mon-Sat) Same day service if you drop off your laundry in the AM.

Libraries
Biblioteca Nacional (Map p79; ☎ 220 1746; Av Miguel de Cervantes near Calle Salvador Corleto; ✆ 7:30am-noon, 12:30-3:30pm Mon-Fri) Houses a good collection of Honduran history books. On-site use only; leave your passport as a deposit.

Medical Services
Farma City (Map p81; ☎ 232 4415; Blvd Morazán near Plaza Criolla; ✆ 9am-9pm Mon-Sat, 9am-7pm Sun)

Farmacia Divel (Map p79; ☎ 237 4064; Av Cristóbal Colón at Calle Los Dolores; ✆ 8am-6pm Mon-Fri, 9am-1pm Sun)

Honduras Medical Center (Map pp72-3; ☎ 216 1201; Av Juan Lindo; ✆ 24hr) Considered one of the best hospitals in the country.

Money
In addition to the places listed below, there is a Unibanc ATM at Tegucigalpa airport, and cash machines of all major banks at the malls.

BAC (Map p81; Blvd Morazán at Av Ramón Ernesto Cruz; ✆ 9am-5pm Mon-Fri, 9am-noon Sat) Changes traveler's checks and has a 24-hour ATM.

Banco Atlántida 6a Av at 11a Calle (Map pp72-3; 6a Av at 11a Calle; ✆ 9am-4pm Mon-Fri, 8:30-11:30am Sat) Downtown Tegucigalpa (Map p79; Parque Central) Changes traveler's checks and has 24-hour ATMs.

Mundirama Travel (Map p81; ☎ 232 3909; fax 232 0072; Edif CIICSA, Avs República de Panamá & República de Chile; ✆ 8am-5pm Mon-Fri, 8am-noon Sat) An American Express representative; issues and replaces traveler's checks.

Post
Comayagüela post office (Map pp72-3; 6a Av btwn Calles 7a & 8a; ✆ 7:30am-5pm Mon-Fri, 8am-1pm Sat) In the same building as Hondutel.

Downtown post office (Map p79; Av Miguel Paz Barahona at Calle El Telégrafo; ✆ 7:30am-6pm Mon-Fri, 8am-1pm Sat)

Mailboxes, Etc. (Map p81; ☎ 232 3184; Blvd Morazán; ✆ 8am-6pm Mon-Fri, 9am-1pm Sat) Offers Federal Express service for international deliveries and Viana for domestic. There's a DHL office nearby.

Telephone
Most Internet cafés (see opposite) also offer domestic and international calling.

Comayagüela Hondutel office (Map pp72-3; ☎ 220 0707; 6a Av btwn 7a & 8a Calles; ✆ 7am-8:30pm Mon-Fri) In same building as the post office.

Downtown Hondutel office (Map p79; ☎ 222 1120; Av Cristóbal Colón at Calle El Telégrafo; ✆ 7:30am-9pm Mon-Sat) Call center and Internet café.

Tourist Information
Administración Forestal del Estado – Corporación Hondureña de Desarrollo Forestal (COHDEFOR; Map pp72-3; ☎ 223 4346; www.cohdefor.hn; Colonia El Carrizal; ✆ 8am-4pm Mon-Fri) Headquarters, offering information on Honduras' national parks, wildlife refuges and other protected areas. It's near the Cemeterio General.

Amitigra (Fundación Amigos de la Tigra; Map p81; ☎ 238 6269; www.amitigra.org; 5a Av Edificio Italia, 4th Flr, office No 6; ✆ 8am-12:30pm & 1-5pm Mon-Fri) Offers information about and manages overnight visits to Parque Nacional La Tigra.

Instituto Geográfico Nacional (Map pp72-3; ☎ 225 0752; 3a Av Barrio La Bolsa; ✆ 7:30am-noon, 12:30-3:30pm Mon-Fri) Sells large detailed maps of Honduras, its regions and several of its cities. Also sells road and topographical maps.

Instituto Hondureño de Turismo (Map p81; ☎ 220 1600, 800/222 8687, in USA 800/460 9608; www.letsgo honduras.com; Edificio Europa, 2nd fl, Av Ramón Ernesto Cruz at Calle República de México; ✆ 7:30am-4:30pm Mon-Fri) Offers brochures and basic information on the country's sites. Staff speak English.

Travel Agencies
There are several reliable travel agencies near the Hotel Honduras Maya; others are downtown on Calle Peatonal near Parque Central. Be aware that some agencies charge just for the *cotización* (trip quote).

Mundirama Travel (Map p81; ☎ 232 3909; fax 232 0072; Edificio CIICSA, Avs República de Panamá & República de Chile; ✆ 8am-5pm Mon-Fri, 8am-noon Sat) Can help

TEGUCIGALPA

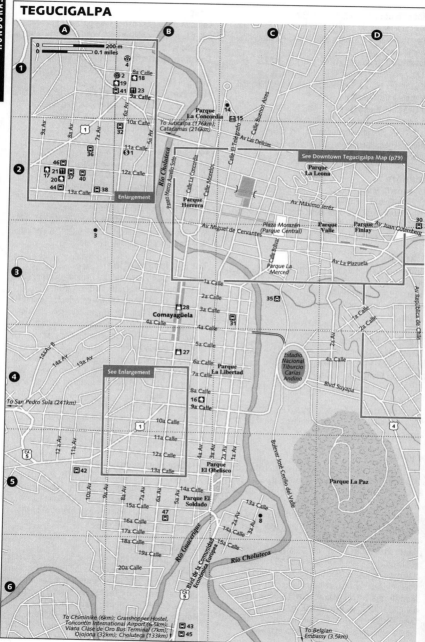

0 — 200 m
0 — 0.1 miles

Enlargement

See Enlargement

See Downtown Tegucigalpa Map (p79)

8a Calle
9a Calle
10a Calle
11a Calle
12a Calle
13a Calle

9a Av
8a Av
7a Av
6a Av
5a Av

Parque La Concordia

To Juticalpa (176km); Catacamas (216km)

Río Choluteca

paseo Marco Aurelio Soto

Calle La Concordia
Calle Morelos

Calle El Telégrafo
Calle Las Delicias
Calle Buenos Aires
Av Las Delicias

Parque La Leona

Parque Herrera

Av Máximo Jerez

Parque Valle

Parque Finlay

Av Juan Gutemberg

Av Miguel de Cervantes
Plaza Morazán (Parque Central)

Calle Bolívar

Av La Plazuela

Parque La Merced

1a Calle
2a Calle
3a Calle
4a Calle
5a Calle
6a Calle
7a Calle
8a Calle
9a Calle
10a Calle
11a Calle
12a Calle
13a Calle

Comayagüela

Parque La Libertad

Estadio Nacional Tiburcio Carías Andino

Blvd Suyapa

Av República de Chile

To San Pedro Sula (241km)

12a Av
11a Av
13a Av
14a Av
15a Av-B

Parque El Obelisco

Parque El Soldado

14a Calle
15a Calle
16a Calle
17a Calle
18a Calle
19a Calle
20a Calle

10a Av
9a Av
8a Av
7a Av
6a Av
5a Av
4a Av
3a Av
2a Av

Parque La Paz

Bulevar José Cecilio del Valle

Río Guacerique

Río Choluteca

Blvd de la Comunidad Económica Europea

To Chiminike (6km); Grasshopper Hostel;
Toncontín International Airport (6.5km);
Viana Clase de Oro Bus Terminal (7km);
Ojojona (32km); Choluteca (133km)

To Belgian Embassy (3.5km)

CA 5

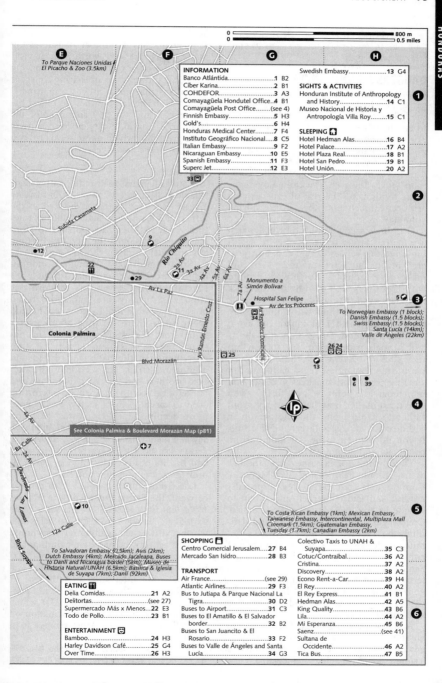

To Parque Naciones Unidas &
El Picacho & Zoo (3.5km)

INFORMATION
Banco Atlántida.....................**1** B2
Ciber Karina..........................**2** B1
COHDEFOR............................**3** A3
Comayagüela Hondutel Office..**4** B1
Comayagüela Post Office........(see 4)
Finnish Embassy.....................**5** H3
Gold's...................................**6** H4
Honduras Medical Center........**7** F4
Instituto Geográfico Nacional....**8** C5
Italian Embassy......................**9** F2
Nicaraguan Embassy..............**10** E5
Spanish Embassy...................**11** F3
Superc Jet.............................**12** E3

Swedish Embassy...................**13** G4

SIGHTS & ACTIVITIES
Honduran Institute of Anthropology
and History.......................**14** C1
Museo Nacional de Historia y
Antropología Villa Roy.........**15** C1

SLEEPING
Hotel Hedman Alas................**16** B4
Hotel Palace.........................**17** A2
Hotel Plaza Real....................**18** B1
Hotel San Pedro....................**19** B1
Hotel Unión..........................**20** A2

Subida Casamata

Río Chiquito

Av la Paz

Monumento a
Simón Bolívar

Hospital San Felipe
Av de los Próceres

Colonia Palmira

Av Ramón Ernesto Cruz

Av República Dominicana

Blvd Morazán

To Norwegian Embassy (1 block);
Danish Embassy (1.5 blocks);
Swiss Embassy (1.5 blocks);
Santa Lucía (14km);
Valle de Ángeles (22km)

See Colonia Palmira & Boulevard Morazán Map (p81)

3a Calle

2a Av

Quebrada Los Lomas

12a Calle

Blvd Suyapa

To Salvadoran Embassy (0.5km); Avis (2km);
Dutch Embassy (4km); Mercado Jacaleapa, Buses
to Danlí and Nicaragua border (5km); Museo de
Historia Natural/UNAH (6.5km); Basílica & Iglesia
de Suyapa (7km); Danlí (92km)

To Costa Rican Embassy (1km); Mexican Embassy,
Taiwanese Embassy, Intercontinental, Multiplaza Mall
Cinemark (1.5km); Guatemalan Embassy
Tuesday (1.7km); Canadian Embassy (2km)

SHOPPING
Centro Comercial Jerusalem....**27** B4
Mercado San Isidro................**28** B3

TRANSPORT
Air France.............................(see 29)
Atlantic Airlines....................**29** F3
Bus to Jutiapa & Parque Nacional La
Tigra................................**30** D2
Buses to Airport....................**31** C3
Buses to El Amatillo & El Salvador
border..............................**32** B2
Buses to San Juancito & El
Rosario.............................**33** F2
Buses to Valle de Ángeles and Santa
Lucía................................**34** G3

Colectivo Taxis to UNAH &
Suyapa.............................**35** C3
Cotuc/Contraibal...................**36** A2
Cristina................................**37** A2
Discovery.............................**38** A2
Econo Rent-a-Car..................**39** H4
El Rey..................................**40** A2
El Rey Express......................**41** B1
Hedman Alas........................**42** A5
King Quality.........................**43** B6
Lila.....................................**44** A2
Mi Esperanza.......................**45** B6
Saenz..................................(see 41)
Sultana de
Occidente.........................**46** A2
Tica Bus..............................**47** B5

EATING
Delia Comidas......................**21** A2
Delitortas.............................(see 27)
Supermercado Más x Menos...**22** E3
Todo de Pollo.......................**23** B1

ENTERTAINMENT
Bamboo...............................**24** H3
Harley Davidson Café............**25** G4
Over Time............................**26** H3

with travel planning. As an American Express representative it issues and replaces Amex traveler's checks. Does not hold mail, unfortunately.

DANGERS & ANNOYANCES

Crime is on everyone's mind in Tegucigalpa, and to read the newspaper, browse the US State Department website, or even to talk to Peace Corps volunteers (who are normally pretty sanguine about traveling in potentially dangerous areas) you may never step out of your hotel, much less explore downtown or go out at night. Using common sense, however, you can enjoy Tegus while minimizing the risk of experiencing any crime, much less violent crime, during your stay.

Criminals aren't stupid: they will watch a potential target to see if they're carrying anything valuable. Cameras and jewelry (real or faux) are sure to be seen, and make easy targets – don't walk around with them. Try doing without a daypack or purse; even if there's nothing valuable in it, a potential thief won't know that. Carry money and ID, of course, but avoid flashing it around. Dress modestly: shorts and sandals many seem fine to you but they stick out like a sore thumb in most Latin American cities, Tegus included. Try wearing pants and sneakers instead. And remember, the point isn't to 'fit in' – you won't, no matter how hard you try – but rather to avoid being the one person in a thousand who gets targeted for crime. If you do happen to be that one person, cooperate and do not resist.

The downtown area is fine during the day, as are Colonia Palmira and Blvd Morazán. Comayagüela can be dodgy, especially around San Isidro Market, and a trip to Parque La Paz (p76) is not recommended. Comayagüela and downtown should definitely be avoided at night – there's not much to do, anyway. If you're at a hotel in either, use cabs to come and go after dark. Same goes if you're going to or from a bus terminal with bags. When waiting for a bus, go inside the terminal, or at least near the ticket booth, and keep a hand on your bags at all times.

And one last thing: relax. The chances of anything happening to any one person at any one time are exceedingly low, even in a 'crime-ridden' place like Tegucigalpa.

SIGHTS

Tegucigalpa has a number of interesting sights, which are well worth a short visit. To be sure, none compare to the amazing museums and galleries, or soaring churches and plazas that make other Latin American cities so special. But they do reflect the resourceful and scrappy character of the Honduran capital, a city no one expects to be great, but which never seems to stop trying to prove nay-sayers wrong.

Museums

The **Museo Nacional de Historia y Antropología Villa Roy** (Map pp72-3; ☎ 222 3470; admission US$1.10; ⏰ 8am-4pm Mon-Sat) is housed in the former home of ex-president Julio Lozano (near Calle Morelos), an opulent two-story mansion overlooking the city. Fascinating, if somewhat intense, the museum traces a chronological path through Honduran history, from independence, through the Liberal reform period, to modern-day Honduras. Displays are long and detailed (and in Spanish only); a close reader could spend hours here learning about everything from the establishment of the national telegraph system to unionization movements in the banana, railroad and mining industries. The section on the Vaccaro brothers and the rise of Standard and United Fruit companies will be interesting even to casual visitors, as few events have more deeply shaped Honduras' past and present. The **Honduran Institute of Anthropology and History** (IHAH; Map pp72-3; ☎ 220 6954; ⏰ 8am-4pm Mon-Fri) operates the museum and has its headquarters and research library near the museum entrance.

Located in what was once a 17th-century convent, the **Galería Nacional de Arte** (Map p79; ☎ 237 9884; fundarte@usa.net; Parque La Merced; admission US$1; ⏰ 9am-4pm Mon-Sat, 9am-1pm Sun) is well worth a visit. Seven exhibition rooms house modern artwork, colonial-era paintings and religious artifacts. There is also a small exhibit of pictographs found in Honduras – all replicas – but interesting nonetheless. At the ticket booth, there is an excellent Spanish-language pamphlet (US$0.55), which provides good background information on the gallery's collection. Most signage is in English and Spanish.

The **Museo del Hombre Hondureño** (Map p79; ☎ 220 1678; Av Miguel de Cervantes btwn Calles Salva-

---

LOCAL LORE: LA VIRGIN DE SUYAPA

In 1747 a farmer named Alejandro Colindres was returning home to Suyapa when he stopped to camp for the night. Settling down, he felt a hard object under his back, which he removed and threw into the brush. Lying back, the lump was still there; he again pried it out but this time placed it in his knapsack. The object turned out to be a 6cm wooden statue of the Virgin Mary, which Colindres' wowed neighbors came to worship for its healing powers. The statue's fame spread; when it cured a wealthy landowner of his kidney stones in 1768 he built a temple in its honor, where it remains today. (The massive Basílica de Suyapa was built nearby in 1954 after the icon was declared Honduras' patron saint; it is moved there for holidays only.) The statue has been stolen twice, most notoriously in September 1986, when it turned up several hours later, wrapped in newspaper, in the men's room of La Terraza de Don Pepe, a popular downtown restaurant. The Feria de la Virgin de Suyapa is celebrated every year on February 3.

---

dor Corleto & Las Damas; admission & hr vary) displays Honduran art, mostly contemporary work. It is often closed, however, open mainly for special events or private parties.

Tegucigalpa's newest museum is the ambitious **Museo para la Identidad Nacional** (MIN; Map p79; ☎ 222 2299; www.min-honduras.org; Av Miguel Paz Barahona btwn Calles Morelos & El Telégrafo; admission & hr to be announced) which is intended to encapsulate the whole of Honduran history, from pre-Colombian civilization to the present day. The museum is housed in the former Palace of Ministries, built in 1880 as a hospital, and will reportedly use the latest audio-visual technology, including a 'virtual theatre' to bring its displays to life. Former President Maduro rushed to inaugurate the museum before he left office, even though it was far from complete; however, it should be open by the time you read this.

The **Museo Histórico de la República** (Map p79; ☎ 237 0268; Paseo Marco Aurelio Soto at Calle Salvador Mendieta; admission US$3, free last Thu of month; ✆ 8:30am-noon & 1-4pm Wed-Sun) is another museum tracing the history of Honduras from independence to the present – the displays are interesting enough, but other museums cover the same ground just as well or better. The building that contains them is the real gem, having served as the *Casa Presidencial* (Presidential Palace) from 1920 until 1992.

Just down the hill from the Basílica de Suyapa (7km south of the city center) is the **Universidad Nacional Autónoma de Honduras (UNAH)**. Typically called Ciudad Universitaria, it houses the **Museo de Historia Natural** (Blvd Suyapa) in the biology building. The museum, however, is a serious downer despite the upbeat listing in *Honduras Tips*.

It houses a sad collection of stuffed birds and animals, many with eyes missing, and feathers and fur coming off in clumps. Only the whale skeleton and petrified dung display are remotely memorable, but still not worth the effort, even for kids.

Also not worth your time is the **Museo Histórico Militar** (Map p79; ☎ 237 9729; Parque Valle; admission free; ✆ 8am-4pm Mon-Fri) which is supposed to be Honduras' military history, but can barely rustle up a few uniforms and old rusty weapons. (The lack of actual military successes on the part of Honduran armed forces may be part of the problem.)

Churches & Plazas

The most important church in Tegucigalpa, and Honduras, is the Gothic **Basílica de Suyapa**, about 7km south of the city center in the suburb of Suyapa, near UNAH, the national university. La Virgen de Suyapa is the patron saint of Honduras; in 1982 a papal decree made her the patron saint of all Central America. Construction of the basilica, which is famous for its large, brilliant stained-glass windows, began in 1954; finishing touches are still being added though.

La Virgen de Suyapa is a tiny wooden statue, measuring only 6cm. Many believe she has performed hundreds of miracles. She is brought to the large basilica on holidays, especially for the annual Feria de la Virgen de Suyapa (p78) beginning on the saint's day (February 3) and continuing for a week; the celebrations attract pilgrims from all over Central America. Most of the time, however, the little statue is kept on the altar of the very simple **Iglesia de Suyapa** (if you squint, you'll see her on the main altar). Built in the late 18th and early 19th centuries, and renovated multiple times, the church stands a few hundred meters behind the impressive basilica.

Buses for Suyapa (US$0.23, 20 minutes) leave from the gas station at 6a Av and 9 Calle in Comayagüela; get off at the university and walk the short distance from there. *Colectivo* taxis leave from a stop a short distance south of Parque La Merced.

At the center of the city is the fine **cathedral** (Map p79) and, in front of it, the **Plaza Morazán**, often just called Parque Central. The domed 18th-century cathedral (built between 1765 and 1782) has an intricate baroque altar of gold and silver. Parque Central, with its statue of Morazán on horseback, is the hub of the city.

Three blocks east of the cathedral is the **Parque Valle**, with the **Iglesia de San Francisco** (Map p79), the first church in Tegucigalpa, founded in 1592 by the Franciscans.

Iglesia Los Dolores (1732; Map p79), northwest of the cathedral, is worth a visit, with a plaza out front and religious art inside. On the front of Los Dolores are figures representing the Passion of Christ – his unseamed cloak, the cock that crowed three times – all crowned by the more indigenous symbol of the sun. Further west is **Parque Herrera**, which seems to attract a somewhat less savory crowd, but the 18th-century **Iglesia El Calvario** (Map p79) is worth a peek, as is the Teatro Nacional Manuel Bonilla, if it happens to be open when you pass by.

Another 18th-century church, **Iglesia La Merced** (Map p79), located next to the Galería Nacional de Arte, faces **Parque La Merced**. In 1847, the convent of La Merced was converted to house Honduras' first university; the national gallery was established there in 1996. The well-restored building is itself a work of art, and is as impressive as the paintings inside. The unusual modern building on stilts next door is the **Palacio Legislativo** (Map p79), where Congress meets.

A couple of blocks west of the Museo Nacional de Historia y Antropología Villa Roy is **Parque La Concordia**, a mellow park full of reproductions of the Maya ruins at Copán, including a pyramid and many stone carvings.

Parks
On the north side of Tegucigalpa is **Parque Naciones Unidas El Picacho** (United Nations Park El Picacho; Map pp72-3; adult/child US$1/0.50; ☺ 8am-5pm), established to commemorate the UN's 40th anniversary. Besides excellent views of the city, there's a soccer field where games are held on Sunday, and a somewhat decrepit **zoo** (adult/child US$0.25/0.10; ☺ 9am-4:30pm Wed-Sun). Food and drink are sold from a small *comedor*.

The park is located about 6km from the center of town, up a winding road past some of the capital's most exclusive real estate (the US Ambassador's residence, for one). On Sundays, buses leave from behind Iglesia Los Dolores all the way to the park gates. Otherwise, take an El Hatillo bus (US$0.35, every 25 minutes; 5am to 10pm; last return bus at 9pm) from Av Juan Gutemberg or Parque Herrera and get off at the junction. It takes about 20 minutes. A taxi from the center costs around US$5.

If you don't want to make the trip all the way to Parque Naciones Unidas, **Parque La Leona** also offers quiet respite from the bustle of downtown and almost-as-good views over the city. It's one of Tegucigalpa's most pleasant (and undervisited) parks, though there could be more shade for the benches. You can walk there, but it's further – and a lot steeper – than it appears on the map. Take Paseo La Leona from the central park and follow it up, up, up. A few small stands sell sodas and chips.

It is not recommended you visit **Parque La Paz**, a wooded hill and park south of the Estadio Nacional. Though the views are impressive, it is a notorious hang-out of delinquent kids, many hooked on glue sniffing, and assaults on visitors are common.

ACTIVITIES
Gym
Gold's (Map pp72-3; ☎ 236 9827, fax 236 8688; Residencial Montecarlo, near Blvd Morazán; day/week/month US$9/30/80; ☺ 5:30am-10pm Mon-Fri, 8am-5pm Sat & Sun) Large well-equipped gym, with weight machines, free weights, spinning, and aerobics. Discounts for children and seniors; annual, group and couples' plans also available. Be sure to bring your own towel.

Hotel Honduras Maya (Map p81; ☎ 220 5000; www.hondurasmaya.hn; near Calzada San Martín, Colonia Palmira) has a swimming pool, gym, spa and sauna that are open to non-guests for US$10 per day, US$5 for children.

QUICK TRIPS

You don't have to pack up your bags and check out of the hotel to see something besides Tegus proper. Here are a couple of day trips that will have you back in time for Happy Hour.

Parque Nacional La Tigra (p91) The park offers hikes of various lengths and difficulties through cloud forest and old growth trees. The Jutiapa entrance is just 22km away.

Valle de Ángeles & Santa Lucía (p90 & p89) Small artsy towns with colonial buildings and cobblestone streets, and just a half-hour from the capital. Busy on weekends, dead on Monday, quiet and serene during the week.

WALKING TOUR

Start in **Parque Central (1)**, aka Plaza Morazán, in the center of town. The **cathedral (2)** is one of Honduras' best, with its spectacular baroque altar. Walk back west a bit and then head south for a block along Calle Bolívar to **Parque La Merced (3)**. The building on stilts in front of you is the federal legislative building (Palacio Legislativo); to your left is another pretty church, Iglesia La Merced. But you're mainly looking for the **Galería Nacional de Arte (4)**, the country's top art museum. Many posted descriptions include English translations, but if you read Spanish there's even better information in a pamphlet available at the ticket counter (US$0.55). When you're done, re-

turn to Parque Central and take Calle Peatonal west to the new **Museo para la Identidad Nacional (5)**, a tech-savvy journey through Honduras' cultural and national formation. Or, for a more traditional museum, walk a bit further (or grab a cab) to the brainy **Museo Nacional de Historia y Antropología Villa Roy (6)**. You may be hungry at this point – along Av Cristóbal Colón you'll find Chinese, Mexican and Honduran food within a few blocks (plus street eats for the adventurous in front of Iglesia Los Dolores). After lunch, stretch your legs by walking up curvy Paseo La Leona to **Parque La Leona (7)**. Grab a Coke and enjoy the view while you catch your breath. Make your way back down to the neighborhood around pretty little **Parque Valle (8)**, east of the center. Cut down a block to Av Miguel de Cervantes; if you're lucky, the **Museo del Hombre Hondureño (9)** will be open, for a quick peek at more Honduran art. If not – it's usually closed – the next two blocks boast a bookstore, a great little café and several **artesanía shops (10)**. Finally, continue along Av Miguel de Cervantes across a small bridge and up the hill into **Colonia Palmira (11)**, where there are excellent restaurants for an end-of-the-day drink or dinner.

TEGUCIGALPA FOR CHILDREN

Chiminike (☎ 291 0339; www.chiminike.com; Blvd Fuerzas Amadas de Honduras; admission US$2.75; ⏰ 9am-noon & 2-5pm Tue-Fri, 10am-1pm & 2-5pm Sat & Sun) is Tegucigalpa's excellent new children's

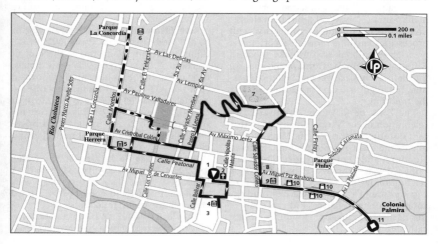

TALK THE TALK

Tegucigalpa's go-to Spanish school offers excellent one-on-one classes that are popular with diplomats, business people and NGO administrators. For travelers, La Ceiba, Western Honduras and the Bay Islands – not to mention Guatemala, the Spanish school mecca – are more likely places to spend a week or two taking language classes.

CONVERSA Language School (Map p81; ☎ 231 1874; aerohond@cablecolor.hn; Paseo República de Argentina 257; ☑ 8am-5pm Mon-Fri, 8:30am-12:30pm Sat) Three types of courses are offered on a monthly basis: Intensivo (120 hours, US$924), Semi-Intensivo (80 hours, US$624), and Diario (40 hours, US$324). Homestays (US$350 per month including two meals per day), all within walking distance of the school, can be arranged.

museum, one of many such institutions that have popped up around Central America in recent years. Situated about 7km south of Downtown Tegus, it accounts for kids of all ages, from a peaceful infant/nursing area to adolescent-level displays on Maya history. And it's refreshingly frank: the area about the human body has exhibits on the hows and whys of farting, vomiting, sneezing and body odor, while a crawl-through digestive tract starts at the mouth and ends with a slide through an oversized rectum. Other highlights are a miniature supermarket and construction site, working TV and radio studios, a bubble room, a bed of nails and a *casa de equilibrio* ('equilibrium house') – a small house built at a 22-degree angle to highlight your sense of balance (separate admission US$1). There's a café-restaurant onsite.

FESTIVALS & EVENTS

Tegucigalpa is virtually deserted during Semana Santa (Holy Week), but the celebration is slowly growing in popularity, with processions and *alfombras* – 'carpets' made of brightly colored sawdust like those in Antigua, Guatemala. Comayagua, just up the highway, has a larger and better celebration, but Tegus is trying to reclaim some of the tradition.

The Feria de la Virgin de Suyapa is a celebration of the Virgin de Suyapa, a tiny cedar statue of the Virgin Mary that is one of the most revered Catholic icons in Honduras and Central America. The actual saint's day is February 3, but the whole celebration lasts a week – masses and processions are held around the city (and the country, for that matter) but especially at the Basílica de Suyapa, Honduras' largest cathedral.

SLEEPING

The city's cheapest lodging is in Comayagüela, which is also where most of the bus terminals are, but the area can be dodgy during the day and downright dangerous at night. Downtown is slightly more expensive, safe during the day (but not at night) and near most of the sights. If you can afford it, Colonia Palmira offers the best quality and safest surroundings, day and night.

Downtown Tegucigalpa

our pick **Nuevo Hotel Boston** (Map p79; ☎ 237 9411; Av Máximo Jérez 321; s/d/tw US$12/16/19) Located in a colonial-style building, the rooms here are very well kept and have high ceilings, talavera tile floors and squeaky clean bathrooms. Rooms facing the street can be noisy but they're big and have nice balconies. Two large and airy common rooms have couches, rocking chairs and TVs for guests to use. Free coffee and cookies are always available too.

Hotel Granada No 2 (Map p79; ☎ 238 4438; fax 237 0843; Subida Casamata 1326; r/tw US$20/28; ⓟ ▣) Comfortable but plain, this is the best of a group of three large 1970s-style hotels; most of the 48 rooms have nicely renovated bathrooms, TV and in-room telephone.

Hotel Granada No 3 (Map p79; ☎ 222 0597; fax 237 0843; Subida Casamata 1325) This is across the street from No 2, and has identical prices but the rooms are somewhat neglected and gloomy.

Hotel Granada No 1 (Map p79; ☎ 237 2381; fax 222 2654; Av Juan Gutemberg 1401; s/d US$16/21) A block away, this place is very clean with small bathrooms and good beds – a good choice if every lempira counts.

Hotel Iberia (Map p79; ☎ 237 9267; Calle Los Dolores near Av Cristóbal Colón; s/d with shared bathroom US$6/8,

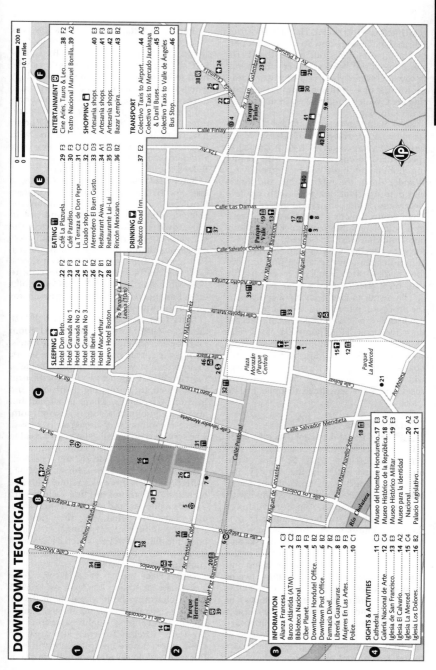

DOWNTOWN TEGUCIGALPA

INFORMATION
Alianza Francesa...........................1 C3
Banco Atlántida (ATM)...................2 C4
Biblioteca Nacional........................3 E3
Ciber Planet..................................4 F3
Downtown Hondutel Office.............5 B2
Downtown Post Office...................6 B2
Farmacia Divel...............................7 B2
Librería Guaymuras.......................8 F3
Mujeres En Las Artes.....................9 E3
Police...10 C1

SIGHTS & ACTIVITIES
Cathedral....................................11 C3
Galería Nacional de Arte................12 C4
Iglesia de San Francisco................13 E3
Iglesia El Calvario.........................14 A2
Iglesia La Merced.........................15 C4
Iglesia Los Dolores.......................16 B2
Museo del Hombre Hondureño......17 E3
Museo Histórico de la República....18 C4
Museo Histórico Militar.................19 E3
Museo para la Identidad
   Nacional..................................20 A2
Palacio Legislativo........................21 C4

SLEEPING
Hotel Don Beto............................22 F2
Hotel Granada No 1......................23 F3
Hotel Granada No 2......................24 F2
Hotel Granada No 3......................25 F2
Hotel Iberia..................................26 B2
Hotel MacArthur..........................27 B1
Nuevo Hotel Boston.....................28 B2

EATING
Café La Plazuela...........................29 F3
Café Paradiso...............................30 F3
La Terraza de Don Pepe................31 C2
Licuado shop...............................32 C2
Merendero El Buen Gusto.............33 D3
Restaurant Aiwa...........................34 A1
Restaurante Lai-Lai.......................35 D3
Rincón Mexicano..........................36 B2

DRINKING
Tobacco Road Inn........................37 E2

ENTERTAINMENT
Cine Aires, Tauro & Leo................38 F2
Teatro Nacional Manuel Bonilla....39 A2

SHOPPING
Artesanía shops............................40 E3
Artesanía shops............................41 F3
Artesanía shops............................42 E3
Bazar Lempira..............................43 B2

TRANSPORT
Colectivo Taxis to Airport.............44 A2
Colectivo Taxis to Mercado Jacaleapa
   & Danlí Buses............................45 D3
Colectivo Taxis to Valle de Ángeles
   Bus Stop..................................46 C2

r US$11; for fan US$1, for TV US$2) Half a block from Iglesia Los Dolores and somewhat hidden by the market stalls out front, the Iberia has some of the cleanest shared bathrooms in town. Upstairs rooms have private bathrooms that open onto a pleasant, sunny sitting area. Watch your pockets in the market when you exit.

Hotel MacArthur (Map p79; ☎ 237 9839; homacart@datum.hn; Av Lempira near Calle El Telégrafo; s/d with fan US$35/40, s/d with air-con US$40/46; P ⛶ ⬜) A spectacularly modern entrance with gleaming floors and high ceilings greets you. Wander down the lobby a bit, and you'll bump into a glorious pool with crystal-clear water, lounge chairs and shaded tables. Then go up to your room. It's as if it were in a completely different hotel; very clean but somewhat worn and dated – a let down for sure. Stay here if you plan to enjoy the common areas, but if you're just looking for a place to sleep, you'll get more bang for your buck elsewhere.

The owner of Grenadas No 2 & 3 was in the process of building another hotel – **Hotel Don Beto** (Map p79; Subida Casamata 1323) – across the street from Hotel Granada No 3. The Don Beto looks as if it'll be a cut above its sister hotels. The building is modern and boasts brand new…everything. The citywide views from the top floor rooms are spectacular. It's scheduled to open in late 2006.

Colonia Palmira

our pick **Hotel Portal del Ángel** (Map p81; ☎ 239 6538; www.portaldelangel.com; Av República de Perú; s/d/ste US$90/105/110; P ⛶ ⬜ ⛶) One of the only boutique hotels in the country, the Portal del Ángel is an upscale and classy place. Rooms are lovingly decorated with Honduran artesanías, plush furnishings and high-end art. All boast polished wood floors – some parquet, some caoba – and have silent air conditioners, heavy desks and large flat-screen TVs. There is a pool in the center of the hotel, with a garden patio and a gourmet restaurant running along two of its sides. Rates include a la carte breakfast and a *merienda* (late afternoon snack) of petit fours and fresh juices. There's also a 24-hour business center, a complimentary daily shoe shine and free shuttle service to and from the airport. It's an excellent place to stay if you want to treat yourself.

Hotel Linda Vista (Map p81; ☎ 238 2099; www.lindavistahotel.com; Calle Las Acacias 1438; s/d US$41/59; P ⛶ ⬜) This cozy, well-run B&B is small – just six rooms – which means it can be hard to get a reservation, though definitely worth trying. The foyer and common area have colonial-style wooden chairs and potted plants, and a grassy backyard and patio offer a truly *linda vista* (pretty view). Rooms have firm beds and ceramic floors, with decorative touches like throw pillows, large wooden headboards, and framed paintings. Rates include continental breakfast.

Hotel Guadalupe 2 (Map p81; ☎ 238 5009; 1a Calle; d/tw US$17/20; P ⛶) The go-to place for Peace Corps volunteers – it's affordable, near the program office and not in downtown or Comayagüela (which the US embassy portrays as only slightly less dangerous than a dark alley in Baghdad). Fourteen no-frills rooms have clean sheets, cable TV and a fan, and you can walk to Blvd Morazán from here. Peace Corps folks often have good travel advice, especially for out-of-the-way places.

Confort Inn (Map p81; ☎ 238 3864; fax 238 9721; Calzada San Martín; r US$50; ⛶ ⛶) An 11-room B&B located among several high-rise hotels. Rooms are spread out over a couple floors, many with a view over the northeast side of the city; all are spotlessly clean, with firm beds, air-conditioning, big bathrooms and in-room telephones. There is a small but appealing pool and a sunny dining room, where complimentary breakfast is served. The service is excellent – staffers try hard to make you feel like you've come home.

Casal B&B (Map p81; ☎ 235 8891; casal@multivisionhn.net; Av República de Perú; s/d US$43/58; ⛶ ⬜) A B&B that feels more like a hotel with free breakfast. The rooms are fine – clean with in-room phones and cable TV but small and charmless (what were they thinking with the industrial carpeting?). It's in a good location, however, which means a lot in this town. A decent place to stay if you're running out of options.

Leslie's Place (Map p81; ☎ 220 7494; www.dormir.com; Calzada San Martín; r with fan/air-con US$69/80; ⛶) A charming B&B where the little details up the rate: luxurious linens, matching furniture sets, quality artesanía on the walls, wireless Internet, and a garden dining area where complimentary breakfast is served. Every afternoon, there also is

COLONIA PALMIRA & BOULEVARD MORAZÁN

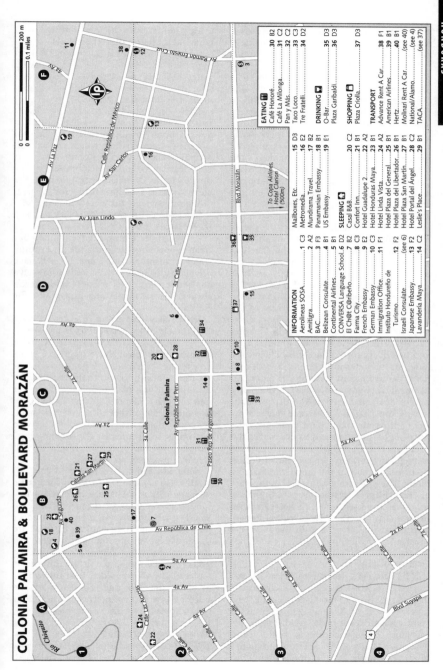

0　　　　200 m
0　　　　0.1 miles

INFORMATION
Aerolíneas SOSA.................................1 C3
Amitgra...2 A2
BAC...3 F3
Belizean Consulate............................4 B1
Continental Airlines...........................5 B1
CONVERSA Language School..........6 D2
El Ch@t C@ribeño.............................7 B2
Farma City..8 C3
French Embassy.................................9 E2
German Embassy..............................10 C3
Immigration Office..........................11 F1
Instituto Hondureño de
  Turismo......................................(see 6)
Israeli Consulate...............................12 F2
Japanese Embassy............................13 F2
Lavandería Maya..............................14 C2
Mailboxes, Etc..................................15 D3
Metromedia.....................................16 E2
Mundirama Travel............................17 B2
Panamanian Embassy......................18 B1
US Embassy.....................................19 E1

SLEEPING
Casal B&B.......................................20 C2
Confort Inn.....................................21 B1
Hotel Guadalupe 2..........................22 A2
Hotel Honduras Maya......................23 B1
Hotel Linda Vista.............................24 A2
Hotel Plaza del General...................25 B1
Hotel Plaza del Libertador...............26 B1
Hotel Plaza San Martín....................27 B1
Hotel Portal del Ángel.....................28 C2
Leslie's Place...................................29 B1

EATING
Café Honoré...................................30 B2
Café La Milonga..............................31 C2
Pan y Más.......................................32 C2
Taco Loco.......................................33 C3
Tre Fratelli......................................34 D2

DRINKING
O-Bar...35 D3
Plaza Garibaldi................................36 D3

SHOPPING
Plaza Criolla....................................37 D3

TRANSPORT
Advance Rent A Car........................38 F1
American Airlines.............................39 B1
Hertz..40 B1
Molinari Rent A Car......................(see 40)
National/Álamo............................(see 37)
TACA...(see 37)

To Copa Airlines,
Hotel Clarion
(500m)

a *merienda* – pastries, coffees, and juices – for guests to enjoy. Popular with business people and expatriates.

Hotel Honduras Maya (Map p81; ☎ 220 5000; www.hondurasmaya.hn; near Calzada San Martín; s/d/t with buffet breakfast US$81/93/100; ✵ P ☎ ⬚) Honduras' first upscale hotel is still a good choice, thanks to regular upkeeping and redecorating. Clean, well-appointed rooms have firm beds and smallish bathrooms; some have great city views, all have modern amenities like coffee maker, hair drier and wireless Internet access (US$10 per day). Just past the welcoming lobby is a mid-sized swimming pool with lounge chairs, and access to the hotel's gym and spa. They haven't been able to update the exterior, though, which screams 1970s with its modular lines and poor approximation of…what are those? Maya glyphs? The bar and restaurant here aren't half bad, as hotels go.

Hotel Plaza del Libertador (Map p81; ☎ 220 4141; www.hotelplazadellibertador.com; Plaza San Martín, s/d US$100/120; P ✵ ⬚) Our favorite of the three sister hotels (soon to be four) clustered at the top of a small hill in Colonia Palmira. The Libertador is the middle sister, and has classy rooms with cozy chalet-like look; junior suites have king-size beds and better bathrooms for just US$20 more. All rooms have a great little terrace; definitely ask for one with a city view. A design snafu means the neighbor's terrace has a view right into your room (and yours into the next one) – pulling the curtains solves the problem, but it's still a bummer. No swimming pool, but there's free wireless Internet in all rooms and in the small comfortable lobby. The other hotels, just across the way, are **Hotel Plaza San Martín** (Map p81; ☎ 238 4500; www.plazasanmartinhotel.com) and **Hotel Plaza del General** (Map p81; ☎ 220 7272; www.hotelplazadel-general.com). Similar pricing to the Plaza del Libertador applies.

Comayagüela

ourpick Hotel Plaza Real (Map pp72-3; ☎ 237 0084; fax 238 8114; 6a Av near 8a Calle; r with shared bathroom US$9; r/tw US$11/16) Overall, this is the best place to stay in Comayagüela. Smallish rooms have decent beds, good linen, ceiling fans – even decorations on the walls. The shared bathrooms are clean and there's always hot water. All the rooms open onto

a leafy courtyard, which is outfitted with tables and chairs, plus there's also a *pila* (laundry station) for guests to hand-wash their clothes. Free coffee and drinking water 24/7. A side door gives direct access to a good restaurant, Todo de Pollo (p85).

Hotel Hedman Alas (Map pp72-3; ☎ 237 9333; www.hedmanalas.com; 4 Av btwn 8a & 9a Calles; s/d with breakfast US$16/19) Another good option, this newish hotel is administered by Central America's best bus line, which has its stop several blocks away. Rooms are small, but very clean. A cool polished lobby and reception area provide welcome respite from the bustle outside. It's a little pricey for the area, though reasonable for what you get.

Hotel Unión (Map pp72-3; ☎ 237 4213; 8a Av btwn 12a & 13a Calle; s/d/tw US$12/13/16) Opened in 2005, the Hotel Unión offers cramped but clean rooms with gleaming tile floors, pine wood furnishings and cable TV. All have private bathrooms, though only some have hot water. Service is friendly and there's always free purified water and coffee for guests.

Hotel Palace (Map pp72-3; ☎ 237 6660; fax 238 0844; 12a Calle btwn 8a & 9a Avs; r US$22; r/tw with air-con US$31/41; P ✵) This is the Fort Knox of Comayagüela: guests have to greet a shot-gun-toting security guard, get through two secured doors and shout to the receptionist through a thick plexiglass window to get into the place. Rooms are distributed over five floors, and although somewhat small, are comfortable with firm beds and private hot-water bathrooms. It's a decent place, although for the price, you might as well stay in a nicer neighborhood.

Hotel San Pedro (Map pp72-3; ☎ 222 8987; fax 222 6783; 6a Av btwn 8a & 9a Calles; s/d with shared bathroom US$5/6; s/d US$8/9, extra for fan US$2-3) Despite saggy beds and brusque service, the San Pedro remains popular with budget travelers. Rooms are relatively clean as are the shared bathrooms, though for the steady stream of guests it receives, you'd think the walls could be re-painted or the thin sheets replaced and they could at least throw fans in under the base rate. The small on-site cafétéria as well as an Internet café next door (p70), however, are nice conveniences.

Other Neighborhoods

ourpick Grasshopper Hostel (☎ 234 2002; www .grasshopperhostel.com; Colonia 15 de Septiembre Bloque 1,

No 39; dm US$12, r US$28) Run by a super-friendly English-speaking family, this brand new hostel has four spacious rooms with bunks and Guatemalan bedspreads, clean shared bathrooms, large lockers, common room with cable TV and Internet access, laundry service, luggage storage, book exchange, free coffee and tea, and no curfew. There's one private room and a nearby commercial center has an ATM, pharmacy, clinic and fast-food joints. But here's the catch: the hostel is about two grasshopper leaps from the airport, which is great for coming or going, but well away from the center. It's about 7km south of Downtown Tegus. Buses and taxis (colectivo and private) pass within steps of the hostel, so getting back and forth is easy enough, but it's not the same as having everything within walking distance.

InterContinental (☎ 231 2727, fax 231 2828; www .gruporeal.com; Av Roble at Blvd Juan Pablo II; r weekend/weekday US$124/149, executive club US$154/179; P ☒ ☒ ☐ ☒) Next to Multiplaza Mall, the InterContinental is Tegucigalpa's top hotel and popular with upscale tourists, businesspeople, visiting diplomats and politicians. The huge air-cooled lobby is a study of marble and muted tones, with low light adding to the effect. Standard rooms feature marble bathrooms, firm beds and the expected amenities: safe, mini-bar, iron, hairdryer, etc. Executive rooms have higher ceilings and extras like free breakfast, free in-room Internet and quick checkout.

EATING

Like any large city, Tegucigalpa runs the gamut in eating options, from street food to five-star gourmet.

Downtown Tegucigalpa

our pick **Café Paradiso** (Map p79; ☎ 237 0337; Av Miguel Paz Barahona 1351; mains US$1-5; ☺ lunch & dinner Mon-Sat) Coffeehouse lingerers will like this coffeehouse/gallery near El Arbolito, one of the coolest spots in the downtown area. Order international food – ham and cheese croissant, yogurt cup with granola, small salads – and check out the goings-on at the extensive bulletin board in front. Artsy, mostly English-language movies are shown Tuesdays at 7pm; Thursdays are for poetry readings or other live cultural performances. High-speed Internet is also available.

La Terraza de Don Pepe (Map p79; ☎ 237 1084; Av Cristóbal Colón 2062; dishes US$2-7; ☺ 8:30am-10pm) A popular second-floor eatery, La Terraza has good *platos del día* (daily specials) and has live crooning most evenings. Tables on the small terrace, or just inside, overlook the busy street and catch nice natural light. While you're here, take a look at the unusual shrine to the Virgin of Suyapa, whose statue was once abducted from the Basilica de Suyapa; it turned up in the men's restroom.

Rincón Mexicano (Map p79; ☎ 222 8368; Av Cristóbal Colón at Calle El Telégrafo; mains US$2.50-4; ☺ breakfast, lunch & dinner) This 'Mexican corner' is indeed a quiet little place where you can escape the noise and exhaust of Av Colón traffic. Small connected dining rooms have just a few cantina-style tables and chairs apiece. The menu has all the usual suspects: tacos, mole, tortas (even 'drowned tortas,' a specialty of Guadalajara), plus American variations like fajitas and burritos. May open late – best for lunch or dinner.

Café La Plazuela (Map p79; ☎ 237 0501; Av Miguel Paz Barahona 1349; dishes US$2-4; ☺ breakfast, lunch & dinner Mon-Sat) Next door to the Café Paradiso, this casual modern eatery has soups and light meals, and a happy hour from 5pm to 7pm. A total interior renovation meant the place was closed when we were in town, but the menu and sharp atmosphere should remain the same. It hosts periodic events, like live music performances or important soccer games on TV.

Restaurante Lai-Lai (Map p79; ☎ 238 7763; Calle Adolfo Zuniga at Av Cristóbal Colón; mains US$2.50-6; ☺ breakfast, lunch & dinner) This Chinese restaurant is housed somewhat improbably in a beautiful converted colonial mansion, with *azulejo* (painted tile) floors and an inner courtyard with filtered sunlight from above. The food is a step up from similar restaurants – not exactly refined, but quite tasty. The 'personal menus' come with three different items and a tall glass of soda for not more than US$3.25, and there are, of course, the mongo 'family' plates typical of many Chinese restaurants. Service is uneven, but at least the building will occupy your eyes while you wait.

Restaurant Aiwa (Map p79; Calle Morelos btwn Avs Máximo Jerez & Paulin Vallardes; mains US$4-7; ☺ lunch &

TEGUCIGALPA & SOUTHERN HONDURAS

dinner) Another recommendable Chinese restaurant with a completely different look. A huge marquee-like sign and swinging glass doors make it easy to mistake Aiwa for a movie theatre; inside, the air-cooled dining room has gleaming tables and floors, and waiters zipping around with huge plates of chop suey, chow mein and more. As usual, portions are enormous – a regular plate serves two, a family plate four or more. Take-out available.

Merendero El Buen Gusto (Map p79; ☎ 238 7767; Calle Hipolito Matute; dishes US$2-3; ☽ breakfast & lunch Mon-Sat) A true Honduran greasy spoon behind the Cathedral, packed with workers of all stripes. Counter-seating only, with quick unceremonious service; food ranges from fried chicken to beef stew and not much further.

There's an awesome **licuado shop** (☽ 8am-6pm Mon-Fri, 8:30am-4pm Sat, 10am-4pm Sun) at the northwest corner of Parque Central next to Little Caesar's pizza. Literally a hole in the wall, there are a couple tables inside, but just as many people take their drinks to go, to enjoy in the park. A thousand combinations are offered, it seems, all made with fresh fruit and a base of either water, milk or fresh orange juice.

At lunch, the **food stands** (mains US$0.50-1.50) in front of Iglesia Los Dolores (Map p79) fill the air with the smoke, sounds and smells of sizzling meats, and people ordering, eating and talking. There's a little of everything here – pupusas, baleadas, soups and, of course, grilled beef and chicken. A must-do if you like street food.

Colonia Palmira

our pick **Café La Milonga** (Map p81; ☎ 232 2654; Paseo República de Argentina 1802; mains US$4-8; ☽ lunch & dinner Mon-Fri, lunch until 6:30pm Sat) This terrific Argentinean grill has much more than just meat – and is much more than just a restaurant, for that matter. First things first: a long lunch and dinner menu includes sandwiches (several veggie options available), thick wedges of quiche (spinach, eggplant, broccoli, Lorraine), empanadas (chicken, beef or spinach) and of course excellent cuts of meat, in 8- or 12-oz portions that are melt-in-your-mouth tender. Judging from the name (la milonga is an Argentinean dance) it's no surprise that music and dance also figure prominently

here: folk singer Karla Lara got her start here and Guillermo Anderson has played here too. Friday nights are for tango, including a short class for beginners. Movies are played Wednesdays at 7:30pm.

Tre Fratelli (Map p81; ☎ 221 6748; Paseo República de Argentina at rear entrance of Plaza Criolla; mains US$6-13; ☽ breakfast, lunch & dinner) A blast of cool air and a huge mural of San Francisco welcome guests to this popular and reasonably priced Palmira restaurant. It's a chain, yes, but one serving reliable Italian food. The long list of pasta includes seafood lasagna and *fettuccini inferno*, made with spicy shrimp and chicken sausage. There are also several main dishes – meat and fish mostly – and pizza. A spacious outdoor patio is nice when it's not too hot.

Pan y Más (Map p81; ☎ 232 4064; Bakery Center, Paseo República de Argentina; ☽ 7:30am-7:30pm) This small first-floor shop has fresh cookies, bread and pretty good bagels – a bag of six costs US$2. There are sodas and coffee, plus light sandwiches – crab, ham or turkey – for around US$3.

Café Honoré (Map p81; ☎ 239 7566; Paseo República de Argentina 1941; mains US$3.50-8.50) Five or eight bucks is a lot for a sandwich, but this may be the only place in Honduras to get the real deal instead of processed ham and Wonder bread. Sandwiches come with combinations of salami, roast beef, prosciutto, roast peppers, mozzarella cheese and more, with a choice of wheat bread, sourdough, baguette or pita. This is also a gourmet deli, for all your pickle and pâté needs.

Taco Loco (Map p81; ☎ 239 7131; Blvd Morazán; mains US$1-5 ☽ lunch & dinner) Orange caféteria-style tables stand opposite an open kitchen and grill in this small smoky taco joint. Hefty tacos come with flour or corn tortillas, and choice of beef, pork or chicken filling; an order of *cebollas lloronas* (grilled, literally 'cry baby', onions) is worth the extra US$1. Delivery available.

Comayagüela

Centro Comercial Jerusalem (Map pp72-3; 6a Av btwn 5a & 6a Calles; ☽ 8am-6pm Mon-Sat, 8am-noon Sun) This small shopping center has a handful of cheap but clean eateries, most offering *típica*, sandwiches and snacks. **Delitortas** (3rd fl; mains US$1-2) is known for its good daily specials like a hamburger, fries and a soda for US$1.50, but be sure to check out the other options.

EATING IN

If you're tired of eating plates of fried chicken with fries, consider busting out of your routine by buying fresh food to prepare at your hotel or hostel. No kitchen? No worries. Even fixings for a sandwich – just like you make at home – is a good change of pace. And while you're poking around the market, look around. See what *capitalinos* are throwing in their baskets. You might be surprised by what you see. Good places to check out include the following.

The **Supermercado Más x Menos** (Map pp72-3; Av La Paz at 4a Av; ☼ 8am-8pm) is an upscale, large supermarket, offering a good selection of fresh food, including nice cheeses and wines.

Todo de Pollo (Map pp72-3; 6a Av near 8a Calle; mains US$2-3.50; ☼ breakfast, lunch & dinner) Todo de Pollo – Everything Made of Chicken – is right. This colorful eatery serves up chicken in every way, shape and form. Eggs are chickens, right? Located next to – and with a side entrance to – the Hotel Plaza Real.

Delia Comidas (Map pp72-3; 8a Av btwn 12a & 13a Calles; mains US$1.50-3; ☼ breakfast, lunch & dinner) A simple buffet-style eatery that also doubles as a pulpería, Internet café (per hr US$1), and call center (US$0.11 per minute to US and Canada, US$0.22 to rest of the world). You'll find *típica* all day long; arrive at regular meal times for the freshest food.

DRINKING

Café La Plazuela (Map p79; ☎ 237 0501; Av Miguel Paz Barahona 1349; ☼ 9am-11pm Mon-Sat) The place to go for football and occasional live music performances. It's also a great place to get something to eat.

Café Paradiso (Map p79; ☎ 237 0337; Av Miguel Paz Barahona 1351; ☼ 9am-8pm Mon-Sat, 9am-9:30pm Tue & Thu) Next door to La Plazuela, screens English-language movies every Tuesday night at 7pm and has poetry readings Thursdays at 7pm. The food's good too.

Tobacco Road Inn (Map p79; ☎ 222 4081; Av Máximo Jérez 1013) A cool little downtown bar that's good for meeting other travelers. Live music most Friday nights.

Plaza Garibaldi (Map p81; ☎ 232 0017; Blvd Morazán at Av Juan Lindo; ☼ 24hr) Great for your karaoke and Mexican music fix.

Ruby Tuesday (☎ 235 3463; Blvd Juan Pablo II; ☼ 11am-11pm Mon-Thurs, 11am-2am Fri-Sat, 11am-midnight Sun) Has two-for-one beer and appetizers on Sundays.

ENTERTAINMENT
Nightclubs

Most of Tegucigalpa's nightlife is found on Blvd Morazán, and is usually open from Wednesday to Saturday.

O-Bar (Map p81; ☎ 235 3437; Blvd Morazán; cover US$5.50; ☼ 7pm-2am Wed-Sat) Situated close to Colonia Palmira hotels and the Peace Corps office, this sleek modern bar and club sees a mixed crowd of foreigners and locals. Low round tables stand in the front rooms and around the edges of the bar area, while a small dance floor pulses with black light and laser machines. Friday is Ladies Night, while Saturday usually sees open bar for rum drinks, 2-for-1 tequila and beer specials.

Bamboo (Map pp72-3; ☎ 236 5391; Blvd Morazán; cover US$6-8; ☼ 9pm-2am Wed-Sat) Formerly the Hipa Hipa, this is still Tegucigalpa's most exclusive nightclub – don't even think of wearing sandals and a T-shirt. The doors are manned by beefy bouncers, while inside, the capital's young and rich and beautiful cram the large sunken dance floor. Expect drink specials from Wednesday to Friday, like free national beers or one-lempira rum and vodka; Saturdays are the most crowded, and occasionally have performances or special events.

Over Time (Map pp72-3; ☎ 963 6703; Blvd Morazán; admission free; ☼ 2pm-midnight) In case you can't get into Bamboo – it happens – you can always nurse your ego at the large bar next door. It's technically a sports bar, hence the odd name and the TVs everywhere showing soccer matches, but its warehouse look and music à la Gwen Stefani and Green Day, make this one of the coolest sports bars you're likely to see.

Harley Davidson Café (Map pp72-3; Blvd Morazán; admission free; ☼ 5pm-2am Mon-Sat) There aren't really enough bikers in Honduras to make a real biker bar, but you get the general idea here. Outdoor tables, buckets of Port Royal and 2-for-1 bar food make for an everyman atmosphere, which can be a welcome alternative to the too-cool scene elsewhere. Friday nights feature live classic rock shows, complete with loaner Harleys

THE HONDURAN SEX TRADE

Sex tourism is not as obvious in Honduras as is in the resort towns of the Dominican Republic or in Costa Rica, where dozens of websites advertise what amounts to sex-tour packages. But that may be simply because the preferred victims are less visible: children.

In May 2006, FBI and immigration agents arrested a 58-year-old Florida man who they accused of arranging trips to Honduras for men interested in having sex with underage girls. The man was a commander of a local US Navy children's program, teaching youngsters the Navy's values of honor, courage and commitment. In 2004, a Brooklyn pediatrician was sentenced to 21 years in prison for having lured children in Honduras and Mexico into sexual encounters.

Casa Alianza, the Latin American affiliate of Covenant House, a NY children's advocacy group, issued a report that said 8000 to 10,000 girls and boys were involved in sex work in Honduras alone. Honduran teenagers are among the most frequently trafficked children in Central America, most going to brothels and resorts in Guatemala, Mexico and El Salvador, where the patrons are mainly American, European and Australian men.

Groups like Casa Alianza have worked to raise awareness of the problem in Central America, which they say has grown in the wake of crack-downs in Thailand and other Asian countries long known for their prostitution and pedophilia rings. In a bitter irony, Casa Alianza fired the 15-year director of its Tegucigalpa office in 2004 after reports surfaced that he had paid a 19-year-old staying in one of the group's youth shelters to have sex. The director, a British citizen, was a well-known children's advocate, and had even been awarded an Order of the British Empire Medal in 2000 for his work with homeless children.

In 2000, advocates across the political spectrum joined in pressing the US to pass a law against human trafficking. The law has been particularly effective in Asia and Eastern Europe, breaking up numerous trafficking rings and returning victims to their homes and countries. Progress has been slower in Latin America, however, and pressure on the issue is still needed.

on a trailer outside and gyrating Harley girls.

Cinemas

Cinemark (☎ 231 2044; www.cinemarkca.com; Multiplaza Mall, Av Juan Pablo II; admission US$2.75) Large mall movie theater showing mostly Hollywood movies; call or check the paper for show times.

Cine Aries, Tauro & Leo (Map p79; ☎ Subida Casamata near Juan Gutemberg; admission US$1) Screening Hollywood and Latin-American films at 7pm and 9pm daily.

Theater

Teatro Nacional Manuel Bonilla (Map p79; ☎ 222 4366; Av Miguel Paz Barahona) Hosts a variety of performing-arts shows, including plays, dance and music. Built in 1912, the theater's interior was inspired by the Athens Theatre of Paris, making it a very enjoyable place to attend a performance.

Live Music

No one would call Tegucigalpa a live music Mecca, but there are a few places to see shows now and again.

Café La Milonga (Map p81; ☎ 232 2654; Paseo República de Argentina 1802; mains US$4-8; ☽ lunch & dinner Mon-Fri, lunch until 6:30pm Sat) Has tango classes on Fridays, sometimes with live music accompanying. Ask about special performances, especially folk music.

Tobacco Road Inn (Map p79; ☎ 222 4081; Av Máximo Jérez 1013, btwn Calles las Damas & Salvador Corleto; r per person US$4.75) A downtown bar with a regular crowd of expatriates and travelers. Live shows most Friday nights.

Café La Plazuela (Map p79; ☎ 237 0501; Av Miguel Paz Barahona 1349; dishes US$2-4; ☽ breakfast, lunch & dinner Mon-Sat) Has occasional shows by local cover bands and singer-songwriters.

Sport

The **Estadio Nacional Tiburcio Carías Andino** (Map pp72-3; 9a Calle at Blvd Suyapa) is across the river from Comayagüela and hosts soccer games and other sporting matches. Tickets sold the day of the event.

SHOPPING

There is a string of **artesanía shops** (Map p79) on Av Miguel de Cervantes a couple of blocks past the bridge that separates downtown from

Colonia Palmira. Browsing them, you'll find the capital's largest selection of Honduran folk art, from Lenca pottery to homemade paper products from the Moskitia.

Bazar Lempira (Map p79; ☎ 237 9436; Av Máximo Jeréz, near Iglesia Los Dolores; ☼ 8am-5:30pm Mon-Fri, 9am-5pm Sat) Although mostly kitsch, this small, over-stuffed shop has a few good buys if you can find them past the replica Maya urns and leather machete scabbards.

In Comayagüela, you can find just about anything for sale in the chaotic **Mercado San Isidro** (Map pp72-3; ☼ 6am-5pm), excellent artesanía included. However, there's a Catch-22: pickpocketing and snatch-and-run theft are common, and the market is the last place you want to carry anything valuable, especially a wad of money.

Tegucigalpa also has a number of large modern malls. **Multiplaza Mall** (Blvd Juan Pablo II; 8am-10pm), a couple of kilometers southwest of Colonia Palmira, is the best of the bunch, a sprawling complex with department stores, some twenty banks and ATMs, bookstores, Internet cafés and a movie theater.

GETTING THERE & AWAY
Air
Tocontín International Airport in Tegucigalpa is decidedly down-scale compared to the modern airport in San Pedro Sula. It's also poorly-marked, with just a short driveway and small parking lot. The airport's reservations area has a single Unibanc ATM and an Expresso Americano coffee shop. However, a planned renovation ought to be at or near completion by the time you read this.

Aerolineas Sosa (Map p81; ☎ 233 5107; at airport 234 0137; www.aerolineas.com; Blvd Morazán; ☼ 8am-noon & 1-4pm Mon-Fri, 8am-noon Sat)

Air France (Map pp72-3; ☎ 236 0029; www.airfrance .com; Av La Paz at Av Juan Lindo; ☼ 8am-5pm Mon-Fri, 8am-noon Sat)

American Airlines (Map p81; ☎ 800 220 1414; toll free in Honduras 220 7585; Edif Palmira across from Hotel Honduras Maya; ☼ 8am-6pm Mon-Fri, 8am-noon Sat)

Atlantic Airlines (Map pp72-3; ☎ 237 8597, at airport 234 9701; www.atlanticairlines.com.ni; Av La Paz at Av Juan Lindo; ☼ 8am-5pm Mon-Fri, 8am-noon Sat)

Continental Airlines (Map p81; ☎ 220 0999; at airport 233 3676; www.continental.com; Av República de Chile; ☼ 8am-5pm Mon-Fri, 8am-2pm Sat)

Copa Airlines (☎ 235 5610; at airport 291 0099; Hotel Clarion, Av República de Chile; 8am-6pm Mon-Fri, 8am-2pm Sun)

TACA (Map p81; ☎ reservation center 234 2422; ☎ office 236 8222; www.taca.com; Blvd Morazán; ☼ 8am-5pm Mon-Fri, 9am-5pm Sat, 9am-2pm Sun)

Bus
Excellent bus service connects Tegucigalpa with other parts of Honduras, but like elsewhere in the country, each bus line has its own separate terminal. Most terminals are clustered in Comayagüela (see map p79), where you should keep a close eye on your bags and belongings while waiting for the bus. The free magazine *Honduras Tips* has a very helpful section on bus routes and schedules.

INTERNATIONAL BUSES
Tica Bus (Map pp72-3; ☎ 220 0579; www.ticabus .com; 16a Calle btwn 5a & 6a Avs, Comayagüela) and **King Quality** (Map pp72-3; ☎ 225 5415; fax 225 2600; Blvd Commanded Economical European near 6a Av) offer international service to El Salvador, Guatemala, Nicaragua and the Mexico border, with a connecting service to Costa Rica and Panama. Note that King Quality has two classes of service in the same bus: 'Quality' which is first class and 'King' which is deluxe with fully reclining seats and added amenities. Service to Costa Rica (both lines) and Panama (Tica only) connect through Managua, Nicaragua.

Guatemala City (Guatemala) Tica Bus US$26 one way, 589km, overnight in San Salvador, 12:30pm; Transportes King Quality quality/king US$53/74 one way, 14 hours with 2hr layover in San Salvador, 6am

Managua (Nicaragua) Tica Bus US$20 one way, 8 hours via Danlí, 9am; King Quality quality/king US$25/37, 7 to 8 hours, 6am and 2pm

San Salvador (El Salvador) Tica Bus US$15 one way, 6½ hours, 12:30pm; King Quality quality/king US$28/41 one way; 6 to 7 hours; 6am and 2pm

Tapachula (Mexico) Tica Bus US$41 one way, overnight in San Salvador, transfer in Guatemala City

GETTING AROUND
Bus
It is not recommended you use local public buses. Petty crime is common, and even gang members have taken to boarding public buses and 'collecting' from everyone on board. This happens mainly in outlying neighborhoods (and almost never on intercity buses) but most travelers won't know when the area has turned from good to bad.

Car & Motorcycle

Rental car rates average US$50 per day, more for a 4WD vehicle, less for an economy car or for longer-term rentals. If your credit card offers rental insurance, you may be able to save US$5 to US$12 per day by declining the insurance provided by the rental agency. Not all agencies allow this, but it's worth trying. Be sure to ask about the deductible (the amount of damages you have to cover before insurance kicks in) as it can be as high as US$1600. Airport desks are open daily, but renting there usually costs 10% to 15% more than in town.

Advance Rent A Car (Map p81; ☎ 235 9531, at airport 233 3927; www.advancerent acar.com; Calle República de México; ☽ 8am-6pm)

Avis (☎ 239 5712; at airport 232 0088; www.avis.com; Blvd Suyapa, Edif Marina; ☽ 8am-6pm)

Budget (☎ 235 9528, 265 8000; www.budget.com; airport only)

Econo Rent-a-Car (Map pp72-3; ☎ 235-8582, at airport 291 0107; www.econorentacar.net; off Calzada San Martín; ☽ 8am-6pm)

LONG-DISTANCE BUSES FROM TEGUCIGALPA

Destination	Bus line	Phone	Fare	Frequency	Duration
Catacamas*	Discovery (Map72-3)	222 4256	US$4.50	Hourly, 6:15am-5pm	3½hr
Choluteca	Mi Esperanza (Map pp72-3)	225 2863	US$2.50	Hourly, 4am-6pm	3½hr
Comayagua	El Rey (Map pp72-3)	237 1462	US$1.60	Hourly, 3am-6pm	2hr
El Amatillo	Various buses	no phone	US$2.50	3½ hr	
Jutiapa*	Discovery (Map pp72-3)	222 4256	US$3.60	Hourly, 6:15am-4:15pm	2½hr
La Ceiba**	Hedman Alas (Map pp72-3)	237 7143	US$21.75	5:45am, 10am, 1:30pm	5½hr
La Ceiba*	Viana Clase de Oro	235 8185	US$15	6:30am & 1:30pm	5½hr
La Ceiba	Cristina (Map pp72-3)	220 0117	US$9.25	7 departures, 6:15am-3:30pm	7hr
La Estrada	Sultana (Map pp72-3)	237 8101	US$8	Hourly, 6am-1:30pm	6hr
Marcala	Lila (Map pp72-3)	237 6870	US$3	6 departures 7-11:30am	3¾hr
San Marcos de Colón	Transportes Mi Esperanza (Map pp72-3)	225 2863	US$3	Frequency unavailable	4hr
San Marcos de Colón*	Transportes El Rey Express (Map pp72-3)	237 8561	US$4	Frequency unavailable	3½hr
San Pedro Sula*	El Rey Express (Map pp72-3)	237 8561	US$6	Hourly, 5:30am-6:30pm	3½hr
San Pedro Sula	El Rey (Map pp72-3)	237 6609	US$3.85	Hourly, 3am-6pm	4hr
San Pedro Sula**	Hedman Alas (Map pp72-3)	237 7143	US$12.25	4 departures daily, 5:45am-4:30pm	3½hr
San Pedro Sula**	Saenz (Map pp72-3)	233 4229	12.25	6-7 departures daily, 6am-6pm	4hr
Santa Rosa de Copán	Sultana (Map pp72-3)	237 8101	US$8.50	Hourly, 6am-1:30pm	7hr
Tela	Cristina (Map pp72-3)	220 0117	US$9.25	7 departures, 6:15am-3:30pm	5hr
Tela**	Hedman Alas (Map pp72-3)	237 7143	Fares unavailable	3 departures	Duration unavailable
Trujillo	Cotuc/Contraibal (Map pp72-3)	237 1666	US$12	7:30am	9hr

*Direct service
**First class/luxury service

GETTING TO & FROM THE AIRPORT

The airport is 6.5 traffic-snarled kilometers south of downtown Tegucigalpa. To get into town from there, walk a few meters to the roadside – the center is to your right, so you don't have to cross the street: to Comayagüela, catch a Loarque or Centro bus (US$0.25, 30 minutes, 5am to 5pm) – the drivers' assistant will be calling out one of those names. The bus goes north through Comayagüela on 4a Av to about 3a Calle – get off at your hotel's cross-street. To downtown, colectivo taxis (US$0.50, 20 minutes, 5am to 6:30pm) pass in front of the airport and go to their stop on Calle Morelos, five blocks west of Parque Central.

To get to the airport, do the reverse: from Comayagüela, catch the Loarque or Río Grande bus headed south to 2a Av, where the bus turns left across the river. Colectivo taxis (Map p79) leave from their designated spot downtown every 15 minutes or so, passing right in front of the airport. The airport is easy to miss – ask the driver to tell you where to get off; it's across from a huge Burger King.

Taking a private taxi (US$8) to or from the airport is recommended from late-afternoon onwards. As usual, it's much cheaper to catch a cab on the main street rather than from the terminal.

Hertz (Map p81; ☎ 238 3772, at airport 234 3784; hertz@multivisionhn.net; Centro Comercio Villa Real; ☻ 8am-6pm Mon-Sat)

Molinari Rent A Car (Map p81; ☎ 237 5335; molinarirentacar@yahoo.com; Centro Comercio Villa Real, off Calzada San Martín; ☻ 8am-noon & 2-6pm Mon-Fri, 8am-noon Sat)

National/Alamo (Map p81 ☎ 220 5000 ext 7814; at airport 233 4962; national.hond@multivisionhn.net; ☻ 8am-5pm Mon-Fri, 8am-3pm Sat & Sun)

Taxi

Private taxis cruise all over town, giving a little honk to advertise when they are available. A ride in town costs around US$2. There is also a system of *colectivo taxis* (collective taxis; see Map pp72-3 & Map p79 for locations) which operate essentially like a bus, following a fixed route and carrying multiple passengers. Convenient routes include those to the airport, Suyapa and the bus stops for Valle de Ángeles or Danlí. The fare is typically around US$0.50.

AROUND TEGUCIGALPA

SANTA LUCÍA
pop 2284

Santa Lucía is a charming old Spanish mining town built on a hillside. Cobblestone lanes and walkways wind around the hillside, leading to small colonial-style homes and businesses. The main plaza, with its fountain and landscaped garden, is a nice place to nurse a licuado. On most weekends, Santa Lucía's restaurants, *artesanía*

shops, and *viveros* (nurseries) fill up with daytrippers from the capital. Come on a weekday, and it's a sleepy little village that's fun to poke around in (except on Mondays, when it's downright comatose).

Information

The **police station** (☎ 779 0476; ☻ 24hr) is located at the entrance to town. Phone calls can be made at **Hondutel** (☻ 8am-8pm Mon-Sat, 10am-4pm Sun), which is a block from the *iglesia*.

Sights & Activities

Santa Lucía has great views of the pine-covered hills and Tegucigalpa in the valley. The 18th-century **iglesia** perched on a hillside is especially beautiful; inside are old Spanish paintings and the Christ of Las Mercedes, given to Santa Lucía by King Felipe II in 1572. If the doors of the *iglesia* are closed, walk around to the office at the rear and ask to have them opened for you.

Sleeping

Two hotels are located just outside Santa Lucía, on the road that leads up to town from the highway.

Hotel Santa Lucía Resort (☎ 779 0540; www.santaluciaresort.com.hn; Calle a Santa Lucía; r US$28, cabin US$50; P) Surrounded by pines a few hundred meters off the road (and 1km from the town), the feeling here is one of peaceful isolation. Stand-alone cabins take the effect further – cozy units with hard-wood floors, sloped ceilings, comfy beds and a space heater (which, if you close your eyes, you can imagine is a fireplace...sort of). A small patio lets you relax and take in the cool mountain air. Rooms in the main building – which is crowned with a terrific bougainvillea bush – have polished brick floors (usually covered with a rug), high ceilings and large bathrooms. The décor seems haphazard in places, but not unpleasantly so. The **restaurant** (mains US$5-16; 🕙 8:30am-8:30pm) has indoor and outdoor seating, a full bar and a menu of mostly meat and seafood dishes.

Hotel Brisas de Santa Lucía Casa de Huespedes (🕿 /fax 779 0597; Calle a Santa Lucía; r with continental breakfast US$28; 🅿) A converted private home, this guesthouse has a very homey feel, with a large common kitchen and living room, and a spacious garden in back with hammocks. Rooms feel like bedrooms more than hotel units, and open onto a large sitting area. You're closer to town here than the Hotel Santa Lucía, but you're also right on the road. Breakfast is buffet, with cereal, toast and coffee set up in the well-equipped kitchen.

Eating

Restaurante Miluska (🕿 231 3905; mains US$3-8 🕙 10am-8pm Tue-Sun) A favorite, with tables indoors and outdoors on a pleasant covered patio. A 'European corner in the heart of Honduras', it serves German and Czech dishes in addition to typical Honduran fare. Look for the signs.

Restaurante Cataipa (mains US$2-5; 🕙 breakfast, lunch & dinner) A pleasant little eatery with painted wood tables and chairs. Overlooking the main plaza, it's great for people-watching over a plate of simple but very good Honduran fare.

Café El Jardín (mains US$1-2; 🕙 breakfast & lunch Tue-Sun) A small, flower-clad place that sells *golosinas*, typical Honduran snacks, like fruit shakes, rice pudding or *empanadas*. Located across the street from the church and run by a friendly local woman.

Getting There & Away

Santa Lucía is 14km northeast of Tegucigalpa, about 2km off the road leading to Valle de Ángeles and San Juancito. Buses leave Tegus every 45 to 60 minutes from 7:30am to 8pm (US$0.35, 30 minutes). Return buses leave Santa Lucía from 7:30am to 8pm. Alternatively, take an *ordinario* bus

headed to Valle de Ángeles from Tegus (see opposite), get off at the crossroads to town, and walk or hitch the 2km or so into town (all uphill).

VALLE DE ÁNGELES

pop 5764

Eight kilometers past Santa Lucía, Valle de Ángeles is another beautiful, historic Spanish mining town. It's been declared a tourist zone, and much of Valle de Ángeles has been restored to its original 16th-century appearance. In front of the town's old *iglesia* is an attractive shady plaza, which has a pretty fountain that is lit up at night. Some of the surrounding streets have been closed to cars and are now pedestrian walkways. The annual fair takes place on October 4.

Artisan souvenir shops line the streets, selling excellent Honduran crafts for less than they cost in Tegucigalpa, including wood carvings, basketry, ceramics, leatherwork, paintings, dolls, and wicker and wood furniture.

Most people come to Valle de Ángeles as a day trip from Tegucigalpa, but it is a quiet place to stay over. The only time it gets busy is on weekends and holidays; otherwise, the town is pretty mellow.

Information

Active Services (Internet per hr US$1.25; 🕙 8am-9pm) International calls to USA and Canada (US$0.08 per minute), Europe (US$0.26 per minute) and Australia (US$0.37 per minute). It's a block from parque central.

Banco de Occidente (parque central; 🕙 8:30am-12:30pm, 1-4pm Mon-Fri) Exchanges US dollars. No ATM.

CESAMO (🕙 7am-4pm Mon-Fri) Basic health clinic with a pharmacy. Located on the road to San Juancito, just past the island triangle.

Police (🕿 766 5121; parque central; 🕙 24hr)

Tourist Office (🕿 996 4477; 🕙 8am-5pm Mon-Fri, 9am-6pm Sat & Sun) Located in the back of a gift shop half a block from parque central. Staff offer basic information on area sights and help coordinate guided hikes. Some English spoken.

Sights & Activities

There's a pleasant and mildly challenging hike from Valle de Ángeles to **Los Golondrinas waterfall**. The hike is mostly uphill on the way there – allow two hours up and an hour to return. There's no need for a guide, as the trail is well-marked; if you're ever in doubt, ask any passerby for *la cascada* (the waterfall). The trailhead is almost impossible to miss: on the left side over 1km from town on the road toward San Juancito.

At the entrance to town from the Tegucigalpa side are a couple of **recreational parks**, with restaurants, swimming pools, soccer fields and volleyball courts; there are also ultra-mellow horseback rides. Catering to city-slicker families, they have little or no appeal for most travelers, but those with kids may appreciate finding a safe friendly place to let the little guys run loose for a while.

Sleeping & Eating

Posada del Ángel (☎ 766 2233; posadadelangel@yahoo .com; s/d US$18/25; P ☀) The only hotel option in town, this budget place has simple, clean – acceptable – rooms. All open onto a large rectangular pool, which is a big plus on hot days. Service is a bit lacking, however. Located two blocks north of parque central.

Villas del Valle (☎ 766 2534; www.villasdelvalle .com; Carr a San Juancito; r/tw/ste/studio US$25/30/50/65; P ☀) A good option just outside of town, Villas del Valle offers several brick bungalows on an ample, green property. The grounds are a bit over-manicured – enough with the gravel already – but the rooms are spotless and comfortable. An overground pool is particularly popular with kids. It's on the same road as Posada del Ángel, heading out of town.

Parque central is the hub of restaurant life in Valle de los Ángeles. Catering to *capitalinos* (residents of the capital) with cash, most of the restaurants are hip and attractive with menus that show off their clients' discerning palates. Some of the favorites on parque central include **Restaurante Jalapeño** (US$3-6; ☀ lunch & dinner Tue-Sun) with good veggie options, **El Anafre** (☎ 766 2942; US$5.50-12; ☀ lunch & dinner) serving up Italian specialties, and **Restaurant Manolo** (☎ 766 2694; US$3-6; ☀ lunch & dinner), a meat lovers paradise. For a more typical – and cheaper – eating experience, try **La Ceibeña** (☎ 766 2855; US$1-3; ☀ breakfast, lunch & dinner), a small eatery one block from parque central.

Getting There & Away

Two bus lines provide service between Valle de Ángeles and Tegucigalpa. In Tegucigalpa, *ordinario* buses come and go from a

BUYING LOCAL HANDICRAFTS

Valle de los Ángeles is a shoppers paradise, with artesanía boutiques on just about every block. Handcrafted leather is made mostly in town but you'll see items from all over Honduras: *junco* (straw weavings) from Santa Bárbara, drums from Garífuna villages, clay pottery from La Ruta Lenca, and *cuadro de tunu* (tree bark art) from La Moskitia. For a sampling of what the town – and country – has to offer, head to **Pabellones Artesanales** (☀ 9am-5pm), a warehouse-sized artesanía market one block east of parque central.

stop (Map pp72–3) on the corner of Av de los Próceres and Av República Dominicana (US$0.50, 45 minutes to 1 hour, hourly). *Rapiditos* depart more frequently and drop passengers a block from the cathedral in Tegus (US$0.75, 30 minutes, every 30 minutes). From Tegucigalpa, both lines have service from 5:30am to 8pm on weekdays, until 7pm on weekends. In Valle de Ángeles, both lines depart from the large paved square east of the central park. The last return bus departs Valle de Valle de Ángeles at 6pm.

PARQUE NACIONAL LA TIGRA

Parque Nacional La Tigra (adult/child US$10/5; ☀ 8am-5pm Tue-Sun, no entry after 2pm) covers 238 sq km of rugged forest a short distance northeast of the capital. The park includes cloud forest and dry pine forest, numerous rivers and waterfalls, and a large and varied (but exceedingly shy) population of mammals, including pumas, peccaries, armadillos and agoutis (a rabbit-sized rodent). Somewhat easier to spy are the park's numerous birds – 350 species in all – making La Tigra the country's best bird-watching spot after Lago de Yojoa. If you're lucky, you may even spot a quetzal, which has a distinctive aqua color and long tail feathers. Impossible to miss is the park's exuberant flora: lush trees, vines, lichens, large ferns, colorful mushrooms, bromeliads and a million orchids (so it seems).

For all its natural beauty, La Tigra bears many scars too: for more than 70 years it was the site of intense mining and logging by the American-owned Rosario Mining

Company. Most of the forest along the trails is actually secondary growth. On the upside, abandoned mines and buildings – even the ruins of a US Consulate – dot the area. And although you should never enter one without a guide, they make for interesting sights, some filled with water, others being slowly reclaimed by the forest. Upwards of US$100 million in gold, silver, copper and zinc were extracted from the mountains between 1880 and 1954, mostly by thousands of exploited Hondurans. The mining company finally pulled out after the Honduran government began talk of instituting corporate taxes and miners began to lobby for better wages. The park was set aside as a forest reserve in 1952 and declared a national park – Honduras' first – in 1980. Today, besides being a major tourist destination, the park provides fresh water for 33 communities around its periphery, and almost a third of Tegucigalpa's water.

Ready access – the closest entrance is in Jutiapa, just 22km from Tegucigalpa – and a series of well-maintained trails of varying difficulty make La Tigra a popular destination for day-trippers. A campground, simple eco-lodges and one terrific mountain retreat (Cabaña Mirador El Rosario, opposite) near the second entrance at El Rosario make staying the night an attractive option too.

The temperature in La Tigra can fluctuate unexpectedly – wear suitable shoes and bring an extra layer of clothing. Long pants and long sleeves are good protection from mosquitoes, which are annoyingly abundant.

Information

Amitigra (Fundación Amigos de la Tigra; Map p81; ☎ 238 6269; www.amitigra.org; Edificio Italia, 4th flr, office No 6; ☒ 8am-12:30pm & 1-5pm Mon-Fri) has friendly staff and complete information about getting to, hiking in, and staying at the national park. You can pay park/lodging fees here or at the park entrance.

You don't really need one, but guides are available at either entrance to point out features of the forest and (if you're lucky) its wildlife. Guides are typically used for large groups, and charge US$5 to US$20 per group, depending on the trail. Couples or solo travelers should negotiate a price.

Dangers & Annoyances

La Tigra is a rugged, mountainous area – wear suitable shoes and know that damp ground can give way unexpectedly. Dense forest and unmarked mine shafts are a good reason to stay *on* the beaten path. It should go without saying – but we will anyway – that you should *never* enter a mine alone or without an experienced guide.

Hiking

Eight trails form a series of intersecting loops through the forest. All are well maintained and relatively easy to follow – be alert for signs. The road to Jutiapa is dull compared to the one to San Juancito and El Rosario; but the Jutiapa side of the park is less deforested. The Amitigra office and both visitors centers have brochures with maps and descriptions of the various hikes. Cabaña Mirador El Rosario (opposite) has even more detailed information available to guests.

SENDERO PRINCIPAL

The main trail is in fact the old road that connected Tegucigalpa with the area's mining operations. It is the most direct route through the park, extending 6km from Jutiapa to El Rosario. From Jutiapa, the first 2km are a dirt road, still used occasionally by park maintenance crews, arriving at Rancho Quemado (Burned Ranch), the highest point of the park trail system. From there, the road becomes more trail-like, descending 4km past abandoned mines, small rivers and a few fine views of the San Juancito valley before reaching El Rosario. This is the busiest trail in the park, and though attractive, it's not the most memorable. It is a good way to 'close the loop' on the longer hikes, like Los Plancitos or La Mina/La Cascada.

SENDERO LA CASCADA

A more appealing trail is to 'the waterfall,' a 40m no-name falls that is impressive in the winter (October–February) but which can dry up considerably in the summer. Coming from Jutiapa, follow the Sendero Principal over 1km to the Sendero La Cascada cut-off, located at a sharp bend in the trail. Descend the steep stone steps and continue another 2km past smaller falls and abandoned mines to a T-intersection:

go straight to reach the falls (10 to 20 minutes), or left to reach El Rosario via Sendero La Mina. You can cool your feet at the falls' base, but there's no real pool for swimming, unfortunately.

SENDERO LA MINA

The 'Mine Trail' is the one to take to reach the waterfall from El Rosario. The trail begins at *el mirador* (the look-out), a short distance along the Sendero Principal from the Rosario visitors center. After 1km of level hiking you'll pass a cluster of abandoned mining buildings and a cement dynamite bunker; a side trail leads up a stone ramp and over a footbridge to the mine. Back at the main trail, continue for more than 1km, past earthen scars caused by landslides during Hurricane Mitch, to a T-intersection; go left to the falls (10 to 20 minutes) or right onto Sendero La Cascada, toward Jutiapa.

SENDERO LOS PLANCITOS

The park's longest and least-trafficked trail forms a rambling 8km half-loop from Jutiapa to an intersection on the Sendero Principal about 25 minutes west of El Rosario. The trail takes hikers through pine forest, past the park's lowest point and along the foot of Mt Estrella. You can use Sendero Principal to make it a loop; from either entrance, it's about 15km, with plenty of up and down. You should be in good shape for this one. And start early.

OTHER TRAILS

The park's remaining four trails all start from the Jutiapa visitors center and, combined with each other or the Sendero Principal, make for relatively easy loop-hikes. Sendero Bosque Nublado (Cloud Forest Trail; 1km) was the park's first trail and probably the most rewarding of these four for its thick, dripping vegetation. La Esperanza (2km) has the park's best stretch of primary forest, including some impressive ancient trees; a good shortish loop from the Jutiapa side would be out on Bosque Nublado and back on La Esperanza. Sendero Jucuara (2km) has a camping area (p94) and forms the first part of Sendero Los Plancitos, while Las Granadillas (600m) is designed for children, seniors and those with limited mobility.

Sleeping & Eating

Cabaña Mirador El Rosario (☎ 987 5835; s/d US$15.50/24.50; breakfast & dinner US$2.25-3.75) Simple charm, amazing views and easy access to the national park make this one of Honduras' most appealing get-aways. There are just two units, side-by-side, one with a queen-size bed and the other with two twins, sharing a detached toilet and hot-water shower. They are built of rough-hewn wood, and have a small common patio with chairs, hammocks and a sweeping view of the valley below. The friendly German owners (Monika and Joerg) live in a separate cabin on-site – meals are served on their patio – and they have detailed information (and plenty of personal experience) on hiking in the park. With room for only four guests and a loyal clientele from Tegucigalpa, the Mirador is often full – definitely call ahead. English, Spanish and German spoken.

Eco-Albergue El Rosario (adult/child US$15/10) The lodge-like visitors center has nine simple rooms for visitors. Three have private bathrooms, while the other six share a toilet and shower. The digs are pretty basic, especially for the price: you can feel the wooden slats through some of the mattresses and the shared shower could use a scrubbing. But the sheets are clean, you're right at the park entrance and anyway it's your best option if Monika and Joerg are full.

Hotelito San Juan (☎ 777 0522; San Juancito; r with shared bathroom US$3.75) A last resort option, this is a tiny, ultra-basic hotel with dark, musty rooms. Be sure to wear your flips flops in the bathroom – the stench should be warning enough but the hearty layer of grime is a good reminder just in case you've got a cold. Located in the village of San Juancito, a block from the main road.

Cabañas & Eco-Albergue Jutiapa (adult/child US$15/10) The Jutiapa visitors center has long had just one cabaña outfitted with two queen-size beds, private bathroom and hot water. (Being so close to Tegucigalpa, it's rare that visitors stay the night.) But a larger eco-albergue, similar to the one at El Rosario, is being built and should be ready by the time you read this. The two-story building will have six simple rooms, each with one queen-size bed and one twin. Some will have a private bathroom, others will share. In both cases, there's hot water. Like at El Rosario the per-person price is the same for all rooms (including the cabaña), so definitely ask if a room with private bathroom is available.

Jucuara campground (per person US$5) Located 1km from the Jutiapa visitors center, with latrine toilets, unpurified water, fire pits. You're only camping option since it's not allowed inside the park.

Both visitors centers have **comedores** (mains US$2.75-3.50; ❧ 7am-6pm Thu-Sun, Jutiapa; ❧ 7am-8pm daily, El Rosario) that serve basic meals to park visitors. They may even make you a pack-lunch to take with you hiking; ask the day before, if possible.

Pulpería El Rosario (❧ 7am-6pm Mon-Sat) has snacks and some basic groceries that you could use for lunch on the trail.

Shopping
Located across from the Pepsi kiosk near the steep road up to El Rosario, the **Bus Fantasma** (Phantom Bus; ❧ weekends) is an abandoned school bus that has been ingeniously converted into an *artesanía* shop. It has a good selection of hand-made items, including paper lamps, clay urns and the famous 'De La Mina' homemade jam. Well worth a quick stop.

Getting There & Away
The western entrance to the park, above Jutiapa, is the closest to Tegucigalpa, 22km away. To get there from Tegus, catch a bus (US$0.80, 1¼ hours, every 45 minutes, first bus between 6am and 7am) toward El Hatillo from the Dippsa gas station on Av Máximo Jérez at Av la Plazuela, across from a Banco Atlántida (or in front of Hotel Granada No 2; Map p79). Tell the driver you are going to La Tigra; most likely you'll be dropped at Los Planes, a soccer field about 2km short of the visitors center, but occasionally drivers take you all the way to the entrance. A little friendly pleading may improve your chances. On the return trip, a few buses leave from the visitors center, but most leave from Los Planes; the first is at 6am, the last around 3pm. It you miss the last one, it's 4km to the next town (Los Limones) where buses run much later.

The eastern park entrance is at El Rosario, a small community perched on a steep hillside. It overlooks San Juancito, once a booming mining town, now a quiet

mountain village. From Tegucigalpa, buses go only so far as San Juancito (US$0.75, 1½ hours); they leave from the Mercado San Pablo (3pm Monday to Friday; 8am, 12:40pm and 3pm Sat; 8am and 12:40pm Sun), Valle de Ángeles bus stop, opposite Hospital San Felipe (5pm Monday to Friday), and Supermercado Más x Menos (4:30pm Sat). Buses on their way back to Tegus from San Juancito leave from the kiosk on the main road (6am and 6:50am Monday to Friday; 6am, 6:40am, 12:30pm and 2:30pm Saturday; 6:20am Sunday).

From San Juancito, it is a very steep, winding 3km dirt road up to El Rosario – typically a 60 to 90 minute walk – it's much harder and sweatier than anything you'll encounter in the park itself. The guy at the Pepsi kiosk opposite Bus Fantasma takes travelers up the hill in his pickup for around US$10; Monika and Jeorg at Cabaña Mirador El Rosario (p93) will do the same for their guests.

OJOJONA
pop 2785
This dusty colonial town is popular among capitalinos on weekend shopping trips, though surely more for its proximity to the city than for any other reason. The town's three 18th- and 19th-century churches are moderately interesting, as is watching *artesanía* being made in local workshops. More intriguing are a set of Maya cave paintings (opposite) outside of town, but overall there's just not a whole lot here.

Ojojona has basic services, including **Ojojona Internet** (main plaza; per hr US$0.95; international calls per min US$0.11; ❧ 8am-8pm Mon-Fri, 8:30am-12:30pm Sat) on the main plaza, **Hondutel** (☎ 767 0113; ❧ 8am-5pm Mon-Fri, 8am-noon Sat) a block north of the main plaza and a **police station** (☎ 777 0174; ❧ 24hr) at the entrance to town. A library which will double as a visitors center is due to open in 2007.

Sights & Activities
Ojojona and the surrounding area is best known for producing simple clay pots, but in fact, has a wide variety of clay handicrafts sold in shops…everywhere. It's almost impossible to turn down a street and not see a gift shop or someone selling their art curbside. There's a fair share of kitsch (who buys those huge clay cats?) but now and again,

you'll run into some very fine work. Most shops are open 9am to 5pm daily. A good place to start your browsing is in **Artesanía Manos Lencas** (☎ 767 0178; main plaza; ✆ 9am-5pm), which sells high-end crafts from all over the country.

A number of storefronts double as workshops and visitors are free to peek inside. There's a leather shop next to Iglesia El Carmen, and several more – seeds, weaving, woodworking – in a row of wooden shacks nearby.

Ojojona has three beautiful late-colonial churches. The oldest is **Parroquía San Juan**, dating to 1783. Straight up the hill from there is tiny **Iglesia El Calvario**, which contains a remarkable painting of *La Sangre de Cristo* (The Blood of Christ), dated 1700. **Iglesia El Carmen** is in the middle of town, opening onto a shady plaza. All are open on Sundays but frequently closed during the week.

A short steep road leads from town to **el mirador** (the overlook) with fine views over Ojojona and the surrounding landscape. There's a small grassy area, good for picnicking. To get there, turn left one block past Arte Halagos, and just keep going up. It's 2km to the top.

Sleeping & Eating

Hotel Ojojona (☎ 914 0375; r/tw US$20/25; **P**) A nice surprise in this dusty little town, this hotel has six brand new rooms with private hot-water bathrooms, cable TV and fans. It is spotlessly clean, the service friendly and has great views from second-story rooms. It's only downside is that it's at the top of a steep hill, a slow walk up a rutted dirt road (there's no way that Kia will make it up). The walk down is a breeze, however, and will take you to the main plaza in about 10 minutes. As you're coming into town, look for the signs after the police station.

If you can't swing the hotel but are interested in staying in town, there are several homestay options; hosts typically charge US$7 per person for a private room with a hot-water bathroom. Stop by the *alcaldía* (city hall) to hook up with one of these places.

Restaurante Joxone (mains US$2-5; ✆ breakfast, lunch & dinner) Serves good basic meals in a large, somewhat dim dining area. Be sure to check out the tree in front, with its amazing tangle of branches.

You can also get a meal at the **food stands** (mains US$1) in the market.

Getting There & Around

Ojojona is 33km from the capital. Buses come and go from a stop in front of Iglesia El Calvario. Service to Tegucigalpa (US$0.50, 1½ hours) is every hour from 4:30am to 5:15pm, and more frequently on mornings and weekends. The Tegus stop is in Comayagüela; if you prefer, you can get off in front of the airport and take a taxi or *colectivo* downtown or to Colonia Palmira instead.

LAS CUEVAS PINTADAS

Opposite the Ojojona turnoff is a dirt road leading to San Buenaventura and, beyond that, the village of El Sauce. From there, an easy hour's walk leads you to the **Cuevas Pintadas** (Painted Caves), a handful of caves in a large rock outcropping. The caves vary in size, from narrow tunnels to large domes, and are filled with dozens of painted images, especially animals. It was believed (or perhaps hoped) that the paintings dated back several millennia, but recent analyses suggest they're closer to 600 years old. Local kids have left some cave paintings spray-painted, but the damage is relatively unobtrusive. For a guide, call or look for Oscar Pineda (☎ 767 0161) at the municipal offices in Ojojona; knowledgeable on the area and proficient in English, Pineada offers guided trips to Cuevas Pintadas and elsewhere for around US$4 per person.

EL PARAÍSO DEPARTMENT

Heading east from the capital, the highway climbs through a series of fertile valleys, ideal for agriculture. Appreciating this in 1943, Wilson Popenoe, the great American agrarian, selected this area to establish the *Escuela Agrícola Panamericana*. Better known as 'Zamorano', today it's one of the premier agricultural schools in the world. Cuban cigar barons also noticed the quality of the land; fleeing their country following the 1959 revolution, many made their way here and opened cigar factories, pushing Honduras into the world of elite cigar-making. Today, travelers can tour a handful of cigar factories, an easy stop on the way to or from Nicaragua. Yuscarán, the department capital, is another highlight. A colonial beauty, it's a charming little town worth exploring.

YUSCARÁN
pop 2375

A cool, colonial, mining town, Yuscarán makes a pleasant place to kick around for a day or two. It is centered around a shady parque central, with cobblestone roads that twist and turn throughout the village. A great place to wander, take in small-town life and just breathe a little. Located 66km from Tegus, it's a real wonder that more people don't visit.

Information

Banco de Occidente (Parque Central; ⊗ 8:30am-4:15pm Mon-Fri, 8:30-11:30am Sat) US dollars exchanged. No ATM.

CCCC Internet (per hr US$0.80; ⊗ 9am-7pm Mon-Sat) Located two blocks from parque central, near the police station.

Hondutel (⊗ 7am-8pm Mon-Sat) Rates per minute are US$0.11 to USA and Canada, US$2.32 to Europe and US$2.12 to Australia and New Zealand. Located just off parque central, next to the post office.

Police (☎ 793 7125; ⊗ 24hr) Located one block from parque central near Casa Fortín.

Post office (⊗ 8am-4pm Mon-Fri, 8am-noon Sat) Located just off parque central.

Sights & Activities

The closest thing in Yuscarán to a regular 'sight' is **Casa Fortín** (free; ⊗ varies), a 19th-century mansion that belonged to one of Yuscarán's wealthiest families that now functions more or less as the town museum. The Fortín family had its finger in many pies, earning a fortune and gathering influence in mining, cattle, agriculture, trading and politics. One son, Daniel, served as Secretary of State in the 1880s. The family lived here until around 1910, when the house was all but abandoned and remained that way until 1979 when it was declared a national monument. Today, it contains a random and mostly unorganized collection of era-pieces; exploring the building itself is far more interesting than the majority of displays. Oscar Lezama (☎ 793 7160, 357 6209) is the de-facto caretaker, and tries to

open the museum from 8am until noon and 2pm to 4pm daily, and give free tours. If it's closed, you can call him, or ask for him at his house, opposite the church.

Yuscarán is home to **Distilería El Buen Gusto**, the manufacturer of Honduras' best-known brand of its best-known drink: *aguardiente*. Plant **tours** (admission free; ⊗ 7am-noon & 1-4pm Mon-Fri, 7am-noon Sat) are short but interesting. You can see the various stages of processing, from fermentation to bottling. There's no formal system for tours, and sometimes no one is available to do it. But ask at the door, and they will at least tell you when to come back.

Festivals & Events

If you've ever wanted to bob for mangos (who hasn't?), look no further than Yuscarán's annual **Festival de Mangos**. Typically held the first weekend in June, it features folkloric dance performances, live music, art exhibits, any number of mango-related games, and one year it featured a polo match on donkeys. A parade kicks off the event complete with a mango queen, her mango entourage and marching children in mango outfits. A popular event, both with locals and capitalinos.

Sleeping & Eating

Casa Colibri (☎ 793 7176; casacolibriyuscar@hotmail.com; parque central; s/d US$15/20) A renovated colonial home right on the parque central, Casa Colibri offers two large rooms with hot water bathrooms, cable TV and lots of hospitality. The rooms have high ceilings and are lovingly decorated with Guatemalan and Honduran *artesanía*. A large common area between the two guestrooms has couches with lots of good books, and a leafy patio makes a good place to write those postcards you've been meaning to get to. Staff speak English and German.

Apart-hotel Ochoa (☎ 265 3912; r per person US$8; P ⊕) This place is a four-room hotel run by a friendly family; accommodations are no-frills but clean. Despite the name, there is nary an apartment but there is a *comal* (a wood-burning griddle) for guests to use as well as three *pilas* (handwashing stations) that are roomy enough for you to put some elbow grease into your dirty laundry. There is also a small wading pool – a little on the green side when LP passed through – but

---

INTO THE COUNTRY NEAR YUSCARÁN

Towering directly behind Yuscarán is the Reserva Biológica Yuscarán, with a triad of (nearly) 2000m-high mountains: Cerro El Volcán, Cerro el Fogón, and Cerro Monserrat. An extremely steep dirt road leads 7km from a small bridge on the way into Yuscarán town to the top of Cerro Monserrat, where Hondutel has a communications antennae. 4x4 trucks can make it, or it's a sweaty three-hour hike. There used to be trails that went from there, wound over and around the mountains before emerging at Ocotal, a small town about 4km north of Yuscarán. However, mudslides from Hurricane Mitch washed out much of the trail system.

Near the town of Oropolí, 25km from Yuscarán, is a set of petroglyphs, whose origin is still unclear. Cascada de Barro and Cascada La Fortuna are two picturesque waterfalls beyond Oropolí, about 90 minutes hiking from the town of La Cienaga.

For these and other excursions, consider hiring a guide in Yuscarán. Oscar Lezama (opposite) at Casa de Fortín or the folks at Fundación Yuscarán (next to the *alcaldía*) should be able to help.

---

promising if it's clean. The hotel is located three long blocks from parque central; take the road to the left of the church.

Comedor Chica (mains US$1.50-3; ☺ breakfast, lunch & dinner) A tiny restaurant set up in what looks like a converted living room, this eatery serves some of the best *típica* (Honduran fare) in town. And lots of it. Popular with travelers and locals alike, it's on the same street as Casa Colibri. Look for the small sign three blocks from parque central.

Getting There & Away

Buses come and go right from the main park. Buses to Tegucigalpa (US$1.25, 2 hours) leave at 5am, 6am, 8am, 9am, 10:45am, 2:45pm, 3:15pm and 4pm. To get to Danlí, there is occasionally a direct bus in the morning, otherwise take any Tegus-bound bus (or one of the frequent microbuses) to the highway intersection, also known as El Palme (US$0.55, 30 minutes). Transfer there to any east-bound bus, which pass every 45 minutes or so.

DANLÍ
pop 45,792

Danlí is the largest town between Tegucigalpa and the border at Las Manos. It was founded by Spanish settlers in 1667 as San Buena Ventura. The name was later changed to Danlí, which reportedly comes from the Nahuatl-Xallili word for 'water running over sand', probably a reference to several shallow rivers in the area. From early on, Danlí was an important commercial hub, with goods carried back and forth to Puerto de Amapala by mule. Commer-

cial traffic dried up in the early 1900s, and Danlí survived by cotton and sugarcane. Following the Cuban revolution in 1959, Cuban cigarmakers made their way to Danlí and turned the area's low-key tobacco cultivation – then producing mostly lowgrade tobacco for cigarettes – into a center for the production of world-class cigars.

Danlí's other claim to fame is as the birthplace of the *Festival Nacional de Maíz* (National Corn Festival). This week-long event is held at the end of August and draws thousands of visitors, for the parade, music and all things corn.

Information

Banco Atlántida (☺ 8:30am-3:30pm Mon-Fri, 8:30-11:30am Sat) Exchanges US dollars and has one 24-hour ATM. Located a half-block from Chat People.

Chat People (☺ 8am-10pm; 1 block from Hotel Apolo; per hr US$0.55) One of numerous Internet cafés near the park; most also have international phone calling.

Farmacia Oriental (☎ 883 2831; ☺ 8am-6pm Mon-Fri, 8am-noon Sat) Located across the street from Chat People.

Post Office (☺ 8am-4pm Mon-Fri, 8-11am Sat) Located a half-block from parque central.

Tourist Office (☎ 763 3456; Calle del Comercio; ☺ 8am-4pm Mon-Fri) The sign reads 'Festival Nacional de Maíz' – the office's main annual undertaking – but it provides good general information as well.

Sights & Activities

The **Museo Municipal** (Parque Central; admission US$0.50; ☺ 8am-3:45pm Mon-Fri), housed in the former city hall building that dates to 1857, is Danlí's municipal museum and makes for a mildly interesting visit, certainly worth the half-hour, tops, that it takes to

A CIGAR MECCA

Danlí stands at the edge of the fertile Jamastrán valley, which is blessed with near-perfect conditions for tobacco cultivation, comparable to the Pinar del Río region of Cuba. Indeed, many master cigarmakers who fled the Communist revolution in Cuba settled here, and have since made Danlí the cigar capital of Honduras.

Honduran cigars, like those in Nicaragua and Cuba, are known for their strong-flavored, full-bodied smoke. They are not novice cigars. Most Honduran tobacco is grown using Cuban seed, including criollo and shade-grown corojo, smuggled out of Cuba in the years following the revolution.

The Honduran tobacco industry was devastated in the 1980s by an outbreak of blue mold, an airborne fungus that leaves tobacco leaves blistered and spotted, even riddled with holes. Certain varieties of tobacco are susceptible to the plague, which is more common in Central America than the Caribbean islands. In 1998, Hurricane Mitch plowed through Honduras killing close to 10,000 people. There was little damage to tobacco plants – the hurricane hit outside of planting season – but hundreds of workers lost their homes; many cigarmakers set up temporary shelters in their factories.

Danlí sees relatively few travelers, but those who come are cigar aficionados on a sort of pilgrimage. **Tabacaleras Unidas** (☎ 763 6072) is a small factory whose owner, Libardo Rico, has given tours to Peace Corps volunteers and other groups and is especially amenable to visitors. **Puros Aliados Cigar** (☎ 763 1486) shows curious visitors around its cigar-rolling plant, located 1km east of town. Tours are free and mainly entail visiting the plant floor, where 150-odd rollers, mostly women, roll the company's signature Puro Indio, Cuba Aliado and Roly Cigars. It's owned by noted cigarmaker Rolando Reyes, Sr. On a whole other scale is **Plasencia Tobacco** (☎ 763 2828), reputedly one of the largest cigar factories in the world, with some two thousand workers turning out tens of millions of cigars a year. It is owned by renowned Cuban tobacco baron Don Nestor Plasencia and his family, which also operates the smaller **Paraíso Cigars** (☎ 763 4918); both plants are on the highway toward El Paraíso and are open to visitors.

get through it. The first floor has displays on the tobacco, cotton and mining trade. Or at least the tools used in those trades, like curved two-headed tobacco knives and large wooden *morteros* used to shell rice and other grains. Upstairs there are bios on notable *Danlidenses* and important events, like the building of Los Arcos aqueduct in 1770 (Honduras' second oldest).

The tourist office has a map and information on a number of short excursions that can be done around town. You'll most likely need a car, your own or taxi, as bus transportation is only along main roads. Ask about visiting **Acuaducto Los Arcos** and **Laguna de San Julian**, a manmade lake 25km from town that was built by mining companies for electricity generation.

Festivals & Events

The **Festival Nacional de Maíz** (National Corn Festival) is a popular celebration of all things corn, held every year during the last week of August. The festival began in Danlí in 1977; it has since spread through-

out the country, but Danlí's is still the largest event, attracting several thousand people at its height. The festival is inaugurated on a Saturday, followed on Sunday by the traditional 'Noche Campesina,' a string concert in Plaza San Sebastián. Music, dance, theater, sports tournaments and other cultural/community events take place throughout the week, and of course vendors sell corn-based food and drink: *pupusas, tamales, montucos* (similar to a tamal), *pozol* (hominy soup), *arroz de maíz* (corn meal with pork ribs or wild hen), *atole* (a hot corn meal drink), and of course *elote* (corn on the cob, served boiled or grilled). The event culminates on Saturday with a huge parade and carnival in the center of town.

Domingo Gastronómico is a newish event in Danlí, held on the last Sunday of every month. Townspeople crowd around tables set up by the city and manned by local women who serve up traditional home-grown specialties, like *mondongo* (tribe soup), *sopa de pata de vaca* (cow's hoof soup), *sopa de olla* (stew), and *arroz de maíz*. It's a great way to spend an otherwise sleepy Sunday in Danlí, especially given the rather limited restaurant selection.

The **Founding of Danlí** is celebrated every April 12, with a small carnival, including music and street food. The highlight is the crowning of the *madrinas*, but instead of just one 'Miss Danlí' there are three: child, young adult and senior citizen. Photos of past winners are posted in the tourist office.

Sleeping

Hotel Esperanza (☎ 763 2106; fax 763 2877; s/d with shared bathroom US$7/12; s/d US$12/24; s/d with air-con US$21/35; P ⊠) With well-kept rooms and friendly service, the Hotel Esperanza is a good choice if you want to stay in town. Many rooms have been recently renovated – look for these near the front – and there's a secure parking lot. Located one block west of the gas stations on the main drag.

Hotel Granada (☎ 763 3225; s/d with fan US$17/26; s/d with air-con US$30/45; ⊠ P) A huge, modern hotel with two types of rooms: older ones that are cramped, with fans, cold-water bathrooms and worn mottled floors; and newer ones with air-conditioning, gleaming tile floors, and matching furniture and bedspreads. Both are very clean but frankly, if you can only afford the older rooms, you're better off at the Hotel Esperanza. It's on the main road into town; just look for the enormous sign.

Eating

Rancho Mexicano (☎ 763 3307; half-block from park; mains US$2-5; ⊠ lunch & dinner) Sombreros on the wall and ranchero on the radio are givens, but this Mexican restaurant goes a step further, with a collection of antique farming equipment in one corner – stirrups, wooden ploughs etc. On the menu are typical Mexican and Mexicanish dishes: tacos (beef, chicken or al pastor), tortas, burritos, full plates of beans, rice and a main dish, and gringas (which are better avoided). Service is fast, though not exactly effusive.

Rincón Danlidense (Half-block from park; mains US$2-5; ⊠ lunch & dinner) It is a measure of just how limited Danlí's restaurant selection is that the next best restaurant is also next door. Smaller than Rancho Mexicano, with plastic tables instead of wood, Rincón Danlidense has loyal clients who come, above all, for the beef soup, a house specialty that's served on weekends only. Weekdays, a potpourri of other dishes are offered: enchiladas, tacos, Honduras *típica*, even hamburgers.

If you're passing though on the last Sunday of the month, skip the restaurants and head to the **Domingo Gastronómico** for some good homecooking at even better prices.

Getting There & Away

Danlí's main bus stop is on the outskirts of town; a taxi there costs US$0.75. **Rapiditos del Oriente** (☎ 736 7411) operates minibuses (US$3.25, 1½ hours, 4:30am to 4:30pm, every 30 to 40 minutes) between Danlí and its terminal is near the Mercado Jacaliapa in Tegucigalpa. A larger 'Discua' bus makes the same trip for about half the price, taking a half-hour longer and departing every hour. There is also service to El Paraíso (US$0.75, 30 minutes, 6am to 5pm, every 20 minutes) where you can catch another bus the rest of the way to the Nicaraguan border.

EL PARAÍSO & CROSSING INTO NICARAGUA

The last town before hitting the Nicaraguan border at Las Manos, El Paraíso offers basic services to travelers on their way in or out of the country:

Hotel Isis (☎ 793 4251; parque central; s/d/tw US$8/12/16; P) A simple, clean hotel with private hot-water bathrooms; rooms near the front have better beds and better lighting. There's also a secure parking lot.

There are a handful of **comedores** (US$1-4; ⊠ breakfast, lunch & dinner) on parque central, all serving decent *típica*. One block from the parque, you'll find **Banco de Occidente** (⊠ 8am-4pm Mon-Fri, 8am-noon Sat), which exchanges US dollars but has no ATM.

Buses to the Nicaraguan border at Las Manos (US$0.50; 30 minutes) leave near Hotel Isis every 40 minutes from 6:30am to 4pm; buses from the border to town operate from 7:50am to 5pm.

TEGUCIGALPA & SOUTHERN HONDURAS

THE FAR SOUTH

Honduras' 124km Pacific coastline is part of the hot coastal plain that extends down the western side of Central America through several countries. It's a fertile agricultural and fishing region; much of Tegucigalpa's fish, shrimp, rice, sugarcane and hot-weather fruits (like watermelon) come from this area. Honduras' Pacific port is at San Lorenzo; the original port at Amapala proved too shallow. But San Lorenzo will soon be eclipsed by the combination of a major modern port being built in La Unión, El Salvador, and what is being dubbed the Central American 'dry canal': a transportation corridor that will expedite the transfer of goods between La Unión, El Salvador on the Pacific and Puerto Cortés, Honduras, on the Atlantic (see p104 for more info). Further inland, past the city of Choluteca, the land rises into the foothills and the mountains, forming the Sierra de la Botija range on the Honduras–Nicaragua border.

CHOLUTECA

pop 77,089

Choluteca, capital of the department of the same name, lies near Río Choluteca, the same river that runs through Tegucigalpa.

It's the largest town in southern Honduras, and the fourth largest in the country. Which is not to say there's a whole lot to do here; it's principally a commercial center for the agricultural region and a stopping-off point between the borders. The hills west of town were once rich with gold and other metals, and small towns grew up around the mines. Today the mining has declined, but communities remain, struggling economically but cool and charming nonetheless. Choluteca's annual festival day is December 8.

Orientation

The streets in Choluteca follow a standard grid, with *calles* (streets) running east–west, and *avenidas* (avenues) north–south. The city is divided into four zones: NO (*noroeste,* northwest), NE (*noreste,* northeast), SO (*suroeste,* southwest) or SE (*sureste,* southeast). Parque central is in the middle.

The bus terminal is in the southeast zone, on Blvd Carranza and 3a Av SE. The Mi Esperanza bus terminal is just over a block north. The old market (Mercado Viejo San Antonio) is just three blocks south of parque central but nine long blocks west and two blocks north of the bus terminal. The old market is the center of activity, and several hotels, restaurants and banks are nearby.

EL SABIO – THE LIFE & TIMES OF JOSÉ CECILIO DEL VALLE

José Cecilio del Valle's role in Central American independence is often overshadowed by that of his contemporary, and sometime rival, General Francisco Morazán (who is known fetchingly as the 'George Washington of Central America'). Born in Choluteca in 1777, del Valle was a judge and law professor, nicknamed *El Sabio* (The Wise) for his carefully crafted opinions. In 1821, he drafted the Central American Declaration of Independence. Later, when Central America was annexed by Mexico, del Valle served as one of the region's representatives in the Mexican Congress. There, del Valle led efforts to limit the authoritarianism of Augustine del Iturbide (who had declared himself emperor, among other abuses), for which del Valle was eventually arrested and jailed. It was a brief detention: Iturbide was exiled shortly thereafter and del Valle rejoined Congress. In 1823 he made a famously impassioned argument before his fellow legislators that Central America be granted independence: 'Free will is the basis of all agreements. The union of two nations demands the freely-given consent of both. For Mexico and [Central America] to unify, it is necessary that both Mexico and [Central America] want to be united.' Mexico ordered the withdrawal of troops, and del Valle returned to Central America in 1824.

Back home, del Valle helped draft the constitution of the new Central American federation, which included the abolition of slavery. Del Valle was narrowly defeated in his bid to be the federation's first president, and again in 1830. He finally won in 1834, but died before he could take office. One of few figures of his time who was esteemed by Liberals and Conservative alike, del Valle received a hero's funeral, with bells tolling across the nation. Honduras' medal for distinguished service is named after him, as is one of its prominent universities.

Information

Banco Atlántida (6a Av NO; 8:30am-3:30pm Mon-Fri, 8:30-11:30am Sat) One 24-hr ATM. Located one block south of parque central.

Farmacia Luar (882 0969; Calle Williams near 6a Av NO; 8am-noon, 1-5pm Mon-Fri, 8am-noon Sat)

Global Cyber (6a Av NO near Calle Williams; 7:30am-6pm Mon-Sat; per hr US$0.80) Web-based international calls also made; US$0.08 per minute to USA and Canada, US$0.11 per minute to Europe and Australia. Located on the second floor of Pasaje Sarita, a small shopping center.

Hondutel (2a Calle NO near 3a Av NO; 7am-9pm)

Police (782 0951; Parque Central; 24hr)

Post Office (2a Calle NO at 3a Av NO; 8am-4pm Mon-Fri, 8am-noon Sat)

Sights & Activities

There isn't much to see in Choluteca, but if you're wandering around town, check out the huge white-washed *casona* on the southwest corner of parque central. Once the family home of José Cecilio del Valle (opposite), it now houses the town's public library.

Sleeping

Hotel Santa Rosa (782 0355; Av La Rosa btwn Calle Williams & Calle Paz Barahona; s/d US$5/7, s/d with TV US$6/9, s/d with air-con & TV US$10/14;) Comfortable and well kept, the simple rooms at this hotel have clean private bathrooms and an overhead fan. Those with air-conditioning have quiet mini-splits. All open onto a colorful courtyard full of plants, hammocks and rocking chairs. It's on the west side of Mercado Viejo San Antonio (right).

Hotel Bonsai (782 2648; 6a Av NO; r/tw US$11/13; r/tw with air-con US$15/17;) A pleasant hotel with rooms that open onto a palm-tree–lined courtyard. Rooms are small but comfortable. The air-conditioned rooms have bathrooms with walls that don't quite make it to the ceiling. Fine if you're by yourself, not so, um…private if you're traveling with a friend. Located one block south of parque central.

Hotel Central (782 0090; Av La Rosa; r/tw US$7/9; tw with air-con US$16;) Four blocks north of Mercado Viejo San Antonio (old market), this is a basic hotel with rooms that are hit-or-miss with when it comes to cleanliness. All have private cold-water bathrooms, cable TV and a fan. They also all open onto a pleasant courtyard with hammocks and chairs. Be sure to check a few out before committing.

Hotel Rivera (782 0828; Blvd Enrique Weddle; r/tw US$180/24;) A step up in quality, the Riviera offers motel-style rooms with hot-water bathrooms and air-conditioning. The hotel is attractive and well-maintained, and the service is attentive. Located on Blvd Enrique Weddle, a busy street with a smattering of fast-food restaurants. Coming into town from Tegucigalpa, take a left at the Banco de Occidente. The hotel is about a 25-minute walk from the *parque central*.

Eating

In addition to the places listed here, you'll find a slew of small *comedores* along the streets bordering the old market.

Paplon's (882 6430; main street; mains US$1.50-4; breakfast, lunch & dinner) A popular restaurant on the main road through town, Paplon's offers *típica* in a leafy open-air restaurant. Service is quite good. The street noise is the only downer.

Cafetería Frosty (Calle Williams near 6a Av NO; mains US$1.50-2.50; breakfast & lunch) Food is served fresh and hot at this caféteria-style diner – just be sure to get there early so you don't get left with the scraps. If that happens, there's an extensive hamburger menu.

Restaurante Yi Kim (782 5578; Av La Rosa; mains US$3.75-8.50; lunch & dinner) Huge portions of Szechuan- and Cantonese-inspired food are served at this paper-lantern–laden restaurant. Food comes out at light speed – how do they make it so fast? Located one block west of parque central.

Tío Rico (Calle Williams; mains US$2-5; 8am-2am) A simple restaurant serving mostly sandwiches, tacos and enchiladas. It doubles as *the* place to head for drinks on weekends. Maybe it's the live music – typically a guy and his electric keyboard. The show starts at 9pm every Friday and Saturday night.

Espresso Americano (6a Av NO near Calle Williams; 8:30am-5:30pm Mon-Fri) This place has the best coffee around. The service is a little gruff but it's worth it for a quick caffeine fix. Cappuccinos, lattes, mochaccinos and chai tea run US$1-2.

Mercado Viejo San Antonio (old market; Calle Williams btwn 6a Av NO and Av La Rosa) You'll find everything you need – and don't need – at this centrally located market. Great for last-minute items or just as a point of reference.

Getting There & Away

Choluteca's bus terminal is on Blvd Carranza, at the corner of 3a Av NE. There are small *comedores* and shops in the bus terminal, if you're just passing through. **Transportes Mi Esperanza** (☎ 782 0841) has its own station a half-block down the street opposite the main terminal, while **Rey Express** (☎ 782 2712) and first-class **Saenz** (☎ 782 0712) have terminals around the block. La Esperanza has a **small hotel** (☎ 782 0759; per person US$5.50) near its terminal but it's grubby enough to make a cab ride into town worthwhile. Service includes the following.

San Marcos de Colón main terminal US$0.90, 1½ hours, 58km, 11 departures, 6:15am to 6:15pm; La Esperanza US$1, 1¼ hours, six departures, 7:30am to 7:15pm; Rey Express US$1.10, 1 hour, 9:45, 2:25pm and 6:25pm; last bus from San Marcos to Choluteca at 4:25pm

San Pedro Sula Saenz US$19.50, 6 hours; take any Tegucigalpa bus and transfer

Tegucigalpa Mi Esperanza US$2.50; 3½ hours, hourly, 4am and 6am to 5:30pm; Rey Express US$3.50, 3 hours, 8:15am, 12:15am and 4:15pm; Saenz US$7.25, 2½ hours, 133km, 6am, 10am, 2pm and 6pm.

Getting Around

Virtually all the listed hotels, restaurants and services are within a few blocks of the central park, and are easily managed by foot. The exceptions – the Hotel Riviera and the bus terminals – are best reached by taxi, which are plentiful in the center of town.

EL CORPUS

pop 1213

Just 17km from Choluteca, El Corpus' cool climate and quaint cobblestone streets seem a world apart from the hot, bustling department capital. Perched on a hillside, the small stone plaza has beds of flowers and benches overlooking the sloping valley below. The fortunes of El Corpus have long depended on those of its on-again, off-again mining industry (mostly gold). It was once one of the richest mining towns in the country but is now much reduced.

There are at least two good hikes around town. The toughest – and most rewarding – is to the top of Cerro Guanacaure, with an amazing 360-degree view from the summit. On a clear day, you can see into Nicaragua, the Gulf of Fonseca and all the way to eastern El Salvador. It's a steep 4km trail to the top, starting from the community of Aqua Fría, about 8km from El Corpus proper.

The other hike is up Cerro Calaire, with views of the Valle de Choluteca and sometimes the Golfo de Fonseca. It's a moderately tough 90-minute hike to the summit, starting from El Corpus. The **tourist office** (☎ 787 3523, Municipal Bldg; 8am-4pm Mon-Fri, ☺ 8-11am Sat) can help arrange a guide. March and April are burning season, pretty much spoiling the view.

You can also hire someone to show you some of the many abandoned mines that pock

---

GETTING TO & FROM THE BORDER: NICARAGUA & EL SALVADOR

Choluteca is within striking distance of three borders crossings: El Amatillo for entering El Salvador, and Guasaule and La Fraternidad/El Espino for entering Nicaragua. A hot, bustling border town is not the sort of place most travelers spend any more time than they have to, and in fact none of these three have recommendable hotels.

El Amatillo (El Salvador) Has more traffic of small-time farmers and merchants than at the other large Honduran–Salvadoran border town, El Poy, so expect longer lines. From the Choluteca terminal, buses (US$1.50, 2¼ hours, 4:30am to 4:30pm) leave every 25 minutes. Entering Honduras, you can take the same bus to Choluteca, or another for Tegucigalpa (US$2.50, 3 hours, 4:30am to 3:30pm, every 30 minutes). If you're just trying to get to Nicaragua, the fastest way is on a microbus to the border at Guasaule (US$4.75, 1¾ hours, 7:20am to 5pm, every 45 minutes). This is a direct service that does not stop in Choluteca.

Guasaule (Nicaragua) Feels distinctly dodgy and you should stay alert for pickpockets or be wary of anyone being overly 'helpful'. From the Choluteca terminal, the directos (US$1.25, 45 minutes, 5am to 9pm) service leaves every 25 minutes and returns until 5pm. Avoid the ordinario service as it can take twice as long. Microbuses (US$4.75, 1¾ hours, 7:20am to 5pm, every 45 minutes) zip from here to the Salvadoran border at El Amatillo.

La Fraternidad/El Espino (Nicaragua) From San Marcos de Colón (opposite), colectivo taxis and microbuses operate between 6am and 7pm and charge around US$0.75 for the 10-minute ride. Both wait until they fill up before leaving; they line-up in front of Mi Esperanza bus terminal. A private taxi costs US$3.25. There's identical service from the border until about 6pm.

the area in and around El Corpus (there's even one right in town). Needless to say this can be an extremely dangerous activity – the tourist office can help arrange a guide with the proper experience and know-how.

Buses to Concepción de María (US$0.70, 1 hour), the next town up, leave Choluteca's bus terminal hourly from 4:30am to 3:30pm, with a stop in El Corpus along the way. There are Corpus-only buses (US$0.70, 1 hour) at 7am, 11:45am and 3pm.

CEDEÑO
pop 1520

Considering it's the nearest beach to Choluteca, it's too bad Cedeño is not more appealing. Picture dark-brown sand leading to even darker brown water, makeshift food stands lining the beach in every direction, garbage strewn about and the water packed ten deep with jean-clad swimmers. Add several sketchy dance halls blasting reggaetón (hip-hop with Jamaican and Latin American influences), and you've got Cedeño. Weekends are particularly awful (unless, of course, this is your sort of scene) but walk down the beach a kilometer or so, and it's not so bad. Just watch your belongings.

Cedeño is located 33km south of the Amatillo–Choluteca highway. Look for the turnoff at a Texaco gas station. Buses ferry passengers to and from Choluteca (US$1.50, 1½ hours, 4am to 4:45pm, every 30 minutes).

SAN MARCOS DE COLÓN
pop 8921

San Marcos sees a steady stream of travelers catching a bus to or from Nicaragua. Very few stay, though, and the riches of this little colonial town – and the mountains around it, teeming with birds and wildlife – remain largely unknown.

Like most Honduran towns, parque central is the center of town. The one in San Marcos de Colón is particularly pleasant with plenty of shady trees, benches and a high-steepled church.

Being a small place, there aren't many traveler services: you'll find **Banco Atlántida** (8:30am-3:30pm Mon-Fri, 8:30-11:30am Sat) one block east of parque central. It doesn't have an ATM so you should plan accordingly (the nearest one is in Choluteca). For medicine, try **Farmacia Familiar** (☎ 888 3410; 8am-noon &

1-5pm Mon-Fri, 8am-noon Sat), which is kitty-corner to the bank. **Hondutel** (7am-9pm Mon-Fri, 7am-2pm Sat & Sun; to USA & Canada per min US$0.11, Europe per min US$2.32, Australia & New Zealand per min US$2.12) is one and a half blocks west of the park; the **police station** (☎ 788 3063; 24hr) is next door.

Sleeping & Eating
Hotel Shalom (☎ 788 3268; r US$12; P) Located in a peach-colored building at the top of steep street overlooking parque central, the Hotel Shalom offers very clean rooms with hot-water bathrooms and cable TV. Many suffer from Stinky Bathroom Syndrome but a plastic bag over the drain should help. The best thing about this place is the view; well above the town, many rooms afford views of its colonial surroundings with a mountain backdrop. A huge breakfast with fresh fruit, eggs and pancakes runs US$2.65.

Hotel Colonial (☎ 788 3822; r US$12; P) Two long corridors lead to several large rooms with high ceilings. Quiet and dark, rooms are spotless, though the beds are a bit squishy. All include private hot-water bathrooms and cable TV. There also is secure indoor parking. Located two blocks from parque central.

La Esquisita (mains US$1-2; breakfast, lunch & dinner Wed-Mon) A pleasant café serving *típica* all day. The menu is about two sentences long, the meals are excellent and are served at picnic-style tables. Service is fast and friendly.

Pollo Campestre (mains US$1.50-4; lunch & dinner) As the name suggests, the 'Country Chicken' specializes in chicken – grilled, fried, rotisserie-style, whole, chopped up. You name it, you'll probably find it. Well, maybe don't ask for *cordon bleu*. Service is at outdoor tables only – they're set up on a cleaned-off dirt lot under a corrugated tin roof. Nothing fancy, but good nonetheless.

Getting There & Away
East of the park, **Transportes Mi Esperanza** (☎ 788 3705) has daily service to Choluteca (US$1, 1 hour) that continues to Tegucigalpa (US$3, 4 hours) at 6am, 7:45am, 10am, 12:30pm, 2:30pm and 4pm. Around the corner, **Rey Express/Blanquita Express** (☎ 788 3972) offers a more direct service on the same route (Choluteca US$1.10, 45 minutes; Tegucigalpa US$4.20, 3½ hours) at 7:15am, 11:15am and 3:15pm. Otherwise, no-name buses shuttle back and forth to Choluteca (US$1, 1½ hours, every 30

minutes) all day; pick them up near Mi Esperanza.

Buses to Duyusupo leave twice a day at 7am and 1pm (US$1.35, 2 hours). The bus stop is in front of a yellow house a block east of Funerales San Martín. Return trips are at 8:30am and 2:30pm.

For info on getting to/from the Nicaraguan border at La Fraternidad/El Espino, see p102.

REFUGIO DE VIDA SILVESTRE OJOCHAL

South of San Marco de Colón, the **Refugio de Vida Silvestre Ojochal** (Ojochal Wildlife Reserve) is a private wildlife reserve within the pristine Sierra de la Botija mountains along the Honduras–Nicaragua border. Precious few travelers make it here; those who do are rewarded with gorgeous pine and tropical forest that's brimming with wildlife, especially white-faced monkeys. There are no organized services for the refuge, and trail maintenance is uneven. The best way to visit is to contact Dr Ángel Enrique Sándoval López (☎ 788 3505, 977 9442) and family, who own La Esquisita restaurant. They grow coffee and vegetables at a large family *finca* (plantation) in the town

of Duyusupo, near the edge of the park. Travelers may be able to stay the night in the family's home, or camp on the grounds. From Duyusupo, it's a two-to-three-hour downhill hike into the protected area at Río Negro – it's a punishing return. You can also climb Cerro de Águila, one of several forest-clad mountains in the area. A shorter hike (30 minutes) is to Chorro de la Mina, a 20m waterfall with a natural swimming hole at the bottom. Ask Dr Sándoval about hiring guides; there's usually someone in Duyusupo or in the neighboring community of Zarzal that can accompany you.

For transportation information, see p103.

AMAPALA & ISLA DEL TIGRE

Amapala is a quiet fishing village on Isla del Tigre, an inactive volcanic island 783m high. Founded in 1833, Amapala was once Honduras' main Pacific port town, before the port was moved to San Lorenzo on the mainland. Visitors come here for holidays during Semana Santa (the week before Easter), and in smaller numbers on weekends, but generally the place is very quiet. There's a picture of Amapala on the back of the two-lempira note.

PLAN PUEBLA–PANAMA

In 2001, Mexican president Vicente Fox announced the launching of 'Plan Puebla–Panama,' a multi-billion dollar development initiative to promote commerce between southern Mexico and Central America (ie from Puebla to Panama). The plan is yet another salvo in the free-trade wars, beginning with NAFTA in 1994 and flaring up more recently with CAFTA–DR, or the Central America and Dominican Republic Free Trade Agreement.

Plan Puebla–Panamá, or PPP, would require building and expanding some 4500 miles of highways, including creating up to four 'dry canals': extra-large highway corridors designed to zip goods from Pacific ports to Atlantic ports, alleviating pressure on the Panama Canal (itself set for a US$6 billion expansion).

One of the proposed dry canals would connect El Salvador's Cutuco port near La Unión with Honduras' Puerto Cortés port. The 'logical' route of such a corridor would be through the border at El Amatillo, skirting Tegucigalpa, along Highway 5 to San Pedro Sula and Puerto Cortés beyond. But the notion of adding hundreds more 18-wheelers to the already-busy Highway 5 is fanciful at best. New highways would have to be built, raising concerns about the impact on Honduras' environment, including Lago de Yojoa.

There is a uniquely post-September 11 element to the plan as well. A dry canal across the Central American isthmus would create a bottleneck, helping stop some would-be immigrants (and terrorists, say US officials) from ever making it to the US border. The glass-is-half-full argument is that the dry canal would create jobs, reducing the necessity of Central Americans to emigrate in the first place. Opponents say that free-trade programs like NAFTA, CAFTA and PPP create overall job losses, if not around the corridor itself, then among small time farmers and merchants in Central America's rural areas.

The few services that are available on the island are in Amapala. For basic information on the island or homestay options, head to the **tourist office** (☎ 895 8555; end of main pier; ☽ 8am-noon & 2-5pm Mon-Fri, 8am-noon Sat); the **immigration office** (☎ 795 8643; ☽ 8am-noon & 1-5pm Mon-Fri) is also on the pier. **Hondutel** (☽ 8am-5pm Mon-Sat; to USA & Canada per min US$0.11, Europe per min US$2.32, Australia & New Zealand per min US$2.12) and the **post office** (☽ 9am-4pm Mon-Fri) sit side by side a block south of the main pier. And while there are no banking services on the island, the folks at Restaurante El Faro de Victoria (p106) will exchange US dollars for a premium.

Sights & Activities

Del Tigre's main draw is its beaches, though none are exactly scintillating. **Playa El Burro** is the nearest beach to Amapala, reachable on foot in about 20 minutes. (It's also closest to Coyolito, and the boat can drop you here directly.) A large clean tawny-sand beach, it faces inland and has almost no waves. At low tide, the shallows are muddy and unpleasant. A couple of restaurants sell simple food.

Playa Grande is the most popular. It doesn't get muddy at low tide, like Playa El Burro, and has a small cave at one end. Unfortunately clapboard eateries have been built right on the sand virtually from end to end, leaving very little actual open beach.

Most travelers prefer **Playa Negra**, which is less built up. Small, with sparkling black sand, the beach is backed by high bluffs. A few stands sell simple meals, or you can eat at the restaurant at Hotel Playa Negra (right), which overlooks the beach. The main trouble with the beach is that it's the furthest from Amapala (6km).

You can also climb **Cerro Vejía** (783m), the distinctive bulge in the middle of the island. The view from the summit includes the entire gulf and three countries. Take the dirt road that starts opposite the naval base, about 3km from Amapala; it winds its way to the top of the Cerro. The road is fairly well-shaded, but the region's oppressive heat makes this a tough hike. Leave as early as possible and bring plenty of water; allow three hours up and nearly the same amount for the return.

Aquatours Marabella (☎ 795 8050; Playa El Burro) offers various boat trips, including around Isla El Tigre, to Isla Exposición, and through the mangrove forests on the mainland.

Sleeping & Eating

Amapala has one hotel and one restaurant in town, plus two hotel-restaurant establishments at Playa El Burro. There are also homestay possibilities in private homes around the island. The hotel's first and best-known hotel, located at Playa Negra, has ridden on its laurels far too long – until it gets a major facelift, the hotel will be hard to recommend for anything other than the beautiful beach it overlooks.

Veleros (☎ 795 8040; Playa El Burro; r/tw US$16/21) A nice surprise, Veleros has spotless rooms with private bathrooms, tile floors and good beds, all overlooking the ocean. The service is friendly and there's a small outdoor patio with tables, chairs and hammocks for guests to share. Too bad there are just three rooms. There is also a **restaurant** (mains US$2.50-8; ☽ breakfast, lunch & dinner) right on the beach.

Hotel Aquatours Marbella (☎ 795 8050; Playa El Burro; r US$32; ☒ ☖) Next to Veleros, this is another pleasant find, offering 11 large clean rooms and a shady beachfront courtyard with hammocks slung between the trees. There's a tiny pool with a huge waterslide; the water is rather murky but nice to have during low tide when the beach is unswimmable.

Mirador de Amapala Hotel (☎ 795 8407; www .miradordeamapala.com; Amapala; r/tw US$40/48; ☒ ☖ ☖) The grounds are nice enough – built into the side of a hill, with lots of vegetation and a pool – and some rooms have fantastic views of the Golfo de Fonseca. The cramped quarters and gruff service can mar the experience though. Still, this is the best of Amapala's hotels, and your best option if you want something a little nicer than average.

Hotel Playa Negra (☎ 795 8026, in Tegucigalpa 238 4323; Playa Negra; r US$70; s/d incl meals US$55/110 per person; ☒ ☒ ☖) Well past its prime, the Hotel Playa Negra makes little effort to fix – or even hide – its deficiencies. The bathrooms have cement floors, the headboards are mismatched, the bedspreads and in-room chairs are raggedy. If that weren't enough, the tennis court has weeds growing on it (and it's not a grass court), none of the rooms have views despite sitting above the prettiest beach on the island, and the cloudy pool is

---

EXPLORE MORE OF THE GOLFO DE FONSECA

The shores of Honduras, El Salvador and Nicaragua all touch the Golfo de Fonseca; Honduras has the middle and largest share, with 124km of coastline and jurisdiction over nearly all of the 30-plus islands in the gulf. In September 1992 the International Court of Justice eased previous tensions by ruling that sovereignty in the gulf must be shared by the three nations, barring a 3-mile maritime belt around the coast. Of the islands in the gulf, sovereignty was disputed by Honduras and El Salvador in three cases. The court found in favor of Honduras regarding the island of El Tigre, but El Salvador prevailed on the other two, Meanguera and Meanguerita.

The European discovery of the Golfo de Fonseca was made in 1522 by Andrés Niño, who named the gulf in honor of his benefactor, Bishop Juan Rodríguez de Fonseca. In 1578, the buccaneer Sir Francis Drake occupied the gulf, using El Tigre as a base as he made raids as far afield as Peru and Baja California. There is still speculation that Drake may have left a hidden treasure, but it has never been found.

In Amapala or Coyolito, you can hire a boatman to take you to **Isla Meanguera**, the largest of the islands in the gulf (and the closest to Honduras); it has pleasant black-sand beaches and a small town where you can stop for lunch. As you drift by, be sure to check out the islet directly in front of it, Meanguerita or **Isla de los Pájaros** (Bird Island), named for the thousands of birds that live there (it's a protected zone, in fact). Towards the northwest, the mountainous **Conchagüita** has good hiking. Just south, the island of **Martín Perez** is uninhabited but great if you're looking for solitary beaches.

The islands are all part of El Salvador, so technically you should pass through Salvadoran immigration before visiting them. That said, there's very little chance you'll be 'caught' while on a day trip from Amapala. If you're considering staying a night or two, however, play it safe and go to the immigration office in La Unión first.

---

surrounded by a chain link fence. Not exactly what you expect when you're paying high-end rates. Perhaps the only reason to come here is to the **restaurant** (US$4-10; ⦿ breakfast, lunch & dinner) for a meal, and to enjoy a meal with a view over the Golfo de Fonseca.

Restaurante El Faro de Victoria (☎ 795 8543; main pier; mains US$2.50-10; ⦿ lunch & dinner) An open-air restaurant with tables overlooking the pier and gulf, El Faro would be hard to resist even if it weren't the only real option in town. The seafood is excellent: try the *pescado sudado* ('sweating fish'; whole fish poached in foil). Hamburgers, chicken and sandwiches also available. El Faro rents rooms in the back of the owners' house, but they're barren, grimy and not worth the price.

Hotel y Restaurante Dignita (☎ 795 8707; Playa Grande; mains US$3-10; ⦿ breakfast & lunch) This is the most popular restaurant on Playa Grande. The seafood dishes here are excellent. Clients sit at long wooden tables just a few feet from the ocean – perfect for throwing back a couple of beers over a plate of *ceviche* (raw fish marinated in lime juice). Avoid the rooms for rent though: they're grubby and the beds look salvaged – overpriced even at US$5.50 per person.

Getting There & Away

Fiberglass lanchas (motorboats) ferry passengers to and from Coyolito and Amapala all day, every day. The ride takes about 15 minutes and costs US$0.75 per person on a *colectivo* boat; you may have to wait a while for one to fill up. If you're in a hurry, a private trip is US$7.50. A private car ferry can be summoned by calling Roberto Mol (☎ 795 8482); the cost is around US$45 each way.

From Coyolito, buses depart for San Lorenzo (US$0.80, 1 hour, 5:30am to 4pm, every 40 minutes). In San Lorenzo, buses to Coyolito leave from the mercado municipal, the last departure being 5:30pm. To get to Choluteca or Tegucigalpa, transfer at San Lorenzo or at the gas station at the Coyolito turnoff.

A bike would be ideal for getting around the island – the road is well-paved and relatively flat all the way around, with beautiful vista points; unfortunately there's nowhere to rent a bike on the island. Otherwise, two buses circle the island six or seven times between 5:30am and 5pm. The fare is US$0.25, and the trip around takes an hour or more. Taxis have amazingly high fares; moto-taxis are a bit more reasonable.

Central Honduras

Honduras' central region, especially the department of Olancho, is known as the 'Wild West' of Honduras. People from the rest of the country view the region with a certain uneasiness, like Americans might view Texas. (Ironically, both the US and Honduras elected cowboy presidents from those very regions.) Like any stereotype, there's a germ of truth – rivalries here are legendary for their longevity and notorious for ending in violence, and many people own guns.

Then again it's easy to put too much emphasis on such stories. Most people you meet in Olancho are perfectly nice (and unarmed) and travelers are very unlikely to be drawn into the region's personal and political machinations. And Central Honduras has remarkable natural beauty with hiking that rivals that in the rest of the country.

The region's blue-ribbon attraction is La Picucha, the highest mountain in Olancho and the centerpiece of the Parque Nacional Sierra de Agalta. It's a challenging multiday hike to the top, passing various microclimates to a summit with commanding views of the surrounding mountain range. There's more great hiking in El Boquerón Natural Monument.

Another attraction is central Honduras' cave systems. In Catacamas, Cueva de Talgua houses the famous 'Glowing Skulls of Talgua' – one of the most important recent archaeological discoveries in Honduras. The Cuevas de Susmay outside of Gualaco are also worth exploring.

Olancho is also the departure point for two of the country's great journeys: rafting down the Río Plátano or Río Patuca. Both trips last a week or more, passing through the largest and most pristine rain forest north of the Amazon, before emerging on the famed Mosquito Coast.

Central Honduras and Olancho present travelers with many obstacles, but those up for the challenge will discover a side of Honduras few ever see, let alone appreciate.

HIGHLIGHTS

- Hike up **La Picucha** (p118) in the Parque Nacional Sierra de Agalta, passing through seven ecosystems, from dripping rain forest to a bizarre dwarf forest at the summit.

- Explore **Monumento Natural El Boquerón** (p113), a huge protected area of cloud forest, river valleys and small-time coffee plantations.

- Take a tour within the **Cueva de Talgua** (p117), where amateur spelunkers discovered dozens of 'glowing skulls' left there three thousands years ago.

- Follow a bone-chilling river to the incredible limestone formations at the **Cuevas de Susmay** (p119) near Gualaco, Olancho.

- Be baffled by the Yoro's legendary **Rain of Fish** (p110).

CENTRAL HONDURAS

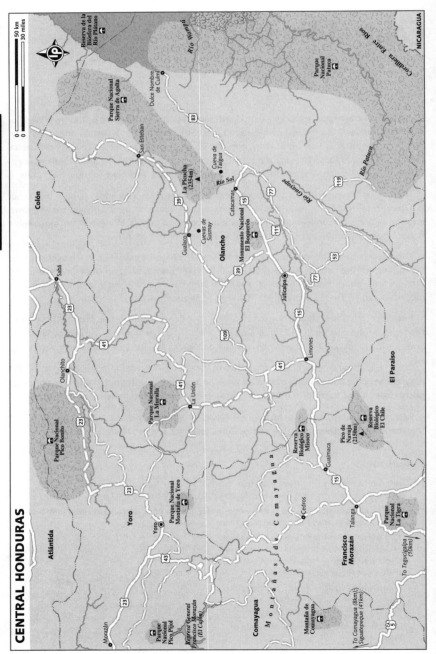

0 — 50 km
0 — 30 miles

Reserva de la Biósfera del Río Plátano

Río Wampú

Parque Nacional Sierra de Agalta

Dulce Nombre de Culmí

84

Parque Nacional Patuca

NICARAGUA

Cordillera Entre Ríos

San Esteban

Cueva de Talgua

Río Sol

La Picucha (2354m)

39

Río Guayape

Río Patuca

119

Colón

Cuevas de Susmay

Gualaco

Catacamas

15

77

Olancho

Monumento Nacional El Boquerón

111

53

Sabá

39

Juticalpa

77

23

15

41

109

Limones

41

El Paraíso

Olanchito

41

23

La Unión

Parque Nacional Pico Bonito

Parque Nacional La Muralla

Reserva Biológica Misoco

Pico de Navaja (2159m)

Reserva Biológica El Chile

Atlántida

Guaimaca

15

Yoro

Yoro

Parque Nacional Montaña de Yoro

Cedros

43

Montañas de Comayagua

Francisco Morazán

Talanga

Parque Nacional La Tigra

Morazán

Parque Nacional Pico Pijol

Represa General Francisco Morazán (El Cajón)

Comayagua

Montaña de Comayagua

To Comayagua (8km); Siguatepeque (41km)

To Tegucigalpa (70km)

5

CENTRAL HIGHLANDS & BEYOND

Heading east from Tegucigalpa, a single paved highway climbs into the country's central highlands to Olancho. Not far from the capital, however, are two biological reserves that see very few travelers. And cutting north from the highway, a country road leads to the former mining town of Cedros then continues over the mountains to the city and department of Yoro. There travelers can explore at least one of two national parks and, with a little luck, witness Yoro's baffling *lluvia de peces* (rain of fish).

RESERVA BIOLÓGICO EL CHILE

This small biological reserve is the first you pass on the highway headed out of Tegucigalpa toward Olancho, at the town of Guaimaca. It's a beautiful and rugged stretch of highland forest, still largely pristine though threatened by pinewood logging, legal or otherwise. The protected area includes several peaks, including Pico de Navaja (2150m) and numerous rivers and important watersheds.

Access to the reserve is through San Marcos, a town of a thousand people about an hour and half by rough dirt road from Guaimaca. There's a small visitors center in San Marcos where you may be able to hire a guide. Two trails leave from San Marcos, a one- to two-hour hike to a set of waterfalls near the village of Piñuela and to a smaller waterfall known as Majastre II.

You may be able to camp at or near the visitors center in San Marcos, or in a small cabin in Piñuela. There are very few travelers here so you'll probably have to ask around for help and information.

The park has a second entrance on its far side via the town of Teupasenti, near Danlí. There, a short but steep hike from the community of El Aguantal leads to an impressive waterfall of the same name. Hiking across the reserve is possible but very difficult – rangers had done it recently on our visit but even they had gotten lost for nearly a full day.

Admission to the reserve is free but it's a good idea to stop in the local **Honduran Corporation for Forest Development** (COHDEFOR; 🕓 8am-noon 1-4pm Mon-Fri) before heading in. The office is 300m off the highway (behind a plywood factory, ironically) about 2km west of Guaimaca.

Getting There & Away

Any bus between Juticalpa and Tegucigalpa can drop you at the turnoff to Guaimaca. From there, buses leave for San Marcos (US$1, 1½ hours) at 1:30pm only; the return bus departs from San Marcos at 7am. Should you choose to hitch, mornings are best.

RESERVA BIOLÓGICA MISOCO

This even-smaller reserve has one maintained trail and is known for its howler monkeys. The turnoff is 750m east from Guaimaca and the reserve itself is at the hamlet of Arenales up an extremely rough road. A visitors center there has simple accommodation where you may be able to hire a guide.

CEDROS

pop 1039

The history of Cedros, which is printed on the side of the kiosk, starts with the town's founding in 1537 by a Spanish captain named Don Alonso de Láceres Guzmán. The country's first *Asamblea Nacional Constituyente* (National Constitutional Assembly) was held here on August 28, 1824. Cedros was the birthplace (in 1839) of pioneering journalist Álvaro Contreras, who is today the namesake of Honduras' top journalism prize. There's very little to do in Cedros, however, other than soak in the sleepy small-town atmosphere. Mining engineers from the US and elsewhere turn up in town now and then, looking for abandoned or unfinished mines that may still be coaxed into production. If you do decide to poke around the surrounding hills, be extremely careful of unfenced, unmarked mine shafts.

The **police** (🕓 24hr) and **Hondutel** (🕓 7:30am-9pm Mon-Sat) are located on the parque central.

Sights & Activities

Across from the police station is the **Casa de Cultura** (🕓 9am-noon & 2-4:30pm Mon-Fri), which occasionally has photo exhibits of the area.

El Cerrito is the name of a small hill in the center of town. At the top, there's a large shady kiosk and a rather obtuse cell phone tower. The view of the town church on one side and the pine-covered valley on the other, is quite nice. The walk there and up only takes a few minutes.

Sleeping & Eating

Doña Elinda (☎ 917 3138; r with shared bathroom per person US$2.75) Located in a simple home behind the *iglesia* (church), this guesthouse is the only place to stay in town. It's a lucky thing that it's comfortable. Five modest but spotless rooms – all with windows overlooking the colonial village – share an equally clean bathroom. There is a *pila* (laundry station) where guests can hand wash their clothes and the owner (who is also the place's namesake) will cook up tasty Honduran meals upon request (US$2 to US$3).

Restaurante Típicos (mains US$2-5; ☺ breakfast, lunch & dinner Mon-Sat) The name pretty much says it all. Located catercorner from the *alcaldía* (city hall), this simple restaurant occupies part of a long low building. A plaque a few doors down informs you that this is the building where the first national constitutional assembly was held.

Just something to think about over your eggs and beans.

Getting There & Away

There are daily buses to Tegucigalpa that leave from Cedros' parque central (US$1.60, 2½ hours, 3am, 4am, 5am and 2pm). From Tegucigalpa to Cedros, buses leave daily at 6am, 7am, 10am, 3pm and 4:40pm (US$1.60, 2½ hours).

YORO

pop 16,221

A dusty, back-country town on the way to nowhere, Yoro is a good place to check out some off-the-beaten-track hikes and spelunking. It is also the site of one of the more bizarre phenomena in Honduras: the rain of fish (below).

Information

On the southeast corner of the park, **Banco Atlántida** (☺ 8:30am-3:30pm Mon-Fri, 8:30-11:30am Sat) has an ATM and does cash advances on Visa cards. **Hondutel** (☎ 671 2116; ☺ 7:30am-9pm Mon-Sat) and **Honducor** (☺ 8am-4pm Mon-Fri, 8am-noon Sat) are side-by-side opposite the bank. Located across the street from the

---

LOCAL LORE: RAIN OF FISH

On a given day in June or July, dark storm clouds will gather over the small town of Yoro and unleash a tremendous summer rainstorm. In the downpour, in the low-lying neighborhood of El Pántano, will appear thousands of silvery fish flopping on the ground. Some residents rush out with baskets to collect the fish (a type of sardine, no more than 11cm long) while others come out just to witness the event. It happens virtually every year and is known as the *aguacero de pescado* or *lluvia de peces* – 'rain of fish'.

Yoreños believe the phenomenon is nothing less than an act of God. They trace its origin to a 19th century Spanish missionary named Manuel Jesús de Subirana, who prayed fervently for three days and three nights for a miracle to feed the local indigenous people, who were facing starvation. God answered his pleas with the rain of fish, which has continued ever since.

Biologists say it can be explained scientifically. Several theories have been proposed, including that the storm conditions briefly create a small waterspout that sucks the fish out of a lake or river and deposits them in El Pántano. However, that would mean smaller fish and other aquatic debris should appear as well, which they do not.

A more widely accepted theory is that this species of fish lives in the ocean but instinctually swims up the Río de Aguán at the end of its life. The same drop in barometric pressure that accompanies the storm season may also signal the fish to begin their upstream journey. As the rain pours down, the low lying fields of El Pántano flood slightly and the fish press onward through the shallow puddles. The water recedes as quickly as it had risen, stranding the fish.

Various teams of scientists have studied the phenomenon, even a film crew from National Geographic. Locals stick to their beliefs. In any case, it's an occasion for a party: since 1997, the annual Festival de la Lluvia de Peces has been held around the middle of June and includes parades, music and, thank God, lots of fried fish.

CENTRAL HONDURAS

DAY TRIP TO PICO PIJOL

Rarely visited by tourists, Parque Nacional Pico Pijol is a lush cloud forest with two imposing peaks – Pico Pijol (2282m) and Cerro El Sargento (1852m). In 1987 it was set aside as a 122 sq km reserve in order to protect its natural resources, namely four rivers, which are a major water source for San Pedro Sula.

The park offers no tourist services or hiking trails, however. The only way to visit it is with a guide and his machete; it's an adventure to say the least. Above 1800m, visitors are treated to the view of an untouched cloud forest heavy with vegetation and teeming with wildlife and tropical birds, including a few families of quetzals.

In Yoro, **Eco-Aventuras No Solo Grotte** (below), offers day trips in the park which can be organized with a couple of days' notice. **AECOPIJOL** (below) manages the park and offers information about visiting the park.

Hotel Marquez, the Internet café **Business Net** (Calle Principal; per hr US$1; 8am-11pm) offers fast connections and web-based calls to the US and Canada (US$0.16 per minute), Europe (US$0.32 per minute) and Australia (US$0.53 per minute).

Activities

Based out of the Tortuga Veloz eatery, **Eco-Aventuras No Solo Grotte** (Not Just Caves Eco-Adventures; 671 0012; nosologrotte@hotmail.com; parque central; 9am-9pm) offers hiking, rapelling and, yes, caving trips in the region. Most tours are to nearby waterfalls and caves, though guides also take visitors to nearby Parque Pico Pijol (above). Most trips last from 7am to 6pm and cost US$35 per person (four person minimum) but overnight camping trips also can be arranged. A guide, transportation and food are usually included in the rates. Call a day or two in advance to book a tour. English and Italian spoken.

If No Solo Grotte is booked, the **Asociación Ecológica para la Protección del Parque Nacional Pico Pijol** (AECOPIJOL; 691 0412; aecopijol@yahoo.es; Parque Central), the management arm of Pico Pijol National Park, can provide general information about the park and help track down a guide.

Parque Nacional Montaña de Yoro lies south of the town of Yoro. It's a small but rugged park with dense forest and numerous caves, as well as a small number of trails. Unfortunately it is also widely known for its illicit marijuana production and the gun-toting men who patrol the area. The **Asociación Ecológica Amigos de la Montaña de Yoro** (AMY; 671 2199; 8am-4pm Mon-Fri) has an office on the 2nd floor of the kiosk in the central park, but they and others tend to discourage casual travelers from visiting the area.

Sleeping & Eating

Hotel Palace (671 2229; Calle Principal; s/d US$9.50/13.25; P) Located on the main road in town, the Hotel Palace offers plain and cramped rooms above one of the biggest pulperías in town. The beds are decent and the breezy common area helps but this is by no means a charmer.

Hotel Marquez (671 2804; fax 671 2815; Calle Principal; r/tw US$19/25; P) Further down the main street, this place looks nicer on the outside than it really is. Rooms are clean, but the beds are saggy, the paint looks slapped on and many of the curtains are holding on by just a thread. There is air-conditioning in all the rooms but overall it's not particularly good value. At least there's a restaurant onsite.

For eats, head to the parque central, where several comedores serve *típica* meals three times a day.

Getting There & Away

Ordinary buses leave for San Pedro Sula (US$3.50, 3½ hours, every 90 minutes, 4:45am to 3pm) from out the front of Supermercado Cabañas on the main drag. A block west of the supermarket, **Transportes Urbina** (671 2532) offers direct service to San Pedro Sula (US$6; three hours) at 4:45am, 7am and 9am. Return buses depart from its terminal at 8a Calle and 1a Avenida in San Pedro Sula at 11am, 1pm and 3pm daily.

Buses to Tegucigalpa leave once daily at 7am (US$6, six hours), or take any bus to

---

LOS TOLUPANES

The Tolupán people of Yoro may be one of the oldest living cultures in the Americas. Many linguists believe their language is descended from the Hokun Sioux tribe of North America, which dates back more than 5000 years. However, other researchers say the Tolupán are part of the Chibcha-speaking migration from South America around 3000 years ago that also gave rise to the Pech, Tawahka and Miskito groups found today in La Moskitia.

What is certain is that the Tolupán territory once extended over most of present-day Honduras. But with the appearance of Spanish colonizers – and the brutality and suffering they brought with them – the Tolupán receded further and further into the mountains and forests of central Honduras.

Today there are only about 19,000 Tolupán left and of those only 700 speak their ancestral language. Deeply reclusive, most live in small villages in the departments of Yoro and Francisco Morazán departments, surviving through subsistence farming, mostly on communal property, growing corn, beans, manioc and coffee.

---

the highway turnoff at Santa Rita (*ordinario* US$3, direct US$4.25, 2½ hours) and catch a Tegucigalpa-bound bus there.

There is somewhat erratic service, usually once or twice per day, to La Unión and to Olanchito. Departures are usually in the morning and depend on the weather and road conditions.

OLANCHO

Olancho is famous throughout Honduras for its cowboy mentality and Wild West ways. But its outdoor opportunities are no less noteworthy. Monumento Natural El Boquerón and Parque Nacional Sierra de Agalta have great one-day and multiday hikes, including caves, waterfalls, cloud forests and more.

JUTICALPA
pop 34,644

The only major town in northeastern Honduras is Juticalpa, the capital of the department of Olancho. There are two bus terminals, across the street from one another, at the entrance to town. From there it's a congested kilometer to the city park, which is surprisingly pleasant, flanked by a huge modern church and filled with trees and benches. There's nothing much to see here – it's mostly a jumping-off point to Gualaco, Catacamas and the Sierra de Agalta – but with a couple of good hotels and restaurants, it's a fine place to spend the night. The annual festival is held on December 8.

Information

Banco Atlántida (parque central; 🕐 8:30am-3:30pm Mon-Fri, 8:30-11:30am Sat) One 24-hour ATM but no currency exchange services.

Farmacia Nueva (☎ 785 2093; 2a Calle near 5a Av NE; 🕐 8am-6pm Mon-Sat, 8am-1pm Sun) Half a block from the parque central.

Graphitech (Parque Central; per hour US$0.80; 🕐 8am-5pm) Web-based calls to the USA and Canada (US$0.11 per minute), Europe (US$0.21 per minute) and Australia (US$0.53 per minute).

Hondutel (5a Av near 1a Calle; 🕐 7:30am-9pm Mon-Sat)

Police (☎ 785 2110; 3a Av SO at 4a Calle; 🕐 24hr)

Post Office (Parque Central; 🕐 8am-4pm Mon-Fri, 8am-11am Sat)

Sleeping

Hotel Posada del Centro (☎ 785 3414; www.olancho web.com; Calle Perulapán at 8a Av SO; r/tw US$22.50/33; 🆒) A true find, the Hotel Posada del Centro is one of the best hotels around. Rooms have all the little details you'd expect in a nice midrange place: recessed lighting, matching bedspreads, good beds, silent air-conditioners, big TVs, in-room phones, even extra towels. Rooms on the 3rd floor open onto a leafy, open-air courtyard with hammocks and comfy chairs – perfect for relaxing after a bumpy bus ride. Breakfast is included. If you can swing the price, it's excellent value.

Hotel Honduras (☎ 785 1331; fax 785 1456; 4a Av SE near 4a Calle; s US$11-12, d US$12-13, s/d with air-con US$17/18.50; P 🆒) Not much to look at on the outside, the rooms at this hotel are a pleasant surprise: high ceilings, spacious, renovated bathrooms and very clean. Most open onto an interior-facing hallway, which makes them dark but quiet.

Hotel Reyes (☎ 785 2232; 7a Av SO near Calle Perulapán; r with shared bathroom per person US$3.25, r per person US$4.25) A sad-looking hotel with a dark cement courtyard and worn but relatively clean rooms. Each room has a sink, which is a nice feature if you've opted to share a bathroom. For three bucks a person, it's tough to complain.

Hotel Antúnez Anexo (☎ /fax 785 2034; 7a Av NO near 2a Calle; s/d with shared bathroom US$4.25/7, s with private bathroom US$6-8, d with private bathroom US$13.25) In the process of being renovated at time of writing, this is (or was?) a small, fairly clean place, with a breezy courtyard in the middle. The renovations looked promising – new tile floors, fresh paint, even talk of air-conditioning – just be sure to get a room with a real bed (as versus a cot).

Eating

Oregano's (2a Calle near 8a Av NO; mains US$4-5; ☺ lunch & dinner Mon-Sat) It would be easy to miss this teeny-tiny restaurant, just 6ft wide and 20ft deep, with a dining area consisting of a single faux-granite counter and six stools. But you know the moment you walk in, beneath an arched ceiling painted with clouds, that you're in for a treat. The menu is a creative and welcome break from *típica*: try the peanut-and-almond-encrusted chicken or *morir soñando*, literally 'to die dreaming,' a Caribbean-inspired dish of shrimp flambé prepared with rum, coconut flakes and coconut milk. A husband-wife operation, the service can be very slow, especially if there are other people ahead of you, but it's well worth the wait.

Restaurante El Rancho (☎ 785 1202; 4a Av SE near 2a Calle; mains US$2-5; ☺ lunch & dinner Mon-Sat) Located directly behind the *iglesia*, the picnic tables are always hopping at this open-air restaurant. Grilled meats are the specialty – try the Pincho al Rancho (US$5) for a mouthwatering beef kabob. The chicken sandwich (US$2.75) is pretty good too, just beware of bones.

Queen's Burger (☎ 785 3518; 1a Calle near 4a Av NE; mains US$1.50-3; ☺ lunch & dinner) A hamburger haven serving up all sizes of beef patties. If you're hungry try the enormous Queen Special burger – roughly the size of a personal pan pizza – with all the fixin's (US$2). Regular hamburgers are a little thin; be sure to order a side of fries so you leave satisfied. Delivery available.

Entertainment

Cine Maya (2a Calle near 3a Av NO; US$1) Despite the odd *problemas técnicos* (technical problems), this old-timer still creaks out Hollywood releases every night.

Getting There & Away

The main bus terminal is about 1km from town on the entrance road from the highway. Buses leave from there for Limones, La Unión, Manguile, Gualaco, San Estéban, Tocoa, Trujillo and La Ceiba. **Transportes Aurora/Discovery** (☎ 785 2237) has its own terminal across the street, with ordinary and 1st-class service to Catacamas and Tegucigalpa. Plenty of taxis run between town and both stations (US$0.80).

Daily service from the two stations include the following.

Catacamas US$1, 40 minutes, 40km, every 30 minutes, 7:30am to 6pm

Gualaco US$2.25, two hours, hourly, 3:30am to 3pm; take any Gualaco-, San Estéban-, or Trujillo-bound bus

La Ceiba US$7, nine hours, 4am and 6am

Tegucigalpa *ordinario* US$2.75, three hours, 170km, hourly, 5am to 6pm, *directo* US$3.75, 2½ hours, 6:15am, 8:30am, 9:15am, 10:15am, 1:15pm, 2:15pm and 5pm

Trujillo US$6, seven hours, 278km, 9:30am; catch on highway

MONUMENTO NATURAL EL BOQUERÓN

Monumento Natural El Boquerón is a 4000-hectare protected zone, anchored by two river canyons and the 1433m Cerro de Agua Buena. The protected area contains primary and secondary tropical forests as well as cloud forests. It also boasts the scenic Río Olancho running through the middle. A number of small farming settlements are found within the protected area, sustained mostly by small plots of corn, beans and coffee, for which parts of the preserve have been cleared or thinned.

The area around present-day El Boquerón town was once known as San Jorge de Olancho and functioned as the department capital in the 16th and 17th centuries. It was a rich and vibrant town, fueled by gold mined from the surrounding hills – locals still uncover tools and other artifacts while plowing their fields. However, legend has it that the townspeople grew miserly and, in an act of divine justice, a volcanic eruption sent a wave of burning lava down the hillside, burying the town and killing its residents. That San Jorge

CENTRAL HONDURAS

de Olancho was mysteriously obliterated is well known, but the volcano story is unlikely – for starters, there are no volcanoes in the area. A more likely scenario, supported by recent geologic surveys, is that a mudslide from Cerro de Agua Buena's steep flanks was responsible for the tragedy.

Information

This is a great place for dayhikes without the need for guides. Following the loop 'backwards' – that is, heading toward El Bambú first – the trail is clear as far as La Avispa. The section along the Río Olancho is harder to follow, faded in places and criss-crossed by hunting trails.

Jose 'Joche' Mendoza and his son Tonito Mendoza are both experienced and recommended local guides. They live in the community of El Boquerón, on the highway at the foot of the protected area. Neither has a phone, but any passerby can help you locate them. Joche doubles as a COHDEFOR park guard and both he and Tonito know virtually every inch of the park. They've guided a number of foreign visitors on daylong and multiday excursions. They typically charge US$5.50 per day per person.

If you do go sans guide, make it a habit to talk with every local you see, to double check that you're headed in the right direction. It's much slower going, but you'll have some good conversations and will be much less likely to veer too far, or for too long, off your path.

Hiking

Trails in the protected area form a large loop. Starting at El Boquerón community, the trail follows the Río Olancho through old-growth forest and passes several swimming holes. A half-hour detour leads to Cueva de Tepisquintle, prickled with stalagmites and stalactites – the path isn't well marked, but any passing local will be able to point you in the right direction. There are numerous butterfly and bird species visible here; while butterflies are most active in the hottest hours, birds emerge mostly at dawn and dusk.

The trail eventually leaves the riverbank and climbs up the main canyon to the small community of La Avispa. There are a few simple comedores there if you get hungry – it takes most casual hikers around three hours to get here from the highway.

Locals in La Avispa can point you to the trail leading to Cerro de Agua Buena and the park's nuclear zone. The ascent is through a thick cloud forest, teeming with birds, including quetzals, toucans and motmots. The summit of Cerro de Agua Buena offers spectacular views of the protected zone.

Along the way you'll pass a temporary settlement, also called Agua Buena. Empty most of the year, the settlement swells between January and March, for the *cosecha de café* (coffee harvest). If you're there then, many workers are happy to chat, even to explain how coffee is cultivated and harvested. You can also buy simple meals of beans-and-rice from local families who have come for the season. From Agua Buena, a pleasant side hike is to the COHDEFOR radio antennae. Campesinos can point you in the right direction; a trail leads away from the coffee areas and deeper into the natural forest.

Otherwise, the trail continues over Cerro Agua Buena and winds down to the tiny hamlet of El Bambú, at last count just three families strong. From there it's a 45-minute walk down a rough dirt road back to El Boquerón.

Sleeping

You can camp for free at a number of points within the protected area. The zone near the community of Agua Buena, or near the summit of Cerro de Aqua Buena, are the most common spots.

Getting There & Away

Monumento Natural El Boquerón is halfway between Juticalpa and Catacamas. Any Juticalpa–Catacamas buses can drop you there (from either side US$0.60, 20 minutes).

CATACAMAS
pop 34,119

At the end of the paved road, deep in Olancho, Catacamas is a small attractive city with a somewhat rough-and-tumble vibe. It is best known for the Cuevas de Talgua, where dozens of skulls left there more than 3000 years ago were discovered by amateur explorers in 1994. The skulls were covered in calcite – the stuff of stalactites and stalagmites – that gave them an eerie iridescent glow when lit by flashlights. The skulls are off-limits but the cave is still a popular sight. More recently, Catacamas has been used as a jumping-off point for a machete-hacking ascent of La Picucha, the tallest mountain in the department and the centerpiece of the impressive Sierra de Agalta national park.

Orientation

There are no street signs in Catacamas; in fact you don't have to go far from the center for the streets to turn from pavement to dirt. The road from the highway into town is Calle Independencia, which quickly bumps into the parque central. A huge beautiful tree spreads its branches over much of the park, providing shade to the benches below. Just before reaching the parque central, Calle Independencia intersects with Blvd La Mora, an impressive paved and divided roadway that extends, well, five or so blocks before turning to dirt. Three blocks down Blvd La Mora is a stoplight; to your right is the *mercado municipal* (city market), to your left is the road that leads to the steps up to La Cruzicita. Continuing straight at the stoplight brings you to the Cuevas de Talgua – a sign at the Independencia–La Mora intersection points the way.

To orient yourself, remember that Blvd La Mora runs east to west and Avenida Independencia north to south.

Information

BGA (8:30am-3:30pm Mon-Fri, 8:30-11:30am Sat) A half-block from Hotel Papabeto, the BGA has an ATM and can extend cash advances on Visa cards.

Clínica Campos (799 5303; 24hr) Located just past the municipal market, opposite Plaza Monise.

COHDEFOR office (8am-4pm Mon-Fri) The director is helpful and very knowledgeable about the area but can be hard to track down.

CyberAs.com (754 7477; Av Independencia; per hr US$0.80; 8am-8pm Mon-Sat) The sign outside has it spelt 'Siberas.com'.

Farmacia Catacamas 2 (799 5106; Av Independencia; 8am-9pm Mon-Sat, 8am-noon Sun)

Post office (Av Independencia; 8am-4pm Mon-Fri, 8am-11am Sat)

Sights & Activities

In town, the main sight is La Cruzicita also known as Cerro de la Cruz. Follow the road straight past the COHDEFOR – you can't miss the long flight of green steps climbing the hillside to the cross and altar. It's a nice enough walk, with a great view of city and surrounding countryside.

Ten kilometers outside of Catacamas is its main attraction, the **Cuevas de Talgua** (US$5, 9am-5pm, no entry after 4pm; closed Mon), a huge limestone cave system made famous by the discovery, in 1994, of hundreds of prehistoric skeletons arranged in chambers deep inside. Over the course of three millennia, water dripping from the roof encased the skeletons in a milky calcite that glows when lit up (p117).

The area of the skeletons is closed to the public, unfortunately, but you can tour the cave up to that point. The 45-minute guided tour of the cave includes a more detailed account of the discovery and of the cave system itself, which is thought to be over 100 million years in the making. There's electric lighting and a walkway over uneven parts. A small museum near the entrance has good displays (in Spanish only) of the area's geology, archaeology and present-day life. There are photos of the glowing skulls, but no actual examples. There is another cave a short distance away which your guide can take you to for a few extra lempiras.

The caves are within the boundaries of the Sierra de Agalta National Park and you can also hike a short distance past the visitors area. Three tiny communities – Talgua Arriba, La Florida and Los Ángeles – are strung along a couple hours' hike from the visitors center. If you take the 6am bus from Catacamas, you can do some hiking and bird-watching before the cave opens; you'll avoid paying the rather inflated park fee, too. Calixto Ordóñez (p117) lives in Talgua Arriba and is an excellent guide. See p116 for information on reaching the caves.

La Cascada de Los Jutes (Snail Shell Falls) is an 80m beauty within the Sierra de Agalta National Park. There are a number of places to swim along the way and the especially adventurous of the group can clamber up the waterfall's sheer rock face. Calixto Ordóñez guides this trip for US$6.50 per group.

You can also climb **Pico La Picucha** from Catacamas, thanks to a new route forged by Peace Corps volunteers and local guides. See p117 for details.

Sleeping & Eating

Hotel Meyling (☎ 799 4746; fax 799 4523; Av Independencia; s/d US$12.25/16, s/d with air-con US$13.75/18.50; ℗ ✗) Opened in 2003, the Meyling is a modern hotel offering plain but spotless rooms with high ceilings, cable TV and in-room telephone. A restaurant onsite offers three meals a day at very reasonable prices; a good option if you arrive late or want to get an early start. Located two blocks south of the parque central.

Hotel Colina (☎ 799 4488; s/d US$9/9.50; ℗) Located half a block south of the parque central. Opening onto a long, sparse courtyard, rooms are dated but very clean. They also come with hot water, cable TV and fans – a good deal.

Hotel Papabeto (☎ 799 5060; hhgarciadiaz@yahoo .com; s/d US$27/32; ℗ ✗ ▤) The best hotel in town, with 10 large rooms, spotless bathrooms and lovely soft beds. There's a pool, complete with a swim-up bar and breakfast is sometimes included in the fare. You gotta wonder what a hotel like this is doing in Catacamas, though it certainly makes a nice splurge after hiking La Picucha.

Hotel Juan Carlos (☎ 799 4212; www.hoteljuan carlos.net; s/d with fan US$12.50/15.50, with air-con US$24.75; ℗ ✗) Located 1km down the road heading to the caves. Popular with conferences and visiting tour groups, the San Juan is large, modern, clean and forgettable. High-ceilinged rooms with ceramic floors and firm beds open onto two long, open-air corridors with a row of greenery in the middle. It's a good alternative for midrange travelers if the Papa Beto is full but the location is inconvenient if you don't have a car.

Comedor Be-Thel (mains US$1.50-3; Parque Central; ☻ breakfast, lunch & dinner) This simple family-run comedor serves exactly what you'd expect it to – hello eggs and beans! – at plastic tables looking onto the central park.

Taki-Mex (mains US$0.50-2; ☻ lunch & dinner) Two blocks west of Blvd La Mora on the road that leads to La Cruzicita, this corner restaurant serves good cheap Mexican and Honduran food in a spotless dining area.

Hotel Papabeto (☎ 799 5060; hhgarciadiaz@yahoo .com; mains US$5-7; ☻ breakfast, lunch & dinner) The restaurant has an oddly sterile dining area – think hospital cafeteria – but the food is highly recommended. The English-speaking chef, who was a tour guide before taking up

cooking, offers a creative and ever-changing menu, from beef fajitas to stuffed bell peppers.

Su Hogar Supermercado (☻ 8am-9pm) Stock up on supplies for a La Picucha climb at this large supermarket. To get here from the central park, go up a block on Av Independencia, turn right at the post office and walk another 2½ blocks.

Drinking

Olancho has a not-undeserved reputation as the 'Wild West' of Honduras, so the drinking scene here is necessarily a bit rowdy. Nights in Catacamas usually begin with tailgating at the Texaco (yes, as in the gas station), which puts up speakers and serves a mean Philly cheese steak. The party eventually moves to **Vaqueros** (Parque Central; ☻ 10pm-2am Thu-Sat) which has a small dance floor that gets packed Friday and Saturday nights. A local Peace-Corps volunteer admitted that there was the occasional, um, shooting or stabbing, but that he regularly took guests there with no problem, especially from 10pm to midnight. After that, alcohol and testosterone start to get the better of some patrons.

Getting There & Away

Transportes Aurora & Discovery (☎ 899 4393) has a terminal on the road leading into town from the highway; it's a 15-minute walk from the center or a US$0.75 cab ride. Direct buses to Tegucigalpa (US$4.50, 3½ hours, every 30 minutes, 5:45am to 4:45pm) pass Juticalpa on the way. Of the two lines, Discovery tends to be more comfortable.

Second class buses shuttle between Catacamas and Juticalpa (US$1, 40 minutes, every 30 minutes, 7:30am to 6pm). It's also pretty easy to catch a *jalón* (hitch) out on the highway.

There is no direct service to Gualaco. Instead take any Juticalpa/Tegucigalpa bus to the Gualaco turnoff (US$0.90, 45 minutes) which is notable for the large 'American' gas station at the corner. From here, wait for buses coming from Juticalpa, which pass hourly from 6am to 3:30pm.

For the Cuevas de Talgua (US$0.75, 30 minutes), a converted school bus leaves Catacamas at 6am, 11am and 3pm from a bus stop near Comercial Palmira, two blocks east and a block north of the stop-

CENTRAL HONDURAS

THE SKULLS OF TALGUA

Two-thousand feet into the dark and then-undeveloped Talgua caves, a group of two Hondurans and two Americans saw what appeared to be a chamber at the top of a wall. Standing on one another's shoulders they clambered up the wall and into history – literally.

What those amateur spelunkers found that April 1994 day was an archaeological treasure trove: a cache of human skeletons, painted red and gathered into small bundles. And when they first trained their flashlights on the remains, the skulls seemed to glow eerily. The effect (besides probably scaring the bejesus out of the foursome) was caused by a layer of translucent calcite that had been deposited over the centuries by water dripping from the chamber's limestone roof – the same way stalactites are formed. The remarkable sight gave the spot its common name: los Craneos Brillantes de Talgua, or the Glowing Skulls of Talgua.

To date, 23 deposits containing more than 200 skeletons have been discovered in these and nearby caves. By analyzing charcoal fragments found with the deposits – probably fallen from wood torches used while preparing the sites – archaeologists believe the remains date back an incredible 3000 years, to around 980 to 850 BC. Many of the bones were painted red and arranged in bundles along with jade and ceramic items. Researchers uncovered evidence of a densely populated village not far from the cave and theorize that the skeletons are the remains of that settlement's elite and were placed there as part of an elaborate secondary burial rite. Ironically, the calcite cap that makes the skeletons so distinctive also makes them extremely difficult to extract and study; most remain where they were found.

---

light on Blvd La Mora. The same bus leaves the caves at 7am, noon and 4pm. A taxi there should cost around US$5.50. You can usually hitch a ride all or part of the way there too.

PARQUE NACIONAL SIERRA DE AGALTA

The Sierra de Agalta range forms a steep mountainous spine down the middle of Olancho, and extends (under a different name) nearly to the Caribbean Sea. Its forested flanks give rise to the Río Guayape to one side and the Río Grande on the other, both of which help nourish the massive Moskitia rain forest. The park protects an amazing range of climates and ecosystems – hiking here is tough, but certainly never dull.

Orientation

There are two main entrances to the Sierra de Agalta National Park – Gualaco and Catacamas – located on opposite sides of the protected area, separated by the jagged mountain spine that runs down its center.

Gualaco is the traditional and more frequently used entrance, especially for climbing La Picucha. The trail is better marked and maintained (though far from perfect) and the ascent is steep but manageable. There are a number of one-day and overnight trips possible as well.

Catacamas is a more recent entry-point; climbing La Picucha from this side is steeper and more overgrown and much of the hike requires hacking through ground cover with a machete. Like Gualaco, the area has several shorter hikes as well.

Information

It is highly recommended that you have a guide for hikes of any length in Sierra de Agalta National Park. The trails are poorly maintained in places, grown over with brush and trees and many paths that are visible are in fact hunting trails that do not lead where you'll be hoping they do. And if following the trail is hard, relocating it once you've gone off is even harder.

In Gualaco, Ramón 'Moncho' Velíz (☎ 789 2377) does most of the guiding; he's a friendly, reliable guy who speaks a little English and knows the park well. Francisco Urbina (☎ 901 3400) is another good choice and as head of the local COHDEFOR office, extremely knowledgeable on the area. However, his second job – evangelical minister – means he's very busy and can be hard to track down. Both charge around US$11 per day, plus food. The folks at Comedor Sharon can help locating either guide.

It's also worthwhile locating the local Peace Corps volunteer – just ask anyone where you can find *el voluntario de Cuerpo de Paz*. They have long served as the de facto tourism contact in town – in fact some bus drivers take it upon themselves to drop arriving backpackers at the current volunteer's front door.

For hikes from the Catacamas side, contact Calixto Ordóñez (calixtoo77@yahoo.com) an extremely reliable and enthusiastic man who has worked with Peace Corps volunteers on developing the Catacamas–Picucha route. Calixto lives in Talgua Arriba, a tiny hamlet about a kilometer past the Talgua caves – enter as you would to visit the park and follow the well-trodden path at the back of the visitors area. His house is across a small river, which you'll actually cross twice before arriving; ask as you go. He typically charges US$7 per day for La Picucha. He also offers a number of other hikes that take in activities including **birdwatching** (US$5), **nearby waterfalls** (US$6.50) and a tour of his own **coffee farm** (US$6).

Dangers & Annoyances

The biggest danger in the park is getting lost which is why guides are recommended for hikes of any length. River and spring water is fairly abundant, at least on the Gualaco side, but you should fill up whenever possible, always using a filter or purification pills. Bring a change of dry clothes including a warm layer for nighttime. Do not attempt this hike if it has rained in the last two days as the trail grows extremely muddy and the rivers may be too high to ford safely.

Sights & Activities

Climbing La Picucha is, of course, the main draw but there are several shorter hikes along the edges of the park, starting from either Catacamas (p115) or Gualaco (opposite) that let you explore the area without taking on such a difficult climb. See those sections for details.

PICO LA PICUCHA

La Picucha is a mother of a mountain and, at 2354m, the highest point in Olancho. It is most commonly climbed from the Gualaco side, a difficult three- to four-day hike. Since 2003, Peace Corps volunteers in Catacamas have worked with local guides to forge a path from there, though it remains a very tough adventure route.

The trail starts about 16km north of town, near the village of El Pacayal. From a small road sign reading 'Sendero a La Picucha', it's an hour and half of level and moderately inclined hiking to the official park entrance. From here, it's another hour and a half – and at least two river crossings – to the first campsite. The site runs alongside the Río Sol (good for a swim) and has a tin-roofed shelter and fire ring.

For those summit-bound, you may want to make it a bit further so the following day isn't so long; however, the second campsite is a good five to six hours further on. Fortunately, there are a number of decent places between the two camps to pitch a tent and refill your water bottle. This part of the trail climbs steadily and is hard to follow in places; the second campsite is also somewhat hidden, below and to the right of the trail. The next day, leave your gear at the second campsite and head for the summit, another two to three hours of tough climbing through a dripping cloud forest. It's beautiful but so steep in places you'll be using branches and tree roots to pull yourself up. At the very top is a bizarre *bosque enano* (dwarf forest) and stunning views of the forested, cloud-wisped valleys below. It's possible to camp on the summit but that would mean dragging your pack and supplies up here as well – no easy task.

The hike from the **Catacamas** side is easier to describe – stay close to your guide and just keep going up. The first day starts at the Cuevas de Talgua, passing the cluster of homes known as Talgua Arriba about 15 minutes past the visitors center (guide Calixto Ordóñez lives here) and La Florida in another hour and a half. From there it's five hours of steady climbing on a well-marked path to the first camp. Dubbed *el Hotel de Lujo*, it is anything but a 'Hotel of Luxury', with rough hewn wood walls, dirt floor and no latrine. The setting, however, could hardly be more beautiful: a thick tropical forest teeming with howler monkeys, toucans, even quetzals.

Day two is when things get tough: a full day of slow steady climbing with all your gear while your guide hacks a path through the underbrush. Starting early, you can get to the summit by 2pm, with time to set up camp amid the dwarf forest and explore the summit area. The following day you should be able to make it all the way back to the Cuevas de Talgua visitor center and the bus back to Catacamas.

Sleeping

Climbing La Picucha takes a minimum of two days and most people take three or four – in any case, you'll be spending at least one or more nights on the trail. Ideally you have your own camping gear; if not, guide Francisco Urbina (p117) rents some basic equipment, but he's hard enough to get a hold of that you can't depend on it. The Peace Corps volunteers in either Gualaco or Catacamas town may be able to help but again it's no sure thing.

On the Catacamas side, you can also stay overnight at guide Calixto Ordóñez's house, where there's a simple room with cement floor, tin roof and room for six (US$5.50), or you can pitch a tent nearby (US$1.75 per person). In either case, it's latrine toilet only; bring a flashlight and candles. Calixto's wife will make simple meals for a few extra lempiras too.

You also can camp at the Talgua Caves visitors center for as many days as you like, for the price of admission. Not as homey as at Calixto's but you do have access to the center's flush toilets.

GUALACO

pop 3666

A tiny dirt-road town that sustains itself by ranching and logging and associated enterprises like wood pulp and butchering (no joke). It lies at the foot of the Sierra de Agalta National Park and has been the site of bitter and sometimes violent conflict between environmentalists and loggers/developers. For travelers, it is most notable as a point of departure for a multi-day hike up La Picucha.

Orientation & Information

At the town entrance is a triangular intersection known simply as *el triángulo*; the parque central is just beyond there. There is an Internet café on the parque central, **Cibermass** (per hr US$1; ⏰ 8am-9m), that also offers telephone service to the US (US$0.21 per minute). Hondutel was just setting up service when we passed through, so there should be more a comprehensive telephone service by the time you read this. Unfortunately there is no bank in town – take out money in Juticalpa or San Francisco de la Paz.

Sights & Activities

Gualaco is best known to travelers as the main jumping-off point for climbing **Pico La Picucha**, the highest mountain in Olancho department. See p117 for details on climbing the peak from Gualaco, or taking an even more challenging route from Catacamas. **La Chorrera** is pretty little waterfall a short distance from the first campsite on the Gualaco–La Picucha trail. A nice one-night trip would be to hike here in the morning, pitch your tent at the campsite and spend the afternoon relaxing by the falls.

Would-be spelunkers can get some thrills at the **Cuevas de Susmay**, a series of caves, each known according to its prevailing feature: Water, Sand and Dry (not to be confused with Earth, Wind, & Fire). The Water cave has a large cavern a short distance inside, but to get there you have to wade and swim through the bone-chillingly cold river that gives the cave its name. Around your ankles swim tiny black fish while overhead sleep thousands of bats – not for the faint of heart, by any stretch. Dry cave is a short but steep clamber above Water cave and has two entrances. Sand cave is also nearby, its floor covered in ankle-deep sand.

Just finding the entrances can be a little tricky – you'll walk about 90 minutes toward the village of Jicalapa, then cut through two pastures to a short forest path that leads to the cave entrances. It's recommended that you go with a guide, especially if you are interested in entering the caves. The local Peace Corps volunteer may well be free to take you, or can set you up with a guide. You can also ask at Comedor Sharon; in fact, one of the pastures you have to cut through belongs to the same family.

North of Gualaco on the road to San Esteban, the **Chorros de Babilonia** were once a beautiful series of eight waterfalls tumbling 50m down; a dam built upriver has left the falls a wisp of their former selves and not really worth the effort. The dam was deeply controversial when it was approved in 2001 – among other things, opponents argued it would ruin the falls while developers insisted it would not. One of the dam's most outspoken opponents, 28-year-old Carlos Roberto Flores, was gunned down in his home in broad daylight.

Sleeping & Eating

The establishments listed are all located on the highway.

Hotel Mi Palacio (☎ 948 9130; r/tw US$6.50/8; P) Opened in 2005, the twelve rooms in this place still seem brand new; they've got gleaming tile floors, nice hot-water bathrooms, firm beds, fans and big TVs. It's run by a friendly couple. Look for the peach building just past el triángulo.

Hotel Los Encuentros (☎ 913 7918; s/d US$7/11, r with air-con US$8.50; P ☒) Just a few hundred meters from Mi Palacio, this hotel has five rooms over a hardware store and several out back around a gravel parking lot. The latter are less appealing, but have air-con. All are smallish but very clean, with new beds and a bright pink paint job. To stay the night – and to buy barbed wire – stop in the hardware store.

Comedor Sharon (mains US$2-3; ☒ breakfast, lunch & dinner) A large, dimly lit eatery serving típica at wood tables covered with red table clothes. Photos of area hikes are mounted on the wall and owners Santiago and Delicias have helped many travelers find guides and make arrangements for climbing La Picucha.

Restaurante El Muelle (mains US$1.50-4.25; ☒ breakfast, lunch & dinner) This new restaurant is fast becoming a favorite among locals, mostly because of the variety. Every day, customers can choose from smoked pork chops, sausage, steak, fried chicken, even fish. The desserts in the display case are tempting too. Located in a bright yellow house with pillars, facing el triángulo.

Getting There & Away

Buses come and go from el triángulo on the highway. Buses to Juticalpa (US$2.25, 2 hours) leave at 6:45am, 7am, 8am, 9am, 10am, noon, 1pm, 2pm and 4pm. There is no direct service to Catacamas; instead take any Juticalpa bus to the highway intersection (US$2.25, two hours, look for the 'American' gas station) and wait for a Catacamas bus there (US$2.25, 45 minutes, last bus at around 5pm).

From Juticalpa, take any Gualaco-, San Esteban-, Trujillo-bound bus from the 2nd-class bus station. Between the three, there's a bus leaving roughly every hour from 5:30am to 3pm.

Two ordinary buses leave daily for Tegucigalpa at 5:40am and 7am (US$4.50; five hours) and at least one bus a day passes by en route from Trujillo. However the quickest route to the capital is to go to Juticalpa first and catch a direct bus from there.

JOURNEY INTO LA MOSKITIA & BEYOND

One of the truly great adventures in Honduras is rafting from Olancho down the Plátano or Patuca rivers, a one- to two-week journey through the heart of La Moskitia. Both trips offer unparalleled wildlife viewing and pristine rain-forest experience, floating for days on end without seeing a single human trace. And the rivers are sights unto themselves – the Patuca is the second-longest in Honduras (after the Río Coco) and the Plátano includes some legitimate Class III whitewater. Omega Tours and La Moskitia Ecoaventuras, both in La Ceiba, offer both tours (p215).

From Dulce Nombre de Culmí, it's a one- to two-day hike to the headwaters of the **Río Plátano**. From there, you paddle downriver for five to six days through the totally uninhabited biosphere reserve, with a good chance of spotting monkeys, river otter, tapir, deer and more. Side hikes to caves and waterfalls are possible. The river varies from wide and slow to narrow and roiling and nights are spent camped on the beach. You eventually arrive at Las Marías, stopping at the petroglyphs along the way. The next day, you'll motorboat to Rais Ta and fly or overland out. Alternatively, you can probably arrange to stay on at Las Marías for extra hiking.

Most trips on the **Río Patuca** start outside of Juticapla, where the Guayape and Guayambre rivers converge to form the Patuca. Paddle for six to seven days through Parque Nacional Patuca and Tawahka Biosphere Reserve. There's great bird- and animal-spotting, spending nights camped on the beach. Arrive at Krausirpe, the largest Tawahka community (all of 300 people!). Switch to a motorized canoe for the trip to Ahuas and catch a flight home. You can extend this by getting off at Wampusirpi, or flying to Belén for additional trips from there.

LA UNIÓN

pop 3114

La Unión is a small, typical Honduran mountain town, nestled into a valley surrounded by pine-covered mountains. It's the gateway to Parque Nacional La Muralla and makes a convenient stopover on the scenic route between Tegucigalpa and Trujillo.

A note of caution: La Unión isn't particularly dangerous, but the long lonely highway on either side of it has a reputation for highway robberies (see boxed text right). Police say the problem has abated, but do not stop for strangers, or drive in the area alone or at night.

Activities

Although the main attraction here is the La Muralla National Park, there are a couple other worthwhile jaunts you can take. **El Chorrón** is a pleasant and refreshing waterfall, only about 6m high but with a fine swimming hole at the bottom. To get there take the road to La Muralla until it crosses a small river, the Río Camote. The falls are 150m along the river from there. You also can hike to the nearby village of **Los Encuentros** (4km) where many houses are decorated with interesting hand-painted designs. If you're there during the sugar cane harvest in March, you may be able to see old wooden *trapiches* (ox-driven sugar mills) in use.

Sleeping & Eating

Hotel Karol (s/d US$2.30/3.50) Basic rooms surround a shady courtyard – brace for avocados crashing onto the corrugated tin roof. Cleanish shared bathrooms have padded seats, perhaps the only ones in the country. There's no sign, but the building is painted purple. It's two blocks south of the *iglesia*, across from BanhCafé. **Hotel La Muralla** (r US$2.50) is another suitable option.

There are a handful of comedores and street food stands around town and the parque central, that serve fried chicken and other standard fare plus hot drinks in the early morning.

Getting There & Away

Bus traffic is decidedly light in La Unión, especially in the afternoon. Arrival/departure times might vary with weather, day

---

EL CAMINO DE LA MUERTE

Olancho's north–south highways have been the scene of numerous roadside assaults; the one via La Unión has the unsettling nickname *camino de la muerte*, or 'road of death.' The problem has abated somewhat – and President Zelaya, an Olanchano, has proposed paving these roads – but avoid driving here if possible and certainly don't do so at night.

---

etc. Wherever you're headed, you'll likely have one to three transfers, so get an early start to avoid getting stuck in the middle of nowhere.

From Tegucigalpa, take a Juticalpa-bound bus and transfer at Limones (US$1.75, two hours). From Juticalpa, only two buses go to La Unión (US$3, 3½ hours, noon and 1pm) or take any bus to Limones and transfer.

To Tegucigalpa, one direct bus leaves La Unión around 5am, or take a Limones bus and transfer. Alternatively, two Tegusbound buses from Sonaguera pass La Unión at 9am-ish and 11am-ish (US$5.50, five hours).

For the north coast, take the 6:45am bus that's bound for Olanchito (US$3.25, 3½ hours); transfer at Mamé to reach La Ceiba (US$1.75, two hours); to reach Trujillo continue to Olanchito, where you can catch a direct bus, or connect through Savá and Tocoa.

PARQUE NACIONAL LA MURALLA

Deep in the heart of Olancho, Parque Nacional La Muralla used to be one of the gems of the national park system – a spectacular virgin cloud forest and a well-organized COHDEFOR office that did a good job maintaining trails, cabins, camping sites, even a youth guide service. For a number of reasons – not the least of which was ongoing and sometimes violent conflict between environmentalists and illegal loggers – the visitors center was closed and maintenance halted.

The park remains a gorgeous piece of the planet. And it is credit to the shipshape condition of the park before the problems started that it is still, in fact, in pretty good shape. Four well-maintained trails start at or near the visitors center – at least one short loop is relatively easy to follow, though the longer trails have started to fade, criss-crossed by fallen trees and branches, or swallowed up by fast-growing bamboo. Toucanettes and quetzals can be seen from certain spots on the trails. February is the best time for seeing birds; you'll see the most wildlife if you come early in the morning.

Information

The COHDEFOR office in La Unión and the visitors center at the park entrance were closed indefinitely at the time of research. It's worth stopping by both, in case they have since reopened. If it's open, the visitors center has photos, maps and other information on hiking in the park, though remember the trails are falling into disrepair. You may be able to hire a guide in La Unión for about US$10 per trip. Be sure to bring along a sweater or jacket, good hiking boots and rain gear; it's quite cool in the park.

Sleeping & Eating

The office will probably discourage you from camping at the sites near the visitors center; inquire about any potential problems, even though numerous travelers and Peace Corps volunteers camped without a hitch. The visitors center once had basic rooms (cots, no electricity), but they were closed at last report; ask in La Unión for the latest. Either way, bring all your own food, water, supplies, etc. There are also simple hotels in La Unión.

Getting There & Away

The park entrance and visitors center is a long 14km from La Unión along a good dirt road. It's uphill the entire way, so allow at least four hours to walk it. If you stay a night in La Unión, you usually can hitch a ride on pickups carrying coffee workers beginning at 5:30am; the stop is several blocks north of the park so ask to be sure you're in the right place. A taxi will cost upwards of US$20. A ride back can be trickier, especially if you're making this a day trip: ask the driver in the morning when the last truck returns, but in general you should be on the road with your thumb out by 1pm or plan on hoofing it.

OLANCHITO

pop 26,867

This tidy agricultural town has very little in the way of tourist attractions but can be a good stopover on your way to or from the interior.

Orientation & Information

Olanchito has a surprisingly pretty parque central, with well-tended plants and paths and benches beneath large leafy trees. A charming little church completes the scene. **Banco Atlántida** (8:30am-3:30pm Mon-Fri, 8:30-11:30am Sat) has an ATM and is located on the main road into town, across from the Esso gas station. There also is an Internet café on the parque central, **Internet Satelital** (per hr US$1; 8am-10pm Mon-Sat, 9am-9pm Sun).

Sleeping & Eating

Hotel Colonial (446 6972; 1a Av NE; r with shared bathroom US$5.50; s/d US$8/8.50, s/d with air-con US$13.75/14.50; P) A simple hotel with two courtyards: one doubles as a parking lot, the other is lined with car seats, which are actually pretty comfy. The 45 rooms are worn but clean. There is a good restaurant onsite, which is perfect if you want to get an early start. Popular with traveling business people; call for a reservation during the week.

Hotel Olimpic (446 2487; 1a Av NE; s/d US$9.25/ 13.25, r with air-con US$16; P) Across the street from the Colonial, this is a decent option if its neighbor is full. The rooms are bigger but the upkeep is hit or miss – some of the bathrooms are notably grubby and the beds are on the saggy side. Definitely check out a few rooms before committing.

Comidas Rapidas El Centro (Parque Central; mains US$1.75-3; breakfast, lunch & dinner) A tiny place serving up quick eats like *baleadas* (tortillas with beans and butter), tacos and enchiladas. The service is a bit gruff but the food is good. Across the street from the *iglesia*.

Pupusería La Unica (mains US$0.50; lunch & dinner) Half a block from parque central and next to Comidas Rapidas, this restaurant serves up hot and fresh Salvadoran *pupusas* (cornmeal mass stuffed with fillings) every day. Choose between the standards: *queso* (cheese), *queso y frijoles* (cheese and beans), *chicharrón* (pork), or *revueltas* (cheese, beans and pork). Two to three *pupusas* plus a fruit shake fill most people up.

Getting There & Away

Christina (☎ 446 2861) has a terminal three blocks south and one block west of the stoplight on the main drag. First class buses to Tegucigalpa (US$12, nine hours) leave at 4:10am and 7am Monday to Saturday and at 7am and 9am on Sunday.

All other buses leave from the main terminal, a half-block from the Dippsa gasoline station on the main drag.

La Ceiba *directo* US$2.75, two hours, *ordinario* US$2.25, three hours, every 30 to 60minutes, 5:30am to 3pm

La Unión Take any Tocoa or Trujillo bus and transfer at desvío Sococo.

San Pedro Sula US$6.75, 5½ hours; 10 departures, 3am to 12:45pm, plus 2pm Sat to Sun

Sava *directo* US$1.50, *ordinario* US$1.25, 45 minutes; take any La Ceiba or Tocoa bus

Tocoa US$2; 1½ hours, 10 departures, 7am to 5:30pm

Trujillo US$2.75, 3 hours, 8:45am only, or take any Tocoa bus and transfer

Yoro US$3.75, 3 hours, 5am, 10am and 3:45pm

CENTRAL HONDURAS

Western Honduras

History is palpable in Western Honduras. The region has been part of the human experience for millennia – it has witnessed the rise and fall of civilizations, the ebb and flow of various people's control over the land and over each other.

History does not seem distant here. Walking through Copán's ruins, it is not hard to picture the valley a bustling city of 20,000. Sitting in a centuries-old church in Santa Rosa de Copán, you can easily imagine a time when the same thick walls were new and the paint fresh. Stand in a Lenca village and you'll see life there as it was generations ago, not much changed.

Certainly the mountains remain: El Cerro de las Minas (the highest in Honduras), Santa Bárbara (the second highest), Montaña de Comayagua and Cerro Azul. Lago de Yojoa still teems with wildlife; sadly, however, the rivers and forest are much changed.

There are pockets of modern life, such as San Pedro Sula, with its gleaming malls and throbbing nightclubs. But these are aberrations – even in San Pedro you might hear a rooster crowing early in the morning – and they emphasize the fact that this is ancient land and we are not so far removed from it as we think.

For many travelers, Copán is the west's main and only attraction. But the ruins, spectacular as they are, are the tip of the iceberg; Western Honduras boasts colonial towns and villages, national parks, lakes, caves, hot springs, indigenous art centers and museums. Stay a few extra days – it may well surprise you.

HIGHLIGHTS

- Feast your eyes on some of the best sculptures and hieroglyphic text in all of Mesoamerica in **Copán Ruínas** (p146), Honduras' only major Maya site
- Lose yourself in beautiful **Lago de Yojoa** (p175), a world-class bird-watching site surrounded by waterfalls, thermal waters and two national parks
- Relax in the cool mountain village of **Gracias** (p159) after climbing Honduras' highest peak in **Parque Nacional Montaña de Celaque** (p163)
- Discover **San Pedro Sula** (opposite) – it may be a bit dodgy but it has a terrific anthropology museum and raucous nightlife
- Join in Semana Santa in **Comayagua** (p187), the country's most traditional celebration, with colorful *alfombras* (colorful sawdust carpets with religious iconography) à la Antigua, Guatemala

★ San Pedro Sula

★ Copán Ruínas   ★ Lago de Yojoa

★ Gracias

Comayagua ★

★
Parque Nacional
Montaña de Celaque

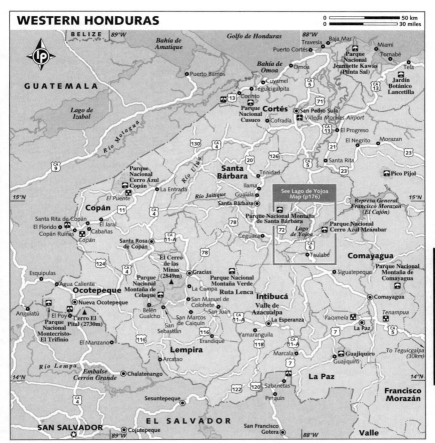

SAN PEDRO SULA

pop 502,939

San Pedro Sula may be second to Teguci-galpa in size, but it is the alpha male in most other respects: Honduras' booming export industry is based here, the major-ity of agricultural products pass through here, the airport is larger and more modern, even the nightlife is better. It is also the capital of Honduras in some less-appealing aspects, including HIV infection and gang violence.

Travelers tend to see San Pedro as a nec-essary evil. Most international flights land here because the city lies right between Honduras' top destinations, Copán Ruínas and the Bay Islands. You wouldn't be alone in trying to get in and out of San Pedro as quickly as possible.

That said, San Pedro does have a very good archaeology and history museum, a pleasant downtown area, some excellent restaurants, and a hopping bar and club scene, includ-ing gay and lesbian spots. If you've been on the road a while, you may appreciate San Pedro's urban amenities, including movie theatres, ultramodern malls, fast food, and clothing and electronics stores.

San Pedro can get extremely hot and humid, especially April to September. The rain starts around May, which helps cool things off.

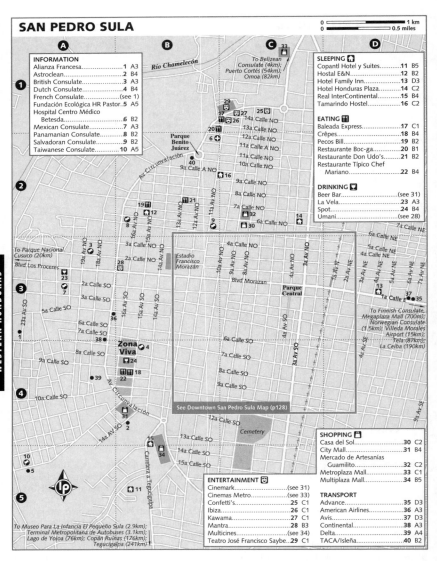

SAN PEDRO SULA

INFORMATION
Alianza Francesa.......................**1** A3
Astroclean...............................**2** B4
British Consulate.....................**3** A3
Dutch Consulate......................**4** B4
French Consulate...................(see 1)
Fundación Ecológica HR Pastor.**5** A5
Hospital Centro Médico
  Betesda.............................**6** B2
Mexican Consulate...................**7** A3
Panamanian Consulate.............**8** B2
Salvadoran Consulate...............**9** B2
Taiwanese Consulate..............**10** A5

SLEEPING 🏠
Copantl Hotel y Suites...........**11** B5
Hostal E&N...........................**12** B2
Hotel Family Inn....................**13** D3
Hotel Honduras Plaza.............**14** C2
Real InterContinental.............**15** B4
Tamarindo Hostel..................**16** C2

EATING 🍽
Baleada Express.....................**17** C1
Crêpes.................................**18** B4
Pecos Bill............................**19** B2
Restaurante Boc-ga...............**20** B1
Restaurante Don Udo's...........**21** B2
Restaurante Típico Chef
  Mariano.............................**22** B4

DRINKING 🍷
Beer Bar............................(see 31)
La Vela................................**23** A3
Spot...................................**24** B4
Umani...............................(see 28)

ENTERTAINMENT 🎭
Cinemark...........................(see 31)
Cinemas Metro.....................(see 33)
Confetti's.............................**25** C1
Ibiza...................................**26** C1
Kawama..............................**27** C1
Mantra................................**28** B3
Multicines..........................(see 34)
Teatro José Francisco Saybe...**29** C1

SHOPPING 🛍
Casa del Sol........................**30** C2
City Mall.............................**31** B4
Mercado de Artesanías
  Guamilito..........................**32** C2
Metroplaza Mall...................**33** C1
Multiplaza Mall....................**34** B5

TRANSPORT
Advance..............................**35** D3
American Airlines...................**36** A3
Avis....................................**37** D3
Continental..........................**38** A3
Delta..................................**39** A4
TACA/Isleña.........................**40** B2

Río Chamelecón

To Belizean
Consulate (4km);
Puerto Cortés (54km);
Omoa (82km)

Parque
Benito
Juárez

Av Circunvalación

WESTERN HONDURAS

To Parque Nacional
Cusuco (20km)
Blvd Los Proceres

Estadio
Francisco
Morazán

Blvd Morazan

Parque
Central

To Finnish Consulate,
Megaplaza Mall (700m);
Norwegian Consulate
(1.5km); Villeda Morales
Airport (15km);
Tela (87km);
La Ceiba (190km)

Zona
Viva

Av Circunvalación

Carretera a Tegucigalpa

See Downtown San Pedro Sula Map (p128)

Cemetery

To Museo Para La Infancia El Pequeño Sula (2.9km);
Terminal Metropolitana de Autobuses (3.1km);
Lago de Yojoa (76km); Copán Ruinas (176km);
Tegucigalpa (241km)

HISTORY

San Pedro Sula – originally named San Pedro de Puerto Caballos – was founded by Pedro de Alvarado in June 1536. Located near the Río Chamelecón, the town was an important commercial center, where goods from the interior – cocoa, indigo, leather, sarsaparilla – were collected before being sent to Spain.

Unfortunately, San Pedro's wealth attracted pirates who repeatedly sailed up the Río Chamelecón to attack and loot the town; it was finally sacked and burned in the 17th century. The town's survivors moved south to Azula, an indigenous village, to restart. The new site – renamed San Pedro Sula – is where the city stands today.

During the 20th century, San Pedro Sula experienced a rapid boom. The population, 5000 in 1900 and 21,000 in 1950, increased to 150,000 by 1975. By 2006 the city had over 500,000 inhabitants. This growth is due to the more than 200 factories that are headquartered in San Pedro Sula; they have attracted Hondurans with little to no job prospects in the rest of the country. The city's population continues to grow at a rate of 5% to 7% each year.

The growth of the city has also brought crime, air pollution and AIDS. San Pedro Sula bears the unfortunate distinction of being the AIDS capital of Central America; whereas Honduras has only 20% of Central America's population, it has 32% of its AIDS cases. A third of these are in San Pedro Sula. Suffice to say that practicing safe sex is extremely important, and nowhere more than here.

ORIENTATION

San Pedro Sula is belted by a highway bypass – Av Circunvalación – a large boulevard that has several shopping centers, gas stations, banks, and fast food restaurants. Inside the beltway, streets are divided between *avenidas* (avenues; abbreviated to Av), which run north–south, and *calles* (streets), which run east–west. The numbering begins where 1a Av and 1a Calle meet in the center of the city. From that point, the numbered *avenidas* and *calles* extend out in four directions: northeast (*noreste*, or NE), northwest (*noroeste*, or NO), southeast (*sureste*, or SE) and southwest (*suroeste*, or SO). As a result, every address in the city is given in relation to a numbered *calle* or *avenida*, and is further specified by the quadrant that it lies in.

Parque central, two blocks west of the 1a Av-1a Calle axis point, is truly the city center. It's a pleasant bustling place, with a number of good places to eat, cool off with an ice cream, or people-watch over a cup of coffee.

INFORMATION
Bookstores

The tobacco shop in the **Gran Hotel Sula** (Map p128; ☎ 552 9999; Parque Central, 1a Calle 0 btwn 3a & 4a Avs NO) sells books and magazines in English, as well as day-old copies of the *Miami Herald* and *New York Times*.

Cultural Centers

Centro Cultural Sampedrano (Map p128; ☎ 553 3911; 3a Calle NO near 3a AV NO; 🕑 9am-noon, 1-6pm Mon-Sat) Sponsors theater productions and art exhibits, and offers long-term art and music courses.

Alianza Francesa (Alliance Française; Map p126; ☎ 553 1178; www.afhonduras.com; 23a Av SO btwn 5a & 9a Calles SO) Offers cultural events and French-language courses.

Emergency

Tourist police (Map p128; ☎ 550 3472; 12a Av NO at 1a Calle 0; 🕑 24hr)

Internet Access

In addition to the places listed here, you'll find internet cafés at all the malls, though prices are higher.

Print-Net (Map p128; 5a Av NO btwn 1a Calle 0 & 2a Calle NO; per hr US$0.85; 🕑 8am-7pm Mon-Sat, 10am-5pm Sun) Also places cheap international phone calls.

Internet y más (Map p128; 5a Calle SO btwn 7a & 8a Avs SO; per hr US$0.55; 🕑 8am-9pm Mon-Fri, 8am-6pm Sat, 11am-3pm Sun)

Cíber Café New Net (Map p128; 2a Calle SO btwn 5a & 6a Avs SO; per hr US$0.55; 🕑 8:30am-6:30pm Mon-Fri, 8:30am-1pm Sat)

Cybercity (per hr US$4; 🕑 5:30am-8pm) At the airport; international calls can also be made.

Laundry

Astroclean (Map p126; ☎ 556 6502; 14a Av SO near Av Circunvalación; per load US$3; 🕑 8am-5pm Mon-Sat) Across from the City Mall.

Lavandería Lavamatic (Map p128; 8a Av NO btwn 2a & 3a Calles NO; per lb US$0.40; 🕑 9am-6pm Mon-Sat)

Medical Services

Hospital Centro Médico Betesda (Map p126; ☎ 516 0900; 11a Ave NO btwn 11a & 12a Calles NO; 🕑 consultations 9-11am & 3-6pm, emergency 24hr)

Super Farmacia Siman (Map p128; ☎ 553 0321; 6a Calle SO btwn 5a & 6a Avs SO; 🕑 8-11am, 2:30-6pm Mon-Fri)

Money

All of the city's malls have banks (open 10am to 6pm Monday to Saturday) with ATMs.

Banco Atlántida (Map p128; Parque Central; 🕑 9am-4pm Mon-Fri, 8:30-11:30am Sat) Changes traveler's checks and issues cash advances on Visa cards; has an ATM.

BAC/Credomatic 5a Av (Map p128; 5 AV NO btwn 1a & 2a Calles NO; 🕑 8am-7pm Mon-Fri, to 2pm Sat); Airport (🕑 9am-5pm Mon-Fri, to noon Sat) Exchanges traveler's checks and has 24 hour ATMs.

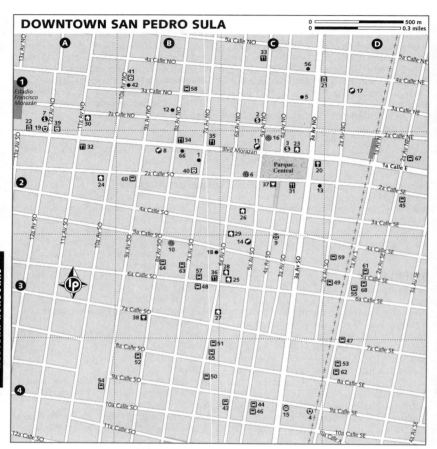

DOWNTOWN SAN PEDRO SULA

Post
Post office (Map p128; ☎ 552 3185; 9a Calle SO at 3a Av SO; 🕑 7:30-6pm Mon-Fri, 8am-noon Sat)

Telephone
Hondutel (Map p128; 4a Calle SO & 4a Av SO; 🕑 7am-9pm)

Print-Net (Map p128; 5a Av NO btwn 1a Calle O & 2a Calle NO; 🕑 8am-7pm Mon-Sat, 10am-5pm Sun) This internet cafés offers domestic and international phone service.

Cybercity (🕑 5:30am-8pm) At the airport. Calls to the USA and Canada cost US$1 per five minutes, while calls to Europe, Australia and New Zealand cost US$3 per minute.

Travel Agencies
Mundirama (Map p128; ☎ 550 0490; www.muntirama travel.com; 2a Calle SO btwn 2a & 3a Avs SO; 🕑 8am-5pm

Mon-Fri, to noon Sat) Full-service travel agency and Amex representative.

Arrecife Tours (Map p128; ☎ 207 4081; www.arre cifetours.com; 7a Av SO btwn 1a Calle O & 2a Calle SO; 🕑 8am-5pm Mon-Fri, to noon Sat)

DANGERS & ANNOYANCES
San Pedro Sula has great restaurants, nightlife, shopping and sights. It also has a serious crime and gang problem. It's perfectly possible to enjoy and avoid the latter, provided you use some basic common sense. The tips are familiar by now: leave expensive jewelry and watches at home, and be discreet when you pull out your money or camera. Be discreet in how you dress and act too – shorts, sandals and loud conversations in English

INFORMATION		SLEEPING ⋂		Buses to Cofradía.....................**43** C4
American Express.................(see 13)		Gran Hotel Sula.......................**23** C2		Buses to Colinas & Trinidad......**44** C4
Arrecife Tours...........................**1** B2		Hotel Ejecutivo........................**24** A2		Buses to El Progreso & Airport
BAC/Credomatic........................**2** C1		Hotel Marina #1.......................**25** C3		Turnoff..................................**45** D2
Banco Atlántida (ATM)..............**3** C2		Hotel Marina #3.......................**26** C2		Buses to Santa Bárbara............**46** C4
Central Police Station................**4** C4		Hotel Real...............................**27** B3		Buses to Yoro & Azacualpa
Centro Cultural		Hotel San Jose.........................**28** C3		(Zacapa)...............................**47** D4
Sampedrano............................**5** C1		Hotel Terraza...........................**29** C2		Casasola..................................**48** B3
Cíber Café New Net...................**6** C2		Los Jícaros Hotel......................**30** A1		Catisa & Tupsa.........................**49** D3
Fundación Ecologista HR				Citracol....................................**50** B4
Pastor....................................**7** A1		EATING ⍰		Citul..**51** B4
German Consulate......................**8** B2		Café Skandia........................(see 23)		Congolón..................................**52** B4
Hondutel....................................**9** C3		Cafetería Pamplona...................**31** C2		Cotuc & Contraibal....................**53** D4
Internet y Más.........................**10** B3		El Fogoncito.............................**32** A2		El Rey Express/Diana Express....**54** A4
Italian Consulate......................**11** C2		Fuente de Salud y Juventud.....**33** C1		Etul...**55** D3
Lavandería Lavamatic...............**12** B1		Nelly's Pizza.............................**34** B2		Euro American/Advantage Rent
Mundirama................................**13** C2		Pizzería Italia...........................**35** B2		A Car....................................**56** C1
Nicaraguan Consulate...............**14** C3		Super Jugos.............................**36** B3		Gracianos & Gama....................**57** B3
Post Office...............................**15** C4		Terraza Restaurant................(see 29)		Hedman Alas............................**58** B1
Print-Net.................................**16** C2				Impala.....................................**59** D3
Spanish Consulate....................**17** D1		DRINKING ⍰		King Quality.............................**60** B2
Super Farmacia Siman...............**18** B3		Espresso Americano...................**37** C2		La Tiga....................................**61** D3
Tourist Police...........................**19** A1		Klein Bohemia..........................**38** B3		Los Norteños.........................(see 48)
US Consulate..........................(see 3)				Molinari Rent A Car...............(see 23)
		ENTERTAINMENT ⍰		Rivera.....................................**62** D4
SIGHTS & ACTIVITIES		Cinemas Geminis......................**39** A1		Saenz.....................................**63** B3
Cathedral.................................**20** C2		Cinemas Tropicana....................**40** B2		Saenz Primera Clase.................**64** B3
Museo de Arqueología e Historia		Multicines Plaza Sula................**41** B1		San José..................................**65** B4
de San Pedro Sula...................**21** C1				Sosa Airlines............................**66** B2
Museo de la		TRANSPORT		Tela Express............................**67** D2
Naturaleza...........................**22** A1		Atlantic Airlines.......................**42** B1		Tima.......................................**68** D3

are a good way to attract attention you may not want. Use taxis! They're cheap, safe and plentiful, and a must late at night (especially when you've been drinking or are by yourself) and a good idea any time you've got all your bags or luggage. And speaking of drinking: it's worth passing on that last round, if it means having your wits about you in the club and, more importantly, on the way home. The parque central gets a little sketchy after 10pm or so, as does the area east and south of it (where the budget hotels are, unfortunately). The fact is, the vast majority of crime in San Pedro Sula is gang related, and is committed by and upon rival gang members; tourists rarely end up in those circles. If you get stuck up, however, the safest thing to do is cooperate and not resist.

SIGHTS & ACTIVITIES

San Pedro's **cathedral** (Map p128; Parque Central; admission free; ☺ various) is worth peeking into. Occupying almost a full city block, it has high, pale-yellow walls and pillars, and an even higher central cupola. The walls are laden with paintings of the saints and other Catholic imagery and hand-carved wooden statues of the same. Like so many huge urban cathedrals in Latin America,

this one offers instant respite from the hustle and bustle on the street.

Don't let its '70s look fool you: the **Museo de Arqueología e Historia de San Pedro Sula** (Map p128; ☎ 557 1496; 3a Av NO at 4a Calle NO; admission US$2; ☺ 9am-4pm Mon-Sat, to 3pm Sun) is an excellent museum that walks visitors through the changes in the Valle de Sula from the pre-Columbian era to the modern day; hundreds of well-maintained archaeological artifacts and antiques are displayed. Signage is in Spanish and English and each room has a bilingual guidebook that visitors can read for more in-depth information.

The **Museo de la Naturaleza** (Map p128; ☎ 557 6598; 1a Calle 0 near 12a Av NO; admission US$1.05; ☺ 8am-4pm Mon-Fri, to noon Sat) has over 80 exhibits that cover the gamut of natural history, from paleontology and human biology to ecology and the universe. The level of detail is on par with a college textbook, which can be somewhat overwhelming on a mellow afternoon. Spanish signage only.

More a children's learning center than a museum, the **Museo Para La Infancia El Pequeño Sula** (☎ 556 5114; sulaykili@yahoo.es; Carr a Tegucigalpa; adult/child US$2/1; ☺ 3-5pm Mon-Fri) offers monthly workshops in the sciences and arts. It's 3km from Av Circunvalación.

DAY-TRIPPING TO PARQUE NACIONAL CUSUCO

Just 45km from San Pedro Sula, **Parque Nacional Cusuco** (admission US$15; ☽ 8am-4:30pm), is a cloud forest nestled in the impressive Merendón mountain range. The park has abundant wildlife, including parrots, toucans and a large population of quetzals, best spotted from April to June. Its highest peak is Cerro Jilinco (2242m). The park's visitors center is the starting point for five different **hiking** trails. Two trails – Quetzal and Las Minas – pass waterfalls and swimming holes. Guides can be hired at the visitors center for around US$5 per trip.

Access to the park is very difficult. From San Pedro Sula, take an early bus west to Cofradía (US$0.60, 45 minutes, from 5:50am, every 10 minutes) in time to catch a pickup at the Parque Central for the rough ride to the village of Buenos Aires (1½ hours, morning only). From there you'll have to hire a car, hitch a ride or walk to the visitors center – it's 20 minutes by car, an hour on foot.

You can camp at the visitors center, though here are no services there. Otherwise, **Fundación Ecologista HR Pastor** (☎ 557 6598; fundeco@netsys.hn; 12a Av NO at 1a Calle; 8am-noon & 1-5pm Mon-Fri, 8am-noon Sat) manages a very simple **cabaña** (r per person US$12) in Buenos Aires. The cabin has two private rooms with cold-water bathrooms, and a small common kitchen. There's no electricity so bring candles. You may reserve by phone but must pay in person at the Fundación office in San Pedro Sula.

Cusuco is beautiful, but the cost – US$15 admission plus US$12 to stay overnight – is somewhat over-the-top. Combine that with the difficulty in getting here and it's no wonder that few foreigners visit.

Merendón Adventures (☎ 984 0719; www.hikinghonduras.com) offers one- and two-day guided excursions in the park.

FESTIVALS & EVENTS

The **Feria Juniana**, a celebration in honor of the city's patron saint, is one of the biggest parties in Honduras. It takes place the entire last week of June, when San Pedranos hit the streets to dance, eat, and watch cultural performances. The height of the *feria* is on June 29, when a huge parade makes its way down Av Circunvalación.

SLEEPING

San Pedro's hotels range from luxury to crap-hole, and you generally get what you pay for. The city's nicest hotels are near the malls but removed from downtown. Several budget options are just south of parque central, but the area can get dodgy at night.

Budget

Tamarindo Hostel (Map p126; ☎ 557 0123; www.tamarindohostel.com; 9a Calle A NO btwn 10a & 11a Avs NO; dm US$8pp, r with bathroom & air-con US$25; P ☒ ☐) One of the best hostels in Honduras, the Tamarindo is an excellent choice if you don't mind cabbing it or taking long walks around town. Rooms have funkadelic murals, fans and extra long bunks; they share plenty of bathrooms so there's rarely a long wait (plus, there's hot water!). Common areas have a boho feel – and it's no wonder, the owners are musicians – with hand-carved furniture, lots of wall hangings and plenty of hammocks. There's also a huge fully equipped kitchen for guests. Linens, towels, soap, a locker and internet access are included in the daily rate. Pickup and drop off at the bus terminals and airport also can be arranged. English and basic German are spoken.

Hotel Real (Map p128; ☎ 550 7929; hotelreal 2002@yahoo.com; 6a Av SO btwn 6a & 7a Calles SO; s/d US$15/18, with air-con US$21/24; ☒) Without a doubt, this is the best downtown hotel for budget travelers. A welcoming place with hand-carved furnishings, Lencan pottery and lots of hanging plants, the rooms are a real surprise. A good one. Few things are better at the end of the day than a comfortable bed, cable TV, a sparkling bathroom and charming décor. And for cheap. The only downer is the location: it's alright during the day but a bit edgy at night. Cab it after sunset.

Hotel Terraza (Map p128; ☎ 550 3108; fax 550 0798; 6a Av SO btwn 4a & 5a Calles SO; s/r/tw with cold-water bathroom US$11.65/16/20, r with hot-water bathroom & air-con US$24; ☒) This old-timer has basic rooms with décor that looks like it's straight out of a 1970s garage sale – Formica floors, bedazzled lamps and busy bedspreads. The 1st floor rooms are dreary, but those on the upper levels are clean and sunny. An excellent breakfast, served in the hotel's popular restaurant, is included in the rate. Just be sure to order it before 9am – you snooze, you lose.

Hotel Marina #1 (Map p128; ☎ 557 2953; 6a Calle SO near 6a Av SO; s/d with shared bathroom US$5.30/6.35, with air-con US$9/10.60; P ⚡) Strikingly clean rooms with checkerboard floors – even the shared bathrooms are spotless – are a real surprise considering the price. Rooms with interior-facing windows are darker but also quieter than the others – decide whether you prefer sunlight or sleep before you plunk down your cash.

Hotel San Jose (Map p128; ☎ 557 1208; 6a Av SO btwn 5a & 6a Calles SO; r/tw US$7.50/10.50) Don't be turned off by the prison-like exterior of this hotel; yes, it's gray, the fluorescent lights don't help, and the long corridor of windowless rooms are utterly charmless but look inside a door and you'll see a simple room that's clean and very quiet (having no windows has its advantages). Considering the location and the price, this is a good option. Just be sure you have a real bed, as opposed to a cot, to sleep on.

Hotel Marina #3 (Map p128; ☎ 557 8722; 3a Calle SO btwn 5a & 6a Avs SO; r/tw with air-con US$13/19; P ⚡) Although the lobby of the Marina #3 is very appealing – bright lights, big windows, attractive furnishings – the rooms are somewhat of a letdown. Frankly, they're cramped and the bathrooms need an overhaul (a showerhead – as opposed to a pipe – would work wonders). At least the rooms have air-conditioning for cheap, which makes the rooms hard to pass up.

Midrange

Hotel Ejecutivo (Map p128; ☎ 552 4289; www.hotel -ejecutivo.com; 2a Calle SO at 10a Av SO; s/d incl breakfast US$50/58; P ⚡ 🖳) This classic businessperson's hotel is spacious, tastefully decorated, sparkling clean and equipped with the amenities you'd expect: cable TV, air-conditioning, in-room telephone, internet access and a small rooftop gym (with a fantastic view of the mountains, no less). Breakfast – choose from over 10 options – is served in a pleasant restaurant. If you like cityscapes, ask for a room on the 5th floor.

Hotel Honduras Plaza (Map p126; ☎ 553 2424; hotelhondurasplaza@sulanet.net; 4a Av NO at 6a Calle NO; r incl breakfast US$50.25; P ⚡ 🖳) Greco-Roman décor – well, columns, heavy gold curtains and overstuffed furniture – make this hotel unique in San Pedro Sula. Fortunately, the theme doesn't go much further. You'll find good-sized rooms with good beds, big bathrooms, air-conditioning, and minibars. There must be a set of Greek statues somewhere…

Hostal E&N (Map p126; ☎ 552 5731; hostaleyn@ amnethn.com; 15a Av NO at 5a Calle NO; s/d US$30/32; P ⚡ 🖳) This converted home is a comfortable option in a quiet upscale neighborhood. Rooms all have hardwood floors, hot-water bathrooms, cable TV and free in-room internet access. Included in the rate is a Continental breakfast, which would be better if there were a place to eat it; instead, guests have their coffee and toast on their feet or crouched around a small coffee table in the lobby.

Hotel Family Inn (Map p126; ☎ 552 2323; fax 552 2432; 1a Calle Este btwn 4a & 5a Calle NE; s/d/t incl breakfast US$40/45/50) An adequate if unmemorable option, rooms here are large, clean and plain; those facing inwards get less street noise but still have good light. Twenty minutes of free internet is included.

Top End

Gran Hotel Sula (Map p128; ☎ 552 9999; www.gran hotelsula-sanpedrosula.com; Parque Central, 1a Calle 0 btwn 3a & 4a Avs NO; s/d US$79/91, ste US$95-107, all incl breakfast; P ⚡ ⚡ 🖳) The Gran Sula is not the newest or fanciest hotel in town, but it's a great place to stay for travelers who want the comforts of a four-star hotel in the hustle-bustle of downtown rather than out by the sleepy neighborhood malls. Right on parque central, south-facing rooms have balconies overlooking the park, city hall and cathedral – ask for a top floor for the best view and least street noise. The view on the other side, overlooking the hotel's pool and leafy courtyard, isn't too shabby either – there you should ask for a room on the 2nd floor, for the double-size balconies.

Los Jícaros Hotel (Map p128; ☎ 550 7003; www .usula.com; 11a Av NO at 2a Calle NO; s/d US$58/70, s/d ste US$70/81; P ⚡ 🖳) Opened in early 2006, Los Jícaros is just six blocks west of parque central – far enough to be in a decent part of town but close enough for it to be an easy stroll there. Everything in the rooms is brand-spanking new – the tiles, the beds, the TVs, the furniture, the bathroom fixtures. It's attractive but also kind of sterile, like a showroom. Perhaps being around for a while will work that out. A continental breakfast is included.

Real InterContinental (Map p126; ☎ 553 0000; www.intercontinental.com; r Mon-Tue US$116, Fri-Sun US$161, executive US$195; P ✕ 🐾 🖳 🖭) President Zelaya was spending the last few days of Semana Santa (Holy Week, the week preceding Easter) here when we passed through, which ought to lay to rest any doubts about which is the top hotel in town. It's not as glamorous as the InterContinental in Tegucigalpa (aka Tegus) but still exudes a cool elegance, from the understated lobby to the thick, crisply folded towels in the bathrooms. The pool is only average – the only surprise in this otherwise first-class hotel. It's just off Av Circunvalación, next to Metroplaza Mall.

Copantl Hotel y Suites (Map p126; ☎ 556 8900; www.copantl.com; Blvd del Sur; s/d/ste US$93/105/116; P ✕ 🐾 🖳 🖭) Behind Multiplaza Mall, Copantl is another high-rise hotel, but at least it's locally owned. Popular with businessmen and well-to-do Honduran vacationers, rooms on the first two floors open onto a corridor overlooking the lobby – if you're a late sleeper ask for something higher. Rooms are comfortable if not glamorous, and many have nice views over the pool, tennis courts and the city beyond.

EATING

San Pedro Sula has a decent range of restaurants downtown, and even more in the Zona Viva (Map p126), at 15a and 16a Avs SO, between 7a and 11a Calles SO. Hondurans do love American fast-food chains, though, which are found just about everywhere.

Budget

Baleada Express (Map p126; 14a Calle NO at Av Circunvalación; mains US$0.60-$2; ⏰ 7am-noon, 4-10:30pm Mon-Sat, 4-10:30pm Sun) Mexico has tacos, El Salvador *pupusas* (cornmeal mass stuffed with cheese and/or refried beans), and Honduras *baleadas* (a stuffed flour tortilla that's folded in half). The *sencilla* (simple) has just beans and melted butter, but the huge

array of options here, including plenty for vegetarians, lets you get creative with the national munchie.

Terraza Restaurant (Map p128; ☎ 550 3108; 6a Av SO btwn 4a & 5a Calles SO; mains US$2.50-6; ⏰ breakfast, lunch & dinner) Don't be put off by the location – inside a budget hotel of the same name, this restaurant is one of the best downtown. Honduran classics like coconut shrimp and chicken tacos are served alongside international faves like BLTs and veggie pasta. The *plato del día* (daily special), however, is hard to beat; typically, this is a meat dish with a couple of sides and a drink for US$2.50.

Cafetería Pamplona (Map p128; Parque Central, 2a Calle SO; mains US$2-7; ⏰ breakfast, lunch & dinner) A good honest restaurant serving good honest meals. There's nothing spectacular about the menu – club sandwiches, chicken and rice, garlic filet of fish, and a few daily specials – but the food is always good and service always friendly. Sometimes it's nice not to have to think too hard about where to eat. Don't be surprised if you come back more than once.

Café Skandia (Map p128; ☎ 552 9999; Parque Central, 1a Calle O btwn 3a & 4a Avs NO; dishes US$3-5; ⏰ 24hr) In Gran Hotel Sula, Skandia is surprisingly pleasant for a hotel restaurant; you can sit in the air-conditioned dining area or at shaded tables by the pool. The menu includes Honduran standbys – eggs, fried fish, roast chicken – plus a bunch of items you rarely see, like waffles, onion rings, apple pie and milkshakes. No wonder it's popular with the business and diplomatic set.

Fuente de Salud y Juventud (Map p128; ☎ 553 7010; 5 Av NO btwn 4a & 5a Calle NO; mains US$1.50-$3; ⏰ lunch Mon-Fri) Mainly a natural goods store (vitamins, supplements etc), the Fount of Health & Youth also prepares a modest vegetarian buffet. The food is pretty underwhelming, but for vegetarians surviving on rice, beans and licuados (smoothies), it's a welcome change. Dishes vary, but expect offerings like lentils, stewed eggplant, carrot *tortas* and *carne de soya* (soy meat).

Super Jugos (Map p128; 6a Av SO at 6a Calle SO; ⏰ 8am-9m Mon-Sat, to 6pm Sun) The motto here is 'the best licuados in Honduras' and who are we to disagree? Try a tall smoothie with any combination of fruit, plus granola or cereal, for under US$1.25.

Midrange

Restaurante Típico Chef Mariano (Map p126; ☎ 552 5492; 9a Calle SO near 15a Av SO, Zona Viva; mains US$7-9; ☺ lunch & dinner) Ask around for a place to get Garífuna food and this is the restaurant most people will recommend. Warm coconut bread is served with excellent main dishes, most of which are seafood based and have intriguing names like *lluvia de róbalo* (bass). Service is top-notch.

Crêpes (Map p126; ☎ 553 5797; 9 Calle SO at 15a Av SO, Zona Viva; mains US$4-8; ☺ lunch & dinner) A great place to get – yes – crepes, but also traditional Colombian food, like soups and *arepas* (corn griddle cakes). Crepes are sweet or salty, ranging from Nutella to beef stroganoff and everything in between.

Nelly's Pizza (Map p128; ☎ 550 2757; 1a Calle O at 8a Av NO; mains US$5-8; ☺ lunch & dinner) A leafy courtyard with potted trees, gurgling fountain and the requisite red-and-white checkered tablecloths make this a great place for a drink or early evening meal. As darkness falls, holiday lights blink on, adding to the ambiance. The food (so-so) and service (slow) don't quite live up to the setting, but if you stick with the pizza, you should go home happy.

Pizzería Italia (Map p128; 1a Calle O & 7a Av NO; dishes US$3-5; ☺ 10am-10pm, Tue-Sun) A block away, this place has great pizza and a funky hole-in-the-wall atmosphere.

El Fogoncito (Map p128; ☎ 553 3000; 1a Calle O at 11a Av NO; mains US$5-10; ☺ lunch & dinner) The best-known Mexican restaurant in town, this cantina-style place offers classic Mexican and Tex-Mex dishes – *tacos al pastor* (spicy pork tacos), fajitas – plus some less frequently prepared specialties like mole (spicy sauce made with chilies and usually chocolate and served with meat) and *cochinita pibil* (Yucatán-style roast pork). The food is good if not spectacular; at least there's a full bar and long hours – till midnight on Thursday, 2am on Friday and Saturday – so dinner can easily stretch into beers.

Pecos Bill (Map p126; ☎ 557 5744; 15 Av NO btwn 6a & 7a Calles NO; mains US$7-10; ☺ lunch & dinner Tue-Sun, lunch Mon) This is the place to come for meat and the game. First the meat: hefty portions of beef, chicken, chorizo or pork chops served with beans and fried bananas on platters for one to four people. And the game: important matches (NFL, NBA, World Cup, whatever) are shown not just on a big TV, but on a huge screen. If there's no game, a movie is shown instead – it's like a drive-in with table service.

Top End

Restaurante Don Udo's (Map p126; ☎ 553 2675; www.donudos.com; 13 Av NO btwn 7 & 7a Calle NO; mains US$7-20; ☺ lunch & dinner) You don't have to be a bigwig to eat here, though plenty do. Don Udo's is one of San Pedro's top restaurants, with excellent food and service and a cool colonial elegance. It's hard to go wrong here – for dinner, the pâté appetizer and tenderloin steak, served with a glass of red wine, are terrific. For lunch, a focaccia sandwich and a beer go down nicely. Live music and a cozy outdoor patio add to the experience.

Restaurante Boc-ga (Map p126; ☎ 991 0077; 11 Av NO at 13 Calle NO; mains US$6-20; ☺ breakfast, lunch & dinner) This is a classy Korean restaurant whose name means 'house of blessing'. Go for Western tables with chairs and table legs, or normal ones, which in here means low to the floor with cushions to sit on. Either way, you've got a grill in the middle for do-it-yourself dishes like Boc-ga teriyaki or *tukpegi bulgogi* (spicy beef), a house favorite.

DRINKING

The bars and lounges in town are great places to start – or end – the night.

Klein Bohemia (Map p128; ☎ 552 3172; www.klein bohemia.com; 7a Calle SO at 8a Av SO; ☺ 4:30pm-midnight Wed, Thu & Sat, to 1am Fri) An artsy bohemian lounge with fantastic drink specials – you can't beat US$0.80 mixed drinks! It's also the heart of the art scene in San Pedro, with photo exhibitions, poetry readings, movie screenings and live concerts. There's no cover most nights.

La Vela (Map p126; ☎ 504 3821; 1a Calle O at 20a Av SO; ☺ 5-11pm Sun-Wed, 5pm-2am Thu-Sat) A small, lively place that's popular with the upper crust, La Vela serves up huge plates of nachos and two-for-one drinks during happy hour (5pm to 8pm). Thursday features live music, usually a local band playing something rockish-funkish.

Umani (Map p126; ☎ 557 3281; 1a Calle NO at Av Circunvalación; ☺ 6pm-3am) This exclusive bar-lounge sits below Mantra, one of the best nightclubs in town. The age minimum (24 for men, 20 for women) and dress code (men must wear a collared shirt and dress shoes; women, well, dress to kill) are strictly enforced. Most people start off their night here, then head upstairs to dance. Popular with young expatriates.

Beer Bar (Map p126; ☎ 580 1343; 3rd fl, City Mall; ☺ 2pm-midnight Tue-Sat, 2-7pm Sun) Yes, it's in a mall, but don't write this place off. As the name suggests, this bar is all about the beer – from Italy, the Czech Republic, South Africa, Peru, Ecuador, Mexico, Panama, El Salvador and Honduras to be exact. Many cost US$2 to US$3 – not cheap – but watching a *fútbol* match with a good pint is priceless.

Espresso Americano (Map p128; Parque Central; coffee US$1-2; ☺ 6:30am-8pm) The cappuccino and mocha here are great, but cold 'frapuccinos' don't have much zing. Whatever you order, take it into the park as the tables are usually packed with old guys yammering.

ENTERTAINMENT

San Pedro has a raucous nightlife, with bars open most of the week and clubs open Thursday to Sunday. The best clubs are scattered along Av Circunvalación, mostly in the northwest (NO) quadrant. The Zona Viva (at 15a and 16a Avs SO, between 7a and 11a Calles SO), on the other hand, mostly has restaurants.

Nightclubs

Mantra (Map p126; ☎ 557 3281; 1a Calle O at Av Circunvalación; ☺ 10pm-3am) The hottest nightspot in San Pedro – and also the most *fresa* (rich or snobby, depending on whom you ask) – don't even think about wearing sneakers or a T-shirt here. The DJ spins mostly salsa, merengue and regguetón (hip-hop with Jamaican and Latin American influences) – prepare to get your groove going on stage alongside the giant Buddha. Thursdays are free cover and half-price drinks; Friday's are US$8 cover with open bar, and on Saturdays it's US$5.50 cover for everyone. An age minimum – 24 for men, 20 for women – keeps the kids out. If you need a break from dancing, head downstairs for a drink at Umani.

Kawama (Map p126; Av Circunvalación, btwn 10a & 11a Avs NO; cover US$2-5; 9pm-3am Tue-Thu, to 5am Fri-Sun) Another hot spot, this discotheque plays mostly recorded Latin music – salsa, merengue, even *punta* (point, a traditional

Garífuna dance involving much hip movement). The place gets hopping around 11pm.

Confetti's (Map p126; Av Circunvalación, near 7a Av NO; cover US$2-5; ☺ 9pm-3am Tue-Thu, to 5am Fri-Sun) Two blocks from Kawama, this club is all about house and techno; there are plenty of people on the dance floor, but it has a good bar scene too.

Gay & Lesbian Venues

Spot (Map p126; 8a Calle SO btwn 15a & 16a Avs SO; cover US$2.75-5.75; ☺ 9pm-3am) San Pedro Sula's only openly gay club, is not only jam packed with men on the dance floor, but also swinging around a stripper pole and shaking it in a cage. Disco and Top 40 rule this place – Madonna, of course, features prominently. Spot is also straight-friendly.

Ibiza (Map p126; Av Circunvalación near 11a Calle NO; ☺ 6pm-3am) An unspoken meeting place for lesbians, this lounge-disco has big couches and lots of tables to kick back, drink and talk. On weekends, the floor gets crowded with dancers moving to a good mix of Latin rock, salsa, merengue and regguetón.

Cinemas

Movies are also popular in San Pedro Sula, and it shows in the number of cinemas. Downtown, **Cinema Geminis** (Map p128; ☎ 550 9060; 1a Calle O at 12a Av NO), **Cinema Tropicana** (Map p128; ☎ 553 0391; 2a Calle SO at 7a Av SO), and **Multicines Plaza Sula** (Map p128; ☎ 557 3860; 10a Av NO btwn 3a & 4a Calles NO) are all small theatres with just a couple of screens. Theaters that are in the malls – **Cinemark** (Map p126; City Mall), **Multicines** (Map p126; Multiplaza Mall), **Cinemas Metro** (Map p126; Metroplaza Mall) – are larger and more modern. Tickets are US$2 to US$2.50, with discounts on Tuesday and Thursday. Look in *La Prensa* newspaper for current listings.

Theater

Teatro José Francisco Saybe (Map p126; ☎ 225 5117; Av Circunvalación, near 11a Av NO) This modern theater near the Universidad de San Pedro Sula hosts San Pedro's finest live performances year-round. Ticket prices vary widely, costing from US$5 to US$53.

SHOPPING

Casa del Sol 6a Calle NO (Map p126; ☎ 557 1371; btwn 8a & 9a Avs NO; 8am-6pm Mon-Sat, to noon Sun); Multiplaza Mall (Map p126; ☎ 550 5711; ☺ 10am-8pm Mon-Sat, to

6pm Sun) This place sells the highest-quality *artesanía* (handicrafts) in town. You'll find every type of Honduran handicraft – pottery, leatherwork, wood carvings, tree-bark pressings, baskets... The shop provides free delivery to your hotel so you don't have to lug your items around town.

Mercado de Artesanías Guamilito (Map p126; 8a & 9a Avs NO btwn 6a & 7a Calles NO; ✆ 7am-5pm Mon-Sat, to noon Sun) Stall upon stall of handicrafts from all over Honduras, Guatemala and El Salvador fill this sprawling market. If you're looking for T-shirts and coconut monkeys, you'll find those too. If haggling makes you hungry, stop by the food stands (open 6am to 1pm) on the opposite side of the building.

Museo de Arqueología e Historia de San Pedro Sula (Map p128; ✆ 557 1496; 3a Av NO at 4a Calle NO; admission US$2; ✆ 9am-4pm Mon-Sat, to 3pm Sun) This excellent museum boasts a fine little gift shop. Items include baskets from Santa Bárbara, pottery from the Ruta Lenca and tree-bark mobiles from La Moskitia. There's also a decent selection of Honduran history books in Spanish and English.

City Mall (Map p128; Av Circunvalación near Carr a Tegucigalpa; ✆ 9am-8pm) An impressive shopping center with an enormous food court, this mall houses high-end boutiques and department stores. It also has several banks with ATMs, internet cafés with calling service, and a movie theater.

Metroplaza Mall (Map p126; ✆ 9am-8pm) is just down the street from City Mall, while the smaller **Multiplaza Mall** (Map p128; ✆ 9am-8pm) and **Mega Plaza Mall** (Map p126; ✆ 9am-8pm) stand guard at the main northern and eastern roads out of town.

GETTING THERE & AWAY
Air
Aeropuerto Internacional Ramón Villeda Morales (15km east of San Pedro Sula) is the country's busiest airport, more so even than Tegucigalpa. Planes come and go from all the major cities in Central America plus several from the US, Mexico and Europe, and of course domestically to Tegucigalpa and La Ceiba. It has conveniences such as a bank, internet and call center, car-rental agencies and even a Hedman Alas bus terminal.

American Airlines (Map p126; ✆ 553 3508, at airport 668 3244; www.aa.com; Av Circunvalación at 5a Calle SO,

Edificio Banco Ficohsa; ✆ 8am-noon & 1-5pm Mon Fri, 8am-noon Sat)

Atlantic Airlines (Map p128; ✆ 557 8088, at airport 668 3251; www.atlanticairlines.com.ni; 10a Av NO btwn 3a & 4a Calle NO, Plaza Monaco; ✆ 8am-noon & 1-5pm Mon-Fri, 8am-noon Sat)

Continental (Map p126; ✆ 557 4141, at airport 668 3208; www.continental.com; Av Circunvalación btwn 7a & 7a A Calles SO, Edificio Versaille; ✆ 8am-noon & 1-5pm Mon-Fri, 8am-noon Sat)

Delta (✆ 550 1616; www.delta.com; 18a Av SO, btwn 9a & 10a Calles SO; ✆ 8am-noon & 1-5pm Mon-Fri)

Sosa Airlines (Map p128; ✆ /fax 550 6545, 550 6548; 1a Calle 0 btwn 7a & 8a Av SO; ✆ 8am-noon & 1-5pm Mon-Fri, 8am-noon Sat)

TACA/Isleña (Map p126; ✆ 516 1061, at airport 668 3183; www.taca.com; Av Circunvalación at 10a Av NO; ✆ 8am-noon & 1-5pm Mon-Fri, 8am-noon Sat)

Bus
San Pedro Sula is a land transportation hub, connecting the north coast to western and southern Honduras. However, if you're not planning to stop, you can sometimes save time by transferring buses at El Progreso instead of going into San Pedro proper.

The city built an enormous **Terminal Metropolitana de Autobuses** (Metropolitan Bus Terminal; 5km south of town) that was designed to bring all the bus lines under a single roof and relieve some of the traffic congestion in town. The opening has been continually delayed, however, and travelers still use the slew of individual bus lots, distributed mostly south and east of downtown.

The free tourist magazine *Honduras Tips* has a very helpful section on bus routes around the country.

For long-distance buses from San Pedro Sula see boxed text p136. You can get additional bus information in *Honduras Tips*, or by calling individual bus lines during working hours.

INTERNATIONAL BUSES
Transportes Hedman Alas (Map p128; ✆ 553 1361; www.hedmanalas.com; 3a Calle NO btwn 7a & 8a Avs NO) has deluxe service to Guatemala City (executive/plus US$45/59, eight hours) that continues to Antigua (executive/plus US$51/66 one way, nine hours), departing daily at 9:50am.

Transportes El Rey Express (Map p128; ✆ 550 8950; www.reyexpress.net; 9a Av SO btwn 9a & 10a Calles SO) has first-class service to Guatemala City (US$26 one way, 6am, 8½ hours). **Transportes King**

WESTERN HONDURAS

LONG-DISTANCE BUSES FROM SAN PEDRO SULA

Destination	Bus Line	Phone	Fare	Frequency	Duration
Agua Caliente	Congolón (Map p128)	553 1174	US$7	6, 8, 10:30am & 1:30pm	5hr
Comayagua	Rivera (Map p128)	no phone	US$3	hourly, 6am-4:40pm	3¼hr
Copán Ruínas	El Rey Express (Map p128)	550 8952	US$4.80	7:30am, 1:30pm, & 3:30pm	3hr
Copán Ruínas	Casasola (Map p128)	558 1659	US$4.80-5.50	6 departures, 7am-2:40pm	2¾-3hr
Copán Ruínas**	Hedman Alas (Map p128)	557 3477	US$13.50	3-4 departures, 7am-2:50pm	2½-3hr
La Ceiba	Catisa & Tupsa (Map p128)	553 1023	US$	hourly, 6am-6pm	3hr
La Ceiba*	Diana Express	552 8952	US$4.25	10am, noon, 4:15pm	3hr
La Ceiba**	Hedman Alas (Map p128)	557 3477	US$13.50	4 departures, 6am-6pm	2¾ -3hr
Peña Blanca & El Mochito	La Tiga or Tima (Map p128)	557 0895	US$1.25	every 30min, 6:20am-5:30pm	2-2½hr
Pto Cortés	Impala/Citul (Map p128)	553 3111	US$1.10-1.60	every 15min, 4:30am-9pm	1-1¾hr
Santa Bárbara	Cotisba	552 8889	US$1.85	every 30min, 5:20am-6pm	2hr
Santa Bárbara*	Cotisba	552 8889	US$2.25	4pm & 5:20pm	1½hr
Santa Rosa de Copán	Congolón (Map p128)	553 1174	US$3.50	6, 8, 10:30am & 1:30pm	2½hr
Tegucigalpa	Saenz (Map p128)	553 4264	US$3.85	every 2hr, 6am-6pm	5hr
Tegucigalpa*	El Rey Express (Map p128)	550 8952	US$6	every 60-90min, 5:30am-6pm	4½hr
Tegucigalpa**	Saenz Primera Clase (Map p128)	553 4969	US$12.25	every 2hr, 6-10am & 2-6pm; 8am-6pm Sun	4hr
Tegucigalpa**	Hedman Alas (Map p128)	557 3477	US$14.50	7 departures, 5:45am-5:45pm	3½hr
Tela	Tela Express (Map p128)	551 8140	US$3	every 2hr, 7am-6pm Mon-Sat, 8am-3:35pm Sun	1½hr
Tela	Catisa & Tupsa (Map p128)	553 1023	US$3.50	hourly, 6am-6pm	1½hr
Trujillo	Cotuc & Contraibal (Map p128)	557 8470	US$7	every 45min, 5:15am-4pm	6hr

*direct service
**luxury service

Quality (Map p128; ☎ 553 4547; www.kingqualityca
.com; 2a Calle SO at 9a Av SO) has deluxe service to
San Salvador (executive/king US$28/41 one
way, six hours, 6:30am and 1pm).

GETTING AROUND
Bus
Avoid taking local public buses in San Pedro
Sula or any large town or city in Honduras.

They are all too often the target of gang attacks and drivers often have to pay 'tax' to
go through certain neighborhoods.

Car & Motorcycle
Driving in San Pedro is a relatively painless
experience. Always check if the street you're
turning into is only one way. Signage is
sparse and the police *will* pull you over for

GETTING TO & FROM THE AIRPORT

San Pedro's Villeda Morales airport, the largest and most modern in the country, is about 15km southeast of town. There is no direct bus to the airport, but you can get on any El Progreso bus and ask the driver to let you off at the airport turnoff. From there, it's a long shadeless walk (25 minutes); if you have heavy bags or it's late, consider springing for a taxi. A taxi ride to/from the airport runs US$10. Coming from the airport, you can get a taxi just to the turnoff ($3) and catch a bus into town.

---

going the wrong way, as our writers learned firsthand. Av Circunvalación is orderly and fast and often better than cutting though town. The areas south and east of the center are busy and chaotic, thanks to the bus terminals and markets there.

Rental-car agencies include **Advance** (Map p126; ☎ 552 2295; at airport 668 0284; www.advance renta car.com; 1a Calle Este btwn 6a & 7a Av NE; ☯ 8am-6pm Mon-Sat, 9am-5pm Sun); **Avis** (Map p126; ☎ 553 0888, at airport 668 3164; avissj2@sulanet.net; 1a Calle Este btwn 6a & 7a Avs NE; ☯ 6am-10pm Mon-Fri, 8am-6pm Sat & Sun), next to Advance; **Euro American/Advantage Rent A Car** (Map p128; ☎ 557 2442, at airport 668 8001; www.euroamericanhn.com; 4a Calle NO btwn 3a & 4a Avs NO; ☯ 8am-noon & 1-5pm Mon-Fri, 8am-noon Sat); **Hertz** (☎ at airport 668 3156; www.hertz.com); and **Molinari Rent A Car** (Map p128; ☎ 553 2639; molinarirentacar@yahoo.com; Parque Central; ☯ 8am-noon & 2-6pm Mon-Fri, 8am-noon Sat), at the Hotel Gran Sula.

Taxi

Taxis are easy to flag down, especially downtown and near the malls. Cabs don't have meters, however, so agree on a price before you get in. Average fares in town are US$1 per person; a trip to the airport costs around US$10.

VALLE DE COPÁN

This broad fertile valley has served as a homestead, an agricultural center and a crossroads for thousands of years. At its peak, the Maya city of Copán wielded influence and control over a wide swath of Central American territory, and traders and

travelers came from near and far, creating a rich commercial and cultural marketplace. Today, political power has shifted elsewhere, but the Copán Valley is still home to many, a vital agricultural zone and a magnet for travelers.

LA ENTRADA
pop 14,893

La Entrada got its name for its position at the *entrada* (entrance) to the humid coastal area from the hotter, drier interior. It remains a crossroads, an overgrown Y-intersection on the highway between San Pedro Sula, Copán Ruínas and Santa Rosa de Copán. Most people blaze right through or stay only as long as it takes for their connecting bus to pull up. La Entrada does have one worthwhile site – a Maya ruin outside of town – and a surprisingly high number of foreign volunteers, mostly from Christian relief organizations, who use La Entrada as a base for projects in outlying villages.

Information & Orientation

La Entrada is a one-road town lined with hotels, restaurants and other services. The main intersection is at the south end of town – coming from San Pedro Sula, bear right for Copán Ruínas and the Guatemalan border, or bear left for Santa Rosa de Copán and the Ruta Lenca.

Farmacia La Milagrosa (☎ 661 2097; ☯ 8am-6pm Mon-Sat) is next door to the Hotel Tegucigalpa. Two-and-a-half blocks north of there is **Banco Atlántida** (☯ 9am-4pm Mon-Fri, 8:30-11:30am Sat), which has an ATM.

Sleeping & Eating

Hotel y Restaurant El San Carlos (☎ 661 2228; hotel-san-carlos@terra.com s/d with fan US$11.25/21.25, with air-con US$17.50/23.50; ⓟ ⓧ ⓡ) Something must have gone wrong for you to be stuck in La Entrada, so why not treat yourself? There's an inviting pool with lounge chairs and shaded tables beneath an enormous bird-themed mural (plus two real macaws squawking nearby). The rooms have spotless hot-water bathrooms, cable TV, drinking water and telephone. There's also a classy restaurant (mains US$3.50 to US$10), open for breakfast, lunch and dinner, which local businesspeople use for lunch meetings. The hotel is 50m from the main intersection, toward Copán Ruínas.

Hotel Alexandra (☎ 661 2263; s/d with fan US$8/13.50, with air-con US$11/19; P ⊠) If all you want is to hole up somewhere cheap, take a hot shower and watch some TV, this is your place. A short walk from the main intersection means you've got easy access to/from all the buses, so you can catch an early morning bus out.

Pollolandia (mains US$3-5; ⊠ breakfast, lunch & dinner) At the main intersection, across from Hotel Alexandra, Pollolandia is the Honduran answer to KFC, except with a better name. Chicken comes fried, roasted or stewed, either buffet style or in a combo plate: a quarter chicken, two side dishes and a drink costs under US$3.50. There's an outdoor dining area, but given the heat and traffic noise, the fan-cooled indoors tables are the way to go.

La Terraza Steak House (⊠ breakfast, lunch & dinner Mon-Sun) Next to Hotel Tegucigalpa, this place is recommended by many travelers for slightly fancier fare; sandwiches cost US$3, steak and other meat dishes US$5 to US$7.

Getting There & Around

The intersection at the south end of town is a good place to catch a bus. Buses to Copán Ruínas, however, stop at a small kiosk under an almond tree about 75m past the Hotel San Carlos, on the turnoff toward the ruins. To get around town, three-wheeled moto-taxis (red and white scooters with a small cab attached) zip around town, charging US$0.30 to US$0.50 per person, depending on the length of the ride. Buses go to the following destinations:

Copán Ruínas (US$1.85, two hours, 6am to 4pm, every 40 minutes)

Nueva Ocotepeque (US$4, 2½ to three hours, 6am to 4pm, every 45 minutes)

San Pedro Sula (*ordinario* US$1.75, one to 1½ hours, 5:30am to 6pm, every 30 minutes; *directo* US$2.20, one hour, 8:10am, 10:10am & 3:10pm)

Santa Rosa de Copán (*ordinario* US$1, 1¼ hours, 6am to 7pm, every 30 minutes; *directo* US$1.60, 45 minutes, 7am to 3pm, every one to 1½ hours)

EL PUENTE

Ten kilometers southwest of La Entrada, **Sitio Arqueológico El Puente** (admission US$2.50; ⊠ 8am-4pm) sees only a trickle of visitors. With one large-ish pyramid and no stelae, El Puente (the Bridge) doesn't begin to compare in size or artfulness to Copán, but having a Maya site all to yourself is a memorable and increasingly rare experience. Unfortunately, there are no buses to the site. If you have a car – or better yet, a bike – it's well worth a trip out there. By taxi, well, you're better off spending that money on a guide at Copán.

El Puente consists of more than 200 structures, though only nine have been excavated. Entering the site, you'll see a well-restored step pyramid in the middle of a long grassy plaza. Along the edges are lower, tree-shaded structures, including what may have been living quarters for the political or religious elite. The west flanking structure has rooms and passages hidden inside – look for the metal access ladder. Behind that is a short nature path, where voracious mosquitoes are poised for attack.

A small but intriguing museum at the entrance displays artifacts uncovered in El Puente's two major excavations (1985–89 and 1990–93). Among them are *líticas* (obsidian blades and tools), which this region is known for, and human remains from several burial sites. Signage is in Spanish only.

Getting There & Away

There is no direct bus to El Puente. The turnoff to the archaeological site is 4.5km south of La Entrada, on the road toward Copán Ruínas, and another 6km from there. You could easily catch a bus to the turnoff but would have to walk the rest of the way, and back, with a large hill in the middle. There's little traffic on this road, so hitching isn't a sure thing. Taxis don't have a fixed price; a ballpark figure is US$20 to US$30 round-trip, including waiting for you while you check out the site.

COPÁN RUÍNAS

pop 6469

Just 1km northwest of Honduras' most famous Maya site, Copán Ruínas is a charming little town with cobblestone streets, white adobe buildings and red-tile roofs. It's a relaxed, peaceful place that envelopes you the moment you step off of the bus. Maybe it's the beauty of the town. Or having a good meal. Or simply being with a community of travelers after a month on the road. One thing's for sure: you'll probably end up staying a day or two longer than you planned.

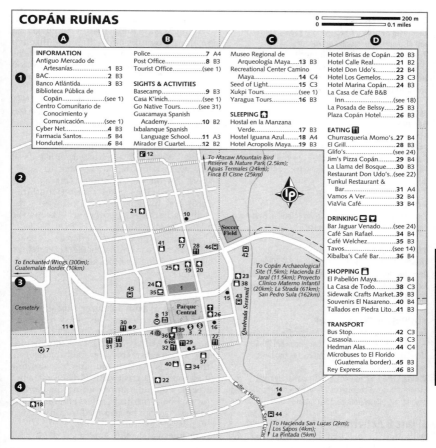

COPÁN RUÍNAS

0 — 200 m
0 — 0.1 miles

INFORMATION
Antiguo Mercado de
 Artesanías..................**1** B3
BAC..................................**2** B3
Banco Atlántida.............**3** B3
Biblioteca Pública de
 Copán..................(see 1)
Centro Comunitario de
 Conocimiento y
 Comunicación..........(see 1)
Cyber Net......................**4** B3
Farmacia Santos............**5** B4
Hondutel........................**6** B4

Police..............................**7** A4
Post Office.....................**8** B3
Tourist Office..............(see 1)

SIGHTS & ACTIVITIES
Basecamp........................**9** B3
Casa K'inich.................(see 1)
Go Native Tours.........(see 31)
Guacamaya Spanish
 Academy..................**10** B2
Ixbalanque Spanish
 Language School.......**11** A3
Mirador El Cuartel........**12** B2

Museo Regional de
 Arqueología Maya....**13** B3
Recreational Center Camino
 Maya.......................**14** C4
Seed of Light................**15** C3
Xukpi Tours.................(see 1)
Yaragua Tours..............**16** B3

SLEEPING
Hostal en la Manzana
 Verde.......................**17** B3
Hostel Iguana Azul........**18** A4
Hotel Acropolis Maya....**19** B3

Hotel Brisas de Copán...**20** B3
Hotel Calle Real............**21** B2
Hotel Don Udo's............**22** B4
Hotel Los Gemelos.........**23** C3
Hotel Marina Copán......**24** B3
La Casa de Café B&B
 Inn.......................(see 18)
La Posada de Belssy......**25** B3
Plaza Copán Hotel..........**26** B3

EATING
Churrasqueria Momo's....**27** B4
El Grill...........................**28** B3
Glifo's.........................(see 24)
Jim's Pizza Copán..........**29** B3
La Llama del Bosque......**30** B3
Restaurant Don Udo's..(see 22)
Tunkul Restaurant &
 Bar...........................**31** A4
Vamos A Ver..................**32** B4
ViaVia Café..................**33** B4

DRINKING
Bar Jaguar Venado.......(see 24)
Café San Rafael.............**34** B4
Café Welchez.................**35** B3
Tavos...........................(see 14)
Xibalba's Café Bar.........**36** B4

SHOPPING
El Pabellón Maya...........**37** B4
La Casa de Todo............**38** C3
Sidewalk Crafts Market.**39** B3
Souvenirs El Nasareno....**40** B4
Tallados en Piedra Lito..**41** B3

TRANSPORT
Bus Stop.......................**42** C3
Casasola.......................**43** C3
Hedman Alas.................**44** C4
Microbuses to El Florido
 (Guatemala border)....**45** B3
Rey Express...................**46** B3

To Macaw Mountain Bird
Reserve & Nature Park (2.5km);
Aguas Termales (24km);
Finca El Cisne (25km)

To Enchanted Wings (300m);
Guatemalan Border (10km)

Soccer
Field

To Copán Archaeological
Site (1.5km); Hacienda El
Jaral (11.5km); Proyecto
Clínico Materno Infantil
(20km); La Strada (61km);
San Pedro Sula (162km)

Cemetery

Parque
Central

Calle a Hacienda San Lucas

To Hacienda San Lucas (2km);
Los Sapos (4km);
La Pintada (5km)

WESTERN HONDURAS

Orientation

Parque central is the heart of town – almost everything is within a few blocks of it. The ruins are 1km outside of town, on the road to La Entrada – a pleasant 15-minute stroll along a footpath alongside the highway. Las Sepulturas archaeological site is 1km further along.

Information
BOOKSTORES

Biblioteca Pública de Copán (Antiguo Mercado de Artesanías, Parque Central; 9am-noon, 1:30-6pm) Offers book exchange of mostly English-language books.
La Casa de Todo (651 4185; www.casadetodo.com; 7am-9pm) Small book exchange tucked into this gift shop, one block east of parque central.

EMERGENCY

Police (651 4060; 24hr) Three-hundred meters west of the park.

INTERNET ACCESS
Centro Comunitario de Conocimiento y Comunicación (Antiguo Mercado de Artesanías, Parque Central; per hr US$0.79; 8am-7pm)
Cyber Net (651 4446; per hr US$1.05; 8am-9:45pm) Web-based calls to USA and Canada only (US$0.11 per minute). Half a block southwest of parque central.

LAUNDRY
La Casa de Todo (651 4185; US$0.42 per lb; 7am-9pm) Same-day service.

MEDICAL SERVICES

Farmacia Santos (☎ 651 4383; ☺ 8am-6pm Mon-Sat) Also open two Sundays per month.

Proyecto Clinico Materno Infantil (☺ 24hr) In El Jaral, the only area hospital specializes in pediatrics and obstetrics, but no one is turned away. Located 20km northeast of Copán Ruínas on Hwy CA-11.

MONEY

BAC (Parque Central; ☺ 9am-5pm Mon-Fri, to noon Sat) Exchanges US dollars, quetzales and traveler's checks; one 24-hour ATM.

Banco Atlántida (Parque Central; ☺ 9am-4pm Mon-Fri, 8:30-11:30am Sat) Offers same services as BAC but has longer lines.

POST

Post office (☺ 8am-noon & 2-5pm Mon-Fri, 8am-noon Sat) Half a block from parque central.

TELEPHONE

Hondutel (☺ 7am-noon, 12:30-6pm & 6:30-9pm) Rates (per minute) for the USA and Canada are US$0.11, for Europe US$2.32, and for Australia and New Zealand US$2.12. Half a block from parque central.

TOURIST INFORMATION

Tourist office (☎ 651 3829; Antiguo Mercado de Artesanías, Parque Central; ☺ 8am-noon & 1:30-5pm Mon-Fri, 8am-noon Sat) Offers brochures and basic information. Spanish only.

ViaVia Café (☎ 651 4652; www.viaviacafe.com) Excellent bulletin board with information on area sites and beyond; 1½ blocks from parque central.

Sights & Activities

Although in need of some updating, the 1970s-era **Museo Regional de Arqueología Maya** (☎ 651 4437; Parque Central; admission US$2; ☺ 8am-4pm Mon-Sat) gives a good overview of the Maya and their presence in the Valle de Copán. The exhibit contains some excellent pieces: painted pottery, carved jade, Maya glyphs and the original Stela B portraying King 18 Rabbit. Don't miss the Tumba de la Bruja, the round tomb of a shamana who was buried with several spectacular offerings, including two human heads (neither of which were hers). English translations have been sporadically taped onto display cases.

Even if you're not traveling with kids, you're likely to enjoy **Casa K'inich** (☎ 651 4105; www.asociacioncopan.org; Antiguo Mercado de Artesanías, Parque Central; admission free; ☺ 8am-noon & 1-5pm).

This fine children's museum explores everything Maya – mathematics, language, astronomy, culture and religion – through games, music, even posing inside of stelae (bring your camera – how often do you get to be Smoke Jaguar?). Exhibits are in English, Spanish and Chortí.

Recreational Center Camino Maya (☎ 651 4648; adult/child US$2.65/1.35; ☺ 8am-5pm Mon-Thu, to 6pm Fri & Sat) This well-maintained recreational area with lush grounds and a pool is just off the road to the Hedman Alas bus terminal. Weekends get packed with kids; if you want some lap time, stick to weekdays. An on-site restaurant (mains US$3 to US$7) serves good *típica* (Honduran fare) and burgers. At night, Tavos – the center's bar and discotheque – keeps the place hopping.

For a fine view over the fertile Copanecan valley, head to the **Mirador El Cuartel**, an abandoned jail five blocks north of parque central.

Courses

Ixbalanque Spanish Language School (☎ 651 4432; www.ixbalanque.com) This newly renovated school offers one-on-one Spanish classes 20 hours per week (US$135). Packages including a homestay (private room/bathroom, three meals per day and laundry) and one area tour are a great value (US$85 extra per week). Volunteer opportunities in elementary schools, medical centers and municipal offices also can be arranged in conjunction with language study.

Guacamaya Spanish Academy (☎ 651 4360; www.guacamaya.com) Virtually the same setup as Ixbalanque – private Spanish classes 20 hours per week plus homestays, extracurricular activities and volunteer opps. Frankly, the main difference is the price – it's a little cheaper here: US$130 per week for classes, US$70 extra per week for the homestay package.

Seed of Light (☎ 651 3779; www.seedoflightcopan.com) If hauling your pack around Honduras has left you aching for a good stretch, drop in on a class (US$7, 1½ hours) at this Krípalu yoga studio. Yoga sessions at the Copán archaeological site; **Hacienda San Lucas** (☎ 651 4495; www.haciendasanlucas.com), 2.5km southeast of town; and Macaw Mountain (p146) are also offered; prices vary depending on the package.

Tours

Copán Ruínas offers much more than an archaeological site, thanks primarily to the large number of creative, quality excursions offered by local tour operators. You can hike, bird-watch, horseback ride or motorcycle ride, or visit Maya villages, natural hot springs and a working coffee plantation. In addition to the tours listed here, see (p145) for additional tours and outings.

Opposite ViaVia Café, **Basecamp** (☎ 651 4695; www.basecamphonduras.com; ☻ 8am-6pm) is the tour-adventure wing of ViaVia Café and easily one of the best operations in Honduras. Belgian Geert Van Vaeck – known around town, without a trace of irony, as 'Gerardo ViaVia' – is co-owner of the café and leads most of the tours. He offers a variety of excursions, from a two-hour walking tour of the 'real' Copán village to an all-day hike through the hills and rural communities around Copán. Geert also offers recommended motorcycle and horseback tours, both for beginning and experienced riders.

The longtime and locally owned **Go Native Tours** (☎ 651 4410; www.copanhonduras.org; gnative4@yahoo.com) offers hiking, caving and horseback-riding trips around Copán, as well as to Lago de Yojoa and Gracias. Some of the local trips involve and benefit local villagers. The office is in Tunkul Restaurant & Bar (p143).

Xukpi Tours (☎ 651 4435) is operated by the ebullient and extremely knowledgeable Jorge Barraza, whose specialized ruins and bird-watching tours are justly famous. He'll do trips to Lago de Yojoa and elsewhere, even into Guatemala.

Just east of parque central, the reliable **Yaragua Tours** (☎ 651 4147; www.yaragua.com; ☻ 7am-10pm) offers various excursions, including tubing and horseback trips along the Copán River, bird-watching, waterfall hikes and coffee plantation tours. Ask for Samuel Miranda.

Festivals & Events

The annual Feria de Copán Ruínas – a huge fair complete with rides and games – is celebrated from March 15 to 20.

Sleeping

A budget travelers paradise, hotels here are cheap and charming. If you've got a little extra cash to spend, though, it'll go a long way.

BUDGET

Hostal el la Manzana Verde (☎ 651 4652; dm US$4) One of the best hostels in Honduras, you'll find hip décor, spotlessly clean rooms and a killer bulletin board with all the information you could possibly need about Copán. Beds are individually named (eg Barbie and Ken for a queen) and match up with food cubbies in the fantastically equipped kitchen. A shady hammock area and lounge serve as comfy common areas. Lockers are included but BYO towel and soap. The hostel is owned and operated by the ViaVia Café, which has five rooms (s/d US$12/14).

Hostel Iguana Azul (☎ 651 4620; www.todomundo .com/iguanaazul; dm US$4, s/d with shared bathroom US$8/10.60) A bit of a trek from parque central, the Iguana Azul offers comfortable and clean private rooms and dorms. All open onto a common room with lots of books and magazines and there is a pleasant garden area as well. No kitchen facilities are available, which is a bummer but not the end of the world considering there are so many options in town.

Hotel Los Gemelos (☎ 651 4077; r with shared bathroom per person US$4; **P**) Run by a very friendly family, this longtime favorite has 14 private rooms with good beds, mosquito nets and a fan; all share clean cold-water bathrooms. There is a beautiful flower-filled interior garden. There is also a *pila* (outdoor laundry station) to hand-wash your threads.

La Posada de Belssy (☎ 651 4680; laposada debelssy@gmail.com; s/d US$12.15/18.50; **P** ☻) The biggest draw of the Belssy – beyond the spotless rooms – is the rooftop lounge. Tables, comfy chairs, hammocks and even a small pool (about the size of a Volkswagen bug) make it one of the best hangout spots in town. The 1st floor also has an open-air common room and a modern kitchen that you may be able to use if you ask first. Tasty meals prepared upon request cost US$2.50 to US$3.50.

Hotel Calle Real (☎ 651 4230; hotelcallereal@yahoo .com; s/d US$9.50/15; **P**) Three steep blocks north of parque central, this hotel is popular for good reason – tile-floored rooms are clean, spacious, and comfortable, flowering bushes and lots of chairs create a welcoming setting, and the service is very good. Be sure to spend some QT in a rooftop hammock – the thatch roof provides plenty of shade so you can enjoy the view. Ask for a *remodelada* (renovated) room to get the best of the lot.

MIDRANGE

La Casa de Café B&B Inn (☎ 651 4620; www.casade cafécopan.com; s/d US$35/45; **P**) This B&B offers 10 understated but classy rooms that open onto a lush garden with tables and hammocks. Each has whitewashed walls, high ceilings with wood beams, mosaic-tile sinks and patchwork bedspreads. Full breakfast is included and served in the garden or the small dining room.

Hotel Acropolis Maya (☎ 651 4634; acropolis@ copanhonduras.org; r US$40; **P** **⊠**) One of the best deals in town, the Acropolis is a colonial-style hotel with 21 very fine rooms. All have been recently remodeled or, in the case of the 2nd floor, constructed; each has two queen-size orthopedic beds, dark-wood furniture, silent air-conditioning and cable TV. A café-bar and rooftop pool are in the works.

Plaza Copán Hotel (☎ 651 4508; Parque Central; www.plazacopanhotel.com; s/d US$49/55; **P** **⊠** **▯** **▣**) This colonial-style hotel offers comfortable though somewhat dated rooms with heavy wood furnishings and flower-print bedspreads. Most rooms also have balconies – rooms 210 through 213 have commanding views over parque central but cost the same as the rest. A small but very well-kept pool is a nice feature, although it's a shame that it opens directly onto the reception area.

TOP END

Hotel Marina Copán (☎ 651 4070; www.hotelmari nacopan.com; s/d US$75/85, ste US$120; **P** **⊠** **▯** **▣**) This classy colonial-style hotel has 51 rooms amid flower gardens, gurgling fountains, koi ponds, and plush seating areas. Rooms are clean and modern, with details like marble sinks, thick linens and old-world furnishings. Ask for one with a balcony, as many of these have spectacular views over the town. An excellent restaurant, live music on weekends, a well-tended pool and a small gym make it especially nice.

Hotel Don Udo's (☎ 651 4533; www.donudos.com; s/d with fan US$35/47, s with air-con US$47-116, d with air-con US$58-140, all incl breakfast; **P** **⊠**) Another upscale colonial-style hotel, this is perfect

if you like the hominess of a B&B but not the intimacy of one. Each room is decorated slightly differently but all have a Guatemalan theme, with whitewashed walls and colorful hand-woven bedspreads. Don't miss the rooftop Jacuzzi and the sauna – they're great places to unwind after a day of exploring the ruins. Breakfast is served at the recommended hotel restaurant.

Hacienda San Lucas (☎ 651 4495; www.hacien dasanlucas.com; s/d/tr incl breakfast US$75/85/95; **P**) This beautifully restored hacienda has eight guestrooms, all built like the original *casa grande*, including high sloped ceilings and ceramic-tile floors. Delight is in the details: redolent cedar headboards, colorful Guatemalan bedspreads, stone showers, fresh flowers and (best of all) candles lit nightly in your room and all over the property, a custom held over from the hacienda's pre-electricity days. The hacienda also offers hiking and horseback-riding excursions and a pricey but terrific restaurant. Hacienda San Lucas is about 2.5km southeast of town; a taxi costs US$2.75.

Eating

If you're craving a change of pace, this is the town to find it – bagels, big salads, pb&j sandwiches, world food – you're sure to find that certain something.

BUDGET

La Llama del Bosque (☎ 651 4431; mains US$1.75-4.25; ☽ breakfast, lunch & dinner) From the outside, this place looks forgettable. But eat one meal here and you're likely to remember it for a long time. The menu is extensive and varied with dishes that are delicious, beautifully presented, abundant and cheap. That combo is hard to find. Add the attractive dining area, including a leafy patio, and you've got a remarkable meal.

El Grill (☎ 651 4809; mains US$1.75-4.75; ☽ lunch & dinner) One of the town's most popular restaurants, El Grill is an open-air eatery serving up Honduran and Mexican dishes. Grilled meats are the focus of the menu; on weekends, consider ordering the *lechón asado* (grilled piglet) for a change of pace.

Vamos A Ver (☎ 651 4627; mains US$2.15-5.30; ☽ breakfast, lunch & dinner) This cozy little patio restaurant dishes up good food: tasty soups, fruit or vegetable salads, homemade breads, a variety of international cheeses and lots of teas. Plus every evening pretend that you're back at camp and make your own smores over an open fire.

ViaVia Café (☎ 651 4652; mains US$1.70-3.70; ⊗ breakfast, lunch & dinner) A hip-boho atmosphere with outdoor and indoor seating; the daily specials are the way to go at this place. Each day, the chef takes a crack at various world-food dishes and often pulls them off with flair.

MIDRANGE
Jim's Pizza Copán (mains US$5.50-9.50; ⊗ lunch & dinner) This thatch-roof restaurant serves some of the best pizza around. Choose from a variety of ingredients – pepperoni, ham, sausage, bell peppers, onion, mushrooms, olives – and it's baked before your eyes in the open-air kitchen. A steady stream of clients keeps the place going late.

Churrasqueria Momo's (☎ 651 3692; mains US$4-7.50; ⊗ breakfast, lunch & dinner) A meat-lover's haven, Momo's, one block south of parque central, serves up beef in four basic styles: *pincho* (kabob), *churrasco* (grilled beef), *puyaso* (grilled beef with the fat left on), and *parrillada* (a sampler, including sausage, beans and tortillas). There are a few chicken, pork, and shrimp dishes, but you might as well go somewhere else for those. Meals are served in an open-air dining area overlooking the Valle de Copán.

Tunkul Restaurant & Bar (mains US$2.65-6; ⊗ breakfast, lunch & dinner) You wouldn't expect it from the outside, but the dining area in this longtime restaurant and bar is quite large and, with a leafy interior courtyard, stone floors and wood tables, downright outdoorsy. (Well, almost.) The food is tasty and the portions large, and there are a number of vegetarian options. Drink specials and a lively crowd make this a good bar, too.

TOP END
Restaurant Don Udo's (☎ 651 4533; mains US$4-10; ⊗ breakfast, lunch & dinner) Overlooking Hotel Don Udo's grassy courtyard, Don Udo's is known as the place to head for seafood. Try the salmon-stuffed ravioli (US$7) or the *camarones pil pil* (white-wine flambé shrimp, US$10) to give your taste buds a treat. Lighter fare like creative sandwiches, crepes, and big salads are also offered. A nice meal without the fancy price tag.

Glifo's (☎ 651 4070; mains US$5.50-12; ⊗ breakfast, lunch & dinner) A bit stuffy but still considered one of the classiest places to eat in town, this restaurant in Hotel Marina Copán offers a wide selection of fine international dishes. The Honduran specialties with a traditional Maya twist, however, are the way to go. Service is excellent.

Hacienda San Lucas (mains US$6-20; ⊗ breakfast & dinner, lunch by request, reservations required) One of Copán's best hotels also offers one of its most memorable dining experiences. Call a day in advance and make a request and the chefs will do their best to accommodate; wood-fired roast chicken, beef, tamales, green salad and fresh tortillas frequently figure in. The view is amazing, including a sliver of the main ruins – come early for a glass of wine and sunset over Templo 21.

Drinking & Entertainment
Café San Rafael (☎ 651 4402; ⊗ 7:30am-8pm) This tiny eatery 1½ blocks south of parque central sells coffee from the family *finca*. You can order the standards – cappuccino (US$1), espresso (US$0.80), and mochas (US$1.35) – with a homemade pastry on the side. Take it to go or enjoy it at one of the garden-side tables.

Café Welchez (☎ 651 4070; Parque Central; coffees US$0.65-1.75, mains US$2.75-3.50; ⊗ 6am-10pm) Although it looks like money, the Café Welchez is a relatively affordable place. Fancy pastries (US$1.75) and frothy cappuccinos sell at just about the same prices as in less high-falutin' places. So enjoy the dark-wood paneling, the antique *azulejo* (glazed ceramic tiles) floors and the track lighting. Heck, splurge a little and get that hazelnut cappuccino shot that you've always wanted. Light meals are served as well.

ViaVia Café (☎ 651 4652; www.viaviacafé.com; ⊗ until midnight) One of the hottest nightspots in town, the ViaVia is a hipster lounge bar-restaurant with low lighting, urban tunes and lots of seating (check out the tree stumps for bar stools). Drinks run a cool US$1 to US$3. Sunday is Oscar day, with an Academy-Award–winning movie shown at 4pm.

Tunkul Restaurant & Bar (⊗ until midnight) Next door, the Tunkul serves up two-for-one drink specials from 7pm to 8pm, sometimes later. Most people bounce a bit between both bars until they close at midnight, then troop down to Tavos for dancing and karaoke.

Xibalba's Café Bar (☎ 651 4182; 🕑 2-10pm Mon-Sat) If this is hell, things are looking up. Borrowing its name from the Maya underworld, Xibalba is a loud lively pub with a young vibe and great music, and even live performances sometimes.

Bar Jaguar Venado (☎ 651 4070; 🕑 11am-10pm) In Hotel Marina Copán, this fancy-pants bar is geared towards an older crowd and offers pricey but stiff drinks. Live marimba music takes over on Friday and Saturday nights from 5pm to 8pm.

Tavos (☎ 651 4648; Recreational Center Camino Maya; cover US$2.65; 🕑 8am-midnight Mon-Thu, to 3am Fri & Sat) A hacienda-style recreational area by day, Tavos becomes a hopping karaoke bar and discotheque by night. It's an upscale place that gets packed on weekends – the DJ gets the crowd going by 10pm. Just 300m south of parque central, it's an easy downhill walk or even easier uphill moto-taxi ride (US$0.25 per person by day, US$1 by trip at night).

Shopping

For a town that sees so much steady tourism, it's a surprise that the shopping isn't much better. There are a fair number of tacky gift shops – even the *artesanía* market got hit with the kitsch stick – but at least there are a handful of hopefuls.

Tallados en Piedra Lito (☎ 651 4138; 🕑 7am-9pm) Perhaps the most enticing souvenirs in Copán are the high-quality Maya replicas made by Don Lito Lara and his son. Third- and fourth-generation sculptors, the Laras create their stone carvings in their modest home. Stop by during the day and you're likely to see one or both of them at work, always willing to tell you about their creations and show you around the workshop. Neither speaks much English, but Don Lito's daughter is often around to translate.

El Pabellón Maya (☎ 651 4066; 🕑 9am-7pm) This warehouse-type store has a variety of *artesanía* from Honduras, Guatemala, and Costa Rica. There's a fair share of kitsch but the Maya replicas are worth a stop. Prepare to have a staff member follow your every move.

Souvenirs El Nasareno (☎ 651 4201; 🕑 8:30am-8pm) Although this small shop may look like one of the pack, the tropical hardwood *artesanías* and the leatherwork are among the best around.

La Casa de Todo (☎ 651 4185; www.casadetodo .com; 🕑 7am-9pm) As the name suggests, the House of Everything has just about…everything: clothing, jewelry, decorations, postcards, a book exchange, café, internet access, international calling center and laundry service. Convenient yes, but not cheap. And kind of snooty too.

Every afternoon, a small sidewalk crafts market sets up just off parque central. You'll see Guatemalan woman sitting side by side with hippyish traveler-jewelers, each loaded down with shell necklaces, bead bracelets, feather earrings – boho wear. There's a fair amount of blah here but browse slowly and you're sure to find a one-of-a-kind piece.

Getting There & Away

Buses to La Entrada (US$1.85, two hours, 5am to 5pm, every 40 minutes) leave from a small dirt lot at the entrance to town, just across the bridge. From there, you can transfer to Santa Rosa de Copán, Gracias or elsewhere on the Ruta Lenca. There's more frequent service from the same stop to Santa Rita (US$0.35, 15 minutes), if you're just headed to El Jaral or Cabañas.

Rey Express (☎ 651 4021; www.reyexpress.net; 🕑 5:30am-7pm) has daily service to San Pedro Sula at 6:10am, 8:10am and 1:10pm (US$4.80, three hours).

Hedman Alas (☎ 651 4037; www.hedmanalas.com; Calle a Hacienda San Lucas; 🕑 4:30am-6pm) has a new terminal a few hundred meters southeast of town, just across the bridge on the road to Hacienda San Lucas. All domestic buses go first to San Pedro Sula (US$14, three hours) with departures at 5:15am, 10:30am, 11am and 2:30pm. From there, you can connect to San Pedro Sula's Villeda Morales airport (US$20, four hours), Tegucigalpa (US$22, seven hours), Tela (US$21, five hours), La Ceiba (US$22, six to eight hours).

Transportes Casasola (☎ 651 4078) has direct service San Pedro Sula (US$5.50, 2¾ to three hours, 5:30am, 6am, 7am and 2pm) from a dirt lot a block east of parque central. You can also buy tickets all the way to Tela (US$9) and La Ceiba (US$9.75); Casasola doesn't go there, but will pay for your taxi in San Pedro Sula to the appropriate bus terminal. And there's no

GETTING TO GUATEMALA

Central American Tours operates a dependable shuttle to Antigua (US$12, six hours, daily at noon) with a stop in Guatemala City. Tickets are for sale at Basecamp and ViaVia Café with no mark-up. Also ask about direct service to Quirigua and Río Dulce (around US$20) as opposed to the old way of just getting off at Río Hondo and catching another bus – it was in the works when we passed through.

You also can get to Guatemala by regular bus, which saves about US$6 over the shuttle but takes three hours longer. Microbuses headed for the border at El Florido leave from a block and a half west of the Parque Central (US$1.25, 15 minutes, 6am to 5pm, every half-hour). On the Guatemala side, buses to Chiquimula leave every 45 minutes from 5:30am to 4:30pm, with connections to Guatemala City and elsewhere.

To go in style, **Hedman Alas** (☎ 651 4037; www.hedmanalas.com; Calle a Hacienda San Lucas; ✆ 4:30am-6pm) has once-daily luxury bus service to Guatemala City (US$35, five hours) and Antigua (US$41, six hours) departing at 1:20pm.

A company calling itself Lonely Planet Tours is *not* run by Lonely Planet Publications, as its operators clearly hope you'll think. In fact, it's the reincarnation of a shuttle company we discouraged travelers from using in a previous edition due to numerous complaints. Needless to say, our opinion hasn't changed.

price mark-up, making it even handier. Trip durations depend on your layover time in San Pedro.

Getting Around

CAR
Driving in Copán Ruínas can be an exercise in frustration. The streets are too narrow for the number of cars on them, and the system of one-way streets has no rhyme or reason – you'll go a dozen blocks out of your way just to get to your hotel garage. Luckily, you don't really need a car for any of Copán's attractions – leave it parked at the hotel and you'll be a lot happier.

TAXI
Moto-taxis run from 6am to 11pm every day. Drivers charge US$0.25 per person in town, US$0.55 to the archaeological site and more for longer distances. As with all cabbies, be sure to confirm the fare before you get in.

AROUND COPÁN RUÍNAS
Finca El Cisne
Known locally as Finca El Cisne, **La Finca Castejo** (☎ 651 4695; www.lafincacastejone.com; ✆ 8am-6pm) is the well-run tourism arm of this century-old family farm; trips to the *finca* combine beautiful scenery with an inside-look at a working *finca* (plantation) and include horseback riding through coffee and cardamom fields, swimming in the

Río Blanco, soaking at Agua Caliente hot springs and a stop at the coffee-processing plants (February to October). Most tours are led by Carlos Castejón, a friendly US- and Zamorano-trained agronomist whose family owns the *finca*. Lodging is in a homey solar-powered cabin. Per person costs (minimum two people) are US$50 (day trips), US$65 (overnight) and US$105 (two-night stays) and include transportation to/from Copán Ruínas and meals. The *finca* shares an office with Basecamp tours, opposite ViaVia Café in Copán Ruínas.

Los Sapos & La Pintada
From Hacienda San Lucas in Copán Ruínas, a pleasant 10-minute walk brings you to Los Sapos, a Maya site purportedly dedicated to women and fertility. Some archaeologists believe it was a place for royal women to conduct fertility ceremonies, or even to give birth. Others say it was simply a place for stonecarvers to practice their trade. In any case, the actual pieces – roughly hewn rocks, one in the shape of a *sapo* (frog), hence the site's name – are significantly eroded but the hike there, with great views over the valley, is half the fun.

From Los Sapos you can continue another 10 minutes to La Pintada, a picturesque Chortí Maya village known for the production of corn-husk dolls. (You may be swarmed by kids trying to sell them to you.) The town has beautiful views, including of

WESTERN HONDURAS

the acropolis at the Copán archaeological site. The name of the town comes from a little-known painted stele nearby. The folks at Hacienda San Lucas can provide a guide to point it out (free, but a tip is expected).

The trails to these sites are maintained by Hacienda San Lucas, and nonguests are charged US$1.50 for their use.

Butterfly Garden
A short distance west of town, **Enchanted Wings** (☎ 651 4133; adult/child US$5.50/1.75; ☻ 8am-4:30pm) has a terrific *mariposario* (butterfly enclosure), bursting with tropical plants and dozens of moths and butterflies flitting about. Come before 11am and you may see new butterflies breaking out of their cocoons (the adults are more active then, too). An attached *orquidiario* has 150 different species of orchids, all native to Honduras.

Bird Reserve
Set on four hectares of tropical forest, **Macaw Mountain Bird Reserve & Nature Park** (☎ 651 4245; www.macawmountain.com; general/student US$10/6; ☻ 9am-5pm) has large enclosures with birds ranging from brilliant Buffon's macaws to manic keel-billed toucans. The ticket price (a bit steep, but good for three days) includes a one-hour guided tour (English and French spoken). There's also a 20-minute nature loop through an adjacent coffee plantation, a small swimming hole and a café. It's 2.5km from town, mostly uphill; a taxi is US$1.10 per person.

Hot Springs
A set of hot springs, **aguas termales** (admission US$1), are 24km north of Copán Ruínas, an hour's drive through fertile mountains and coffee plantations. There are a couple of artificial pools or you can sit in the river, where the boiling hot-spring water mixes with the cool river water. The area has recently been bought by Italian developers, who have visions of a larger-scale resort or attraction but still no firm plans. Bring warm clothes if you come in the evening.

Cabañas
Just a few minutes east of Copán is the cheerful little farming community of Cabañas. Peace Corps volunteers have helped community members organize a day-long **rural tour** (per person US$20); highlights include hiking or horseback riding through coffee fields and tiny farming communities, visiting traditional houses 'painted' with colored mud, a 25m waterfall, and lunch at a campesino home. Visitors can also stay overnight with a family in Cabañas. There's even a website with hotels and descriptions: www.cabanascopan.com. It is vital that you call in advance, so the trip can be organized. Come the afternoon before, stay the night and start the tour early. Doña Magaly Alvarado (☎ 656 7004), who operates the Comedor Calle Real, is the contact person.

Cabañas has a few basic services, including an **internet café** (per hr US$1; ☻ 9am-noon & 2-8pm), one block from parque central, and a **pharmacy** (Medicinas y Novedades Nicole; Parque Central; ☻ 7am-8pm). **Comedor Calle Real** (Parque Central; mains US$2-4; ☻ breakfast, lunch & dinner) serves good *típica* and is operated by Doña Magaly.

To get to Cabañas from Copán Ruínas, take any Santa Rita, La Entrada or San Pedro Sula bus to Santa Rita (US$0.35, 15 minutes); get off at the gas station and walk to parque central, where buses leave for Cabañas (US$0.25, 10 minutes) every half-hour until 4:30pm.

Hacienda El Jaral
The large, rather cheesy **Hacienda El Jaral** (☎ 986 5665; www.haciendaeljaral.com; admission US$4.25; ☻ 9am-5pm Mon-Fri, 9am-6pm Sat & Sun) resort-hotel-waterpark-museum-food-court-minimall-movie theater (did we miss anything?) is what Disneyland might have been if it had US$10,000 in seed money rather than US$10 million. The water park has several high tubular slides that wind down to a somewhat dated pool, while the movie theater has one screen showing Hollywood flicks (US$1.75, 4pm Saturday, 2pm and 4pm Sunday). Both are the only ones of their kind near Copán Ruínas, and the best reason to make the trip (and then only if you are really jonesing for some soft-serve diversion). The much-hyped **Museo de la Vaca** (Museum of the Cow; admission free) is a glorified gift shop, while the hotel is way overpriced.

COPÁN ARCHAEOLOGICAL SITE
Honduras has only one major Maya ruin, but it's a true gem. A Unesco World Heritage site since 1980, Copán archaeological site is known for its remarkable stone sculptures,

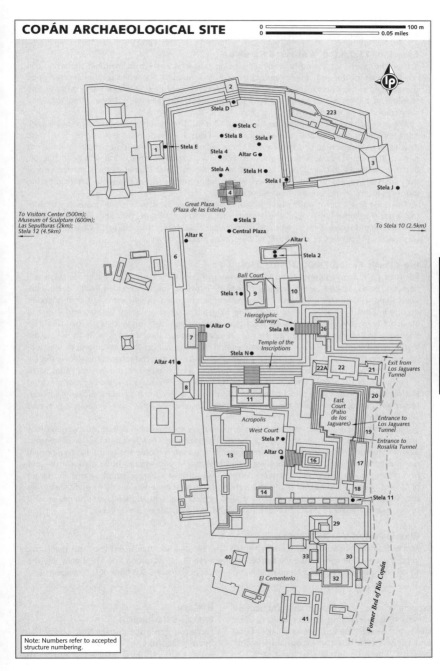

COPÁN ARCHAEOLOGICAL SITE

0   100 m
0   0.05 miles

2

Stela D

Stela C

Stela B

Stela F

1 — Stela E

Stela 4

Altar G

Stela A

Stela H

Stela I

3

Stela J

223

Great Plaza
(Plaza de las Estelas)

4

To Visitors Center (500m);
Museum of Sculpture (600m);
Las Sepulturas (2km);
Stela 12 (4.5km)

Stela 3

Central Plaza

To Stela 10 (2.5km)

Altar K

6

Altar L

Stela 2

Ball Court

Stela 1

9

10

Hieroglyphic
Stairway

7

Altar O

Stela M

26

Temple of the
Inscriptions

Stela N

Altar 41

22A

22

21

Exit from
Los Jaguares
Tunnel

8

11

20

East
Court
(Patio
de los
Jaguares)

19

Entrance to
Los Jaguares
Tunnel

Acropolis

West Court

Stela P

17

Entrance to
Rosalila Tunnel

13

Altar Q

16

14

18

Stela 11

29

40

33

30

El Cementerio

32

Former Bed of Río Copán

41

WESTERN HONDURAS

Note: Numbers refer to accepted
structure numbering.

WESTERN HONDURAS

THE RISE & FALL OF THE MAYA

Creation (13.0.0.0.0, 4 Ahaw, 8 Kumk'u)

It took the gods four attempts to create a being powerful enough to maintain the world. On the first attempt the gods made deer, birds and other animals, but when the gods called upon the animals to pronounce the names of their creators, they only squawked and grunted and roared. Not being able to speak properly to honor the gods, they were deemed unworthy and condemned to be eaten.

The second attempt was a human made out of mud. The mud person spoke 'without knowledge and understanding' and soon he fell apart and dissolved back into the mud. The gods' third attempt was a person carved from wood. These were better than the mud people, but still not perfect. They could speak, walk around, and even began to populate the world with their children. But they 'walked without purpose,' and did not remember their Framer or their Shaper, and so they were destroyed, ground up on their own grinding stones. The survivors became chattering monkeys found in trees throughout Mesoamerica.

The gods finally got it right when they discovered maize, from which they made the flesh of mankind. The Popul Voh, one of the great religious texts of all time, describes the event: 'Thus their frame and shape were given expression by our first Mother and our first Father. Their flesh was merely yellow ears of maize and white ears of maize...'

Pre-Classic Period (2000 BC–AD 250)

For their part, archaeologists (mud people?) say the Copán Valley had its first proto-Maya settlers by about 1100 BC, and a century later settlements on the Guatemalan Pacific coast were developing a hierarchical society. Without question, the most significant event of this period occurred about 1000 BC, not in the traditional Mayan lands, but in nearby Tabasco and Veracruz, Mexico. The mysterious Olmec people developed a hieroglyphic writing system, perhaps based on knowledge borrowed from the Zapotecs of Oaxaca. They also developed what is known as the Vague Year calendar of 365 days. Although aspects of Olmec culture lived on among their neighbors, paving the way for the later accomplishments of Maya art, architecture and science, the Olmecs themselves disappeared; historians assume they were overpowered by waves of invaders.

From 800 BC to 300 BC, known as the Middle Preclassic Period, rich villages already existed in Honduras' Copán Valley and trade routes flourished, with coastal peoples exchanging ever-important salt for highlanders' tool-grade obsidian. There was a brisk trade in ceramic pots and villages were founded at Tikal, in northern Guatemala.

Improved agricultural techniques led to surpluses, an accumulation of wealth, class divisions and monumental construction projects, particularly temples. The first temples were modest affairs, consisting of raised-earth platforms topped by a thatch-roofed shelter similar to a normal *na*. In the lowlands, where limestone was abundant, the Maya began to build platform temples from stone. As each succeeding local potentate had to have a bigger temple, more and larger platforms were put over other platforms, forming huge step pyramids with a na-style shelter on top. More and more pyramids were built around large plazas, with working class homes around the outskirts. The stage was set for the flourishing of Classic Maya civilization.

Classic Period (AD 250–800)

Armies from Teotihuacán (near modern Mexico City) invaded and conquered the Maya highlands, imposing their rule and culture for a time, but were eventually absorbed into Maya daily life. The so-called Esperanza culture, a blend of Mexican and Maya elements, was born of this conquest and

especially the enormous and intricately carved stelae depicting former leaders. The site is not as lofty or grandiose as, say, Tikal or Chichén Itzá but the artisanship is impressive. The museum is also top-notch.

History
PRECLASSIC PERIOD

Ceramic evidence shows that people have been living in the Valle de Copán since at least 1300 BC and probably before that.

acculturation. It was during this period that the Maya produced the western hemisphere's most brilliant ancient civilization. Stretching from Copán, through Guatemala and Belize to Mexico's Yucatán Peninsula, they constructed great ceremonial and cultural centers including Quiriguá, Tikal, Uaxactún, Río Azul and Yaxhá in Guatemala, Caracol in Belize, Yaxchilán and Palenque in Chiapas and Calakmul, Uxmal and Chichén Itzá in the Yucatán. Maya astronomers could predict lunar eclipses, and their calculation of the orbit of Venus was off by less than one day for every thousand years.

At its peak, most Maya lands of the Late Classic Period were ruled as a network of independent, but interdependent, city-states. Each city-state had its noble house, headed by a king who was the social, political and religious focus of the city's life. The king propitiated the gods by shedding his blood in ceremonies where he pierced his tongue, ears or penis with a sharp instrument. Not blood shy, he also led his soldiers into battle against rival cities, capturing prisoners for use in human sacrifices.

Post-Classic Period (AD 800–1500)
Beginning in AD 800, Maya civilizations entered a rapid and mysterious decline. The ruling dynasties apparently lost power, the construction of new structures and stellae halted, and the population dropped, likely by a combination of death, migration and lowered birth rate. The once mighty Mayan cities of Tikal, Yaxchilán, Copán, Quiriguá, Piedras Negras and Caracol all reverted to little more than villages. Over the centuries, the people living in those villages – still Maya, of course – lost all collective memory of their fabled past. By the time European explorers arrived, the ruins had been swallowed by their jungle surroundings and were as much a mystery to the local people as to the explorers themselves.

Why Classic Maya civilization crashed so suddenly is still a matter for debate. Most researchers agree that a combination of factors are to blame, mostly related to a population boom that taxed the food supply and exhausted fertile farmland. Devastating droughts, each of several years' duration, around 810, 860 and 910 would have exacerbated the problem. Maya royalty derived its legitimacy, to a large degree, on a divine connection with the gods. When kings and priests proved unable to induce the gods to improve the increasingly desperate situation, disenchantment and even rebellion may have swept the region. In any case, when Toltec invaders arrived from Central Mexico, the Maya could do nothing but retreat into their villages.

An End is Near (Present–23 December 2012)
When discussing the 'Maya Collapse' it is often assumed that the Maya disappeared altogether. In Honduras, the Chortí Maya are descended from the builders of Copán, and remain mostly subsistence farmers. They, like indigenous people everywhere, contend with an array of modern challenges, including cultural preservation and land rights (p153).

But there is solace in knowing the end, or at least rebirth, is near. The Great Cycle of the present age will last for 13 baktun cycles, which in mud people's time ends December 23, 2012. Death and life must dance together for the succession of days to continue, so while 2012 may well be the end of us, it will not be for the cosmos. In fact, there are stelae that refer to a period of time 41,341,050,000,000,000,000,000,000,000-years long. By comparison, the chattering monkeys say the Big Bang occurred a mere 15,000,000,000 years ago. And even that incomprehensibly long cycle will be repeated, over and over, infinitely.

With contributions from Dr Allen J Christenson

WESTERN HONDURAS

Copán must have had significant commercial activity since early times; ceramics dated to that period show clear influence from El Salvador, Guatemala and even Mexico.

The Preclassic was a period of rapid and fundamental change in many Maya regions, but Copán seems to have lagged behind in that important era. Archaeologists aren't sure why: occupying a small self-contained valley with rich agricultural lands, the city had the fundamental elements needed for physical and cultural expansion. Instead Copán experienced a decline in population between 400 BC and AD 100.

CONSOLIDATING POWER

Around AD 426 a mysterious king named Mah K'ina Yax K'uk' Mo' (Great Sun Lord Quetzal Macaw), came to Copán, ruling until AD 435. Archaeological evidence indicates that he was a great shaman; later kings revered him as the semidivine founder of the city. His dynasty ruled throughout Copán's florescence during the Classic period (AD 250–800).

Of the early kings who ruled from about 435 to 628 we know little. Only the names of some of the rulers have been deciphered: Mat Head, the second king; Cu Ix, the fourth king; Waterlily Jaguar, the seventh; Moon Jaguar, the 10th; and Butz' Chan, the 11th.

Among the greatest of Copán's kings was Smoke Imix (Smoke Jaguar), the 12th king, who ruled from 628 to 695. Smoke Imix was wise, forceful and rich, and he built Copán into a major military and commercial power in the region. He might have even taken over the nearby princedom of Quiriguá, as one of the famous stelae there bears his name and image. By the time he died in 695, Copán's population had grown significantly. At its peak, Copán is thought to have supported about 20,000 people.

Smoke Imix was succeeded by Uaxaclahun Ubak K'awil (18 Rabbit; 695–738), the 13th king, who willingly took the reins of power and pursued further military conquest. In a war with his neighbor King Cauac Sky, 18 Rabbit was captured and beheaded, to be succeeded by Smoke Monkey (738–749), the 14th king. Smoke Monkey's short reign left little mark on Copán. In 749 Smoke Monkey was succeeded by his son Smoke Shell (749–763), one of Copán's greatest builders. He commissioned the construction of the city's most famous and important monument, the great Hieroglyphic Stairway, which immortalizes the achievements of the dynasty from its establishment until 755, when the stairway was dedicated. It is the longest such inscription ever discovered in the Maya lands.

Yax Pac (Sunrise or First Dawn, 763–820), Smoke Shell's successor and the 16th king of Copán, continued the beautification of Copán, though it seems that the dynasty's power was declining and its subjects had fallen on hard times.

THE DECLINE

Until recently, the collapse of the civilization at Copán has been a mystery. Now, archaeologists are starting to understand what happened. Apparently, near the end of Copán's heyday, the population grew at an unprecedented rate, straining agricultural resources. In the end, Copán was no longer agriculturally self-sufficient and had to import food from other areas. The urban core expanded in the fertile lowlands in the center of the valley, forcing both agriculture and residential areas to spread onto the steep slopes surrounding the valley. Wide areas were deforested, resulting in massive erosion that further decimated agricultural production and flooding during rainy seasons. Skeletal remains of people who died during the final years of Copán's heyday show marked evidence of malnutrition and infectious diseases, as well as a decreased lifespan.

The Valle de Copán was not abandoned overnight – agriculturists probably continued to live in the ecologically devastated valley for another 100 or 200 years – but by 1200 even the farmers had departed, and the royal city of Copán was claimed by the jungle.

EUROPEAN DISCOVERY

The first known European to see the ruins was Diego García de Palacios, a representative of Spanish King Felipe II, who lived in Guatemala and traveled through the region. On March 8, 1576, he wrote to the king about the ruins he found here. Only about five families were living there and they knew nothing of the history of the ruins. The discovery was not pursued, and almost three centuries went by until another Spaniard, Colonel Juan Galindo, visited the ruins and made the first map of them.

Galindo's report stimulated Americans John L Stephens and Frederick Catherwood to come to Copán on their Central American journey in 1839. When Stephens published the book *Incidents of Travel in*

Central America, Chiapas, and Yucatán in 1841, illustrated by Catherwood, the ruins first became known to the world.

DIGGING UP HISTORY

The history of the ruins continues to unfold today, as archaeologists continue to probe the site. The remains of 3450 structures have been found in the 24 sq km surrounding the Principal Group, most of them within about 500m of the Principal Group. In a wider zone, 4509 structures have been detected in 1420 sites within 135 sq km of the ruins. These discoveries indicate that at the peak of Maya civilization here, around the end of the 8th century, the valley of Copán had over 20,000 inhabitants – a population not reached again until the 1980s.

In addition to examining the area around the Principal Group, archaeologists are continuing to explore and make new discoveries at the Principal Group itself. Five separate phases of building on this site have been identified; the final phase, dating from AD 650 to 820, is what we see today. But buried underneath the visible ruins are layers of other ruins, which archaeologists are exploring by means of underground tunnels. This is how the Rosalila temple was found, a replica of which is in the Museum of Sculpture; below Rosalila is yet another, earlier temple, Margarita.

Orientation

There are three buildings at the entrance to the archaeological site: the visitors center, the Museum of Sculpture, and the cafeteria-gift shop. Behind the visitors center are signs for the ruins themselves and the Yax Ché nature trail.

Information

Admission to the **Copán archaeological site** (☎ 651 4108; admission US$10; ⏰ 8am-5pm, museum closes 4pm) includes entry to Las Sepulturas (p152). The tunnels (p152) cost an additional and exorbitant US$12, while the extra US$5 fee for the Museum of Sculpture (p153) is totally worth it. Near the ticket booth are a small gift-shop, restrooms and a booth where you can arrange a guide. Across the parking lot, near the Sculpture Museum, is a much larger *artesanía* shop, and a small *comedor* that sells simple meals,

plus chips, Gatorade, and other snacks; both places are surprisingly good.

Dangers & Annoyances

The biggest safety concern at Copán is falling down the steep stone steps, which, besides being endlessly embarrassing, can be quite painful, even bone-breaking. Copán doesn't have the high pyramids other ruins do, but wear good shoes and watch your step at all times.

Sights

THE GREAT PLAZA

The Principal Group is a group of ruins with huge, intricately carved stelae portraying the rulers of Copán. It's about 400m beyond the visitors center.

STELAE OF THE GREAT PLAZA

Most of Copán's best stelae date from AD 613 to 738, during the reigns of Smoke Imix (628–95) and 18 Rabbit (695–738). All seem to have been painted; a few traces of red paint survives on Stela C. Many stelae had vaults beneath or beside them in which sacrifices and offerings were placed.

Many of the stelae on the Great Plaza portray King 18 Rabbit, including Stelae A, B, C, D, F, H and 4. Perhaps the most beautiful stele in the Great Plaza is Stela A (AD 731); the original has been moved inside the Museum of Sculpture; the one outdoors is a reproduction. Nearby, and almost equal in beauty, are Stela 4 (AD 731); Stela B (AD 731), depicting 18 Rabbit upon his accession to the throne; and Stela C (AD 782), with a turtle-shaped altar in front. This last stele has figures on both sides. Stela E (AD 614), erected on top of Structure 1 on the west side of the Great Plaza, is among the oldest stelae.

At the northern end of the Great Plaza, at the base of Structure 2, Stela D (AD 736) portrays King 18 Rabbit. On its back are two columns of hieroglyphs; at its base is an altar with fearsome representations of Chac, the rain god. In front of the altar is the burial place of Dr John Owen, an archaeologist with the expedition from Harvard's Peabody Museum who died during the work in 1893.

On the east side of the plaza is Stela F (AD 721), which has a more lyrical design, with the robes of the main figure flowing around to the other side of the stone, where there are glyphs. Altar G (AD 800), showing twin serpent heads, is one of the last monuments carved at Copán. Stela H (AD 730) might depict a queen or princess rather than a king. Stela 1 (AD 692), on the structure that runs along the east side of the plaza, is of a person wearing a mask.

BALL COURT & HIEROGLYPHIC STAIRWAY

South of the Great Plaza, across what is known as the Central Plaza, is the ball court (AD 731), the second-largest in Central America. The one you see is the third one on this site; the other two were buried by this construction. Note the macaw heads carved at the top of the sloping walls. The central marker in the court was the work of King 18 Rabbit.

South of the ball court is Copán's most famous monument, the Hieroglyphic Stairway, the work of King Smoke Shell. Today it's protected from the elements by a roof. This lessens the impact of its beauty, but you can still get an idea of how it looked. The flight of 64 steps bears a history – in several thousand glyphs – of the royal house of Copán; the steps are bordered by ramps inscribed with more reliefs and glyphs. Unfortunately, when archaeologists uncovered the stairway, its upper section had collapsed. The bottom 15 stairs are in their original position, but the rest of the stones were jumbled and replaced with no way of knowing the correct order. As a result only about 45% of what's written on the steps is decipherable, and the overall story is far from clear.

At the base of the Hieroglyphic Stairway is Stela M (AD 756), bearing a figure (probably King Smoke Shell) in a feathered cloak; glyphs tell of the solar eclipse in that year. The altar in front shows a plumed serpent with a human head emerging from its jaws.

Beside the stairway, a tunnel leads to the tomb of a nobleman, a royal scribe who might have been the son of King Smoke Imix. The tomb, discovered in June 1989, held a treasure trove of painted pottery and beautiful carved jade objects that are now in Honduran museums.

THE ACROPOLIS

The Acropolis is a collection of imposing structures at the south end of the site that, in

Copán's heyday, would have been the heart of the city and government. The lofty flight of steps to the south of the Hieroglyphic Stairway is called the Temple of the Inscriptions. On top of the stairway, the walls are carved with groups of hieroglyphs. On the south side of the Temple of the Inscriptions are the East and West Courts. In the West Plaza, be sure to see Altar Q (AD 776), among the most famous sculptures here; the original is in the Museum of Sculpture. Around its sides, carved in superb relief, are the 16 great kings of Copán, ending with the altar's creator, Yax Pac. Behind the altar was a sacrificial vault in which archaeologists discovered the bones of 15 jaguars and several macaws that were probably sacrificed to the glory of Yax Pac and his ancestors.

TUNNELS

In 1999 archaeologists opened up two tunnels that allow visitors to get a glimpse of preexisting structures below the visible structures. The first, Rosalila tunnel, is very short and takes only a few visitors at a time. Behind thick glass, the famous Rosalila temple is only barely exposed. The other tunnel, Los Jaguares, was originally 700m in length, but a large section has been closed, reducing it to about 80m, running along the foundations of Temple 22. This tunnel exits on the outside of the main site, so you must walk around the main site to get back in again. While interesting, it's hard to justify the US$12 extra you pay to get in.

Rosalila, dedicated in AD 571 by Copán's 10th ruler, Moon Jaguar, was apparently so sacred that when Structure 16 was built over it the temple was not destroyed but left completely intact.

The original Rosalila temple is still in the core of Structure 16. Under it is a still earlier temple, Margarita, built 150 years before, as well as other earlier platforms and tombs.

LAS SEPULTURAS

Excavations at Las Sepulturas and other outlying areas have shed light on the daily life of the Maya of Copán during its golden age.

Las Sepulturas, once connected to the Great Plaza by a causeway, might have been the residential area where rich, powerful nobles lived. One huge, luxurious residential compound seems to have housed some 250 people in 40 or 50 buildings arranged around

WESTERN HONDURAS

11 courtyards. The principal structure, called the House of the Bacabs (officials), had outer walls carved with the full-size figures of 10 males in fancy feathered headdresses; inside was a huge hieroglyphic bench.

To get to the site, you have to go back to the main road, turn right, then right again at the sign (2km).

MUSEUM OF SCULPTURE
Whereas Tikal is renowned for its tall temple pyramids and Palenque for its elegant design and limestone relief panels, Copán is unique in the Maya world for its sculpture. Some of the best pieces are displayed at the site's excellent museum, built in 1996 and a highlight of any visit to Copán. Entering the museum is an impressive experience in itself: you enter through the mouth of a serpent and wind through the entrails of the beast before suddenly emerging into a fantastic world of sculpture and light. The centerpiece of the museum is a huge true-scale replica of the Rosalila temple, the ornate brightly painted structure found at the core of Structure 16, the central building of the Acropolis. Two floors of wide corridors connected by long ramps open to the middle for better views of the Rosalila. On the walls are examples of Copán incredible stonework, with well-organized displays explaining the icons, imagery and hieroglyphics found there. Part of the museum's roof collapsed in 2005; no visitors were hurt or pieces damaged, but INAH (Instituto Nacional de Antropología e Historia) officials took advantage of the temporary closure to give the museum a major facelift. It reopened in 2006.

STELAE 10 & 12
Dating to AD 652, Stelae 10 and 12 are found on two hills approximately 2.5km

---

FIGHTING FOR SOME LAND TO STAND ON

In September 2005 some 1500 Maya-Chortí indigenous people marched onto the Copán archaeological site, blocking the entrance and demanding the Honduran government complete the land reforms it promised almost a decade ago. The occupation, which lasted five days, was one in a series of such actions: in June 2005 around 3000 Chortí occupied the site for 14 hours and in November 2001 a protest by almost 1000 people was broken up by police officers wielding tear gas and batons; dozens were injured and at least 17 hospitalized. The site has been blocked at least two other times, in 2000 and in 1998.

The immediate conflict stems from an agreement reached in 1997 that the government would buy the Chortí around 14,000 hectares of privately owned land, worth around US$6 million. Only 2700 hectares had been distributed by 2005.

The root of the matter is considerably older, of course. The Maya Chortí – descended from the builders of Copán ruins – have lived in the Valle de Copán for generations as subsistence farmers. In the 1950s, wealthy landowners bought up thousands of acres of traditional Chortí farmland, forcing the Chortí into plantation labor. They and other poor farmers eventually organized into large peasant unions, whose actions, sometimes militant, prompted the adoption of Honduras' agrarian reform laws in the 1960s and '70s.

But even as laws gave poor farmers more rights, intimidation and repression increased. In 1997 Chortí leader Cándido Amador was brutally murdered – he was stabbed, shot, scalped and dumped by the side of the road – in a crime many say was orchestrated by local landowners. It remains unsolved. Amador was the 25th indigenous leader to be killed in a period of just five years, and one of dozens over the preceding decades. His murder galvanized Chortís and gained international attention; thousands marched on Tegucigalpa a month later, which led to the land distribution agreement that Chortí activists today say remains unenforced.

Chortí communities today are desperately poor, and alcoholism and drug addiction are rampant. Sadly, travelers' first interaction with Chortís may well be in Copán village, where aggressive teenagers harangue tourists into unredeeming horseback rides. Cándido Amador himself was critical of foreign tourism, which he called 'a mercenary commerce controlled by the State and local landed gentry.' Local business owners, even those sympathetic to Chortí concerns, are of mixed mind about the takeovers. Most argue that tourism, done well, will help the Chortí in the long run.

apart and 4.5km from the archaeological site. These monoliths measure around 3m, each with inscriptions on all four sides. On two days a year – April 12 and September 7 – the sun sets directly behind Stela 10 as you look at it from Stela 12. No one knows the meaning; some believe they are a calendar for planting and harvesting, others think that they have an astronomical significance. In any case, both make pleasant hikes, with sweeping views of the valley. It's best to go with a guide – most agencies in town offer day trips that include a visit to one or both sites.

Tours

Independent travelers are often loath to hire guides, but those at Copán Ruínas tend to be better than most. All guides go through a one- to two-week training; some have been working at Copán for years and are remarkably well versed in the history, mythology and archaeology of the site. Fees are steep at US$35 per group for the ruins and tunnels, or US$25 per group for the ruins only. Tours last about two hours; don't be shy about asking other travelers if they want to go in together for a guide. Between a small group, the cost is less prohibitive and the experience considerably more educational. Guides speaking Spanish, English, French and Italian are available.

You can also pick up a copy of the booklet *History Carved in Stone: A Guide to the Archaeological Park of the Ruins of Copán,* by William L Fash and Ricardo Agurcia Fasquelle, which is usually available for a couple of dollars at the visitors center.

Getting There & Away

The archaeological site is about 1km outside of Copán Ruínas on the road to La Entrada – a pleasant 15-minute stroll along a footpath to one side of the highway. Las Sepulturas is 1km further along.

LA RUTA LENCA

The Ruta Lenca (Lenca Route) is a series of rural towns in southwestern Honduras, strung like pearls through the heart of traditional Lenca territory. The route officially starts in Santa Rosa de Copán, and includes

Gracias, San Juan, La Esperanza and others, continuing to Marcala, nearly to the Salvadoran border. The route has excellent hiking and other outdoors opportunities – Honduras' highest mountain is outside Gracias – plus museums, traditional Lenca *artesanía* and festivals, and all-around small-town charm.

SANTA ROSA DE COPÁN
pop 28,223

Santa Rosa de Copán is a small, cool, very Spanish mountain town, with cobblestone streets, clay-tiled roofs and a lovely colonial church with *azulejo* floors. There's not a ton to do here, but with a bustling city center and vibrant festivals throughout the year it provides a wonderful window into everyday Honduran life.

History

Since the early 1700s, Santa Rosa has been key to the region's prosperity because of its tobacco production. In 1765 the Spanish crown chose the town as the site of La Real Factoría del Tabaco, a government office responsible for setting tobacco prices, marketing the product and distributing the seeds and equipment necessary for its production. This official presence helped to market the region's cash crop even more, which in turn increased the wealth of this city. It became such an economic force, in fact, that by 1812 Santa Rosa de Copán was declared the capital of what is now the Lempira department. Today, although the department capital has moved to Gracias, Santa Rosa remains a strong presence in the tobacco industry; cigars produced here are considered among the best in the country and, some say, the world.

Orientation

Santa Rosa is up on a hill, about 1km from the bus terminal on the highway. From the highway, follow the 'Centro Histórico' signs, which lead travelers on 4a Av NO to the city center. Parque central is three blocks west of 4a Av NO and bordered by 1a Calle NO, Calle Real Centenario, 1a Av NO and 1a Av NE. (As with most towns in Honduras, *avenidas* run north–south, and *calles* run east–west.) Almost everything you'll need is within walking distance of parque central.

WESTERN HONDURAS

Information

Banco Atlántida (Parque Central; 8am-4pm Mon-Fri, 8:30-11:30am Sat) Exchanges traveler's checks and US dollars. One 24-hour ATM.

Casa de Cultura (662 0800; Av Alvaro Contreras at 1a Calle SO; 8am-noon & 2-5pm Mon-Fri) Occasionally presents art exhibits and theater productions; long-term exercise, music, and art courses too.

Farmacia Central (662 0465; Parque Central; 8am-noon & 2-6pm Mon-Sat)

Hondutel (Parque Central; 7am-9pm) Rates (per minute) for the USA and Canada are US$0.11, for Europe US$2.32 and for Australia and New Zealand US$2.12.

Hospital del Occidente (662 0112; Barrio El Calvario; 24hr)

Lavandería Wash & Dry (1a Calle NE near 4a Av NE; per load US$4.25; 7am-9pm)

Pizza Pizza (662 1104; Calle Real Centenario near 6a Av NE; 11:30am-9pm, Thu-Tue) Decent book exchange of mostly English-language books.

Police (662 0019; Parque Central; 24hr)

Post office (Parque Central; 8am-noon & 2-5pm Mon-Fri, 8am-noon Sat)

Tourist office (662 2234; turismosrc@yahoo .com; Parque Central; 8am-noon & 1:30-6pm Mon-Sat) In the kiosk in parque central; has good information on area sights and services. Also has internet access (US$0.80 per hour) and free CD-burning. English is spoken.

Zona Digital (1a Calle NE at 3a Av NE, Plaza Saavedra; per hr US$0.85; 8am-10pm) Internet access; also offers international calls, starting at US$0.10 per minute.

Sights & Activities

Fine hand-rolled cigars are produced in **La Flor de Copán** (662 0185; Carr a Nueva Ocotepeque; 8:30am-4:30pm Mon-Fri) factory, just 2km from town. You can learn about the entire process – from the trimming of the tobacco to the packaging of *puros* – by taking a tour (US$2, 10am and 2pm); call to reserve a spot. If you want a smoke without a tour, stop by the factory outlet store in town (Calle Centenario near 3a Av Norte), open from 8am to noon and 2pm to 5pm Monday to Friday, 8am to noon Saturday.

Learn how coffee is roasted, classified, and prepared for export at **Beneficio Maya** (662 1665; www.cafécopan.com; Colonia San Martín; 7am-noon & 2-5pm Mon-Fri, 7am-noon Sat), a coffee processing plant. Visitors are welcome year-round but tours are only offered during the coffee season (November to February).

At the western end of town, **Parque El Cerrito** (8a Av NO to 12a Av NO btwn Calle Real Centenario & 1a Calle NO) has a nice lookout point – 105 steps to the best view around. Skip the sad-looking playground.

Courses

Although it's mainly dedicated to teaching English to Hondurans, **International Language Institute** (ILI; 662 1378; 3a Av SE btwn 2a & 3a Calles SE; 1-6pm Mon-Fri) also offers Spanish courses. Classes are one-on-one and cost US$6 per hour. Homestays, including three meals per day, can be arranged for an additional US$60 per week.

Tours

Lenca Land Trails (662 1128; max@Lenca-Honduras .com; Calle Real Centenario near 3a Av NO) offers personalized day trips and multiday excursions to the colonial villages on the Ruta Lenca and the Parque Nacional Montaña de Celaque. Contact Max Elvir, a well-respected local guide, to book a trip.

WESTERN HONDURAS

LOCAL LORE: LA SUCIA

One of the most widely told tales in Honduras is of La Sucia, or 'the Dirty Woman.' The story varies widely, but the basics stay the same: a man encounters a woman, usually by a river or lake. Usually her face is obscured, whether because it's nighttime or because she's just washed her hair. The woman seduces the man, or attempts to, and soon begins to cackle loudly. The man looks at her to discover she is in fact a toothless old hag. She has gargantuan breasts, which she thrusts at him, crooning *'Toma tu teta, toma tu teta!'* (a vulgar way of saying, 'Drink your milk, drink your milk!') Horrified, the man runs off.

The story often involves a soon-to-be-married groom or a wayward son. A version of La Sucia is told by the Lenca, who call the woman the *ciguanaba;* by English-speaking blacks, who call her Bubbly Susan; and by Garífunas, who call her Agayuma and often set the story to music. The story must be intended to dissuade men from cheating on their wives, lest they end up with La Sucia, but is told with such relish and humor that it's hard to detect much moralizing in it.

Festivals & Events

Santa Rosa de Copán is known for its religious processions during **Semana Santa**. Beginning on Thursday, re-enactments of the six processions surrounding Jesus' death and resurrection take place. The most spectacular is the Holy Cross Procession, where Jesus – under the weight of a cross and the eyes of guards – is led on a 2km walk over *alfombras* (intricate, colored carpets made of sawdust, flowers and seeds) that are created overnight by townspeople. The Holy Cross Procession takes place on Friday morning in the historic town center. Be sure to find a place to stand before 9am so you can check out the artwork before it's trampled.

La Feria de los Llanos is an artisanal fair that showcases crafts made in and around Santa Rosa. Music and cultural presentations are also sponsored and there's a fair share of *típica* (Honduran fare) too. It is held three times a year: Semana Santa, August 25 to 30 and the second week in December.

A lively event, the **Noche de Fumadores** (held the third Friday of August) is an evening dedicated to fine cigars. A variety of locally produced stogies are offered by La Flor de Copán and sampled by festival-goers. If you're not into blowing smoke, there's plenty of Honduran food and drink to keep you busy.

Sleeping

BUDGET

Hotel Blanca Nieves (☎ 662 1312; 3a Av NE near 2a Calle NE; s/d with shared bathroom US$4/7, r with bathroom US$8.50) Rooms at the Snow White are not the fairest of them all, but they're relatively clean. If you can swing it, opt for a private bathroom; otherwise prepare to wear flip flops in the shared shower.

Hotel El Rosario (☎ 662 0211; 3a Av NE near 2a Calle NE; r with shared bathroom per person US$4, r per person US$6.60; **P**) Two doors down, El Rosario is even simpler than its neighbor. A long corridor offers relatively clean rooms with squishy beds, water pipes for shower heads and exposed light bulbs.

The tourist office can also arrange **homestays** (r with breakfast/breakfast & lunch US$10.50/16), which may be the best option for budget travelers.

MIDRANGE

Posada de Carlos y Blanca (☎ 662 0236; posadacb@hotmail.com; Calle Real Centenario near 4a Av SO; s/d incl breakfast US$20/26; **P** 🖳) Run out of a converted home, this cozy hotel has five rooms with firm beds, hot-water bathrooms and cable TV. There's a welcoming living room with lots of table games and books too. Breakfast is served in the homey dining room.

Hotel VIP Copán (☎ 662 0265; hotelcopan@hotmail.com; 1a Calle NE at 3a Av NE; s/d US$14.15/25.15, s/d with air-con US$27/36.25; **P** 🍴 🖳) Though the 34 rooms here are cramped and dark, this a fairly decent hotel. The 'VIP' in the name seems to only apply to the eight spacious suites, which have cherry-wood furnishings, gleaming tile floors, bathtubs and windows that actually let sunlight in. There's a pleasant pool on the premises – it borders the parking lot but the landscaping hides it well.

Hotel Elvir (☎ 662 1374; hotelelvir@hondudata.com; Calle Real Centenario near 3a Av NO; s/d US$36/45, ste US$110; **P** 🍴) The entrance and common areas of the colonial-style Elvir are by far the most appealing in town – a leafy stone courtyard, endless columns and arches, lots of beautiful ironwork. Unfortunately, the charm ends there. Accommodations are clean but stark, with particle-board furniture, dated décor and poor lighting – all in all a disappointment given the price and grand surroundings.

Eating

BUDGET

Pizza Pizza (☎ 662 1104; Calle Real Centenario near 6a Av NE; mains US$1.50-5.75; 🕙 lunch & dinner, Thu-Tue) A popular pizzeria that serves brick-oven pizza made with hand-tossed dough, homemade sauce and any number of toppings. It's owned by Warren Post, a friendly American who is a great source of information if you can catch him.

Tio Kike (☎ 662 3249; 1a Av SE near 1a Calle SE; mains US$1-3; 🕙 breakfast, lunch & dinner) An unexpectedly appealing hole-in-the-wall that serves up good *típica*. The roasted chicken (US$3) and fruit smoothies (US$1) are particularly good.

Hemady's Típico (☎ 662 1124; Calle Real Centenario near 2a Av NO; mains US$1.50-4.50; 🕙 breakfast, lunch & dinner Mon-Sat, lunch & dinner Sun) Housed in a renovated colonial building with original *azulejo* floors, this place serves reliable Honduran fare, sandwiches and hamburgers. It's a 'family friendly' establishment, which means no booze.

Ten Napel Café (☎ 662 3238; Calle Real Centenario near 4a Av NO; ☺ 9am-noon & 1:30-7pm) Next to the Hotel Elvir, this cozy coffee shop is perfect if you need a caffeine or sugar fix (or both). Coffee drinks start at US$0.50, homemade desserts at US$0.65.

Every afternoon, street vendors sell steaming corn tamales and sweet breads (US$0.50 to US$1) from their baskets and Tupperware on parque central. A fine way to pull together a meal.

Manzanitas Supermarket (Calle Real Centenario near 2a Av NO; ☺ 8:30am-7pm Mon-Sat, to noon Sun) is a full-on supermarket in the center of town., while the **Mercado Central** (1a Calle NE at 2a Av NE; ☺ 6am-4pm Mon-Sat, to noon Sun), behind the church, sells everything from carrots to clothing. It's a good place to pick up fresh veggies or fruit, though you can also enjoy a meal in the dining area, which is lined with food stalls selling a variety of *típica*.

MIDRANGE

El Rodeo (☎ 662 0697; 1a Av SE btwn 1a & 2a Calles SE; mains US$5-8; ☺ lunch & dinner) This cavernous steakhouse doubles as a boho-bar Thursday through Saturday nights. Meals are well prepared and portions are hefty; they always come with a complimentary *anafras* (bean fondue) for the table too. There are a few options if meat isn't your thing, but if it is, definitely go for it – you'll leave satisfied.

Restaurante Flamingos (☎ 662 0654; 1a Av SE near 1a Calle SE; mains US$4.75-6; ☺ lunch & dinner) Considered one of the best restaurants in town, Flamingos has a pleasant atmosphere and good food. Seafood is the specialty here – the conch soup (US$5) and fish in garlic sauce (US$5.50) are mouthwatering. There's live music on Sundays.

Drinking & Entertainment

El Rodeo (☎ 662 0697; 1a Av SE btwn 1a & 2a Calles SE; no cover; ☺ 10:30am-midnight) You'd never guess that a restaurant called the 'Rodeo' would be the best boho bar in town. This dimly lit steakhouse is the place to head Thursday, Friday and Saturday nights if you want to listen to live music and rub shoulders with the lefty crowd. It gets packed by 9pm; if you want a place to rest your beer, be sure to arrive early.

Luna Jaguar Disco (3a Av SE near Calle Real Centenario; cover US$5.50; ☺ 9pm-4am Wed-Sat) A DJ keeps the

regguetón and electronic thumping at this 20-something nightclub. The dance floor is big enough to get your groove on but the stage sees a fair share of solo dancers too. Women get in free on Thursdays.

Xtassi's Discotec (1a Av SE near 2a Calle SE; cover US$5; ☺ 9pm-4am Wed-Sat) Just down the street from El Rodeo, this disco attracts a young – as in teen – crowd on weekends. Not much of a scene unless you're into braces and cliques.

Cinema Don Quijote (☎ 662 2625; Plaza Saavedra; 1a Calle NE at 3a Av NE; tickets US$1.85) Late-release Hollywood films are shown on one screen at 7pm every night.

Getting There & Away

Buses from Santa Rosa de Copán come and go from the Terminal de Transporte on the main highway, about 1km from the center of town – look for the large 'JM Restaurante' sign. **La Sultana de Occidente** (☎ 662 0940) has a ticket office behind JM for express buses to San Pedro Sula, La Entrada, Agua Caliente (at the Guatemalan border) and San Salvador, with connections to Copán Ruínas and Tegucigalpa. Toritos & Copaneca has a stop two blocks down the highway, with buses to San Pedro Sula and Tegucigalpa (direct and ordinary) plus Gracias and Belén Gualcho. Destinations include the following.

Agua Caliente Guatemalan border; US$3.75, 2½ hours, 110km, 5am, 9:30am, 10:30am, noon, 1pm, 2:30pm, 3:30pm, 5pm & 6pm

Belén Gualcho US$2, two to three hours, 10:30 and 11:30am, 4pm from San Pedro Sula

---

CROSSING INTO EL SALVADOR

Transportes San José operates buses from Nueva Ocotepeque to both borders from its dirt-lot terminal two blocks north of the park, near the Toritos & Copaneca office.

Buses to the Salvadoran border at El Poy (US$0.50, 15 minutes, 7km) leave every 20 minutes from 6:30am to 7pm; coming from the border, the same buses depart from a lot 200m from the border during the same hours. A private taxi in either direction costs US$2.75, or US$0.55 per person (minimum four people) for a *colectivo* (shared taxi or minibus). This border is secure and orderly, as borders go.

CROSSING INTO GUATEMALA

Buses to the Guatemalan border at Agua Caliente (US$0.75, 30 minutes, 22km) leave every half-hour from 6am to 6pm. Once past Honduran immigration, catch a truck or moto-taxi to the Guatemalan post (US$0.55, 2km). Entering Honduras, buses for Nueva Ocotepeque leave on the same schedule from in front of the Honduran immigration office. Congolón also operates direct buses from the border to San Pedro Sula (US$7, five hours, 3am and hourly from 5:30am to 4:30pm) with stops in Santa Rosa de Copán (US$3.50, 2½ hours) and La Entrada (US$3.75, 3½ hours). The border area is tense and crowded with pushy money changers and paper-runners; watch your pockets and belongings.

Copán Ruínas US$2, three hours, 107km, 11:30am, 12:30pm and 2pm, or take any bus heading to San Pedro Sula and transfer at La Entrada

Gracias US$1.60, 1½ hours, 47km, 7:10am to 6pm, every 45 minutes

La Entrada *directo* US$1.60, 45 minutes; *ordinario* US$1, 1¼ hours, 28km, take any San Pedro Sula bus

Nueva Ocotepeque US$3.25, two hours, 95km, take any Aqua Caliente bus

San Pedro Sula *ordinario* US$2.75, 3½ hours, 152km, 4:30am-5pm, every 30 minutes; *directo* US$4, 2½ hours, 6am, 7:30am, 9am, 10am, 11am and 1pm on La Sultana; 8am, 9:30am & 2pm on Toritos and Copaneca

San Salvador via El Poy; US$10, four hours, 8:30am only

Tegucigalpa US$8.50, 6½ hours, 393km, take any San Pedro Sula morning bus and transfer

Getting Around

CAR & MOTORCYCLE

All of the streets in downtown Santa Rosa are one lane and one way; before you turn down any street, check to see if you'll be going with the flow of traffic – checking to see if parked cars are facing away from you is a good trick.

TAXI

From 7am to 7pm, taxis circle the city or are at taxi stands at parque central and the bus terminal. To book a cab call the **Asociación de Taxis Copán** (☎ 983 9892). Rides within town and to the bus station cost US$0.75; for destinations further afield, be sure to agree on a price before you get in.

NUEVA OCOTEPEQUE

pop 8894

In the southwest corner of Honduras, Nueva Ocotepeque is surprisingly mellow for having not one but two different international borders a short distance away. Buses to/from Agua Caliente (Guatemala) and El Poy (El Salvador) pass through frequently, and most travelers spend only the time that they need to transfer lines here. Hotels, restaurants and services are either on or near the main street, Calle Intermedio.

Information

Banco Atlántida (Calle Intermedio; ◯ 9am-4pm Mon-Fri, 8:30-11:30am Sat) Next to Hotel Internacional; has no ATM.

Immigration (☎ 653 2162; Calle Intermedio; ◯ 7:30am-3:30pm) Across from the Congolón bus terminal.

Online World (per hr US$0.80; ◯ 8am-8pm) Next to Hotel Maya Chortí.

Police (Carr a Santa Rosa de Copán) Located 500m from the town entrance.

Sleeping & Eating

All the places to stay and eat in Nueva Ocotepeque are on or near Calle Intermedio, which runs right through town.

Hotel Internacional (☎ 653 2357; Calle Intermedio; s/d with fan US$12/18, with air-con US$16/24, all incl breakfast; P ⬚) Rooms here are clean and modern but rather sterile. Perhaps it's the white ceramic flooring that extends from the lobby and hallway right into the rooms, like a hospital. That said, the beds are firm and the bathrooms spotless – a perfectly reliable place.

Hotel Maya Chortí (☎ 653 3377; Av General Francisco Morazán; s/d with fan US$11/19, with air-con US$14/24, incl breakfast; P ⬚) The lobby and staff are definitely welcoming here and the rooms spacious, but the hotel has a certain shabbiness that comes with age: bedspreads are beat, air-conditioning noisy and bathroom fixtures need to be replaced. It's not bad – you just expect better from the outside.

Hotel Turista (☎ 653 3639; Av General Francisco Morazán; s/d/tw with shared bathroom US$3.25/5/6.50, s/d/tw US$4.25/6.50/8.50) The best of several cheapies clustered around the Toritos &

Copaneca and Transporte San José bus stops. Rooms are very simple but relatively clean. The shared bathrooms are in the lobby, right next to the reception counter, which is awkward to say the least.

Servi Pollo (mains US$3-4; ⏰ 9am-7pm) This bright, glossy joint specializes in fried and roast chicken, but also has hot dogs and hamburgers. A big-screen TV counts as ambiance, usually with a movie playing. Go south from the local bus stop, left at the Banco Occidente, then take the second right.

Getting There & Away

Nueva Ocotepeque has two long-distance bus companies, charging almost identical prices. **Congolón** (☎ 653 3064) is half a block south of parque central, on the road to El Poy (El Salvador). **Toritos & Copaneca** (☎ 653 3405) is two blocks north of the park, near the entrance of town. Buses run to various destinations, including the following.

San Pedro Sula US$3.25, 4½ hours, 247km; Toritos & Copaneca 3am, 4am, 6:30am, 7:15am, 8am, 8:40am, 10am, 10:40am, 12:30pm, 1:45pm, 2:30pm, 4:30pm and 5:30pm; Congolón midnight; 3am, 5:30am, 6am, 9:30am, 11:30am, 12:30pm, 1pm and 3:30pm

Santa Rosa de Copán US$2.40, 1½ hours, 95km, take any San Pedro Sula bus

La Entrada US$4, 2½ hours, 123km, take any San Pedro Sula bus

Tegucigalpa US$11, nine to 10 hours, take any San Pedro Sula bus midnight to 10:40am and transfer; one Toritos & Copaneca direct bus at 11pm, US$13

AROUND NUEVA OCOTEPEQUE
Parque Nacional Montecristo-El Trifinio

This magnificent park straddles Honduras, Guatemala, and El Salvador, whose borders join at the peak of the park's showcase mountain, Cerro Montecristo, also known as El Trifinio. The three countries manage the park jointly, but only El Salvador has made it reasonably accessible to the public, from the town of Metapán.

GRACIAS

pop 8236

Gracias is a peaceful mountain town with cobblestone streets, colonial churches and a sense that time here moves at a slower pace. It is an important stop on the Ruta Lenca, a collection of western towns with strong Lenca indigenous communities and influence. Gracias itself has a new museum with some fine pieces, and is the gateway to smaller towns like La Campa and San Manuel Colohete, which are just beginning to appear on travelers' radar.

But Gracias is perhaps best known for its proximity to Parque Nacional Montaña de Celaque, a rugged swath of dense forest that's home to the country's highest peak. A challenging ascent can be done in one long day or in a more leisurely fashion in two or three, camping beneath the towering canopy of one of Honduras' best cloud forests.

History

Gracias was founded in 1526 by Spanish captain Juan de Chávez; its original name was Gracias a Dios (Thanks to God). The Sede de la Audiencia de los Confines, the governing council for all Central America, was established here on April 16, 1544; the buildings that the council occupied are still here. The town was important and grew for several years, and for a short time served as the capital of the Spanish empire in Central America. It was eventually eclipsed in importance by Antigua (Guatemala) and Comayagua, and slowly returned to its small-town roots.

Information

There are no ATMs in Gracias. The nearest one is in Santa Rosa de Copán.

Banco de Occidente (Parque Central; ⏰ 8:30am-4:30pm Mon-Fri, to 11:30am Sat) Exchanges traveler's checks and US dollars.

Hondutel (⏰ 7am-6:30pm & 7-9pm) Rates (per minute) for the USA and Canada are US$0.11, for Europe US$2.33, and for Australia and New Zealand US$2.09. Next to the post office.

Hospital Dr Juan Manuel Galvez (☎ 656 1100; Carr a Santa Rosa de Copán; ⏰ 24hr) Near the entrance to town, across from a Texaco station.

Internet Ecolem (per hr US$1.05; ⏰ 8am-9:30pm) Also offers web-based calls to the USA and Canada (per minute Monday to Friday US$0.08, Saturday and Sunday US$0.05).

Lavandería La Estrella (per load US$2.65; ⏰ 8am-5pm Mon-Sat) Two blocks west of Iglesia Las Mercedes.

Medicinas Alessandra (☎ 656 1275; ⏰ 7:30am-12:30pm, 1:30-8pm) This pharmacy is two blocks west of Hondutel.

Police (☎ 656 1326; Parque Central; ⏰ 24hr)

Post office (⏰ 8am-noon & 2-5pm Mon-Fri, 8-11am Sat) One block from parque central.

WESTERN HONDURAS

Tourist office (Parque Central kiosk; ☾ 8am-noon & 1:30-4:30pm Mon-Fri) Information binders are more helpful than the well-meaning staffers. Spanish only.

Sights & Activities

Gracias has several **colonial churches**: San Marcos, Las Mercedes and San Sebastián (at last check, closed and falling apart in a dirt park surrounded by enormous trees). Next door to the Iglesia de San Marcos, the Sede de la Audiencia de los Confines is now the *casa parroquial,* the residence for the parish priest.

Built in response to the tumultuous times of the 18th century, the striking **Fuerte de San Cristóbal** (San Cristóbal Fort; admission free; ☾ 8am-

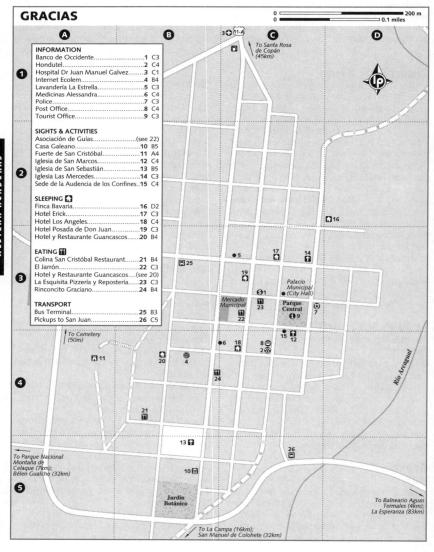

GRACIAS

0   200 m
0   0.1 miles

INFORMATION
Banco de Occidente..........................1 C3
Hondutel...2 C4
Hospital Dr Juan Manuel Galvez......3 C1
Internet Ecolem...............................4 B4
Lavandería La Estrella......................5 C3
Medicinas Alessandra.......................6 C4
Police...7 C3
Post Office.......................................8 C4
Tourist Office...................................9 C3

SIGHTS & ACTIVITIES
Asociación de Guías.....................(see 22)
Casa Galeano..................................10 B5
Fuerte de San Cristóbal..................11 A4
Iglesia de San Marcos.....................12 C4
Iglesia de San Sebastián.................13 B5
Iglesia Las Mercedes......................14 C3
Sede de la Audencia de los Confines..15 C4

SLEEPING 🛏
Finca Bavaria..................................16 D2
Hotel Erick......................................17 C3
Hotel Los Angeles..........................18 C4
Hotel Posada de Don Juan..............19 C3
Hotel y Restaurante Guancascos....20 B4

EATING 🍴
Colina San Cristóbal Restaurant.....21 B4
El Jarrón...22 C3
Hotel y Restaurante Guancascos....(see 20)
La Esquisita Pizzería y Repostería....23 C3
Rinconcito Graciano........................24 B4

TRANSPORT
Bus Terminal...................................25 B3
Pickups to San Juan........................26 C5

To Santa Rosa
de Copán
(45km)

To Cemetery
(50m)

To Parque Nacional
Montaña de
Celaque (7km);
Bélen Gualcho (32km)

Jardín
Botánico

To La Campa (16km);
San Manuel de Colohete (32km)

To Balneario Aguas
Termales (4km);
La Esperanza (83km)

Río Arcagual

Palacio
Municipal
(City Hall)

Parque
Central

Mercado
Municipal

LENCA TRADITIONS: PAST & PRESENT

Traditional Lenca *cosmovisión* (an explanation of the origin and operation of the universe), includes numerous deities and spirits. Interaction and communication with the different entities was (and is) a central preoccupation of many Lenca communities. Some deities are represented in stone and clay figures, others are associated with natural phenomenon, such as wind, rain or lightning. The existence of elves and other fantastical creatures is a given, though as tricksters you can never be sure of their intentions. Many beliefs, like 'Father' and 'Mother' creators loosely coincide with those espoused by Catholic missionaries.

Animals are thought to represent different qualities or personalities. A tradition that has faded but is still practiced in some isolated communities is sprinkling ash around the house where a child is born; the animal that leaves its prints there will be the child's *nahual* (companion and protector for life).

Shamans, healers and other spiritual leaders play important roles in Lenca communities, with each empowered to perform specific rituals and ceremonies. Animal sacrifice is still practiced; Lencans were deeply influenced by the Aztecs of central Mexico and may have performed human sacrifices in a distant past. Many modern Lenca communities have municipal governments, as well as an Alcaldía Auxiliar de la Vara Alta – an auxiliary mayor who is responsible for conducting Lenca ceremonies and serves as a liaison between Lencans and the 'official' city government. (Vara Alta, literally 'Tall Staff', is a rotating political-religious position from within traditional Lenca society.)

A fascinating pre-Hispanic custom that has survived in a few Lenca towns is the *guancasco*, an annual ceremony that confirms peace and friendship between neighboring communities. *Guancascos* take many forms and have adopted many Catholic symbols along the way, but typically include traditional costumes, processions and an elaborate exchange of greetings, statues of saints and other symbolic rites (not to mention a fair amount of revelry). The towns of Yamaranguila and La Campa, both on the Ruta Lenca, host *guancascos*.

WESTERN HONDURAS

4pm) has fantastic views of Gracias and the San Marcos church below. Beyond that, there's not much else to see up there, save the tomb of Honduran Juan Lindo, the former president of El Salvador (1841–42) *and* Honduras (1847–52). That, and a few teenage couples looking for a quiet corner to make-out. It's five blocks west of parque central.

Lenca pottery is arguably the best and most widely recognized *artesanía* in Honduras. Yet the country has long lacked a first-class museum to exhibit and preserve this unique folk art. Now there are two: one in Gracias – the **Casa Galeano** (slated to open at the end of 2006) – and the other in La Campa (p165).

The **Jardín Botánico** (admission free; 8am-5pm Mon-Sat, to noon Sun) is at the southern end of town, five blocks south of the Mercado Municipal, and takes up half a city block. Local flora can be admired all year long from a sidewalk that meanders through the park.

The hot springs at **Balneario Aguas Termales** (admission US$1; 6am-8pm) are one of Gracias' main attractions. Four kilometers

southeast of town, the hot springs have several pools at various temperatures. You can walk there in one to 1½ hours: take the road to La Esperanza until you reach the right-hand turnoff for the Aguas Termales, then follow the road or take the first right onto a footpath, which is a shortcut but requires fording a (usually) small river. You should be able to hitch a ride back – everybody does. Cabs don't usually come here; hiring a private truck costs around US$10, with an hour at the springs (ask at Hotel Guancascos).

Tours

A one-man guiding operation but arguably the best one in town, **Puma Trail Tours** (656 1113; waltermurcia@hotmail.com) is run by Walter Murcia, who offers specialized hikes through Parque Nacional Montaña de Celaque, historical and church tours of the region, as well as *artesanía* excursions along the Ruta Lenca. Tours cost US$60 per day (up to four people). English is spoken.

Based out of El Jarrón restaurant, the newly organized **Asociación de Guías** (656

0627) comprises a group of guides who also offer tours to area villages and Parque Nacional Montaña de Celaque. Prices depend on the length of the tour and the number of people. Ask for Marco Aurelio.

Sleeping

Hotel y Restaurante Guancascos (☎ 656 1219; www .guancascos.com; s/d/tw/tr US$12/14.50/20/21.50; **P**) Fifteen comfortable, thoughtfully decorated rooms, all with hot-water bathrooms and some with terrific views (especially rooms 12, 13, and 14), make Guancascos hard to beat. A terrace restaurant has excellent food and views, and is a good place to meet travelers heading to – or returning from – Parque Nacional Montaña de Celaque. You can leave bags here while you're hiking; there are sleeping bags (but no tents) for rent. Ask too about Cabaña Villa Verde, a fully equipped house at the entrance to Celaque.

Hotel Posada de Don Juan (☎ 656 1020; hotelposadadedonjuan@yahoo.com; s/d/tw with fan US$11/16/19, tw with air-con US$21; ✻) Right in the middle of town, with an internet café and restaurant, this hotel is convenient. Rooms are modern and clean but lack the mountain charm of Guancascos. For most, this is a solid second choice.

Finca Bavaria (☎ 656 1372; d/tr US$9/11) Set on a peaceful 35,000-sq-meter *finca de café* (coffee plantation) at the edge of town, the Bavaria's eight large guestrooms each have a hot-water bathroom and two to three firm beds. The German-Honduran couple who owns it had been living in Germany for several years when we last passed through, and it was unclear when (or if) they'd return. A caretaker was still renting the rooms but the restaurant, bar and lively conversation are on hiatus for the time being. Camping is available, too.

Hotel Erick (☎ 656 1066; s/d without hot water US$3.50/5.50, tw with hot water/TV US$8/10; **P**) A longtime favorite of budget travelers, rooms here are basic but clean, with little niceties like complimentary drinking water and a small table to make up for the saggy beds and flat white light. Guests can leave their luggage here while camping in the national park – a big plus. Service is gruff but well-meaning.

Hotel Los Angeles (☎ 656 1433; s/tw US$5.50/11) This is a decent shoestring option if you can

score a room with hot water and cable TV, but the service can be dodgy. If the gate is closed, ask in the store below.

Eating

Rinconcito Graciano (mains US$1-2.65; ☻ breakfast, lunch & dinner) This artsy place with Lencan art on the walls, handmade menus and rustic clay dishes, has a menu rife with traditional Lencan food – *ticucos* (cornmeal patties, stuffed with beans), *anafres* (bean fondue with tortilla chips), *mulitas* (corn tortilla filled with beans, eggs, avocado and cheese) and *chilate* (a sweet drink). Eat indoors at one of the simple wood tables or outdoors in the small garden courtyard. It's one of those places you're always searching for.

Colina San Cristóbal Restaurant (☎ 656 1543; mains US$1-5; ☻ 7am-9pm) Known mostly for its outstanding pizza, La Colina also offers grilled meats, hamburgers, sandwiches and *comida típica* (Honduran fare). The two dining rooms are understated and classy, with huge windows, muted colors and silk flowers. It's well worth the long walk from parque central.

La Esquisita Pizzería y Repostería (mains US$1.50-3; ☻ breakfast, lunch & dinner) Almost always jam packed with locals, this pizzeria is half a block west of parque central. The $2 daily special – whatever it is – is the way to go; it's served fast and comes loaded with a couple of sides and a drink. À la carte meals – there's no menu but the waitress will list items until you stop her – are pretty good too, just a little skimpy. Be sure to get a piece of chocolate cake for dessert.

El Jarrón (☎ 656 0627; mains US$1.50-3; ☻ breakfast, lunch & dinner Mon-Sat, breakfast & lunch Sun) Next to the market, this cozy eatery serves *típica* at a handful of tables. Service is very friendly and the food good, which makes it a popular spot around midday. Get there early for a seat. Tour guides and camping rentals are also available; ask for Marco Aurelio.

The rambling **Mercado Municipal** (two blocks west of Parque Central; ☻ 6am-4pm Mon-Sat, to noon Sun) has vendors selling fresh fruits and vegetables, dried food stuff, clothing and housewares. It's a good place to stock up on supplies if you're planning an overnight trip into Parque Nacional Montaña de Celaque.

Shopping

Hotel y Restaurante Guancascos (☎ 656 1219) One wall of this restaurant doubles as a small gift shop. You'll find regional *artesanía*, books in English and Spanish, and a few T-shirts too.

Rinconcito Graciano (◷ 7am-9pm) Lencan pottery, cigars and honey are sold in the tiny gift shop of this artsy restaurant.

El Jarrón (☎ 656 0627; ◷ 7am-9pm Mon-Sat, 7am-2pm Sun) The crafts sold at this eatery definitely veer toward the kitschy but if you can look past the loud key chains, you just might find a woodcarving worth taking home.

Getting There & Away

Gracias is 45km from Santa Rosa de Copán and 37km from San Juan, on good paved roads. From the terminal, numerous buses go to Santa Rosa de Copán (US$1.50, 1¼ hours, hourly, 5am to 5pm) and four *directos* to San Pedro Sula (US$4, four hours, 5am, 6am, 8:30am, 9:50am); otherwise transfer at Santa Rosa de Copán. For Copán Ruínas, take the San Pedro bus and transfer at La Entrada. The whole trip takes three to four hours and costs about US$5.

The best way to get to San Juan is by *jalón* (hitchhiking); just wave down a pickup truck on the road toward San Juan. Be sure to offer the driver some money when you arrive – US$1 to US$2 is fair.

Buses for La Campa, San Manuel Colohete and that region leave the terminal daily around noon. See each town for prices and information on return buses.

PARQUE NACIONAL MONTAÑA DE CELAQUE

One of Honduras' most impressive national parks, the Montaña de Celaque is a lush, steep, cloud forest, just over 6km from Gracias. It boasts El Cerro de las Minas (2849m), the highest peak in Honduras – a good, tiring hike.

Celaque, which means 'box of water' in the local Lencan dialect, is an appropriate name: Celaque's 11 rivers supply water to all of the surrounding communities, northern Honduras, and parts of El Salvador. It also has a majestic waterfall that is visible from the entire valley.

The park is rich in plant and animal life: 232 plant, 48 mammal, 269 bird and 18 reptile species make Celaque their home. Jaguars, pumas, ocelots and a number of rare endemic species have been spotted by lucky hikers. More common, but still elusive, are spider monkeys and quetzals. You have to be very quiet, and up very early, to see much wildlife, but if you don't see many animals, the rugged pine and cloud forests are still rewarding.

Information

The entrance fee (US$2.65) is payable at the visitors center, as is the additional cost of staying overnight – US$2.65 per person regardless of whether you stay in the dorm or in a tent.

For information on hiking in Celaque, Walter Murcia is a knowledgeable guide with lots of experience in the park. He willingly shares information – even a free hand-drawn trail map – without giving you a hard sell for his services. He can be tracked down through **Puma Trail Tours** (☎ 656 1113; waltermurcia@hotmail.com) or **Hotel Guancascos** (☎ 656 1219; www.guancascos.com) in Gracias.

Dangers & Annoyances

Although it may be tempting to follow that spider monkey into the mist, don't wander off the trail. The forest is so dense that it can be hard, even impossible, to find your way back. A Dutch hiker disappeared here in 1998 and was never found; a Honduran hiker got lost and died in 2003.

Temperatures in the park are much chillier than in Gracias, so bring warm clothes. Also be prepared for dampness and rain; it's a cloud forest after all and the park gets around 2000mm to 4000mm of annual precipitation.

Hiking

The main hike in Celaque is to Cerro de las Minas (2849m) – a 1449m ascent from the visitors center. It is a steep, challenging hike that takes most hikers two to three days to complete. Many people misjudge the time they need for the climb. Some do the whole thing in a single day, but it's a very long haul. Even spreading it over two days, you should start hiking early. The trail is somewhat unclear in places – look for the colored ribbons.

The original nameless trail (it should be called Switchback Heaven), heads up the

WESTERN HONDURAS

northern side of Río Mecatal, directly to Campamento Don Tomás; it passes over several streams, through a dense pine forest, with switchback upon switchback until it reaches the campsite. After about two hours, you'll come to a fork in the trail – continue left (south), as the trail to the right goes to Santa Lucia Waterfall. It takes about 4½ to five hours to get to the campsite.

A second trail – Rooster Trail – heads up the southern side of Río Mecatal, passing a waterfall vista and taking hikers through Monkey Valley, an area known to be inhabited by spider monkeys (keep your eyes peeled – they're fast little buggers). It also leads to Campamento Don Tomás in about 3½ hours.

Most hikers set up camp at Don Tomás but if you can handle a couple more hours of steep climbing – literally, pulling yourself up the mountain by tree roots and rocks – it's worth the sweat to get to Campamento El Naranjo to set up for the night. From there, it's another 1½ to two hours on a beautiful rolling trail through the cloud forest to the summit. Because of clouds and tree cover, you might not see anything from the top, but there's a sign there all the same.

A third steep trail leads to Santa Lucia Waterfall, a majestic cascade emerging from the cloud forest. It's a four- to five-hour hike from the visitor center; follow 'Switchback Heaven' until you reach a fork in the trail, about two hours up; go right (north) to reach the falls. There's no campsite along this trail, so start early to be sure you'll be back before dark. With a lunch break, it could take you nine to 11 hours to complete.

There are a couple of short trails from the visitors center – one to a little waterfall due north, the other east down Río Arcagual. It'll be very tempting to jump into the latter after a long grueling hike; however, the river provides drinking water downstream, so swimming is strictly prohibited.

Tours
Puma Trail Tours (☎ 656 1113; waltermurcia@hotmail .com) and the **Asociación de Guías** (☎ 656 0627) both offer trips of varying length and difficulty in Celaque. Trips must be arranged at least one day in advance.

Sleeping & Eating
At the visitors center, there is a simple but clean dorm with bunks that can sleep up to 15 people. Half of the bunks have mattresses, while the rest are just wood frames; either way, bring your own bedding. There's also a decent communal kitchen.

The good folks at Gracias' **El Jarrón** (☎ 656 0627) restaurant rent out tents/sleeping bags (US$3.25/2.65 per night) and they can also track down binoculars and walkie-talkies for you.

From the visitors center, a four-hour uphill walk along a well-marked trail leads to Campamento Don Tomás (2060m). The camp has a sketchy two-bunk shack reminiscent of the abandoned house in *The Blair Witch Project*; you're better off just camping. There's also a small latrine onsite but no running water. Remember to collect some from the streams that you pass on your way up (be sure to purify it with tablets or a filter).

A second campsite, El Naranjo (2560m), is only 500m away, but the trail up is very steep (one to two hours). It's a pretty camp though – just inside the cloud forest – and worth staying at if you can handle carrying your gear up.

Comedor Doña Alejandra (mains US$1.50; ⏲ breakfast, lunch & dinner) is the only place to get food if you don't bring it yourself. Run out of Doña Alejandra's home, just northeast of the visitors center, this basic eatery offers simple and tasty food.

Getting There & Away
From Gracias, it's a 6.5km steady climb to the park entrance; it takes around one to two hours to get there – look for the well-marked shortcut for those *a pie* (on foot). From there, it's another half-hour uphill to the park visitors center.

If you opt to get a lift to the park entrance, the cheapest option is a bumpy ride in a moto-taxi (US$3.75 per person). Otherwise, you can either cab it (US$13.50) or arrange a ride through **Puma Trail Tours** (☎ 656 1113; 1–2 people US$13.25, 3/4 people US$17.50/21.25, 5 or more per person US$4.50).

Another option is to enter the park at Belén Gualcho, but there are no park services available at that entrance; besides, the forest is much more pristine on the Gracias side.

LA CAMPA

The first town you reach headed south from Gracias is La Campa, a scenic little community at the bottom of a steep-walled river valley known for its handmade pottery. La Campa's natural beauty and proximity to Gracias (16km) make it a good place for travelers to stop. Two new hotels, a good museum and two *artesanía* cooperatives make it even better. Hiking and other excursions are possible as well, though travel here still requires a fair amount of improvising.

Information & Orientation

The road from Gracias descends through several switchbacks before reaching the bottom. There, a large grassy field is effectively the parque central, with a pretty colonial church on the near side and municipal buildings across the way. Passing the center, the road crosses a bridge and climbs abruptly, up and out of town.

On the park, there's a building with a sign advertising '*información turística*' but no tourist information as yet. The *alcaldía* (city hall), also on the park, is a logical place to ask for help, though results will vary. For internet access, head to the **Centro Comunitario de Conocimiento y Comunicación** (CCCC; per hr US$1; 🕑 9am-9pm Mon-Fri) behind the large municipal building.

Sight & Activities

The Lenca region, and La Campa in particular, is known for its *alfarería* (handmade pottery). The **Centro de Interpretación de Alfarería Lenca** (admission US$1.50; 🕑 4am-4:30pm) is a museum dedicated to this art form, complete with several excellent displays of pottery and historical information. It's housed in a beautiful colonial-style building overlooking the center of town.

Local workshops have long been open to drop-in visitors. **Doña Desideria Pérez' workshop** (🕑 8-11am & 1-4pm), 700m past the church, specializes in giant *cántaros* (urns), made entirely by hand without the use of a wheel. The pieces take a week to make and sell for around US$55 each. Most are used as decoration in gardens and outdoor patios, though traditionally they served as storage for corn, beans or water. Doña Desideria is a charming woman who's been making pottery for over four decades and is happy to chat with visitors; occasionally she's taken on volunteer assistants/apprentices for a month or two.

The nearby community of **Cruz Alta** has two artisan collectives, one making pots, mobiles, and other clay items, the other *tejado de pino* (pine-needle basketry). The artwork is modest and is made and sold in private homes amid chickens, children and other trappings of everyday life; ask for Suyapa Pérez or Máximo Velásquez. Cruz Alta is 4km from La Campa, up an extremely steep dirt road past the basketball court. There is no regular transport.

There are also a couple of guided area **hikes** (US$3.25/4.25/5.50/6.50 for one/two/three/four people): one to Cuevas del Gigante, a trek through the countryside to a set of caves; and another to El Cañon de la Mujer Cabra, a relatively easy hike through a lush canyon. Both trips can be done on **horseback** (US$6.50/10.50/14.50/19 for one/two/three/four people) and can include lunch (US$1.50 to US$2 extra). Hikes last approximately three hours; contact Neftaly García at Hostal J.B. for more information.

Sleeping & Eating

Hostal J.B. (🕿 551 3772 in San Pedro Sula; hostal_jb@yahoo.com; s/d/tr US$6.50/8/10) One of the best hotels on the Ruta Lenca, this is more like a huge house with five rooms for rent. All have new queen-size beds with thick comforters and hot-water bathrooms; guests share a fully equipped kitchen and a spacious living room with sofas, folk art and high wood-beamed ceilings. Internet access is in the works too. It's at the hairpin turn just before the church and run by Neftaly García, a friendly English-speaking local who lives next door. He's also a guide and can take you on area hikes.

Casa de Huespedes María Marta (r with shared/private bathroom US$5.50/6.50) Run by a terrific young family, this *hospedaje* next to the CCCC offers simple cement-block rooms with three-quarter bathroom walls and a small window overlooking the town. All open onto the plant-filled property, which has hammocks that are perfect for digging into a good book. It's perfectly nice, but not able to compete with Hostal J.B.

Getting There & Away

The once-daily bus from Gracias to San Manuel Colohete (US$1, one hour) passes La Campa at around 1pm. Going in the other direction, the bus passes around 6:30am (US$0.75, 45 minutes). It's also possible to hitch a ride in either direction.

SAN MARCOS DE CAIQUÍN
pop 2000

Six kilometers past La Campa is the turnoff to San Marcos de Caiquín, commonly shortened to just 'Caiquín'. The road winds another 5.5km through a gorgeous pine forest, a rich green in the rainy season and carpeted in red fallen needles in the dry months. The town has a brilliant whitewashed church, and simple cement and adobe houses.

Information

Check your email at the municipal **Sala de Computo** (9am-noon & 2-9pm, per hr US$0.55), a surprisingly modern computer center in the building next to the alcaldía (city hall). The town's **teléfono comunitario** (community phone; ☎ 640 4900; domestic per min US$0.25, international per min from US$1.15; 7am-8pm) is in a private home facing the park – it's the one with the red, white and blue lion logo of the Olimpia soccer team in front.

Sights & Activities

There's not a lot to do in Caiquín, beyond soaking in the small-town atmosphere. The interior of the **Iglesia de San Marcos de Caiquín** was recently restored and is quite beautiful, but it's all but impossible to get in (even for insistent guidebook writers) on any day other than Sunday.

It is possible to **hike** from here across the mountains to Erandique, which takes you through small towns, pine forest and areas once controlled by Lempira, the famous 16th-century Lenca chieftain. The road appears on some maps, though it's very rough in places, passing through Cualaca and Arcamón, then over the mountain to the community of Santa Cruz and down into Erandique. Budget at least two days; the alcaldía may be able to locate a guide.

There's a shorter hike along the dirt road that connects Caiquín to Cruz Alto, the small artistically inclined aldea (hamlet) of La Campa.

Sleeping & Eating

In a pinch, you can stay the night in the **casa de Doña Josefina Santos** (☎ 915 4347; r US$5.50), 1½ blocks from the church, but the conditions

are pretty basic: the kids are kicked out of their room whenever a backpacker shows up, and everyone shares a rather gross coldwater bathroom. Doña Josefina, a gruff but friendly lady, also runs a comedor (a basic and cheap eatery) and pulpería.

You may also be able to camp somewhere in or around town – there's certainly no shortage of open space. Ask at the alcaldía for advice and permission.

There are just three comedores in town, including Doña Josefina's place, so finding them isn't a problem. Comedor Daniela and a no-name eatery in a quaint adobe building opposite the church both serve cheap típica meals.

Getting There & Away

There's just one bus daily in and out of Caiquín. It leaves from in front of the church at 6:30am bound for Gracias, returning at 12:30pm (US$1.25, 1½ hours). An ordinary car can easily make it in the dry season, but you'll need a 4WD vehicle in the winter to cross over the mud, especially after a heavy rain.

SAN MANUEL DE COLOHETE

The road continues another steep and winding 15km to San Manuel Colohete, which is literally in the shadow of the Parque Nacional Montaña de Celaque and the largest town in this neck of the woods. There are a number of good hikes along the town's periphery to Belén Gualcho.

The landscape changes dramatically with the seasons, becoming lush and green in the rainy season (April to November) and hot and brown in the dry season. The best time to come is the end of the rainy season, when the trees are still green but the roads and trails have started to dry out.

It's impossible to get lost in San Manuel, though it's easy enough to get disoriented on the narrow curving streets. There's no post office or internet café in town. The small pharmacy and health clinic have no signs or regular hours. Jack Simpson, a friendly American expatriate, is a great source of information; ask anyone in town to point you toward his house.

Sights & Activities

San Manuel is justly known for its **colonial church** (Sun) a beautiful colonial structure with 400-year-old fresco paintings inside; its altar and wood columns were recently restored by a Spanish NGO.

On the 1st and 15th of every month, the town hosts a large **market** (☯ 6am-noon), similar to the one held in Belén Gualcho. People come from all over the region to buy and sell domestic and farm goods; you won't find much *artesanía*, but it's a good place to stock up on rubber boots, machetes, tin buckets and the like. You never know when you'll need an extra colander.

For a nice day hike, follow the road past parque central out of town up to San Antonio, a small community on the edge of the national park, with a nice little plaza and school.

A longer **hike** goes from San Manuel to Belén Gualcho. Take the road toward San Antonio that veers off across a swinging bridge and onto a trail over the ridge. Alternatively, take one of two trails off the road to San Sebastián, one 2.5km west from San Manuel at a small river, the other 2km further on at the community of San José. No matter how you go, take time to ask around San Manuel about the latest conditions. On the trail, ask locals you pass if you're headed in the right direction; there are plenty of side trails that can take you off track. Plan on staying the night in Belén Gualcho – it's a good six to seven hours each way.

It's also possible to climb **Pico Celaque** from here, but you'll need an experienced guide. Ask Jack Simpson for help on locating someone suitable.

Sleeping & Eating

It's slim pickings on the hotel and eatery front in this town. Jack Simpson was planning on building a backpackers hostel when we passed through, but until then there is only one option in town.

Hotel Emanuel (Calle Principal; s/d with shared bathroom US$2.25/5.50, r US$3.75/7.50) Nine clean simple rooms – three with private bathroom, one of which has hot water – occupy this two-story building on Calle Principal. Room 6 is the best: spacious, with a private bathroom and a view of the valley below. The entrance is easy to miss – there's just a small wooden sign next to a large black gate, and there's no formal reception.

For meals, ask at the front desk of the hotel; they'll help set something up. You also can get snacks at Pulpería Giselle in the center of town.

Getting There & Away

The bus from Gracias to San Manuel (US$1.50, 1½ hours) leaves between noon and 1pm, dropping passengers at the center of town before continuing to San Sebastián. The return bus passes San Manuel between 6am and 6:30am. Travel times can be considerably longer in the rainy season.

SAN SEBASTIÁN

Another 12km brings you to San Sebastián, a small, somewhat tense town, and the end of the road for all but the hardiest of vehicles. From here, a decrepit dirt road continues to Belén Gualcho, a scenic and moderately tough hike that takes four to six hours. Other than doing that hike (or finishing it) there's not much reason to come here.

The road to Belén Gualcho begins about 750m outside of San Sebastián, right where the road from San Manuel makes a sharp left and starts up a hill into town. Look for a barbwire fence with wood posts. The hike is very doable on your own, but you can also hire the services of Victor Manuel Pasqual, a friendly local farmer and sometime guide who lives in the first house on the right past the Belén Gualcho turnoff.

You may need to stay a night in San Sebastián, either to get an early start or if you arrive late from the other direction. The best option are four **rooms for rent** (with shared/private bathroom per person US$2.25/2.75) owned by Don Adrian, who is typically at a *pulpería* near parque central. The rooms are cramped and a bit grubby but adequate. Opening the window helps, though passersby can look right in. The other hotel in town, **Hotel Mejilla Melgar** (r per person US$1.75), looks kind of cool from the outside, but is seriously not cool on the inside. Dank rooms and dirty beds are bad enough, but the shared toilet will give you the dry heaves.

You can get snacks and simple meals at Don Adrian's or head down to parque central where Doña Alicia runs a small *comedor* (no sign). There's also a fruit-and-veggie shop on the park.

Buses to San Sebastián (US$2, 3½ hours) leave Gracias between noon and 1pm. Return buses leave from San Sebastián's parque central, near the Hotel Mejilla Melgar, at 5:30am.

BELÉN GUALCHO
pop 2405

Belén Gualcho is a picturesque colonial village on the other side of Parque Nacional Montaña de Celaque, known for the Lenca market held there every Sunday morning. Perched on the side of a mountain at 1600m above sea level, the village is cool and fresh, its residents reserved but friendly.

There are only four phone lines in Belén Gualcho. Three of them are for the community calling center operated by **Hondutel** (☎ 651 9600, 601 5030, 601 5029; domestic per min US$0.10-0.25, USA per min US$1.20; ☺ 7:30-noon & 1-5pm;), half a block from parque central, and the other is at the **alcaldía** (☎ 655 8055; Parque Central). To reach someone in Belén Gualcho, call the Hondutel office and they'll send a kid to find the person. There also is one internet café, **Internet Cecob** (per hr US$0.80; ☺ 11am-1:30pm & 4-10pm Mon-Fri, 11am-10pm Sat & Sun), next to the Hotel Olvin. **Farmacia El Carmen** (Parque Central; ☺ 8am-5pm Mon-Sat, to noon Sun) has basic medicines and supplies.

Activities
There's an entrance to Parque Nacional Montaña de Celaque on the outskirts of Belén Gualcho. There's no checkpoint and no services but the one trail starting here follows the southern edge of the mountain to San Sebastián and San Manuel Colohete. It's a steep four-hour hike but a beautiful one. Just be sure to stay on the trail – even locals can get lost in the area.

A picturesque hike to a set of waterfalls, the **Cataratas de Santa María de Gualcho**, is also a good way to explore the area. From Belén Gualcho, walk to the hamlet of Lentago, which is on a turnoff from the dirt road that leads to the highway; you should get there in about 10 minutes. Once there, ask someone to point you in the direction of the *sendero* (trail) to the falls. About a 30-minute trek will take you right there.

Sleeping & Eating
Hotels fill up on Saturdays with market vendors; if you plan to stay over that night, check in early to guarantee a spot.

Hotelito El Carmen (s/d with shared bathroom US$2.25/4.50, s/d US$3.25/6.50; ℗) Belén Gualcho's best hotel is a very simple but surprisingly pleasant place, two blocks downhill from the church and parque central. Rooms are small and boxy but clean and comfortable – a few have square windows with swinging wood shutters with a view of town and the valley beyond. Hot water would be an added bonus, but no such luck. The shared bathrooms are kept reasonably clean.

Pulpería y Hotel Olvin (main street; r with/without bathroom US$5.50/3.25) If the Hotelito El Carmen is full, this is the only other option in town. Not a particularly welcoming place, the hotel's rooms are on the sketch side of clean but they'll do for a night. At least there's electricity and running water 24 hours a day. The reception desk doubles as the cashier counter for the family's *pulpería*.

There are three basic eateries in town within a couple of blocks of each other on the main drag – Pulpería y Comedor Onan, Comedor y Golosinas Raquel and Pollera Lety. All serve cheap *típica* for breakfast, lunch and dinner.

Getting There & Away
To get here, two daily buses arrive from Santa Rosa de Copán; a third also comes from San Pedro Sula. To return, buses to Santa Rosa de Copán (US$2, two to three hours, 3am to 8am, hourly) leave from the church. On Sundays, the schedule is 4am, 5am, 7am, 9:30am, noon and 1pm. You may also be able to hitch a ride on a pickup.

SAN JUAN
A slowly improving highway and the dogged efforts of at least two generations of Peace Corps volunteers and a local tourism committee are helping put this tiny mountain town on the tourist map. Once little more than a crossroads between La Esperanza and Gracias, San Juan is now a popular stop on the Ruta Lenca, offering guided hikes and a chance to interact with local families and farmers.

Information
Cesamo (☺ 8am-4pm Mon-Fri) Basic health clinic; five blocks from parque central.

Internet Access (Parque Central; per hr US$1; ☺ 8:30am-7pm Mon-Fri, to noon Sat)

Police (☎ 754 7126; Parque Central; ☺ 24hr)

Telephone (☎ 783 1716; ☺ 7am-8pm) Near Hotelito La Posada de Rosario; standard domestic rates but higher-than-usual international, starting at US$0.80 per minute. You can also buy a prepaid Tigo card and borrow a cell phone (per minute from US$0.05) from Gladys Nolasco at the visitors center.

Visitors center (☎ 754 7150; sanjuan_turismo@yahoo .com; main street) Lots of good information offered about area sights; guided tours also can be arranged. It's run out of Gladys Nolasco's home and paper store. Spanish only.

Activities

Local guides can take you on a number of interesting hikes in the region. The most worthwhile include the **Cascada de los Duendes**, a trek through a cloud forest with a small set of waterfalls that ends with a *finca de café* tour (the best time for this hike is between December and March, when coffee is in full production); and **El Cañon Encantado**, a hike in the lush San Juan Valley complete with legends of the ghosts who inhabit it (Spanish only). Both hikes are moderately difficult but have decent trails. Prices are kind of steep (US$21/26/30/35 for one/two/three/four people) but the trips last from 8am to 4pm and include lunch. The same excursions can also be taken on horseback (US$28/35/43/64 for one/two/three/four people). A hike to **Piedra Parada**, the enormous rock where the famous Lencan chieftain Lempira was killed, can also be arranged for US$64 (up to six people); it includes transport to the hamlet of La Laguna and a hike to Congolón, one of the highest peaks in the country. All tours must be reserved a day in advance.

San Juan also has two cultural tours: a **coffee roasting and tasting** demonstration in a local home (translation: watch a tourist official's mother, Doña Soledad, roast coffee beans on her wood-burning stove and then try it yourself) and a **clay artisan** demonstration (head 5km south of town to watch and learn how to make a terracotta brick or tile – ask for Don Amadeo). Not the most scintillating activities but a great way to interact with locals and learn a little about daily life in a Lencan village. Both tours cost US$1.35 per person; no advance notice needed.

If you're in the mood for a swim, head to **La Piscina de Don Nicho** (adult/child US$1/0.50; ☺ sunrise-sunset), a set of spring-fed pools 5km south of town near the road to Esperanza. It's nothing fancy, but it's refreshing.

Bicycle rentals (half/full day US$1.35/2.65), perfect for exploring the town and surrounding area on your own, can be arranged through the visitors center.

Sleeping & Eating

Posada de Doña Soledad (Calle Principal; r per person US$3.25) Meeting Doña Soledad, a straight-talking octogenarian, is surely the best reason to come to this otherwise simple guesthouse. The two rooms – one large, one small – are reasonably comfortable with hot-water bathrooms and separate entrances. Home-cooked meals are an extra US$2.25. It's half a block from the visitors center.

Hotelito La Posada de Rosario (☎ 953 6818; r with/without bathroom per person US$6.50/3.75; **P**) The next best thing, if Doña Soledad is full or you just want something not so guest-housey. Boxy, mid-size rooms are brightly painted, but could use a scrubbing. Ditto for the bathrooms. Coming from Gracias, the hotel is on your left near the entrance of town.

Cabaña en el Campo (r per person US$3.75) This simple wood-construction guesthouse, with outdoor toilet and shower, is near the Opalaca Biological Reserve, about a half-hour's walk from San Juan. Reservations are required and can be made at the visitors center.

Comedor Yamilet (Calle Principal; mains US$1.75-2; ☺ breakfast, lunch & dinner) Opposite the visitors center, this cool, spacious eatery has a sign on the counter inviting diners and travelers into the kitchen to watch and help the food be prepared – their own dish, presumably. Whoever makes it, the food is simple and tasty, with the day's offerings written on a dry-erase board.

Getting There & Away

Buses to La Esperanza pass through the center of town at 6am, 7:30am, 8:20am and 9:30am daily (US$1.58, 1½ hours). For the same fare, there is also a *busito* (minivan) that heads to La Esperanza at 1:30pm every day.

There is iffy bus service to Gracias that sometimes passes through town between 6am and 8am (US$1.60, one hour); if you prefer not to hold your breath (and pass out) waiting, it's easy to get a *jalón* from drivers headed there. Stand on the main road and just wave a pickup truck down. Also, be sure to offer the driver some money for the ride – US$1 to US$1.50 is fair.

ERANDIQUE
pop 1918

An attractive colonial town 24km south of San Juan, Erandique has some good hiking but is most famous for its opals, which are extracted from three mines in the area. A number of valuable varieties can be found here, including black seam, black matrix and white opals. You are sure to be approached by locals selling them, some rather aggressively.

There are two internet cafés in town, one in Barrio Gualmaca (per hour US$0.85) and one near parque central (per hour US$1.05); the latter also has domestic and international phone service, or try Hondutel. And FYI, Erandique is a 'dry' community – no alcohol is permitted.

Sights & Activities

One of Erandique's three **mines** is a half-hour walk from town, in the direction of Gualguire. As with any mine, you should never venture beyond the entrance without an exceptional guide or companion. Another good half-day hike is to **Las Cuatro Chorreras** (the Four Waterfalls), 3km to 4km away.

For something more challenging, **Peñol de Cerquín** and **Piedra Parada** – the fortress of 16th-century Lenca chieftain Lempira and the place where he was assassinated – can be reached from here, though the trip is at least two days round-trip on foot.

Sleeping & Eating

Erandique has three hotels. All have basic rooms with cable TV and private bathrooms with hot water: **Hotel Steven** (Barrio Gualmaca; s/d/tr US$5.50/8/11; P), **Hotel Sinai** (Barrio Gualmaca; s/d US$5.50/8; P), and **Hotel Torre Fuerte** (Barrio Centro; r/tw/tr US$4.25/5.50/8; P), one block south of the church.

Comedor Rossie (Barrio Gualmaca) and **Comedor Los 3 Reyes** (Parque Central) are both open for all three meals and serve good cheap Honduran *típica*, plus sandwiches and snacks.

Getting There & Away

The bus to Gracias (US$2.75, two hours) leaves from Barrio Gualmaca at 5am; to return, the same bus leaves Gracias at noon, from the bridge opposite the electricity company (EENE). The bus to La Esperanza (US$3, 2½ hours) leaves Erandique's parque central at 5am, while the return bus leaves La Esperanza at noon. The bus is marked 'San Francisco' and leaves from behind the soccer stadium.

LA ESPERANZA
pop 7347

La Esperanza is Intibucá's capital and largest city, though you'd never guess from the dusty streets and small-town atmosphere. The town is best known for its Sunday market, when Lencans from the surrounding area buy, sell and trade goods of all sorts. In the heart of one of Honduras' poorest regions, La Esperanza also attracts an unusually large number of foreign volunteers, either Christian groups building latrines or general practitioners helping out in area clinics.

Orientation & Information

Most of La Esperanza's restaurants, hotels and services face or are within a few blocks of its parque central, either on the road that runs between the park and the police station, or one street over (Av Los Próceres), which eventually turns into the main highway, connecting La Esperanza to Siguatepeque and Gracias.

Banco de Occidente (8:30am-4:30pm Mon-Fri, to 11:30am Sat) Near parque central; traveler's checks exchanged from 9am to 2pm weekdays, US dollars exchanged anytime. No ATM.

Explored (Plaza María; Internet per hr US$0.65; 9am-11pm) Across from Hotel Mejia Batres; offers cheap international phone calls too.

Farmacia Santa Isabel (783 0427; 8am-noon & 2-6pm Mon-Sat, to noon Sun) Behind the church.

Hondutel (Parque Central; 7am-noon, 12:30-6pm & 6:30-9pm)

Police (783 1007; Parque Central; 24hr)

Post office (Parque Central; 7:30am-4pm Mon-Fri, to noon Sat)

Sights & Activities

A number of very interesting sights are found outside of La Esperanza, including the Lenca town of Yamaranguila and the

Valle de Azacualpa, which make for excellent day trips.

Closer to town, **Cicai** (Centro Indigenista de Capacitación Artesanal Intibucano; ☎ 783 0565; Calle a Azacualpa; ☻ 7am-3pm Mon-Fri, Feb-Nov) is a semiboarding school, 1.5km north from the center, where around 80 indigenous students learn folk art and vocational skills. Students learn a little of all disciplines – weaving, leatherwork, carpentry, welding and others – but select one that they spend three years mastering. The school welcomes visitors – some of the teachers are foreign volunteers – and you can sit in on a class or talk with the students or teachers. Mornings are best; check in at the administrative office first. Sadly, the school is often without enough supplies or materials.

Ask about things to do in La Esperanza, and you'll invariably hear about the **bosque enano** (dwarf forest), a few kilometers from town. It sounds intriguing, but the 'forest' is actually a low bulge of hard earth dotted with tiny gnarled shrubs (and not a small amount of litter). It's right alongside the road, in view of a large earth-excavation project. Tree enthusiasts may derive some enjoyment from the sight, but a more typical response is 'Huh?'

Sleeping

La Posada de Clelia Margarita (☎ 783 0856; posada clelia52@hotmail.com; Barrio Lempira; r US$11; apt per week US$27; **P**)) This family guesthouse is run by the delightful Doña Clelia, a fulltime teacher, part-time guide and sometime surrogate mother for the innumerable volunteers who have stayed here. All units have hot water, a private bathroom and telephone and are comfortable in a homey worn-in way; guests can also arrange for meals to be included, served at the family table. To get here, turn north (away from the park) at Banco Nacional de Desarrollo Agrícola and continue 300m.

Hotel Mina (☎ 783 1071; r/tw/ste US$10.75/16/ 29.75; **P**)) Two blocks east and one block south of the bus terminal, this hotel offers spotless rooms with exposed brick walls and heavy wood furnishings. Cheaper rooms are tiny but still have private hotwater bathrooms and cable TV. An on-site restaurant (mains US$2.50 to US$4), open for breakfast, lunch and dinner, serves good *típica* and snacks.

Hotel Mejia Batres (☎ 783 0051; s/d with shared bathroom US$4.25/7.50, s/d US$6.75/10.75, cable TV US$5.25; **P**)) Although suffering from seriously stinky bathrooms, this is a clean hotel offering basic, somewhat worn rooms. Its location is prime – one block west of parque central. Just be sure to keep the bathroom door shut tight.

La Esperanza also has an on-again, offagain system of **homestays** (s/d US$4.75/6.95, with 3 meals per day US$10.25/17.95). **Casa de Luz** (☎ 783 1142, 783 0414), **Casa de Eneyda** (☎ 783 0124) and **Casa de Leyda Villanueva** (☎ 783 1169) all offer a room with a queen-size bed and private hot-water bathroom.

Eating

Café Jardín Colonial (☎ 783 0988; Av Próceres; mains US$1-3; ☻ breakfast, lunch & dinner) This great little café, three blocks from parque central, will assuage the pain of anyone missing their favorite coffee spot back home. Cappuccinos, espressos and cool licuados are served in a sunny courtyard with a handful of metal tables shaded by canvas umbrellas. The menu also includes fresh sandwiches and a long list of crepes, from chicken and ham to jam, banana or *melacatón* (passionfruit), served with a scoop of ice cream.

Papapua's (Av Próceres; mains US$3-6; ☻ breakfast, lunch & dinner) Two blocks from parque central, this smallish, goodish Mexican restaurant is popular with La Esperanza's large volunteer crowd, both for its food and its nightlife. An open-air patio in back has shaded wood picnic tables, which go well with the *tortas*, taco plates and burritos. There's music and dancing Thursday and Saturday, karaoke on Friday.

El Recreo (mains US$2-6; ☻ breakfast, lunch & dinner) Another favorite among young volunteers, El Recreo has a friendly owner who serves a fixed menu for breakfast, mostly *baleadas* for lunch, and dishes like coconut chicken or a barbecue sampler for dinner. There's music and dancing Friday and Saturday. It's a block south and a block west of parque central.

Opalaca's Restaurant (☎ 783 0503; mains US$5-9; ☻ breakfast, lunch & dinner) Ask for the best restaurant in town and most people will point to this one. It certainly looks the part, housed in a colonial-era building with high wood-beamed ceilings, and offering cloth napkins and real water glasses. All of which makes the menu that much more surprising, with grilled beef, grilled pork chops, Honduran barbecue, plus hamburgers and sandwiches. The food is reliable, just not as refined as the restaurant's reputation and décor would lead you to believe.

Getting There & Away

Most buses leave from the *mercado quemado* (burned market) a huge dusty lot south of the park. Some depart from *el estadio* (the stadium, located near the bridge on the highway to Siguatepeque) and others from individual terminals down the main drag. You can always catch buses to Siguatepeque, San Pedro and Tegucigalpa at the Texaco station at the edge of town – be sure to take a *directo*, which takes half as long and costs only pennies more. Taxis around town cost US$0.70 per person or slightly more at night.

Gracias US$4.35, four hours, morning departure, time varies, pickup service might be available

Marcala US$1.75, 1½ to two hours, three departures daily, roughly 8am, noon & 3pm, stops in front of Hotel La Esperanza

San Juan US$1.58, 1½ hours, 11:30am, 1pm, 2:45pm and 4:45pm

San Pedro Sula US$4.25, 3½ hours, 4:15am to 12:15pm, every two hours, Sunday at 12:15 and 1:30pm only

San Juan US$1.60, 1½hours; 6am, 1pm, 2:20pm, 3:30pm and 4:45pm

Siguatepeque US$2.25, *directo*, one hour, take any San Pedro Sula or Tegucigalpa bus

Tegucigalpa US$3.50, 3½ hours, 4:40am to 2pm, every one to 1½ hours

AROUND LA ESPERANZA
Yamaranguila
pop 1212

Yamaranguila is a quaint, predominantly indigenous, mountain town 9km from La Esperanza. It is notable for preserving a system of traditional Lenca governance that coexists with the 'modern' elected municipal government. The Vara Alta is the post held by a local Lenca elder, who is responsible during his term for maintaining Lenca traditions. This includes planning and overseeing traditional rituals and ceremonies, especially the *guancascos,* a pre-Hispanic ceremony designed to promote peaceful relations between neighboring communities. Yamaranguila is one of a dwindling number of indigenous communities that celebrate *guancascos*, usually held around the first week of December. Yamaranguila also celebrates not one, but two patron saints' days: San Francisco in early October and Santa Luca in mid-December.

The other attraction of Yamaranguila is a tall wispy waterfall that's an easy walk from town. From the park, all roads lead downhill to the school; there, hop the small creek that runs between the road and the soccer field, duck through the barbed-wire fence and continue downstream through the pine forest less than 1km to the falls. The viewing area is at the top of the falls – at the lip of a huge sinkhole. Ask around town for someone to show you how to get to the bottom. It's a long, roundabout route and a steep climb back out.

Buses run from La Esperanza to Yamaranguila daily (US$0.35, 20 minutes, every one to 1½ hours, 6am to 5pm). They return at the same frequency from 6am to 2pm.

Valle de Azacualpa

If you have a car – or better yet, a mountain bike – a great way to spend a day is exploring the Valle de Azacualpa, a fertile rolling valley over 300 hectares big and only a short distance from La Esperanza. The valley is mostly populated with Lenca families who get by on farming and *tejido y hilado* (weaving and stitch work), the latter aimed at their neighbors as much as visitors. That's because Lenca women here wear traditional clothing, including brilliant pink, blue and scarlet blouses and equally bright headscarves. Driving or riding through the valley, it is common to see women working in the fields, their distinctive clothing set against the dark browns and greens of the landscape.

Following Calle Azacualpa out of town, you'll pass Cicai (p171); 6.5km later you'll reach a fork in the road. Turning right, the road winds 2.5km through fringe forest and beside fields and flower nurseries, to **Laguna Chiligatoro**, a pretty little pond with a stout white church just beyond. On Sundays after service, the grounds are a sea of color, filled with churchgoers in traditional clothing. Another 4km brings you to the hamlet of **Cacao**, where a local cooperative produces handkerchiefs, tablecloths and other woven items. There's no formal store or workshop, but a *pulpería* on the left is run by one of the cooperative's member families, who may show you their modest loom and supply of products. More importantly, it's a chance to interact with local residents; other families are nearby. From Cacao, the road continues into the mountains, growing steeper and rougher until only 4WDs can reliably pass to the community of Río Grande. **Cascada Río Grande** is an impressive 60m waterfall a short distance from town. The view is even better if you hire a local to show you the way to the bottom.

The road makes a long rough loop, but for most it's easier to turn around at Cacao and head to **Cerro de los Hoyos**. The 'Hill of Holes' is a tree-covered hill pocked with holes, more like wells, 1m wide and up to 20m deep – keep your eyes on the ground when you walk! No one seems to know who made them or why, or even when, but scratching away some of the topsoil reveals a clue: obsidian. The hill seems to be a huge bubble of volcanic glass, and the holes may have been used to gather large, unbroken pieces. The hill is near the hamlet of Los Olivos, about 10km (and three turnoffs) down the left-hand fork back at the first intersection – ask as you go, it's part of the fun.

MARCALA
pop 10,388

Marcala, the southern end of the Ruta Lenca, is a quiet mountain town with a strong indigenous history and character. The town is known for producing world-class coffee beans. In fact, coffee from Macala was the first in Central America to receive the prestigious 'Denomination of Origin' stamp, protecting the authenticity of beans from this region. An organic coffee and produce cooperative – the first of its kind in Honduras – offers tours of its member plantations and processing plants. There are a few mildly interesting hikes in the area, as well.

Orientation

There are no street names in Marcala, but you can orient yourself according to the tourist kiosk in parque central: it's on the southeast corner.

Information

There are no ATMs in Marcala; the nearest one is in La Esperanza.

Banco de Occidente (⌚ 8:30-4pm Mon-Fri, to noon Sat) Two blocks north of parque central; exchanges US dollars only.

Clínica Moreno (☎ 764 5478; ⌚ 9am-9pm Mon-Sat, to 2pm Sun) Medical clinic near the police station.

Farmacia Lamar (☎ 764 5214; ⌚ 8am-8:30pm) One block north of parque central.

Global Online (☎ 764 5562; per hr US$0.95; ⌚ 7am-9pm) Internet access; half a block west of parque central.

Hondutel (☎ 764 5398; ⌚ 7am-9pm) On the main road into town; calls (per minute) to the US and Canada cost US$0.11, to Europe US$2.32, and to Australia and New Zealand US$2.12.

Lavandería Bourcas (⌚ 8am-6pm Mon-Fri, 8am-noon Sat) Charges by the piece; typically US$3 to US$5 per load; 1½ blocks north of parque central.

Police (☎ 764 5715; ⌚ 24hr) Across the street from the Biblioteca Municipal (public library). Five blocks northeast of parque central.

Post office (⌚ 8am-noon & 2-4pm Mon-Fri, 8am-noon Sat) On the main road into town.

Tourist office (Parque Central; ⌚ 8am-noon & 1-4pm, closed Wed) Kiosk with helpful staff offering information, brochures and maps on area sights. English is spoken.

Sights & Activities

The tourist office has pamphlets describing eight different hikes in the area as well as detailed descriptions of getting there and back.

Among the options is **La Estanzuela**, a short hike to a pretty waterfall and swimming area, and a large cavern (La Cueva del Gigante) with a few prehistoric paintings on its walls 1km further. By bus, it's a 2.2km walk to the town of La Estanzuela and another 2km to the falls. With a car, you should have enough time to combine this with the nearby **Cascada de Santa Rita** or **La Isla** hikes.

RAOS (☎ 764 5181, 911 5315; cooperativaraos@yahoo .com; ⌚ 8am-noon & 1-4pm Mon-Fri, 8am-noon Sat), half a block north of parque central, is Honduras' first organic farming cooperative. RAOS produces mainly coffee, but also lettuce, squash and other vegetables. **Finca tours** (per person US$5-13.50) include visiting two to three plantations, learning about organic farming and talking to the farmers. From November to March, you can visit the *beneficio húmedo* (wet processing plant, where coffee beans are depulped) and the *beneficio seco* (dry processing plant, where the beans are dried before toasting). The tour can also include a lunch break at El

Chiflador waterfall. Stop by the RAOS office or tourist information kiosk to arrange a visit.

Festivals & Events

The long-shelved **Feria de Café** was resuscitated in 2006 by local coffee producers and the municipal tourism committee. Held at the beginning of April, festival-goers can partake in coffee-tasting competitions, check out displays on the picking and processing of coffee, and buy some great coffee too. The *fiesta patronal* (patron saint festival) is held during the last two weeks of September.

Sleeping & Eating

Hotel Jerusalén Medina (☎ 764 5909; r/tw US$11/ 13.25; P) This two-story motel has several simple, clean rooms with private hot-water bathroom, a fan and cable TV. A huge gated parking lot makes it popular with truckers. It's two long blocks east of parque central.

Hotel San Miguel (☎ 754 5793; r US$8; P) Near the police station, this hotel's small, clean rooms (with one queen or two twin beds) open onto a dirt courtyard that doubles as a parking lot. Rooms have private hot-water bathrooms and cable TV – an unexpectedly good deal. There's also a small café (mains US$1 to US$3), open for breakfast, lunch and dinner, that serves good, cheap *típica*.

Casa Gloria (☎ 764 5869; mains US$3-6; lunch & dinner) Sure it's *comida a la vista* (buffet), but Casa Gloria is still the most pleasant of Marcala's eating options, occupying a high-ceilinged colonial-style building right on parque central. A large and ever-changing selection of lunch and dinner options, from fried eggs to stewed chicken, are served

from a colorful serving area in front and eaten in the main dining room or at a small patio-bar area in back.

Restaurante Riviera Linda (☎ 764 5630; mains US$1.50-5; breakfast, lunch & dinner) One block north of parque central, this airy restaurant comes with an extensive menu – you'll find everything from sandwiches to chop suey here. The food is just OK and the service frustratingly slow, but there are only so many options in town.

Centro Comercial Junior (8am-6:30pm Mon-Sat, to 5pm Sun) A good-sized supermarket with all the basics and then some. It's on the main drag into town, one block north of parque central.

Mercado de Marcala (7am-4pm Mon-Sat, 7am-noon Sun) Near Hondutel and the supermarket, this market sells a good variety of fruits, vegetables and grains.

Shopping

RAOS (☎ 764 5181, 911 5315; cooperativaraos@yahoo .com; 8am-noon & 1-4pm Mon-Fri, 8am-noon Sat) In addition to offering tours of its coffee plantations, this organic farming cooperative has a small office and storefront just north of parque central where you can buy great organic coffee, honey, fruit and veggies, and so-so *artesanía*.

Artesanía de la Ruta Lenca (☎ 393 9061; 8am-noon & 1-6pm) One block east of parque central, this folk-art store has a little of everything from the Lenca region (and some from beyond).

Getting There & Away

Buses leave from various points, but all pass the Texaco gas station at the east end of the main road in and out of town, making it a

---

GETTING TO PERQUÍN, EL SALVADOR

There's twice-daily bus service to Perquín, El Salvador (US$2.50, three hours, 5am and noon) continuing to San Miguel, El Salvador (US$3.50, five hours). Unfortunately, due to a long-standing border dispute, there is no Salvadoran immigration post at this border. This may not be a problem if you are only interested in going to Perquín and coming back the same way – technically you will be in El Salvador illegally, but it is unlikely you'll be checked and several travelers and Peace Corps volunteers have reported doing this with no problem. However, if you plan to travel further into El Salvador or leave from a different border, you may be fined for having entered illegally once your status is discovered – even going directly to the immigration office in San Miguel or San Salvador won't help. The only sure alternative is to exit or enter through another location, ie El Amatillo. That said, definitely ask in Marcala about the latest – local businesses and NGOs on both sides of the border frequently lobby the Salvadoran government to rectify the situation.

good de facto bus stop. Buses to El Salvador leave from behind the *alcaldía*.

Tegucigalpa Transportes Lila US$3.50, 3½ to four hours, 4:30am, 5:30am, 8:45am, 10:30am, 1:30pm and 2pm; Transportes Vanesa US$3, 3½ to four hours, 5:50am

San Pedro Sula Transportes Lila US$4, five hours, 5:15am; Transportes Vanesa US$4, five hours, 4:45am

Comayagua US$2.25, three hours, 6:30am, 8am, 11am, 1pm and 3pm

La Esperanza (US$1.50, 1½ to two hours, 6:30am and 8:30am, plus 7:30am Saturday and Sunday

La Paz US$2, two hours, 7:15am to 3:45pm, eight departures daily

THE WESTERN CORRIDOR

The western corridor stretches 241km along the Valle de Comayagua between Tegucigalpa and San Pedro Sula. It's a four-hour bus trip, passing Comayagua, Siguatepeque, Parque Nacional Cero Azul Meámbar and Lago de Yojoa along the way. Also on this route are turnoffs for two archaeological sites, two cave systems, the thermal waters at Azacualpa, the colonial region around Santa Bárbara, and the national park of the same name. In short, there's a lot to do.

This region has long been an important commercial corridor. Settled at least 3000 years ago, it was an important trading route for early indigenous groups. Today, the valley is transected by the ever-improving CA-5 Hwy, the jugular vein of the Honduran economy, connecting the country's two largest cities, its government and business capitals, even – extending the route to its natural ends – the Pacific and the Atlantic.

LAGO DE YOJOA

Honduras' largest natural lake and surely its most beautiful, Lago de Yojoa (89 sq km) is slowly emerging as a new tourism nexus in Honduras. It has long been a favorite among bird-watchers, who have recorded over 375 species around the lake. The lake is also a good base for exploring two national parks: Cerro Azul Meámbar, with well-marked, moderately challenging trails, and Santa Bárbara, with the country's second-highest peak and an adventurous two-day hike to the summit. A number of easy day trips are also possible, including boat rides

on the lake, a Lenca eco-archaeological site, and the impressive Pulhapanzak Falls.

Orientation

Lago de Yojoa is 157km north of Tegucigalpa and 84km south of San Pedro Sula. Peña Blanca (pop 3662), a small town near the lake's north shore, is the best place to base yourself, with two adequate hotels in town and several better options a short distance away. From the CA-5 Hwy, the turnoff to Peña Blanca is 200m north of the town of La Guama – look sharp, as it's very easy to miss.

Information

Most of the lake region's basic services are in Peña Blanca, 15km northwest from the highway turnoff at La Guama.

Asociación de Municipios del Lago de Yojoa y su Área de Influencia (Amuprolago; ☎ 988 2300; www .lagodeyojoa.info; CA-5 Hwy; ☼ 8am-4pm Mon-Fri) Detailed information about the lake and the surrounding area; guide services can be arranged with advance notice. An excellent glossy map of the area is also for sale (US$1). It's 300m south of Honduyate Marina.

Banco Occidental (Peña Blanca; ☼ 8am-3:30pm Mon-Fri, to noon Sat) No ATM or currency exchange. At the eastern end of Calle Principal.

Clínica Santa Cecelia (☎ 650 0010; ☼ 24hr) Medical clinic near the turnoff to Los Naranjos.

Medicinas Marantina (☎ 650 0106; Peña Blanca; ☼ 8am-5pm) At the western end of Calle Principal.

Peña Blanc@net Café (Peña Blanca; per hr US$0.70; ☼ 8am-9pm) At the western end of Calle Principal; web-based calls (per minute) to the USA and Canada are US$0.21, and to Europe and Australia US$0.27.

Police (Peña Blanca; ☎ 650 0026; ☼ 24hr) Opposite Hotel La Maranata.

Sights & Activities

Besides what's listed here, Lago de Yojoa is also a good jumping-off point for Cerro Azul Meámbar and Santa Bárbara national parks.

PARQUE ECO-ARQUEOLÓGICO DE LOS NARAJOS

On the northwest side of the lake, the **Parque Eco-Arqueológico de los Naranjos** (☎ 650 0004; admission US$5; ☼ 8am-4pm) is a Lencan archaeological site dating to approximately 700 BC. The ruins themselves are not terribly interesting; they're made of clay so have only been semi-excavated (to protect them from environmental damage). The main reason to visit, however, is the wildlife. The park has 6km of trails that wind through the forest over hanging bridges and on a lakeside boardwalk, providing fantastic opportunities for spotting birds. A small museum at the visitors center gives a general overview of Lencan civilization, which is mildly interesting. The park is 5km south of Peña Blanca.

BOATING ON LAGO DE YOJOA

If you have a hankering to get on the lake, Robert Dale at D&D Bed & Breakfast (☎ 994 9719) can arrange for you to rent a **rowboat** (per day US$2.25) from a local fisher-

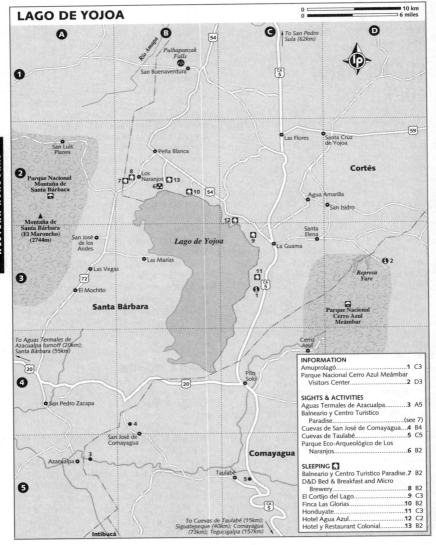

LAGO DE YOJOA

0 — 10 km
0 — 6 miles

INFORMATION
Amuprolagó...1 C3
Parque Nacional Cerro Azul Meámbar
    Visitors Center..2 D3

SIGHTS & ACTIVITIES
Aguas Termales de Azacualpa.............3 A5
Balneario y Centro Turistico
    Paradise..(see 7)
Cuevas de San José de Comayagua...4 B4
Cuevas de Taulabé................................5 C5
Parque Eco-Arqueológico de Los
    Naranjos..6 B2

SLEEPING
Balneario y Centro Turistico Paradise.7 B2
D&D Bed & Breakfast and Micro
    Brewery...8 B2
El Cortijo del Lago.................................9 C3
Finca Las Glorias................................10 B2
Honduyate...11 C3
Hotel Agua Azul..................................12 C2
Hotel y Restaurant Colonial..............13 B2

VISITING THE PULHAPANZAK FALLS

Centro Turístico Pulhapanzak (☎ 995 1010; admission US$1.60; ☯ 6am-6pm) is a magnificent 43m waterfall on the Río Amapa surrounded by a lush and well-kept park. This is a popular swimming spot, and there also are guides who will take visitors to a small cave behind the falls. It takes just a few minutes to get there – and anyone can do it – but it feels like something out of Indiana Jones: jumping off boulders, swimming across roiling pools, inching around rocks amid a maelstrom of crashing water and swirling air, and finally squeezing up the narrow passage into the cave. There's no set price, but it's worth a good tip: US$2 to US$3 per person is fair.

If you like it enough to stay, there is a simple **hospedaje** (r US$21.25). If you bring gear, **camping** (per person US$1.60) is permitted in a grassy area surrounded by *monticulos* (unexcavated pre-Columbian mounds). For meals, a simple eatery (mains US$2 to US$4) serves *típica* and snacks until nightfall.

From Peña Blanca or Los Naranjos catch any San Pedro Sula bus (or pickup headed in that direction) and ask to be let off at the San Buenaventura turnoff (10km). From there, it's a little more than a kilometer down a dirt road to the village and the falls just beyond.

---

man. For another US$2.25, a kid will come along to row, and if you arrange it for the early morning, he'll be able to guide you to the best places to see birds.

Hotel Agua Azul (☎ 991 7244) rents out **kayaks** (per hour single/double US$5.50/8) as well as **pedal boats** (4-person maximum, per hour US$11). If you want a little more wind in your hair, the hotel also can arrange for a **guided motor boat tour** (5-person maximum, per hour US$18.50) of the lake.

Ask at either place about including fishing in your boat trip. The lake is famous for its bass.

BALNEARIO Y CENTRO TURÍSTICO PARADISE

Almost 5km south of Peña Blanca, the **Balneario y Centro Turístico Paradise** (☎ 357 0469; ☯ daylight hours) is a beautiful coffee and flower plantation with a river running through it. It doubles as a recreational area with picnic spots and plenty of swimming holes to jump into the cool, refreshing river. Although it's free most of the year (a small admission is charged during Semana Santa), it's far enough off the beaten track to keep visitors to a minimum. There are also a few rooms for overnight guests.

AGUAS TERMALES DE AZACUALPA

Most hot springs are a trickle of hot water burbling quietly out of a rock, but not at **Aguas Termales de Azacualpa** (☯ 7am-5pm; admission US$0.55; Ⓟ). Here, superheated water spits and boils out from the ground – one spot whistles like a teapot. A natural stone

arch over the site conveniently contains the thick sulfurous steam, and there's a makeshift sauna made of tarp if you really want to sweat. The water streams into the nearby Río Jaitique, forming shifting semi-hot pools. Upstream are large swimming holes flanked by high stone cliffs that are perfect for cooling off – there's even a wee sandy beach. Parking costs US$2.25.

From the hot springs it's possible to **hike** to caves on the Río Ulua. Ask the attendant about guides.

A Honduran NGO has a large dorm and camping area next to the hot springs; if it's not being used, the caretaker, Juan Ramón Henríquez, aka Muncho (☎ 608 9781), will let you camp (per tent US$4.25). He is also building two adobe casitas (small houses) to rent, which should be ready by the time you read this. On the other side of Azacualpa, 1km from town, the **Centro Turística Acosta** (☎ 608 7204; admission US$0.50) has cabins in the works, plus three very nice swimming pools (use of pools US$1) and a soccer field with sheep grazing on it.

Azacualpa is 25km southwest of Pito Solo, at the southeastern edge of Lago de Yojoa; the springs are a 1.5km walk from town. To get to Azacualpa, catch a *rapidito* (microbus) at Pito Solo. They generally leave at 8:30am, 11am and 1pm (US$1.25, 45 minutes). Others go as far as Zacapa, where you may be able to hitch the rest of the way.

Buses from San Pedro Sula pass Pito Solo around 2:30pm and 5:30pm, and there's direct service from Santa Bárbara. To return, buses leave Azacualpa for San Pedro Sula at 6:30am and noon, and for Santa Bárbara at 6:30am and 8am. You may also be able to hitch to the Santa Bárbara–Pito Solo road, where the last bus to Santa Bárbara passes the turnoff at 5:30pm, and the last to Pito Solo at 3pm.

Sleeping & Eating
AROUND THE LAKE
D&D Bed & Breakfast and Micro Brewery (☎ 994 9719; dndbrew@yahoo.com; camp sites/hammock per person US$2.25, s/d US$8.50/11.75, tw cabins US$17, with Jacuzzi US$20, extra person US$2.25; P 🐕) American Robert Dale says he started D&D because he wanted a place to get a real hamburger and a real beer, and listen to good music. He's done all that and added rooms for travelers of various budgets: hammocks and campsites, simple cement rooms, and newer cabins that sleep up to four. Add a small clean pool and lush grounds and it's no wonder D&D has such a loyal clientele. The beer is home brewed, by the way, and the restaurant menu goes way beyond burgers: try the tilapia (a type of fish) for dinner and the blueberry pancakes for breakfast. D&D is off the road to El Mochito.

Hotel Agua Azul (☎ 991 7244; hotelaquaazul@emv .hn; r with fan/air-con US$20/29, 2-bedroom cabin US$35.75; P 🐕) Past its glory days but still just fine, Agua Azul offers simple wood cabins with painted cement floors and no view. Considering it's right on the lake, it seems like an architectural blunder but perhaps the point is to have guests enjoy the views from the pool, the excellent restaurant (mains US$2.50 to US$7), or from a boat on the lake itself. It's 3km from the highway on the north side of the lake.

Balneario y Centro Turístico Paradise (☎ 357 0469; r US$18.50-37; P 🐕) A beautiful coffee and flower plantation that doubles as a recreational area, the Paradise, 2.7km south of Peña Blanca, has two bungalows on stilts with glorious views over the *finca*, each with a small lounge, cable TV and hot-water bathroom. There are rooms in the main house but they're not much value: worn and a bit forgotten. If you have gear, ask about camping on-site, as the management occasionally allows it.

Hotel y Restaurante Colonial (☎ 380 5266; s/d US$16/21.25; P 🐕 🐕) One kilometer from Parque Eco-Arqueológico Los Naranjos,

this brand-new hotel is good for birders who want to be at the park at dawn. Five smallish but comfortable rooms have gleaming hot-water bathrooms and cable TV. A teeny, immaculate pool faces the driveway, but is refreshing nonetheless. The restaurant serves mostly Mexican dishes.

Hotel Finca Las Glorias (☎ 566 0461; www.hotel lasglorias.com; r US$40-50, ste US$56, cabins US$110-150; P) One of the best-known resorts on the lake, Las Glorias caters to large groups, with large comfortable cabins and a slew of activities like boating, biking, horseback riding, volleyball and a huge new water park (US$5). Solo travelers or couples have better options elsewhere.

El Cortijo del Lago (☎ 608 2901; johnachater@ yahoo.com; dm US$5.50, cabañas US$11-16, r US$22-27) The grounds are the highlight here: right on the lake, carpeted with pine needles, with canoes and sailboats available for rent. The dorms are simple and clean with bunks and cots. Upstairs, rooms are plain for the price but share a great sunroom overlooking the lake. The rest feel half-done, especially those in a strange octagonal building. El Cortijo is 2km from La Guama turnoff.

Honduyate (☎ 990 9387; www.honduyatemarina.net; CA-5 Hwy; r US$70, extra person US$10; P 🐕 🖥 🐕) Catering to the yacht-owning crowd, rooms here are large and clean, with amenities like air-con and TVs with DVDs, but the décor is seriously foofy and the prices high, especially given what's available elsewhere around the lake. The restaurant (mains US$4 to US$10) and bar, open 9am to 7pm Sunday to Thursday, and to 10pm Friday and Saturday, can be lively and popular; there's also a public internet café.

PEÑA BLANCA
Hotel La Finca (☎ 650 0131; www.hotellasglorias.com; r/tw US$13.25/18.50; P) A sister hotel to Finca Las Glorias, this is the better of the two options in Peña Blanca proper. Occupying a converted townhouse, with a large yard and fountain as remnants of a more glamorous youth, the hotel has six comfortable but plain rooms and a common area with sofas. Reception is in the pill-box office at the entrance.

Hotel La Maranata (☎ 650 0160; r with/without bathroom US$11/5.50) The cheapest rooms in town are about what you'd expect – small, spongy beds and cold-water bathrooms –

but adequate and convenient if you're on a tight budget.

La Copaneca (mains US$1-3; ☽ breakfast, lunch & dinner) A few tables set up in the front room of this family home, at the western end of Calle Principal, make up a good *pupusería* and *típica* eatery. Food is abundant and cheap.

Mini-Super Eben Ezer (☽ 7am-6:30pm) is a very well stocked minimart where the road to El Mochito meets the Calle Principal.

Getting There & Away

From San Pedro Sula, the 'El Mochito' bus passes through Peña Blanca – get off there for hotels in town, or catch a second bus toward La Guama and hotels along the lake (US$0.50, 10 minutes, every 20 minutes). For D&D and Balneario y Centro Turístico Paradise, stay on the Mochito bus past Los Naranjos to the signed access road. The last bus back to San Pedro Sula leaves at 4:30pm.

From the CA-5 Hwy, ask the bus driver to let you off at the *desvío* (turnoff) to Peña Blanca – it's just north of La Guama and very easy to miss. From there, buses to Peña Blanca run until 5pm. To get to D&D or Balneario y Centro Turístico Paradise, take a cab from Peña Blanca (US$0.25 to the access road, US$1 to their front gates).

To access Parque Nacional Santa Bárbara, take a bus from Peña Blanca to San Luis Planes (US$0.80, one to 1½ hours, 10:30am only) or to Los Andes.

PARQUE NACIONAL CERRO AZUL MEÁMBAR

Just east of Lago de Yojoa, Parque Nacional Cerro Azul Meámbar (Panacam) is easily one of the country's best-equipped – and most underappreciated – national parks. A lush cloud forest measuring 312 sq km and reaching 2074m at its highest point, the park is a key source of the region's water, providing 70% of Lago de Yojoa's water, 20% of Francisco Morazán hydroelectric reserve, and drinking water for over 40 communities. All that water means waterfalls, green surroundings and lots of wildlife, including over 334 species of birds. Add some 15km of well-maintained hiking trails, an excellent visitors center (including guest rooms and a *comedor*), affordable fees and relatively easy access, and you have a true gem of a park.

Information

A US$1 park fee is payable at the **visitors center** (☎ 608 5510, in Tegucigalpa 773 2027; www .paghonduras.org/pancam.html). Staffers are very knowledgeable and can help arrange guide services (US$8 to US$11). There's also a rudimentary but useful trail map available.

A second entrance is planned for the small community of Cerro Azul, 7km east of the main highway. The turnoff is 5km south of Lago de Yojoa, marked by a sign for the national park; one bus passes daily (US$0.50, 15 minutes, noon) and hitching is easy. A 10km trail, due to be completed in 2008, will connect the two entrances. There are basic accommodations in Cerro Azul; ask at the coffee *pulpería* in the center of town.

Hiking

The park has three main trails totaling 15km. They form intersecting loops, making it possible to hike on several without returning to the visitors center. The intersections are mostly well marked and the trail map is handy in clearing up any confusion.

Sendero El Sinai (8km, about four hours) is the hardest of the three trails, climbing from 750m at the visitors center to the system's highest point (1060m). The trail can be hiked in either direction; making a counterclockwise loop, it starts out with a moderate incline, up to an observation tower. Then it turns much steeper, shadowing a river (you'll cross at least four bridges) to Cascada El Sinai, a pretty 10m waterfall at about the 90-minute mark. As tempting as it will be, swimming is not allowed as the water is used for drinking. From the waterfall, the trails climbs more evenly, cresting at 1060m in about an hour. Heading down you'll come to a mirador (975m) with terrific views of Lago de Yojoa, the Represa Yure (Río Yure Dam), and the surrounding countryside. A steep winding descent follows; just before the visitors center you'll intersect with Sendero El Venado – turn left for that trail, or right to return to the center.

Sendero El Venado is only 1.2km long but it's moderately difficult. Following it

GONE SPELUNKIN'

South of Lago de Yojoa are two caves systems, one very well developed, the other down and dirty.

The **Cuevas de Taulabé** (CA-5 Hwy, Km 140; adult/child incl guide US$2/0.55; ☺ 8am-5pm), located alongside the highway, 25km north of Siguatepeque, were discovered in 1969 when the highway was being built, and have been explored to a depth of 12km, with no end in sight. The first several hundred meters have lights and a cement pathway; guides lead you on a 30-minute tour, describing the formation of the cave and pointing out stalagmites and stalactites with recognizable shapes (Jesus, Buddha etc). Tipping the guide is customary; for a bit extra, they'll take you to deeper, less-visited areas.

Not far away, **Cuevas de San José de Comayagua** are two completely undeveloped caves. The first cave has a narrow crawl-through entrance, with spectacular stalactites and stalagmites. The second has a dramatic high-ceilinged entrance, huge formations and a crystalline river through the middle, which you have to wade through in places (1m to 1¼m deep). You can explore 300m into each cave; the first has no bats, the second does. Guides are required; tours (US$10, one to three people) last four hours, including two hours' hiking and an hour in each cave. The trip can also include lunch and a stop at a swimming hole on the Río Jaitique (extra US$5 per person). Flashlights, a hard hat, gloves and rope are provided; wear shoes that can get wet. The caves are 3km from the town of San José de Comayagua, which can be reached by bus from Taulabé (45 to 60 minutes, several departures daily) or by hitching. This same road connects with the thermal waters in Azacualpa. **Daniel Espinoza García** (☎ 922 0232; dedaniesp@yahoo .com) is one of several guides; the 20-something is also San José's vice-mayor and can often be found at the city hall.

clockwise, the trail intersects with the end of the Sinai trail, climbing through predominantly secondary forest before intersecting with the Sinai trail again, this time the first part. Continuing straight on, you'll descend steeply to the river, where the trail dead-ends into the third trail, Sendero Los Vensejos.

Turning left, you'll cross a hanging bridge to Cascada Los Vensejos, a small falls pouring from a stone chasm into a welcoming pool. This one you can swim in – there's even a makeshift changing area. The other direction is the first part of Sendero Los Vensejos, which loops around less than 1km before emerging at the visitors center playing field.

Sleeping & Eating

The accommodations here are among the best in the country's national-park system. Visitors can choose between simple and spotless **cabins** (US$5.50 per person) with bunk beds, hot-water bathrooms, and linens (and even soap); or **camping** (US$1 per person) on a grassy field overlooking a beautiful valley. The visitors center also rents camping gear (US$1.60 per night for a tent and sleeping bag) and sells basic toiletries.

The park can provide meals in the cafeteria as long as two prerequisites are met: at least seven people are interested and advance notice is given. That probably means you're on your own for food. Plan to bring your own eats and either enjoy them raw or rent the cafeteria kitchen (US$8 per day) to cook them up.

Getting There & Away

The park entrance is at the end of a dirt road that starts at La Guama, just off CA-5 Hwy. Pickups typically head part of the way up every five to 11 minutes (6am to 7pm), shuttling locals to their villages. For a sure bet, call Junior Molina (☎ 924 8448), who regularly takes visitors to the park in his van. The one-way trip costs US$8 per vanload (up to 15 people).

An alternative entrance is being established from the town of Cerro Azul (p179), along the southwestern edge of the park.

PARQUE NACIONAL MONTAÑA DE SANTA BÁRBARA

Overlooking Lago de Yojoa, the Parque Nacional Montaña de Santa Bárbara is home to the majestic Montaña de Santa Bárbara, or El Maroncho, as many locals call it. At 2744m, it is the second-highest peak in Honduras – and looks absolutely mammoth from afar. A protected area since 1987, the park is a 321 sq km combination of tropical, pine and cloud forest. It also is composed entirely of limestone – the only one of its size in Central America – which means there are lots of caves and tunnels, and no visible water at higher elevations, as it is absorbed by the porous rock.

The park is accessible through the villages of El Playón (southside), San Luis Planes (northside), and San José de los Andes (eastside) There is no direct access through the town of Santa Bárbara, but you can still catch a bus from there to one of the entry points.

Information

Santa Bárbara National Park does not have any tourist infrastructure – trails are unmarked, there are no campgrounds and no park services. But it is free.

For general information about the park, and for help with the logistics, contact Sandra Barahona in the Santa Bárbara **tourist office** (☎ 643 2338; turismosb@yahoo.com).

Hiking

There are several unmarked trails ranging in difficulty from intermediate to challenging. It takes most hikers two to three days to hit the summit, depending on where they enter the park. Along the way, visitors will have the opportunity to see almost four dozen orchid varieties, 407 bird species, 15 endemic plants, and animals like spider monkeys, anteaters and, if you're incredibly lucky, jaguars.

As there is only minimal development, a guide is essential. Fortunately, each of the three villages that border the park have highly recommended ones: Mario Orellana (☎ 904 4457) in El Playón; Adán Teruel (☎ 674 3304) in San Luis Planes; and Marcos Chavez in Los Andes. Most charge between US$8 to US$10 a day for their services; if you enjoy the trip, a tip is also appreciated.

Sleeping & Eating

Visitors have to bring their own gear and food to camp in the park. If you need equipment, Mario Orellana (☎ 904 4457) in El Playón rents tents and sleeping bags for a nominal fee. For food, its best to stock up in the villages before you head out; it's also customary to buy food for the guide.

Getting There & Away

To enter the park through El Playón, take a bus from Santa Bárbara (US$0.95, 45 to 60 minutes) at 6:30am, 11:30am and 2pm Monday to Saturday; it returns at 6:30am, 7:30am and 2pm. To San Luis Planes, a bus leaves from Peña Blanca at 10:30am daily (US$0.80, one to 1½ hours); to return, take the daily 6am bus back to Peña Blanca. There is also a bus from Santa Bárbara at 11:30am (US$1, 1½ to two hours); there is a return at 6:30am daily. Finally, to head into the park through Los Andes, take a bus from Peña Blanca.

TRINIDAD

pop 4308

The largest of the villages north of Santa Bárbara, Trinidad is a small colonial town with big-time charm – cobblestone streets, whitewashed homes and a beautiful old church. Be sure to check out the spectacular view from the hilltop cemetery. There

---

EXPLORING THE VILLAGES AROUND SANTA BÁRBARA

Several small towns between Santa Bárbara and the CA-4 Hwy are worth a short stop, whether for their *artesanía*, colonial churches or simple small-town appeal. Between Gualala and Ilama, several roadside *junco* (basket-weaving) stands have a good selection of hats, bags and hammocks.

- San José de los Colinas (22km from Santa Bárbara) is a picturesque village set in the hills and has one of the oldest churches in the country.
- Gualala (400m from CA-4 Hwy) features whitewashed homes with red-tile roofs, and lots of bougainvillea and *junco* products sold in front of local homes.
- Ilama (300m from CA-4 Hwy) is built into the hillside, and is bigger and less picturesque than other villages but has a few nice shops.

aren't many services in town, but you can check your email at **Tec@net** (☎ 608 2479; per hr US$1; ☻ 9:30am-9pm Mon-Fri, 9:30am-7pm Sun), three blocks west of parque central.

Sleeping & Eating

Hotel y Pulpería López (☎ 933 7814; Calle Principal; r with fan/air-con US$8/10.75; ☒) Two blocks behind the main church, this pleasant and clean hotel – the only one of its kind in town – has good beds, cable TV and spotless bathrooms.

Outside of town, **Estancia El Pedregal** (☎ 552 6359, 608 1150; www.estanciaelpedregal.com; r US$40-56; **P** ☒) is a comfortable lodge 7.5km up a dirt road from Hwy 20, with horseback riding and views of Pico Santa Bárbara.

For meals, stop in the modest *comedores* on parque central.

Getting There & Around

Buses traveling between Santa Bárbara and San Pedro Sula stop alongside the highway at the entrance to town. Once here, walk or use moto-taxis (in town US$0.30 per person, to El Pedregal US$11).

SANTA BÁRBARA
pop 15,431

About 53km west of Lago de Yojoa, Santa Bárbara, capital of the department of the same name, is a medium-sized colonial town known for its *junco* handicrafts. (It is not the jumping-off point for Parque Nacional Santa Bárbara, however.) The town has a pleasant old-fashioned air – many evenings, teenagers in school uniforms circle parque central in a courting ritual reminiscent of the 1950s.

As a point of reference, the cathedral is on the east side of parque central, Betty's is on the west.

History

Santa Bárbara was founded in 1761 by Spanish families from the towns of Gracias and Tencoa. Its residents are nicknamed *pateplumas* (winged feet), a reference to their speedy withdrawal into the mountains during the civil unrest that followed the dissolution of the Central American Federation in the late 1830s. Though the name was probably first used pejoratively, locals have embraced it as evidence of their peace-loving nature.

Information

The town maintains an impressive bilingual website (www.santabarbara.gob.hn) with history, photos and area attractions. Bus and events information is out of date, however.

Andromeda.com (☎ 643 2678; per hr US$1; ☻ 8am-9pm Mon-Sat, 8am-12:30pm Sun) Half a block south of the cathedral; web-based calls (per minute) to the USA and Canada cost US$0.13, to Europe US$0.26, and to Australia US$0.53.

Banco Atlántida (☻ 8:30am-3:30pm Mon-Fri, to 11:30am Sat) Half a block north of the cathedral; traveler's checks are exchanged and there's a 24-hour ATM on-site.

Farmacia Santa Bárbara (☎ 643 2022; ☻ 8am-9pm Mon-Fri, to noon Sat) Across from the Universidad Tecnológica de Honduras.

Hondutel (☻ 7am-noon, 12:30-5pm & 5:30-9pm) Next to the post office.

Hospital Integrado Santa Bárbara (☎ 643 2721; ☻ 24hr) At the entrance to town.

Police (☎ 643 2647, 643 2120) Downhill from parque central.

Post office (☻ 8am-4pm Mon-Fri, 8-11:30am Sat) One block south of the cathedral.

Tourist office (☎ 643 2338; turismosb@yahoo.com; ☻ 8am-noon & 2-5pm Mon-Sat, 8am-noon Sun) Two blocks east of parque central; has good information on area sites, including Parque Nacional Santa Bárbara.

Sights & Activities

Santa Bárbara's colonial parque central is the heart of the town, with a strikingly white church and a number of popular eateries around its edges.

It's definitely not a reason to stop in Santa Bárbara, but if you're in town and can't stand the heat, visit **Balneario La Torre** (☎ 643 2440; adult/child US$2.25/1.15; ☻ 7am-6pm Sat & Sun), three blocks east of parque central. It has three river-fed public pools – two kiddie, one adult – that get packed with people. Arrive early before the water gets murky.

To get sweeping views of the valley, head to **Castillo Bográn** (2.8km southeast of town), a steep hike to the shell of what was once a colonial-style building. The property itself is enclosed in barbed-wire and the structure isn't particularly interesting but the view is nice. Be sure to bring a hat and bottled water – there's little shade and no *pulperías* along the way.

Sleeping

Gran Hotel Colonial (☎ 643 2665; r with fan/air-con US$12/18, new bldg r/tw with air-con US$24.50/29.25;

P X) Most travelers who stay in Santa Bárbara end up here – while no Ritz, it's an affordable, reliable choice close to the center, with enclosed parking if you have a car. Rooms in the new building are larger and have better bathrooms, but are not necessarily worth the extra cash. It's 1½ blocks east of parque central.

Hotel Ejecutivo (☎ 643 2206; s/d/tr with fan US$11/16/19) Next to the Junqueños bus stop, this quiet hotel feels as much like a home as a hotel. Rooms are simple and clean, with fans and cable TV but no hot water. The best part: the hotel reception doubles as an ice-cream shop, so all guests get a free cone, 1L of water and a juice box. Thanks, Mom!

Hotel Boarding House Moderno (☎ 643 2203; Calle El Progresso; s/d with fan US$8/12, with air-con 13.25/19; P X) This old-fashioned hotel has a spacious tiled lobby and large, rather plain rooms. Beds and bathrooms could use a face-lift, but overall it's a fine option. Upstairs rooms are a bit cheerier.

Eating

Mesón Casa Blanca (mains US$2.50-4.50; ☾ breakfast, lunch & dinner) With a converted living room that has knick-knacks galore, a couple of mounted deer heads, oil paintings and plants, this colonial-style restaurant is known as one of the best in town. Food is *típica* and served buffet-style for lunch and à la carte for breakfast and dinner. If it looks closed, just ring the bell; someone is almost always home. It's three blocks southeast of parque central.

Cafetería y Repostería Betty's (☎ 643 3006; Parque Central; mains US$1-2.50; ☾ breakfast, lunch & dinner) An air-conditioned hole-in-the-wall, Betty's has quick service, huge portions and cheap food. If you see an open table, nab it; otherwise take your order to go and enjoy it in parque central.

Behind the cathedral, the **Mercado Municipal** (☾ 6am-5pm Mon-Sat, to noon Sun) is a rambling city market with a huge variety of fruit and vegetable stands, butcher shops and household wares. You'll also find an entire clothing and shoe section.

Drinking & Entertainment

Billares Berpsha (☾ 10am-10pm Mon-Fri, 8am-10pm Sat & Sun) Definitely a guy's guy scene – pool halls generally are in Honduras – but if

you're looking to shoot a game or two, this is a relatively friendly place for travelers to go. Heck, at US$0.15 per game, play a whole dollar's worth. It's behind the cathedral.

Getting There & Away

Los Junqueños (☎ 643 2113) buses to Tegucigalpa leave from 1½ blocks north of the plaza, past Banco Atlántida. All other buses leave from or near the main terminal, a block west of parque central. Buses go to various destinations, including the following:

Tegucigalpa US$5.30, four hours, Los Junqueños has two to three morning departures and one 2:30pm departure

San Pedro Sula *directo* US$2.25, 1½ hours, 8am-5am, every 30 minutes; *ordinario* US$1.85, two hours, 4am to 5pm, every 30 minutes

Santa Bárbara National Park El Playón US$0.95, 45 to 60 minutes, 6:30am, 11:30am and 2pm Monday to Saturday; San Luís Planes US$1, 1½ to two hours, 11:30am

Azacualpa/Aguas Termales US$1.25, 1½ hours, 10am and 4pm, or take a Tegus-bound bus and transfer; be sure to take the bus to Azacualpa, Zacapa, not Azacualpa, Valle

Copán Ruínas or **Santa Rosa de Copán** take an *ordinario* toward San Pedro Sula and transfer at La Ceibita

Ilama US$0.50, 30 minutes, 6:30am to 9:30pm, until 5pm Saturday and Sunday, every 15 minutes

Colinas US$0.55, last at 7pm, every 15 minutes, take any Ilama bus and transfer

SIGUATEPEQUE

pop 44,192

Siguatepeque is about halfway between Tegucigalpa (117km) and San Pedro Sula (124km) – a two-hour drive in either direction. There's no real reason to stop in here, frankly, except if it's getting late and you want to get off the road. If you want to break up the trip between Tegucigalpa and San Pedro, Comayagua is a more pleasant stop.

History

Siguatepeque was founded by Spanish colonists in 1689 as a center for religious and monastic training. Some of the vows were evidently optional though, as the town's population grew quickly from the extensive intermixing of colonists and Lencans. The name Siguatepeque reportedly means 'town

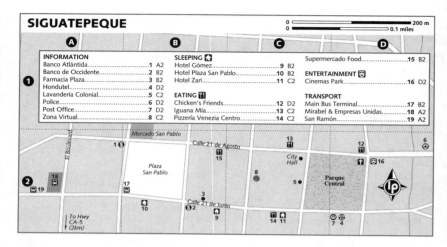

WESTERN HONDURAS

of beautiful women' in Nahuatl, which may have had something to do with it.

Orientation

Siguatepeque has two large plazas with the town's hotels, restaurants and services nearby. The pleasant parque central has trees and shady benches with a huge spider-like structure in the center. Plaza San Pablo, three blocks west, is ratty and unappealing and has been for years. Calle 21 de Junio and Calle 21 de Agosto connect the two.

Information

Banco Atlántida (Plaza San Pablo; ☒ 8:30am-3:30pm Mon-Fri, 8:30-11:30am Sat) Exchanges traveler's checks; ATM only accepts Visa/Plus cards.
Banco de Occidente (Plaza San Pablo; ☒ 8:30am-4:30pm Mon-Fri, to 11:30am Sat) One 24-hour ATM.
Farmacia Plaza (☎ 773 0259; Calle 21 de Junio; ☒ 7:30am-6pm Mon-Fri, 8am-noon Sat)
Hondutel (Parque Central; ☒ 7am-9pm)
Lavandería Colonial (Parque Central; per 10lb US$3; ☒ 7am-5pm Mon-Sat)
Police (☎ 773 0042; Calle 21 de Agosto; ☒ 24hr)
Post office (Parque Central; ☒ 8am-noon & 2-4pm Mon-Fri, 8am-noon Sat)
Zona Virtual (per hr US$0.80; ☒ 8am-8:30pm Mon-Sat) Internet access plus web-based calls.

Sleeping

Hotel Zari (☎ 773 0015; hotelzari@yahoo.com; Calle 21 de Junio; s/d US$8.50/12; P) The best value in town, this hotel near parque central offers good-sized but stark rooms that are spar-

kling clean. Each room has hot water, cable TV and a strong fan. Secure parking is also available. Service is friendly too.

Hotel Gómez (☎ 773 2868; Calle 21 de Junio; s/d US$8/12) Although it's showing some wear and tear, the Gomez is a clean place with decent beds and private bathrooms. There is secure courtyard parking, a cafeteria (mains US$1 to US$3) open for breakfast and dinner Monday to Saturday, and free drinking water. Not bad for a cheapie.

Hotel Plaza San Pablo (☎ 773 4020; www.hotel plazasanpablo.com; Plaza San Pablo; r with fan US$15.50, r/tw with air-con US$26.50/53; P ☒ 🖵) If you can get past the King Arthur castle motif, rooms here are really very comfortable and spacious with hot-water bathrooms and cable TV. It's popular with business travelers, so you'll need a reservation most weekdays.

Eating

Pizzería Venezia Centro (☎ 773 2999; Calle 21 de Junio; mains US$3-8; ☒ lunch & dinner) One of Siguatepeque's longest-running restaurants, the Venezia serves fresh, thick-crust pizzas with just about any combination of meats and veggies. A medium pie easily serves two (US$6), though you may find yourself wanting more.

Iguana Mía (☎ 773 4955; Calle 21 de Agosto; dishes US$2-6; ☒ breakfast, lunch & dinner) A favorite hangout of Siguatepeque's expatriate crowd, this reliable restaurant has colorful walls decorated with amateur celebrity portraits and Mexican travel posters – an odd combination until you see the menu: enchiladas and egg muffins, tortas and pancakes.

Chicken's Friends (☎ 773 1122; Parque Central; dishes US$2-3; ☺ lunch & dinner) Chicken could really use some new friends: the ones he's got let him get chopped up, fried and served to backpackers for three bucks a plate. (Pretty tasty, though.)

Entertainment
Cinemas Park (Parque Central; tickets US$1.75) Once-a-night shows start at 7:15pm.

Getting There & Away
Siguatepeque's buses leave from west of Plaza San Pablo. Most leave from a large walled lot at the corner of El Boulevard and Calle 21 de Junio, or just outside of it. You can also catch Tegucigalpa- and San Pedro Sula-bound buses at the highway.

Tegucigalpa US$2.25, 2½ hours, 5:15am to 5pm, hourly

San Pedro Sula US$2.50, 2¾ hours, 4:40am to 4:10pm, every 45 minutes

Comayagua US$1.05, 40 minutes, 6am to 5:15pm, every 15 minutes, use 'Directos Rapiditos'

La Esperanza US$2, 1½ hours, 5:30am & 7am, in front of the Hospedaje Central, a half-block from the terminal. After that, take a taxi (US$1) to La Esperanza turnoff, where buses leave at 8:30am, 9:30am, 11am and noon.

COMAYAGUA
pop 60,174

Comayagua, 84km northwest of Tegucigalpa, is the historic first capital of Honduras and was a religious and political center for over three centuries, until power shifted to Tegucigalpa in 1880. The town's colonial past is evident in its several fine old *iglesias*, an impressive cathedral, colonial plazas and two interesting museums. A very Catholic city, it's also considered the best place

in Honduras for visitors to witness Easter celebrations.

History
The city was founded as the capital of the colonial province of Honduras in 1537 by Spanish captain Alonso de Cáceres, fulfilling the orders of the Spanish governor of Honduras to establish a new settlement in the geographic center of the territory. The town was initially called Villa de Santa María de Comayagua; in 1543 the name was changed to Villa de la Nueva Valladolid de Comayagua.

Comayagua was declared a city in 1557, and in 1561 the seat of the diocese of Honduras was moved from Trujillo to Comayagua because of its more favorable conditions, central position and proximity to the silver- and gold-mining regions.

Orientation
As in most Honduran towns, life and essential services focus around parque central, which has been tastefully refurbished with gardens, benches and even piped-in music. Comayagua is a very walkable city, though the area between parque central and where most of the hotels are can feel very lonely after dark. Solo travelers, especially women, should consider taking a cab home if it's late.

Information
EMERGENCY
Police (☎ 772 3040; ☺ 24hr) At the eastern end of 5a Calle NO.
Red Cross (☎ 195, 772 1997; ☺ 24hr)

INTERNET ACCESS
Media Net (1a Av NO btwn 5a & 6a Calles NO; per hr US$0.65; ☺ 8am-9:30pm) Cheap web-based calls too.

LA PALMEROLA

Fifteen kilometers from Comayagua is the Soto Cano air base, better known as La Palmerola and a longtime nerve center of US military presence in Central America. Up to 2000 US soldiers were stationed here during the 1980s, when the US was waging the Contra war in Nicaragua. Since then, it's been converted to a Honduran base – on paper, anyway – and the force reduced to around 550 American soldiers. Periodic reports have called the mission at Soto Cano 'not critical,' but after the pullout of US forces from Panama in 1999, La Palmerola now represents the 'front-line' of US forces in the Americas. Far from scaling back, in 2005 the US Air Force underscored its intention to remain at La Palmerola by replacing hundreds of old soldier barracks with modern new apartments.

COMAYAGUA

0 — 400 m
0 — 0.2 miles

INFORMATION
Banco Atlántida...........................1 B3
Banco Atlántida...........................2 A3
Centro Médico Comayagua
    Colonial................................3 C2
Farmacia Santa Fe.....................4 C3
Hondutel.....................................5 C2
Lavandería Ebenezer.................6 C3
Media Net...................................7 B2
Police...8 C2
Post Office..................................9 C2
Tourist Office...........................10 B2

SIGHTS & ACTIVITIES
Catedral de la Inmaculada
    Concepción...........................11 B2
Iglesia Nuestra Señora de la La
    Caridad.................................12 A1
Iglesia Nuestra Señora de la
    Merced..................................13 C3
Iglesia San Sebastián..............14 D5
Iglesia y Ex-Convento de San
    Francisco...............................15 B2
Museo Colonial de Arte
    Religioso................................16 B3
Museo Regional de
    Arqueología..........................17 B2

SLEEPING
Hotel América Inc....................18 B3
Hotel Casagrande Bed &
    Breakfast...............................19 B2
Hotel Emperador......................20 B4
Hotel Halston............................21 B3
Hotel Norimax Colonial..........22 C4

EATING
Casa Castillo.............................23 B2
Repostería y Cafetéria La
    Económica............................24 C3
Restaurante Mang Ying...........25 A1
Restaurante Plaza Colonial....26 B2

ENTERTAINMENT
Cine Valladolid.........................27 B2

SHOPPING
Metro Plaza..............................28 A4

TRANSPORT
Buses to La Paz........................29 B4
Buses to Marcala......................30 B4
Buses to San Pedro Sula..........31 B4
El Rey Bus Stop.........................32 B5
Pickups to Río Negro/Parque
    Nacional Montaña
    de Comayagua......................33 B3

LAUNDRY
Lavandería Ebenezer (Parque La Merced; per 1kg US$1.05; 7am-6:30pm Mon-Sat, noon-6:30pm Sun)

MEDICAL SERVICES
Centro Médico Comayagua Colonial (772 1126, 772 4026; 3a Calle NE; emergency 24hr, pharmacy 8am-5pm Mon-Fri, to noon Sat)

Farmacia Santa Fe (772 2459; 1a Av NE at 2a Calle NO; 8am-12:30pm & 1:30-5:30pm)

MONEY
Banco Atlántida El Bulevar (at 4a Calle NO; 8:30am-3:30pm Mon-Fri, 8:30-11:30am Sat); 1a Av NO (btwn 2a & 3a Calles NO) Both branches are open the same hours, have an ATM and change traveler's checks.

POST

Post office (1a Av NE btwn 4a & 5a Calles NO; ☼ 8am-4pm Mon-Fri, to 11am Sat)

TELEPHONE

Hondutel (1a Av NE btwn 4a & 5a Calles NO; ☼ 7am-noon, 12:30-6pm & 6:30-9pm)

TOURIST INFORMATION

Tourist Office (☎ 772 2080; www.comayagua.hn; Parque Central; ☼ 8am-noon & 2-5pm Tue-Sat, 8am-noon Sun) Offers brochures and bare-bones information on area attractions.

Ecosimco (Ecosistema Montaña de Comayagua; ☎ 772 4681; ecosimco@hondutel.hn; Camara de Comercio; ☼ 9am-noon & 1-5pm Mon-Fri) Manages the Montaña de Comayagua National Park; 500m north of town.

Sights

The **Catedral de la Inmaculada Concepción** (Parque Central; ☼ 7am-8pm) is a colonial gem. Built between 1685 and 1715, it contains fine art in the Renaissance, baroque and neoclassic styles, both inside and out. The impressive three-paneled altar is similar to that of Tegucigalpa's cathedral; both are believed to have been made by the same (unknown) artist. The clock in the *iglesia* tower is the oldest in the Americas and one of the oldest in the world. The Moors built it around 1100 for the palace of the Alhambra in Granada. It was donated to the town by King Phillip II of Spain.

Other fine *iglesias* include the 1584 **Iglesia y Ex-convento de San Francisco** (1a Av NE btwn 6a & 7a Calles NO; ☼ 7am-8pm), which has a newly remodeled plaza; the 1585 **San Sebastián** (3a Av NE near 6a Calle SO; ☼ 7am-8pm), at the south end of town; and the 1730 **Nuestra Señora de la Caridad** (7a Calle NO at 3a Av NO; ☼ 7am-8pm). Comayagua's first *iglesia* was **Nuestra Señora de la Merced** (1a Av NE at 1 Calle NO, Parque La Merced; ☼ 7am-8pm), built from 1550 to 1558; it has a great little plaza in front. Another colonial *iglesia*, San Juan de Dios (1590), was destroyed by an earthquake in 1750, but samples of its artwork, along with artwork from all the other *iglesias*, are on display in the Museo Colonial de Arte Religioso. If you read Spanish, look for a small book entitled *Las Iglesias Coloniales de la Ciudad de Comayagua*, which contains an interesting history of Comayagua and its churches. It's available at both museums in town.

Housed in the former presidential palace, the **Museo Regional de Arqueología** (☎ 772 0386; 6a Calle NO near Av 2o de Julio; US$1; ☼ 8:30am-4pm) has six excellent exhibits displaying artifacts from ancient Lenca communities, including pottery, *metates* (stone on which grain is ground), stone carvings and petroglyphs. The seventh and final hall is reserved for temporary exhibits, which can range from ancient history to modern art. Signage is in English and Spanish.

Opened in 1962, the **Museo Colonial de Arte Religioso** (☎ 772 0169; Av 2a de Julio near 3a Calle NO; admission US$1.85; ☼ 9am-noon & 2-5pm Tue-Sun) was once the site of the first university (1632) in Central America, which operated for almost 200 years. Priests have occupied the building even longer, since 1558. Totally renovated in 2005, the museum contains artwork and religious paraphernalia culled from all five churches of Comayagua, spanning the 16th to 18th centuries. The price of the ticket includes a guide.

Festivals & Events

If there is one time of the year to visit Comayagua, it's **Semana Santa**. One of the most Catholic cities in Honduras, Comayagua holds religious processions and special masses the entire week leading up to Easter. The height of the celebration is on Good Friday morning, when the Vía Crucis – the procession representing Jesus carrying the cross down the streets of Jerusalem – makes its way around the historical center. The procession walks upon *alfombras*, which townspeople create throughout the night; watching these being made can be as interesting as the procession itself. The procession takes place from 8am to 2pm but be sure to arrive early so that you get a good look at the *alfombras* – and a couple of photos – before they're trampled by thousands of feet.

Sleeping

If you're planning to visit during Semana Santa, be sure to call a couple months in advance to reserve a room.

Hotel América Inc (☎ 772 0360; hotel_americainc@yahoo.com; 1a Av NO near 1a Calle NO; s/d US$10/18, s with air-con US$13.75-20, d with air-con US$22.25-30.25; P X X 🗔 🗟) The best deal in town, the rambling Hotel América offers spacious,

WESTERN HONDURAS

spotless rooms with cable TV, hot-water bathrooms and orthopedic beds. Most of the rooms have been redone with wrought-iron and heavy wood furnishings, brand-new floor tiles, and refurbished bathrooms. There is also a well-kept pool on-site, a restaurant (mains US$2 to US$6) open for breakfast, lunch and dinner, and secure parking.

Hotel Casagrande Bed & Breakfast (☎ 772 0512; www.casagrande-hotel.com; 7a Calle NO near 1a Av NO; r US$47-57; P 🕸) A B&B set in a restored 19th-century *casona* (colonial-style mansion), the Casagrande is a class act. Rooms are simple but elegant with handcrafted furnishings, warm earth tones and *azulejo* tiles. All open onto a lush central courtyard that leads to an outdoor dining area. A buffet breakfast is included.

Hotel Norimax Colonial (☎ 772 1703; Calle Manuel Bonilla near 1 Av NE; r/tw US$10.75/16, with air-con US$13.25/18.50; P 🕸) Just half a block from charming Parque La Merced, the Norimax Colonial has clean, airy rooms, with high ceilings and lots of sunlight; be sure to ask for one facing away from the busy street. A sister hotel, called simply Norimax, is nearby but the tiny rooms and surly service make it a far inferior choice – be sure you're at the right one.

Hotel Emperador (☎ 772 0332; Calle Manuel Bonilla near El Bulevar; r US$13-14, tw with air-con US$14.25-20.50; 🕸) Despite the lofty name, the 'Emperor' is a basic, no-frills place far from the center of town. It is well kept, however, and rooms with air-conditioning have cable TV and an in-room telephone. Consider spending a bit extra to have an interior facing room; they're super dark but the noise from the interminably busy boulevard in front is muffled by a room with a balcony, a lobby and a couple of thick walls.

Hotel Halston (☎ 772 0755; 3a Calle NO near 1a Av NO; tw with shared bathroom US$4.75, r US$8-9.50; 🕸) The cheapest rooms in town are also among the best located. Definitely ask for one on the 2nd floor; while all the rooms are worn, those on the 1st floor feel and smell like a basement.

Eating
Restaurante Plaza Colonial (Parque Central; mains US$3.50-7; 🕃 breakfast, lunch & dinner) This cute little café-bistro has metal tables and chairs right on parque central. The menu includes *golosinas* (traditional snacks), a hefty club sandwich, as well as beef, chicken and seafood dishes. Even if you're not hungry, it's a nice spot for coffee, postcards or evening beers.

Casa Castillo (☎ 772 3528; Parque Central; mains US$3-8; 🕃 lunch & dinner, Tue-Sun) The Casa Castillo has two dining areas: a courtyard in back and a high-ceilinged foyer that looks onto the park. The pasta is bland but the seafood and other dishes – like sweet-and-sour chicken with tartar sauce – are reasonably tasty. Head to the ice-cream shop next door for dessert.

Repostería y Cafetería La Económica (☎ 772 2331; 1a Av NE at Parque la Merced; mains US$2-5; 🕃 breakfast & lunch Mon-Sat) This small pastry shop serves typical Honduran dishes at tables behind a display case full of cakes. The windows let in plenty of light, but a nicer option is when they set up tables out front, with a view of the church and Parque La Merced.

Restaurante Mang Ying (7a Calle No at El Bulevar; dishes US$5-8; 🕃 10am-10pm) If you're hungry – really hungry – order the Chop Suey Mang Ying. A mound of noodles, veggies, chicken, beef and shrimp, it's gotta weigh at least a couple of kilos. It's not the tastiest Chinese food in the world, but it definitely fills you up.

Entertainment
Cine Valladolid (2a Av NO at 7a Calle NO; tickets Tue-Sun US$1, Mon US$0.50) Although it has seen better days, this old movie house still cranks out a feature every night at 7pm.

Getting There & Away
Comayagua's town center is about 1km east of the highway. To/from Tegucigalpa, Transportes El Rey stops at the Texaco gas station at the highway turnoff, roughly a kilometer from the center of town (US$1.75, 1½ hours, 5am to 7pm, hourly). Another bus line, Transportes Catruchos (same price), has a convenient terminal in the center of Comayagua, but drops you on the outskirts of Tegucigalpa in a rather sketchy area; better to use El Rey.

Transportes Rivera has service to San Pedro Sula (US$3, 3¼ hours, hourly, 5am to 4pm) from its terminal on 1a Av SO at 2a Calle SO. Buses to Marcala (US$2, three hours) park just outside the Rivera terminal wall, with departures at 6:15am, 8am, 10am, noon and 2pm. Buses to La Paz (US$0.50, 30 minutes, 5:40am to 6pm, every 15 minutes) leave from around the corner.

Pickup trucks to Río Negro (US$1.75, four hours) leave from the south side of the market at 11am, noon and 1pm. It's a long bumpy road, with no benches in the truck to sit on.

Getting Around
Taxis around town cost US$0.60 per person, but cost more at night or for longer trips.

PARQUE NACIONAL MONTAÑA DE COMAYAGUA
Spanning more than 30,000 hectares of primary and secondary forest, Parque Nacional Montaña de Comayagua (Panacoma) provides the bulk of fresh water used by some 60 communities, including Comayagua. A full 25% of the water in the Francisco Morazán dam/reservoir, aka El Cajón, also comes from the park.

Information
The national park is managed by **Ecosimco** (☎ 772 4681; ecosimco@hondutel.hn; ⚐ 9am-noon & 1-5pm Mon-Fri), which operates out of a small office next to the Camara de Comercio about 500m north of Comayagua; look for the big green gates. Admission to the park is US$1.75, payable at the Ecosimco office. That said, no one in the park collects your ticket, so it's a strictly karmic exercise.

Hiking
The park has two official trails in it. Both start from near the village of Río Negro, a small cluster of homes along the road 42km north of Comayagua – you'll pass the trailhead, marked Paseo de los Leones, about 1km before the village. The first trail is to Cascada de los Ensueños, a 75m waterfall about an hour's hike away through mostly secondary forest. The trip takes longer if you stop to read the more than 20 placards along the way, explaining the flora, fauna and ecology of the area. The second trail veers off the first just before reaching Los Ensueños, and leads to another waterfall, El Gavilán. Swimming is not permitted in either falls, however, as they both provide drinking water for several communities downstream.

A guide is recommended and can be hired in Río Negro. Local teenager Dania Morales Alvarado is very knowledgeable about the park's ecology and leads most hikes. To go to Los Ensueños/El Gavilán for one to three people costs US$8/13.25 per person, or US$13.25/16 for up to 10 people). The Morales Alvarado house is on the left in Río Negro, just before the road goes steeply downhill. In addition to hiking, there is a pool with a waterfall (and a cave behind it – ask any kid to show you how to access it) abut 300m from the Morales Alvarado home.

Sleeping & Eating
Simple **accommodations** (☎ 990 0802; r US$3-6) are available at the house of Don Avilio Velásquez, which also serves as the de facto visitors center. They're basic eco-casitas with four bunks apiece, cold-water bathrooms, sturdy wooden furniture and no electricity. There are also places to camp and simple meal service. A Peace Corps volunteer is sometimes stationed here, and can be a good resource for information on the park. It's a short walk from Dania Morales Alvarado's place.

Getting There & Away
Pickup trucks bound for Río Negro leave from the south side of the market in Comayagua at 11am, noon, and 1pm (US$1.75). From Río Negro, they leave at 5am and 6am only. It's four long, bumpy hours, standing the whole way, since there are no seats in the truck.

YARUMELA
Located on the Río Humuya between Comayagua and La Paz, Yarumela is a mostly unexcavated archaeological site with mounds that simply look like hills covered in brush. Lencans occupied the city from 1000 BC until AD 250, when it was abruptly abandoned. Because of the number of administrative and religious buildings, it also is believed to have been a seat of government.

The site has two major mounds worth checking out. The central structure is 20m high; archaeologists believe it was the residence of a chieftain. From the top, the view of the Valle de Comayagua is fantastic. The smaller mound sits right beside the river; it has been reconstructed on one side, revealing a step pyramid with several platforms and a stairway going up the middle. The remaining half of the mound looks like a grassy knoll. '

Getting There & Away

Yarumela is accessible by cab or private vehicle only. From Comayagua, take CA-5 Hwy toward Tegucigalpa. Take the turnoff to La Paz and go over the Río Humuya. Just before you come to a roundabout, take a right on the dirt road. Stay on it until you come to the large mound on the right-hand side of the road. This is the site. There are no set prices for a cab ride from Comayagua. A taxi from La Paz costs around US$11 round-trip.

TENAMPUA

Tenampua sits on a large hill and was constructed between AD 900 and 1000 – a time of war in the valley. Its structure reflects the era: it is both well protected and easy to defend. The sweeping views it had of the entire valley allowed the inhabitants to see approaching enemies; the ascent is very steep on three sides, and on the fourth side, a high, 2m-thick wall was constructed. Features that can be seen today include a handful of unexcavated mounds, walls and a ball court, an example of the influence that the Maya had over the region.

Getting There & Away

Tenampua is about 20km south of Comayagua. Take a Tegucigalpa-bound bus and ask to be let off at the *sendero* for Tenampua; it's on the east side of the highway, just north of the Restaurant Aquarios. It's a steep climb and takes one to 1½ hours.

LA PAZ

pop 17,983

La Paz is a gateway to La Esperanza and the Ruta Lenca, though Comayagua, just 20 minutes away, serves the same function and is much more pleasant.

Orientation & Information

This small town has basic services for travelers. There is a **Banco Atlántida** (Parque Central; 8:30am-3:30pm Mon-Fri, to 11:30am Sat), which exchanges traveler's checks and dollars. For internet access, try **Lovrytino Café Internet** (per hr US$1; 8am-noon & 2-5pm) at the entrance to town. The **post office** (8am-4pm Mon-Fri, 8-11:30am Sat), is three blocks from parque central and Dr Leonardo Selaya (774 2281) has a general medicine clinic attached to Valle de Piedras B&B and is on call 24 hours.

Sleeping & Eating

Valle de Piedras B&B (774 3713; Blvd Los Pinos; s/d with fan US$11/13.50, with air-con US$18/21; P) A great little place, this B&B has just seven rooms a short distance from the main square. Upstairs air-conditioned rooms are clean and bright, with ceramic floors and large TVs. The fan room – there's just one – is downstairs so it doesn't get the same natural light, but is still clean and roomy. The second 'B' in 'B&B' must stand for something other than breakfast, but fresh coffee plus a fridge, microwave and sunny little terrace are available to guests upstairs.

Hotel B&F (774 2581; fax 774 3355; s/d US$9.50/ 13.25) Half a block from the market, this friendly place offers five clean, spacious rooms all with hot water, cable TV and a fan. Each opens onto a leafy courtyard with tables, chairs, and hammocks – an unexpectedly pleasant place to relax with a book or a few postcards.

Comedor y Golosinas La Chalupa (mains US$1-3; breakfast, lunch & dinner Mon-Sat) An old school eatery, this *comedor* has high ceilings, shutters pulled to keep the heat out, and a menu replete with Honduran *típica*. It's two blocks from parque central.

Las Champas (mains US$1-3; breakfast, lunch & dinner) Although it doesn't look like much (maybe a converted auto-parts shop?) this small restaurant at the back of a dirt lot, 1½ blocks from the market, is often packed with locals. They come for the fast, friendly service and cheap lunch specials: fried fish or chicken plates with sides of rice, beans or salad for a couple bucks.

Getting There & Away

Buses come and go from the busy intersection at the entrance to town. Buses to Marcala (US$1.50, two hours, 5am to 4pm, every 30 minutes) and Comayagua (US$0.50, 40 minutes, 5am to 6pm, every 15 minutes) park right on the shoulder. Buses to Teguci-galpa (US$1.50, 1½ hours, 4:30am to 4pm, every 30 to 60 minutes) leave from a small terminal next to the Shell gas station. Buses to San Pedro Sula (US$3.50, three hours) originate in Marcala and pass the Tegus terminal at around 5:30am and 6:30am; be sure to arrive 30 minutes early.

A taxi in town costs US$0.65 per person, or US$0.80 at night.

The North Coast

The north coast is all about eco-travel: you can hop, skip and jump down the long, straight Caribbean coast, hiking on the beach here, kayaking through mangroves there, rafting rivers, biking backroads, snorkeling and diving off deserted islands that you swear were plucked from a postcard (and you'd be right). With almost a dozen protected areas between Omoa and Trujillo, the outdoor offerings are more than plentiful.

If the adrenaline starts to go to your head, the north coast has some notable cultural features as well. The region is the home of Honduras' Garífuna people, descendents of Arawak Indians and West Africans who escaped from slave ships in the 16th century. Garífuna communities dot the coast, ranging from isolated hamlets to large towns, some quite insular, some open and welcoming to travelers. Other cultural options include museums, colonial-era forts, Spanish schools, annual festivals and the famously raucous nightlife in La Ceiba.

For all that Caribbean shoreline, one thing the north coast does not have is good beaches. Cayos Cochinos, Tela and Trujillo are your best options. Regardless, during Semana Santa (Holy Week) the north coast fills up way, way, way beyond reasonable capacity with beach worshippers from around the country. It is a scene unto itself – arguably the mother of all contemporary Honduran cultural events. But if you're not into crowds (or don't have a hotel reservation, made several weeks in advance) consider spending Holy Week inland.

THE NORTH COAST

HIGHLIGHTS

- Feast your eyes on white beaches, black howler monkeys and a big blue seascape at **Parque Nacional Jeannette Kawas** (Punta Sal; p204), west of Tela
- Get below the surface at **Cayos Cochinos** (p227) a diver's and snorkeler's paradise – just as beautiful above the water as beneath it
- Kayak through **Refugio de Vide Silvestre Cuero y Salado** (p222), home to monkeys, birds and even manatees
- Master the finer points of *punta* (traditional dance) at the Garífuna Festival at **Baja Mar** (p195), the largest of its kind
- Raft the **Río Cangrejal** (p225), Central America's best white-water river, right along the edge of the lush Pico Bonito national park.

DANGERS & ANNOYANCES

There are occasional reports of travelers being accosted and robbed on beaches along the north coast, typically by groups of young men. Most of the incidents have happened on lonely stretches of beach outside La Ceiba and, to a lesser degree, Tela. Some people have reported having belongings swiped from the beach while they were in the water. The simple solution, of course, is not to walk along these beaches without company and certainly never at night, and to not leave valuables unguarded.

The north coast also has a very high rate of HIV infection: plan accordingly.

PUERTO CORTÉS & AROUND

Puerto Cortés is one of the busiest deepwater ports in the Americas, its port area bustling with trucks, containers and huge transoceanic ships. Just 64km north of San Pedro Sula, it is also a popular getaway for city-dwellers, though travelers searching for an idyllic Caribbean getaway won't find it here – the beaches are drab and the cranes on the horizon kind of spoil the illusion.

Things improve considerably outside of Puerto Cortés proper. The little town of Omoa has a somewhat better beach, though it can still get crowded on hot summer weekends. East of Puerto Cortés are Travesía and Baja Mar, two isolated Garífuna towns, each with a surprisingly good hotel. The latter hosts the annual Garífuna festival, a raucous celebration that brings Garífunas from around the country for dance competitions and general revelry.

PUERTO CORTÉS

pop 49,050

Puerto Cortés has a large and not unattractive plaza, but the town is mainly useful as a way to get to more appealing places to the east or west. Another reason to come is for the twice-weekly boat service to Belize, the only regularly scheduled boat transportation between the two countries.

Puerto Cortés' annual fair is held on August 15.

History

More interesting than the town itself is its history. Puerto Cortés was founded in 1524 by Spanish colonizers drawn to its potential as a deepwater port. The port was originally called Puerto Caballos (Port of Horses); as the story goes, when explorer Gil González Dávila arrived, a powerful storm blew in and he had to throw several horses overboard in order to survive. How throwing the poor horses in the ocean improved the situation remains unclear, but the name stuck until 1869, when it was changed to Puerto Cortés.

The port quickly became one of the region's most important ports, and remains so today. Over half of the country's exports – mostly bananas, pineapples and other produce – pass through here. The port has also fueled the explosion of *maquilas* (factories) along the corridor between Puerto Cortés and San Pedro Sula. Thousands of Hondurans work here, especially sewing clothes and producing textiles for major US brands.

Information

Banco Atlántida (2a Av near 4a Calle Este; 9am-4:30pm Mon-Fri, to noon Sat) Exchanges traveler's checks; ATM accepts Visa cards only.
Centro Medico Bahía (☎ 665 4325; 2a Av at 7a Calle Este; 6:30am-5pm Mon-Fri, to noon Sat) Emergencies handled 24/7.
Farmacia FarmaUNO (☎ 665 1579; 4a Av btwn 2a & 3a Calles Este; 7am-6pm Mon-Fri, to noon Sat)
Hondutel (1a Calle btwn 1a & 3a Av; 7:30am-8:30pm)
Munguinet (2a Av near 6a Calle Este; per hr US$0.65; 8am-8pm) International calls (per minute) to the USA and Canada are US$0.05, to Europe US$0.21 and to Australia US$0.53.
Police (☎ 665 0420; 24hr)
Post office (1a Calle btwn 1a & 3a Av; 8am-4pm)

Dangers & Annoyances

As a port town goes, Puerto Cortes has its fair share of roughnecks and shady characters. It's perfectly fine during the day, but exudes a certain toughness at night, especially anywhere drinking is going on.

Sights & Activities

Puerto Cortés is a hugely popular beach destination for Hondurans, who zip up from San Pedro Sula on summer weekends. Although the city beaches are drab, the one at **Hotel Playa** (☎ 665 0453; www.hotelplaya.hn), Playa de Cienaguita, is clean and open to everyone.

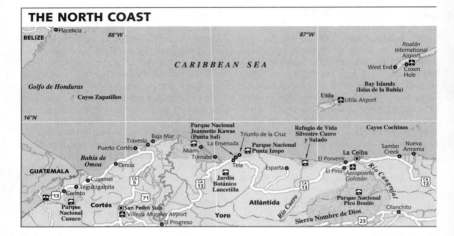

THE NORTH COAST

Sleeping

Hotel El Centro (☎ 665 1160; fax 665 3250; 3a Av btwn 2a & 3a Calles Este; r/tw US$13/18.50, with air-con US$18/23.25; 🅿 ✲) Near the bus terminals, this well-kept hotel has gleaming tile-floored rooms. Each has a cable TV and hot-water bathroom. The rooms are a little small but not oppressively so – the framed posters on the walls help a lot.

Hotel Buenos Aires (☎ 665 4580; 5a Av btwn 12a & 13a Calles Este; r/tw US$13/18.50, with air-con US$18/23.25; 🅿 ✲) The sister hotel to El Centro, has more of the same – clean, well-priced rooms with cable and hot water. The biggest difference is the location; the Buenos Aires is in a quiet neighborhood nine blocks from parque central – a shortish walk by day, but one that you should cab at night.

Mr Ggeerr's Hotel (☎ /fax 665 4333; 9a Calle Este btwn 1a & 2a Avs; tw with fan US$21.25, tr with air-con US$26.50; ✲) A favorite for many years, this hotel remains a friendly though sagging version of what it once was. Rooms have hot-water bathrooms and air-conditioning and are reasonably clean, but it's hard to overlook the worn carpet, chipped tiles and musty smell.

Eating

Repostería y Comida Buffet Plata (3a Av at 2a Calle Este; mains US$1.50-4; ✲ breakfast, lunch & dinner Mon-Sat) Near the bus terminals, this bustling cafeteria serves tasty *típica* (Honduran fare) and tempting baked goods. Come at the height of each meal – 8am, 12:30pm and 6:30pm – to get the best selection of food.

Parrillada Joché (3a Av at 11a Calle Este; mains US$2-4; ✲ lunch & dinner) This popular barbecue place serves grilled meat and chicken. Seating is on the front lawn of a private home. Arrive early for a seat on weekends – it's hopping with customers at peak hours.

Pupusería La Bendición de Cristo (7a Calle Este near 3a Av; mains US$0.45-1; ✲ lunch & dinner) A simple outdoor eatery serving Salvadoran *pupusas* (stuffed cornmeal patties). *Queso* (cheese), frijoles (cheese and beans), *chicharrón* (pork rind), and *revueltas* (combo of cheese, beans and pork rind) are standard offerings. If you're lucky, *loroco* (a popular herb) will be thrown in for variety. Two to three should fill you up.

Entertainment

Cinema Vicenta (Parque Central; US$1.50) This old movie theater cranks out Hollywood and Latin American releases.

Getting There & Away
BOAT

Boats to Belize leave Barra La Laguna, near Puerto Cortés, twice a week – Mondays they go to Dangriga (US$35, two hours) and Tuesdays to Belize City (US$55, 3½ hours). Departure is at 9am, though it is often delayed for up to two hours. You must come with your passport the day before to sign up (yes, it's a pain). The office is about 3km west of Puerto Cortés – take any

Omoa-bound bus and get off at La Laguna. The office is in the fish market, under a bridge about 200m from the highway. Contact **Gulf Cruz** (☎ 984 9544, 982 6985) for more information and tickets.

BUS

Two bus companies service Puerto Cortés from side-by-side terminals on 4a Av between 3a and 4a Calles. Between them, buses leave for San Pedro Sula every five to 10 minutes from 4am to 9pm. Both have direct (US$1.60, one hour) and ordinary service (US$1.35, 1½ hours).

For transportation information to Travesía and Baja Mar see right.

Citral Costeños (☎ 655 0888; 3a Calle Este) provides daily service to Omoa (US$0.50, 30 minutes to the turnoff) every 20 minutes from 5am to 5:40pm. It also has service to Corinto (US$2.10, two hours) every 15 minutes from 6am to 8pm.

TRAIN

The passenger train between Puerto Cortes and Tela is no longer operating.

TRAVESÍA & BAJA MAR
pop 2420

Just east of Puerto Cortés, Travesía and Baja Mar are traditional Garífuna villages with houses built along the shore and fishing boats pulled up onto the sand. The beach at Travesía is cleaner than the one at Baja Mar. Beyond Travesía and Baja Mar and

a good distance inland, is a non-Garífuna town called Brisas del Chamelcón, although very few visitors make it that far.

Festivals & Events

Baja Mar is best known as the home of the **Garífuna Festival**, held here every year between July 9 and 24. Members of the three dozen or so Garífuna communities in Honduras come together, making it one of the best opportunities to experience Garífuna culture. The height of the party is typically July 16, when an all-night dance competition keeps everyone moving until the sun rises.

Sleeping & Eating

Hotel Frontera del Caribe (☎ /fax 665 5001; r US$13.25; ℗) Right on the beach, at the western entrance to Travesía, this is the most pleasant place to stay near Puerto Cortés. Seven upstairs rooms (sleeping up to three people each) have hardwood floors with private bathrooms and ceiling fans. They're simple but clean and every room has a window that lets in the sea breeze. Downstairs there is a restaurant (mains US$1 to US$7), open for breakfast, lunch and dinner, that serves *típica* and seafood specials in a pleasant coconut tree garden overlooking the ocean. The beach in front is kept clean, which makes staying here – or even just spending the day – a treat.

Hotel Victoria (☎ 922 5616; eastern end of Baja Mar; r/tw US$8/10.75; ℗) This pink hotel offers two different types of basic rooms: smaller ones that are a bit musty and spacious ones that are housed in what was once a discotheque. If given a choice, definitely go for the latter – the disco ball is gone, but the rooms are airy and have relatively new furnishings. It's right on the beach, which would be nicer if there were less trash on it.

Getting There & Away

The road to Travesía is so-so, worse to Baja Mar, and awful to Brisas. In the summer an ordinary car can make it to all three, driving carefully; otherwise only 4WDs can manage the mud. Accordingly, departure times and durations may vary considerably.

Buses from Puerto Cortés to Travesía (US$0.25, 15 minutes), Baja Mar (US$0.40, 30 minutes) and Brisas del Chamelecón (US$0.75, 45 minutes) normally depart from a stop at the corner of 5a Calle Este and

4a Av at 7am, 9:30am, 10:30am, 12:15pm, 2pm, 4pm and 5:30pm. The bus returns from Brisas, in front of the Pulpería Lester, at 8am, 11am, noon, 2pm and 4pm.

A taxi will take you between Puerto Cortés and Travesía for US$3.40.

OMOA
pop 5036

Omoa is a sleepy seaside town, 18km west of Puerto Cortés. A weekend getaway for San Pedro Sulans, Omoa also attracts a steady stream of backpackers. It's a bit baffling, frankly, as the beach is humdrum at best and there's not a whole lot to do. (A dive shop just opened here, however, which may change things.) For many, Omoa is a convenient stopover before or after crossing the Guatemalan border, so you don't arrive in either Puerto Barrios or San Pedro Sula at night. And once in Omoa, the hostels (though imperfect), beachside fish shops, and pervasive shorts and flip-flops atmosphere can definitely be soporific. Ironically, the road to the border is now fully paved, making it less likely that you'll need to lay up here before or after crossing. Omoa's annual festival is held on May 30.

Information

Buses to/from Omoa stop on the main highway, 1km from the beach. There is a cluster of shops and services at the highway intersection and on the road to the beach.

Bahía de Omoa (☎ 658 9076; per load US$2.25-4.25) Hotel that offers laundry service to non guests.

Banco de Occidente (☺ 8:30am-4pm Mon-Fri, 8:30-11:30am Sat) Just west of the Omoa turnoff; exchanges traveler's checks but has no ATM.

Dr Jorge Mejia (☎ 658 9070; ☺ from 5pm) Recommended by locals and expatriates; 40m west of the Farmacia San Antonio.

Farmacia San Antonio (☎ 658 9198; ☺ 8am-6pm Mon-Sat, to 1pm Sun) At the highway turnoff.

Internet & Video Club (☎ 933 0271; per hr US$1.05; ☺ 8am-10pm) Located 150m from the highway.

Space Cyber (☎ 602 1750) Across from the Omoa turnoff; per-minute domestic calls cost US$0.30 to US$0.45, to the USA US$0.20, and to the rest of the world US$0.25 and up.

Sights

Omoa's claim to historical fame is the **Fortaleza de San Fernando de Omoa** (☎ 658 9167; admission US$2; ☺ 8am-4pm Mon-Fri, 9am-5pm Sat & Sun), on the main street. The fort was built under King Fernando VII of Spain between 1759 and 1775 by enslaved Indians and

---

PIRATES OF THE CARIBBEAN

Pirates played a significant and tangible role in the history of Honduras and Central America, and still loom large in the language and culture of many Hondurans. In La Moskitia, the city of Brus Laguna derives its name from 'Brewers Lagoon,' after the notorious pirate Bloody Brewer, who had his hideaway there. Likewise, the name 'Miskito' comes from 'musket,' which the Miskito obtained from British pirates to use against Spanish colonizers. Up to 30% of the Miskito language comes from English, also a result of contact with British pirates. Several Honduran cities also have forts, built to repel pirate attacks. Trujillo – where Columbus first landed on the American mainland – built several forts but was still abandoned for a century after being sacked repeatedly by pirates. Sir Francis Drake is said to have left a treasure hidden on one of the islands in the Gulf of Fonseca, and the Bay Islands (Islas de la Bahía) are believed to be haunted by ghosts protecting hidden pirate loot.

In his book *Villains of All Nations* (Beacon Press, 2004), University of Pittsburgh professor Marcus Rediker debunks the popular conception of pirates as ruthless killers and plunderers – or at least as *only* killers and plunderers. He points out that life for sailors on lawful merchant ships was no picnic. A standard merchant ship might have 15 or 20 miserably overworked crew members, while a pirate ship of similar size might have 80 or 90. Sailors who were injured on board commercial ships were jettisoned at the nearest port, if not before. The semicomical picture of a pirate with peg-leg and eye-patch may more accurately portray destitute crippled sailors, scores of whom could be found begging on the streets of Atlantic port cities. On pirate ships, injured crew members were still entitled to a portion of the booty – an early form of welfare. Moreover, captains were elected democratically. Those who abused their crew could be removed, punished or even killed. And captains never received more than twice what the ordinary sailors got – propose *that* to the average oil-company CEO.

DUKES UP

Travelers should know about – but pay no attention to – the bitter feud between two longtime expatriates in Omoa: Roli, of Roli's Place, and Pia, of Bahía de Omoa. God knows how or where it began, but to speak to either is to hear tales of verbal abuse, psychological torment, immigration violations, predatory business tactics, illegal dealings, corruption and outright insanity about the other. The inspired passion with which they seem to hate each other would be comical if the charges were not so serious: the last time LP passed through, there were accusations of a knife attack, this time around, arson. The police, municipal government, immigration service and various embassies have been involved, to no avail. Local residents usually just shrug and shake their heads. LP has ignored the feud in past editions – this has been going on for years – but has received enough letters (from readers and, lately from Roli and Pia themselves) to warrant mentioning it, at least so readers aren't sucked in unwittingly. Suffice to say that nothing either says about the other can be taken at face value – whether true, partly true or totally false, both will try to dissuade you from associating with the other. Both offer decent accommodations, with pros and cons depending on your style and budget. And both also have considerable knowledge about Omoa and the surrounding area and can be quite helpful to travelers when not griping about the other.

---

later, enslaved Africans. It was constructed to protect the coast and the region's treasures – gold, silver and indigo – that were shipped out from there. The plan worked only for four years; in 1779 the fortress was captured by the British after a two-day battle. Still in good shape today, the fort features 31 rooms, about three dozen cannons and hundreds of cannonballs.

Activities

Omoa has a pretty waterfall and swimming hole about 2km to 3km south of the highway turn-off. To get there, follow the road past the bank, bearing right until you reach a small garbage dump. Bearing left, stay on the road until it crosses the river, where you turn left and walk along the river to the falls. There were some much-publicized assaults on this hike several years ago, though reportedly none of late. Definitely check at your hotel, and leave valuables at home.

Omoa Divers (☎ 909 5592; www.omoadivers.com), at Restaurante Macarela at the east end of the beach, opened in 2005 and is Omoa's first and only dive shop. It may be just to get the word out, but owner-instructor Lars Benn offers cut-rate diving: US$179 for Open Water, and US$20 per tank fun dives, including equipment rental. Omoa Bay doesn't have the variety of coral that Roatán or Utila, two of the Bay Islands, do, but you'll have the place to yourself. Benn also can arrange trips to **Cayos Zapatillos**, a collection of eight spectacular Belizean islands 45km offshore.

Sleeping

Flamingo's (☎ 658 9199; flamingosomoa@yahoo.com; on the beach; s/d/tw incl breakfast US$37/40/46.50; Ⓟ Ⓧ) The top dog in town, Flamingo's has large modern rooms, with spotless floors and bathrooms, high ceilings and brightly painted walls. The restaurant has views over the beach and pier. Service is friendly and professional.

Roli's Place (☎ 658 9082; roli@yaxpactours.com; hammocks US$2.75, campsites per person US$2.75, dm US$3.75, s/d with shared bathroom US$7.50/8.50, r US$10.75; Ⓟ Ⓧ) There are two good reasons to stay in this grassy compound: the new air-conditioned rooms and the nice camping spots (BYO gear). Anywhere in between, you're kind of SOL: the rooms with shared bathroom are musty and dark and the dorm is pretty grim (think corrugated tin roof, no fans and flimsy mattresses). The place is run by Roli Gassmann, a no-nonsense Swiss national who takes his rules very seriously – No socializing after 11pm! Bicycles back by 6pm! No visitors! – and guests have been thrown out for breaking them. If you can live with that – and eight-minute-long hot-water showers during the cold season (no joke) – you'll appreciate the communal kitchen, kayaks and bicycles. Laundry service (US$0.40 per pound) is available too.

Bahía de Omoa (☎ 658 9076; r with/without air-con US$24/13.25; Ⓟ Ⓧ) This hotel has four 2nd-floor rooms with high ceilings, hot-water bathrooms and cable TV. Beds are hit or

THE NORTH COAST

miss but the rooms are clean. Little details like *artesanía* (handicrafts) and posters on the walls add a bit of personality. Bicycles are free for guests. Pia, a Dutch expatriate, and her German husband run the hotel and live on the ground floor.

There are a number of additional hotels, built in a row along the beach. Most have adequate but nondescript rooms, one not terribly different from the next. On the budget end, try **Hotel Julie** (☎ 658 9174; r with shared bathroom US$6, s/tw US$10/12) or pay a bit more for **Sea View Hotel** (r US$11-16), run in conjunction with Omoa divers, or more again for **Hotel Tatiana** (☎ 658 9186; s/d with fan US$16/22, with air-con US$27/37; ❄).

Eating

Omoa has a gaggle of beachside restaurants – just walk around and pick the one that most fits your fancy.

Comedor Doña Rafa (main street; mains US$1-2; ❤ breakfast, lunch & dinner) Serves up huge portions of good *típica* in a mini outdoor eating area. It's near the bend in the main road, 200m from the beach.

Punto Italia (☎ 658 9125; mail@puntaitalia.com; mains US$6-15; ❤ lunch & dinner Wed-Sun) Punto Italia serves tasty slow-cooked Italian specialties and well-prepared pizza and pasta. A grocery is attached, with gourmet items like anchovies, olives and wine, plus everyday stuff like rum, sunscreen and condoms. It's halfway between the fort and the highway.

Longtime favorites include **Champa Johnson** (mains US$4-9; ❤ lunch & dinner) and the somewhat funkier **Jardín Romántico** (mains US$3-8; ❤ breakfast & dinner)

Getting There & Away
BUS
Buses to Omoa depart from Puerto Cortés every 20 minutes from 5am to 5:40pm (US$0.50, 30 minutes) from the **Citral Costeños terminal** (☎ 655 0888; 3a Calle Este). It stops on the highway, a 15-minute walk from the fort and beach. From Omoa to Puerto Cortés, buses depart every 20 minutes from 5:20am to 6pm.

If you're headed to Guatemala, jump on a bus headed to Corinto; the green and yellow buses pass Omoa every hour from 6:50am to 3:50pm (US$1.60, 1¼ hours). Just flag one down on the highway. In Corinto, be

sure to get your exit stamp (US$3) and then jump into the back of a *colectivo* (shared) pickup for the 10km ride to the border.

Roli's Place (☎ 658 9082; roli@yaxpactours.com) runs a shuttle to La Ceiba (US$20 per person, 3½ hours, minimum eight people), which leaves early enough to catch the ferry to Utila or Roatán. Shuttle service to Puerto Barrios (US$15 per person, 1½ hours, minimum eight people) is also offered.

Bike taxis – and more recently mototaxis (red and white scooters with a small cab attached) – ferry people back and forth from the highway to the town and beach. A ride in either direction is US$0.55 – way better than lugging your pack down that long hot road.

TELA & AROUND

Honduras does not stand out for its beaches, but Tela has the best of the bunch, at least on the mainland. It's also got several very worthwhile outings – you can rent a bike and ride to Jardín Botánico Lancetilla, or hire a boat (or book a trip) out to Punta Sal in Parque Nacional Jeannette Kawas. The city of Tela is mellow and manageable – and the small villages nearby even more so – while San Pedro Sula or La Ceiba are an easy bus ride away.

TELA
pop 29,635

A quiet coastal town, Tela has a fine beach and several good hotels and restaurants. The central park has benches and shade trees, but a more pleasant spot to take a break is along the boardwalk, where you can enjoy a beer or a coffee with a view of the ocean. While the main drag occasionally gets snarled with cars and mototaxis, Tela is usually quite mellow, even soporific. The exception is during Semana Santa when Tela (and the rest of the north coast) is deluged with vacationers from all over the country.

History

Tela was founded in 1524 by Cristóbal de Olid, one of several Spanish conquistadores who vied for dominance in the new-found colony. In fact, not long after founding Tela, Olid was betrayed by his own men to his main rival, Gil González Dávila, who had Olid beheaded.

The precise day of Tela's founding was May 3 – the day of the Holy Cross, so the town was named Triunfo de la Cruz, which was eventually shortened to Tela. (Later, a Garífuna community established east of the city adopted the full original name, which it still has today.) Through the early 1900s, Tela survived largely on small-time banana farming. In 1913 the United Fruit Company acquired the Tela Railroad Company and in exchange for building the railroad was awarded rights to most of the farmland around Tela. For the next half century, workers – eventually organized in unions –

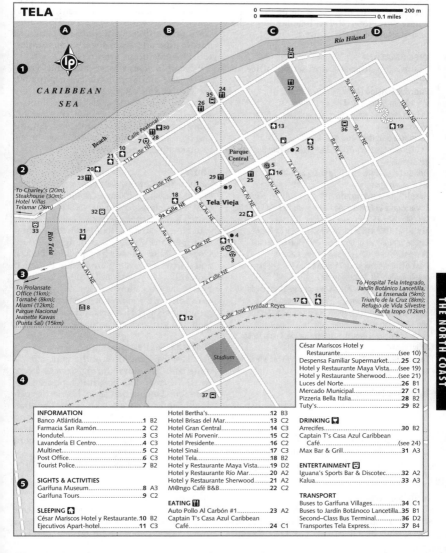

César Mariscos Hotel y
Restaurante.............................(see 10)
Despensa Familiar Supermarket.....25 C2
Hotel y Restaurante Maya Vista.....(see 19)
Hotel y Restaurante Sherwood......(see 21)
Luces del Norte..............................26 B1
Mercado Municipal..........................27 C1
Pizzeria Bella Italia........................28 B2
Tuty's...29 B2

DRINKING 🍸
Arrecifes.......................................30 B2
Captain T's Casa Azul Caribbean
Café...(see 24)
Max Bar & Grill...............................31 A3

ENTERTAINMENT 🎭
Iguana's Sports Bar & Discotec.......32 A2
Kalua...33 A3

TRANSPORT
Buses to Garífuna Villages..............34 C1
Buses to Jardín Botánoco Lancetilla..35 B1
Second–Class Bus Terminal.............36 D2
Transportes Tela Express.................37 B4

INFORMATION
Banco Atlántida..............................1 B2
Farmacia San Ramón.......................2 C2
Hondutel..3 C3
Lavandería El Centro........................4 C2
Multinet...5 C2
Post Office......................................6 C3
Tourist Police..................................7 B2

SIGHTS & ACTIVITIES
Garífuna Museum............................8 A3
Garífuna Tours................................9 C2

SLEEPING 🛏
César Mariscos Hotel y Restaurante.10 B2
Ejecutivos Apart-hotel....................11 C3

Hotel Bertha's................................12 B3
Hotel Brisas del Mar........................13 C2
Hotel Gran Central...........................14 C3
Hotel Mi Porvenir............................15 C2
Hotel Presidente.............................16 C2
Hotel Sinai.....................................17 C3
Hotel Tela......................................18 B2
Hotel y Restaurante Maya Vista......19 D2
Hotel y Restaurante Río Mar...........20 A2
Hotel y Restaurante Sherwood........21 A2
M@ngo Café B&B...........................22 C2

EATING 🍴
Auto Pollo Al Carbón #1..................23 A2
Captain T's Casa Azul Caribbean
Café...24 C1

battled with United for better wages and working conditions. It is a fight workers are still waging, though international oversight has improved workers' rights considerably.

Orientation

The town is divided into two sections: Tela Vieja, the 'old town,' on the east bank of the Río Tela where the river meets the sea; and Tela Nueva, on the west side of the river, where the Hotel Villas Telamar hugs the best stretch of beach around.

INFORMATION

There's no tourist information office in Tela.

Banco Atlántida (4a Av NE at 9a Calle NE; 8:30am-3:30pm Mon-Fri, to 11:30am Sat) Has an ATM and can exchange travelers' checks and give cash advances on Visa cards.

Farmacia San Ramón (☎ 448 1007; 9a Calle NE; 7:30am-6pm Mon-Fri, to 2pm Sat) Opposite the Texaco gas station.

Hondutel (4a Av NE btwn 7a & 8a Calles NE; 7:30am-9pm)

Hospital Tela Integrado (☎ 442 3176; 24hr)

Lavandería El Centro (4a Av NE btwn 7a & 8a Calles NE; per 10lb US$3.75; 7am-5pm Mon-Fri)

Multinet (☎ 448 0119; cnr of 9a Calle & 6a Ave NE, Parque Central; per hr US$0.95; 7:30am-7:30pm Mon-Sat, 9:15am-7:15pm Sun) Internet access.

Post office (4a Av btwn 7a & 8a Calles NE; 8am-noon & 1-4pm Mon-Fri, 8am-noon Sat)

Prolansate (☎ 448 2042; www.prolansate.org; Edificio Kawas, Calle del Comercio; 8:30am-noon & 1:30-5:30pm Mon-Fri, 8:30am-noon Sat) Offers brochures and other material about the protected areas. It also oversees Parque Nacional Jeannette Kawas, Punta Izopo national park and Jardín Botánico Lancetilla.

Tourist police (☎ 448 0253, 448 2079; 11a Calle NE at 4a Av NE; 24hr)

Dangers & Annoyances

Several years ago, travelers suffered a spate of assaults, especially on the beaches in and around Tela. While the problem has diminished significantly with the inauguration of a tourist police force, it is still not advisable to walk on the beaches around town after dark.

Sights & Activities

Tela's main attraction is its **beaches**, which stretch around the bay for several kilometers. The beach in town is OK, though

sometimes littered; the one at Hotel Villas Telamar is worlds better and open to the public; it has clean, tawny, powdery sand and a huge grove of coconut trees. Beach chairs and umbrellas can be rented by nonguests (US$1.40 each) from the hotel's *palapa* (thatched, palm-leaf–roofed shelter) snack bar.

An interesting stop if you find it open, the **Garífuna Museum** (8a Calle near 1a Av NE; admission free) has good exhibits on Honduras' Garífunas. A decent gift shop sells paintings and handicrafts from these communities, too. Opening hours are irregular.

Several **Garífuna villages**, including Tornabé (p206) and Triunfo de la Cruz (p209), are also within easy reach of Tela. All are right on the coast, with simple houses shaded by coconut trees and tiny restaurants serving typical Garífuna food. And all can be visited as a day trip, and have hotels to make it an overnight stay.

Tours

Garífuna Tours (☎ 448 2904; www.garifunatours.com; 9a Calle at 5a Ave; 7:30am-6:30pm) offers all-day boat excursions to Parque Nacional Jeannette Kawas (per person US$27); birdwatching excursions to Los Micos Lagoon (per person US$27); kayaking in Punta Izopo wildlife reserve (per person US$22); and horseback riding in Jardín Botánico Lancetilla (per person US$35). Garífuna Tours has trips almost every day, which is convenient if you're not traveling with a group of people. However, prices are rather high and groups can be huge – 50 or more.

Festivals & Events

Tela is somnolent most of the year, but it's quite another story during **Semana Santa**, when the town fills up with Honduran vacationers. During that time, hotel rates can double and advance bookings are essential. In July and August, North American and European travelers descend upon the town and things get busy then too, though room rates remain unchanged.

Tela's annual festival is held on June 13.

Sleeping
BUDGET

Hotel Bertha's (☎ 448 3020; 2a Av NE near 7a Calle NE; r/tw US$11/22, r with air-con US$16;) Housed in a relatively new building near the Tela

Express bus terminal, this hotel is kept very clean – spotless, really – and has lots of plastic hanging plants and framed posters. The rooms are small but not suffocating and all have private bathrooms.

Hotel Sinai (☎ 448 1486; fax 448 3195; 5a Av NE at Calle José Trinidad Reyes; s/d/tw with shared bathroom US$6/7/11, s/d/tw US$11/14/16, air-con US$3; ⊠) Near the train tracks, the Sinai is an excellent budget option. A basic hotel with exposed brick walls, its 19 rooms have good beds and clean bathrooms. Service is especially friendly, too. The only down side is that it's a ways to the beach.

Hotel Tela (☎ 448 2150; 9a Calle NE btwn 3a & 4a Avs NE; s/d US$16/28) Fine wood construction with lots of air and light lend a certain elegance to this old building. There's a large rooftop terrace and spacious rooms with cold-water bathrooms. The on-site restaurant (mains US$2 to US$5; open for breakfast, lunch and dinner) looks like a dance hall straight out of the 1940s with its long bar, hardwood floor and high ceiling.

M@ngo Café B&B (☎ 448 0388; www.mangocafé .net; 8a Calle NE at 5a Av NE; s with fan US$12-15, d with fan US$16-18, s/d with air-con US$19/24; ⊠) This charmless but clean place is operated by Garífuna Tours and is popular with backpackers because of its central location and rates. Room 1 is by far the most spacious and it has a TV too. Don't be confused when breakfast isn't served – despite the name, none is included. Service is a bit uppity.

Ejecutivos Apart-hotel (☎ 448 1076; 8a Calle NE at 4a Av NE; r/studios US$21.25/27; ℗ ⊠) Consider staying here if you plan to stay a while – having even a small kitchen can help you save on going out for every meal. The plain but adequate studios also have air-conditioning, two double beds, cable TV and hot-water bathroom. There's 24-hour security too.

Hotel Brisas del Mar (☎ 448 2486; 7a Av NE at 10a Calle NE; r/tw US$8/19) A totally acceptable, if somewhat drab, hotel; the rooms here are breezy, clean and near the beach. The more expensive rooms are bigger and in slightly better condition.

Hotel y Restaurante Río Mar (☎ 448 0639; 11a Calle NE at 2a Ave NE; r US$16, r/tw with air-con US$31/43; ℗ ⊠) Named after its location – where the Río Tela and the Caribbean meet – the Río Mar is the only acceptable budgetish hotel on the beach. The place has seen better

days, for sure, but the rooms are clean and the service friendly. It's pretty empty during the week, which makes it kinda creepy in *The Shining* sort of way, but if you can get past that, it's a decent place. Although its right on the beach, there is no direct access to it from inside the hotel; you have to go round the corner to get there.

Hotel Mi Porvenir (☎ 448 1459; 9a Calle NE btwn 7a & 8a Avs NE; s/d/tw US$4/8/13) This three-story cement hotel offers several small rooms with fans. The bathrooms could definitely use a scrub down, though the rest of the place is relatively clean. Rooms in the front of the building are especially breezy; just prepare to be woken up by the early morning hustle and bustle.

MIDRANGE

César Mariscos Hotel y Restaurante (☎ 448 2083; www.hotelcesarmariscos.com; Calle Peatonal at 3a Av NE; r/tw US$45/49, 2-bedroom apt US$72, all incl breakfast; ℗ ⊠ 🖳 🖳) Charming rooms with a modern beachy feel open onto two sunny decks and a mezzanine-level infinity pool with Jacuzzi. Most rooms have balconies and the view from the pool – well, it's classic Caribbean. Right on the boardwalk, César Mariscos also has a beachfront restaurant.

Hotel Gran Central (☎ 448 1099; www.grancentral .com; Calle José Trinidad Reyes at 5a Av NE; s/d/ste incl breakfast US$40/50/60; ⊠) A true charmer, the Gran Central offers seven artsy rooms on the 2nd floor of a renovated colonial building. Each is decorated differently, with details like handcrafted light fixtures, checkerboard floors and hand-painted designs on the walls. Downstairs there is a classy bar-café open from 4pm to 10pm and a small reading room with English, French and German books. There also is a small but lush garden patio, where guests often take breakfast. It's a fabulous place to stay, but just a little too far from the action to call perfect.

Hotel y Restaurante Maya Vista (off 8a Calle NE between 9a and 10a Avs NE; ☎ 448 1497; www.mayavista .com; r with fan US$25, r with air-con US$40-50, tw with air-con US$50, ste US$55-65; ℗ ⊠ 🖳) Wake up to one of the best views in Tela. Built on a hill and climbing several stories into a windswept sky, this hotel seems to have acres of patio space to take in the ocean vistas. Rooms have warm, tasteful décor and some have private patios. The restaurant is a bit pricey but the food is excellent.

Hotel y Restaurante Sherwood (☎ 448 1065; www.hotelsherwood.com; Calle Peatonal at 3a Av NE; s US$25-43, d US$36-54, ste US$62-83; P ✗ ☒) The 3rd-floor rooms are definitely the way to go at this place – hardwood floors, wood paneling and great views. The other rooms are comfortable and clean but they're standard tile-floored, white-walled rooms that you'd find anywhere. A well-maintained pool and a breezy beachside restaurant are nice features.

Hotel Presidente (☎ 448 2821; www.hotelpresidentetela.com; Parque Central; r/tw US$30/40, 2-bedroom apt US$87; P ✗ ☐ ☒) A rambling hotel smack dab on parque central, the Presidente is reminiscent of Holiday Inn – pleasant but impersonal. Rooms boast air-conditioning, furniture sets, matching bedspreads and big bathrooms. Features like a pool, game room and gym (even if it is an oversized closet) are nice surprises. There's also a decent restaurant (mains US$2 to US$6), open for breakfast, lunch and dinner. An excellent value.

TOP END
Hotel Villas Telamar (☎ 448 2196; telemar@simon.intertel.hn; s/d with garden view US$82/88, r with ocean view US$129, 1-/2-bedroom apt US$117/146, 2-/3-/4-bedroom villas US$187/262/297; P ✗ ☒) Tela's heavy hitter, this mega resort offers brand-spanking-new hotel rooms, well-maintained Caribbean-style bungalows and villas, and the best stretch of beach around. There are two pools – a quiet, shady one frequented by magazine-toting adults, and an enormous lively one with fountains, bridges and slides where most of the kids hang out. Although it's not an all-inclusive, it is set up like one; there's daily programming (dance classes, water aerobics, beach-volleyball competitions), two restaurants (including a buffet, of course), and on weekends guests wear wrist bands to keep the riff-raff out. The resort also boasts three tennis courts and an 18-hole golf course, all complimentary for guests. It's 2km west of town.

Eating
Seafood is plentiful, delicious and inexpensive around Tela. Seafood soups are a particular delicacy of the town; fish, shrimp, lobster and *caracol* (conch) are found in many restaurants. Another specialty of the town is *pan de coco*; you'll see Garífuna women and children selling it around town. Try it – it's delicious.

BUDGET
Luces del Norte (☎ 448 1044; 11a Calle NE at 5a Av NE; dishes US$2.50-8; ☺ breakfast, lunch & dinner) This longtime favorite has a casual atmosphere, inexpensive meals and a postcard stand to boot. The menu has all the standard breakfasts and *platos fuertes* (main dishes) plus great sandwiches – fish, chicken, BLT, even peanut butter and banana – and a long list of soups, like vegetable clam and one called Queen's Seafood Soup.

Tuty's (9a Calle NE at 5a Av NE; dishes US$2-3; ☺ 6am-10pm) This gleaming air-cooled pastry and licuado (smoothie) shop and the hot cramped chicken place next door are one and the same – a culinary Dr Jekyll and Mr Hyde. The chicken place serves up good greasy meals; the breakfast and lunch specials – US$2 and US$1.60 respectively – are a steal. Just sit where the industrial-strength fans hit you, so you don't sweat off everything you just ate. A licuado from next door also helps.

Auto Pollo Al Carbón #1 (11a Calle at 2a Av; ☺ breakfast, lunch & dinner) Just a wishbone's throw from the beach, this simple open-air chicken shack serves up good roast chicken.

In New Tela, two side-by-side restaurants near Kahlua's (a bar-disco) offer good hefty meals in a lively atmosphere. **Charley's** (mains US$5-12; ☺ lunch & dinner) and **Steakhouse** (mains US$5-12; ☺ lunch & dinner) have excellent, moderately priced steaks, plus chicken and pork dishes and sandwiches.

Despensa Familiar (Parque Central; ☺ 7am-7pm Mon-Sat, 7am-6pm Sun) is a large supermarket on parque central. The **Mercado Municipal** (8a Av NE btwn 10a & 11a Calles NE; ☺ 7am-5pm Mon-Sat, to 2pm Sun) is a small but packed public market selling fresh fruits, veggies, breads, dried foods and seafood. You'll also find cheap clothing, shoes, toiletries and bootleg CDs.

MIDRANGE
Captain T's Casa Azul Caribbean Café (☎ 415 3072; 11a Calle NE at 6a Av NE; mains US$3-10 ☺ lunch & dinner, Thu-Tue) Under new ownership, this longtime favorite now has a mostly Caribbean-Garífuna menu, with some southern Florida flare, like deep-fried fish, and holdovers

from the old restaurant, like pizza and spaghetti.

Pizzería Bella Italia (☎ 448 1055; 4a Av NE at Calle Peatonal; mains US$4-12; ☻ lunch & dinner, Tue-Sun) The friendly Italian owners spent almost a decade in Santa Rosa de Copán before moving to Tela to be near the beach. Pizza here is terrific – from *personal* to 16-piece *gigantes* (extra large) – but the specialty is the *panzerotti*, a variation of calzone stuffed with salami, ham, mushrooms and more.

Hotel y Restaurante Maya Vista (☎ 448 1497; mains US$3-11.50; ☻ breakfast, lunch & dinner) Off 8a Calle NE between 9a and 10a Avs NE, this restaurant has friendly service, excellent home-cooked dishes and a spectacular view from its breezy outdoor dining area. A full meal will set you back a bit but the seafood dishes are well worth it. The view is at least worth a coffee and cake in the afternoon.

César Mariscos Hotel y Restaurante (☎ 448 2083; Calle Peatonal at 3a Av NE; mains US$4-10; ☻ breakfast, lunch & dinner) A bustling open-air restaurant right on the boardwalk, this place is known for serving up great fresh seafood – it's regarded by some as one of the town's best restaurants. Service is slow but then again, what's the rush?

Hotel y Restaurante Sherwood (☎ 448 1065; Calle Peatonal at 3a Av NE; mains US$2-8; ☻ breakfast, lunch & dinner) Offering reliable meals overlooking the beach, the Sherwood has a classic hotel-restaurant menu – there's something for everyone: *típica,* sandwiches, pasta, grilled meats and seafood. There's live music on weekends.

Drinking

A number of restaurants around town stay open late on weekends for bar service. A good place to start out the night, **Max Bar & Grill** (10a Calle NE btwn 1a & 2a Avs NE; ☻ open late Thu-Sat) has US$1 beers and rum and tequila drinks, plus late-night food service if you get the munchies – pizza, sandwiches, even Sloppy Joes. It's next door to Iguana's Sports Bar & Discotec and a short walk from the other clubs. **Captain T's Casa Azul Caribbean Café** (☎ 415 3072; 11a Calle NE at 6a Av NE) and the **Hotel y Restaurante Maya Vista** (☎ 448 1497; off 8a Calle NE btwn 9a & 10a Avs NE) both have mellow bar scenes. On the boardwalk, Arrecifes serves cheap beers and sometimes

has a guy with his keyboard belting out tunes.

Entertainment

Tela has several discos, most clustered on 11a Calle NE. Some can get a little rough though, so ask around about the current situation before you venture into one. **Iguana's Sports Bar & Discotec** (10a Calle NE near 2a Av NE) in town and **Kahlua** (11a Calle NE) just across the 11a Calle NE bridge are both popular spots for travelers. Iguana's also posts upcoming shows and events on a chalkboard outside its front door.

Getting There & Away
BUS

Direct buses to La Ceiba (US$2.50, 1½ hours) don't enter Tela proper; instead, take a taxi to the Dippsa gasoline station on the highway, where buses from San Pedro Sula on the way to La Ceiba pass every 30 to 45 minutes. Alternatively, ordinary buses to La Ceiba (US$1.60, 2½ hours) leave from the second-class bus terminal on 9a Calle NE every 25 minutes from 4am to 6pm.

Transportes Tela Express (2a Av NE) operates direct buses to San Pedro Sula (US$3, 1½ to two hours) from its terminal a block past the train tracks; departures are at 6am, 7am, 8am, 10am, 12:30pm and 2pm Monday to Saturday and at 7am, 8am, 10:30am, 1pm, 2:30pm, 3:30pm, 4:30pm and 5:30pm on Sunday.

Buses to various Garífuna villages leave from a dirt lot at the corner of 8a Av NE and 11a Calle NE. Buses go to Triunfo de la Cruz (US$0.50, 30 minutes) and continue to La Ensenada (US$0.75, 45 minutes) hourly from 9am to 5pm (until 4pm only on Sunday). Buses to San Juan (US$0.45, 25 minutes) and Tornabé (US$0.50, 30 minutes) leave from the same lot on roughly the same schedule.

Buses to Jardín Botánico Lancetilla leave from the corner of 6a Av NE and 11a Calle NE.

Garífuna Tours (☎ 448 2904; www.garifunatours .com; 9a Calle at 5a Ave), half a block from parque central, runs shuttles from Tela to San Pedro Sula city and airport (per person US$15), La Ceiba city and airport (per person US$15), and Copán Ruínas (per person US$39). There's no fixed schedule, but at least three people are required to make a trip. Advance reservations are required; there's an additional cost for travel at night.

TRAIN
The passenger train between Tela and Puerto Cortés no longer operates.

Getting Around
BICYCLE
M@ngo Café B&B (☎ 448 0388; 8a Calle NE at 5a Av NE) rents bicycles for US$4/7 per half-/full day.

TAXI
Tela abounds with taxis; a ride in town costs US$0.55.

JARDÍN BOTÁNICO LANCETILLA
One of the largest tropical botanical gardens in the world, **Lancetilla Botanical Garden & Research Center** (www.lancetilla.org; admission US$6; ☯ 7:30am-5pm, no entry after 4pm) spans some 1680 hectares with 1200 species of plants from four continents. The garden has hundreds of bird species and generates 60% of Tela's fresh water.

Lancetilla was founded in 1926 by American botanist Wilson Popenoe, who was hired by the United Fruit Company to research banana plant diseases and identify new crop possibilities. In his first year, Popenoe oversaw the introduction of the African palm, still one of Honduras's most important agricultural products. One of Popenoe's most important collaborators was his wife, Dorothy, herself a botanist and archaeologist. In a tragic irony, Dorothy died in Tela in 1932 after accidentally eating the fruit of an ackee tree, an infamously poisonous tree and one of several African species the Popenoes had brought to the garden. She is buried at Lancetilla.

Visiting the Garden
Well-marked trails wind through the main garden and arboretum areas. The trees are divided and labeled according to their major characteristic: ornamental, medicinal, fruit-bearing, timber and poisonous. At the far end of the garden is a long tunnel formed by an arch of bamboo, leading to a swimming hole. Guides are not required, though most are quite knowledgeable; an hour-long tour is only US$5 per group, and most visitors consider it well worth the price.

Lancetilla is also famous for its birds, with some 365 recorded species. Special bird-watching tours (US$16) can be arranged in advance directly with the guides at the bus stop, or by calling the information office ahead of time; tours typically start at 5:30 am or 6am and include three to four hours' hiking through the garden's deeper reaches. Migratory species are present from November to February.

Sleeping
If you're interested in taking a bird-watching tour, which starts at dawn, consider staying a night or two in the park itself. Eight cabins and 12 hotel-like rooms near the park's visitors area are open to the public when they're not filled with visiting researchers and university students. The **cabins** (US$20; ✷) have three individual beds, private bathrooms and air-conditioning. The **rooms** (with fan/air-con US$13.25/15; ✷) are modern in style and occupy the upper floor of a large building behind the *comedor* (a basic, cheap eatery). Call the **visitor information office** (☎ 448 1740; 7am-4pm Mon-Fri, 8am-noon Sat) ahead of time to make reservations.

Getting There & Away
Small buses, from Tela to the gardens, leave from the corner of 6a Av NE and 11a Calle NE, opposite Captain T's Casa Azul Caribbean Café, at 6:30am (Monday to Friday only) and 8am, 10:50am, 1:30pm and 3:30pm (US$0.80, 20 minutes) daily. The return is at 6:20am (Monday to Friday only) and 9am, 11:30am, 2pm and 4pm daily. The bus stops at the ticket kiosk for anyone who needs to pay (many of the passengers are workers) and continues to the main garden and hiking area.

A great way to get to the gardens is by bike, which can be rented in Tela (left). Be extra careful riding on the highway, as there's not much shoulder in places. The dirt road into the park is well-maintained and has little traffic.

PARQUE NACIONAL JEANNETTE KAWAS (PUNTA SAL)
Standing on the beach at Tela, you can look to the west and see a long arc of land curving out to a point. This point, Punta Sal, is part of the Parque Nacional Jeannette Kawas, one of the most scenic places on the north coast. The park has several white-sand beaches, the prettiest and most popular being Playa Cocalito.

JEANNETTE KAWAS

Born in Tela in 1947, Blanca Jeannette Kawas Fernández did not become involved with environmentalism until late in life. In 1992, having returned to Tela after many years of living in the US, Kawas was approached by a Peace Corps volunteer to participate in an ecological organization. She accepted and eventually became president of the group, known as Fundación Prolansate (the Foundation for the Protection of Lancetilla, Punta Sal & Texiguat).

By all accounts, Kawas was a tireless advocate for the environment and a stickler for the law. She would personally patrol the park at night, looking for poachers. Among the people caught by Prolansate and fined for environmental violations were cattle ranchers, former military officers, even a former congressman turned resort owner (who was fined US$1000 for illegally catching dolphins).

In 1995 Kawas and Prolansate were embroiled in a bitter three-way struggle over development in the park. The Unión Nacional de Campesinos (UNC), the country's largest campesino organization, had been granted rights to clear a huge portion of the then Punta Sal Marino National Park to turn it into agricultural land for thousands of poor farmers. At the same time, the palm-oil company Hondupalma had secured a concession to clear part of the park to grow oil-palm trees.

Kawas, who sympathized with the farmers if not with Hondupalma, opposed both concessions, arguing they were shortsighted and would destroy the park. Among other efforts, she organized a 200-person march against the projects, in which she was photographed with a sign that read *No prostituyan el decreto del parque* – 'Don't prostitute the park decree'. Two days later, on February 6, 1995, gunmen shot Jeannette Kawas through an open window in her home. A bullet struck her in the head as she sat doing paperwork at her kitchen table.

Kawas' murder was one in a string of assassinations of environmental and indigenous-rights activists, including Carlos Luna in 1997, Carlos Escaleras in 1998, and Carlos Flores in 2001. Of the four murders, only one has resulted in an arrest. Kawas has been compared to Chico Mendes, the Brazilian environmentalist whose killing brought international attention to efforts made to save the Amazon rain forest. Kawas' legacy certainly lives on – the UNC and Hondupalma projects did not go forward, and Punta Sal was renamed in her honor. More importantly, Fundación Prolansate continues its work protecting natural areas on the north coast.

A lone family there prepares basic meals. Offshore are coral reefs that make for fine snorkeling, and in the forest live troops of howler monkeys. The park was formerly known as Parque Nacional Marino Punta Sal; it was renamed after Jeannette Kawas, a former director of Fundación Prolansate, who was murdered in 1995 during a bitter struggle to protect the park from development. There is a US$3 fee to enter.

On the park's east side is the Laguna de los Micos (Lagoon of the Monkeys), containing extensive mangrove forests. It's a habitat for hundreds of species of birds (especially from November to February, when migratory species flock here) and for the monkeys that the lagoon is named for.

Getting There & Away

There are a few ways to visit the park. Most day trips leave at 8am and return at 3pm – returning much later means fighting high waves on the way back. **Garífuna Tours** (☎ 448

2904; www.garifunatours.com; 9a Calle at 5a Ave) in Tela has trips to Parque Nacional Jeanette Kawas (Punta Sal) almost daily, including hiking, snorkeling and hanging out on Playa Cocalito (per person US$27). This is definitely the easiest way to go, though groups can be big and the tour can feel prepackaged.

Local *lancheros* (boat operators) can provide more personalized service but it can be hard for independent travelers to pull together enough people to make the trip affordable. Don Ardon (☎ 448 2217) is a reliable and recommended boatman and guide, charging US$105 to US$135 for groups of up to 12 passengers. You can also ask at the **Bahía Azul restaurant** (☎ 448 2381; ⏰ 7am-11pm), opposite the Hotel y Restaurante Río Mar in Tela, whose owner does the Punta Sal trip for around US$20 per person for groups of six or more. Otherwise, you can negotiate a trip with one of the boatmen who tie up under the bridge between old and new Tela.

It's also possible to make the trip from the town of Miami. From there you can do a day trip by boat or even walk to Punta Sal and camp there, which, among other things, means you have the beach to yourself after 2pm.

REFUGIO DE VIDA SILVESTRE PUNTA IZOPO

Standing on the beach at Tela and looking to the east, you can see another point: Punta Izopo, namesake of the Punta Izopo Wildlife Reserve. Rivers flowing through the wildlife refuge splinter out into a tangled network of canals and thick mangrove forests. Many animals make their home here, including monkeys, crocodiles, turtles and many species of birds, including toucans and parrots.

Garífuna Tours (☎ 448 2904; www.garifunatours .com; 9a Calle at 5a Ave; Tela) offers kayak trips to the refuge (US$21.50 per person), though it leaves too late to really have a chance at seeing much. On the other hand, independent boatman are unlikely to have kayaks (and exploring the reserve in a motorboat would defeat the purpose).

TORNABÉ

pop 1476

The largest and most developed of the Garífuna villages in the area is Tornabé, around 8km west of Tela. The name comes from 'Turn Bay,' a name given to this inlet by English pirates in the 16th century.

Sights & Activities

The best beach in the area is outside of town at **Pelican Resort** (☎ 366 3550; ◐ 8am-7pm, Tue-Sun), which nonguests are welcome to use, free of charge. The resort keeps it tidy and clean, and the waves are usually pretty mellow. A large pool and water slide (US$4/5.50 per child/adult) is nice for those with kids. A taxi from Tela runs US$2, or less from Tornabé.

The Hotel Last Resort can arrange a day trip to Parque Nacional Jeanette Kawas (Punta Sal) for around US$135 for up to 12 people.

Sleeping & Eating

Hotel The Last Resort (☎ 995 2695; victorresort@ yahoo.es; tw/tr US$27/43; ℗ ℀) There is a whole genre of hotels for people who don't want

to spend top-dollar for a resort, but still want a place to relax for a week, eat their meals, drink some beers, have some easy conversation. The Last Resort fits that description but the grubby cabins and so-so beach leave plenty to be desired.

Getting There & Away

Buses leave Tela for Tornabé every hour; see p203 for details. If you're driving or cycling, you can get to San Juan on the beach road heading west from Tela and continue on to Tornabé. Be careful when you cross the sandbar at the Laguna de los Micos between San Juan and Tornabé; vehicles regularly get stuck. You can also get to Tornabé from Hwy 13; it's longer but it is paved. The turnoff is 5km west of Tela and marked by a sign for 'Hotel The Last Resort.'

MIAMI

Miami is often described as a 'pure' Garífuna village, a cluster of thatched huts at the end of a long sandy road, free of outside influence. There's only one catch: it's not a Garífuna town! It's a designated Garífuna area, and many of the lots are owned by Garífuna people, but almost all of Miami's full-time residents are ladinos who have moved here from Tela, some recently, some generations ago. Most of Miami's Garífunas spend most of their time in Tornabé, where there are jobs, shops, schools and bars (not to mention electricity and running water).

This is not to say Miami isn't a worthwhile place to visit. The beach is scenic and the village appealingly rustic, assuming you don't mind latrine toilets, dirt floors and no electricity. It's also a great jumping-off point for trips, by boat or by foot, to Parque Nacional Jeanette Kawas (Punta Sal) (p204) and the Laguna de los Micos.

Activities

Miami native Alejandro Alas (☎ 950 6853) is one of a half-dozen boat operators in Miami who take travelers on day drips to Punta Sal for US$80 per boat (up to seven people) and Laguna de los Micos for US$27 per boat (up to six people). It is also possible to walk from Miami to Punta Sal and camp there, if you've got camping gear. There is a US$3 park fee for all visitors.

THE NORTH COAST

Trips to Parque Nacional Jeanette Kawas (Punta Sal) by boat should start as early as possible because you have to return no later than 2pm; after that, the wind and waves pick up, and the boat passage can be dangerous. The boat ride to/from Miami takes about 30 minutes. Trips to Parque Nacional Jeanette Kawas (Punta Sal) has a number of beaches, the most scenic of which is Playa Cocalito, where there is a family that serves simple meals. All the tour groups from Tela come here, but if you time your trip, you can avoid them, at least somewhat. From Cocalito, a number of trails, both marked

---

THE GARÍFUNA

In May 2005 the National Garífuna Council of Belize sent a letter to the Walt Disney Company, which was preparing to film sequels to its hit film *Pirates of the Caribbean*. The council objected to the scripts' portrayal of Carib islanders as cannibals, arguing there is no evidence that Caribs regularly ate humans (though roasting a prisoner or two probably did figure into certain warrior rituals). Disney demurred, saying cannibalism was too integral to the plot to change.

The Garífuna Council cares, of course, because Garífuna people – also known as Garínagu – are descended from the Caribs. Originally from South America, this tribe was known for its fighting skills and use of poison darts, and migrated to the Caribbean in the 13th century. The Caribs mingled with the Arawak, an Amerindian group that had made the same northward journey 1000 years prior, to form the Calinago, or Island Caribs.

Columbus' arrival in 1492 heralded disease, enslavement and near extermination for the Calinago – but never total subjugation. Over the next three centuries, the Calinago mixed with escaped African slaves to form a new race known as Black Caribs. British soldiers finally conquered the group in 1796 and, fearing an uprising, deported 5000 of them to the island of Baliceaux, then to Roatán. More than 2000 died in the process, while the survivors became the first Garífunas. April 12 – the date in 1797 when they were ignominiously abandoned on Roatán – is today celebrated as 'Arrival Day.'

The Garífuna settled the Bay Islands and then the coast, establishing communities from La Moskitia to Belize. When banana jobs dried up in the 1930s, many Garífuna men joined the US and British merchant marines. Today there are about 300,000 Garífuna people around the world. The largest number still live in Honduras – around 100,000 – but almost the same amount live in the US, especially Houston, Chicago, Los Angeles, Miami, New York City and New Orleans.

Garifuna life and culture has evolved with the times, but certain elements have survived from antiquity. Yucca was a staple of the Arawak Indians in the 2nd century AD, and of the Caribs after them, and present-day methods of cultivating and preparing the starchy root have changed little over the millennia. (The word Garífuna comes from a Carib phrase meaning 'people who eat yucca.') The most famous yucca product is *ereba*, better known by its Spanish name of *casabe*, a large wafer-like cake made from yucca flour. The yucca must first be grated and dried, and it is traditional for women to sing while doing so, their distinctive and melancholy songs harkening back centuries. The Garífuna are also well known for their dances – the *coreopatea*, *hunguhungu*, *wanaragua* – which often portray ancient fables.

In May 2001 Unesco named the Garífuna language and culture as one of its inaugural 'Masterpieces of the Oral and Intangible Heritage of Humanity.' Storytelling is a deeply important custom among the Garífuna – and *urugas* (storytellers) are much revered – but it was only recently that Garífuna stories were written down. Garífuna language is a mixture of Arawak, Carib and West African words, and there is still no official orthography: Garífunas from English-speaking Belize and Spanish-speaking Honduras and Guatemala disagree on how to properly spell numerous words, such as *gifity* versus *guifity* (a traditional drink), or *hana* versus *jana* (a mortar for mashing plantains).

Garífuna communities face very modern challenges as well, from AIDS to the lasting impact of Hurricane Mitch. Unemployment is high in many communities, something that remittances from abroad both mitigate and perpetuate. There are few definitive works of Garífuna history and culture; online, www.garinagu.com, www.stanford.edu/group/arts/honduras and www.ngcbelize .org have good basic information.

national-park trails and unmarked ones, lead to less-visited beaches, including Puerto Caribe and La Ensenada; you may spot howler monkeys on the way. There is also terrific snorkeling, though you'll need to bring your own gear.

On foot, cross the mouth of the lagoon and continue 7km along the beach – budget two hours – before passing a marked national park trail. Rather than take that, however, look for an unmarked trail a short distance further that leads over the sea cliffs to Playa Cocalito, about another half-hour of hiking. You can camp on Playa Cocalito – after 2pm the tour groups leave and you'll have it all to yourself. To get back, try hitching a ride with one of the tour groups, which ought to cost US$5 to US$7.

We have heard secondhand reports of assaults on this hike – it's a lonely stretch between Miami and Playa Cocalito. Others have done it with no problems, but still it's best not to go alone. And be sure to bring camping gear: if you don't manage a boat ride back, you'll have to stay the night and try the following day.

If you're going by boat to Laguna de los Micos, it's best to leave early, for the best bird and wildlife viewing. The trip lasts about an hour (or more if you can negotiate it) and includes a short hike on a small island and a stop at an observation town.

Sleeping & Eating

Alejandro Alas (☎ 950 6853) also has three extremely simple cabins – dirt floors, thatched roofs, mud-plastered walls – with two beds apiece and generator power until 9pm. Alas provides candles and linens, but no *mosquitero* (mosquito net) – definitely bring one of your own. There are latrine toilets and a cup-and-bucket shower, naturally. It's at the far end of town. Simple meals are also available (US$2 to US$4).

It's also possible to camp; just be sure to find out who owns the plot you're looking at and ask their permission. You may want to arrange to have use of the latrine and shower, as well, for which you should offer a small fee.

You should be able to buy water and snacks in Miami for everyday use, but if you're planning to hike to Parque Nacional Jeanette Kawas (Punta Sal), stock up in Tela or Tornabé.

Getting There & Away

Miami is 8km northwest of Tornabé down a narrow sand road, passable by car in the summer, but by 4WD only in the winter. Pickups leave Tornabé for Miami (US$1, 45 minutes) at 6am and 1pm, and leave Miami for the return trip at 7:15am and 2pm, daily except Sunday. You may be able to hitch a ride, if one happens by, or even walk, though the road is hot and exposed most of the way – bring a hat and plenty of water.

LA ENSENADA

The closest village to Tela is La Ensenada, 5km east along the arc of the beach, just before you reach Punta Triunfo, which is crowned by the Cerro El Triunfo de la Cruz. La Ensenada is a charming little village with seafood restaurants (although most are only open on the weekend, when it can get pretty crowded). The beach here isn't bad.

Activities

Local resident Gerardo Colón can take travelers in a horse-drawn *carreta* (a type of carriage, with a sun shade) to various points along the beach, most commonly to Punta Izopo. Trips cost US$15 per person and last about four hours.

Sleeping & Eating

Hotel Leoduvis (☎ 935 3507; r with fan/air-con US$14/19; P ☒) A surprisingly well-maintained hotel, Leoduvis has eight clean and appealing rooms with good beds and cold-water showers. There is a good beach just in front with a parade of palm trees on it that help keep things cool. The hotel is on the main street, in front of the beach.

Hotel Budari (☎ 365 2957; r US$27, cable TV US$5; P ☒) At the far west end of the main street, this place is definitely a step up from the rest – you get hot water, at least – but it's pretty pricey. Rooms have large, clean bathrooms, ceramic floors and firm foam-core mattresses and that's about it. For US$27, you expect a little more.

Hotelito Mirta (☎ 984 6551; tw/bungalows US$8/11; P) Also on the main street in front of the beach, several meters behind the Leoduvis, this hotel has very rustic accommodations. Rooms here are seriously worn and just kind of clean. It's an option of last resort,

LOCAL LORE: THE FOUNTAIN OF YOUTH

A growing body of historical research calls into question the accuracy of the famous tale of Don Juan Ponce de León's 'discovery' of Florida in his quest for the fountain of youth. In fact, that search may have been conducted by another sailor altogether, Juan Díaz de Solís, and focusing on the north coast of Honduras. While de León was certainly the first European to land on Florida (where he was fatally wounded by a Native American's arrow) records of his journey mention nothing of a search for a fountain of youth – he was there to look for gold and 'wealthy land.' The mistake seems to have stemmed from misreadings of coordinates in the original documents, and a comment by 16th-century Spanish historian Gonzalo Fernández de Oviedo, who snickered that de León's ill-advised adventuring must have been done in search of a fountain of youth to cure his *enflaquecimiento del sexo* (flaccid member). They don't seem to mention that theory at the 'Fountain of Youth' theme park in St Augustine, Florida. For his part, Solís searched the Golfo de Honduras as far as Belize, with no luck.

mainly because it has running water and 24-hour electricity.

Getting There & Away

From Tela, buses headed to La Ensenada (US$0.75, 30 minutes) leave from a dirt lot at the corner of 8a Av NE and 11a Calle NE hourly from 9am to 5pm (until 4pm only on Sunday). The last bus back to Tela leaves La Ensenada at 3:30pm.

If you're driving, the turnoff to La Ensenada (and Triunfo de la Cruz) is 5km east of Tela on the coastal highway. From there, take the road 500m until you come to a fork in the road: La Ensenada is 500m down the left prong.

TRIUNFO DE LA CRUZ

Triunfo de la Cruz is larger and more developed than La Ensenada, and as a result has lost some of the peaceful, somnolent air of the smaller villages. At the same time, food, lodging and services are better and more abundant here, and the pretty, grey beach is good for swimming, with waves neither too strong nor too wimpy.

Sleeping & Eating

Cabañas y Restaurante Colón (☎ 986 5622; tw US$11-16, r with air-con US$24; P ⌘) In the center of town, this charming and well-kept hotel is made up of several cabañas. Most are thatch-roofed but all have cold-water bathrooms and are just feet from a well-maintained beach. The ones with air-conditioning also have cable TV. A sister hotel, next door, has cheaper rooms, but they're much less appealing. The hotel restaurant (mains US$3.25 to US$10.75, open

for breakfast, lunch and dinner) specializes in seafood.

Caribbean Coral Inn (☎ 994 9806; www.caribbean coralinn.com; s/d incl breakfast US$51/62) This small hotel at the eastern end of town offers rustic but comfortable bungalows. All open onto the beach and have queen beds and hot-water bathrooms. A continental breakfast is served beachside at the hotel eatery, La Banana Restaurant (mains US$3 to US$10), which is also open for lunch and dinner. The rate is a bit high for what you get – it's pretty basic after all – but the beach is clean, the food good, and there always seems to be a hammock available. All-inclusive packages (US$25 extra per person) and day passes (adult/child US$9/30) are available too.

Getting There & Away

Buses (US$0.50, 30 minutes) leave roughly every hour from a dirt lot at the corner of 8a Av NE and 11a Calle NE in Tela.

The turnoff to Triunfo de la Cruz is 5km east of Tela on the coastal highway. Take this road 500m to a fork in the road (look for the dilapidated 'Bienvenidos' sign). Triunfo de la Cruz is 700m down the right-hand road.

LA CEIBA & AROUND

La Ceiba could hardly be better situated: the city stands at the foot of Parque Nacional Pico Bonito and the towering Sierra Nombre de Dios. To the west is the Cuero y Salado Wildlife Reserve, home to monkeys, tropical birds and even manatees.

East of town is the Río Cangrejal, serving up some of Central America's best rafting, from Class II rollers to Class V white water. Further east are the Garífuna villages of Nueva Armenia and Sambo Creek, and the jumping-off point to the remarkable Cayos Cochinos. La Ceiba is where you come to catch the ferry to Roatán and Utila, and is a good place to organize (and begin) trips into La Moskitia, Honduras's final frontier.

For all its natural wonders, this area is still just learning how to cater to foreign travelers. A number of entities, including the government, eco-lodge owners, tour operators, NGOs, USAID, and the Peace Corps, have been working in and around La Ceiba to develop its infrastructure and tourism potential.

LA CEIBA
pop 134,449
La Ceiba is a convenient base camp for a slew of good outdoor excursions, including hiking, canoeing, rafting, canopy tours and butterfly farms. Sure, it's not the most attractive city in the world – the hotels are so-so and the beach is mediocre – but hopefully you'll be out and about all day and have energy to check out the city's justly famous nightlife. You're certain to pass through La Ceiba anyway, on your way to/from the Bay Islands or La Moskitia. Rather than making a beeline from bus station to the ferry pier, stop here a while – it's well worth it.

History
Pech indigenous people occupied much of the north coast before – and well after – the arrival of Spanish explorers. The first non-Indians to settle in present-day La Ceiba arrived in 1810 and were not Spanish, but Garífunas from Trujillo. They were followed by waves of immigrants from Olancho, who were fleeing the violence that broke out there in 1828 and lasted a half-century. The Spanish finally showed up in 1846, followed by French settlers in 1857. The city – officially chartered in 1872 – was long known as La Ceiba for a large ceiba tree that stood near the coast, used as a mooring and a community gathering place. (The tree was cut down in 1917 to make room for a new customs house.) Cuban and

Arab wayfarers also settled here before the end of the century.

La Ceiba's modern history began in 1899, with the arrival of the Vacarro brothers, who founded a banana exporting business that would become the Standard Fruit Company, today known as the Dole Food Company. La Ceiba was its longtime headquarters, and much of the city's early infrastructure, including the port, railroad tracks, electrical system, hospitals, parks, housing and the first bank, was built by Standard to support its massive operations. Today, Dole Fruit Company, and its main competitor, the United Fruit Company, now Chiquita – continues to provide thousands of jobs for area residents, even while many of its corporate and labor practices are denounced by labor unions and environmental organizations.

Orientation
Most travelers find all they need in La Ceiba's center. The shady central park has a cathedral on one corner and a Pizza Hut on another. Av San Isidro is the main north–south corridor; it runs alongside parque central, north to the ocean and south to the highway. Along the ocean is 1a Calle, which extends east across a small inlet to Barrio La Isla, a mostly Garífuna neighborhood that's also home to the Zona Viva, La Ceiba's nightlife district. Two blocks south of the park, 11a Calle turns into Av 15 de Septiembre and runs west 2km to the main bus terminal; you can also catch passing buses on the highway. The airport is 10km west of town, the ferry pier 8km to the east.

Information
BOOKSTORES
Rain Forest Gifts (Map p211; ☎ 443 2917; rain_forest _hn@yahoo.com; Av La Bastilla; ☼ 9am-noon & 2-5:30pm Mon-Fri, 9am-noon Sat) A gift shop with a wide selection of used English-language books for sale and exchange.

EMERGENCY
Red Cross (☎ 195, 443 0707; Carr Muelle Cabotaje near Av 14 de Julio; ☼ 24hr)
Tourist police (☎ 441 0860; Residencial El Toronjal; ☼ 24hr) Three blocks south of Carr a Tela.

IMMIGRATION
Immigration office (Map p213; ☎ 442 0638; 1a Calle near Av 14 de Julio; ☼ 7:30am-3:30pm Mon-Fri)

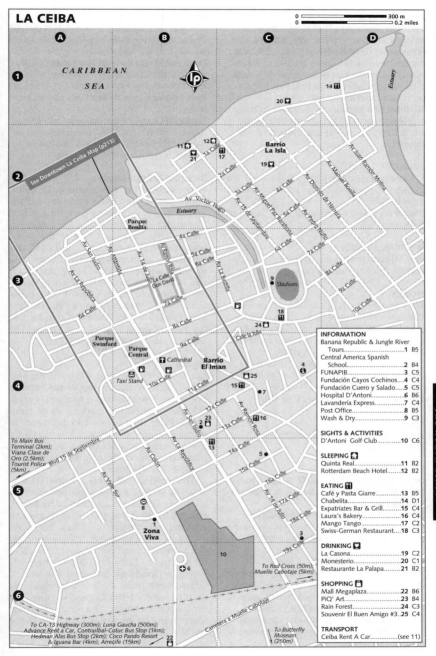

LA CEIBA

0 — 300 m
0 — 0.2 miles

CARIBBEAN SEA

Barrio La Isla

Estuary

Barrio El Iman

Parque Bonilla

Parque Swinford

Parque Central

Cathedral

Taxi Stand

Zona Viva

Stadium

To Main Bus Terminal (2km);
Viana Clase de Oro (2.5km);
Tourist Police (5km)

To CA-13 Highway (300m); Luna Gaucha (500m);
Advance Rent a Car, Contrailbal-Cotuc Bus Stop (1km);
Hedman Alas Bus Stop (2km); Coco Pando Resort
& Iguana Bar (4km); Arrecife (15km)

To Red Cross (50m);
Muelle Cabotaje (5km)

Carretera a Muelle Cabotaje

To Butterfly Museum (250m)

THE NORTH COAST

INFORMATION
Banana Republic & Jungle River
   Tours.....................................**1** B5
Central America Spanish
   School.................................**2** B4
FUNAPIB.................................**3** C5
Fundación Cayos Cochinos....**4** C4
Fundación Cuero y Salado.....**5** C5
Hospital D'Antoni...................**6** B6
Lavandería Express................**7** C4
Post Office.............................**8** B5
Wash & Dry............................**9** C3

SIGHTS & ACTIVITIES
D'Antoni Golf Club...............**10** C6

SLEEPING 🏠
Quinta Real...........................**11** B2
Rotterdam Beach Hotel........**12** B2

EATING 🍽
Café y Pasta Giarre..............**13** B5
Chabelita..............................**14** D1
Expatriates Bar & Grill.........**15** C4
Laura's Bakery......................**16** C4
Mango Tango........................**17** C2
Swiss-German Restaurant....**18** C3

DRINKING 🍷
La Casona.............................**19** C2
Monesterio............................**20** C1
Restaurante La Palapa..........**21** B2

SHOPPING 🛍
Mall Megaplaza....................**22** B6
PiQ' Art.................................**23** B4
Rain Forest...........................**24** C3
Souvenir El Buen Amigo #3..**25** C4

TRANSPORT
Ceiba Rent A Car...............(see 11)

INTERNET ACCESS

Cyber City (Airport; per hr US$1.85; ☉ 5:30am-7pm) Also offers web-based telephone service to the USA.

Miramar Café Internet (Map p213; ☎ 443 2666; Av San Isidro btwn 5a & 6a Calles; per hr US$0.80; ☉ 8am-9pm) Web-based telephone service too (per-minute calls to the USA and Canada cost US$0.08, to Europe US$0.16 and to Australia and New Zealand US$0.16).

Multi-net (Mall Megaplaza, Carretera a Muelle Cabotaje at Av Morazán; per hr US$1.25; ☉ 9am-8:30pm Mon-Sat, 10:30am-8:30pm Sun) Personal laptops can also be plugged in.

LAUNDRY

Lavandería Express (Map p211; Barrio El Iman; per 10lb US$2.65; ☉ 7:30am-noon & 1-5pm Mon-Sat) Near the end of 12a Calle.

Wash & Dry (Map p211; per 10lb US$2.65; ☉ 8am-noon & 1-5pm Mon-Sat)

MEDICAL SERVICES

Hospital Eurohonduras (Map p213; ☎ 443 0244; Av Atlántida; ☉ 24hr) Between 1a Calle and the beach.

MONEY

BAC Av San Isidro (Map p213; at 5a Calle; ☉ 9am-5pm Mon-Fri, to noon Sat); Mall Megaplaza (Carretera a Muelle Cabotaje at Av Morazán; ☉ 10am-6pm Mon-Fri, to 5pm Sat); Airport (☉ 9am-5pm Mon-Fri, to noon Sat) All have 24-hour ATMs and exchange traveler's checks.

Banco Atlántida Av San Isidro (Map p213; btwn 6a & 7a Calles; ☉ 9am-4pm Mon-Fri, 8:30-11:30am Sat); Mall Megaplaza (Carretera a Muelle Cabotaje at Av Morazán; ☉ 10am-6pm Mon-Fri, to 5pm Sat) Both have 24 hour ATMs.

POST

Post office (Av Morazán at 14a Calle; ☉ 8am-4pm Mon-Fri, to noon Sat)

TELEPHONE

Centro de Llamadas Café @ Café (Map p213; btwn 6a & 7a Calles; ☉ 7:30am-6:15pm Mon-Sat, 8am-1pm Sun) Inexpensive web-based calls.

Hondutel (Map p213; Av Ramón Rosa near 6a Calle; ☉ 7am-9pm) International telephone service is cheaper at most internet cafés but this will do in a pinch.

TOURIST INFORMATION

Tourist office (Map p213; ☎ 440 3044; proyectoturismo@caribe.hn; 8a Calle near Av San Isidro; ☉ 8am-6pm Mon-Fri, to noon Sat) Offers a bunch of brochures and maps on area sites and has a small gift shop. Some English is spoken.

Tourist information kiosk (Map p213; ☎ 440 1562; Parque Central; ☉ 8am-6pm Mon-Sat) Dispenses basic information and brochures.

Fundación Cuero y Salado (Map p211; ☎ /fax 443 0329; www.cueroysalado.org; Av Ramón Rosa at 15a Calle; ☉ 8am-noon & 1-5pm Mon-Fri, 8-11am Sat) Manages the Cuero y Salado Wildlife Reserve.

Fundación Parque Nacional Pico Bonito (Funapib; Map p211; ☎ 442 0618; www.picobonito.org; Av 14 de Julio at 19a Calle; ☉ 7:30am-5pm Mon-Fri, 8-11am Sat) About 19km out of town. Manages Parque Nacional Pico Bonito.

Fundación Cayos Cochinos (Honduras Coral Reef Fund; Map p211; ☎ 442 2670, 443 4075; www.cayoscochinos.org; 13a Calle, Barrio El Iman; ☉ 8am-5pm Mon-Fri) Manages the Cayos Cochinos Marine Reserve.

Dangers & Annoyances

Crime against tourists is rare in La Ceiba. Police patrol the center of town and the Zona Viva, and travelers have little reason to wander into the less-secure neighborhoods. That said, La Ceiba is the country's third-largest city and you should take the same common-sense precautions you would in any urban area. The Zona Viva is safe overall, but has its fair share of drugs, prostitutes and pickpockets. Fights break out now and then, and some tourists have been hassled by local drunks. Consider taking a cab home at the end of the night. The beach is also unsafe at night.

Sights

Created by the Standard Fruit Company, the beautifully manicured **Parque Swinford** (Map p213; Av La República btwn 7a & 8a Calles) is arguably the prettiest city park in all of Honduras. Palm trees tower over hundreds of plants and flower beds, small bridges lead to gleaming bronze sculptures, and antique train cars remind visitors of the city's role in the banana industry.

The one-room **Museum of Butterflies & Insects** (☎ 442 2874; www.hondurasbutterfly.com; Etapa 2, Casa G-12, Calle Escuela Internacional, Colonia El Sauce; adult/child $3/1.50; ☉ 8am-5pm Mon-Sat) houses an amazing collection of butterflies, moths and other insects – 13,000 creepy-crawlers in all, stuck with pins and preserved in glass cases on the walls. Almost 10,000 of these are native to Honduras, including the world's largest moth (with a 30cm wingspan), the most iridescent butterfly, and the one with the longest proboscis. The remaining come from over 110 countries and include the world's largest scorpion and heaviest insect – a quarter-pounder beetle (no cheese).

You don't have to be crazy about insects to appreciate the variety and beauty of the myriad species and specimens here, all part of the private collection of schoolteacher and master bug-catcher Robert Lehman. There's a free guided tour (if someone's available) and an interesting 25-minute video about butterflies and moths.

A **city tour** (☎ 440 7562; per person US$1.60; 🕒 6–10pm Mon-Wed, Fri & Sat) on a caboose pulled by a tractor (a cabractor? a traboose?) takes visitors to La Ceiba's highlights – Parque Swinford, the Zona Viva and Barrio La Isla – while a somewhat garbled recording relates the town's history. The tour lasts 30 minutes and is mildly interesting while giving you a good idea of the lay of the land.

Tickets are sold at the information kiosk in parque central; the tour leaves from just in front.

Activities

The main reason to stop in La Ceiba is to partake in the outdoors activities all around it. All can be reached as a day trip from town, but definitely consider one of the many lodging options outside of town, whether a community-run *hospedaje* (guesthouse) or a luxury eco-lodge. Not only is the setting more scenic, but you can start hikes and canoe trips at dawn – a big advantage for spotting birds and other wildlife. In fact, Omega and Jungle River Tours both operate 'jungle lodges' and offer a free night's lodging with every trip.

DOWNTOWN LA CEIBA

INFORMATION	
BAC	**1** A3
Banco Atlántida	**2** A3
Centro de Llamadas Café @ Café	**3** A3
Hondutel	**4** B3
Hospital Eurohonduras	**5** B2
Immigration Office	**6** B2
Miramar Café Internet	**7** A3
Tourist Information Kiosk	**8** A3
Tourist Office	**9** B3

SIGHTS & ACTIVITIES	
Garífuna Tours	**10** A2
La Moskitia Ecoaventuras	(see **6**)
Tourist Options	**11** A4
Turtle Tours/Caribbean Travel	**12** A3

SLEEPING 🏠	
Gran Hotel Paris	**13** A3
Hotel Caribe	**14** A3
Hotel Ceiba	**15** A2
Hotel Iberia	**16** A3
Hotel Italia	**17** B3
Hotel Monserratte	**18** B4
Hotel Principe	**19** B3

EATING 🍴	
Cafetería Cobel	**20** B3
Comidas Royale	**21** A3
Mixers	**22** B3
Pizza Hut	**23** A3
Pupusería Univeritaria	**24** B2
Ricardo's	**25** B4
Super Ceibeño Supermarket	**26** A3
Super Ceibeño Supermarket #2	**27** B3

DRINKING 🍷	
Espresso Americano	**28** A3
Espresso Americano	**29** A3
Mangos	**30** B3

SHOPPING	
Tourist Office Gift Shop	(see **9**)

TRANSPORT	
Aerolineas Sosa	**31** A4
Atlantic Airlines	**32** A4
Molinari Rent–a–Car	(see **13**)

THE NORTH COAST

HIKING

The primary hikes in the area are to two waterfalls in the buffer zone of Parque Nacional Pico Bonito. (The park's core is closed to hiking.) See p225 for details.

Another option for hikers is through **Guaruma Servicios** (☎ 442 2673; www.guaruma.org), a new community-based tour operator in the small town of Las Mangas, on the Río Cangrejal, that offers inexpensive guided hikes. See p225 for details.

WHITE-WATER RAFTING

The Río Cangrejal forms the eastern border of Parque National Pico Bonito and is considered by many to offer the best white-water rafting in Central America. The river tumbles down a narrow river gorge, with plenty of swimming holes, ledges to clamber up and leap off, and short hikes into the park's buffer zone. Omega Tours and Jungle River Tours both offer trips; the standard outing includes two to three hours on the water and covers Class II to Class III water. Omega Tours, which costs a bit more but generally receives higher marks for service, also offers a three- to four-hour trip from further upriver, where Class IV to Class V rapids form in high water. Trips run US$35 to $45, and both outfits include lunch and a free night's stay at their jungle lodges. Be sure to ask what stops you'll make – some travelers have written to say the trips felt too short.

CANOEING & KAYAKING

Experienced kayakers can take on the Río Cangrejal; Omega Tours has rentals and organized trips. The most popular flat-water boat trips are in the Refugio de Vida Silvestre Cuero y Salado (p222), which can be arranged either independently or through most tour operators in town. Omega Tours also offers paddling trips in the less-visited Cacao Lagoon (US$46), 24km east of La Ceiba, which may well turn up more birds and howler monkeys than in Cuero y Salado.

CANOPY TOURS

Jungle River Tours opened the north coast's first canopy tour, an eight-cable circuit that begins at Jungle River's lodge on the Río Cangrejal and ends with a 660ft (200m) slide across the river (US$35 per person, two to three hours, reservation required). Like all Jungle River's tours, a free night at the river lodge is included. **Canopy Tours** (☎ 355 5481) then came along and opened an even longer tour, a 20-cable system about 500m past Sambo Creek, east of La Ceiba. The 20-cable tour (US$35 per person, two to three hours, open 8am to 5pm) starts with a 35-minute horseback ride up a steep road to the first station and includes a stop at a natural hot springs, where you can smear yourself with the possibly therapeutic, definitely sulfur-smelling mud there. Any east-bound bus from La Ceiba can drop you at the entrance; a cab there will cost around US$30.

MOUNTAIN BIKING

Jungle River Tours offers a handful of guided mountain-bike trips, ranging from mellow to challenging. The most difficult is a five-hour trip west of La Ceiba, through the Pico Bonito buffer zone to a picturesque waterfall. The ride is mostly on single-track path, and includes a stop in a small community for lunch (US$58 per person). Other trips follow the dirt road upriver from the jungle

---

IF YOU HAVE A FEW MORE DAYS

There are a number of tawny-sand beaches near La Ceiba that are easy to explore by bus (and even easier with a rental). Most are 1km or 2km off the highway, usually down dirt roads. They're empty during the week but often see action – *fútbol* games, food vendors, bodysurfing and general ocean- and sun-worshipping – on weekends. As always, be aware of your surroundings and your belongings; don't take valuables as they have a way of walking while you're practicing your synchronized swimming moves just a few meters away.

Although this coast is sprinkled with decent beaches, try these to get started: the windswept **Playa de Peru** (9.5km east), the town beach at **Villa Nuria** (17km east), the ocean and river beaches at **El Porvenir** (15km west) and the often-packed **Cuyamel** (18.5km west) with its spectacular barbecued-fish stands.

lodge, and include excellent views of the Río Cangrejal valley and/or a stop at the Colorado petroglyphs. Jungle River also rents out **mountain bikes** (per hour/day US$6/18) that you can take down the same road, stopping in villages or at vista points along the way.

HORSEBACK RIDING

Omega Tours offers excellent, one- to three-day horseback riding trips (US$), a step up from the plodding nonadventures you may have been suckered into elsewhere. Trips start on the beach west of La Ceiba, and cross through the lowland lagoons and waterways to the town of El Pino. Multiday trips include an overnight stay at a private home – or the Lodge at Pico Bonito (p219), if you want to treat yourself – and either return the next day via an alternative route or continue another day into the Pico Bonito buffer zone.

GOLF

If you're itching to play a round of golf, the **D'Antoni Golf Club** (☎ 440 2736; Carr Muelle Cabotaje near Av San Isidro; ☾ 6am-sunset) is your only option. While not a very challenging course – it's pretty flat and most greens are a straight shot from the tee – it's a fine way to spend a morning. Caddies are required (US$6) but the green fees are reasonable enough (US$10.60). Club rentals are available.

Courses

Central America Spanish School (Map p211; ☎ 440 1707; www.ca-spanish.com; Av San Isidro btwn 12a & 13a Calles) offers intensive Spanish classes for students of all levels. Classes (US$150 per week) include 20 hours per week of one-on-one instruction, weekly excursions and cultural events like Latin dance or Honduran cooking classes. Homestays (US$70 per week, including meals) and other housing options can be arranged.

Tours

Based at Hotel Palma Real, an all-inclusive resort 25km east of La Ceiba, **Dive in Caribik** (☎ 361 6584, 373 8620; www.dive-in-caribik.com) is a German-run dive shop that offers recommended diving and snorkel trips to Cayos Cochinos.

    Garifuna Tours (Map p213; ☎ 440 3252; www.garifunatours.com; Av San Isidro at 1a Calle) runs several excursions on the north coast. Most

trips are based on a four-person minimum, though this is rarely a problem, since large tour groups are the norm (and kind of a bummer).

    Based in Banana Republic Guesthouse, across from the Hospital D'Antoni, **Jungle River Tours** (☎ 440 1268; www.jungleriverlodge.com; Av Morazán) offers white-water rafting trips, canopy tours, mountain biking and hiking. A free night at their jungle lodge is included with every trip.

    Run by Jorge Salverri, an expert birder and one of the most knowledgeable guides to La Moskitia, **La Moskitia Ecoaventuras** (☎ 440 2124; www.honduras.com/moskitia; Av 14 de Julio) has tours ranging from five to 12 days that are the cheapest around, though some complain about corner cutting. Based at Hotel Plaza Caracol, Ecoaventuras also offers rafting and other day trips around La Ceiba.

    Operated by a young German couple, **Omega Tours** (☎ 440 0334; www.omegatours.hn; Omega Jungle Lodge; Calle a Yaruca, Km 9) runs top-notch tours, with licensed professional guides and impeccable service, including to La Moskitia. All trips include a free night at their jungle lodge.

    One of the recipients of Conde Nast's prestigious Green List Award in 2006, **Rare Conservation** (☎ 443 1276; www.larutamoskitia.com; Col El Sauce, 3a Etapa, Calle del Enano), a non-profit organization, offers quality, eco-friendly tours through La Moskitia. All proceeds go directly to Moskitia communities.

    The family-run **Tourist Options** (Map p213; ☎ 440 0265; www.hondurastouristoptions.com; Blvd 15 de Septiembre near Av República) arranges personalized trips throughout Honduras, including tours of Garífuna villages, hiking in Pico Bonito and kayaking in Cuero y Salado.

    German-run **Turtle Tours** (Map p213; ☎ 414 5368; www.turtle-tours.com; Av San Isidro btwn 5a & 6a Calles) has a reputation for professionalism. Formerly based in Trujillo, it is best known for guided trips into La Moskitia and multiday motorcycle tours.

Festivals & Events

Though none are the size of the Feria de San Isidro (p216), La Ceiba does have a number of other celebrations. **Semana Santa** certainly rivals the *feria* in sheer numbers; all of Honduras is on vacation and hankering to cool off on the beach, making La Ceiba one of the country's major Holy Week destinations.

FERIA DE SAN ISIDRO

La Ceiba is known to be a party town, but no ordinary Saturday night in the Zona Viva compares to the one during the city's patron saint festival, **La Feria de San Isidro**. Also known as the Gran Carnival Nacional (Great National Carnival), it is the largest celebration in Honduras and, some say, all of Central America. Nearly a quarter of a million visitors descend on La Ceiba for a weekend of live music, cultural performances and all-night food and drink stands. It culminates with a huge parade of horses, floats and dancers in costume down Av San Isidro. The party continues that night in the Zona Viva, where the bars and clubs are crammed to the rafters. The official festival and parade takes place the third Saturday in May, but crowds start arriving midweek and mini-celebrations in neighborhoods around town start a week prior. The festival is known to be friendly and safe, but be on the alert for pickpocketing and the occasional drunken brawl.

The **Carnaval del Aniversario de La Ceiba** is held in the third week of August and celebrates the founding of the city with live music and other street performances in the Zona Viva. The **Festival del Amor y Amistad** (Festival of Love & Friendship) is held in February around Valentine's Day, and also entails live music, plus contests and other activities 'all alluding to love and friendship,' according to the organizers. Finally, the city's peaceful **Festival Navideño** (Christmas Festival) is held in the first week of December in parque central.

Sleeping

La Ceiba has some terrific nature lodges outside of town (p219), with easy access to the area's many outdoor attractions. Unfortunately, the options in town are less than appealing, with average rooms for above-average prices in below-average neighborhoods. It's still worth stopping here, but most travelers won't be wowed by where they stay.

BUDGET

La Ceiba's cheapest bunks are the ones you get free – in a riverside jungle lodge, no less – when you book a trip with Omega Tours or Jungle River Tours (p215). In town, the budget options have their ups and downs, but will do for a couple days.

Banana Republic Guesthouse (☎ 441 9404; www.jungleriverlodge.com; Av Morazán; dm US$6, r US$19; P ⊠ ⬚) Only the second hostel in La Ceiba, the Banana Republic is a welcome, if imperfect, addition for budget travelers. The rooms are fine – three private units with fan and cold water, and two spacious dorms with six beds apiece, lockers and plenty of windows. A shaded patio has tables for the

free continental breakfast and a grassy yard with hammocks is perfect for chilling out. However, it's a bit of a trek from downtown and even further to any sort of nightlife. And some travelers complain about surly service from the managers and their family, who live on site. The hostel is run by Jungle River Tours, so you can get info and book tours here too.

Hotel Italia (Map p213; ☎ 443 0150; hotel@carrion .hn; Av Ramón Rosa near 6a Calle; r US$19.25-22.25, tw US$25-28; P ⊠ ⬚) Comfortable, clean and well-kept sums up the Italia pretty well. Add air-conditioning, hot water, cable TV, and in-room phones and it's a steal. Weigh in the sparkling garden-side pool and welcoming bar-lounge and it's downright dreamy. The only drawback is that it's smack dab in the middle of the outdoor market, which is fine during the day but kind of sketchy at night. Consider cabbing it after sunset.

Hotel Iberia (Map p213; ☎ 443 0401; www.hotel iberia.com; Av San Isidro btwn 5a & 6a Calle; d/tw US$22/25; P ⊠) Friendly service and clean air-conditioned rooms make the Iberia a good choice for those on the cusp of budget and midrange – the Italia is in the same category and is slightly better value, but the location here is better. Some rooms have balconies overlooking the street, which lends some natural light, but the traffic noise starts pretty early. Internet and banks are steps away, food and nightlife just a bit further. Bad plumbing can make the bathrooms stinky – a plastic bag over the shower drain works wonders.

Rotterdam Beach Hotel (Map p211; ☎ 440 0321; Av Miguel Paz Barahona at 1a Calle, Barrio La Isla; r/tr US$10/15) Clean, medium-sized rooms open onto a small garden at this quiet Barrio La Isla hotel. It's better value than a like-priced room in town, and you're near La Ceiba's nightlife, but the area is dead during the day and you're a solid 20-minute walk from the center.

Hotel Caribe (Map p213; ☎ 443 1857; 5a Calle btwn Avs San Isidro & Atlántida; s/tw US$6/10, with TV US$8/11, r with air-con & TV US$14; ☒) Upstairs rooms at this midsized hotel are a decent deal. They're huge (so big they look a little barren), with heavy-duty fans, and open onto a broad exterior corridor where you can hang hand-washed clothes. The bathrooms leave much to be desired – a good cleaning, for starters – but it's still not bad for under 10 bucks. Main-floor rooms are dark and unpleasant.

Hotel Principe (Map p213; ☎ 443 0516; 7a Calle btwn Avs Atlántida & 14 de Julio; s/tw/tr US$17/21/24; ☒) This is an adequate choice for those who are on a budget but will pay a bit extra if it means they don't have to wear flip-flops in the shower. Plain rooms with ceramic floors and clean sheets and bathrooms come in either hospital white or bright blue. The best rooms (105, 106, 145 and 146) have large windows facing a wide outdoor passageway. (You'll definitely get traffic noise in the morning, though.)

Another budget alternative, **Finca El Eden** (bertiharlos@yahoo.de; Carr a Tela, Km 158) has been recommended for its camping, basic cabins and options for hiking and horseback riding. It's 32km west of La Ceiba and run by a German-Honduran couple.

MIDRANGE

Hotel Ceiba (Map p213; ☎ 443 2747; www.hotelceiba .com; Av San Isidro at 5a Calle; s/d US$25/30; ☒ ☒ ☒) The cool classy lobby is a welcome refuge from the busy street corner just outside. Rooms have large bright bathrooms and clean ceramic floors, though the beds can be a bit spongy. Almost all have nice private balconies overlooking the street and north over town to the ocean; there are better views and less street noise on the upper floors. This is a good alternative to the Gran Paris, if you can do without the pool and park-front location.

Gran Hotel Paris (Map p213; ☎ 443 2391; hotel paris@psinet.hn; Parque Central; s/d US$36/46; ☒ ☒ ☒ ☒) The Paris was long La Ceiba's go-to spot for upscale digs; although it's been eclipsed recently by the Quinta Real, it is still a comfortable and centrally located choice. The large lobby opens onto an interior courtyard where a clean kidney-shaped pool is surrounded by a handful of tables and lounge chairs, and a small *palapa* bar. Many rooms have aging air-conditioning units and spongy beds, but there are a few renovated units worth asking about.

Hotel Monserrate (Map p213; ☎ 440 4133; monse 2703@aol.com; 9a Calle; s/d US$35/53; ☒ ☒ ☒ ☒) Another new hotel – it opened the week we passed through – the Monserratte exudes cool upscale class. Rooms are decorated in mellow reds and oranges and have firm beds and modern amenities. There's a small clean pool tucked in the back and a gym too.

Coco Pando Resort & Iguana Bar (☎ 969 9663; in the US 866 463 6959; www.cocopando.com; Colonia Ponce; r/tw US$50/60; ☒ ☒ ☒) Four kilometers west of town, the Coco Pando can be inconvenient if you don't have a car; then again, many guests come not so much to explore the area as to just sit back and relax for a while. And for that it's well suited: large, comfortable rooms, with fridge, purified water, free internet and use of kayaks and hammocks. The beach is so-so at best, but the restaurant is excellent and the hotel offers free pick-up and drop off. Owner Charlie Meador is a regular on LP's Thorntree forum (http://thorntree.lonelyplanet.com), and the resort website has lots of good info.

TOP END

La Ceiba's top hotels are Las Cascadas and the Lodge at Pico Bonito, both outside of town along the periphery of Pico Bonito National Park. For a more central location, there's only one option.

Quinta Real (Map p211; ☎ 440 3311; www.quinta realhotel.com; Av 15 de Septiembre at 1a Calle; Barrio La Isla; s/d US$75/104, ste US$104-162, incl breakfast; ☒ ☒ ☒ ☒ ☒) Opened in December 2005, this hotel has all the modern comforts you'd expect for the price, including spa, business center, pool, restaurant, shops and pool-side bar. A curving stairway leads from the lobby to 81 comfortable rooms, with hot water, air-conditioning, high-speed internet (in most), hair drier etc; the suites have nice ocean views from private patios. There's plenty of nightlife nearby, though rooms facing the back may get some unwelcome noise from a boisterous bar a half-block away. Too bad the beach isn't better.

Eating

La Ceiba has a large, if not totally remarkable, selection of restaurants and small eateries. Outside of town, The Lodge at Pico Bonito and Omega Tours Jungle Lodge (see boxed text, opposite) both serve terrific food and are open to nonguests, provided you call in advance.

BUDGET

Pupusería Universitaria (Map p213; ☎ 440 1070; 1a Calle near Av 14 de Julio; pupusas US$0.70; ☽ lunch & dinner) Honduras and El Salvador don't agree on much but they do agree on the merits of corn-dough patties stuffed with cheese and *chicharrón* (fried pork rind) and grilled to piping-hot perfection. Honduran *pupusas* tend to be larger (and more expensive) than the Salvadoran originals, but no less tasty.

Cafetería Cobel (Map p213; ☎ 442 2192; 7a Calle near Av Atlántida; mains US$1.50-3; ☽ breakfast & lunch Mon-Sat) Always jam-packed with regulars, the Cobel is an institution in La Ceiba. And for good reason – *típica* is served hot and fast and it's a steal. Try the hearty *pollo con arroz* (chicken with rice), crispy enchiladas, or if you're feeling adventurous, the *sopa de mondongo* (tripe soup), which is popular enough to make it a regular daily special. Service is decent but prepare to flag someone down at the height of the lunch hour.

Mixers (Map p213; ☎ 443 4166; Centro Comercial Panayotti, 7a Calle near Av 14 de Julio; mains US$1.50-3; ☽ breakfast, lunch & dinner Mon-Sat) Cafeteria-style eating is what you'll get at this locale. Every day a new variety of *típica* is served up – there's always beans, rice and a vegetable dish though – so you won't get bored if you eat here more than once. It's on the 2nd floor of a peach-colored shopping center.

Comidas Royale (Map p213; ☎ 443 2391; Parque Central, Av La República at 8a Calle; mains US$2.75-4; ☽ breakfast, lunch & dinner) Right on parque central, this is one of the best buffets in town. Not only is it open all day, every day, but the trays always seem to be brimming with fresh food. Dishes vary by the hour – *típica* of all sorts is served up alongside Honduran-style chow mein, fried rice, sweet-and-sour chicken, and ribs. Portions are large and there's always a good daily special that includes a drink and a couple of sides.

Swiss-German Restaurant (Map p211; Av La Bastilla; mains US$2.50-4; ☽ breakfast & lunch Mon-Sat) The name says it all. Popular with expatriates, the menu is replete with meat and sausage dishes plus a lion's share of potatoes and cabbage. Try the *chuleta ahumada* (smoked pork chop) for something a little different. Look for this sunny place a couple blocks south of the stadium.

Laura's Bakery (Map p211; ☎ 443 1494; 13a Calle; ☽ 7am-6:30pm Mon-Fri, to 5pm Sat) This bakery is known for its breads – most notably the wheat and French loaves – sold piping hot in the mornings. The pastries, however, are hard to resist too. There is another located in the Mall Megaplaza.

Outdoor market (Map p213; ☽ 6am-5pm Mon-Sat, 7am-noon Sun) This noisy market winds its way along 6a Calle, Av 14 de Julio, and the area in front of the Hondutel office. There you'll find anything and everything: fruits and vegetables, grains and sun-dried food, fresh meats and fish, clothing, shoes, sunglasses, bootleg CDs and DVDs, toiletries, toys, kitchen utensils…you name it, it's probably there.

Super Ceibeño Supermarket #2 (Map p213; Av 14 de Julio at 6a Calle; ☽ 7am-6:45pm Mon-Sat, to noon Sun) This is full-on supermarket is in the heart of the open-air market district. It's great for one-stop shopping. There is a second store across from the Parque Swinford, which is good for picking up a few items for a picnic in the park.

Supermercado Mesa (22a Calle at Av Morazán; ☽ 9am-9pm) Inside the Mall Megaplaza, this is a convenient place to shop for goodies, if you've got a car.

MIDRANGE

Café y Pasta Giarre (Map p211; ☎ 443 1400; Av San Isidro at 13a Calle; mains US$5-10; ☽ lunch & dinner Mon-Sat) This European-style café serves a wide range of homemade pastas, freshly made Italian desserts and good espresso drinks. Customers can choose between eating indoors in an intimate dining area or outdoors at sidewalk tables with big umbrellas.

Expatriates Bar & Grill (Map p211; ☎ 440 3373; 12a Calle; dishes US$6-10; ☽ dinner Thu-Fri, lunch & dinner Sat & Sun) Aptly named, this is a longtime favorite of foreigners living in La Ceiba. The specialty is barbecue chicken wings, but just about everything is grilled and good – ribs, shrimp, chicken breasts, veggies. There's also a full bar, large-screen TV with major sporting events, high-speed internet and a large selection of top Honduras cigars. It's at the eastern end of 12a Calle.

Chabelita (Map p211; ☎ 440 0027; 1a Calle; mains US$5-10; ☽ lunch & dinner Tue-Sun, dinner Mon) This Garífuna-style restaurant, at the far end of the Zona Viva, is well worth the walk. Seafood is the specialty – try the hefty fish fillet or Chabelita's famous *sopa marinera* (seafood soup). The dining area is unremarkable,

but a little patio in back is perfect for a late-afternoon or evening meal and a cold beer.

Mango Tango (Map p211; 1a Calle at Av Miguel Paz Barahona; mains US$4-10; ☽ dinner Wed-Sun) Across the street from Amsterdam 2001 and the Rotterdam Beach Hotel, this breezy restaurant-café-bar is a good place to start any Zona Viva outing – for many, it's the main destination. Its claim to fame is the well-stocked salad bar, one of the few in Honduras. The rest of the menu it typical north coast and

---

LA CEIBA'S ECO-LODGES

La Ceiba has four 'eco-lodges': three along the Río Cangrejal and another near the town of El Pino, 19km west of La Ceiba. They run the gamut in price and amenities, but all offer respite from the city and easy access to the area's impressive natural riches.

Lodge at Pico Bonito (☎ 440 0388, in US 888-428-0221; www.picobonito.com; Carr a Tela, El Pino; per two people May-Dec US$225-320, Dec-Jan US$277-385, Jan-April US$295-395, extra person US$40; Ⓟ ⊠ 🐾 💻 🏊) The first resort in Honduras to be included on the Small Luxury Hotel of the World list, this was a La Ceiba institution from the day it opened its doors in 2000. The hotel boasts a whopping 300 hectares of private forest with terrific hiking on guest-only trails. There's also a butterfly and reptile enclosure, observation tower, library and pleasant swimming pool. Cabins are spaced well apart for privacy, and have polished wood floors, tile bathrooms and a private patio with hammock. While the Lodge is no longer the area's most luxurious digs – that would be Las Cascadas on the Río Cangrejal – it still offers first-class service and installations in a gorgeous setting. Meal plans cost US$39 to US$49 per day.

Las Cascadas Lodge (☎ 419 0030; www.lascascadslodge.com; Calle a Yaruca, Km 6; s/d US$225/320 incl meals & wine; Ⓟ ⊠ 💻 🏊) With just three rooms, expertly prepared meals and a no-kids policy, Las Cascadas offers supreme comfort and relaxation in a beautiful setting. The lodge is built beside a gurgling creek with three scenic waterfalls – the namesake *cascadas* – surrounded by thick forest. Large rooms have canopy beds, hardwood floors and stone showers, while the high-ceilinged common area has sofas and chairs – and a beautiful wood table for family-style eating. Outside are nooks and crannies with wood chairs, perfect for relaxing. The Canadian owners offer friendly, personalized service; they prefer to rent to groups of six, making this more a private vacation home than a hotel. Rafting, hiking and other excursions can also be arranged.

Omega Tours Jungle Lodge (☎ 440 0334; www.omegatours.com; Calle a Yaruca, Km 9; s/d with shared bathroom US$10/14, cabins US$25-75) Nestled in a 40.5-hectare lot a few hundred meters from the road and river, this friendly well-managed lodge has something for every budget. Backpackers can stay for cheap – or free, if you book a trip – in large no-frills rooms with shared bathrooms. For a bit more, two new split-level cabins sleep five and have hot water, firm beds and nice views from upstairs. Or ask for the cozy Creek Cabin, built right over a creek, which will babble you to sleep every night. There's a small pool and a great outdoor shower, and guests can hike up behind the lodge for views of Cascada El Bejuco, across the river. The kitchen specializes in awesome German food like Kasespatzle (Spaetzle cheese noodles) and German roast beef but also has veggie lasagna, fish fillets and more.

Jungle River Lodge (☎ 440 1268; Calle a Yaruca, Km 7; r with/without bathroom US$20/15) The Río Cangrejal tumbles by just meters from this simple but attractive lodge, operated by Jungle River Tours. Wood-constructed rooms feel somewhat cramped but are free if you book a tour. Two private rooms offer a bit more space. The restaurant-bar serves family-style meals at open-air tables (breakfast and lunch US$4, dinner US$5). But the best reason to come is for the young, mellow atmosphere and easy access to the river, which is wonderfully swimmable when the water isn't too high. Canopy tours, hiking trips and mountain-bike rides all start here. To get here, take a Yaruca bus from the main bus terminal and look for the sign on your right.

THE NORTH COAST

Ceibeño fare – lots of seafood – served fresh at *palapa*-shaded tables. The bar stays open late, with sports playing on large TVs.

Pizza Hut (Map p213; ☎ 443 7492; Parque Central; mains US$3-5; ☼ lunch & dinner) In a town where fast-food restaurants seem to be the only places open on Sundays, they're hard to ignore. Of all of them (and there are lots), Pizza Hut offers the best options – pizza, pasta, sandwiches, salads – plus free refills on drinks. Prices are surprisingly reasonable and there are weekday specials. It's open late too.

TOP END

Ricardo's (Map p213; ☎ 443 0468; Av 14 de Julio at 10a Calle; mains US$8-21; ☼ lunch & dinner Mon-Sat) Reputed to be one of the finest restaurants in northern Honduras, Ricardo's offers a quiet and classy respite from the hubbub outside. Choose between eating in a comfortable air-conditioned dining room or a leafy garden courtyard. Seafood is the specialty but steak and pasta dishes also are very good. If you like spicy food, the Pescado Ricardo's (US$9) – broiled fish topped with jalapeño sauce and Parmesan – is divine.

Arrecife (Carr a Trujillo; mains US$10-15; ☼ lunch & dinner Tue-Sun) Watch your back Ricardo's: local food buffs and hotel concierges have started calling Arrecife the best restaurant in town. An upscale but understated place 15 km east of town, it offers terrific seafood dishes and a good wine list. Classy service completes the experience. The only drawback is the location – if you don't have a car, you may end paying more in taxi fare than you do for dinner.

Luna Gaucha (Colonia Toronjal; mains US$7-12; ☼ lunch & dinner Tue-Sun) Uruguayan food, with strong influences from Brazil and Argentina, is emerging in many countries as a unique and satisfying cuisine. Luna Gaucha is La Ceiba's first of such restaurants and serves tasty grilled dishes, both individual and traditional family-style platters, in a friendly atmosphere. Good value.

Drinking & Entertainment

La Ceiba is famous for its nightlife, most of which is found in the Zona Viva in Barrio La Isla. The bars and clubs are all within walking distance of each other so you can crawl from place to place. It's relatively safe, but robberies and pickpocketing occur now and then – keep your radar on and take a cab home at the end of the night.

La Casona (Map p211; ☎ 440 3471; 3a Calle btwn Av Miguel Paz Barahona & Dionisio de Herrera, Barrio La Isla; cover US$5.50; ☼ 9pm-late Wed-Sat) On a dirt road two blocks off the main drag, this huge wood-paneled building may look more like a ski lodge than a nightclub, but it's a favorite destination for La Ceiba's late-20s and early-30s set. The music is mostly regguetón (hip-hop with Jamaican and Latin American influences) and techno, though you'll hear a little bit of everything over the course of the night. Women often get in for free, and there are regular drink specials.

Monesterio (Map p211; ☎ 440 1700; 1a Calle at Av Manuel Bonilla; cover US$5.50; ☼ 9:30pm-late Thu-Sat) This is the preferred club for La Ceiba's moneyed, mostly 20-something crowd. The turreted exterior says King Arthur more than John the Baptist, but the inside is pure LA, with a raised dance floor, mezzanine VIP area and sleek tables and high stools in a cavernous bar area. Friday is usually ladies' night (free entrance, free rum and free domestic beer). Regguetón rules, of course, but the DJ usually plays some hip-hop, reggae and even merengue now and then. Dress sharp.

NEED A BREAK?

Mangos (Map p213; 7a Calle near Av 14 de Julio; licuados US$1-2; ☼ 8am-6:30pm Mon-Sat) A local smoothie spot, Mangos is a small, yuppy-ish juice bar in the center of town. Choose from over 35 licuados or make up one of your own. A few tables and air-conditioning make this a nice stop on a steamy afternoon.

Espresso Americano (Map p213; Av San Isidro near 7a Calle; coffee drinks US$1-3; ☼ 8am-6pm Mon-Sat) Serving up some of the best coffee in the country, this Honduran chain is well worth a stop. You'll find drinkable goodies of all kinds – espresso (of course), cappuccino, mochaccino, flavor-infused coffees, frozen drinks, even chai. It's a good way to jump-start your day. There's another branch on parque central.

THE NORTH COAST

Restaurante La Palapa (Map p211; ☎ 443 3844; 1a Calle at Av 15 de Septiembre, Zona Viva; no cover; ☺ 9pm-late Wed-Sat) In front of the Quinta Real hotel, this breezy bar-restaurant has a large dancing area on one side, wooden tables encircling a bar on the other, and the namesake *palapa* roof high above. Saturdays are the most fun, when crowds turn out for live bands playing a combination of salsa, merengue, reggae and rock. The food here isn't bad either – try the Parrillada Palapa, a two-person platter of chicken, pork, sausage and beef, with beans and tortillas. Hailing a waiter can be a challenge, though.

Cine Milenium (Mall Megaplaza, 22a Calle at Av Morazán) Two screens feature Hollywood films daily; tickets cost US$1.60 before 7pm, or US$2.15 afterwards.

Shopping

PiQ' Art (Map p211; ☎ 440 4041; piqart@yahoo.com; Av San Isidro btwn 12a & 13a Calles; ☺ 1-6pm Mon-Fri) A gem of a place, this tiny yellow house is brimming with beautiful works of Honduran art: the walls are laden with dozens of oil paintings, the floors are lined with intricately carved sculptures and furniture, and long tables display finely crafted pottery and a few pieces of seed jewelry too. It may be pricey but it's the best value in town.

The Rain Forest Gifts (Map p211; ☎ 443 2917; rain_forest_hn@yahoo.com; Av La Bastilla; ☺ 9am-noon & 2-5:30pm Mon-Fri, 9am-noon Sat) This boutique has a wide variety of handicrafts from around Central America. Don't miss the Garífuna rag dolls or the colorful tree-bark mobiles from La Moskitia. The prices are pushing the upper limit of reasonable, but the quality is good. Be sure to check out the English-language book exchange in back.

Souvenir El Buen Amigo #3 (Map p211; ☎ 442 0716; Barrio El Iman; ☺ 8am-6:30pm Mon-Sat) Don't be discouraged by so-so sister shops #1 and #2 – this is the best of the Buen Amigo lot. Although somewhat out of the way (near the eastern end of Calle 12), you'll find a great selection of Honduran *artesanía*: Lencan pottery, junco art, woodcarvings and Maya replicas, and coffee. And if you're in the market for kitsch, no worries – there is a fine selection of loud T-shirts, 18-Rabbit shot glasses and coconut monkeys.

Tourist Office Gift Shop (Map p211; ☎ 440 3044; 8a Calle near Av San Isidro; ☺ 8am-6pm Mon-Fri, to noon Sat) A corner of this city office houses a gift shop with a small selection of quality crafts from around the country. It's worth a peek if you haven't found what you're looking for in the bigger shops.

Mall Megaplaza (22a Calle at Av Morazán; ☺ 10am-9pm) Near the entrance to town, the Megaplaza is a two-story giant with the classic mall players: big department stores, teen-clothing boutiques, shoe shops, record stores, knick-knack islands, an arcade (open from 9:30am to 9:30pm Sunday to Thursday, to 10pm Friday and Saturday) and a food court with just under a bazillion eateries. There's also a movie theater, a supermarket, an internet café and a handful of banks with ATMs.

Getting There & Away

AIR

La Ceiba's **Aeropuerto Golosón** (☎ 443 3925) has frequent flights to/from San Pedro Sula, Tegucigalpa, the Bay Islands and La Moskitia. Services include a bank, an internet café and several car-rental agencies. There are various airline companies in La Ceiba:

Aerocaribe de Honduras (☎ 442 2565; Aeropuerto Golosón; ☺ hours vary)

Aerolineas Sosa (Map p213; ☎ 443 1894, at airport 440 0692; Av San Isidro btwn 8a & 9a Calles; ☺ 7am-5pm Mon-Fri)

Atlantic Airlines (Map p213; ☎ 440 2343, at airport 440 1220; www.atlanticairlines.com.ni; 11a Calle at Av República; ☺ 8am-noon & 1-5pm Mon-Fri, 8am-noon Sat)

TACA/Isleña (☎ 441 3191, at airport 443 2683; www.taca.com, www.flyislena.com; Mall Megaplaza, 1st fl, 22a Calle at Av Morazán; ☺ 9am-6pm, 9am-1pm Sat)

BOAT

Two comfortable, air-conditioned ferries ply the water between La Ceiba, Roatán and Utila. For Roatán, the **Galaxy Wave** (☎ 443 4633, in Coxen Hole 445 1795) leaves at 9:30am and 4:30pm daily, taking 1¼ hours (coach/first-class US$21/26.50; children aged 5-10 half price). For Utila, the **Utila Princess** (☎ in Utila 425 3390; US$22) leaves at 9:30am and 4pm daily and takes one hour. In the low season, the Utila ferry often runs just once a day at 4pm. La Ceiba's main pier (Muelle Cabotaje) is about 8km east of town; a taxi to/from town costs US$1.60 per person. There is no regular passenger service to Guanaja or Cayos Cochinos, nor are there direct boats between Roatán and Utila.

BUS

Most buses – but not all – leave from the **main bus terminal** (Mercado San José, Blvd 15 de Septiembre), about 2km west of the center. **Cristina** (☎ 441 2028), **Diana Express** (☎ 441 6460) and **Catisa-Tupsa** (☎ 441 2539) have offices there, serving Tela and San Pedro Sula. **Contraibal-Cotuc** (☎ 441 2199) stops at an office on the main highway, with service to/from Trujillo and San Pedro Sula. **Hedman Alas** (☎ 441 5347; www .hedmanalas.com) is located next to the Supermercado Ceibeño #4 on the main highway near the eastern end of town and has luxury service to Tela and San Pedro, with connections to Tegucigalpa and Copán Ruínas. Another luxury line, **Viana Clase de Oro** (☎ 441 2330), uses the Esso gas station 500m west of the main bus terminal and serves San Pedro Sula and Tegucigalpa. Buses go to various destinations, including the following.

Corozal US$0.45, 30 minutes; take any Sambo Creek bus

Copán Ruínas Diana Express US$9.50, 6½ hours, 8:15am and 9:40pm, with a 10- to 20-minute layover in San Pedro Sula; Hedman-Alas luxury service, US$21.50, 5:15am and 10am; transfer in San Pedro Sula

El Naranjo/Río Cangrejal US$0.65; 15 minutes, last return bus at 2pm; take any Las Mangas and Yaruca bus.

El Porvenir US$0.55, 45 minutes, 15km; same buses as to La Unión

La Unión/Cuero y Salado US$0.75, 1½ hours, 20km, 6:30am to 6:00pm Monday to Saturday, every 45 minutes, 8am to 5pm Sunday hourly, last return bus at 4pm

Las Mangas/Río Cangrejal US$0.70, 20 minutes, 9am, 11am, noon, 2:30pm and 4pm, last return bus at 2pm; use Yaruca bus

Nueva Armenia US$1.30, 1½ hours, 40km, 9:30am, 10:30am, 12:30pm, 2:30pm, 3:30pm and 4:30pm; last return bus at 11am

Olanchito US$0.2.75, *ordinario* 3¼ hours, *directo* two hours, 6:45am to 4pm, hourly

Savá US$2.15, *ordinario* one hour, *directo* 45 minutes; take any Olanchito bus

Sambo Creek US$0.50, 45 minutes, 6:10am to 6:10pm Monday to Saturday, 8am to 5pm Sunday, every 35 minutes, last return bus at 4pm

San Pedro Sula Diana Express and Catisa-Tupsa US$4.25, 3½ hours, 202km; Hedman-Alas luxury service, US$13, three hours, 5:15am, 10am, 2pm and 5:45pm; Viana Clase de Oro US$10, 6am and 3pm

San Pedro Sula Airport Hedman-Alas, US$19.50, four hours; take any San Pedro Sula bus

Tegucigalpa Cristina US$9.25, seven hours, 397km, 6:15am, 7:30am, 9:30am, 11am, 12:30pm and 5:30pm; Hedman Alas luxury service, US$21.50, 6½ hours, 5:15am, 10am and 2pm; Viana Clase de Oro US$15; 6:30am and 3pm

Tela Diana Express and Catisa-Tupsa, US$2.50, 1½ hours, 103km, 5:30am to 6:30am, hourly

Tocoa US$2.50, 2½ hours, 4:30am to 5:30pm, every 30 minutes; for faster service, catch any Trujillo-bound bus at the Cotuc-Contraibal stop on the main highway, US$3.75, 1½ hours, 8:30am to 7pm, every 45 minutes

Trujillo Cotuc-Contraibal, US$4.25, three hours, 8:15am to 7am, every 30 to 45 minute; nonstop departures at 4:15pm and 6pm

Getting Around
TO/FROM THE AIRPORT

Taxis from the airport cost US$5.30, but you should be able to get a ride for half that just by walking about 100m outside the airport gate. Chances are a taxi will be waiting there; otherwise walk to the highway – another 100m – and flag one down there.

CAR & MOTORCYCLE

Most of La Ceiba's attractions can be reached fairly easily by taxi or bus, but a rental car saves some time and planning. Daily rates average US$40 to US$60, but you can get discounts for economy cars and long-term rentals, and if your credit card provides car insurance.

Advance Rent A Car (☎ 441 1105; www.advancerent acar.com; Carr a Tela; ☉ 8am-6pm Mon-Fri)

Ceiba Rent A Car (☎ 440 3312; Av 15 de Septiembre at 1a Calle; Barrio La Isla; ☉ 8am-5pm) At the Quinta Real hotel.

Molinari Rent-a-Car (☎ 443 0055; molinarirentacar@ yahoo.com; 8a Calle btwn Avs San Isidro & República; ☉ 8am-noon & 2-5pm Mon-Fri, 8am-noon Sat) At the Gran Hotel Paris.

TAXI

Taxis in La Ceiba are easy to find; in fact, they normally find you. The cost of a ride depends on the distance and time of day. In town, a cab costs (per person) US$0.80 from 5am to 8pm, US$1.05 from 8pm to 11pm, and US$1.50 from 11pm to 5am. Rides to the airport run about US$5.30 for up to four people and US$1.60 per person to Muelle de Cabotaje (the main pier). For other destinations, prepare to negotiate and be sure to agree upon a price before you get in.

REFUGIO DE VIDA SILVESTRE CUERO Y SALADO

On the coast about 30km west of La Ceiba, the Cuero y Salado Wildlife Refuge takes its name from two of three rivers, Cuero and

MANGROVE ECOLOGY

Mangrove forests – often referred to as swamps – are vital to the protection of coastal lands. Providing a buffer zone between the ocean and the land, their extensive root systems slow waves, which ultimately prevents erosion. They are also home to a rich and varied wildlife; in Honduras, this includes birds like snowy egrets, neotropic cormorants and yellow-crowned night herons as well as larger creatures like American crocodiles, Caribbean manatees, leatherback turtles and howler monkeys.

The trees and bushes that make up mangroves grow along coasts and have developed the unique ability to withstand daily inundation and high levels of salinity. They survive – and thrive – by having an exposed root system that allows them to get oxygen directly from the air during low tide. They do so either by having roots that elevate them above the low tide level or by having roots that stick out of the muddy silt that they grow in.

Today, the biggest threat to mangrove forests is agricultural development. More and more farmers are settling in coastal regions, clearing lands and draining wetlands to create plots suitable for planting or ranching. The result has been the destruction of key wildlife habitats and the increased vulnerability of the mainland, and its swelling population, to the wrath of tropical storms and hurricanes.

There are several mangrove forests on Honduras' coastlines; those that are protected include Parque Nacional Jeannette Kawas, Refugio de Vida Silvestre Cuero y Salado and Refugio de Vida Silvestre Laguna de Guaimoreto.

Salado (the third is San Juan), which meet at the coast in a large estuary, creating waterways, mangrove forests and coastal lagoons along the way. A reserve since 1987, it protects varied and abundant wildlife; manatees are the most famous and most elusive, but there are also (among others) howler and white-faced monkeys, sloths, otters, iguanas, caimans and 196 species of birds.

Orientation

Cuero y Salado is 9.5km northwest of La Unión. Visitors must take a train from there to the visitors center (see p224) in Salado Barra, which is in the heart of the reserve.

Information

A brand-new **visitors center** (☎ 440 1990) in Salado Barra overlooks the estuary at the end of the railroad track; all guests must pay the park fee here (adult/child US$10/5) and can book a tour, eat at the cafeteria or reserve a bed for the night. Also inside is a small but very good exhibition on the refuge, and its flora and fauna. Signage is in English and Spanish.

For information on the refuge before you arrive, contact La Ceiba-based **Fundación Cuero y Salado** (☎ /fax 443 0329; www.cueroysalado .org; Av Ramón Rosa at 15a Calle, La Ceiba; ☺ 8am-noon & 1-5pm Mon-Fri, 8-11am Sat), which manages the reserve.

If you stay overnight and want to check email, La Unión has one **internet café** (per hr US$1.35) that doubles as an **international call center** (per min US$0.21) and pulpería. Ask for Ana Meléndez's *ciber*.

Sights & Activities

To see the most wildlife, visit the reserve early in the morning or late in the afternoon. During the heat of the day, animals hide from the sun. Also, be sure to bring plenty of water, sunscreen and insect repellent. For tours, make a reservation a day in advance so that guides can be ready for your arrival.

Just 500m from the visitors center, **Coco Beach** is a rustic but relatively clean gray-sand beach. It's not classic Caribbean, but being in the reserve you're likely to get it all to yourself.

BOATING

Without a doubt, the best way to see the wildlife in this reserve is on the water. Guided **canoe tours** (1-2 people US$8) lasting 3½ hours take visitors silently down the rivers and through mangroves, which is perfect for spotting birds, monkeys, crocodiles, and sometimes even a manatee. Guided two-hour **motorboat tours** (1-2 people US$20, per person for more than 3 people US$5.50, plus guide US$5.50) are also offered. Although they take visitors to lagoons and channels further afield, the noise of the outboard motor can startle animals into flying or scurrying away before you can admire them. Tours can be arranged at the visitors center; for early morning tours, make a reservation a day in advance.

BIRD-WATCHING

Experienced guides offer two-hour **bird-watching tours** (per person US$8) in the wetlands. Tour groups are small and leave early in the morning. With over 25% of all of the Honduran bird species represented in this reserve, you're bound to see some beauties.

TOURS

Learn how *casabe,* a yucca-based Garífuna flat bread, is made on a tour of the **Casa de Casabe** (admission US$1; ⊙ 8am-6pm), a community production center. It's in a yellow house, 3km from La Unión on the railroad track.

With advance notice a **Garífuna cultural tour** (up to 8 people US$45; 2½hrs) can be arranged, complete with a guided tour of the community, a stop at the Casa de Casabe, and dance and musical performances. Ask at the visitors center for details.

Sleeping & Eating

A wooden-plank building on stilts houses a very well-maintained **dorm** (per person US$7) about 200m from the visitors center. Each room is spacious, has large windows with screens, and two to three bunk beds apiece – linens included. The shared bathroom is clean and has running water 24/7. No worries about the house full of soldiers next door; they're posted on the reserve to protect against poachers. **Camping** (per person US$3) is also permitted. Tents can be rented for US$6.75 (no sleeping bags, unfortunately).

Breakfast, lunch and dinner (mains US$1.50 to US$3) are prepared and served in the airy cafeteria at the visitors center; you'll get standard Honduran fare – mostly chicken, eggs, fried bananas, rice and beans. It's run by the friendly Doña Fátima.

If you're waiting for a ride to/from the reserve and want to get a meal in La Unión, head to **Sandra's** (☎ 352 1612; mains US$1.50-3; ⊙ breakfast, lunch & dinner), a simple eatery three doors west of the *trencito* (railcar) station.

Getting There & Away

To get to the reserve, you can either take a bus from La Ceiba's main terminal to La Unión (US$0.50, 1½ hours, 6am to 4pm, every 45 minutes) or spring for a taxi (US$16 to US$21). From La Unión, jump on the *trencito* for the 9.5km ride on the old banana railroad to the visitors center in Salado Barra (one person US$10.50, two or more people US$5 each, 45 minutes, 7am to 2pm, every 1½ hours). If you arrive between *trencitos,* consider taking a *burra,* a railcar basket pushed gondola-style by a couple of men with poles (US$5.30 per person, one hour). Be sure to tell the *trencito* or *burra* drivers when you'd like to return; the last bus from La Unión to La Ceiba is at 4pm. You also can walk along the railway tracks to the visitors center; it takes about 1½ hours at a brisk pace.

PARQUE NACIONAL PICO BONITO

One of Honduras' best-known national parks, Pico Bonito national park has the country's third-highest peak (Pico Bonito; 2436m) and an unexplored core area of 500 sq km. It was already the largest national park in Honduras when additional forest territory was included in July 1992. Its magnificent and varied terrain includes thick forests, rivers, waterfalls and abundant wildlife, including jaguars, armadillos, wild pigs, *tepezcuintles* (pacas), monkeys, doves, toucans and more.

Now for the bad news: the vast majority of the park is off-limits to intrusion of any kind, including hiking. Fortunately, trails to two waterfalls on the park's perimeter make for great day hikes, and still offer a glimpse into this rugged and pristine area.

There are two entrances to the park, at **El Pino** and at **Río Cangrejal**. Almost every tour agency in La Ceiba offers Pico Bonito tours, mostly to the El Pino side, though others can be arranged. Entrance to Pico Bonito National Park is US$6 – be sure to ask if admission is included or separate from the tour price.

For additional information about the park, contact the **Fundación Parque National Pico Bonito** (Funapib; ☎ 442 0618; www.picobonito .org; Av 14 de Julio at 15a Calle, La Ceiba; ⊙ 7:30am-5pm Mon-Fri, 8-11am Sat). And in case you're wondering, climbing Pico Bonito itself requires technical climbing experience and takes several days and special permissions. Few groups have attempted it, even fewer have made it.

El Pino

The original entrance to Pico Bonito is at the town of El Pino, 19km west of La Ceiba on the highway toward Tela.

INFORMATION

El Pino Tourism Committee (☎ 386 9878) offers several guided trips. The prices are surprisingly high for day hikes – as much as US$26 per person – but this has partly to do with the fact that the park charges foreigners a US$6 entry fee. The committee also works to provide guides with a competitive wage, around US$8 to US$11 per trip. The tourism committee does not have an office, but you can call, or get information and arrange tours a day in advance, at **Vivero Natural View** (☎ 368 8343, 371 9631) in El Pino.

The **Lodge at Pico Bonito** (☎ 440 0388, in US 888-428-0221; www.picobonito.com; Carr a Tela) also has a number of trails in its private protected forest at the foot of the mountain. Access is free for guests, but day trips for nonguests can be arranged.

HIKING

The park's first trail is still a favorite, with a moderately difficult three-hour hike to **Cascada Zacate** (per person incl guide, transport & park entrance fee US$11). You'll hear the falls before you see them – in fact, they are also known as Cascada Ruidoso, or 'noisy falls.' When the water is high, it thunders through a narrow chasm, throwing up a thick cloud of vapor. The pool at the base is enticing, but a community downstream uses the water for drinking so swimming isn't allowed. Fortunately, there's a smaller waterfall, with an equally appealing swimming hole, at the trailhead.

Other options, not in the park, include **Sendero La Montura** (per person US$17), a tough eight-hour hike that forms a loop through varied forest, stopping at a small waterfall and passing overlooks with views of Parque Nacional Cayos Cochinos and Refugio de Vide Silvestre Cuero y Salado; a three-hour **cacao and butterfly tour** (per person US$16); and a three-hour hike along the **Río Coloradito** (per person US$9). The folks at Vivero Natural

View have booklets detailing all the available outings.

SLEEPING & EATING

The Lodge at Pico Bonito (☎ 440 0388, in US 888-428-0221; www.picobonito.com; Carr a Tela) This is certainly the nicest option in El Pino and not far from the Cascada Zacate trailhead.

Posada El Buen Pastor (Carr a Tela; r US$16-22) El Buen Pastor has four surprisingly comfortable rooms, all with private bathroom, fan, hot water and homey décor. There's a common TV room, a garden in back and a patio in front. Noise from passing buses and trucks is the main drawback here, but traffic is fairly light at night. Morning toast and coffee are included.

Centro Ecoturístico Natural View (☎ 368 8343, 371 9631; r US$11) Two kilometers north of the highway, this place has a couple simple rooms that sleep two, and camping is possible on the large grassy plot. It's also a good place to eat and relax après-hiking, with *palapa*-covered tables and shady hammocks.

GETTING THERE & AWAY

Any bus headed toward Tela or San Pedro Sula can drop you at El Pino. To get to **Vivero Natural View** (☎ 368 8343, 371 9631) look for the purple tourist information sign on your right.

Río Cangrejal

Access to part of Parque Nacional Pico Bonito is also available along the Río Cangrejal, a narrow, lively river that forms much of the park's eastern border. The most common way to experience the river is to raft it, a popular excursion offered by a number of outfits (see p214) that usually includes stopping for a short hike or two into the park. You can stay at any of three jungle lodges along the river (p219) – two of the lodges are operated by the rafting operators, which offer a free night with any trip.

For a more cultural experience, there is a nascent ecotourism project involving the communities of Las Mangas and El Naranjo, with guided hikes, community tours and a stay at a guesthouse (see below).

INFORMATION

Guaruma Servicios (☎ 442 2673; www.guaruma .org; Centro Cultural, Las Mangas; ◷ 7am-7pm) is a guide service run jointly by students and community members, with help from the local Peace Corps volunteer. Its ecotourism programmes are designed to support its primary projects: environmental education, computer education and photography. Guaruma is based in the Centro Cultural in Las Mangas, which is part of the local school. The community guesthouse is also located there.

In the town of El Naranjo, the **Centro de Información Turística** (Tourist Information Center; ☼ 7am-7pm) has simple displays and photos about the hikes and other activities available in the area.

SIGHTS & ACTIVITIES

On the Río Cangrejal side, the one main trail leads to **Cascada El Bejuco**, a 60m falls that's a good one- or two-hour climb from the river, depending on the condition of the trail. You'll pass several smaller falls along the way that are nice for swimming.

Guaruma Servicios offers two guided **hikes**. The longer hike (per person US$6, four hours) takes you to the village of La Muralla, stopping at a swimming hole to take a dip, while the shorter hike (per person US$3, two hours) starts just beyond the river bridge south of town and winds through thick forest before reaching a pleasant swimming hole. Tours start at the Centro Cultural, where, if you're interested, you can have a quick introduction to the various community programs, from computer training to photography lessons.

El Naranjo is a timber town, and groups of men hike far into the forest to cut tropical hardwoods. They hew the logs with handsaws and carry them on their shoulders back to town. The leftover scraps used to be discarded, but a few enterprising residents have learned to turn them into *artesanía*, sold along the roadside. El Naranjo also has a very modest orchid garden containing about 15 species of orchids.

Guaruma rents **bicycles** (half-/full day US$2.50/5), – a great way to explore the area and other communities along the main road.

SLEEPING & EATING

Cabañas Aventuras del Bosque (r US$15) Consisting of three cabins and a *comedor*, this place is jointly owned and operated by a group of three families. The cabins have two rooms apiece, each with a hot-water bathroom. They are rustic, built of handhewn wood slats that add to the charm but leave gaps here and there – a mosquito net would come in handy. A large terrace has hammocks, and the *comedor* (open for breakfast and lunch) serves simple fish, chicken and pork dishes (mains US$2 to US$4).

Expatriates Cangrejal (☎ 440 3373; ☼ lunch Fri-Sun) A sister restaurant of the popular La Ceiba watering hole of the same name, this place serves up weekend comfort food, like barbecued food and burgers.

GETTING THERE & AWAY

Take a Yaruca-bound bus from the main bus terminal, departing at 9am, 11am, noon, 1pm, 2:30pm and 4pm. The bus can drop you anywhere along the road, including El Naranjo (US$0.60, 30 minutes) and Las Mangas (US$0.70, 40 minutes). A taxi from La Ceiba will cost US$12 to US$14.

Getting Around

Just about everything here is built on or near the main dirt road, which itself hugs the river, climbing steadily from the highway turnoff. (Whether on foot or bike, it's always easier headed south.) Buses pass every couple of hours, and you can always hitch a ride with a passing pickup truck.

SAMBO CREEK
pop 2573

This Garífuna fishing village 21km east of La Ceiba is most notable as a jumping-off point to Cayos Cochinos.

Sleeping & Eating

The first two hotels listed here are reached via a dirt road, 200m past the main Sambo Creek entrance. The others are in Sambo Creek proper.

Helen's Hotel & Restaurant (☎ 440 2303; www.dive.to/honduras; r/tw/ste US$24/29/32, 1-bedroom apt US$43-53, 2-bedroom apt US$64; (P) ▨ ▣ ▨) The rooms here are homey in a dowdy sort of way with hot-water bathrooms, air-conditioning and small refrigerators. The lush, well-tended grounds, however, are very appealing: it's on the beach and has two pools (one for adults, one for kids). There's also a popular thatch-roofed restaurant (mains US$2.75 to US$6.50), open for breakfast, lunch and dinner, that serves seafood and pasta dishes and sandwiches.

Hotel Canadien (☎ 440 2099; www.hotelcanadien .com; s/d US$30/35; P ⚅ ⚆) Somewhat dated rooms have two air-conditioned areas: a sitting room with a futon and a bedroom with a low-lying bed. There's a pool that was bright green when we passed through; if it's cleaned, it would probably make a nice place to hang out. The rooftop restaurant (open for breakfast and lunch Sunday to Thursday, and for dinner also on Friday and Saturday) is the best thing about the place – it has a spectacular view over the Caribbean and Cayos Cochinos in the distance. The menu (mains US$3 to US$11) has a little bit of everything.

Hotel El Centro (r/tw with shared bathroom US$8/16) A simple, super-clean hotel on the main street in the middle of Sambo Creek, El Centro's rooms have nice details like curtains, brightly painted walls and good beds. The four shared bathrooms are large and strikingly clean. There's 24 hours of electricity and running water too.

Hotel Hermanos Avila (r/tw with shared bathroom US$6/7, r with private bathroom US$8) A beachfront hotel at the eastern end of the main street, this place has 16 pink rooms with squishy beds. The shared bathroom is reasonably clean; steer clear, however, of the room with the private bathroom – it's pretty grim. The hotel runs the discotheque next door; if you want to sleep on weekends, stay elsewhere.

Restaurante Sambo Creek (mains US$3-10; ⚆ breakfast, lunch & dinner) A wizened Massachusetts transplant, the owner of this long-time watering hole in the center of town is a good source of information and can also organize trips to Cayos Cochinos. You can usually find him holding court at the restaurant's open-air dining area, where friends, kids and passersby far outnumber diners. The whole fish and fresh jumbo shrimp are tasty. Rooms for rent (US$8 to US$13) are homey – in fact, they're used by the kids in the house until a tourist shows up and then the kids get the couch for a couple days.

Champa Kabasa (☎ 440 3360; mains US$5-11; ⚆ lunch & dinner) This popular restaurant at the entrance to town has branches in La Ceiba and San Pedro Sula, and menus in English. Garífuna and seafood dishes are the specialty: the seafood sampler makes a good appetizer, while the *sopa marinera* is a classic. Grab a table right on the beach, or head to the 2nd-floor patio for views of the ocean.

Golosina Ethel (☎ 429 1039; mains US$2.50-7.25; ⚆ lunch & dinner) Doña Ethel serves up excellent Garífuna cuisine – you can eat just about anything cooked in coconut milk here and you won't be disappointed. Look for the yellow-and-blue clapboard building just up the block from Hotel El Centro.

Getting There & Away

Local buses connect Sambo Creek with La Ceiba (US$0.45, 45 minutes, 5:30am to 7pm, every 35 minutes).

CAYOS COCHINOS

A classic Caribbean beauty with white-sand beaches, impossibly turquoise water and palm trees galore, Cayos Cochinos are two small islands and 13 cays. It was designated a Marine National Monument in 2003 after 10 years of hard lobbying by the **Fundación Cayos Cochinos** (Honduras Coral Reef Fund; Map p211; ☎ 442 2670, 443 4075; www.cayoscochinos.org; 13a Calle, Barrio El Iman, La Ceiba; ⚆ 8am-5pm Mon-Fri). As a result, commercial fishing is not allowed in Cayos Cochinos and instead the 489 sq km reserve is filled with pristine reefs and a flourishing marine life that make for excellent diving and snorkeling. The islands are also known for their unique pink boa constrictors, which aren't dangerous.

As a protected reserve, there is a fee to visit any part of the Cayos Cochinos; it's US$10 per person if you come with a tour operator, US$5 if you come with an independent boatman – payable at the Fundación Cayos Cochinos research station at Cayo Menor.

Sights & Activities

Most people visit Cayos Cochinos as a day trip; Garífuna Tours and other operators (see p215) offer day-long excursions from La Ceiba that include snorkeling and lunch at the village of Chachauate, on the cay of the same name. Alternatively, contact Omar Acosta (☎ 383 8031) in Sambo Creek, who offers a similar but less-packaged trip (per person US$35, minimum five people). Unlike most independent boatmen, Acosta's boats are equipped with life jackets and flares, although you should bring your own snorkeling gear.

THE NORTH COAST

Cayos Cochinos have spectacular **diving** and **snorkeling**. There are over 60 named dive sites, and hundreds more unnamed ones, of all descriptions: black coral reefs, sea mounds, walls, drift dives, shallow, deep, even a two-engine Cessna in 17m (55ft) of water. See below for dive packages.

Fundación Cayos Cochinos (Map p211; ☎ 442 2670, 443 4075) coordinates various **volunteer programmes** at its research facility on Cayo Menor, the smaller of the two main islands in Cayos Cochinos. The center is used by scientists to monitor the flora, fauna, and reef in the reserve; volunteers can participate in projects like reef surveying (Open Water dive certification required), sea-turtle watching and studying the islands' pink boa constrictors.

Sleeping & Eating

Plantation Beach Resort (☎ 442 0974; www.planta tionbeachresort.com; r per night/week US$110/750, non-divers US$100/650, plus 16% tax; 🖵) Opened as a fishing camp in the 1960s, Plantation Beach is still the only resort and dive shop based in Cayos Cochinos. Dive packages include lodging, meals, three boat dives per day, unlimited shore diving, and use of kayaks and snorkels. It's no Hilton, of course. While there is a set of newly built rooms with a beachy modern feel, most are older, a little worn, and look like they haven't been significantly updated in 40 years. The setting, however, is one of a kind.

Dive in Caribik (☎ 361 6584, 373 8620; www.dive -in-caribik.com) In 2006 this well-regarded dive shop, based at the Hotel Palma Real 25km east of La Ceiba, began offering overnight accommodations and diving at a private home on one of the smaller cays. The home is a classic wood-frame beach house – comfortable but not luxurious, with boxy rooms and a large common area. Dive packages are a good deal: five nights with full board, 10 dives and transfer to/from La Ceiba are under US$460 per person (double occupancy). Customized packages are available too.

The tiny Garífuna village of Chachauate, named after the cay it lies on, has lodging with several families who will happily rent you a room, or in some cases, their entire house. Homes are rustic – sand floor, no running water, no electricity, a communal town latrine – so don't expect much beyond a thin foam mattress and a thatch roof over your head. Rates run between US$3 and US$ 10 per night. There is also a handful of simple eateries on the cay; a standard meal (US$2 to US$3) includes fried fish, rice, beans and a side of *plátanos* (plantains).

You may be able to stay at the **Fundación Cayos Cochinos** (Map p211; ☎ 442 2670, 443 4075) research station on Cayo Menor, if they aren't already booked with scientists and volunteers. It offers three simple dorms with foam-mattress bunk beds and indoor bathrooms that open onto the beach. They're way overpriced – US$25 per person – and the staff seems to much prefer hosting volunteer groups over independent travelers. For meals, there's a hilltop eatery that offers *típica*.

Getting There & Away

Day trips and dive packages typically include transportation to/from the islands. If you're just interested in getting there on your own, René Arzá (☎ 937 1674) in Nueva Armenia charges around US$25 per person (depending on the size of the group), including pickup on another day. Omar Acosta (☎ 383 8031) in Sambo Creek can provide similar service (and has more experience) but his rates may be higher. If all else fails, you can simply go to Sambo Creek or Nueva Armenia and arrange a ride with the local fishermen, who make the trip daily.

TRUJILLO & AROUND

Not long ago, Trujillo and the surrounding area were very popular weekend destinations, the pale beaches, glassy water and seaside restaurants an easy drive or flight from La Ceiba and San Pedro. Then came Hurricane Mitch in 1998, which destroyed homes and roads and, along with it, Trujillo's tourism business. The airport closed, the tourists stopped coming and a sense of dejection settled over the city, which, truth be told, has not yet fully lifted. But things are improving – Trujillo has always been a natural base for overland trips to/from La Moskitia, and now that the trip can be done in a day, more travelers are coming and, once here, staying a while.

TRUJILLO

pop 30,000

Capital of the department of Colón, Trujillo sits on the wide arc of the Bahía de Trujillo. It's famous for its coconut palm–lined beaches and gentle seas. At the end of that long arm is Puerto Castilla, another of Honduras' major deepwater ports. There's nothing much to see out there, but the seaward side of the peninsula has fine rustic beaches.

History

It was near Trujillo that Christopher Columbus first set foot on the American mainland, on August 14, 1502, on his fourth and final voyage. The first Catholic Mass on American mainland soil was held on the spot where he

and his crew landed. Trujillo was founded two decades later, in 1525, and served as Honduras' provincial capital until 1537.

Trujillo's deepwater port was used by ships carrying gold and silver to Spain, and was attacked numerous times by pirates, including A-list scallywags like Nicolas Van Horn and Henry Morgan. The Spanish built fortresses – including Fortaleza Santa Bárbara – to repel the pirates but to no avail. After being sacked by Dutch pirates in 1643, the city was abandoned for over a century.

Orientation

Trujillo is much smaller and quieter than many people expect, and the center is easy to

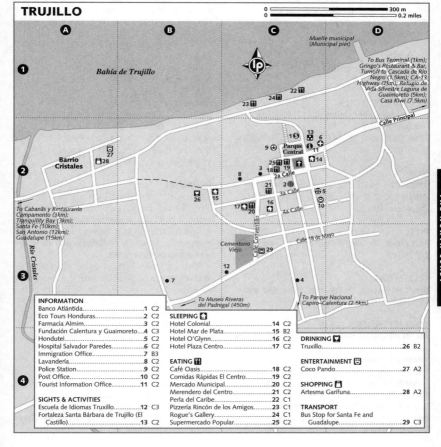

INFORMATION
Banco Atlántida...1 C2
Eco Tours Honduras...2 C2
Farmacia Almim...3 C2
Fundación Calentura y Guaimoreto...4 C3
Hondutel...5 C2
Hospital Salvador Paredes...6 C2
Immigration Office...7 B3
Lavandería...8 C2
Police Station...9 C2
Post Office...10 C2
Tourist Information Office...11 C2

SIGHTS & ACTIVITIES
Escuela de Idiomas Truxillo...12 C3
Fortaleza Santa Bárbara de Trujillo (El Castillo)...13 C2

SLEEPING
Hotel Colonial...14 C2
Hotel Mar de Plata...15 B2
Hotel O'Glynn...16 C2
Hotel Plaza Centro...17 C2

EATING
Café Oasis...18 C2
Comidas Rápidas El Centro...19 C2
Mercado Municipal...20 C2
Merendero del Centro...21 C2
Perla del Caribe...22 C1
Pizzería Rincón de los Amigos...23 C1
Rogue's Gallery...24 C1
Supermercado Popular...25 C2

DRINKING
Truxillo...26 B2

ENTERTAINMENT
Coco Pando...27 A2

SHOPPING
Artesma Garífuna...28 A2

TRANSPORT
Bus Stop for Santa Fe and Guadalupe...29 C3

navigate on foot. However, the bus station is 1km from town and a few popular hotels are further still. Taxis are plentiful and hitching is very common.

Information

EMERGENCY
Police (☎ 434 4038; Parque Central; ☯ 24hr)

IMMIGRATION
Immigration office (☎ 434 4451; ☯ 7am-5pm Mon-Fri) South of Barrio Cristales; can extend visas for US$20. It's also open some nights and weekends.

INTERNET ACCESS
Eco Tours Honduras (☎ 434 4780; per hr US$0.80; ☯ 7am-10pm Mon-Sat, 9am-10pm Sun) Offers telephone service too; calls (per minute) to the USA are US$0.15, to Canada US$0.21, to Europe US$0.31 and to Australia US$0.53. Despite the name, tours are rarely offered. It's a half block south of the church.

LAUNDRY
Lavandería (2a Calle; per 10lb US$2.80; ☯ 8am-5pm Mon-Fri)

MEDICAL SERVICES
Hospital Salvador Paredes (☎ 434 4093; Calle Principal; ☯ 24hr)
Farmacia Almim (☎ 434 4526; 2a Calle; ☯ 8am-8pm Mon-Sat)

MONEY
Banco Atlántida (Parque Central; ☯ 9am-4pm Mon-Fri, 8:30-11:30am Sat) Exchanges traveler's checks; one 24 hour ATM.

POST
Post office (4a Calle; ☯ 8am-noon & 2-4pm Mon-Fri, 8-11am Sat)

TELEPHONE
Hondutel (3a Calle; ☯ 7am-9pm Mon-Fri, 8am-noon Sat & Sun)

TOURIST INFORMATION
Tourist information office (Parque Central; ☯ 8:30am-noon & 1-5:30pm) Moderately helpful place. Look for *El Navegante*, a pamphlet produced by local Peace Corps volunteers, which is chock-full of info and tips about Trujillo.
Fundación Calentura y Guaimoreto (Fucagua; ☎ 434 4294; 7am-noon & 1:30-5pm Mon-Fri) On the road toward Parque Nacional Capiro-Calentura; manages the national park and the Laguna de Guaimoreto Wildlife Reserve.

Sights
Trujillo is best known for its attractive **beaches**, with pale sand fronting a glassy, waveless ocean. Some of the best are near the airstrip, over 1km east along the beach from town. Several beachside open-air thatched-roof restaurant-bars provide shade, food and a cool drink for beachgoers, and keep the beaches clean.

Often called El Castillo (the Castle), **Fortaleza Santa Bárbara de Trujillo** (☎ 434 4535; Parque Central; admission US$3, free last Thu of every month; ☯ 9am-5pm) is a 17th-century Spanish fortress with a small museum containing pre-Columbian artifacts, religious relics, slave chains, Garífuna masks, and antique weaponry – each item a glimpse into the area's history. The grounds have excellent views of the coast, several old cannons and a stone marker of the execution site of adventurer and would-be conqueror William Walker (opposite).

The **Museo Riveras del Pedregal** (☎ 434 3245; adult/child US$2.25/US$1.10; ☯ 7am-5pm) has a huge collection of antiques and artifacts, ranging from wacky to sublime. There are pre-Columbian figurines and jade jewelry, old pirate treasure chests, farming supplies, even part of a plane that crashed into the bay in 1985. There's little ceremony or signage (and what there is may not be reliable, like the one that reads 'Maya pieces – 10,000 years before Christ').

Activities
The most 'substantial' excursions around Trujillo are an all-day hike to the upper reaches of **Parque Nacional Capiro-Calentura** or a bird-watching trip through the tangled mangrove channels of **Refugio de Vida Silvestre Laguna de Guaimoreto**.

The bay has several good places to go **snorkeling**. Cayo Blanco and the Banco de Estrellas Marinas (Sea Star Bank) are the best spots, with a healthy coral reef teeming with fish, starfish (of course) and the occasional turtle. The folks at C&R Campamento offer snorkeling trips for US$53 for up to eight people, equipment included. Or you can organize it at Casa Kiwi, where guests can rent snorkel gear – walk 2km east along the beach to a sunken boat; its rusted hull sticks partway out of the water just a short distance from shore.

The short hike to **La Cascada de Río Negro** is another pleasant excursion. On the road

WILLIAM WALKER – THE GRAY-EYED MAN OF DESTINY with contributions by Paige Penland

It's tempting, if a cliché, to accuse Tennessee-born William Walker of a Napoleonic complex – at 5'2", he had suffered childhood taunts of 'missy' while caring for his ailing mother. His social life thus lacking, by age 22 he spoke several languages and had degrees in medicine and law. Walker became editor of the left-wing San Francisco Herald, where he spoke out against slavery, but after the death of both his fiancée and his beloved mother, Walker decided to pursue other interests.

Filibustering, a word derived from an old Dutch term for pirate, became the Spanish verb for invading another country as a private citizen, then unofficially receiving aid from your home government. Walker's first filibustering gig targeted La Paz, Mexico, where he pulled off a stunning, if short-lived, victory against the larger, better-equipped (but totally unprepared) Mexican army. The venture played well in the press and two years later, in 1854, Walker was invited by liberals in Nicaragua to help defeat conservatives for control of the country. Dubbed 'the Immortals', Walker's army easily took Granada and before long he had installed himself as dictator, abolished Spanish and reinstated slavery. The rest of Central America seemed to pooh-pooh the development – some liberals even hailed it – until Walker declared his intention to conquer the whole region and launched an attack on Costa Rica. Neighboring countries joined together and fell on Walker who, after a year of bloody fighting, accepted a US-brokered truce and retreated to New Orleans.

Walker returned to the USA a hero, and immediately began planning his return. In 1860 he and 200 soldiers set sail for Roatán, but discovering the island was still controlled by Britain, landed in Trujillo instead and captured the fort. Walker intended to unite with liberal commander Trinidad Cabañas, but after sailing up the Río Negro Walker found Cabañas' camp abandoned. By then British and Honduran forces were closing in; after five days of fighting, Walker surrendered to the British, assuming he'd be returned to the US. But Britain handed him over to Honduran authorities in Trujillo, who promptly had him executed.

Walker is buried in Trujillo, though the cemetery is usually locked. To learn more, check out Guillermo Yuscarán's Gringos in Honduras or the critically panned and somewhat hallucinogenic movie Walker, directed by Alex Cox (of Sid and Nancy and Repo Man fame).

into Trujillo, turn at the 'Mahogany & Cacao Reforestation & Research Facility' sign, circle behind the stadium and then turn right down a dead-end street. Veer right down a dirt road and through a gate; where the road bends rights, look for a small path with a water tube partially buried in the middle. Follow the path (and the tube) about 1km to the falls.

Courses

The **Escuela de Idiomas Truxillo** (☎ 434 4135; 20hr per week US$100, with homestay US$170, incl materials), 50m east of Hotel Trujillo, offers one-on-one classes, four hours per day.

Festivals & Events

Every other Sunday a Garífuna Mass, including traditional singing, is held at Iglesia San Juan Bautista at 6:30pm.

The annual fair in honor of Trujillo's patron saint, San Juan Bautista, takes place the last week of June.

Sleeping

While staying in town is a good way to get to know Trujillo, it's small enough that most travelers prefer to visit it on a day trip from one of three outlying hotels. Each is just a short jalón (hitch), bus or cab ride away.

IN TOWN

Hotel Plaza Centro (☎ 434 3006; Calle Conventillo; r/tw with fan US$10/12, with air-con US$14/16; P ⚡) Two floors of rooms surround a long interior courtyard; newer upper units have air-conditioning, comfy beds, huge hot-water bathrooms with groovy slanted shower doors (and possibly higher prices). The lower units are plain but adequate.

Hotel O'Glynn (☎ 434 4592; 4a Calle; tw/tr US$24/29; P ⚡) A Trujillo institution, the Hotel O'Glynn has friendly service and a good location but, after more than a dozen years in operation, it is starting to show its age. Large clean rooms have white-tile

THE NORTH COAST

floors and spare décor, almost to the point of sterility. Those on the 2nd and 3rd floor share a large balcony – there's no view, but the natural light has a warming effect.

OUTSIDE OF TOWN
Cabañas y Restaurante Campamento (☎ 991 3391; torsteinson83@hotmail.com; hammocks US$3, camping d US$6, cabaña with fan/air-con US$35/37; P ⊠ ⍰) There are eight modern bungalows on this beachfront property 3km west of Trujillo; each has a hot-water bathroom, good bed and porch that faces the ocean. If camping is more your style, set up under any number of palm trees (BYO gear) or just string up a hammock so that you have a view of the Caribbean. There's also a thatch-roof restaurant (mains US$3.75 to US$15, open for breakfast, lunch and dinner) at one end of the property, overlooking a well-maintained pool. All in all, this is a hideaway paradise for just about everyone.

Tranquility Bay (☎ 928 2095; in USA 303-954 4915; www.tranquilitybayhonduras.com; cabañas US$45; P) An adults-only establishment (as in no kids allowed, so keep your shorts on), 3km west of Trujillo, Tranquility Bay offers sunny cabañas, all charmingly decorated with Guatemalan bedspreads and Maya prints. They are sprinkled on a grassy lot overlooking a well-kept stretch of beach. Guests are welcome to use the pool at Cabañas Campamento next door and often have their meals there, too.

Casa Kiwi (☎ 434 3050; www.casakiwi.com; Calle a Puerto Castilla; dm US$4, r with fan US$7-9, d/tw cabin with air-con US$27/32; P ⊠) Although it's over 7 km east of Trujillo, the isolation here has its advantages: guests get to know each other over beers and billiards in the airy dining area and the beach out front is almost entirely yours. Dorms are clean but cramped, private rooms are a bargain for couples (get one on the ocean side), and cabins are pricey for what you get but a worthwhile splurge if you prefer some anonymity. Bikes, beach gear and snorkel gear are for rent (guests only). A cab from town or the bus terminal is US$4.25. Hitching is possible too.

Eating
Merendero del Centro (☎ 434 3034; mains US$1-3; ☽ breakfast & lunch) Near 3a Calle, this popular place serves up *típica* hot and fast. The

baleadas (flour tortilla filled with beans and melted butter) and *pasteles* are particularly tasty although the daily lunch specials (US$1.35) are hard to resist.

Café Oasis (2a Calle; mains US$2-3; ☽ breakfast, lunch & dinner) Although more like a cave than an oasis, the food here is still reliable. There's a good variety of *típica* – from tacos to fried fish platters – and the licuados can't be beat. The air-conditioning is a plus in the summertime too.

Comidas Rápidas El Centro (☎ 434 4567; Parque Central; mains US$2-5.50; ☽ breakfast, lunch & dinner) A standard cafeteria-style eatery, this place has outdoor tables that it shares with an ice-cream shop next door. Be sure to get there early to get the freshest food; platters sit out until they're finished – not very appetizing at the end of a hot day.

Gringo's Restaurant & Bar (☎ 434 4277; mains US$4-7; ☽ breakfast, lunch & dinner) Sunday barbecue is famous here, where ribs and chicken are grilled in converted 55-gallon drums and served dripping in barbecue sauce with all the fixings for US$3.50. True to its name, the menu includes hamburgers, hotdogs, buffalo wings, nachos and pancakes. Gringo's is at the airstrip, 1.5km east.

Just below the main plaza, there are over a dozen virtually identical **beachside restaurants** (mains US$3-7; ☽ breakfast, lunch & dinner). All offer *típica* with a focus on seafood and have similar prices. Favorites include **Rogue's Gallery** (☎ 434 4668), **Perla del Caribe** (☎ 434 4486), and Pizzería Rincón de los Amigos.

For groceries, try **Supermercado Popular** (Parque Central; ☽ 7:30am-7:30pm Mon-Sat, 8am-noon Sun) or the **Mercado Municipal** (3a Calle; ☽ 6am-4pm Mon-Sat, 6-11:30am Sun), where you'll find a little of everything (including a few mangy dogs).

Drinking & Entertainment
Truxillo (2a Calle; cover US$2.15) Regguetón, merengue and Latin rock keep the locals moving from 8pm until the early morning hours. Thursday night is karaoke night.

Coco Pando (☎ 443 4748, Barrio Cristales; cover US$1; ☽ from 9pm Fri-Sun) This is a popular dance spot on the beach, in a mostly Garífuna neighborhood.

Shopping
Artesma Garífuna (☎ 434 3583; Barrio Cristales; ☽ 7am-11pm) This place offers a good selection of Garífuna handicrafts and souvenirs.

Be sure to check out the handmade yucca graters and drums.

Getting There & Away

AIR

Trujillo's airport has been closed for several years; there are no plans to reopen it.

BOAT

It's theoretically possible to get a ride on one of the many cargo or fishing ships going to the Bay Islands or La Moskitia. Go to the pier and try your luck. Definitely check out the vessel (and the weather) before you sign up.

BUS

Buses arrive and depart from the main terminal about 1km east of town. The two main bus lines – Contraibal (☎ 434 4932) and Cotuc (444 2181) – rotate service, so ask which is leaving next.

Buses for San Pedro Sula (US$7, six hours) making a stop in La Ceiba (US$4.25, three hours) leave the terminal every 45 minutes from 1:45am to 1:45pm. There's a 2:30pm bus to La Ceiba only, where you can transfer to the San Pedro Sula bus that originates there.

Although both are technically direct, you can usually get off at any of the intermediate points, including Corocito (US$1.25, 30 minutes), Tocoa (US$1.75, 45 minutes), Savá (US$2.50, 1¾ hours), and Tela (US$6.25, five hours).

Direct buses to Tegucigalpa (US$12, nine hours) leave at 1am and 4:45am.

If you're only going as far as Corocito, in order to catch a bus to Iriona and La Moskitia, a Trujillo–Tocoa bus leaves every hour from 5am to 5pm (US$1.05, 30 minutes).

Buses for Puerto Castilla (US$0.65, 30 minutes), passing Casa Kiwi (US$0.35) along the way, leave the Trujillo terminal at 7:15am, 9:30am, 10:30am, 12:30pm, 2pm, 4pm (usually) and 6pm Monday to Saturday; Sunday departures are at 8am, 1pm and 5pm only. Return buses depart Puerto Castilla at 6am, 7:30am, 9am, 11am, 12:15pm, 2pm and 4pm Monday to Saturday, and at 6am, noon and 4pm on Sunday.

For Santa Fe (US$0.75, 45 minutes) and Guadalupe (US$0.80, 55 minutes) buses leave from in front of the Cementerio Viejo (old cemetery).

Getting Around

Cabs out of town generally cost US$2.75 to US$4.25. If you hitch – very common here – definitely offer the driver money, though most likely they won't accept it.

AROUND TRUJILLO

West of Trujillo are three pleasant Garífuna villages, all with houses stretching along the beach.

Santa Fe

pop 1251

Ten kilometers west of Trujillo, Santa Fe is a mellow Garífuna village with a decent swath of beach. It doesn't receive much tourism except during its annual fair, Feria de Santa Fe (July 15 to 30), when the town bursts at the seams with party-goers. The last three days are especially frenetic.

SLEEPING & EATING

Hotel Mar Atlántico (☎ 429 0593; r/tw US$8/11) A motel on the western end of town; rooms here are basic but will do for a night or two. All seven rooms have cold-water bathrooms and a fan. It's one block from the beach, near Hotel Las Tres Orquidias.

Hotel Las Tres Orquidias (☎ 429 9297; tw US$13.25) A small white two-story building on the beach, this place offers just four rooms, each with two queen beds and a cold-water bathroom. The rooms are simple, like the ones at the Mar Atlántico. The main difference between the two *hospedajes* is that Las Tres Orquidias is on the beach.

There are a handful of small eateries along the road as you come into town. Of all of them, **Comedor Caballero** (mains US$2-12; ☯ breakfast, lunch & dinner), on the main street, is considered the best restaurant around. It's a simple eatery with five rickety tables, typically full of fishermen and friends of Pete, the owner. Seafood is absolutely the way to go; if you can swing it, this is the place to treat yourself to a house special (huge dishes start at US$7).

GETTING THERE & AWAY

Buses to Santa Fe (US$0.75, 45 minutes) leave from the old cemetery in Trujillo at 9:30am, 10:30am, noon, 1pm, 3pm and 5pm (Monday to Saturday) and continue to San Antonio and Guadalupe (US$0.80,

THE NORTH COAST

1¼ hours). On the return trip, buses leave Santa Fe at around 7am, 7.30am, 8.30am, 10.30am, 12.30pm and 2.30pm. On Sunday, there's just one bus that leaves Santa Fe at 7.30am and returns from Trujillo at noon.

San Antonio & Guadalupe

These two very small, very isolated villages (12km and 15km, respectively, from Trujillo) sit on opposite sides of a wide river. They are classically Garífuna, with little outside influence, evidenced in the people's dress, their language, their faces and the watchful but not unwelcome attitude toward newcomers.

At the eastern end of the main street in Guadalupe, **Hotel Franklin** (☎ 429 9046; r/tw US$5.50/8) offers dark, cramped rooms that are, frankly, pretty grim. Limit your time in the bathroom too – it's dry-heave city. You'll want to wear your flip-flops just about everywhere in this place: the floors don't look like they've been scrubbed in, well, ever. Unfortunately, the Hotel Franklin is the only option in the Guadalupe and San Antonio area. At least there's electricity 24 hours a day. Look for it on the main street, along the river. If it's closed, head to the Pulpería Franklin – someone there will let you into the hotel.

GETTING THERE & AWAY

Buses ply the dirt road to Guadalupe, leaving from the old cemetery in Trujillo at 9:30am, 10:30am, noon, 1pm, 3pm and 5pm (Monday to Saturday), passing Santa Fe (US$0.75, 45 minutes) and continuing to San Antonio and Guadalupe (US$0.80, 1¼ hours). On the return trip, buses leave Guadalupe at 6:30am, 7am, 8am, 10am, noon and 2pm, passing Santa Fe about a half-hour later. On Sunday, there's just one bus that leaves Guadalupe at 7am and returns from Trujillo at noon.

Parque Nacional Capiro-Calentura

The mountain behind Trujillo, Cerro Calentura (1235m), is part of the Parque Nacional Capiro-Calentura. A dirt road leads all the way to the top, about 10km, with a number of side trails cutting into the forest along the way. A hike to the top takes about four hours, the return about three.

On the way up the hill, you'll pass through a couple of distinct vegetation zones. At around 600m to 700m the vegetation changes from tropical rain forest to subtropical low-mountain rain forest, and you'll find yourself in a zone of giant tree ferns, with lush forest, large trees, vines and flowering plants. About a third of the way up, a couple of trails diverge off from the road to the left, leading to a waterfall and a tiny reservoir; although they're not marked, you can see them distinctly from the road.

While it might be sunny, clear and warm in Trujillo, it might be cloudy and much cooler at the top of the hill. If the weather isn't cloudy, you can get a great view from the summit over the beautiful Valle de Aguán, along the coast as far as Limón, and across to the Bay Islands and Cayos Cochinos. There is a radar station at the summit.

Fundación Capiro-Calentura Guaimoreto (Fucagua; ☎ 434 4294; ☼ 7:30am-noon & 1:30-5pm) oversees the park and ostensibly provides information, though service can be pretty hit-and-miss. You'll pass the office, clearly marked on your left, on the road to the park.

Refugio de Vida Silvestre Laguna de Guaimoreto

Five kilometers east of Trujillo, Laguna de Guaimoreto is a large lagoon with a natural passageway into the bay. About 6km by 9km, the lagoon is a protected wildlife refuge; its complex system of canals and mangrove forests is home to abundant animal, bird and plant life, including thousands of migratory birds between November and February.

Ask at the tourist office in Trujillo or at **Casa Kiwi** (☎ 434 3050; www.casakiwi.com; Calle a Puerto Castilla), 7km east of Trujillo, about arranging an early-morning bird-watching trip. The going price is around US$60 to US$80 for up to six or eight people. You also can rent a dugout canoe from a fisherman and paddle yourself through the long channel toward the lagoon. Go early – or better yet, the evening before – to arrange it with a fisherman. A few hundred lempira ought to do it.

More information on the lagoon is available at the **Fucagua office** (☎ 434 4294;

(☼ 7:30am-noon & 1:30-5pm), on the road toward Parque Nacional Capiro-Calentura.

Santa Rosa de Aguán
pop 1335

Paul Theroux's remarkable novel, *The Mosquito Coast,* which was later made into a movie starring Harrison Ford, featured this small pleasant town. Just 40km from Trujillo, Santa Rosa de Aguán is a good place to get a taste of La Moskitia, if you don't have the time or the money to go all the way out there. The town was severely damaged during Hurricane Mitch, when 44 people drowned, and evidence of the destruction remains. Still, it has an engaging, frontier-like atmosphere, and you can hire boats to take you up the Río Aguán, where you might catch sight of 4.3m (14ft) alligators.

There's an annual **Garífuna festival** here from August 22 to 29. Two very basic hotels charge US$3.50. Buses to Santa Rosa de Aguán leave Trujillo daily at 10:30am.

SAVÁ
pop 9896

There's no real reason to stop at this dusty roadside town that has grown into a city unless you're transferring buses or it's getting late and you're ready to get off the road.

Information

There is no ATM in town, but either **Banco de Occidente** (☼ 8:30am-4:30pm Mon-Fri, to noon Sat), on the main street, or **Banco Atlántida** (☼ 9am-4pm Mon-Fri, 8:30-11:30am Sat) around the corner, will exchange traveler's checks. For

---

INSIDE THE BANANA BUSINESS

It would be hard to underestimate the impact that the banana industry has had on Honduras, and Central America as a whole, in the last century. In virtually every arena – political, economic, military, social, environmental, health – American fruit companies have left their mark.

In the early part of the century, banana companies gobbled up land as quickly as they could. Banana baron Samuel Zemmuray helped orchestrate a 1908 coup in order to win a concession for more land. In 1913 the United Fruit Company secured a deal under which it would complete and operate two new national railways in exchange for huge tracts of land along the route. The railroad never extended more than a few hundred kilometers, but thousands of small-time farmers were left landless.

Despite having acquired so much land, the banana companies used only a fraction of what they had. In 1954 Guatemalan president Jacobo Arbenz undertook a plan to buy back unused land from the United Fruit Company – at the value United itself had declared for tax purposes – in order to distribute it to landless peasants.

But land reform was an idea whose time had come. In 1962 Honduran president Ramón Villeda Morales signed into law an ambitious agrarian reform – the country's first – designed to redistribute unused land to poor farmers. The law was undermined by the fruit companies, and Villeda Morales was ousted by the military a year later, but an even more aggressive law was put into effect 10 years later by the same military government. Standard Fruit, followed by United, could see the inevitability of reform, and began voluntarily returning some lands. The companies turned the situation to their favor, of course. Entering into exclusive contracts to buy bananas from the small farmers and collectives, the fruit companies reaped nearly the same profits but assumed none of the political or economic risk of owning the land.

In recent years, the environmental and health impact of the banana industry has gained more attention. Researchers estimate that plantations in Central America use 10 times more pesticides than those in industrialized countries. One pesticide, a soil fumigant called Nemagon, was banned in the US in the 1970s after it was shown to cause migraines, vision loss, infertility, cancer and birth defects.

In Honduras, as elsewhere, landless farmers have been forced to clear and cultivate undesirable plots, namely on Honduras' steep mountain slopes, thereby contributing to deforestation. Others have migrated to cities like San Pedro Sula and Tegucigalpa, living in shanty towns along riverbanks and unoccupied hillsides. When Hurricane Mitch hit in 1998, thousands of Hondurans died in mudslides on those very same denuded hillsides and overcrowded shantytowns.

THE NORTH COAST

internet access, check out **Digit@l Cibercafé** (per hr US$0.80; 🕑 8am-9:30pm Mon-Sat), also on the main street; calls to the USA can be made for US$0.11 per minute. There is a **Hondutel** (🕑 7:30am-3:30pm Mon-Fri) down the street for calls to other destinations. The **police station** (🕑 24hr) is outside of town, at the highway turnoff to La Unión.

Sleeping & Eating

M&S Hotel (☎ 424 8487; Barrio El Centro; r/tw US$12.25/16; P 🗙) An excellent excuse to stay the night, this hotel is nothing fancy but it is one of the best budget values in the country. It's a charming and absolutely spotless place with brand-new everything – floors, furniture, mattresses, linens, TVs, framed posters. Plus all of the rooms have air-conditioning and hot-water bathrooms. There's a gated parking lot as well.

Cafeteria La Cascada (main street; mains US$1.50-3.50; 🕑 breakfast, lunch & dinner) Near the M&S Hotel, this simple eatery serves *típica*, sandwiches and lots of fried chicken.

Getting There & Away

Contraipal (☎ 424 8616) has an office in the middle of town, on the road that leads to La Ceiba, opposite Mercadito Jorg. Buses to San Pedro Sula (US$5.50, 4½ hours) that stop in La Ceiba (US$2.25, 1¼ hours) pass by this office every 45 minutes from 2:30am to 3:15pm. To Trujillo (US$2.50, 1¾ hours), buses pass every 45 minutes from 10am to 8:30pm. Buses to Tegucigalpa (US$10, eight to nine hours) depart twice daily, at 2am and 6:30am.

Buses coming from Sonaguera and continuing to La Unión (US$4.50, four hours) stop opposite the Contraipal station, at the Mercadito Jorg, at around 7am. You can catch the same bus west of town at the La Unión turnoff (aka Desvío Sacoco). There, the bus stops briefly at 8am before continuing to La Unión (US$3.75, three hours) and Tegucigalpa (US$9, seven hours). Another bus, originating in Olanchito, stops at the turnoff at 12:15pm, going to La Unión.

To Olanchito (US$1.50, 45 minutes) buses pass roughly every 90 minutes.

The Bay Islands

Honduras is filled with natural treasures – biosphere reserves, national parks, wildlife refuges – but most travelers come here for the mother lode: scuba diving on the Bay Islands. The three Islas de la Bahía – Roatán, Utila and Guanaja – lie along the southern end of the Mesoamerican Barrier Reef, the second-longest coral reef in the world. Beneath the clear turquoise waters is a trove of unbelievable riches: vibrant coral, massive sponges, multicolored fish and large pelagic species, like manta rays, sea turtles and whale sharks. Yet prices remain remarkably low, making the Bay Islands a great place to learn, and in turn love, scuba diving.

Even before Jacques Cousteau popularized diving, the Bay Islands attracted treasure hunters of a more literal sort. Pirates and buccaneers used the islands as a base for attacking Spanish galleons laden with precious metals, woods and other New World bounty bound for Andalusia. Roatán, the largest of the islands, was scallywag central, with as many as 5000 living (and hiding their booty) there in peak years. Much later, British ships dumped more than 2000 rebellious Black Caribs on Roatán; descendents of Arawak Indians and escaped African slaves, the indomitable Caribs morphed into the more mellow but equally resilient Garífuna people of today, found in seaside communities in Roatán and along Honduras' north coast.

For modern-day wayfarers, the Bay Islands offer three distinct experiences. Roatán has a bit of everything: budget and luxury hotels, independent dive shops and all-inclusive resorts, tangled mangroves and easy eco-parks, as well as activities for divers and non divers alike. Utila is a classic backpackers' haunt with sand roads, cheap digs and cheap food. Guanaja is the least visited, with an off-the-beaten track feel and just a handful of hotels and restaurants. Repeat visitors tend to develop favorites: 'Which island should I go to?' is a much-debated issue on LP's Thorn Tree. Some travelers will definitely find one more suitable than another, but don't sweat the decision too much – you'll strike gold, no matter which island you dig into.

HIGHLIGHTS

- Learn to **dive in Utila** (p266), still the best way to find underwater peace and above-water parties
- Find out why you can't beat the **diving in Roatán** (p247), with fun sites like Hole in the Wall and Texas just minutes from West End
- Soak up the sun on Roatán's **West Bay beach** (p254), with thick white sand, clear blue water, and amazing sunsets
- Go **whale-shark spotting** (boxed text, p239) off Utila's north shore from March to May and August to October
- Head to the island of **Guanaja** (p273) for terrific diving and snorkeling, and an off-the-beaten-path feel you won't find on Roatán or Utila

THE BAY ISLANDS

www.lonelyplanet.com

THE BAY ISLANDS

THE BAY ISLANDS

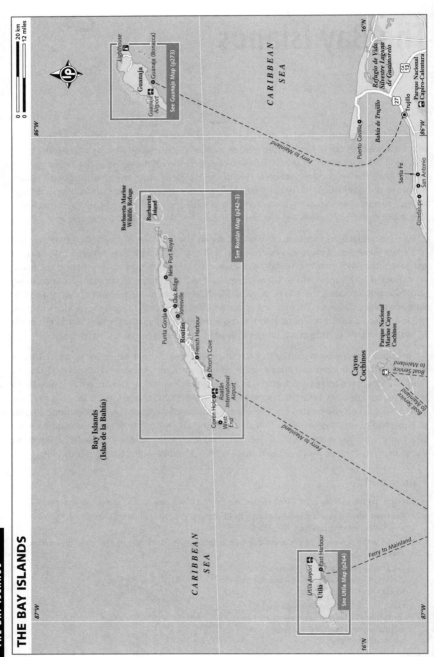

HISTORY

Little is known about life on the Bay Islands before the arrival of European explorers in the 16th century. All three islands were surely inhabited by AD 1000, and perhaps as early as AD 600, but who those early island inhabitants were and where they came from remains unclear.

Christopher Columbus, on his fourth and final voyage to the New World, landed on the island of Guanaja on July 30, 1502. Alerted to a large indigenous population there and on the other islands, Spanish slave-traders kidnapped the islanders and sent them to work on plantations in Cuba and in the gold and silver mines of Mexico.

Meanwhile, English, French and Dutch pirates (including English buccaneer Henry Morgan) established hideaways on the islands, and used them as bases to launch raids on Spanish cargo vessels laden with gold and other treasures bound for Europe.

By the mid-17th century as many as 5000 pirates were ensconced on Roatán alone.

In March 1782, after many attempts, the Spanish captured the town of Port Royal, killing most of the pirates and selling the rest off as slaves. The islands were left largely unoccupied until 1797, when British marines dumped over 2000 Black Caribs, the surviving participants of a massive uprising on the island of St Vincent, on Roatán. That group became known as the Garífuna, and Punta Gorda, where they settled, the first Garífuna village.

The Bay Islands were controlled by the British until 1859, when Great Britain finally ceded the territory to Honduras.

PEOPLE

The population of the Bay Islands is very diverse. Most *isleños* (islanders) have a mixed heritage that includes African, Carib and European. English, spoken with a broad Caribbean accent, is the dominant language,

BOUNTY & BEAUTY UNDER THE SEA: WHALE SHARKS

You put your snorkel gear on, slip into the water and when the bubbles clear and your eyes adjust, before you is a truly massive creature: dark-gray, white spots, long bony ridges down its body, and the fixed pectoral fins and slow sweeping tail that scream *SHARK*. A whale shark to be exact, and no matter what you've heard – they are, in fact, totally harmless – you'd have to be cold-blooded not get a certain stomach-in-the-throat feeling. Because once you're in the water, you're in the shark's realm, and between that very big animal and the very big sea all around, you suddenly feel very small.

Whale sharks (*Rhincodon typhus*) have been spotted around all the Bay Islands, including Cayos Cochinos, but they are far more prevalent in Utila than anywhere else. Underwater currents around Utila stir up seabed nutrients that support plankton, the whale shark's favorite food. The sharks are present year round, but, as migratory animals, tend to be most numerous from March to May and August to October.

The biggest fish in the sea, whale sharks can grow up to 16m (50ft) and weigh 15 tons. Fishermen in Utila tell of a resident whale shark that's 60ft long and known as Old Tom. The name may be quite apt, as whale sharks can live to be 150 years old. Whale sharks are filter feeders, swimming at or near the surface straining plankton out of the water with structures called 'gill rakes'. When not feeding, they dive: scientists now believe whale sharks spend two-thirds of their life at depth, possibly as far down as 1000m.

But there is a lot scientists do not know about whale sharks. The first order of business is simply determining whale shark populations and migration routes. To that end researchers on Utila and elsewhere have been tagging sharks and using their spots – captured with underwater cameras – to create a database of individual animals. On Utila, the Whale Shark & Oceanic Research Center (WSORC; p265) leads much of the current research and has a number of ways divers and snorkelers can be involved.

WSORC has also developed guidelines for shark encounters, such as not touching or grabbing a shark, no flash photography, no more than eight snorkelers in the water at a time, only one boat within 100m of a shark at a time and more. It's vital that travelers know and follow the rules, and insist their guides and boat captains do the same.

THE BAY ISLANDS

with Spanish following as a distant second. On Roatán, there is a Garífuna settlement at Punta Gorda, where Garífuna, English and Spanish are all spoken.

There are still some descendants of early British and Irish settlers, especially on Utila. You're likely to meet people who look like they just got off the boat from England, Scotland or Ireland, though their ancestors came to the islands over a century ago.

More recently, there has been a large influx of ladinos from the mainland, especially to Roatán, where the tourism boom has created lots of new jobs in the construction, service, and security industries. The ladino migration is changing the language on the island; you will hear much more Spanish spoken here now than even just a few years ago.

There is also a significant population of foreign whites, mostly from Europe and the US. Most work at dive shops and other tourist-oriented businesses; in these establishments, you'll hear a variety of languages, including German, Italian, French and Hebrew.

COSTS

The Bay Islands are much more expensive than the mainland. Guanaja is the most expensive of the three islands, and well out of backpacker range. Roatán is more reasonable, but food, accommodations and Internet can add up fast. Keep costs down by renting a place with a kitchen so you don't have to eat out every meal. Diving prices on Roatán and Utila are about the same, but Utila has cheaper hotels and restaurants, and many dive shops offer free or discounted accommodation packages.

Visiting the islands will eat into your budget for sure, but if you want to dive, it truly doesn't get any cheaper (or much better) in the Caribbean. If you can only afford to dive a few times, or not at all, you can snorkel and kayak cheaply, or swim and sunbathe for free.

DANGERS & ANNOYANCES

The islands are generally safer than the mainland, although a few assaults have been reported on the beach between West End and West Bay; discarded beer bottles and the occasional needle might explain the problem. Water taxis are a faster and safer option than walking. Also, when swimming or snorkeling, don't leave valuables unattended on the beach – they have a way of walking. Better not to bring them at all.

Mosquitoes and sand flies are voracious on the islands, especially during the rainy season. You'll need plenty of repellent. It's also very important that you take antimalarial medication – five different strains of the disease have been identified on Roatán alone. Mosquitoes also carry dengue fever; see the Health chapter, p322, for more information on both malaria and dengue fever.

Sand flies don't carry diseases, but they're tiny – the size of a grain of sand – and can turn your back and legs into a forest of red welts in one afternoon on the beach.

DIVING

Diving is by far the most popular tourist activity on the Bay Islands, and it's known as one of the cheapest places in the world to get certified. Most dive shops offer a range of courses and recreational dives, from an introductory resort course (basic instruction plus a couple of dives) to a full PADI-certification course qualifying you to dive worldwide. Most dive shops are affiliated with PADI, but NAWI and SSI courses are also available. An open-water diving certification course will last from three to four days and includes two confined water and four open-water dives. Advanced diving courses are also offered. Despite the low cost, safety and equipment standards are reasonable.

Utila used to have the lowest certification and fun-diving prices of the three Bay Islands, but prices on Roatán are about the same now. Guanaja is more expensive. When comparing prices, check whether study materials are included; ask about reef taxes too. On Utila, see if courses include free lodging or a couple of free fun dives. Rental equipment is usually included in all the rates; if you have your own, ask about discounts.

Don't make the mistake of selecting a diving course purely on the basis of price though – you'll find the differences are small, anyway. Instead, find one that has a good record and where you feel comfortable (see boxed text, opposite).

GUIDELINES FOR SAFE DIVING

Diving safety must be taken very seriously. Do not let the laid-back atmosphere of the Bay Islands translate into a blasé attitude toward safety guidelines. That goes for all aspects of the sport, from setting up your gear, to riding on the boat, to entering and exiting the water, to floating on the surface, to exploring the depths below. It's true that the Bay Islands have an excellent safety record, and diving itself demands relatively little physical prowess or technical know-how. But it is vitally important that you do not skip or hurry basic safety measures, nor dive with a shop or instructor that does.

The single biggest concern for a student diver should be quality of instruction and supervision. Turnover of divemasters and instructors can be very high – at any given time, even a highly recommended shop might be short on instructors. Understaffing can lead to larger groups and less attentive supervision. Ask how many people will be in your course; eight is the maximum allowed by PADI, less is better. If the number is high, consider going to a different dive shop or starting a day later.

You should like and trust your instructor. Ask other divers for recommendations, not just for shops but for specific instructors and divemasters. It's perfectly OK to ask instructors how long they have been teaching and how long they have been on the island. Ask to see the equipment – as a beginner there's not a lot you'll be able to determine, but you'll get a sense of your instructor's attitude toward you and your concerns. If you're uncomfortable with a particular instructor, ask to move to a different course or simply go to a different shop.

Quality of equipment is also important. While it takes training to truly assess equipment, you can and should check certain things, like the O-ring on your tank isn't broken or frayed and whether your regulator hisses when you turn on the air. Arrive early to check your gear; if you're uncomfortable with something – even if the instructor assures you it's OK – ask for a replacement. Being comfortable and confident in the water is a crucial part of safe, enjoyable diving. Shops should also have their air analyzed three to four times per year, and have a certificate prominently displayed to prove it. If you don't see one, ask about it.

There are certain boat safety guidelines that shops should follow as well. All boats should have a captain who stays on board (make sure the captain is not also your divemaster). All boats should have supplies of oxygen, usually carried in a green first aid kit, and a VHF radio – cell phone service is not reliable. Don't be afraid to ask about each of these things, and to have the instructor actually show you the items on board – if enough divers did so, more shops would follow the rules; in the rare case of an emergency, they can make the difference between life and death.

Finally, no matter where you sign up, do not rely on your instructor or divemaster to anticipate every problem. Check your own equipment, assess your comfort level and be vocal about your concerns. Actively monitor your own safety using the following guidelines:

- Accept responsibility for your own safety on every dive. Always dive within the limits of your ability and training.
- Use and respect the buddy system. It saves lives.
- Do not surface if you hear the motor of a boat, unless you are pulling yourself slowly up by the dive-boat mooring line. Accidents have occurred when boats have hit divers who were on the surface or just under it.
- Do not go into caves unless you're certified to do so. Go through tunnels and 'swim-throughs' only with qualified guides.
- Don't drink or use drugs and dive – it's stupid and can kill or injure you or the people around you.
- If you haven't dived for a while, consider taking a refresher course before you jump into deep water. It takes about an hour and only costs around US$15. It's much better to discover that you remember all your diving skills in 3m of water than to realize you don't in 20m.

Qualified divers also have plenty of options, including fun dives, 10-dive packages, night dives, deep dives, wreck diving, customized dive charters and dives to coral walls and caves. There is a great variety of marine life, the water temperature is balmy, and the visibility is hard to beat. The waters between Roatán and Utila are also among the best places in the world to view whale sharks, which are typically in the region between May and September.

GETTING THERE & AWAY

You can reach all three Bay Islands by airplane or by ferry. All flights come and go from La Ceiba (p221), as do the ferries for Roatán and Utila. For Guanaja, the ferry leaves from Trujillo. For some reason, the ferry companies have never offered direct service between Roatán and Utila – you've always had to go via La Ceiba. But more and more private boat owners are making the trip, and the price, frequency, and reliability are improving. It's certainly something that's long overdue – ask on either island for the latest.

GETTING AROUND
Boat

Water taxis are used on Roatán and Guanaja. On Roatán, they are useful for getting between West End and West Bay, and for exploring Oak Ridge, which is set around a small bay. On Guanaja, you'll need a water taxi to get between the main village, which is on a small cay, and the island proper.

Car & Motorcycle

You can rent cars on Roatán and motorcycles on all three islands. However, rentals are not cheap – around US$50 per day plus fuel costs.

Taxi

Taxis ferry people all around Roatán, and to a lesser degree Utila. *Colectivo* (public transportion) fares are reasonable (US$1 to $2), but private rates can be high (US$10 or more). Be sure to establish the type of service you want – and how much it's going to cost – before you get in the car. On Roatán, taxi prices go up whenever a cruise ship is in dock and after 6pm.

ROATÁN

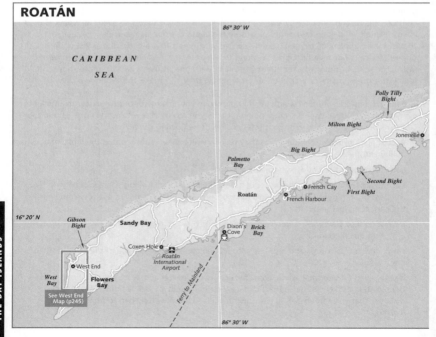

ROATÁN

pop 65,000

Roatán is the largest and most popular of the Bay Islands. About 50km long and just 2km to 4km wide, it is surrounded by a rich living reef, making it a paradise for divers and snorkelers. It's also big enough to keep non-divers interested, with botanical gardens, butterfly and iguana farms, family recreational areas, canopy tours, and winding dirt roads leading to small villages and isolated bays. And if you just want to relax, parts of Roatán, especially West End and West Bay, are as idyllic as any tourist brochure, with clear turquoise water, colorful tropical fish, powdery white sand and coconut palms.

Getting There & Away

AIR

Roatán's **Aeropuerto Juan Ramón Galvez** (RTB; ☎ 445 1880) is located a short distance east of Coxen Hole.

Isleña/TACA (☎ 445 1088, reservations 443 0179; www.flyislena.com), **Sosa** (☎ 445 1658; www.aerolineas sosa.com) and **Atlantic Airlines** (☎ 445 1179; www .atlanticairlines.com.ni) all have offices in Roatán's airport; they offer daily flights between Roatán and La Ceiba (all charge around US$42 each way), with domestic and international connections. At the time of research, **Continental** (☎ 445 0224; www.continental .com) operated nonstop flights from Houston to Roatán on Saturday and Sunday, and **Delta** (☎ 550 1616; www.delta.com) had flights from Atlanta on Saturday only.

BOAT

Safeway Maritime's (☎ Roatán 921 7695, La Ceiba 445 1795) new Galaxy Wave catamaran ferry provides a fast, comfortable ride between Roatán and La Ceiba (economy/first class US$21/26.50, 1¼ hours). There are daily departures from La Ceiba to Roatán at 9:30am and 4:30pm, and from Roatán to La Ceiba at 7am and 2pm

Getting Around

BICYCLE

Captain Van's Rentals (p254) rents mountain bikes for US$10 per day.

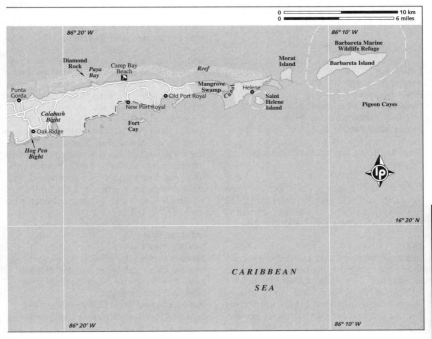

BOAT

Water taxis are most commonly used between West End and West Bay (US$2, 10 minutes) and for getting around Oak Ridge, which is built up along both sides of a long inlet. You can hire the same boat drivers to take you on a private tour of the island, or to reach places inaccessible by car, like Barbareta Island. There are no fixed or standard prices for such excursions, however, so be prepared to negotiate.

BUS

Roatán has two bus routes, both originating in Coxen Hole.

Bus 2 is the one most visitors use. It travels west from Coxen Hole past Sandy Bay and on to West End. Minibuses depart from both ends and take about 25 minutes in each direction (US$0.80, every 15 minutes from 6am to 6pm).

Bus 1 travels east from Coxen Hole past the airport to French Harbour, past Polly Tilly Bight, through Punta Gorda and on to Oak Ridge (US$0.70 to US$1, every 30 minutes from 6am to 5:30pm); the cost depends on the destination. Travel time varies by driver, taking up to a painful one hour to get to Oak Ridge.

CAR & MOTORCYCLE

Car rental agencies on Roatán include the following:

Best Car Rental (☎ 445 1494; www.roatanbestcarrental.com; airport; ☽ 7am-5pm)

Caribbean Rent a Car (☎ 455 6950, at airport 455 1430; www.caribbeanroatan.com; ☽ 8am-6pm)

Roatán Island Rental (☎ 455 6759; www.roatanislandrental.com; French Harbour; ☽ 8am-5pm).

Sandy Bay Rent a Car (☎ 445 1710; Sandy Bay; ☽ 7am-5pm)

In West End, Captain Van's Rentals rents out 125cc and 200cc motorcycles for US$52 to US$64 per day plus insurance, as well as two-stroke scooters for US$45 per day.

TAXI

Plenty of taxis operate around the island. Many are *colectivos* during the day, which means they stop along the way to pick up additional passengers and don't charge much more than buses. Cabbies will assume you want a taxi *privado*, or direct service, so be sure to let the taxi driver know what type of service you want before you get in. Unfortunately, there are no *colectivos* between West End and the new ferry terminal in Dixon Cove; if you are short on lempira and long on time, catch a *colectivo* between West End and Coxen Hole (US$1.75), then take a private cab between Coxen Hole and Brick Bay(US$5). Otherwise, a private cab from West End to the ferry terminal costs around US$15. As with everywhere in Honduras, always clarify the price of the ride before you get in. Fares are higher after 6pm

WEST END

Curled around two small turquoise bays and laced with coconut palms, West End is a busy but pleasant village on the western end of the island. This is where virtually all the independent travelers come (as opposed to those headed to all-inclusives) and the town's one sandy road is packed with restaurants, hotels and dive shops.

Orientation

Roatán's east–west alignment makes it easy to assume that West End is oriented the same way. In fact, the road through West End runs almost exactly north-to-south – a good thing, too, as it makes for spectacular sunsets from anywhere in town. The road from Coxen Hole intersects West End's main road at the east side of Half Moon Bay, the first of West End's two small bays. Buses and taxis to Coxen Hole wait at that intersection. To the north (your right as you enter town) is a handful of hotels, restaurants and dive shops. South (left) of the main intersection, the road curls around Half Moon Bay, passes the First Baptist church and continues to where most of West End's restaurants, bars and dive shops are concentrated. The road continues south until the buildings eventually end at an expansive beach that leads to West Bay.

Information

BOOKSTORES

Barefoot Charlie's (☎ 403 8721; ☽ 9am-9pm) A big collection of beach trash, but not much else; offers two-for-the-price-of-one or buy one, get the second one at half-price. Opposite Foster's Bar.

Mariposa Lodge (☎ 403 8728) A one-for-one book exchange of English-language books is offered at the reception kiosk of this lodge (see p249).

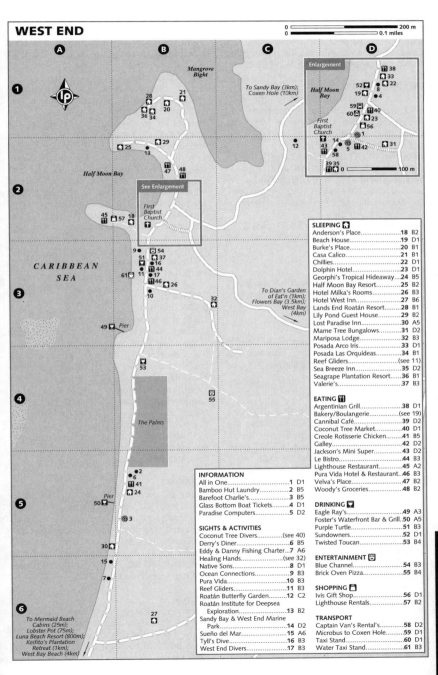

WEST END

SLEEPING		
Anderson's Place	18	B2
Beach House	19	D1
Burke's Place	20	B1
Casa Calico	21	B1
Chillies	22	D1
Dolphin Hotel	23	D1
Georphi's Tropical Hideaway	24	B5
Half Moon Bay Resort	25	B2
Hotel Milka's Rooms	26	B3
Hotel West Inn	27	B6
Lands End Roatán Resort	28	B1
Lily Pond Guest House	29	B2
Lost Paradise Inn	30	A5
Mame Tree Bungalows	31	D2
Mariposa Lodge	32	B3
Posada Arco Iris	33	D1
Posada Las Orquídeas	34	B1
Reef Gliders	(see 11)	
Sea Breeze Inn	35	D2
Seagrape Plantation Resort	36	B1
Valerie's	37	B3

EATING		
Argentinian Grill	38	D1
Bakery/Boulangerie	(see 19)	
Cannibal Café	39	D2
Coconut Tree Market	40	D1
Creole Rotisserie Chicken	41	B5
Galley	42	D2
Jackson's Mini Super	43	D2
Le Bistro	44	B3
Lighthouse Restaurant	45	A2
Pura Vida Hotel & Restaurant	46	B3
Velva's Place	47	B2
Woody's Groceries	48	B2

DRINKING		
Eagle Ray's	49	A3
Foster's Waterfront Bar & Grill	50	A5
Purple Turtle	51	B3
Sundowners	52	D1
Twisted Toucan	53	B4

ENTERTAINMENT		
Blue Channel	54	B3
Brick Oven Pizza	55	B4

SHOPPING		
Ivis Gift Shop	56	D1
Lighthouse Rentals	57	B2

TRANSPORT		
Captain Van's Rental's	58	D2
Microbus to Coxen Hole	59	D1
Taxi Stand	60	D1
Water Taxi Stand	61	B3

INFORMATION		
All in One	1	D1
Bamboo Hut Laundry	2	B5
Barefoot Charlie's	3	B5
Glass Bottom Boat Tickets	4	D1
Paradise Computers	5	D2

SIGHTS & ACTIVITIES		
Coconut Tree Divers	(see 40)	
Derry's Diner	6	B5
Eddy & Danny Fishing Charter	7	A6
Healing Hands	(see 32)	
Native Sons	8	D1
Ocean Connections	9	B3
Pura Vida	10	B3
Reef Gliders	11	B3
Roatán Butterfly Garden	12	C2
Roatán Institute for Deepsea Exploration	13	B2
Sandy Bay & West End Marine Park	14	D2
Sueño del Mar	15	A6
Tyll's Dive	16	B3
West End Divers	17	B3

Labels on map:
- Mangrove Bight
- To Sandy Bay (3km); Coxen Hole (10km)
- Enlargement
- Half Moon Bay
- First Baptist Church
- Half Moon Bay
- See Enlargement
- First Baptist Church
- CARIBBEAN SEA
- To Dian's Garden of Eat'n (1km); Flowers Bay (3.5km); West Bay (4km)
- Pier
- The Palms
- Pier
- To Mermaid Beach Cabins (25m); Lobster Pot (75m); Luna Beach Resort (800m); Keifito's Plantation Retreat (1km); West Bay Beach (4km)

EMERGENCY

The nearest **police station** (☎ 445 3438) is in Coxen Hole, though pressure is mounting to have a station opened in West End.

INTERNET ACCESS

Internet speeds have increased in West End, thanks to satellite connections, but the prices remain astronomical. More and more hotels are offering free wireless Internet for those with laptops.

All in One (☎ 403 8238; Half Moon Bay; per hr US$6.25; ☼ 8:30am-9pm Mon-Sat, 10am-6pm Sun)

Barefoot Charlie's (☎ 403 8721; per hr US$6.25, unlimited access 2/3/4 week US$10/15/20; ☼ 9am-9pm) Very slow connection, but the unlimited-access plans are a steal. Opposite Foster's Bar

Paradise Computers (Half Moon Bay; per hr US$12.75; ☼ 8am-10pm) Prepaid Internet accounts available (1/9hr US$10/60).

LAUNDRY

Bamboo Hut Laundry (per pound US$0.80, minimum 5lb) Same-day service if you drop off in the morning. Next to the Palms condos.

MONEY

There's an ATM in the lobby of the **Dolphin Hotel** (☎ 445 4499; Half Moon Bay; ☼ 9am-9pm) and another in the **Coconut Tree Market** (Half Moon Bay; ☼ 7am-8pm).

TELEPHONE

Most Internet cafés in West End also place national and international calls. Rates are relatively uniform (and uniformly high): domestic fixed line per minute US$0.25, domestic cell phone per minute US$0.55, international calls per minute US$0.75. It's much cheaper to call from Coxen Hole (p259).

Sights

Half Moon Bay has a small, clean beach and good snorkeling if you get past the sea grass. It is a popular spot for kayaking and sunbathing too. While you're there, check out **Sandy Bay & West End Marine Park** (☎ 349 4138; www.roatanmarinepark.com; Half Moon Bay; ☼ 8am-noon & 2-6pm Mon-Sat), a marine preservation office with a small exhibit on the marine park and island ecology. It is located above a gift shop.

Nearby **West Bay beach** (p254) is one of the most beautiful beaches in the country and is great for snorkeling too. Frequent water taxis (p256) make it a quick and easy trip over. You can also walk there – just keep heading south along the beach – although it's not recommended to do so alone or at night (see p240).

Lady Slipper, Queen and Sunset Langwings, Helicopter, Common Owl and Orange Dog are just a few of the 30-plus species of moths and butterflies at the **Roatán Butterfly Garden** (☎ 445 4481; www.roatan butterfly.com; adult/child US$5/3; ☼ 9am-5pm, Sun-Fri), a 3000-sq-ft enclosure a few hundred meters from the West End turn-off. The best time to visit is noon or early afternoon, when the sun is hottest and the butterflies are most active. The garden also has a large collection of orchids and other tropical plants, as well as bird enclosures with keel billed toucans, collared aracari, and several species of parrots – one can sing 'Happy Birthday' and squawk, rather aptly, 'Help! Help! Let me out!'

Activities

SNORKELING

Many dive shops loan snorkel gear to their students for free; non students can rent for US$5 a day. Otherwise look for signs advertising snorkel gear – reliable options include **Ivis Gift Shop** (Half Moon Bay; ☼ 7am-6pm) and **Lighthouse Rentals** (☎ 363 6727; ☼ hours vary) near Lighthouse Restaurant. Just past the Palms condos, **Derry's Diner** (☎ 445 4404; ☼ 8am-10pm) takes groups of four or more on hour-long snorkel trips (US$5). You don't go far – just to Blue Channel or Canyon Reef in front – but it's nice to snorkel from a boat and you can't beat the price.

KAYAKING

There are plenty of places to push off in West End; Half Moon Bay is one of the easiest – and prettiest – places since it's so well protected. A few hotels – Posada Arco Iris, Sea Breeze Inn, and Casa Calico – provide kayaks for their guests to use. **Lighthouse Rentals** (☎ 363 6727; ☼ hours vary) rents one- and two-person kayaks.

HIKING

A loop starting in West End heading to Flowers Bay, then continuing south almost to the tip of the island, over the ridge to West Bay and back up the beach to West End, makes a good five- to six-hour hike.

THE BAY ISLANDS

Limerick
County Library

Tack on a couple of hours enjoying the beach at West Bay, and it's a whole day's excursion. For a shorter trek, simply do the West End–Flowers Bay leg – when you reach the ridge, look out over both sides of the island. In either case, bring plenty of water to stay hydrated and adequate repellent to ward off the numerous ticks and sand flies.

MASSAGE

If carrying tanks on and off the dive boat has put a kink in your neck, book a massage at **Healing Hands** (☎ 403 8728; per hr US$40). Located at Mariposa Lodge (p249) and recommended by local expatriates, owners Susan Deduk and Mike Dewar offer shiatsu and European massages as well as reiki treatments in a private studio.

Dive Shops

Roatán is a diver's paradise, with near perfect Caribbean conditions and innumerable dives, from wrecks and reefs, to swimthroughs and drift-dives. There is plenty of great diving within a few minutes' boat ride of West End, including spots like Hole in the Wall, Texas, Sponge Emporium, Black Rock, and Lighthouse. Most shops offer three single-tank dives per day, starting at 9am and spending their surface interval back at the shop.

Dive shops in West End have worked hard to standardize prices for courses and fun dives, and to end the destructive price wars of past years. Prices have gone up, yes, but only because they were ridiculously low before. At the time of research, Open Water courses cost from US$200 to US$240 per person depending on the number of people in your group, plus US$30 for PADI-required materials. An advanced course costs US$200, rescue US$225, and divemaster US$500 and up, plus materials. Fun dives cost from US$20 to US$35 per tank, depending on whether you book a package of one, five, or ten dives. Night dives and two-tank trips to the south side cost a bit more. Finally, most shops – but not

---

ROATÁN'S TOP DIVE SITES

Roatán has dozens of dive sites and most shops do a good job of making sure divers who buy multidive packages don't end up going to the same place again and again. If there's a site you are keen to try, don't be afraid to ask. At the same time, weather and water conditions dictate most site selection, and some aren't practical or able to be dived for days at a time. Some favorites – among many, many others – include the following:

Mary's Place Fissures in the coral form a deep, sheer-faced maze at this one-of-a-kind site. Winding through, you'll likely see jacks, lobsters and crabs, and huge schools of silversides; near the mooring, keep an eye out for seahorses. Mary's Place is near French Harbour, and is usually combined with another south-side dive and lunch at Hole in the Wall restaurant.

Texas Part of the same area known as West End Wall, Texas is so called for its wide open terrain and Texas-sized barrel sponges. A deep, strong current means you can sometimes fly over the reef at three to four knots without lifting a fin. It's not uncommon to see free swimming morays, large groupers, and even the occasional hammerhead. You may even spot the elusive sargassum triggerfish.

Hole in the Wall Another amazing dive: dropping through a hole in the reef at 20ft, you descend through a narrow sloping channel before it spits you out 100ft down. Be sure to look up at the spectacular vertical vista above you.

El Águila Wreck Scuttled in 1997 just opposite Anthony's Key Resort, the Águila was a good dive until Hurricane Mitch came along and broke the ship into three pieces – and now it's even better! As you descend, you may draw a crowd of huge groupers looking for a snack, and resident moray eels may join in the swim-about. (Cool to see, but a good reason not to feed animals while diving or snorkeling since they can get annoying – and sometimes even aggressive.)

Blue Channel A 30ft-deep channel running parallel to shore just off West End, Blue Channel has some easy swim-throughs and an incredible array of fish and reef life, including triggers, damselfish, grunts and barracuda.

Overheat A shallow dive site that's good for novice divers. Its proximity to the Águila wreck makes it a good place to spot giant groupers.

all – have joined the Sandy Bay & West End Marine Park, and voluntarily charge all divers a one-time US$10 park fee. The money goes toward anti-poaching and reef-protection programs. Please only use shops that are part of this effort – there's a list of member shops at the marine park's website (www.roatanmarinepark.com). It costs a little more, but one dive will show you why it's so important.

Coconut Tree Divers (☎ 445 4081, 403 8782; www .coconuttreedivers.com; next to Coconut Tree Market) The only shop to regularly offer advanced two-tank dives in the morning. Experienced instructors lead most dives; after-dive beers draw a younger crowd.

Native Sons (☎ 445 1214; natives@hondutel.hn; at the entrance to Chillies hotel) A solid professional outfit run by Alvin Jackson, a local instructor with almost three decades of experience. Fast modern boats mean this shop is more willing than most to go to distant dive spots.

Ocean Connections (☎ in US 305-767 4225; www .ocean-connections.com; across from Blue Channel) Caters to a slightly older crowd, with small classes and a friendly, noncompetitive atmosphere. Operated by the same dog-loving British couple for more than a decade.

Pura Vida (☎ 445 4110, 403 8798, in US 786-319 4571; www.puravidaresort.com; Pura Vida Hotel & Restaurant) Another shop with a good, long-standing reputation.

Reef Gliders (☎ 403 8243; www.reefgliders.com; next to Purple Turtle) Under new ownership, and capably managed by a young American-Canadian couple who used to work in Utila; known for friendly service and small groups. Dorms are offered for divers (see opposite).

Seagrape Plantation Resort (☎ 445 4428; www.sea graperoatan.com; at the northern end of town) A hotel dive shop that gets good reviews.

Sueño del Mar (☎ 445 4343, in US 800-298 9009; www.suenodelmar.com; near Lost Paradise Inn) Friendly, professional dive center with excellent gear – in fact they service equipment for several competitors in town. Hotel and retail shop on-site.

Tyll's Dive (☎ /fax 455 5322; near Blue Channel) Old Tyll hasn't run the shop since 2003, but the current management maintains a relaxed, friendly shop.

West End Divers (☎ 368 0616; www.westenddivers .com; opposite water taxi pier) A small shop catering to a younger crowd.

Tours
The **Roatán Institute for Deepsea Exploration** (RIDE; ☎ 359 2887, in US 305-720 2821; www.stanley submarines.com; Half Moon Bay) is the fancy name for an American kid with a homemade submarine, which he uses to take tourists into the deep sea trenches just off Roatán's

north shore. This is one of only two operations in the world that take Joe Public deeper than 300ft. And the *Idabel*, as the sub is called, goes much deeper than that – more than 2000ft down, for as long as seven hours. There is no vegetation after 300ft (and no light after 1700ft) and only the strangest of life forms: bioluminescent sponges, swimming sea cucumbers, six-gilled sharks, all amid huge limestone boulders and fossilized coral formations. The sub's 30-something creator, Karl Stanley, got into submarine building with no formal engineering training, or even advanced welding, for that matter. He admits he has no special insurance (nor the international certification he'd need to secure it); if anything happens, says Karl, he's not coming up either. The sub does have redundant safety systems and three days' worth of air and supplies, and has had no major incidents in hundreds of outings. Up to three passengers can take trips of varying lengths: two hours to a maximum depth of 1000ft (US$500), three hours to 1500ft (US$800), four hours to 2000ft (US$1200), or a five- to seven-hour night dive in search of sharks (US$1500).

At the far end of town, **Eddy & Danny Fishing Charter** (☎ 445 4015; west of Sueño del Mar; ⏰ 8am-9pm) is a friendly family operation that takes groups trolling (for tuna, dorado, barracuda, and sometimes wahoo and marlin in season), deep sea fishing (for grouper, snapper) and flat fishing (catch-and-release bone fish). On a full-day trip (US$350 to US$600 depending on the boat), you can combine different types of fishing, and even stop for snorkeling or lunch on a deserted beach. Half-day trips cost from US$200 to US$350. At the end of the day, you can have your catch cooked up, along with potatoes, garlic bread and veggies, for an extra US$5 per person.

Glass-bottom boat rides (per person US$20) at a small kiosk across from the Beach House at Half Moon Bay. There is no fixed schedule, but at least two people are needed to take the 45- to 60-minute trip.

Sleeping
With such a steady number of tourists arriving in West End every day, there is an excellent selection of hotels. Be aware that some taxi drivers will try to shepherd you

to ones where they get a commission – if you have a place in mind, insist on stopping at it.

BUDGET

Georphi's Tropical Hideaway (☎ 445 4104, in US 508-854 1356; www.roatangeorphis.com; just south of The Palms condo complex; dm US$5; r with/without air-con US$25/12; r with shared bathroom & kitchen per person US$13; P ✗) This is a collection of small, well-kept cabins on a sloping, tree-filled lot. Most are on stilts and all have mosquito screens and small refrigerators. They also have private porches that are perfect for whiling away an afternoon. Ask for a re-modeled cabin for the best of the litter.

Burke's Place (☎ 445 4146; r with/without air-con US$30/20, studios US$25; P ✗) This is one of West End's best kept secrets. They don't look like much on the outside, but the simple rooms in these wood-plank cabins are very well maintained; each opens onto a grassy area and shares long porches. The communal kitchen, in its own large cabin, is one of the best on the island; this is one place you won't have to worry about critters. Located on the northern end of town, towards Seagrape Plantation Resort

Chillies (☎ 445 4003; www.nativesonsroatan.com /chillies.htm; behind Native Sons; r with shared bathroom US$18, cabins with shared bathroom & kitchen US$22, cabins US$27) Affiliated with Native Sons dive shop (p247), Chillies offers simple clapboard rooms and cabins on a tidy lot. All the rooms are decent; the US$27 rooms are the newest, but the US$22 ones are the best deal – slightly larger, they're in duplex cabins so you share a bathroom and a kitchen with just one other room. The rest use the communal – and somewhat sketchy – kitchen in the main house.

Dolphin Hotel (☎ 445 4499; dolphinhotels@cable color.hn; near Coconut Tree Market; s/d US$25/30; P ✗) This is a basic but clean hotel in one of the most coveted locations in West End – on the main drag overlooking Half Moon Bay. Of the 10 rooms, only three have been recently renovated and these also happen to be the only ones with a view – a great deal if you can score one. The others are dark and showing some wear and tear but they're adequate.

Hotel Milka's Rooms (☎ 445 4241; dm US$10, r US$20) Owned by a local family, this new hotel is a decent option for travelers on a budget. Dorms are set up in two split-level houses; each floor has its own spacious kitchen and big porches – great for hanging out. Private rooms are in a ranch-style building next door. The rooms are cramped – there's barely enough space to set down your pack – but they're clean and have cable TV. It's located on the road to Mariposa Lodge, just a few steps from the main drag.

Reef Gliders (☎ 403 8243; www.reefgliders.com; next to Purple Turtle; dm US$5) This dive shop's new owners previously ran a dive shop on Utila, so it's no surprise that one of their first moves was to open a dorm exclusively for their students. Just four beds, it has an in-room bathroom and a small deck with excellent views. It's right over the classroom, so you can stumble out of bed and be calculating surface intervals within seconds.

Anderson's Place (☎ 403 8753; r with/without shared bathroom US$15/10) This is a collection of a few rundown wood-plank cabins with unobstructed views of the Caribbean – what Sandals would give for this plot! As it is, however, the bathrooms could use a scrub down (as could the rooms), but the view doesn't get better than this. The owner, who's a bit gruff, lives in a small house behind the First Baptist church; the cabins themselves are further back, on the path to Lighthouse Restaurant.

Valerie's (☎ 403 8757; www.roatanonline.com /valeries; dm US$5; r with shared bathroom US$12-16) A longtime favorite with backpackers, this labyrinth has certainly seen better days. The dorms are ramshackle, the kitchens are functional but seriously grubby, and the shared bathrooms…well, suffice it to say, wear flip flops. So, why bother? The private rooms. They're not bad, and cheap too – relatively new, they have decent beds, and some indication of a cleaning staff.

MIDRANGE

Mariposa Lodge (☎ 403 8728; www.mariposa-lodge .com; r with air-con US$40, r with shared bathroom US$25 1-bedroom apt US$35; P ✗) Often full – and with good reason – the Mariposa is the best deal in West End. Accommodations are set up in three buildings: the main house has five modern apartments with fantastically equipped kitchens; a small annex houses two private rooms with air conditioning – they're a little plain Jane but are spotless and comfortable nonetheless; and the Mariposa Pequeña is a cottage with three private rooms that share a kitchen and bathroom. The rooms in the cottage are small, but the common area more than makes up for it. The Canadian owners are friendly hosts and have tons of information about the island. Located down a side road, just east of Pura Vida Hotel & Restaurant.

Posada Arco Iris (☎ 445 4264; www.roatanposada .com; Half Moon Bay; r US$35, studio US$40, 1-/2-bedroom apt US$50/55, air-con extra US$10; ❄ 🖳) One of West End's nicest places, the rooms and apartments here are set in two-story buildings on a lush and well-maintained lot. All have private porches and are charmingly decorated with Guatemalan bedspreads and Honduran handicrafts. It is also one of the only hotels in town that offers lounge chairs on the beach for its guests as well as free use of one- and two-person kayaks.

Posada Las Orquídeas (☎ 445 4387; next to Seagrape Plantation; r with fan US$35-40, studio with fan US$40-45, air-con extra US$10; ❄) The owner of Posado Arco Iris also recently opened this place – 18 comfortable rooms with balconies and ocean views. Regardless of where you stay, you won't be disappointed.

Seagrape Plantation Resort (☎ 445 4428; www .seagraperoatan.com; r & cabin US$50, r with shared bathroom per person US$10; P ❄) At the far northern end of town, Seagrape is an old-timer that's holding on strong. The oceanfront bungalows are the best of the lot: standalone wood cottages, with private porches, and beautiful views. The hotel rooms, unfortunately, lack character – they're shiny and new but that's about it; big tour groups tend to favor these anyhow. There's also an ultra-budget section that's geared toward backpackers; these rooms are kind of drab, but they have access to a small kitchen. The one surprise – perhaps, even a bummer – is that there's no beach. Instead of sand in front, it's ironshore, a sharp, black rock made of coral, mollusk shells, and limestone. Not exactly a great tanning spot, but it is dramatic.

Half Moon Bay Resort (☎ 445 4442; in US 800-989 9970; www.halfmoonbaycabins.com; s/d US$38/55, with air-con US$50/65; P ❄) On the quiet end of Half Moon Bay, this small resort offers 14 wood bungalows dotting the water's edge. The rooms are no frills – except for the air-con – but are clean. A huge plus is a deck

right on the water. Frankly, if this hotel was anywhere else, it'd be half the price. Location is everything though.

Sea Breeze Inn (☎ /fax 445 4026; www.seabreeze roatan.com; r with fan/air-con US$25/$30, studio with fan/air-con US$40/45, ste with fan/air-con US$55/65; ❄) An attractive three-story building behind Cannibal Café, Sea Breeze Inn is generally cramped and dark, but the suites (for four, with separate bedroom and full kitchen) are a good deal. A small playground out the back is a plus for people traveling with kids. There's free use of kayaks too.

Keifito's Plantation Retreat (☎ 978 4472; www .keifitos.com; s/d with fan US$30/35, with air-con US$50/55; P ❄) Although a bit weathered, Keifito's offers six comfortable cabins perched above a quiet stretch of beach. Accommodations are stark – a bed, a fan, and a porch with hammocks – but offer peace and lots of quiet. A defunct restaurant turned fantastic communal kitchen and dining area is open for guests to cook their own meals; right on the cliff's edge, the views here can't be beat. A steep staircase leads straight to the beach and good snorkeling (BYO gear). It's located about a kilometer south of West End, around the bend from Luna Beach Resort.

TOP END

Mame Tree Bungalows (☎ 403 8245, in US 718-710 4392; www.mametreebungalows.com; 2-bedroom bungalows US$89-99; P ❄ 🖳) Perched on a verdant hill overlooking Half Moon Bay, the Mame Tree offers two beautiful bungalows that each sleep up to four people. Each has boutique flair and a theme: the Moroccan has lots of purples, reds, and flowing curtains, while the Caribbean is all about blues, whites, and shells. Both are identical in size, with two bedrooms, a stone-inlaid bathroom, and a fully equipped kitchen. They also have all the amenities you'd expect from a high-end place: cable TV, DVD/mp3 player, wireless Internet, central air-conditioning, and a safety box. Wraparound porches have hammocks, chairs, and fantastic views – the sunset here is hard to beat. All that plus free calls to the USA and Canada, free floaties and snorkeling gear, 24-hour security, and – get this – complimentary laundry service. Really, there's not much more you could ask for. It's a great deal, especially if you're traveling with a couple of friends.

Lily Pond Guest House (☎ 403 8204; www.lilypond guesthouse.com; Half Moon Bay; r US$95-120; ✗ ☐) Owned and run by two British expatriates, this lovely B&B features four classy rooms, each built on top of the other in a renovated island home. All have hardwood floors, silent air conditioners, fully stocked mini-fridges, and lots of windows. Common areas include a spacious rooftop deck and a tropical garden with the namesake lily pond. Airport transfers and breakfast are included in the rate.

Luna Beach Resort (☎ 445 4025, in US 866-710 5862; www.lunabeachresort.com; d US$87-97, q US$101-117, 3-bedroom house US$217-247, 4-bedroom house US$277; P ✗ ☐ ☒) Offering comfortable beachside hotel rooms and enormous hillside homes, you can see the money here. It's not super fancy, but the details stand out: nice furnishings and fixtures, well-kept beach and pool, a good restaurant, a fully equipped dive shop. It's all A-OK, but lacks character and depth, like a megachain hotel or a bad TV show. In fact, *Temptation Island* has been filmed here seven times.

Lands End Roatan Resort (☎ 372 4120; www .landsendroatan.com; r US$50-90; P ✗ ☐ ☒) Ten simple but classy rooms make up this modern hotel. Rooms are spacious, spotlessly clean, and most have a balcony with a hammock. Although the hotel is alongside the ocean, it doesn't have a beach; ironshore is where you'd expect the sand to be. Still, guests can enjoy the ocean – and the fantastic reef in front – via a swim ladder. Or, if you opt to stay out of the Caribbean, you can still wade in its waters in the saltwater infinity pool that lines the front of the property.

Casa Calico (☎ 445 4231; www.casacalico.com; r US$40-50, 1-bedroom apt US$70, 2-bedroom condo US$125; P ✗ ☐) Also known as the Tanglewood Resort, Casa Calico's accommodations are hit and miss. The apartments in the new buildings get two thumbs up; they're nicely decorated, have fully equipped kitchens, and are very well-kept. Rooms in the main building, however, are dark and aging – certainly not worth the price. A big breakfast is included in the rate, as is the use of kayaks. Service is begrudgingly given.

Other acceptable options include **Hotel West Inn** (☎ 445 4087; hotelwestinn@globalnet.hn; r/tw US$41/53; P ✗), **Mermaid Beach Cabins** (☎ 445 4335; r US$41, with air-con US$58; P ✗ ☐), **Lost Paradise Inn** (☎ 445 4210; www.lost-paradise.com; s/d US$79/99; P ✗), and the **Beach House** (☎ 445 4260; r US$175, studios US$200; P ✗ ☐). All are fine hotels, but they're simply overpriced – the last, spectacularly so.

Eating

With such a good variety of restaurants, eating out in West End can be a real delight. Just be aware that prices are much higher here than on the mainland.

BUDGET

Creole Rotisserie Chicken (next to Georphi's; mains US$2.75-8; ✗ 3pm-midnight, Tue-Sun) Super tasty roast chicken is served in quarter-, half-, or whole-bird portions at this small open-air eatery, along with large sides of rice, beans, potato salad or coleslaw for a buck and change each. The fish fingers don't disappoint, either. This is a longtime backpacker haunt, but you don't have to be on a budget to appreciate good food.

Galley (behind Paradise Computers; mains US$3-8; ✗ lunch & dinner) Another great place for good cheap meals; nothing on the menu here is more than US$8, including Thai curry and a three-meat BBQ plate. Most dishes are a lot cheaper, like fried rice and a killer carbonara. As it's just a small wood shack a dozen or so meters off the road, it's easy to miss – look for the gravel path next to Paradise Computers.

Velva's Place (✗ 7am-10pm Mon-Sat) This low-key outdoor restaurant is away from the hubbub of West End's main strip. An 'Island breakfast' of eggs, bacon, beans and toast costs US$3, burgers are about the same, and fish and shrimp dishes go for US$6 to US$8. It's two minutes north of the intersection.

Bakery/Boulangerie (☎ 445 4260; Beach House; mains US$0.80-3.50; ✗ breakfast & lunch, Tue-Sun) Along with freshly baked breads and croissants, this casual place offers decent breakfasts and sandwiches. Daily specials like turkey burgers and falafel are worth a stop. Eat on the back porch with a view of Half Moon Bay or take your treats to go.

Cannibal Café (☎ 445 0020; mains US$3-10; ✗ lunch & dinner, closed Sun & Tue) While most of us have a policy against eating at any nonvegetarian restaurant with the word

THE BAY ISLANDS

'cannibal' in its name, the meals at this open-air eatery are big enough and good enough to warrant an exception. Mexican food is the specialty, with the burritos turning many into repeat customers.

There are three markets/grocery stores in West End. None are cheap or have the selection of HB Warren in Coxen Hole or Eldon's in French Harbor, but will do for supplies and making simple meals. **Coconut Tree Market** (Half Moon Bay; 7am-8pm) and **Jackson's Mini Super** (near First Baptist church; 7am-8pm) are the best stocked; **Woody's Groceries** (past Posada Arco Iris; 7am-6pm Sun-Thu, to 5pm Fri) is less so. You can also get fresh fruit and veggies from a **produce truck** (7am-6pm) that is usually parked near the First Baptist church.

MIDRANGE

Argentinean Grill (☎ 445 4264; Posada Arco Iris; mains US$3.50-13; 3-10pm, Thu-Tue) The hottest restaurant in town, this is the place to splurge if your lemps are burning a hole in your wallet. As the name suggests, steaks are the specialty – the filet mignon is spectacular – but, if red meat isn't your thing, the seafood and chicken dishes are just as good. Be sure to save room for dessert – the Argentinean crêpe is a mouthwatering concoction stuffed with coconut and caramel and served with vanilla ice cream. There's also an extensive wine list, featuring Argentine and Chilean labels. The ocean view isn't bad either.

The Lobster Pot (☎ 916 7165; mains US$4-15; breakfast, lunch & dinner) Right on the beach, this mellow restaurant serves fine Caribbean cooking. It's not cheap (or fancy for that matter) but it's worth the splurge. For breakfast, the Lobster Pot omelette (a two-egg affair with thick lobster chunks, sweet peppers, cheddar cheese and tomatoes, US$8), is a fine way to start the day; for dinner try the rum-roasted shrimp (US$13). The dessert choice is killer – key lime pie, yucca cake or coconut brownies (US$3).

Le Bistro (☎ 403 8854; mains US$7-15; dinner) Never mind that the dining area is actually the wood walkway between a couple of closed-up shops, Le Bistro serves superb French-Vietnamese dishes with a care and style that belies its haphazard setting. Try the spring rolls or wontons as an appetizer, and the ginger shrimp and chicken

served over crispy noodles for the main course. Pricy, but divine.

Lighthouse Restaurant (☎ 445 1209; near Anderson's; mains US$2.75-14; breakfast, lunch & dinner) Everyone loves an inside tip, and Lighthouse Restaurant is that easy-to-miss 'secret spot' that hoteliers like to recommend to their guests. *Condé Naste* magazine even got into the act, recently rating the seafood here the best in West End. That may be going too far, but it's definitely good: the coconut prawns and Thai-style seafood bowl are reliable, and the daily specials usually have some intriguing items. The setting is the real highlight: it's hidden from the main road and (amazingly enough) is one of only a couple of restaurants with seating right on the water. Service is uneven.

Pura Vida Hotel & Restaurant (☎ 445 4110; turnoff to Mariposa Lodge; mains US$4-15; breakfast, lunch & dinner) There's no shortage of Italian food to be had in West End, including Tre Fratelli, the strip's first chain restaurant, but Pura Vida still takes the cannoli for quality and service. For lunch, the grilled veggie focaccia sandwich is humongous and terrific, while the black fettucine with shrimp is a delectable departure from the typical spaghetti and meatballs dinner (though they have that too). For something more familiar, the pizza doesn't disappoint, and the restaurant was installing an open-air grill at the time of research, with plans to serve imported T-bone and New York strip steaks.

TOP END

Dian's Garden of Eat'n (☎ 368 1098; road btwn West End & West Bay; mains US$8-20; dinner Tue-Sat) After years of operating out of a tiny kitchen and torch-lit garden dining area on Half Moon Bay, gravel-voiced Florida-transplant Dian Lynn has finally moved her wildly popular Thai-Caribbean fusion restaurant to a 'real' locale. You won't be able to just mosey in anymore – the new shop is a three-minute drive or taxi ride from the West End turnoff toward West Bay – but a meal here remains well worth the effort and expense. The menu includes creative dishes like wasabi garlic shrimp, mango ginger wahoo, cilantro lime lobster, and a terrific Thai curry made from spices that Lynn grows herself. Credit cards are not accepted.

THE BAY ISLANDS

Drinking & Entertainment

Sundowners (across from Native Sons; ☼ to 10pm) This is a small, easy-going bar – more a kiosk, really – right on the beach at Half Moon Bay. The view makes this a popular place to start the night before migrating to Purple Turtle or Twisted Toucan. Happy hour is from 5pm to 7pm.

Purple Turtle (☼ 7am-10pm Sun, to midnight Mon-Thu, to 2am Fri & Sat) Formerly the Mango Verde, this tiny bar reopened in 2005 under the current name and has never looked back. It's packed almost every night.

Twisted Toucan (across from Eagle Ray's) Somewhat eclipsed by upstart Purple Turtle, this longtime West End bar still knows how to throw a party. As the fad bars come and go, the Twisted Toucan seems to stick it out. Look for drink specials (happy hour is from 4pm to 7pm) and an occasional big smoky BBQ on the patio.

Eagle Ray's (☎ 445 4283; on pier across from Twisted Toucan; ☼ 11am-late) Wilma whipped some West End ass in October 2005, especially this bar-restaurant built on stilts over the water. The dive shop that occupied the ground floor has since moved, and the bar's front patio had to be completely rebuilt. But rebuilt it was, and Eagle Ray's is back serving US$1.50 tequila shots, screw drivers and other drink specials during happy hour (4pm to 6pm) and well into the night.

Foster's Waterfront Bar & Grill (☼ 11am-midnight Sun-Thu, to 2am Fri & Sat) One of two bars-on-a-pier jutting out over the water, Foster's (formerly Monoloco's) has live music just about every Friday, Saturday and Sunday, mostly of the bluesy-acoustic sort befitting the new owner's and manager's southern backgrounds. Drink specials vary nightly, but at last check were two-for-one beer on Tuesday and 100-lempira beer buckets on Thursday. Come early for dinner – the ribs and steak (US$10 to US$15) are imported and grilled to perfection.

Movies are a popular diversion in West End, especially on nights when you're wiped from multiple dives and you're not up for another all-nighter at the Purple Turtle. **Brick Oven Pizza** (past Twisted Toucan; mains US$8-15; ☼ dinner, closed Tue) shows recent-release movies almost every night, usually at 5pm and 7pm. Schedules are on those white flyers plastered all over town. The pizza here is decent, but overpriced. **Blue Channel** (☎ 445 4133; across from Ocean Connections; mains US$5-10; ☼ breakfast, lunch & dinner) has a huge screen and shows movies most nights at 8pm. The schedule is posted in front; admission is free with consumption, US$2.75 otherwise.

Shopping

Ivis Gift Shop (Half Moon Bay; ☼ 7am-6pm) The very friendly proprietor here has packed her small wood-shack shop with Honduran, Salvadoran and Guatemalan *artesanías* (handicrafts), plus T-shirts and other knick-knacks – some are good, some not so good, but worth a browse if you're in the market for souvenirs.

Getting There & Away

Microbuses shuttle between West End and Coxen Hole (US$0.80, 25 minutes, 12km), leaving from the corner near Coconut Tree Divers every 10 minutes from 6am to 6pm. Taxis make the same route. *Colectivo* taxis (per person US$1.50) and *privado* taxis (per car US$5.50) also travel the same route.

GETTING TO WEST END

From the Airport

Taxis inside the airport gate charge a whopping US$15 (US$20 at night) to West End. Walk just outside the gate – about 50m from the door – and an ordinary cab will make the same trip for US$2.75 to US$5. As always, be sure to agree on a price before getting in.

From the Pier

A taxi is the quickest and easiest way to get to West End from the pier, especially if you buddy up with other travelers. The official rate is US$10, but two people can usually get a ride for US$6 (which is what you'd pay coming from West End to here) or four people for US$9. You can also walk 100m (turn left from the pier) and catch a minibus (US$0.80).

THE BAY ISLANDS

There's no *colectivo* service between West End and West Bay, and the fixed price is US$10 – highway robbery. Better to take a water taxi, which is US$2 per person. If you're catching the 7am ferry from Dixon Cove, your only choice is to spring for a private cab (US$15) since *colectivos* and minibuses don't travel between West End and the ferry terminal. It's possible to take public transportation to Coxen Hole and transfer to a private cab (US$5) from there, but you likely won't make the 7am ferry since you need about an hour and a half to get there this way and neither *colectivos* nor minibuses start running until 6am

Getting Around

Captain Van's Rentals (☎ 403 8751, 445 4076; opposite church; ⓨ 9am-4pm) rents full-size motorcycles (125cc/200cc US$52/64 per day), scooters (US$45 per day) and mountain bikes (US$10 per day). Helmets are included, but insurance is extra (US$6 per day). Dollars, lempira and traveler's checks are all accepted; credit cards have an 8% surcharge.

WEST BAY

The beach at West Bay, about 4km southwest of West End village, is the most beautiful beach on Roatán and one of the finest in Honduras. Several houses and high-end resorts and restaurants line the beach; at the Mayan Princess, a US$10 day pass gets you a fancy little bracelet and access to the beach chairs. Otherwise, bring a blanket and set up under the palms at the far end. There's excellent snorkeling at the western end, though the reef is starting to show damage.

Sights & Activities

West Bay has three dive schools, which by mutual agreement charge the same amount

---

DON'T TOUCH THE CORAL

Coral comes in many shapes, sizes and colors, especially in the Bay Islands. Some coral, such as fan coral, resembles a plant. Other coral, such as brain coral, looks more like a rock. But coral is neither a plant nor a rock, it's an animal.

'Don't touch the coral' is a refrain you will often hear in the Bay Islands, where thousands of divers and snorkelers come every year to explore the magnificent reefs just a few yards offshore.

Coral is fascinating and beautiful, and many divers – beginner and experienced – are tempted to touch it. Even if you resist that temptation, it's easy to accidentally brush the coral with your fin or tank, either as you swim past or if you are still learning to maintain neutral buoyancy.

Avoiding such contact is extremely important. Coral has an invisible covering of slime that protects it, much like skin on other animals. Touching the coral can damage this protective covering, exposing it to infection and disease. Large segments of coral can be killed by a single brush of a diver's fin.

If you hit it hard enough, you can even break it; some places are littered with coral fragments, broken by divers or heavy surf. Under ideal conditions, most coral grows about 1cm (less than half an inch) per year; even the fastest growing sponges grow only an inch per year. The coral and sponge formations you see in the Bay Islands are the result of centuries of growth.

Another good reason not to touch the coral is that it will sting you. Fire coral is the most famous for this – you'll feel like you're on fire if you touch it. Even coral that doesn't sting can be surprisingly sharp or prickly, and cuts from it are notoriously slow to heal. (If you are stung by coral, vinegar will help stop the stinging and anti-bacterial cream will help it heal; no such luck for the coral, though.)

Historically, the reefs around the Bay Islands have been healthy and pristine, thanks to the low number of divers and inhabitants on the islands. But both of those numbers increased dramatically in recent years, and the coral began to show signs of damage. So much so that in 1998, the Honduran government invited the nonprofit Coral Cay Conservation to study the reef and propose solutions to sustaining it, and initiatives have now been adopted by island communities and businesses to secure the reef's health. So far, the effort is slowly working. It remains crucial – especially with even more divers expected (not to mention legions of snorkeler-toting cruise shippers) – for everyone to help preserve the coral reef.

for courses and fun dives. Courses cost more here than they do at West End (US$325 for Open Water, US$265 for advanced), catering mostly to resort guests. Fun dives are comparable to West End, costing from US$35 for one dive, to US$250 for a package of 10. Prices do not include the 16% tax and the one-time US$5 reef tag. Whereas shops in West End are pretty firm in their prices, those in West Bay seem more willing to extend discounts, especially on fun-dive packages.

Octopus Dive School (☎ 403 8071; www.octopus diveschool.com; north end of beach; ☼ 8:30am-4:30pm) is a friendly multilingual shop operating out of a wooden kiosk at the north end of the beach. Ask about accommodation-dive packages.

Bananarama Diving Center (☎ 403 8021; www .bananaramadive.com), West Bay's first dive shop, is also the largest and busiest. It offers a number of good lodging-diving packages, but you may have to contend with large groups.

Las Rocas (☎ 403 8046, in US 877-379 8645; www .lasrocasresort.com; north end of bay) is a small professional shop, befitting the more intimate setting of the hotel it's a part of.

A family recreation park, **Gumbalimba Park** (☎ 987 4082; www.gumbalimbapark.com; ☼ 9am-4pm) has something for everyone: beach, kayaking, canopy tour, snorkeling, SNUBA, nature path, botanical garden, monkey and bird enclosures, and, of course, restaurants and gift shops. Aimed squarely at cruiseshippers, it can still be a fun outing for independent travelers with kids. The park is only open to the general public on days when there are no cruise ships on the island. Even more strange, the park does not have set individual admission prices – they negotiate package deals with cruise ship companies – so be sure to call the day you plan to go to see what the fee is

Festivals & Events

The **Bay Islands International Triathlon** (www.bay islandstriathlon.com) is an Olympic- and sprint-distance event that takes place every March. An International Triathlon Union (ITU)–rated race, it is considered a challenging course primarily because of the steep cycling section that includes 16%, 18%, and 20% grades. The race starts and finishes on West Bay beach and makes several loops,

and extends as far east as Anthony's Key Resort. Cash prizes are given to the top seven athletes. A beach party is typically hosted at the close of the race.

Sleeping

West Bay has a reputation for being Roatán's 'resort capital', but in fact there are as many nontraditional options as traditional ones. Prices aren't cheap, of course, but it is possible to get a nice little place on Honduras' best beach, without paying the premium that brand-name places charge (or suffering the cookie-cutter treatment).

Island Pearl (☎ 445 5001; www.roatanpearl.com; 2-bedroom condo d/q US$150/180; **P** 🖳) A study in relaxation, the villas at Island Pearl are fully equipped for a comfortable stay: porches with hammocks and chairs, nooks with loungers, spacious bedrooms with luxurious linens, beautiful mosaic bathrooms, and kitchens you can really cook in. Add gorgeous West Bay beach right in front and you've got a fine place to vacation.

Las Cupulas West Bay Village (☎ 403 8022; www.westbayvillage.com; 1-/3-bedroom house US$93/285; **P** 🍴 🖳) This set of six luxury homes is right on West Bay beach. Each house has a different owner, which accounts for the vastly different styles. All, however, are modern and come fully equipped with all the amenities you'd expect: cable TV, DVD player, stereo, hot water, and air-conditioning. Breakfast, beach loungers, purified water, and Internet access are included in the rate. It's a great deal, especially if you're traveling in a group.

Bananarama Resort & Diving Center (☎ 403 8021; www.bananaramadive.com; s/d cabins US$54/64, s/d ste US$69/79; **P** 🍴 🖳) The old school cabañas are the way to go at this place; they've got rustic Caribbean charm, with brightly painted walls, hardwood floors, private porches, and lots of sunlight. The hotel rooms are fine, but they just lack any sort of character – tile floors, white walls, and a bed – and might as well be in the middle of Nowhere, Honduras. Breakfast is included in the rate and is served in an outdoor dining area, just steps from the Caribbean. There's also a fully equipped dive shop on-site; ask about package deals.

Las Rocas (☎ 403 8046, in US 877-379 8645; www .lasrocasresort.com; north end of bay; s/d incl breakfast US$55/85; **P** 🍴 🖳 🐾) With just 13 units,

Las Rocas is the sort of place where guests really get to know each other: over breakfast, on the dive boat, at the bar. Bungalows are simply but comfortably appointed, with polished wood floors, mini split air conditioners and firm beds (too firm in some cases); superior rooms have peaked ceilings, king-size beds and (in some cases) terrific ocean views. True to its name, Las Rocas is built on a rocky outcrop and doesn't have a beach of its own. West Bay beach is a short walk away, and the hotel has a small saltwater pool and a waterfront wooden deck for sunbathing, but hardcore beach-hounds may be disappointed. Airport transfers are included in rates, but the 16% tax isn't.

Casa Carnival (☎ in US 913-897 6263; www.bayislandsroatan.com; next to Henry Morgan; 1-4 person per week low/high/holiday season US$1250/1450/1650, extra person per week US$250; ❄) From your bed to the beach in a dozen steps: that is the main appeal of this large stand-alone West Bay home. A full kitchen, large living room, two bathrooms, two bedrooms, and a sunroom with pullout bed (room for eight in all) make this a good choice for a group of friends or a large family. The facilities aren't deluxe, but you've got free access to beach chairs, kayaks, paddleboats, and, of course, the beach on your doorstep. Air-conditioning costs extra, though most people make do with ceiling fans. The caretakers live in the ground-floor unit, and can help arrange diving and island tours.

Casa de Paradise (☎ 403 8052, in US 913-440 4144; www.casadeparadise.com; behind Casa Carnival; units per week US$350-$1450; ❄) Just behind the Casa Carnival, this five-unit complex is definitely more modern and stylish, but isn't right on the beach (OK, 50 steps instead of a dozen). Units range from a studio to a four-bedroom apartment; the caretakers at Casa Carnival handle bookings here.

Eating

Bite on the Beach (mains US$5-15; ❄ lunch & dinner Tue-Sat, closed Sep) Perched on a rocky outcrop at the north end of the beach, this was West Bay's second establishment, and the first restaurant, when it opened in 1996. (How times have changed!). The friendly American owners, who took over in 2001, serve an eclectic menu, from hamburgers and blue-cheese-and-sundried-tomato chicken to Thai curry and conch soup. Their large

garden salads are made with vegetables from Roatán's hydroponic garden, and the key lime pie is divine. The view isn't too shabby either – from the restaurant's raised two-level eating area, the bay and ocean spread out below you, both endlessly blue.

Las Rocas (☎ 403 8046; north end of bay; mains US$5-12; ❄ breakfast, lunch & dinner) This establishment has a fine restaurant, open to guests and nonguests alike, just a few steps from Bite on the Beach. Seafood is the specialty – surprise, surprise – and comes in various incarnations: fish fillet, grilled shrimp sandwiches, shrimp and gorgonzola, seafood linguini, even seafood pizza (which is terrific, by the way).

Out of the Blue Mini Mart (north end of beach; ❄ 8am-10pm) This small expensive bodega right on the beach is good for water, soda, and snacks, and has a limited selection of canned foods. The shop may be closed when the owner is out running errands.

Drinking & Entertainment

Bite on the Beach (left) stays open relatively late for drinking, with a happy hour between 4pm and sunset. The bar at Las Rocas (p255) can also be lively. It's easy to stagger between one and the other.

Getting There & Away

A regular taxi from West End to West Bay costs an outrageous US$10 each way. Unless you're in a large group, a better option is a water taxi, which charges US$2 per person. The ride is more interesting too. In West Bay, you can flag down a driver at any of the piers or right from shore, if you don't mind sloshing through the shallows. The last boat in either direction is around 6pm. You can also walk along the beach between West End and West Bay. It takes about 45 minutes, but isn't recommended at night or by yourself (see p240).

SANDY BAY

About 4km before you reach West End is Sandy Bay, a quiet bend of seashore with several homes and hotels tucked away in the trees. There aren't any services here, except for an Internet café, **Sandy Bay Internet** (west end of bay; per hr US$9.50; ❄ 9am-7pm Sun-Fri), that is often closed despite posted hours. You can also make international calls here (US per minute US$0.55).

Sights & Activities

Across the road from Anthony's Resort, the **Carambola Botanical Gardens** (☎ 445 3117; carambolabg@yahoo.com; admission US$5, incl guided tour US$10; ☺ 7am-5pm Mon-Sat) has well-maintained trails through 40 acres of protected forest, extending up a hillside known as Carambola Mountain. It's about 1km to the 'summit', where you can see all the way to Utila on a clear day and, at the right time, down into the dolphin show at Anthony's Key Resort. Along the trail you'll encounter dozens of species of native plants, including orchids, spice plants, medicinal plants, and fruit trees. You'll also pass Iguana Wall, a cliff favored by iguanas and parrots, as well as remnants of pre-Colombian settlements. Reservations are required for guided tours.

Anthony's Key Resort (right) has a resident population of some 20 bottlenose dolphins, and offers a number of programs for both guests and nonguests. It's worth checking out the **dolphin show** (resort guest free, nonguest US$4) held daily at 10am and 4pm. For more interaction, you can sign up for one of several 'dolphin discovery' programs; from the **Dolphin Beach Encounter** (guest/nonguest US$73/84) where you wade and interact with a single dolphin in waist-deep water to a **Dolphin Snorkel** (US$73/84) or **Dolphin Dive** (US$84/112), which include interacting with a group of dolphins in the open water. Dolphin programs like these definitely vary in their quality (especially for the dolphins), but Anthony's Key does a good job of treating its dolphins humanely and as something more than just show animals.

Anthony's also houses the **Roatán Museum** (admission incl dolphin show US$5; ☺ 8am-5pm), a smallish historical center with displays spanning island history from prehistoric times to Maya occupation to Columbus' arrival and the beginning of the colonial period. There's surprisingly little on Garífuna history though, in which Roatán played an important role (see boxed text p207). Overall, however, the artifacts and displays (in Spanish and English) are quite good. A visit takes about 30 to 45 minutes.

Sandy Bay has excellent **windsurfing** conditions, including warm water, a broad obstacle-free bay, and strong steady wind. Advanced sailboarders may wish there was a bigger swell, but the flat shallow water is ideal for those just learning the sport. Run by a young friendly Chilean couple who live on-site, **Wind & Fun Windsurf School** (☎ 445 3292; jm_carvajal@yahoo.com; west of Blue Bahía Resort; ☺ 9am-5pm Tue-Sun) offers one-on-one lessons for US$20 per session (1½ to two hours, including equipment); equipment rental only is US$20 per hour. You may also be able to arrange accommodations in a two-bedroom, two-bathroom apartment with kitchen (per night US$70 to US$80).

Island's Gym (☎ 445 3123; www.islandsgym.com; day/week/month pass US$20/49/89; ☺ 10am-8pm Tue-Sun) is a spectacular gym offering state-of-the-art exercise machines and free weights. Personal trainers are available too. It's located next door to Rick's American Café.

Massage and personalized treatments of various kinds are available at **Spa at Baan Suerte** (☎ 445 3059, 931 7975; ☺ 9am-9pm), a small private spa at Baan Suerte resort. Swedish, deep tissue, and other massages cost US$30/60/85 for 30-/60-/90-minute sessions; a 90-minute Mayan stone massage costs US$90. Have a quick touch up – manicure, pedicure or waxing – or go for the deluxe two-hour exfoliation and healing body wrap plus massage for US$120. Appointments required.

Sleeping & Eating

Anthony's Key Resort (☎ 445 3003; www.anthonyskey.com; 7-night all-inclusive dive package s/d US$1220/2085, snorkelers US$1100/1855; P ✗ ☐) Anthony's Key Resort has long been the premier dive resort on Roatán, while also offering plenty of options for nondivers, like kayaking, snorkeling and the island's only dolphin encounter programs. (There's no beach, however). Week-long dive packages include lodging and meals, plus three single-tank dives, two night dives, and limited shore diving, all supported by a well-respected crew of boat captains and dive guides/instructors, not to mention the island's only hyperbaric chamber. Accommodations are in individual bungalows that, while not exactly luxurious, are quite comfy, all with a sundeck; the best ones have king-size beds, air-conditioning and ocean views. Ask about alternative rates for children, groups, honeymooners, and the low season.

Inn of Last Resort (☎ 445 1838; www.innoflastresort.com; s/d per person US$150/120; P ✗ ☐) If there were summer camp for families, it would look something like this: an all-inclusive resort with simple woodsy rooms, each with air-conditioning and private hot-water bathrooms. It's set on wild, lush grounds and guests also have direct access to a private lagoon with clear turquoise waters. A huge lodge with a game room, lounge, and dining area is a popular spot for guests to hang out, meet each other, and just relax. With a fully equipped dive shop, the resort also offers dive packages, which include three dives per day, unlimited shore diving, and room and board for seven nights (per person US$795).

Mayoka Lodge (☎ 445 3043; www.mayokalodge.com; 6-12 person per week US$14,400-22,500; P ✕ ☒ ▯ ☒) No, that isn't a typo: for a couple of grand each, you and the other jurors can deliberate in style at this stunning six-bedroom, 6500-sq-ft beachfront home, surely one of the most beautiful houses (and most luxurious accommodations) in the whole country. Overlooking Sandy Bay, the home features a wine cellar, cigar humidor, infinity pool, 25in and 45in flat-screen TVs, multilingual book and DVD library, pool and poker tables, tennis courts, kayaks, sea scooters, wireless Internet, dedicated maid, chef and chauffeur service…the list goes on and on. But it's the details that make the Mayoka special: the massive wood table where you take gourmet meals, the crystal clear infinity pool, the gorgeous woodwork, the four-clawed porcelain tub in the master bedroom, the fresh flowers every day. Truly a step above the rest, and (for better or worse) a glimpse of Roatán in years to come. Rates include meals and most drinks, but not taxes.

The Sanctuary (☎ 362 0954; cabins per week US$300-500; P ▯) The five cabins here range in size from one to two bedrooms and are priced accordingly. All have fully equipped kitchens, including gas stove, fridge, even a juicer. Large semi-shaded decks are perfect for taking in the sea breeze (or making use of the wireless Internet). The Sanctuary isn't as fancy-pants as the name and sign on the main road may lead you to believe – the years and salt exposure are starting to show a bit – but it's still a comfortable and reasonably priced place to stay.

Rick's American Café (☎ 445 3123; www.ricksamerican.com; mains US$11-26; ☽ dinner Tue-Sun) This is a pricey restaurant with a fine view, superb meats and big salads. The specialty is the baby back ribs (US$15), though the lamb (US$19) is a favorite among regulars. During the NFL season, this is the place for Sunday brunch. It's located west of Anthony's Key Resort.

Getting There & Away

Anthony's Key marks the eastern end of Sandy Bay, while a small dirt road with a sign for the windsurfing school marks the western end. Taxis and buses pass right by and drop you at either end.

COXEN HOLE

Coxen Hole is the largest town on Roatán. It's home to government offices, three banks, a large grocery store, and the post office, not to mention having the airport and ferry terminal just outside town. Despite the activity – or perhaps because of it – Coxen Hole is not an attractive town. It's hot and muggy and although it's right beside the sea, there's no beach. Now that there are ATMs in West End, there's one less reason to come. Avoid walking around Coxen Hole at night, as discos and bars can get rowdy.

LOCAL LORE: DUPPIES IN THE BUSH

Ghosts, or *duppies* as they're known on the Bay Islands, are very much a part of island culture. They are said to live in the forests and mangroves, stuck on earth because of unfinished business. With a history so rich with pirates – the Bay Islands, after all, were a refuge for those famous for looting Spanish galleons – it is no wonder that the *duppies* who walk these shores are said to be guarding hidden treasure. It's only when they tire of protecting their stash and are ready to move to a higher plane that they reveal where their treasure is, typically by visiting a descendant in a dream. Father Red Cape, a *duppy* well-known in West End, used to be spotted often, but locals say it's been a while since he's appeared. Some speculate that the development on Roatán has run him deeper into the bush. Others think that perhaps Father Red Cape just spilled the beans.

THE BAY ISLANDS

Orientation

The commercial section of Coxen Hole is only a few short blocks. The HB Warren supermarket, with the teeny-tiny city park beside it, is at the center of town; just about everything of interest is situated nearby or on the road leading into town. Buses and taxis arrive at and depart from in front of the city park. The main road through Coxen Hole is one-way; if you are driving a rented car, be careful as there are no signs alerting you to this fact.

Information

Coxen Holes banks are located on Front street, have ATMs, and exchange traveler's checks

Banco Atlántida (🕙 9am-4pm Mon-Fri, 8:30-11:30am Sat)

Burgo Store/Farmacia (☎ 445 1480; near city hall; 🕙 8am-6pm Mon-Fri, to 5pm Sat)

Casi Todo Bookstore (☎ 445 1944; averyl@globalnet .hn; 🕙 9am-4pm Mon-Fri) New and used English-language books to buy or trade. Located at the west entrance to town.

Hondutel (☎ 445 1329; 🕙 7am-8:30pm) On the same passageway as Martínez Cyber Center.

Martínez Cyber Center (☎ 445 0396; 🕙 8am-10pm Mon-Sat) Internet costs US$2.15 per hour, while phone calls cost US$0.25 to US$0.50 for national calls, US$0.30 to USA, and US$0.55 to the rest of world. The centre is located down a narrow passage between BGA bank and city hall.

Migración (☎ 445 1326; Parque Central; 🕙 9am-noon & 1:30-4pm Mon-Fri)

Paradise Tours (☎ 445 1747; 🕙 8:30am-3:30pm Mon-Fri, to noon Sat) Handles domestic and international plane tickets. Second-floor office west of HB Warren.

Police (☎ 445 3438; Parque Central; 🕙 24hr)

Post office (🕙 8am-noon & 2-4pm Mon-Fri) East of HB Warren.

Wood Medical Center (☎ 445 1080; near old ferry pier; 🕙 24hr) Largest private clinic with an emergency room, pharmacy, on-site laboratory and English- and Spanish-speaking staff.

Sleeping & Eating

Hotel Cay View (☎ 445 1202; near ferry pier; s/d US$20/25; 🛏) Unless you really hate West End (or love Coxen Hole) it's hard to imagine a good reason why anyone would stay here. It's not that the rooms are awful – they're small and worn, but have hot water bathrooms, air conditioning and cable TV – but for the same price (a short bus or cab ride away) you can stay in a better place in a better location. The hotel restaurant

(mains US$4 to US$8 open for lunch and dinner, Mon to Sat) has a nice patio out the back overlooking the water, and serves typical Honduran fare, plus a few specials like garlic or coconut milk shrimp.

Tito's Chicken (Front St, two doors from Wood Medical Center; mains US$2-5; 🕙 breakfast & lunch Mon-Sat) This great greasy-spoon chicken joint serves fried and roast bird at red plastic tables in a one-room cement-floor dining area. It's popular with locals, which is always a good sign.

HB Warren (☎ 445 1208; 🕙 7am-7pm Mon-Sat) The largest supermarket on this end of the island, this is a good place to stock up on groceries. It also has a popular cafétria (mains US$0.50 to US$3) with counter seating, low prices and possibly the best fried chicken on the island.

¿Qué Tal? Café (☎ 445 1007; below Casi Todo Bookstore; 🕙 breakfast & lunch Mon-Fri) The perfect place to dig into the book you just scored upstairs, this café has good coffee, salads, sandwiches and baked goods.

Shopping

Yaba Ding Ding (🕙 9am-5pm Mon-Sat) Located on the ground floor of a two-story commercial center next to HB Warren, this friendly shop has a surprisingly complete selection of Honduran *artesanías*, including Lenca pottery, Garífuna paintings, glasswork from Tegucigalpa, junco baskets from Santa Barbara, even some talavera dishes and clay masks from El Salvador, for good measure. Also on display – but not for sale – are several pieces of *yaba ding ding*, an island term for pre-Colombian artifacts.

Getting There & Away

Taxis and minibuses line up near HB Warren supermarket for West End (private taxi US$5.50, *colectivo* taxi US$1.50, minibus US$0.80).

FRENCH HARBOUR

French Harbour is the second-largest town on Roatán. An important port, it's home to a large fishing, shrimp and lobster fleet, but has relatively little to offer most travelers.

Information

Banco Atlántida (☎ 455 7484; main hwy, 100m from turnoff to French Harbor center; 🕙 9am-4pm Mon-Fri, 8:30-11:30am Sat) Has an ATM and exchanges traveler's checks.

THE BAY ISLANDS

Martínez Cyber Center (☎ 455 5228; per hr US$2.15; ⏲ 8am-10pm Mon-Sat) National and international phone calls offered too.

Police (☎ 455 5099; ⏲ 24hr) Located at the entrance to town, 250m past Eldon's supermarket.

Sights & Activities

The area's main attraction is the impressive **Arch's Iguana Farm** (☎ 975 7442; admission US$5; ⏲ 8am-3:30pm) in French Cay, just outside of town. It is a worthwhile stop. Less a farm than the house of a serious iguana-phile, everywhere you look you see iguanas – on the driveway, in the trees, under bushes, everywhere. In all, around 3000 iguanas live here, some as long as 1.5m. Midday is feeding time, and the best time to visit. There's also an enclosed pool with a school of huge fish, several small sea turtles, and dozens of conches.

Sleeping & Eating

El Faro Inn Hotel (☎ 455 5214; Calle Principal; s/d/t US$40/45/50) Upstairs from Gío's Restaurant (and owned by it too), this hotel doesn't stand out the way the restaurant does (see right). Rooms are adequate but unremarkable; all with hot-water bathroom, air-conditioning, and cable TV, but very little character and a somewhat musty, worn-out feel. Room 5 is the largest and the best, with three large beds and a view of the harbor.

Roatán's Yacht Club (☎ 455 5233; www.roatan yachtclub.com; r with fan US$76, with air-con US$87-99, ste US$128; P ⛌ ⛤ ▤ ☂) This is a comfortable hotel with a pool and restaurant that's simply overpriced. Accommodations are modern and clean with nice views of the harbor, but on this island, 80 bucks ought to give you some bang; this place is more like a sparkler. Worth it, perhaps, if you've arrived by yacht – there is a private marina where you can park your boat.

Casa Romeo Hotel y Restaurante (☎ 455 5518; www.casaromeos.com; mains US$9-20; ⏲ lunch & dinner Mon-Sat) A fine Italian restaurant right on the harbor's edge, Casa Romeo offers excellent, though pricey, meals. Seafood is the focus – the conch chowder and Caribbean king crab are superb. A wine list featuring Italian, French, Chilean, and Californian wines rounds out the menu nicely. Next door, Casa Romeo's hotel (rooms US$52.25, twins US$64) is a disappointment: saggy beds, thin walls and marginal cleanliness don't merit the price.

Gío's Restaurant (☎ 455 5214; Calle Principal; mains US$6-20; ⏲ lunch & dinner Mon-Sat) Long considered one of the best restaurants on the island, Gío's specializes in seafood – especially crab and lobster, for which they issue bibs – but serves up a pretty mean *churrasco* (Argentinean-style beef) or filet mignon too. All dishes come with salad and garlic bread, and are served in the air-cooled dining room or on a patio overlooking the harbor.

Eldon's (☎ 455 7484; ⏲ 7am-7pm Mon-Fri, to 8pm Sat, 8am-1pm Sun) The island's largest supermarket is on the access road to French Harbour, just off the main cross-island highway. Dollars, traveler's checks and credit cards (no commission) are all accepted.

Getting There & Away

Bus 1 (US$0.70, 20 minutes) runs once or twice an hour between Coxen Hole and French Harbour from 6am to 5:30pm daily. *Colectivo* taxis to Coxen Hole cost US$1.50, while a private one runs around US$6.

AROUND FRENCH HARBOR
Brick Bay

This sheltered bay on Roatán's south side has a large secure marina frequented by long-range sailors and yachters. Those folks seem to leave their boats only rarely, and the community's one hotel, **Hotel Brick Bay** (☎ 445 1127; Brick Bay Rd; r with air-con US$50; P ⛤), is a dark lonely place, made even creepier for almost always having no clients. Worse, an American expatriate was killed in his home here in 2005 by would-be burglars. All in all, it's hard to imagine the average traveler having much interest or reason to come here.

Palmetto Bay

Palmetto Bay Plantation (☎ 991 0811; www.palmetto bayplantation.com; 7-night all-inclusive d US$2100-2400, family of 4 US$3000-3150) There aren't many places left on Roatán where you have a whole beach to yourself, and even fewer that don't assault the shoreline with their gaudy buildings, giant pools and matching lounge chairs. Palmetto Bay is one of those select few, an understated luxury resort hidden several kilometers down a dirt road, sharing a beautiful stretch of beach with hundreds of palm trees and not much else. The resort has 31 bungalows (with two to three bedrooms, one to two bathrooms), all with gorgeous hardwood floors, high-peaked ceilings, and spacious kitchens with gas ranges and full-size stainless steel refrigerators. Sliding doors open onto a large deck, most with partial views of the ocean. An infinity pool, free kayaks, wireless Internet, and airport pickup and drop-off are all included in the rates (which vary by season, number of guests, and category of lodging). The resort's **bar & restaurant** (mains US$7-20; ☽ lunch & dinner) is popular with guests and nonguests alike, with live music Friday and Saturday night. Reservations are recommended.

Subway Watersports (☎ 359 4190; www.subway watersports.com) operates out of the resort, but is open to the public. Open Water courses cost US$350, while fun dives are US$28. The resort can also arrange **sunset horseback rides** (per person US$35), which last from 1½ to 2½ hours (advance reservations required), or if you're feeling brave, try the 1½-hour **Canopy Tour** (per person US$35), located near the main road.

Santé Wellness Center

A great way to pamper yourself is at the **Santé Wellness Center** (☎ 991 0474, in US 510-455 4232; www.santewellnesscenter.com; Parrot Tree Plantation; ☽ 9am-4pm, or by appointment), a full day spa located on a tiny private island about 5km east of French Harbour. Specialty massages (US$50 per hour), facials (US$50), and body treatments (US$30 to US$55) are offered daily; afterwards, spend some time sunning yourself by the pool or snorkeling on the reef in front. If you find it hard to leave, you don't have to – there is a high-end **bed & breakfast** (d per person US$48) here as well. Base prices include breakfast, but all-inclusive packages including meals, spa treatments, and diving are also available.

EASTERN ROATÁN

Eastern Roatán has almost none of the rapid, large-scale development that has consumed the other side of the island. Here, paved roads turn to dirt and construction sites and crowds of suntanned foreigners give way to grassy bluffs and solitary fishermen plying rough coastal waters. It is a much poorer area, too, visible in the shanty houses of towns like Oak Ridge and Punta Gorda. A

drive out to eastern Roatán is, in many ways, a drive into its past, when island residents lived isolated island lives, before the arrival of planes, resorts and foreigners.

Oak Ridge

Oak Ridge is a port town on Roatán's eastern side, a somewhat more appealing town than French Harbour or Coxen Hole. It's officially called José Santos Guardiola, but almost no one calls it by its Spanish name. The tiny town hugs a protected harbor, with wooden houses on stilts all along the shore and colorful boats plying the waters. More homes and shops are on a small cay just a two-minute motorboat ride from shore. Water taxis take passengers around the harbor and across to the cay for about US$1; they dock in front of the bus stop.

SIGHTS

Water taxis at the Oak Ridge dock take visitors on a pleasant tour through mangrove canals to **Jonesville**, a small town on a nearby bight. A 45- to 60-minute boat tour costs US$20 for up to eight people. You can stop and eat at the famous Hole in the Wall restaurant, which has an all-you-can-eat shrimp feast on Friday and Sunday (Sunday only during low season); if you do, be sure to give your boat driver an extra large tip for waiting.

SLEEPING & EATING

Oak Ridge has two of the oldest dive resorts on the island, both offering very affordable packages. Both are quite isolated from the rest of the island, and are for those who want to do a lot of diving, a lot of relaxing, and not much else. Dive sites here receive a fraction of the traffic of those around West End, making them that much more pristine.

Reef House Resort (☎ 445 2297; www.reefhouse resort.com; 7-night package s/d per person US$900/799, plus 16% tax) This is a comfortable hotel, restaurant and diving center, featuring large rooms with two queen-size beds, private bathroom, air-conditioning and cable TV. Most guests come on seven-night packages, which include a room, meals, three dives a day, unlimited shore diving, a night dive and transport to or from the airport. Snorkel and room-and-board only packages are also available.

THE BAY ISLANDS

GETTING THERE & AWAY
Oak Ridge is 25km east of Coxen Hole. Buses leave from Coxen Hole for Oak Ridge every half-hour from 6am to 5:30pm (US$1, one hour). *Colectivo* taxis are rare; rates for a private cab must be negotiated.

Punta Gorda
Punta Gorda was the first ever Garífuna village, where a band of over 2200 Black Caribs from St Vincent settled after they were dumped in 1797 by British colonizers fearful of a slave uprising (see boxed text, p207). Unfortunately, the town's historic significance has not preserved it from the degradation and decay so many Garífuna communities have suffered; it is run down, with few job prospects and an inadequate social service network.

SIGHTS & ACTIVITIES
The **Punta Gorda Festival** is the main reason for travelers to visit. The festival, which typically runs from April 8 to 12, includes a re-enactment of the arrival of the first Caribs on Roatán, the crowning of a Garífuna queen, and lots of Garífuna music and dancing. Beyond this, however, there is little reason for tourists to come here, and few do.

Outside of Punta Gorda is a new attraction that is either an economic boon for the town or a gross reduction and repackaging of Garífuna culture for material gain. Maybe both. **Yübu – The Garífuna Experience** (☎ 455 6713; www.garifunaexperience.com; admission US$5; ☻ 10am-3pm Tue-Fri) is an utterly artificial cultural center that was built as a tourist trap for cruise-shippers, and which seems to be working its magic perfectly well. The experience begins with a 30- to 35-minute historical talk about the Garífuna's beginnings and their brutal passage to Roatán. After that, a dance demonstration ought to be uplifting, but the dancers are obviously not having much fun. You can also shop in the gift shop, learn to make *casabe* (a traditional yucca flatbread) or eat Garífuna specialties at the small *comedor*, but the food, like the overall experience, is pretty bland.

GETTING THERE & AWAY
Buses do not go beyond Oak Ridge. Most travelers interested in exploring the far east rent a car or hire a taxi for the day.

Paya Bay & Camp Bay
Eight kilometers beyond Oak Ridge, Paya Bay and Camp Bay see very few visitors, local or foreign, despite their dramatic cliff lines and rustic golden sand beaches. Both are reachable by car or taxi, even by bike or walking if you're up for it. The lack of visitors makes the one hotel there – Paya Bay Beach Resort – all the more attractive. Guests have access to a private beach on the west side of the hotel, but anyone can eat at the restaurant and make use of Paya Beach proper.

Camp Bay is further east, and has calmer water and an even more isolated feel. It's

---

WANARAGUA – THE MASKED WARRIOR DANCE

The story goes like this: Barauda, the wife of Satuye, an important Black Caribe chieftain on the island of St Vincent, was berating her husband for his army's inability to rid the island of British invaders once and for all. Working up a head of steam, she declared that the women may as well do the fighting while the men, who evidently lacked the *cajones* to get the job done, could dress in their wives' clothing and hide. (Ouch!) But this gave Satuye an idea. The next time the British invaded, they found the Carib men gone. When they let down their guard, the men, disguised as women, fell upon the unsuspecting Redcoats, defeating them soundly.

The *wanaragua* dance recounts the tale of the cross-dressing army, and is one of the most beloved and memorable of Garífuna dances. The dance is performed by men only, and is notable for its extremely elaborate costumes – a long woman's dress decorated with ribbons, a headdress made of feathers and mirrors, and a mask made of painted metallic mesh set on an oval frame. The dancers wear shell rattles on their legs, and are accompanied by a drummer.

The dance is performed rather half-heartedly for visiting cruise-shippers at Yübu – The Garífuna Experience (above), hardly doing it justice. To see the real thing, visit the Garífuna village of Punta Gorda or a Garífuna town on the mainland.

EXPLORING THE EAST-END ISLANDS

Paya Bay Beach Resort (below) offers day-long tours to Roatán's eastern islands with their beautiful deserted beaches and clear, snorkel-friendly waters. Excursions typically include Pigeon Cayes and Barbareta Island and cost approximately US$200 for one to four people.

---

reachable by car, though for a bit of adventure you can borrow a hotel kayak (guests free, nonguests US$5) and paddle there.

After being walloped by Hurricane Mitch in 1998, **Paya Bay Beach Resort** (☎ 435 1712, 435 1498, in US 866-323 5414; www.payabay.com; r US$125, full board per person US$120, plus 3 tanks per day per person US$160; P ☒), a friendly, locally owned enterprise, has been resurrected as a great little hotel and resort, with just 11 rooms and two virtually private beaches. It's similar to Palmetto Bay in its seclusion and isolation, but not nearly as fancy (or expensive). Rooms are understated and comfortable, with polished wood floors, peaked ceilings, and small porches; twin-bed rooms have dramatic cliff and ocean views, while king units look over the beach. The hotel has a recommended dive shop, and being the only resort this far east, the coral is pristine and you can go for a whole week without seeing another dive boat. Tours to Roatán's eastern islands are also offered.

UTILA

pop 8500

Utila is a slow, welcoming place, where locals and visitors interact regularly, mainly because almost everyone is in the same small town. There is only a handful of cars on the island and no buses; most people ply the few streets in flip flops and on bicycles, though you will see an occasional golf cart and scooter. Diving costs about the same here as on Roatán – and is just as good – but food and lodging are cheaper, which can make a huge difference if you're on a budget. Utila does not have the classic Caribbean beaches you might expect, but the combination of a strong local presence and a mellow youthful energy make for a unique, refreshing island experience.

EAST HARBOUR (UTILA TOWN)

Utila has one small town, officially called East Harbour, though most people use 'Utila' to refer to both the town and the island. Virtually everything travelers need – hotels, restaurants, dive shops, Internet, banks, bars, medical service and the ferry pier – is located here. It's also where most of the island's residents live, though their homes are found more on the outskirts rather than in the tourism-oriented center.

Orientation

The public jetty, where the ferries arrive and depart, is at the intersection of the town's two main roads. Facing away from the pier, you can turn right (east) or left (west) on the main road, or go straight onto Cola de Mico Rd (north). If you turn left on the main road, you'll run into a third road, Mamey Lane, which runs north from the fire station. It's nearly impossible to get lost. There used to be a notion that shops and restaurants were better or worse depending on their direction from the pier, but that's irrelevant now – you'll find good (and not so good) places in all directions.

Information

BOOKSTORES

Bundu Café (east main st; ⊙ 8am-9pm) Decent selection of books for sale or exchange, including a range of pre-loved Lonely Planet titles.

EMERGENCY

Police (☎ 425 3145; Mamey Lane; ⊙ 24hr) Facing the soccer field.

IMMIGRATION

Migración (☎ 425 3365; main st; ⊙ 9am-noon & 2-5pm Mon-Fri) Extend visas here. Located on 1st floor of the Palacio Municipal building next to the public jetty.

INTERNET ACCESS

Utila has numerous Internet centers, and some dive shops also offer Internet access to their students. Most Internet centers allow you to download pictures from digital cameras and burn them onto a CD for a small fee.

Hideout Internet (☎ 425 3478; east main st; per hr US$1.25; ⊙ 9am-8pm Mon-Sat) Near Alton's Dive Shop.

Mermaids Internet (east main st; per hr US$1.85; ⊙ 9am-10pm Sun-Thu, to 5pm Fri, 6-10pm Sat) Near Reef Cinema.

THE BAY ISLANDS

UTILA

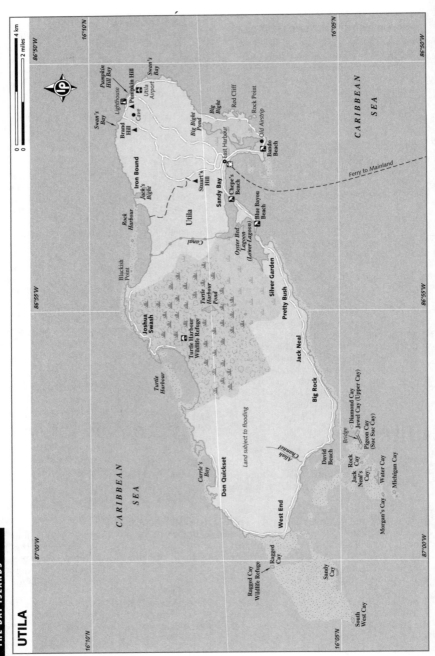

Caye Caulker Cyber Café (☎ 425 3525; east main st; per hr US$1.85; ☺ 8am-9pm Mon-Sat) Next to the Central American Spanish School. Also places inexpensive international calls.

JC's Internet (☎ 425 3772; west main st; per hr US$2.15; ☺ 9am-7pm Mon-Sat, 10am-6pm Sun) Next to Tranquila.

LAUNDRY

There are a number of private homes that will wash clothes; most charge per piece (pants and shirts US$0.30, socks and underwear US$0.10). Look for handwritten signs along the main street, especially in the vicinity of the Central American Spanish School.

MEDICAL SERVICES

Bay Islands College of Diving (☎ 425 3376, 425 3291; west main st) Housing Utila's only recompression chamber.

Utila Community Clinic (☎ 425 3147; west main st; ☺ 8am-noon Mon-Fri, 9-11am Sat) Run by Dr John McVay, an eccentric but well-regarded American doctor. There's also a pharmacy on site.

Utila Centro de Salud (☎ 364 6254; ☺ 9am-noon Mon-Fri) Frequented by the island's Spanish-speaking residents. It's inland, past Bar in the Bush.

MONEY

Most dive shops and many hotels accept lempira, US dollars, traveler's checks and credit cards (usually with a service fee).

BGA (☎ 425 3117; main st, facing pier; ☺ 8am-3:30pm Mon-Fri, 8:30-11:30am Sat) Changes traveler's checks and gives cash advances on Visa cards. Also has Utila's only ATM machine. Don't wait until your last lempira to withdraw – it regularly runs out of money.

Banco Atlántida (east main st; ☎ 9am-4pm Mon-Fri, 8:30-11:30am Sat) Gives cash advances on Visa cards for no commission, but has an awful exchange rate. No traveler's checks exchanged.

Reef Cinema (☎ 425 3254; east main st) Near Rubi's Inn. Will process a 'purchase' on your Visa, MasterCard, or Amex card and give you the cash, less a 7% commission. No limit; does not appear as a cash advance on your statement.

TELEPHONE

Utila Telephone Company (west main st; ☺ 8am-8pm Mon-Sat, noon-8pm Sun) Domestic fixed line per minute US$0.20, domestic cell US$0.55, USA and Canada US$0.25, rest of world US$0.30 to US$0.70. Located across the street from Bay Island College of Diving.

TOURIST INFORMATION

Captain Morgan's Dive Centre (☎ 425 3349; www .divingutila.com; main st, facing pier) Across from the pier, offers straightforward info and advice, and you can even leave your backpack there while you look for a hotel.

TRAVEL AGENCIES

Morgan's Travel (☎ 425 3161; utilamorganstravel@yahoo.com; at pier opposite ferry office; ☺ 8am-noon & 2-5:30pm Mon-Sat) Arranges plane tickets off the island and taxis to and from the airport.

Sights & Activities

Utila doesn't have much in the way of beaches, so someone finally took matters into their own hands and made one. **Bando Beach** (☎ 425 3190; east main st; admission US$3; ☺ 9am-5pm), at the old airport, doesn't have the deep soft shoreline of a natural beach, but it's pleasant enough, with beach chairs wrapping around a small point nicely shaded by low tangled trees. The admission fee is credited toward snorkel or kayak rental; kayaks cost US$2.75 per hour, oldish snorkel gear US$5 per visit. The main drawback is the *regguetón* (hip-hop with a blend of Jamaican and Latin American influences) that blasts all day long.

Located just beyond the western edge of town, **Chepes Beach** is a white sand beach with a few shade trees and lots of shallow, clear water. It's a pleasant place, made even better by a handful of simple beach-side restaurants and a new thatch-roofed bar-discotheque.

A scientific center that is open to the public, the **Iguana Research & Breeding Station** (☎ 425 3946; www.utila-iguana.de; east of Mamey Lane; admission US$2.15; ☺ 2-5pm Mon, Wed & Fri) is dedicated to studying, protecting, and breeding the island's endangered iguana, known locally as 'swamper' or 'wishiwilly'. Over-hunting of eggs, and development on the island has led to the iguanas' near demise. Visitors get a tour of the research station, learn about the species, and see lots of wishiwillies. If you're interested in volunteering, check the website for information.

Based out of the Bay Island College of Diving, the **Whale Shark & Oceanic Research Center** (WSORC; ☎ 425 3291; www.wsorc.com; west main st; ☺ 8am-7pm) is one of the only programs in Honduras that is 100% dedicated to advanced whale shark research. Divers

THE BAY ISLANDS

EXPLORING THE REST OF THE ISLAND

Hiking

If island life is making you a little claustrophobic, you can stretch your legs on a walk or hike to Pumpkin Hill Bay, about 3km across the island. Pumpkin Hill itself has some caves; one was supposedly a hideout for the pirate Henry Morgan. As with any cave, do not venture in beyond the opening without a guide. The Iguana Research Station (see p265) occasionally offers guided hikes around the island as well.

Snorkeling

There's excellent snorkeling at both ends of the main road: at Airport Reef, just past the old landing strip and at Blue Bayou on the far western end of the road. Airport Reef is somewhat better, but Blue Bayou has a nice pier and a small patch of sand (fee US$1.60). In either case, beware of the rocky shallows – they're loaded with sea urchins, whose needles deliver a painful sting. Look for the white buoys, which mark diving spots, and be sure to watch for boat traffic. You can also make your way across the island to Turtle Harbour, part of a like-named marine reserve and protected turtle nesting area, for fine snorkeling.

Many dive shops will loan or rent snorkel gear to their students, some to nonstudents as well. **Deep Blue** (☎ 425 3211; www.deepblueutila.com; west main st) rents snorkel gear (half-/full-day US$3/5) and offers snorkel tours at 7:30am and 1:30pm daily (southside/northside US$8/16, including gear and two stops).

Kayaking

Kayaking to Rock Harbour, a beautiful white-sand beach that is only accessible by boat or foot, is also a good way to spend the day. Start by paddling into Oyster Bed Lagoon, then continue into the mangrove canal, which will lead you straight to Rock Harbour. A round-trip from town, with a couple of hours at the beach, takes about four hours.

Utila Water Sports (☎ 425 3264; www.utilawatersports.com; east main st) offers enjoyable half-day kayak trips (per person US$10, students and fun divers US$5) exploring Lighthouse reef, the eastern shore and the mangrove-fringed inland lagoon, where you're likely to spot the iguana species endemic to Utila, known as 'wishiwilly.'

and snorkelers can participate in various whale shark programs, ranging from one-time shark-spotting trips (US$40), to in-depth three- to six-day courses on theory, ecology, and research methods, plus training in spear guns, whale identification and 'big blue' dive training (US$600, including PADI distinctive specialties). Just visiting the WSORC office is fascinating, with its numerous displays about whale shark biology, identification, safe diving practices, and more. **Deep Blue Resort** (p269) also offers programs in whale shark identification to its guests. See its website or call for more information.

Utila finally has a full service public gym, **Ocean Fitness** (☎ 425 3935; west main st, Sandy Bay; per day/month US$3.50/35; ☺ 6am-noon & 2-8pm Mon-Fri, 6am-2pm Sat), with free weights, machines, and treadmills – in all, there's enough space for 20 people to work out at a time.

Dive Shops

Like Roatán, dive shops on Utila have gotten together to standardize prices and avoid the recurrent price wars that made running a shop so difficult in the past. Under the Utila Dive Safety & Environment Council (UDSEC), shops agreed to charge US$229 for Open Water and Advanced courses, including materials and equipment rental, and US$22.50 per tank for fun dives or US$200 for a package of 10, rentals included. Most shops offer from two to four nights of free lodging with every course (usually in a dorm), or two free fun dives.

UDSEC also implemented a mandatory reef tax (per day US$3, or two months for US$30), with a dollar going to support the hyperbaric chamber, a dollar to the municipal government for garbage collection and the planned desalination plant, and a dollar for UDSEC projects, like repairing buoys and paying for tourist police. Everyone pays this, divemasters and instructors included. There is still fierce competition for divers – witness the crowd of flyer-toting Divemasters-in-Training that meets every ferry – but price control at least means travelers choose shops on something more substantial than price.

Most dive shops start Open Water and other courses almost every day, and offer Advanced courses up to Divemaster. Specialty courses, including Nitrox and technical diving, are also available. For more guidance, see boxed text p241.

Recommended dive shops:

Alton's Dive Shop (☎ 425 3704; www.altonsdiveshop .com; east main st) Longtime local shop – 'Alton' is Alton Cooper, Utila's mayor until 2010 – with good equipment and a laid-back atmosphere. Accommodations are in little rooms right at the shop; cheap but very basic – towels aren't even included (dm/r US$3/4).

Bay Islands College of Diving (☎ 425 3291; www .dive-utila.com; west main st) Well-established shop that appeals especially to nervous first-time divers. Its policy is to have only four divers per course or fun dive, but the shop's popularity can stretch the staff thin at times. Recompression chamber (the only one on the island) and dive training pool are both on site. Discounts at nearby hotels.

Captain Morgan's Dive Centre (☎ 425 3349; www .divingutila.com; main st) Small operation with an office at the intersection, but its dive shop and lodging are on Jewel Cay (Upper Cay), a 20-minute boat ride from Utila. Rooms (US$5 per person) are clean and comfy, with kayaks and good restaurants nearby. A good, mellower alternative to staying on Utila proper.

Cross Creek (☎ 425 3397; www.crosscreekutila.com; east main st) What a difference new management makes. Friendly multilingual staff, professional instruction. Rooms and dorms are small, clean, and can get very hot in the sun (dorms US$3, rooms with fan/air-con US$4/16). Cabins are a decent deal, with cable TV and private hot-water bathroom (doubles/triples US$28/33). All guests can use the big shared kitchen and lounge.

Gunter's Ecomarine (☎ 425 3350; http://ecomarine gunters.blogspot.com/; west main st) Low-key and unpretentious, with small classes and solid instruction. Located in a residential area a 10-minute walk west of the center, which can be a bummer or a blessing. Backpacker lodge across the street has a small shared kitchen and even smaller rooms (dorms/rooms US$2/5, nondivers US$4/10).

Underwater Vision (☎ 425 3103; east main st) Friendly local shop founded by Jernigan Cooper, father of Mayor Cooper, and run by members of the family. Lodging in nearby Hotel Trudy (dorms/rooms US$3/4, nondivers US$5/6), which is supposed to be renovated by 2007, with kitchen and new bathrooms. Suites are overpriced. Centrally located, but still low key.

Utila Dive Center (UDC; ☎ 425 3326; www.utiladive centre.com; east main st) Utila's first and biggest dive shop, UDC issued more Open Water certifications in 2004 than any other shop in the world. Groups can get big – up to 12 people – but there's at least one staff (whether instructor, assistant or divemaster) for every two students. Caters to backpackers, but some may prefer a shop with less jostling. There's good, cheap lodging at Mango Inn (p269).

Utila Water Sports (☎ 425 3264; www.utilawater sports.com; east main st) Co-owned and operated by the high-end Laguna Beach Resort, has excellent gear and a well-trained and well-supported staff. Classes are small and noncompetitive. Does not have its own dorm or accommodation, and tends to attract a slightly older, post-backpacker crowd.

DIVING NEAR UTILA

Utila's south shore has warm crystal-clear water filled with tropical fish, coral, sponges and other marine life. On the north side, a plunging wall makes for great drift- and deep-diving. Utila is famous for the huge magnificent whale sharks that gather here from March to May and August to October.

Blackish Point Drift along the sheer wall at 20m, checking out pillar coral and huge rope and tube sponges. Caves and crevices shelter spotted drum, porcupine fish and blue Creole wrasses, peculiar because they swim nose down.

CJ's Dropoff Another wall dive featuring numerous outcrops and caves, pillars and overhangs. Schools of damsel fish and sergeant majors forage among massive barrel sponges.

The Maze A series of deep canyons with steep walls, home to huge Goliath groupers and dainty peppermint shrimp. Divers can also explore several large caverns, including Willy's Hole.

Black Hills A beautiful sea mound rising from 40m to 10m with a truly stunning array of sea life, from giant tube and barrel sponges to huge schools of jack, snapper and spadefish, plus hawksbill turtles and even whale sharks in the right season. Drop to 25m and just wind your way up.

THE BAY ISLANDS

Courses

Utila isn't the most logical place in the world to take Spanish classes – most of the locals speak English – but all of the professors at the **Central American Spanish School** (☎ 425 3788; www.ca-spanish.com; east main st, opposite Rubi's Inn; per week US$125; ⏰ 8am-noon & 1-9pm) are native speakers from La Ceiba, and there are more and more mainland transplants working and living here. Homestays aren't available yet, but with a little effort you should have no trouble finding people to practice your skills on. Classes are offered for all levels, usually one-on-one, four hours per day, five days per week. All books and materials are included, along with five hours of Internet access per week, and the school can help arrange long-term lodging.

Sleeping

Utila has a bunch of cheap places to stay, but there is a good selection of midrange and top-end options too. It doesn't take long to walk around and find something that suits your needs. Most dive shops offer free lodging while you're taking a class, though the quality of the lodging varies considerably. Be sure to book ahead during the high seasons (July to August and mid-December to Easter).

BUDGET

Hotel Bavaria (☎ 425 3809; petrawhitefield3@hotmail .com; Cola de Mico Rd; s/d/tr US$10/13/16) A simple place with six rooms on the 2nd floor of a big house, accommodations here are small, spotless, and boast polished hardwood floors and tile bathrooms. All rooms share a wrap-around porch, which is great for relaxing after a day of diving. It's one of the best deals around. German is spoken. Look for the Bavarian flag near Mango Inn.

Margaritaville Beach Hotel (☎ 425 3366; fax 425 3266; west main st, Sandy Bay; r with fan/air-con US$15/30, cabañas with air-con US$50; 🗙) About 100m from Chepes Beach, Margaritaville is a two-story Caribbean-style house with two wrap-around porches. Rooms are simple (two beds, a fan and a cleanish bathroom) while across the street, the cabañas are a slight step up – updated furnishings, private porches, and on the bay. If you don't feel like walking to the action in town, there's a decent on-site **restaurant** (mains US$2.50-11; ⏰ breakfast, lunch & dinner).

Hotel Roses Inn (☎ 425 3283; fax 425 3183; Mamey Lane; r US$12, with shared bathroom US$8) This is a stand-alone house on stilts with a flower garden, a welcoming front porch, and a small shared kitchen. Rooms are pretty small, but each has a decent bed or two and a window that lets in a good breeze. Bathrooms – private and shared – are in good condition and have hot water to boot.

Bayview Hotel (☎ 425 3114; in US 423-443 4143; bayviewinternet@yahoo.com; west main st; r with fan/air-con US$16/35, 1-bedroom apt with fan/air-con US$30/40; 🗙 🖵) Opening onto a well-kept lawn facing the bay, the simple accommodations at this place are kind of stuffy but very clean. Fortunately, the private pier lures people out of their rooms for afternoon beers and sunbathing. If you want a private kitchen, this place is about as cheap as it gets.

Tony's Place (☎ 425 3376; Cola de Mico Rd; s/d with shared bathroom US$6/8) Two buildings with breezy porches house eight acceptable rooms here. The walls need a coat of fresh paint, or at least a scrubbing, but this place isn't bad for a night or two. There's a *pila* (handwashing station) in the yard and plenty of clothesline to dry your clothes on. Located kitty corner from Mango Inn.

Freddy's Place (☎ 425 3142; east main st; d with fan/air-con US$16/35; 🗙) You can't miss this place, a big boxy building on stilts just across the bridge on the way to Airport Reef. Four apartments have two rooms apiece, with a small kitchen and bathroom between them. Beds are a bit saggy and the whole place could use a facelift, but it's not bad for the price, especially if you're keen on a kitchen. The wrap-around patio is slung with hammocks and gets great ocean breezes.

Sharkey's (☎ 425 3212; east main st; d/apt US$45/50, extra person $10; 🗙) Run by a friendly American/Honduran couple, this longtime guesthouse has five rooms and two studio apartments, all with air-conditioning, cable TV, wood paneling and interesting tile work – kind of a mix of '70s den and mid-Atlantic beach house. Rooms have two queen beds and sleep up to four, while apartments have a kitchenette. It's a bit removed, but a nice location if you want to get away from the 'scene' in town.

Holland's Inn (☎ 425 3206; hollandsinn@yahoo .com; east main st; r US$15, with TV US$18, apt with fan/air-con US$25/30; 🗙) This place is clean and comfortable, although a little stuffy and overpriced. Apartments have TV and kitchen and aren't a bad deal for three to five people, but are often rented long term.

MIDRANGE

Rubi's Inn (☎ 425 3240; rubisinn@yahoo.com; east main st, next to Reef Cinema; s/d with fan US$16/20, r with air-con US$35, r with air-con & ocean view US$45; 🛌) One of the best deals in town – and therefore often full – this low-key hotel offers clean comfortable rooms, a nice sundeck, mini-fridges in all the rooms and a new common kitchen and dining area in the works. The friendly hosts live in the home in front. Laundry and towels are changed every two days, save Saturday, when the family is at church. Machine-washed and line-dried laundry costs US$2.75 per load.

Colibri Hill Resort (☎ 425 3329; www.colibri-resort .com; west main st; s/d US$32/35, with air-con US$43/45, 1-bedroom apt US$65-100; 🛌 🛋) The new kid on the block, the Colibri hit the hotel scene running. Located on a hilltop overlooking the bay – but still just a minute's walk to the main drag – rooms have polished wood floors, white-washed walls, and nice tile bathrooms; they're modern in a stark sort of way. A welcoming pool and a full bar sit in the middle of the hotel's lush garden, both popular with guests in the afternoon.

Mango Inn (☎ 425 3335; www.mango-inn.com; Cola de Mico Rd; dm US$8, r US$41-52, cabins US$64-87; 🛌 🛋) Straight up the hill from the pier, the Mango Inn sits on lush grounds with two sundecks and a great three-tiered pool with hot tub. Rooms and cabins are clean and comfortable, with polished hardwood floors, hot-water bathrooms, and air-conditioning. The dorms are slightly cramped, but they're breezy and the shared bathroom is clean enough. Dive packages are available through Utila Dive Center.

TOP END

Jade Seahorse (☎ 425 3270; www.jadeseahorse.com; Cola de Mico Rd; r/tw US$50/72; 🛌) A fantastical place straight out of *Alice in Wonderland*, the Jade Seahorse features five oddly shaped but comfortable bungalows, each eclecti-cally decorated with bottle art, mosaic tiles, and iridescent glass stones, and painted all different colors. The lush grounds are an

extension of the rooms – pod-like steps, ocean tunnels, glass bubbles with funka-delic masks – it's a trippy place. There's also a popular bar-restaurant at the front of the property (see p271).

OUTSIDE EAST HARBOUR

On the west end of the island are Utila's higher-end resorts. There are just two mod-est establishments for now, and Utilans have so far rebuffed large-scale development there, partly to preserve the island's low profile and partly because Utila's water and power supplies would be severely strained. But as Roatán gets bought up, the pressure to build more and bigger resorts will keep growing

Deep Blue Resort (☎ 425 3211; www.deepblue utila.com; d low/high/peak season US$850/1200/1795, plus 16% tax & reef fees) This low-key 10-room dive resort is one of just a handful of es-tablishments – more surely to come – on the mostly uninhabited west end of the island. Rooms are comfortable if not luxu-rious, with dark wood floors, hot-water bathrooms, air-conditioning and a private patio. The common area, including a bar, dining area, and pool table, is distinctly lodge-like. Meals here are just OK, but then few resorts offer gourmet dining. The hotel owners and staff help out with rides in and out of town, but some guests may be frustrated by not having easier access to Utila town. Others prefer it that way. Deep Blue Resort is also a Whale Shark Re-search Center and offers special programs and packages for those interested in the world's biggest fish.

Laguna Beach Resort (☎ in US 800-668 8452; www.utila.com; dive-package d per person US$940-970) Utila's best resort has 13 bungalows set on a narrow peninsula across from Blue Bayou Beach, with the ocean on one side and the lagoon on the other. Cabins are clean and quaint, with hot water, air-conditioning, and a covered porch overlooking the la-goon. Guests can use the kayaks and bicy-cles, and the resort provides a free water taxi service into town. Dive equipment and staff are top notch, but the meals can get a little monotonous. Dive packages include full board, three dives per day, two night dives, and unlimited shore diving.

Ask here or at **Utila Water Sports** (☎ 425 3264; www.utilawatersports.com; east main st) about the new

Utila Agressor live-aboard (☎ in US 800-348 2628; www.agressor.com), which had a rainy maiden voyage in February 2006.

Eating

There's a surprisingly good selection of eateries considering the size of Utila. If you plan on cooking your own food, however, remember that fruit and vegetables are more expensive here than on the mainland; consider bringing a small stockpile over on the ferry.

BUDGET

Zanzibar Café (east main st; mains US$1-4; ☺ breakfast, lunch & dinner, breakfast & lunch Wed, dinner Sat) A half-dozen rickety wood tables are set up on an equally rickety raised wood patio, but luckily appearances aren't everything – in fact, it's part of the charm here. Zanzibar serves excellent *típica* breakfast (eggs, beans, ham and a stack of toast) and extra tall glasses of fresh-squeezed orange juice and blended licuados. The latter are a steal at US$1 to US$2, and are worth stopping in for even if you're not hungry.

Seven Seas Restaurant (☎ 425 3377; east main st; mains US$2-4; ☺ breakfast, lunch & dinner Tue-Sun) Across from Utila Water Sports, this friendly, low-key eatery opens at 6am – in time for a quick bite before those 7am northside dive trips. The US$2.50 breakfast is simple and fast: eggs, beans, flour tortilla, cheese and 'bacon' (actually fried bologna). For lunch, *baleadas* (flour tortillas smeared with beans and melted butter) are US$0.50 for the classic bean and cheese, more for chicken or ham.

RJ's BBQ (east main st; mains US$4-6; ☺ 5:30-11pm Wed, Fri & Sun) Huge, cheap, well-prepared dishes attract a crowd here – it's lucky for the other restaurants in town that RJ's is only open three days a week. Choose from BBQ chicken, wahoo, kingfish, pork or beef, all of which are served with mashed potato and salad. The selections are written on a chalk board near the cash register, and erased one by one as the night wears on and the food runs out. Needless to say, come early. It's across from Alton's Dive Shop.

Dave's (east main st; mains US$4-6; ☺ dinner, closed Wed & Sun) Hidden from the main drag behind Cross Creek dive center, Dave's is run more like a street stand than a proper restaurant, serving hefty helpings of chicken, seafood, BBQ, and usually a vegetarian dish or two. Getting here before 7pm ensures you the best selection and the shortest lines.

Munchies (☎ 425 3168; west main st; mains US$2.75-5; ☺ breakfast, lunch, & dinner Mon-Sat) Located on the 1st floor of an old island home, this restaurant has a great Caribbean vibe, with pleasant outdoor seating on the front porch and in the back. The food is a bit uneven, but includes good vegetarian options and big breakfasts, which keeps it busy with travelers.

Bundu Café (east main st; mains US$5-10; ☺ breakfast, lunch & dinner) This longtime Utila watering hole is packed most nights. Dishes are a bit bland, but come in huge portions (which is sometimes all that matters after a day of diving). The large book exchange has a few good finds, if you search for them.

Thompson's Café Bakery (Cola de Mico Rd; ☺ 6am-noon) Don't leave Utila without stopping here at least once to try the famous Johnny cakes – a doughy biscuit that is like manna from heaven when fresh from the oven and smeared with butter. For something heartier, have it with egg and ham: a Ferrari to the Egg McMuffin's Pinto. Thompson's opens early (and starts baking even earlier) so you can snag breakfast before an early dive. Good egg-and-bean breakfasts, fresh bread, and cinnamon roles are also served.

La Dolce Vita Pizzeria (dishes US$3-7; ☺ breakfast, lunch & dinner) In the courtyard of Mango Inn, this place serves great brick oven pizza and decent seafood pastas, as well as breakfasts. It's a good place to come for drinks, too, before Tranquila and Coco Loco get fired up.

There is a handful of simple **beachside restaurants** (mains US$2.50-5.50; ☺ breakfast, lunch & dinner) on Chepes Beach that serve snacks, *típica*, and good seafood dishes. They're great places to escape the heat of the sun over a couple of beers and a plate of ceviche (seafood marinated in lemon or lime juice, garlic and seasonings).

Bush's Supermarket (east main st; ☺ 6:30am-6pm Mon-Sat, to 11am Sun) is the island's largest and best-stocked grocery store, while **Supermarket Rose** (main st; ☺ 8am-noon & 2-8pm, Mon-Sat) is run by the folks at Hotel Roses Inn.

THE BAY ISLANDS

MIDRANGE

La Piccola (☎ 425 3746; west main st; dishes US$5-12; ❤ 5:30-10pm Tue-Sun) Also known as Kate's, after its ebullient owner and chef, this classy restaurant serves excellent homemade Italian food. Most of the pasta is made fresh by hand and served at tables with candles and tablecloths.

Ultralight Café (☎ 425 3514; west main st; mains US$3-7; ❤ breakfast, lunch & dinner Sun-Thu, breakfast & lunch Fri) An Israeli restaurant run by a Utila native named after a doomed flying machine – you know there's a story here. Joya, the owner, leased her burger joint to an Israeli couple, who switched from hamburgers to hummus, but were mainly interested in flying their ultralight. They were better chefs than pilots though: the ultralight crashed (no one was hurt) while the restaurant took off – the aircraft's propeller still hangs in the little wood eatery. Joya returned, the Israelis left, and Joya planned to go back to burgers. But the Israelis' kitchen assistant had memorized all the recipes and convinced Joya to stick with *shakshuka* (a popular Israeli egg dish), falafel, *sabich* (a pita sandwich) and what is still the best fresh pita bread in Central America. By the way, the conch soup – one of a few island dishes on the menu – is terrific.

Jade Seahorse Restaurant (☎ 425 3270; Cola de Mico Rd; mains US$4-10; ❤ lunch & dinner) This restaurant is just as eclectic as the hotel it's a part of. The rambling artsy dining area has groovy tile work, unexpected colors, and hardly a symmetrical shape in sight. The menu is nearly as creative, consisting mostly of vegetarian, seafood and pasta plates.

Drinking

Super Jugos (west main st; drinks US$0.80-1.25; ❤ 9am-10pm) Located just past the radio tower, this tiny white house packs a punch when it comes to smoothies and freshly squeezed juices. A couple of dozen combinations are on offer or just make one up yourself.

Tranquila (west main st) Perched on a wood jetty over the water, this is the place to start your night before migrating all of 15 steps to Coco Loco.

Coco Loco (west main st) Just meters away from Tranquila and virtually identical in appearance, it would be easy to stagger out for a pee and return to find yourself in the other bar without realizing it – which is maybe just what happens, because at some point Tranquila starts to empty and the party moves to Coco Loco.

Bar in the Bush (Cola de Mico Rd) Also popular, but this place can get rowdy. Lone travelers should take care at night, since the pathway to the bar is unlit. It's located past the Mango Inn.

Thatch-roofed bar-discotheque (admission free, drinks US$1-2.50; ❤ 2pm-3am) Facing Chepes Beach, this is a great place to strut your stuff on a starry night. Cheap beers and good mixed drinks make it even better.

Café Barracuda (west main st) This newish sports bar is upstairs from the Bay Island College of Diving and that whale shark place. Six large-screen TVs carry whatever major sporting event is on.

Entertainment

Reef Cinema (☎ 425 3254; east main st; tickets US$2.50; ❤ video store 11:30am-6pm Mon-Sat, cinema 7:30pm Sun-Fri, 6:30pm & 8:30pm Sat) Next to Rubi's Inn, this cinema plays a creative selection of recently released movies every night and twice on Saturday. The video store rents videos and DVDs for US$2 with a one-time membership fee (US$11), or for US$2.25 per night with a refundable deposit (US$16).

Shopping

Gunter's Driftwood Gallery (☎ 425 3113; west of Cola de Mico Rd) The gallery and gift shop of Gunter Kordovsky – multimedia artist, accomplished diver, and Utila institution – is worth a stop. Most of Gunter's art is made from materials he's found on the beach or in the ocean – driftwood, shells, shark jaws – which are reworked and then shellacked to hell. The most impressive piece is an enormous whale shark made out of one piece of mahogany, which Gunter found on the beach after Hurricane Mitch. Open every afternoon except Sunday, look for it near the Mango Inn.

Bay Island Originals (east main st; ❤ 9am-noon & 1-6pm Mon-Fri, 9am-noon Sat & Sun) Across from Reef Cinema, this small shop has a good selection of *artesanías*, clothing and souvenirs.

Getting There & Away

AIR

At last check, flights between Utila and La Ceiba were only offered by **Aerolíneas Sosa**

(☎ 445 3161; www.aerolineassosa.com). Tickets cost US$43 one way from Utila (6am Monday, Tuesday, Thursday, and Saturday) or La Ceiba (3:30pm Sunday, Monday, Wednesday and Friday). Double-check the schedule if you are thinking of flying, and bear in mind that even marginally bad weather can cause the flight to be cancelled. Utila has an airstrip, but no terminal; buy tickets at **Morgan's Travel** (☎ 425 3161; utilamorganstravel@yahoo.com; at pier opposite ferry office; ◷ 8am-noon & 2-5:30pm Mon-Sat), which can also arrange an early morning taxi to the airstrip. It's a small plane and fills up fast, so book a spot as early as possible and always reconfirm the day before.

BOAT

The *Utila Princess* ferries passengers between La Ceiba and Utila's main pier every day (US$21, one hour). The ferry makes two trips each way, leaving Utila at 6:20am and 2pm, and returning from La Ceiba at 9:30am and 4pm. During the low season, the schedule is sometimes reduced to one trip per day (leaving Utila at 6:20am and returning from La Ceiba at 4pm). Regardless of the season, plan on arriving 20 to 30 minutes before departure to be sure there's a boat and that you're on it; tickets are good any day of the year. There is no regular direct ferry service between Utila and Roatán – you have to go to La Ceiba first and transfer – though you may see signs around town for charters.

Getting Around

A few golf-cart taxis ply the streets of Utila, charging a standard US$1 for any distance. You can usually find one at El Paisano Restaurant (next to Bundu Cafe on east main street), Bush's Supermarket, or near the pier (ask at Morgan's Travel). Bicycles can be rented at several places in town – look for signs.

Car rental places include the following:
Lance Bodden Rentals (☎ 425 3245; behind BGA, main st; ◷ 8am-noon & 1-5pm Mon-Sat) Rents vehicles by the hour/half-day/full-day, including ATVs (US$15/40/60), motorcycles and scooters (US$12/30/45), electric golf carts (US$12/30/45) and gas carts (US$15/40/60). Gas included in price. Bikes also available for US$5 to US$8 per day.
Rita's Club Car Rental (☎ 425 3692; east main st; ◷ 9am-noon & 2-6pm Mon-Sat) Rents golf carts for around US$40 a day. At Rita's Boutique.

UTILA CAYS

Several cays on Utila's southwest shore make nice day trips. Jewel and Pigeon Cays, connected by a small bridge, are home to a charming village of just 600 residents (and five churches!). Captain Morgan's Dive Centre (p267) operates from here, and loans kayaks and snorkel gear to students.

Water Cay, just beyond Pigeon and Jewel Cays, is a beautiful 3-acre island covered with palm trees and surrounded by warm turquoise waters. It's uninhabited, but there's a caretaker who keeps it clean and charges US$1.35 per visitor for the upkeep of the island. The best snorkeling is off the southeastern shore, but watch for boat traffic.

Festivals & Events

What started out in 1997 as a 50-person party on Water Cay, is today a 1500-person event known as **Sun Jam** (www.sunjamutila.com), an all-day-all-night party with a troupe of bad-ass DJs spinning tunes for a dancing, drinking, and general mayhem-creating crowd of locals and travelers. Held every August, information is released just a few weeks before the party; check the website early and often to secure a spot.

Sleeping & Eating

Hotel Kayla (r free with dive course, fun divers per person US$5) Located on Jewel Cay (Upper Cay) and operated exclusively for Captain Morgan's students and fun divers, Hotel Kayla is a large, airy, wooden building with a long foyer framed with arches that's kind of southern belle-ish. Rooms are large and clean.

Susan's Restaurant (◷ lunch & dinner) Susan's is famous for its fish burgers, served hot with fries and soda or coffee. Whenever possible, dive boats spend their surface interval here.

Myrna's Cafe (◷ breakfast, lunch & dinner) Open early for a quick breakfast before diving, *baleadas* here start at US$0.25 and *típica* meals are offered for less than two bucks.

Getting There & Away

Ask at Captain Morgan's in town about arranging transport to the cays; chances are you'll travel with 'Mister Donald' who goes most days at 11am and returns at 4pm. (Ask about going earlier if you want more time.) The fare is usually US$5.50 per person for the 30-minute trip (minimum four people).

Getting Around

If you stay on Jewel Cay (Upper Cay), you can easily kayak or hire a boat to Water Cay or to some of the cays further out. Each of the Utila Cays can be covered by foot in just a few minutes.

GUANAJA

pop 11,500

The easternmost of the three Bay Islands, Guanaja is a small island, roughly 18km long and 6km wide. It is covered in a forest of Caribbean pine; when Christopher Columbus landed on the island in 1502, he named it the *Isla de Pinos* (Island of Pines). About 90% of the island has been declared a national forest reserve and marine park.

A vibrant coral reef encircles the island and its 15 or so cays; it's this reef – and the ships it has sunken – that makes Guanaja attractive for snorkeling and diving. Although several dive resorts have appeared on the island, the diving and tourist boom that has hit Roatán and Utila has yet to reach Guanaja.

There are a few tiny settlements on the main island, including one on Savannah Bight and another on Mangrove Bight; the latter was badly hit by Hurricane Mitch in 1998 and is still showing signs of recovery.

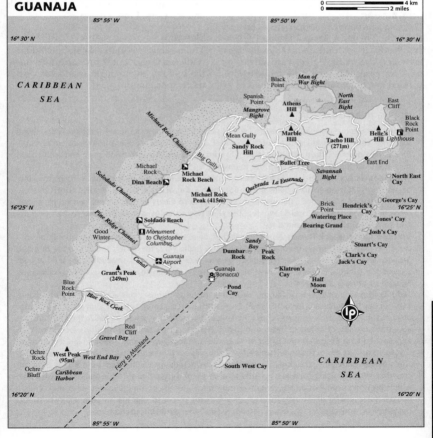

GUANAJA

THE BAY ISLANDS

GUANAJA TOWN (BONACCA)

The island's principal town, Guanaja – called Bonacca by the locals – is on a small cay just off the island's east coast. Every inch of the cay has been built on: wooden houses with sloping roofs stand on stilts at all different heights. There are no roads on the cay and therefore no cars; walkways wind around and narrow canals allow the residents to pull their boats right up to their houses. In fact, Bonacca is sometimes called the Venice of Honduras, which is a stretch for sure, but evocative nonetheless.

Guanaja is not a haven for budget travelers. Most lodging options are upscale resorts; even basic hotels start at US$32. And with no ferry service, even getting here can be expensive.

Information

Guanaja's few public services are located in Bonacca. There's a **Banco Atlántida** (9am-4pm Mon-Fri, to noon Sat), which exchanges traveler's checks and gives cash advances on Visa cards; however, the bank uses a manual machine, so your card should have

raised numbers (the smooth 'electronic use only' cards won't work). There's also a post office, and telephone calls can be made at **Hondutel** (7am-9pm Mon-Fri, to 4pm Sat).

Sights & Activities

Snorkeling, diving and visits to the cays and beaches are the main activities on Guanaja. Most hotels on the mainland have dive shops, and offer courses, fun dives and multidive packages. Dive gear can be rented (usually for an additional fee) if you don't have your own. It's possible to snorkel right off Bonacca, although it's much better off Black Point on the main island, and around South West and Jones Cays. Surprisingly, snorkeling gear is not readily available on the island; you should bring your own. The main island has a number of hiking trails and a waterfall too.

Sleeping

There are a few places to stay in Bonacca (Guanaja town), but if you can afford them, the options on the main island are worlds more appealing.

DIVING NEAR GUANAJA

Declared a marine reserve, the waters around Guanaja are home to 38 terrific dives sites, most teeming with marine life and a flourishing reef. The northside sites are known for their coral forests and dramatic drop-offs, the southside sites for being shallower and sprinkled with channels. Some of the top sites include the following:

The Pinnacle Located in Pine Ridge Channel near Soldado Beach, this pinnacle rises from the ocean floor 135ft down to a point about 55ft below the ocean's surface. Known for its incredible varieties of black coral, divers will also be treated to views of gorgonians, sea whips, arrow crabs, flamingo tongues, and seahorses. The best way to enjoy it is to descend to 80ft or 90ft, and slowly spiral up and around it.

Volcano Caves (Black Rocks) An excellent drift dive, this site is made up of hundreds of volcanic caverns and tunnels that extend along a 1½-maile wall. There isn't much sponge or coral growth here, but lots of fish – silversides, glassy sweepers, grouper, barracuda – are seen in and around the tunnels. Some divers have also been lucky enough to come across sleeping sharks. Be sure to bring a dive light.

Jado Trader One of the most famous dive sites in the Caribbean, this is a 240ft freighter lying 110ft under the surface on a sandy shelf. Next to the wreck, there is a wall that rises to a depth of about 45ft and a bit further off, a 70ft volcanic chimney. Scuttled in 1987, the ship has an abundant growth of coral, sponges and algae. Fish are often fed here, so don't be alarmed if approached by a 6ft green moray eel frisking you for food. Grouper and yellowtail are common fish to spot, and the occasional hammerhead shark is seen here as well.

Jim's Silver Lode An excellent drift dive, this site begins at a 70ft-deep tunnel that is often crowded with silverside sardines. It leads to a large sandy bowl covered in fans and lush coral where grouper, yellow goatfish, stingrays, and moray eels are commonly seen. Be sure to check out the holes and crevices along the wall; they're prime places to spot black durgon, fairy basslets, butterflyfish, and bigeyes. It's a top-notch site for underwater photographers.

IF YOU HAVE A FEW MORE DAYS

After you've spent a few days unwinding, consider booking a boat to take you beach-hopping along the north side of the island (it's mostly uninhabited). Start at **Dina Beach**, just west of Michael Rock, an empty tawny-sand beach with patches of seagrapes and a backdrop of pines. From there, hike or take the boat to **Soldado Beach**, the site where Columbus is reputed to have landed in 1502. There's a ramshackle monument commemorating the event, but far more striking is the pretty inlet with clear turquoise blue waters – be sure to bring your snorkel gear. Finally, set off for **West End Bay**. Located on the southwestern end of the island, it's a long white-sand beach with a lush pine and deciduous tree forest alongside it – it's absolutely perfect for beachcombing.

Hotel Miller (☎ 453 4327; Bonacca; r US$32; ✹) This is a simple hotel with cable TV, private hot-water bathroom, air-conditioning and an on-site restaurant. In addition to this hotel, the Miller family owns half of South West Cay, an excellent spot to spend the day snorkeling, swimming, and beach combing. Ask at the front desk for details about trips.

West Peak Inn (☎ 377 6114, in US 831-786 0406; www.westpeakinn.com; southwest side of island; all-inclusive per person US$95) Situated on three miles of pristine, secluded beach, the all-inclusive West Peak Inn specializes in sea kayaking packages around Guanaja. There's good hiking nearby, and diving, snorkeling and fishing trips can also be arranged. Individual cabins are comfortable and appealing in a simple, beachy sort of way. Service is very good.

Villa at Dunbar Rock (☎ 453 4506, in US 952-953 4124; www.usdivetravel.com/R-HONDURAS-Nautilus .html; Dunbar Rock; all-inclusive s/d US$188/330) This four-room hotel, located on a strikingly beautiful rocky outcrop directly across from Sandy Bay, has basic rooms but phenomenal views – the Caribbean sea in every direction and the lush main island directly in front.

Nautilus Dive Resort (☎ 453 4506, in US 952-953 4124; www.usdivetravel.com/R-HONDURAS-Nautilus.html) There are also great dive packages available through Nautilus Dive Resort, Villa's sister hotel located just 500m away on Sandy Bay.

Bo Bush's Island House (☎ 991 0913; www.bos islandhouse.com; north side of island; all-inclusive per person per week US$500) This small, laid-back resort offers basic but clean rooms in a hillside building with great views of the Caribbean. It's owned by islander Bo Bush who knows the island – and its reefs – like

the back of his hand. All-inclusive dive packages are also available for an additional US$150 per week.

Eating

Many of the hotels on the mainland provide meals to guests, either à la carte or as part of a package. On Sunday, the West Peak Inn holds a popular BBQ.

Best Stop (☎ 453 4523; Bonacca; ✹ breakfast, lunch & dinner Mon-Fri, dinner 6:30-11pm Sat & Sun) Facing the basketball court on Bonacca, this place is good for hamburgers, sandwiches, and freshly baked pastries.

Mexi-Treats (Bonacca; ✹ breakfast, lunch & dinner) The chef here is a Mexican transplant, bringing a variety of Mexican food to this tiny island.

Getting There & Away

AIR

Isleña Regional (☎ 453 4208; www.flyislena.com), **Aerolineas SOSA** (☎ 453 4359; www.laceibaonline .net/aerososa/sosaingl.htm), and **Atlantic Airlines** (☎ 453 4211; www.atlanticairlines.com.ni) all offer a 25-minute flight between Guanaja and La Ceiba. There's a dock near the airport where a motorboat meets incoming visitors for the five-minute ride to Bonacca. For departing flights, a water taxi meets passengers at the pier near the joint airline office in Bonacca to take them to the airport. If you're staying at one of the resorts, transportation to and from the airport is typically provided.

BOAT

There's a twice-weekly **ferry service** (☎ in Guanaja 371 0373, in Trujillo 434 3421; www.teammarin travel.com) to Guanaja from the city of Trujillo. The air-conditioned 250-passenger boat leaves from the municipal pier in

SWAN ISLANDS

Located approximately 156km from mainland Honduras, the Swan Islands are a chain of three rocky islets measuring a mere 8 sq km. Stumbled upon by Christopher Columbus in 1502, they were later occupied by the filibuster William Walker (see p231). After Walker's execution in 1860, Honduras claimed the chain of islands as its own. The US, however, also laid claim to them in 1863 under the Guano Islands Act, a legislation 'enabling' the US to take possession of any island caked in guano – a fancy word for bird shit, which was highly valued as fertilizer at the time – as long as the island wasn't inhabited or owned by another country. In 1971, over a hundred years later, the US relinquished its claim to them.

The Swan Islands are most famous for having housed Radio Swan (later called Radio Americas), which began broadcasting during the period leading up to and after the US invasion of Cuba at the Bay of Pigs. Believed to be owned by a private steamship company, it was eventually discovered that the radio station was owned by the US government and allegedly operated by the CIA to transmit coded messages to Cubans who were going to support American forces during the invasion. Radio Swan was closed in the late 1960s and its main transmitter relocated for use in the Vietnam War.

Today, the Swan Islands are uninhabited except for a small Honduran military base.

Trujillo on Tuesday at 3pm and Saturday at 9am, and returns on Wednesday at 9am and Sunday at 3pm (US$30 one way, 2½ to three hours). Reservations are not required.

Getting Around

Wherever you stay in Guanaja, travel is by boat. Almost everyone has one so rides are easy to arrange; ask at the front desk of your hotel for information on a trusted driver.

La Moskitia

The Moskitia, which spans most of eastern Honduras and across into Nicaragua, is the largest rainforest in Central America, indeed, the largest north of the Amazon Basin. It is a vast area of tropical rainforest, tortuous rivers and huge saltwater lagoons. It abounds with wildlife – monkeys, crocodiles and tapirs – and is also abundant with bird life, from toucans and macaws to egrets and herons. Manatees and jaguars are present too, though are very difficult to spot.

Five different ethnic groups – three indigenous, two of more recent extraction – have homes and communities in the Moskitia. Most live alongside the lagoons and rivers and live by fishing and small-time agriculture.

Travelers have long been drawn to the Moskitia's pristine natural beauty, cultural uniqueness and off-the-beaten-path quality. Fortunately, getting here is now easier, with regular flights and a more predictable overland route. Travel here hasn't changed much though – there are few roads, so you'll be getting around by boat, by foot, and by air, if you've got the nerve.

Visiting the Moskitia is not cheap, whether you come with a tour or on your own. Gas is almost twice as expensive here as in the rest of Honduras – over US$5 per gallon at last check – and NGOs have worked hard to insure guides and boatmen are paid competitive wages.

All told, this is a true highlight in Honduras and one of the last frontiers in Central America, a region whose ecological riches have been severely trampled. Environmentalists say that La Moskitia offers one last chance to get it right. And gliding down the river in a dugout canoe, past mud houses backed by vine-heavy trees, you can't help but hope they – we – do.

HIGHLIGHTS

- Take a three-day hike up **Pico Dama** (p291) into the heart of the Reserva de la Biósfera del Río Plátano.
- Release baby turtles on a moonlit beach with the **Turtle Preservation Program** (p287) in the Garífuna village of Plaplaya.
- Paddle 10 days down the **Río Patuca** (p297) through the Tawahka indigenous reserve to the Caribbean Sea.
- Forget Venice – try a **pipante ride up the Río Plátano** (p291) instead. Taking poling canoes to new extremes, you'll travel upriver, through rapids, in search of wildlife and petroglyphs.
- Visit quiet **Miskito villages** like Rais Ta (p284) and Belén (p285), where children learn to swim before they walk and the soccer field doubles as an airstrip.

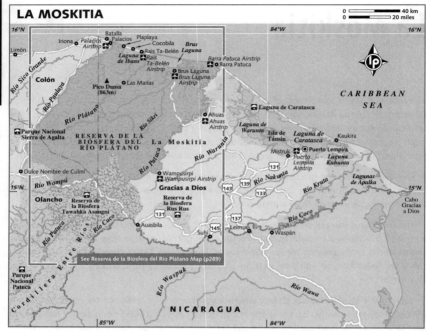

LA MOSKITIA

HISTORY

La Moskitia was inhabited as many as 3000 years ago by Chibcha-speaking Amerindians who migrated here from present-day South America. Today's Pech and Tawahka indigenous groups are descended from those early migrants, and speak variations of Chibcha dialects. The pre-Hispanic population reached its peak between AD 800 and 1200, around the time groups to the west, especially the Maya, were in near collapse.

Christopher Columbus was the first European to reach La Moskitia, on his fourth and last voyage in 1502. Sailing east from the Bay Islands, he landed briefly near the mouth of a large river – which one is unknown, though it was likely the Patuca or the Sico – before rounding the cape (which he dubbed Cabo Gracias a Dios, or 'Thank God Cape', reportedly after weathering a fierce storm). But the unforgiving terrain and environment of La Moskitia prevented any serious exploration for over a century. A cursory exploration in 1564 was not followed up until 1607 and 1609, and the first

church – the point of early expeditions – was not founded until 1610. However, that church, and another founded a year later, were both sacked and burned, and their occupants killed, by Tawahka Indians. It took another 80 years for Spanish missionaries (supported by Spanish troops) to gain a foothold in the jungle.

In the 1700s, Spanish influence waned as that of English pirates (and some Dutch and French) rose. The slow-moving Spanish galleons laden with precious metals and raw materials made easy targets for pirates, who found refuge in La Moskitia's lagoons and river inlets. The English made little attempt to convert the indigenous people to Christianity – one supposes the pirates were not themselves big church-goers – but rather formed alliances with them against the Spanish. In fact, it was arming one group with muskets that gave rise to the term *mosqueteros* and eventually 'Miskito' and 'Moskitia'.

Britain maintained control over eastern Honduras until 1786, when, through a treaty with Spain, it essentially traded the

Moskitia for present-day Belize. But having gained nominal control of the territory, Spain did little to exert any real influence there. The status of the colony was in constant flux: the Central American Federation came and went, and a meddlesome British government briefly recognized the Moskitia as a sovereign nation, before Honduras finally became an independent republic in 1838. Through it all, life in La Moskitia stayed relatively unchanged. Moravian missionaries began arriving in the late 1920s, setting up schools, clinics and churches. The Honduran government didn't take up true civic responsibility in La Moskitia until the 1950s, around the same time indigenous rights organizations began forming to focus on land rights and other issues.

In the 1980s, the Moskitia was used as a base for the Contra war, the US-supported effort to unseat the new Sandinista government in Nicaragua. Puerto Lempira had major military installations, as did many of the small border towns. Countless indigenous people, especially Miskitos, whose traditional lands spanned the Honduran–Nicaraguan border, were killed and displaced during the conflict.

PEOPLE

With five distinct ethnic groups – Miskito, Pech, Garífuna, Tawahka, and ladino – the Moskitia is arguably the most culturally diverse region in the country. The single largest ethnic group in the region is the Miskito, whose present members arose from a mixing of a landed indigenous group and escaped African slaves, and later English

pirates. Historically, they occupied areas along the coast and around the Moskitia's three large lagoons, as well as along the Río Coco. They form the majority in all of the towns frequented by travelers, including Brus Laguna, Belén, Rais Ta, Ahuas, Wampusirpi, and a large part of Las Marías.

Another group, the Pech, once occupied large parts of what is now the Reserva de la Biósfera del Río Plátano, and as far south as the Sierra de Agalta mountains in Olancho and west to the Valle de Aguán. However, a longtime rivalry with the Miskitos along the coast and encroachment by ladino formers in Olancho squeezed the Pech into the middle reaches of the Río Plátano, where they remain today. Even Las Marías, once a vital Pech village, now has a large number of Miskito residents thanks to migration and intermarriage. In 1990, about 40 Pech people moved from Olancho to Las Marías, in part to reestablish Pech presence in the area.

Even more isolated than the Pech are the Tawahka, who live mostly along the Río Patuca and number about 1000 people (see p296). They, too, once controlled large portions of present-day Moskitia, but are today concentrated in just five communities, the largest being Krausirpe, in the Tawahka Asangni Biosphere Reserve. The Tawahka were the last of the indigenous groups in the Moskitia to be contacted by Europeans, and fiercely resisted their intrusion. The first two missionary expeditions to the region, in 1610 and 1611, both ended when Tawahka Indians attacked and killed the interlopers and the soldiers accompanying them.

LOCAL LORE: SEARCH FOR THE WHITE CITY

In 1519, Hernán Cortés first heard reports of La Cuidad Blanca (The White City), a glorious city named after elaborately carved white stones that were said to exist there. Stories of its immeasurable wealth in gold spurred Cortés to find the city, but, hidden deep in the jungles of La Moskitia, he never did.

Many Pech legends refer to The White City as the birthplace of gods and a city filled with golden idols. The basis of countless expeditions, these stories have been fueled by 'sightings' as early as 1544, when Cristóbal de Pedraza, the then bishop of Honduras, wrote to the king of Spain to tell him about an impressive metropolis that he had seen from a mountaintop in La Moskitia; his guides assured him, he related, that nobles there ate from plates of gold.

In modern times, pilots and hunters have reported seeing or stumbling upon this elusive city; expeditions to find it have increased considerably since the 1940s because of this. Many treasure-hunters, in fact, claim to have already discovered it. No proof or directional coordinates, however, have ever been revealed.

The Moskitia has a small number of Garífuna people, living along the coast in the towns of Plaplaya, Batalla and Iriona. Descended from Carib indigenous people and African slaves on the island of St Vincent, and then deported by Britain to Roatán in the late 1700s, the Garífuna did not reach the Moskitia until the turn of the 20th century. Nevertheless, Plaplaya is considered one of the 'purest' Garífuna villages in Honduras, isolated from many modern-day intrusions.

Ladinos, considered 'mainstream' Hondurans, have moved to La Moskitia in ever-increasing numbers, mostly drawn by the availability of land for farming and ranching. A great deal of controversy surrounds ladino occupation of Moskitia lands, especially in areas traditionally used by the region's indigenous groups. Environmentalists worry, too, that ladino clear cutting, to make room for cattle, is contributing to the erosion of the region's rivers and leading to flooding downstream.

DANGERS & ANNOYANCES

As in any large swath of rainforest or wilderness, travel in the Moskitia has a unique set of difficulties, dangers and annoyances.

First and foremost, never venture into the rainforest without a guide. Trails are faint and overgrown, and even experienced hikers can become hopelessly lost within a matter of minutes.

Traveling at night (by boat, truck or foot) can be dangerous, so avoid trying to do too much in any one day. Boats can break down, paths can be washed out, rivers can become impassable: you should always leave yourself several hours of daylight as a cushion in case problems arise. Remember that guides and boatmen – eager to please – may go along with an overly ambitious plan, assuming you understand the risks.

Likewise, avoid crossing Laguna de Ibans and especially Brus Laguna and Laguna de Caratasca late in the day – afternoon winds create large waves that can swamp or sink a boat. Though such incidents are rare, it's even rarer for boats to have lifejackets or radios in case of an emergency. Better to plan ahead so your crossings are in the morning, even if it means having to wake up extra early or 'losing' an afternoon along the way.

And remember, all plans in the Moskitia are provisional. Planes, boats, trucks and buses can all be delayed for hours or days. On the same note, you may well find you want more time than you planned for. Build flexibility into your itinerary to account for unexpected changes of either sort. Changing tickets or plans is usually fairly easy, as all the towns are connected by radio.

TOURS

A prearranged tour is definitely worth considering, especially if your time (or Spanish speaking ability) is limited. Tours have the advantage of having all the transport and lodging planned ahead of time, something that can take a lot of time and energy for indy travelers. Most outfits offering tours to the Moskitia have good guides and track records – it's rare to get suckered into a total fiasco. The cost is higher, though not by as much as you might think. Going independently can be a terrific experience if you have the time, language skills, and, to a certain degree, the money, to take things as they come. Otherwise, a tour can take the guesswork out of going to the Moskitia, letting you sit back and enjoy it.

Recommended tour operators include the following.

Jungle River Tours (☎ 440 1268; www.jungleriver lodge.com; Banana Republic Guesthouse, Av Morazán, La Ceiba) Across from Hospital D'Antoni, offers multiday hiking and rafting trips.

La Moskitia Ecoaventuras (☎ 440 2124; www .honduras.com/moskitia; Hotel Plaza Caracol, Av 14 de Julio, La Ceiba) Run by Jorge Salverri, an expert birder and one of the most knowledgeable guides to the Moskitia. Tours range from five to 12 days and are cheap, though sometimes rough around the edges.

La Ruta Moskitia (☎ 443 1276; www.larutamoskitia .com; La Ceiba) A nonprofit tourism initiative started by Rare Conservation and selected for the 'Green Travel' list of Condé Nast Traveler in 2006. Sort of 'tour-lite': you don't travel with a dedicated guide, but transportation is prearranged and you are told who to ask for in each town. Every penny goes to the guides, guesthouse owners and boatmen you use. The website includes a feature for people looking for others to form a group.

Mesoamérica Travel (☎ 557 8447; 8a Calle 709 at 32a Av NO, Col Juan Lindo, San Pedro Sula) Recommended among more upscale outfits.

MC Tours (☎ 551 8639; www.mctours-honduras.com; Col Tara Local No 3 Adobe 30, San Pedro Sula) Another upscale outfit.

Omega Tours (☎ 440 0334; www.omegatours.hn; Omega Jungle Lodge, Calle a Yaruca Km 9) German owned and operated, offering highly recommended multiday rafting trips down the Plátano and Patuka rivers. It's located along the Río Cangrejal on the way to the town of Yaruca.

Turtle Tours (Caribbean Travel; ☎ 414 5368; www .turtle-tours.com; Av San Isidro, La Ceiba) German-run tour operator with an established reputation for small groups and professional service.

GETTING THERE & AWAY
Air
All flights to the Moskitia depart from La Ceiba. At the time of research, Aerolineas Sosa and Atlantic Airlines had daily flights to Puerto Lempira (US$100 one way), while only Sosa flew to Brus Laguna (US$90 one way) and only on Monday, Wednesday and Friday. There was no scheduled service to Palacios, though SAMI occasionally connects to and from La Ceiba through there.

Aerolineas Sosa (☎ in La Ceiba 443 1894, in Puerto Lempira 433 6432, in Brus Laguna 433 8042; www .aerolineassosa.com; Av San Isidro btwn 8a & 9a Calles, La Ceiba; ☼ 7am-5pm Mon-Fri)

Atlantic Airlines (☎ in La Ceiba 440 2343; in Puerto Lempira 433 6016; www.atlanticairlines.com.ni; 11a Calle near Av República, La Ceiba; ☼ 8am-noon & 1-5pm Mon-Fri, 8am-noon Sat)

SAMI (☎ in La Ceiba 442 2565, in Brus Laguna 433 8031)

Overland
From the north coast, there are two slightly different land routes into the Moskitia, both ending at the sister communities of Rais Ta and Belén, from where you can arrange trips deeper into the rainforest. While Tocoa is the 'official' departure point of both routes, it's possible to make the trip in one long day from either La Ceiba or Trujillo.

From La Ceiba, there are ordinary buses to Tocoa from the main bus terminal from 4:30am to 5:30pm (US$2.50, 2½ hours, every 30 minutes) while direct buses on their way to Trujillo pass the COTUC office on the main highway from 8:15am to 7pm (US$3.75, 1½ hours, every 45 minutes). Though it takes longer, the ordinary bus gets you to Tocoa much earlier and is recommended. See p222 for more info.

From Trujillo, take the 5:45am bus as far as Corocito (US$2, 30 to 45 minutes, every 45 minutes), where you can transfer to either of the two options coming from Tocoa (see following).

Before setting off, check out **La Ruta Moskitia** (www.larutamoskitia.com) for up-to-date land and air information.

VIA BATALLA
At the Tocoa bus terminal, ask for the next *paila a Batalla* – a modified pickup headed to Batalla, a small Garífuna town that was badly damaged in November 2005 by flooding on the Río Sico, caused by tropical storm Gamma and exacerbated by clear-cutting upstream (US$21.50, four to five hours). They leave hourly from 7am to noon every day; try to get the early truck to be sure to reach Belén and Rais Ta before dark. You can catch the same trucks in Corocito, if you started in Trujillo.

At Batalla, *colectivos* (shared boats) usually wait for the arrival of the trucks. The boats make many stops – tell the driver you want to go to Rais Ta or Belén (US$8, one to two hours). If you catch the 7am pickup in Tocoa, you should arrive by early afternoon.

This is the 'primary' route, but is occasionally suspended when storms wash out the roads into Batalla. In that case, the route via Iriona is a good alternative.

VIA IRIONA
From Tocoa, big yellow buses with 'Tocoa–Iriona' painted on the front leave the bus terminal every morning, starting between 6:30am and 7:30am. The schedule varies so you'll have to ask when the next one leaves. The bus passes through Corocito – take the 5:45am bus from Trujillo to catch the first one. The bus to Iriona takes between four and six hours (US$5). Arriving in Iriona around noon, get off the bus at the main pier and catch the next speedboat to Belén (US$19, two hours).

The speedboats go via the ocean, instead of the lagoon, and may be cancelled if conditions are too windy or choppy. In that case, there's an alternative route via the inland channels. From Iriona, hire a motor boat to the town of Tocamacho (per person US$5.50, 45 minutes). From there, you'll walk about an hour to the town of Grasspis, where you can catch another motor boat to Palacios (US$11, 1½ hours). Finally, take a boat the rest of the way to Belén or Rais Ta (*colectivo* US$8, two to three hours; private US$43, 1½ hours). The problem with this option is you may get stuck spending the night in Palacios, which can be unpleasant and even somewhat dangerous, so consider overnighting in Iriona and continuing the next morning.

RETURNING

To return, an early morning boat – 3am to 4am – picks up passengers in Belén, Rais Ta, Cocobila, and Ibans daily. You can get off at Batalla (US$8, one to two hours) for a 6am truck to Tocoa, or continue to Palacios (US$8, one to two hours) and catch the 6am speedboat to Iriona, where the bus to Tocoa will be waiting. Either way, get off at Corocito if you're headed to Trujillo, or go all the way to Tocoa to catch an onward bus to La Ceiba.

GETTING AROUND

Different seasons present different challenges in terms of getting around the Moskitia. The rainy reason is probably the most difficult, especially November through January, as the rivers get swollen with debris and the trails and roads get muddy. Plus, getting caught in the rain while hiking or on a five-hour boat ride is no fun. During the driest months (February to April) some rivers may get too shallow in places to navigate.

Air

Within the Moskitia, **SAMI** (☎ in Brus Laguna 433 8031, in Puerto Lempira 433 6016) has semi-regular flights to and among all the main towns: Puerto Lempira, Brus Laguna, Palacios, Belén/Rais Ta, Ahuas, Wampusirpi, and Barra Patuca. Using tiny propeller planes, these flights are not for the faint hearted, but can be a convenient way to cut your travel time. That said, the flights do not follow a regular schedule – planes arrive and depart any time between 7am and 4pm, with no advance notice, and you may end up waiting a day (or more) for your flight. Fares vary widely, but average from US$30 to US$60 each way. SAMI is at the Atlantic Airlines office in Puerto Lempira.

Boat

Most transportation in and around the Moskitia is by boat. Way upriver, the most common boat is a *pipantes*, a flat-bottomed boat made from a single tree trunk that's propelled by a pole or paddle. However, for longer trips or those on the lagoons, a *cayuco,* a wood planked boat with an outboard motor, is more commonly used.

There are two types of service: *expreso* is like a private taxi and can be fairly expensive depending on the route; and *colectivo*, which is like a bus following a set route picking up passengers as it goes. Prices are somewhat more manageable on *colectivo* services; common routes include Río Plátano to Brus Laguna (US$11, 1½ hours) or Batalla to Rais Ta (US$8, one to two hours).

Truck

A single dirt road along the Laguna de Ibans runs from the town of Ibans west through Cocobila, Rais Ta, and Belén, and east to the town of Río Plátano (at the mouth of the same). Pickup trucks ply the route several times a day; the entire trip takes about an hour and costs US$2.75.

WESTERN MOSKITIA

The western portion of La Moskitia is no longer the major staging area for trips into the rainforest that it once was – that torch has passed to Rais Ta/Belén and Brus Laguna. Palacios is still the second largest town in the region, but air traffic has all but ended and the town has grown steadily less charming and more dodgy. With regular flights to Brus Laguna and improvements in the land route that make getting deeper into La Moskitia in a single day relatively easy, many people either skip this region altogether or just pass through quickly.

IRIONA

This quiet Garífuna village occupies a picturesque stretch of coastline, with palm trees growing amid a loose collection of homes, some made of cement, others of traditional mud walls with thatched roofs. Halfway along the overland route to/from the Moskitia, most travelers spend only the time they need to catch an onward boat or bus from here.

Sleeping & Eating

Iriona has just one hotel and it's pretty dodgy. The rooms are dark and the bathrooms don't

THE MISKITO

The Miskito indigenous group – the namesake of La Moskitia, aka the Mosquito Coast – occupies coastal and inland areas in the state of Gracias a Dios and parts of Olancho. Although they are arguably the most 'modernized' of the ethnic groups in the Moskitia, most essentially still subsist as they have for centuries, through small-time agriculture and fishing.

How the Miskito came to be is not fully understood. Fairly dark skinned, the Miskito are almost certainly descended from an as-yet-unknown indigenous group and escaped or shipwrecked African slaves. The name definitely did not come from 'mosquito' as Paul Theroux led us all to believe, although its true origin is disputed. There was an early king named Miskut, and some argue Miskito is derived from a phrase meaning 'people who follow Miskut'. A more widely accepted theory is that it comes from the English word 'musket,' which the Miskito were given (and quickly mastered) by British meddlers seeking to erode Spanish control of mainland Honduras. In fact, Miskitos probably have a fair amount of British blood, too. Some 30% of Miskito words come from English, including *landing, kitchen, work,* and the days of the week. Some say Miskito culture is so mixed – indigenous, African, English – that it lacks a core identity. Yet it may be their multi-ethnicity that has made the Miskito so well prepared to adapt to the many challenges and changes they face.

Traditional Miskito territory straddles the Nicaragua–Honduras border, marked by the Río Coco. Through the colonial and early independence periods – even to modern times – the Miskito passed back and forth freely, whether for family, fishing or farming. The border became intensely militarized, however, following the Sandinista revolution in Nicaragua, when US-funded Contras launched incursions from camps just across the border. The CIA recruited untold numbers of Nicaraguan Miskitos as guides, translators, foot soldiers, even platoon leaders, while the Sandinista government killed and imprisoned Miskitos they suspected of colluding with the Contras. The US seized upon the deaths as evidence that the Sandinistas would kill their own people to stay in power. Whether Miskito deaths amounted to a massacre, as the US claimed, or were ordinary casualties of war exaggerated by American propaganda, as the Sandinistas said, may never be officially determined.

Miskito people on both sides of the border have returned to a more ordinary existence, still surviving largely on fishing, small-time farming, and, increasingly, tourism. In both countries, but especially Honduras, Miskito men have been drawn to quick money as lobster divers, but hundreds have been crippled or killed by decompression sickness, stemming from a lack of proper training and the failure of boat owners and the government to enforce basic safety regulations.

appear to have been scrubbed in, well, ever. Better to stay at **Hospedaje Don Tino** (r US$5) located in San José de la Punta, a friendly Garífuna village a kilometer or so west of Iriona. Located by the soccer field, the hotel has very simple but adequate rooms and a small **comedor** (mains US$2-5; breakfast, lunch & dinner). It's operated by the man who drives the Tocoa–Iriona bus, and he can probably drop you off there if it looks like you'll have to spend the night.

Getting There & Away

The main *muelle* (pier) is at the mouth of the canal, where it empties into the ocean. Arriving on the bus from Tocoa, ask the driver to drop you off right at the pier, since you pass it before entering Iriona proper. See p281 for more details.

PALACIOS

Palacios was once the hub of travel into and out of La Moskitia, a vibrant Miskito town and the best jumping-off point for trips into the Reserva de la Biósfera del Río Plátano. It is no longer any of those things, and is in fact an increasingly dangerous place. Palacios has long been an important layover for South American drug traffickers, especially those from Colombia. At one time, major players had homes here, and huge speedboats moored alongside local canoes were a peculiar but not uncommon sight. Ironically, the situation worsened – at least for local people – when anti-drug efforts drove out the cartels, which at least had had a stabilizing influence. The city and region are still a major drug corridor, but Palacios has developed a distinctly tense and lawless atmosphere (not to mention very loud), as smaller brokers jockey for dominance.

Unfortunately, the overland route to or from the Moskitia sometimes involves stopping or transferring boats in Palacios; if the weather or boat schedules don't cooperate, you may even have to stay the night here. This possibility should not deter travelers from visiting La Moskitia or from taking the overland route. As in other somewhat dodgy places, only a fraction of people have any problems, and most incidents can be traced to unnecessary risks, like staying out late or hitting up the local bars (or 'businessmen').

Sleeping & Eating

The best and safest lodging in town is the **Hotel Río Tinto** (☎ 966 6465; r US$8), located near the old airstrip. Rooms have private bathrooms and a view of the lagoon. The hotel is run by Doña Ana, a friendly and knowledgeable host who can help guests with travel arrangements, as well as day trips to the coastal Garífuna village of Batalla. Another option is the nearby **Hotel La Moskitia** (☎ 978 7397; r US$21), more modern but with a somewhat dodgier clientele. Both hotels have small restaurants.

Getting There & Away

SAMI (☎ in La Ceiba 442 2565, in Brus Laguna 433 8031) is the only airline with services to and from Palacios. There is no regular schedule, so it's essential to call or radio in advance. You may have to wait a day or more for a flight; there are more regular services from Belén and Brus Laguna.

Lancha (boat) is the most common mode of transport in and out of Palacios. There are several trips per day from Palacios to Belén, and at least one early morning speedboat trip to Iriona, from where you can catch the bus to Tocoa and Trujillo.

AROUND LAGUNA DE IBANS

Laguna de Ibans is the smallest of the three lagoons in the Moskitia, and yet the one with the most tourist infrastructure. Along the low narrow strip of land that separates the lagoon from the ocean is a string of classic coastal villages, comprising simple wood homes built on stilts, separated by patches of sandy grass or small plots of yucca and beans, and connected by small footpaths. Each village is a little different from the next, not only ethnically – Plaplaya is Garífuna, the rest are not – but also in look and feel. In each town, though, an easy atmosphere prevails, the kind that only seems possible in towns where everyone knows everyone else.

RAIS TA

Everywhere you turn in this quiet Miskito village there's an image worth remembering: narrow dirt paths beneath a canopy of high leafy trees; the airstrip used as the soccer field (or is it the other way around?); and wood houses, most on stilts, scattered across the strip of land between the lagoon and the ocean.

Sights & Activities

A few different excursions can be arranged in Rais Ta. These are by no means a *National Geographic* jungle expedition; they're mellow and easy, a chance to see some rainforest, talk with the guide, and get your shoes dirty. The Raista Eco Lodge (opposite) is the best place to make arrangements, whether or not you're a guest there. Visiting early morning is best, not only for animal spotting, but because by afternoon the lagoon gets windy and rough, making your return journey tougher (and a whole lot wetter).

A popular half-day trip is to **Paru Creek** (per person US$10). Taking a *cayuco* across the lagoon, a guide leads you on a mild winding hike through the rainforest, checking out the multitudinous varieties of trees, flowers and insects. Two troops of howler monkeys live in this area, but spotting them is never guaranteed. You end up at Paru Creek, where the *cayuco* will be waiting. Shedding everything but your swimsuit – you may want to keep your shoes on too – you then float down the creek in inner tubes, the water clear and cold, the canopy swaying overhead, before returning to Rais Ta. Similar options are the **Brans Jungle Hike** and a trip to the community of **Banaka**, where you'll see ancient petroglyphs.

A new **butterfly farm** was in the works at the time of research, to replace one that closed in 2003 due to a lack of funding. RARE helped organize a loan, and the assistance of the owner of Enchanted Wings butterfly farm in Copán, to reopen the farm.

Sleeping & Eating

None of the guesthouses in Rais Ta have telephones, so it's all but impossible to make a reservation from outside La Moskitia. Within La Moskitia, ask your hotel owner to call by radio to the next town to let them know you're coming. All that said, it's very rare that every single room is filled, especially in Rais Ta. But if so, arrangements can surely be made with local families – ask one of the guesthouse owners for help.

Raista Eco Lodge (r with shared bathroom per person US$10) Opened in January 2006, this new eight-bedroom wood lodge is run by Doña Elma, whose late husband, Eddie Bodden, was a longtime community leader and pioneer of eco-tourism in La Moskitia. Bodden drowned in a tragic boat accident on the lagoon in May 2005, but the new lodge is evidence that his family is taking up the torch. Rooms are rustic, but well built and comfortable, with sturdy beds, mosquito nets, and small porches; older rooms may also be available (per person US$4 to US$5). Some of the latrine toilets are gag-inducing, but there are several to choose from. You may encounter tour groups here, as it's the only place with enough rooms to house them. Doña Elma also cooks large tasty meals (US$2 to US$4).

Doña Exy (road to airstrip; r with shared bathroom per person US$5) A huge bougainvillea bush greets visitors as they enter the humble grounds of this *hospedaje* (small hotel). The rooms themselves are basic – wood-plank walls with a tin roof and squishy beds – but clean. Meals are served upon request (mains US$2.25). The on-site generator, which runs from 6pm to 9pm nightly, is a plus.

Doña Mendilia (on airstrip; r with shared bathroom per person US$3) A beautiful and well-tended garden is the highlight of this huge old place, the 2nd floor of which houses the guestrooms. Each room has a foam bed with clean linens and is divided from the others by paper-thin walls. Located right on the airstrip, the rickety balcony has great views of the puddle jumpers making their high-speed landings just a few feet away –

very cool in a please-don't-crash-into-us sort of way.

Doña Cecilia (road to beach; r with shared bathroom per person US$6) A cleared grassy lot with two simple buildings – Doña Cecilia's home and the guesthouse – this place has a handful of rooms for visitors. Accommodations are no-frills, but then again, that's pretty much standard around here. Meals, unfortunately, are not offered.

Getting There & Away

There is a landing strip/soccer field at the eastern end of town that is the dividing point between Rais Ta and Belén. Half-way down one side of it is a small wood building that houses the **SAMI office** (6:30am-5pm Mon-Sat). Be sure to check in at 6.30am since flight departures change on a whim. Prepare to wait anywhere from half an hour to a day or two.

An early morning *colectivo* boat takes passengers from Rais Ta to Palacios, in time to catch the first speedboat to Iriona. For Río Plátano, a *colectivo* pickup truck passes every hour (US$2.75, 45 minutes); another passes in the other direction at the same frequency, making stops in Cocobila, Ibans, and Plaplaya. For Brus Laguna, you can take a *colectivo* boat (US$16, two to three hours) or hire an *expreso* (US$80, two hours). You may have better luck finding a *colectivo* by taking the truck to Río Plátano first.

BELÉN

Belén is essentially an extension of Rais Ta (and itself bleeds into the next town, Nuevo Jerusalén). The airstrip and tall water tower mark the division. Like its neighbor, Belén is quiet and bucolic, though more spread out and without Rais Ta's thick canopy of trees. Then again, Belén's lone sleeping option is one of the area's best, and just steps from a beautiful windblown beach.

A community telephone and a couple of general stores are located a short walk from Pawanka Beach Cabins. There are no signs, but most are pretty self evident. When in doubt, locals are invariably happy to help. At some point, the town of Belén ends and Nuevo Jerusalén begins – the difference is imperceptible to most visitors, but worth mentioning as you may be directed there for services. Just keep walking – it's impossible to get lost!

The **teléfono comunitario** (community phone; 8am-7pm Mon-Sat) is in a large building, unmistakable for the antennae and satellite dishes on its roof. Rates are US$0.25 to US$0.50 per minute for domestic calls, US$0.40 and up for USA and the rest of the world. Several **pulperías** (general stores; 7am-6pm Mon-Sat) sell basic groceries and snacks.

Sights & Activities

A very nice walk – which Mario Miller of Pawanka Beach Cabins is likely to take you on as a matter of course – is from the cabins through Nuevo Jerusalén to the beach. Mario has numerous stories to tell about the town, various people and events, all in all presenting an interesting snapshot of the area. You can return via the beach, collecting shells and driftwood. Ships are often moored offshore; many are lobster ships, which Mario can also describe, having been a lobster diver himself. You can do the same trip on horseback – there's nothing quite like galloping on the beach with the wind in your hair. Ask Mario for details.

Mario can also arrange any of the hikes mentioned in Rais Ta (see p284) and has other outings in the works, including manatee-spotting and nighttime crocodile-spotting. None had been finalized at the time of research, but are worth asking about.

Most guests are treated to – or roped into, depending on your taste for these things – a bonfire on the beach with traditional music, singing and dancing by local community members. Of course, the foreigners are always pulled up to dance, usually several times over the course of the hour-long gathering. You can try feigning a sprained ankle, but it's easier to just go with the flow. The rough folksy songs, accompanied by a guitar and washboard, are the highlight of the evening. Kids often perform a dance that appears to be a Miskito version of 'London Bridge is Falling Down', which can be fun.

Sleeping & Eating

Pawanka Beach Cabins (per person US$10; meals US$4) Too bad there are only two cabins here, because these are the nicest ones around. They're identical in design to the Yamari Cabañas outside Brus Laguna, with screen walls, mosquito nets, thick firm mattresses and crisp linens. The ocean waves lull you to sleep at night, while Pico Baltimore, off in the distance, greets you in the morning. And Pawanka has real flush toilets and even a standup shower with shower head if you could use some creature comforts.

Getting There & Away

A *colectivo* boat headed to Palacios passes Belén at around 3am to 3:30am (US$8, two hours). The pier is about 10 minutes on foot to/from Pawanka Beach Cabins; the airport is about the same distance, toward Rais Ta. Mario can help arrange transport to Las Marías from here; the trip takes five to six hours (US$190 round trip), and costs slightly more if you stay longer than two nights.

COCOBILA

The tidiest of the towns on this stretch of coastline, Cocobila's brightly painted wood houses are spaced widely along the main road with large grassy lots between them. As you walk down the road, you can spot the ocean to one side and the lagoon to the other, as breezes push gently across the thin peninsula. There is precious little to do in Cocobila – it has none of the tourist infrastructure that other towns have – but for many travelers its refreshing change of pace is a perfectly good reason to visit. You can easily walk here and back from Belén or Rais Ta if you find yourself with a day or afternoon to kill – plan on 30 to 45 minutes walking each way – or stay a night or two in the simple *hospedajes*. The beach is scenically unkempt.

There is a basic medical clinic in town, **Clínica Privada Judith** (24hr); it is run by Judith Sandoval, a nurse trained in Tegucigalpa with over three decades of experience (her diplomas and licences are prominently displayed to prove it). Look for the green-and-white striped building on the main road.

There are two **community telephones** (per min national US$0.50, USA US$1.60, rest of world US$2.15, incoming call per min US$0.15; 7:30am-8pm Mon-Sat, noon-8pm Sun) located several hundred meters apart on the main road. One is in a private home next door to Hospedaje El Nopal (☎ 401 5060-2) and the other is at nearby Hospedaje & Comedor Ethelinda (☎ 433 8219).

Sleeping & Eating

Hospedaje & Comedor Ethelinda (☎ 433 4219; per person US$5.50) Walking from Rais Ta you'll pass this guesthouse first, comprising four very basic rooms at the back of a private home with a small comedor in front. Rooms have a single cot (you can request another to be added), wood floors, and slat windows looking onto the family's cluttered backyard. A new *servicio* (toilet) was in the works at the time of research, but until it's ready the latrine is across the street – bring a flashlight if you tend to wee in the wee hours, so to speak. The existing toilet's on a nice piece of property actually: you can see the beach through the wood slats and sea breezes keep it odor-free.

Hospedaje El Nopal (r US$5.50) A couple of hundred meters further on is this small hotel with a huge nopal cactus in front – totally out of place in this tropical town, but thriving nonetheless. Rooms are clean and well kept, with cement floors, candles, even lace curtains. The latrine and shower – rainwater or well water, depending on the season – are out the back. The one big drawback here is the rock-hard beds. If no one is around when you arrive, ask for René or Ana at the wooden building across the street and just east of the hotel.

Merendero Baltimor Payaska (mains US$2-3; ☺ breakfast & lunch) Across from the elementary school, this eatery is run out of a small wood-plank home. You can get a mean plate of fried chicken pretty much any day of the week. Tasty *baleadas* (flour tortillas smeared with beans and melted butter) and *pasteles* (small pastries stuffed with meat and veggies) are often served as well.

There are two *pulperías* between Hospedaje Ethelinda and Hospedaje El Nopal, both open roughly from 6am to 9pm daily.

Getting There & Away

The nearest airport is in Belén, which you can walk to in 30 to 45 minutes. As with all the towns on this spit of land, a Palacios-bound boat passes around 3:30am (US$8, two hours) and *colectivos* headed the other direction pass periodically through the day. Pickup trucks shuttling passengers between the towns of Ibans and Río Plátano, and points in between, pass every hour or two (US$1 to US$2.75).

PLAPLAYA

pop 700

Plaplaya is Honduras' easternmost Garífuna community, a quiet disparate community spread out between the lagoon and a scenic ocean beach. Simple wood homes with thatched roofs and dirt floors are sprinkled along the narrow peninsula, connected by dirt paths that angle through small yucca plots. It is common to see women planting, harvesting, grating or compressing yucca, or in their homes standing before a hot wood-burning stove turning the flour into huge, slightly toasted, white *casabe* wafers.

Many consider Plaplaya to be the most traditional of Honduras' Garífuna villages. People here still live by fishing and yucca and banana cultivation, and have not suffered the outside encroachment or massive emigration, especially of young men, common in other communities. (Not that there is no emigration at all – many Plaplayans live and work in La Ceiba, the Bay Islands, San Pedro Sula and the United States.) The center of town has a growing problem with public drunkenness, but there are efforts afoot to ban cantinas, or to restrict them to certain hours. A visit to the turtle protection project is well worth doing, as is just walking around town and speaking with local people.

You can make national and international phone calls at **Pulpería Yohanna** (☎ 433 8221; per min domestic US$0.10-0.45, USA US$1, rest of world US$2.40; ☺ 7am-noon & 1-7pm). It is located a five-minute walk west of Hospedaje Doña Sede.

Sights & Activities

Visitors to Plaplaya should try to track down Doña Patrocinia Blanco, an extremely friendly and capable woman who lives in Barrio Berijales, west of the center. Doña Patrocinia happens *not* to be Garífuna, but moved to Plaplaya from Tegucigalpa more than 30 years ago after marrying a Garífuna man. Her house serves as the de facto visitors center, and she can help you to see (and participate in) *casabe* being made, Garífuna dancing, and the turtle project.

Plaplaya maintains a very successful **sea turtle preservation program** (☺ Feb-Sep), which brings many foreign tourists to the small town and is the source of no small amount of pride for local residents. The project was

LA MOSKITIA

WHAT TO BRING

Pack as you would for any outdoor excursion, including good shoes and lightweight rain gear. In addition, here are a few items that you'll appreciate having on any trip to the Moskitia.

Heavy-duty plastic bags for your backpack All that boat travel means you'll get at least one good soaking. Bring some extras to double-bag or replace ones that get torn.

Ziploc bags Same idea, for your camera, wallet etc.

Wide-brimmed hat and sunscreen You'll be spending a lot of time in an uncovered boat and the sun can be intense.

Lightweight long-sleeve shirt and pants Good for the sun, as well as mosquitoes.

Insect repellent Slather it on – mosquitoes and other buggers are active day and night.

Flashlight and extra batteries Most places you'll stay don't have electricity.

Small bills Bring more money than you think you'll need, and in small bills. It'll be a thick stack, but getting change (let alone extra money) can be impossible.

Water bottle and purification tablets Some guesthouses have jugs of purified water you can fill up from, but these are always good to have, especially on overnight trips in the rainforest.

Toilet paper You never know when you'll need it – an extra roll can go a long way.

Malaria pills Recommended in the Moskitia, and through the north coast of Honduras.

---

started in 1995 with the help of a peace corps volunteer, and protects up to 50 turtle nests every year. Four different species nest here: *caray*, *verde* (green), *caurama* (*Caretta caretta* or loggerhead) and *baula* (leatherbacks, the largest sea turtles in the world). Between February and September, travelers can accompany volunteers on nightly patrols, in search of new nests and turtles laying their eggs. The turtles are measured and the eggs removed to a large nursery, where they have 24-hour protection against other animals and poachers. In 65 days – usually between June and August – the eggs begin to hatch and visitors can help release them into the ocean. The project also goes to schools in various communities to educate children on turtle preservation. *Día de la Tortuga* (Day of the Turtle) is celebrated every year on May 22, in commemoration of the day, in 1995, when the project's first turtles were born.

There's not much to see or do outside of the nesting season, unfortunately. A sea-turtle mural at the local school is worth a peek, though.

Sleeping & Eating

Hospedaje Doña Sede (main rd; r with shared bathroom US$6) This *hospedaje* offers three basic rooms with cement floors and a corrugated tin roof. Beds have mosquito nets and there is a generator on-site (which means rooms get electricity until 10pm) – both huge pluses. As with every hotel around, the bathroom is located in an outhouse; the

shower, in this case, is a hose with a pail. *Típica* meals are provided upon request (US$2.25 to US$3.25).

Doña Vazilia (on lagoon; r with shared bathroom per person US$4) Just down the way from Doña Sede's place, this is a very simple, two-room structure with worn beds. The outhouse is pretty basic – prepare to hold your breath. Meals are provided upon request (US$2.25).

Pulpería Yohanna (☎ 433 8221; ☺ 7am-noon & 1-7pm) A five-minute walk west of Doña Sede's, this place has a limited selection of pasta and canned foods, plus water, soda, and light snacks.

Getting There & Away

From almost any pier on the lagoon, you can wait for a passing collective boat to go east to Belén (US$8, 45 minutes) or to any of the points along the way, including Ibans, Cocobila, and Rais Ta. The boat to Palacios (US$3.25, 45 minutes) passes around 4am.

RESERVA DE LA BIÓSFERA DEL RÍO PLÁTANO

The Río Plátano Biosphere Reserve is surely the most magnificent nature reserve in Honduras. A World Heritage site established jointly in 1980 by Honduras and the UN, it is home to abundant bird, mammal and aquatic life, including a number of exotic and endangered species in the river and surrounding jungle. The best time of year for travelers to visit is between November and July, and the best time for seeing birds is between February and March, when many migratory birds are in the area.

LAS MARÍAS

Las Marías occupies a broad patch of rainforest formed by a loop in the Río Plátano. It is a town of mixed ethnicity, with around 100 Miskito and Pech families living in relative harmony. The Pech population had declined significantly, but the arrival of several families from upriver in Olancho has

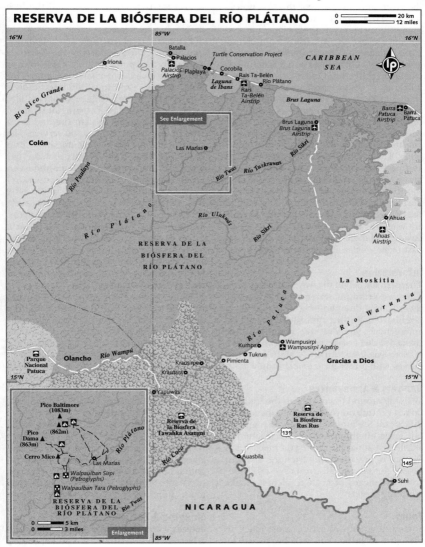

RESERVA DE LA BIÓSFERA DEL RÍO PLÁTANO

LA MOSKITIA

reinvigorated the normally reticent group. Men and women from both communities participate in the guide program – if your guide is Pech, they'll likely let you know.

Orientation

Two of the main *hospedajes* – Doña Diana and Doña Rutilia – are side-by-side along the river, and are some of the first houses in Las Marías you'll reach coming upriver; many travelers stay at these places for convenience's sake. A path leads from behind Doña Diana's up a small rise to a third guesthouse – Doña Justa – that is definitely worth checking out. One of the town's two *pulperías* is a short distance from the entrance to Doña Justa's. Continuing on the path you'll reach the center of town – so to speak – a grassy and little-used airstrip with the clinic on one side and another guesthouse, Hospedaje Don Ovidio, on the other. The path meanders on, over a bridge, and past two churches and a fourth guesthouse (Don Luís), before reconnecting with the river near the put-in for *pipante* trips upriver. The path forms a loop – touted as the 'Village Trail' – that makes for a pleasant walk if you have some free time. Bring a flashlight if there's any chance you'll be out past dusk – when it gets dark it gets *dark*.

Information

There isn't much in the way of services here. There's no running water or electricity, and there is only one phone in town (see Hospedaje Doña Rutilia, opposite). For medical emergencies, you'll receive treatment at the **Clínica de Salud** (center of town; ☺ 7:30am-3pm Mon-Fri, emergencies 24hr), which is staffed by two nurses with a meager medical supply.

Dangers & Annoyances

Walking around town, stay on the trail and do not venture on your own into the forest – this is still the jungle, after all. At night, do not leave anything outside, even laundry. While just about everyone you meet in Las Marías is gracious and friendly, modern shoes, clothes and electronics – so far beyond the means of most residents – make tempting targets.

Tours

Sometime after you arrive, most likely in the early evening, you will be visited by the current *sacaguía,* or head guide. Elected every six months, the *sacaguía* is responsible for greeting newly arrived visitors, helping you determine what tours you'd like to take, and assigning the necessary guides. The *sacaguía's* fee is US$3.75 per group per tour, which you typically pay on the spot. They'll probably also ask for a small donation for trail maintenance and the like; it's not required, but a couple of dollars is definitely appreciated.

Prices for a given tour depend on the number of guides required – the Cerro de Zapote tour requires just one guide for one day, while Pico Dama takes three guides for three days. On any tour, the lead guide is paid US$11 per day, while secondary guides receive US$8 per day. You are not required to pay for the guides' food or supplies, but a 10% tip is customary for good service. The cabins en route to Pico Dama and Cerro Baltimore cost US$3.75 per person per night. Ask the owner of your guesthouse in Las Marías about stowing gear you won't need on your hike. It should be perfectly fine, but do put a lock on your rucksack, and bring along especially important items, like your passport, plane tickets and cash. This can start to add up – all told, a Pico Dama trip costs almost US$100 – so be sure you bring enough cash, always in small bills. Neither the prices nor the number of required guides is negotiable.

Finally, 8am is the standard departure time, which, after introductions, gathering up gear, walking to the boat or the trailhead, and explaining one thing or another, can easily turn into 9am – way too late for bird- or animal-spotting. If you're up for it, tell the *sacaguía* you want to start at 5:30am or 6am; with any luck you'll be on your way no later than 7am and have a better chance of seeing creatures. See boxed text, opposite, for more details.

The only informal tour in town is the **Crocodile Tour** (per group US$16) – a two-hour twilight walk around a crocodile-infested lagoon. Sounds a little edgy, but no one has gotten hurt so far. Plus, the photo opps are excellent. Stop by Hospedaje Doña Justa to set it up.

Sleeping & Eating

Hospedaje Doña Justa (center of town; r with shared bathroom per person US$5) This is a thatch-roofed building with several airy rooms overlooking a huge flower garden. Each room is well-kept and has decent beds with mosquito nets. There's a big patio with lots of hammocks, perfect for whiling away an afternoon with a book. Meals are prepared upon request (mains US$2 to US$3).

Hospedaje Doña Rutilia (on the river; r with shared bathroom per person US$6) Twenty-one beds distributed in several private rooms make up this rambling guesthouse. Some beds have outright mattresses (as opposed to foam cushions) and rooms are relatively clean. The only generator and telephone in town are here too – both pluses if you need, or just like to have, these modern conveniences. Breakfast, lunch and dinner (US$2.50 to US$3) are also offered.

Hospedaje Doña Diana (on the river; r with shared bathroom per person US$5) Two plank wood buildings overlooking the Río Plátano house four private rooms here. Each has a couple of foam beds with mosquito nets and is kept reasonably clean. Meals can be prepared

---

INTO THE WILD: TOURS FROM LAS MARÍAS

There are half a dozen different tours available from Las Marías, of varying lengths and difficulty. Some involve rigorous hiking, others only moderate; some have lots of boat time, others none at all. If you're up for it, Pico Dama and Cerro Baltimore are truly terrific hikes, and afford the best chance of seeing birds, animals, and primary forest (which is why you came, right?). Cerro Mico and Cerro de Zapote are good if you want something less strenuous. The one-day petroglyph tour is very popular, especially with groups, but involves an awful lot of boat time, especially considering you just spent five hours on a *cayuco* to get here and will spend another five to return.

Pico Dama (3 days; 3 guides; difficult) The toughest tour starts with a two-hour *pipante* ride upriver, then a mild three- to four-hour hike through primary and secondary forest to a cabin with simple beds and an area for camping (linens and mosquito nets can be rented in Las Marías for US$2.25 per night). Day Two is a steep three- to four-hour hike through thick vegetation to the base of Pico Dama's distinctive rock pinnacle. Views are spectacular, and the bird and animal life abundant throughout. You return to camp that afternoon, and hike out the following day. For an even longer trip, add the second half of the Cerro Mico tour with a stop at the lower petroglyphs.

Cerro Baltimore (2 days; 2 guides; moderate to difficult) This hike begins from Las Marías with a rolling five- to seven-hour hike through primary and secondary forest, teeming with wildlife. You overnight at a rustic camp-house then wake up early to climb the summit – a two-hour hike with incredible views of Laguna de Ibans and the Caribbean Sea beyond. Return to Las Marías on the same day via a different route.

Cerro Mico (2 days; 3 guides; moderate) This tour begins as the petroglyph tours do, making your way by *pipante* and foot to Walpaulban Sirpi. Camp along the river or stay at a nearby *hospedaje*, and the next day climb Cerro Mico – which is not called 'Monkey Hill' for nothing – returning on a different path to the river where the *pipante* is waiting to take you downstream to Las Marías. You could add a day to this trip by continuing upriver to Walpaulban Tara, the second set of petroglyphs.

Cerro de Zapote (1 day; 1 guide; moderate) This up-and-back hike is essentially the first part of the Cerro Baltimore trip. Starting from Las Marías, you hike through fairly flat terrain, with only one steep hill before turning back. This hike has good bird-watching opportunities without having to stay the night outside of Las Marías – be sure to start early!

Walpaulban Sirpi (1 day; 3 guides; easy) Las Marías' most popular tour begins with a two-hour *pipante* ride upriver before disembarking at the beginning of the Kuyuzqui trail. A moderate 1½- to two-hour hike includes stopping at a new observation tower (still under construction when we hiked by) – the support beams were hand cut, and it took 50 men to carry each one up. Birds and animals are relatively rare, owing to the foot traffic and because you get here relatively late. After seeing the petroglyphs and lunching by the river, you return to Las Marías.

Walpaulban Tara (2 days; 3 guides; easy) Start out as the Walpaulban Sirpi tour does, but rather than return, camp or stay the night at the nearby *hospedaje*. The next day is similar, continuing upriver in the *pipante*, with short hikes along the way. Return to Las Marías in the afternoon.

LA MOSKITIA

upon request (US$2 to US$3) and are served on the porch outside your room; it's convenient and pretty, but, unfortunately, can attract roaches.

Hospedaje Don Ovidio (center of town; r with shared bathroom per person US$5) This is a thatch-roofed building with several private rooms, all with squishy beds and no window screens (lather on the bug repellent). The bathroom facilities are a serious highlight: there's a toilet seat and the outdoor shower is attached to the main building. Meals are prepared upon request (mains US$2.15).

Hospedaje Don Luís (toward the river; r with shared bathroom per person US$5) The *hospedaje* of last resort in town, the rooms here are on the wrong side of clean and the beds are so saggy, you might as well sleep on the floor. The cement bathroom with ceramic toilet bowl would be a plus if you didn't have to push pigs out of the way to get to it.

Hospedaje Wehnatara (r with shared bathroom per person US$4) Located a 35-minute canoe trip upriver, this is an alternative place to stay if you want to explore the petroglyphs, Cerro Mico or Pico Dama. It offers two rooms in a wood building that overlooks the river. Accommodations are basic but adequate. All meals are prepared upon request (US$2.25).

Pulpería Yehimy (center of town; 5am-6pm Mon-Sat) Basic foodstuffs and medicines are sold at this tiny bodega.

Getting There & Away

An *expreso* from Rais Ta to Las Marías has a fixed price of US$190 (five to six hours) – ouch. There are no *colectivos*, though you can often join up with other travelers, or even a tour group, to share the cost. The fare is for a round-trip, with two nights at Las Marías included. The boatman waits in Las Marías, so after the second night it'll cost you an extra US$8 per night.

BRUS LAGUNA & AROUND

The name Brus Laguna (pronounced 'Bruce', as in Springsteen) comes from 'Brewer's Lagoon', after the pirate Bloody Brewer who used it as his hideaway. Today, Brus Laguna (the town) is tucked into a sheltered corner of Brus Laguna (the lagoon) and is one of two towns in La Moskitia receiving regular flights from La Ceiba (the other is Puerto Lempira).

BRUS LAGUNA TOWN
pop 4195

Brus Laguna is a dusty, one-road town, notable mainly for the thrice-weekly Sosa flights that land at its narrow dirt airstrip. Most people go straight from the airport to the boat dock, bound by motorboat for Rais Ta or even straight to Las Marías. However, if you're not crunched for time, consider spending a night at Yamari Cabañas (p294), a new set of cabins outside of town, built on a broad grassy savannah. There is also world-class flat fishing in and around the lagoon, including snook, grouper and record-size tarpon.

Orientation & Information

Brus Laguna has one main drag, a wide dirt road that extends uninterrupted from the pier to the airport, several kilometers away. Just about everything you need is on or near the main road, within a few blocks of the pier. If you're ever unsure, just ask the first person to pass – locals are very friendly, and every year more accustomed to backpack-toting foreigners in their midst.

CESAMO (443 8082; 7:30am-noon & 2-5pm Mon-Fri) is the only medical center in town; services are very basic, but there is always a doctor and nurse on staff. It's located in a blue-and-white building next to the **police** (443 8015; 24hr). On the other side of the main drag is **Hondutel** (7:30am-3:30pm Mon-Fri), where you can make national and international calls.

Sleeping & Eating

Stay in town if you're here just to catch a flight; otherwise, the best accommodations are a short boat ride away (see Yamari Cabañas, p294). A third hotel was being built in town when we passed through, and may be worth asking about when you arrive.

Hotel La Estancia (433 8043; main st; r/tw US$14/16, with shared bathroom US$8/11) This is an out-and-out hotel in the middle of the bush. OK, it's not exactly a fancy hotel and Brus Laguna isn't exactly the bush, but La Estancia is a far cry from roughing it. Rooms are clean, if a bit worn, and have a fan and even cable TV. Second-floor rooms get a nice breeze too. From the main dock, take the first left; it's located just a few doors down on your right.

Laguna Paradise (☎ 433 8039; r/tw US$11/16) Located over Pulpería Vanesa, this is a decent option if La Estancia is full. Beds are a little saggy and the cement walls and floors could be better kept, but it'll do for a night or two. All rooms have fans, cable TV, and private bathrooms – a welcome change after you've spent a few weeks wearing the same two T-shirts and bathing in a river.

Cafetería Doña Nohemy (main st; mains US$2.25-3.25; ☺ breakfast, lunch & dinner) The only restaurant in town, Doña Nohemy will feed you every day of the week as long as you're not picky about what you get. Just be sure it's freshly made – items sit around until they're eaten. Scrambled eggs and sandwiches are safe bets.

Pulpería Vanesa (main st; ☺ 6am-7pm) The biggest *pulpería* in town, this place also has the best variety of goods. Apart from lots of foodstuffs, you will also find mosquito repellent, mosquito nets, rain gear, and batteries (but no sunblock, unfortunately). It's a good place to shop if you've forgotten something from home.

Entertainment

Brus Laguna has a **movie theater** (admission US$0.25; ☺ 7pm daily, 1pm, 3pm & 7pm Sun) – sort of.

It's a digital projector connected to a DVD player, with a dozen or so plastic chairs set up in a private house on the main drag. (It's run by the same family that operates the bus to the airport, in fact.) Most movies are dubbed in Spanish and action-oriented: *King Kong*, yes, *Capote*, no.

Getting There & Away
AIR

At the time of research, **Aerolineas Sosa** (www.aerolineassosa.com) had flights from La Ceiba to Brus Laguna (US$89 one way, one hour) at 10am on Monday, Wednesday, and Friday, returning from Brus Laguna the same days at 11am. You can reserve and purchase Sosa tickets (cash only) at the **general store** (☎ 433 8042; ☺ 6am-7pm Mon-Sat, to noon Sun) near the main pier. They're small planes, so it's recommended you make reservations well in advance (and double-check fares and schedules while you're at it).

SAMI (☎ 433 8031; ☺ 6:30am-5pm Mon-Sat) has even smaller planes – taking six to nine passengers – and serves towns within the Moskitia, including Puerto Lempira (US$44 one way), Ahuas (US$30), Belén (US$30), Wampusirpi (US$53), and Palacios (US$33). The ticket office accepts cash only and is at a bodega several blocks up the main drag from the pier. Flights leave anytime between

---

CANNON ISLAND

In the southwest corner of Brus Laguna (the lagoon) is Cannon Island, a small island that has seen its fair share of history. British marines occupied the islet in the 1700s and fortified it with cannons, which, still there, gave the island its name.

Later, it was a temporary camp for around 250 Scottish settlers who arrived in 1822 and 1823, lured by tales of fertile lands, pliant natives, even government jobs in a newly formed nation called Territory of Poyais. It was all an elaborate self-indulgence of Scottish adventurer Gregor MacGregor (what a name!), who evidently believed he had been given sovereign rights to some 34,500 sq km at the mouth of the Río Negro by the Miskito king. The settlers soon realized the folly of their situation and ensconced themselves on Cannon Island, refusing to venture into what was then unconquered indigenous territory. They were eventually evacuated by British ships from present-day Belize, but not before disease and despair had taken root – at least one settler committed suicide and 180 died of various causes stemming from the ordeal. MacGregor managed to escape blame – survivors even defended him in the British press – and he concocted several similar schemes before retiring to Venezuela, where he died in 1845.

More recently, Cannon Island became known among anglers for its snook and tarpon flats. Record tarpon have been landed here, including several 200-pounders. A fishing camp opened on the island in 1995, but has since changed hands, and disputes over leasing rights have stalled its reopening. Some tours include a stop here to check out the cannons and a small museum created by the original fishing camp operators. Some tour guides and boat drivers can arrange a brief stop on the island. You may need to negotiate a fee.

7am and 2pm (Monday to Saturday only); plan on waiting around all day, and cross your fingers the wait's not two or three days. The flight may make a few stops along the way, depending on where you and the other passengers are headed.

Brus Laguna's airport – a narrow dirt strip with a kiosk on one side for passengers to wait under – is several kilometers from town. A small school bus ferries passengers to and from all Sosa flights (per person US$2.75 – ouch!), while the SAMI guy usually takes passengers there in his pick-up (and charges the same).

BOAT

Motor boats carry passengers from the town pier to various points in and outside the lagoon. *Colectivos* from Brus Laguna to Belén leave the main pier between 5am and 6am daily (per person US$16, three hours). An *expreso* for the same trip costs around US$80 for up to six people.

You can also arrange a boat straight from Brus Laguna to Las Marías. The trip takes five to six hours and costs around US$185 roundtrip, including two nights in Las Marías. The boat holds up to eight people, but costs the same if there are only two. To stay longer in Las Marías, it's US$11 per night. It's important you hire a reliable boat driver, as the trip across the lagoon and up the Río Plátano can be tricky. Juan Membreno and 'El Chele' are recommended, or ask the Woods (see Yamari Cabañas, below) for more suggestions.

Whether you're headed to Rais Ta/Belén or Las Marías, you may be able to get a ride (for a fee) with a tour group; there's likely to be one on the plane from La Ceiba. If you go the same day, don't dally, as wind and waves on the lagoon grow dangerously strong in the afternoon.

OUTSIDE BRUS LAGUNA

An hour's boat ride from Brus Laguna, **Yamari Cabañas** (per person US$10) are two rustic but very comfortable wood cabins built on stilts on a broad grassy savannah. The grassy expanse is bisected by a long meandering creek, and studded here and there with clusters of small tique palms. It is an unusual landscape – you almost expect a giraffe to appear – certainly not what most people would expect when they plan a trip to La Moskitia. And there's

nothing else out here, save a few ranchers and the occasional cow. The cabins are operated by Macoy and Dorcas Wood, a serious but friendly couple who will go out of their way to make your stay pleasant.

A visit to Yamari Cabins typically includes a long walk through the savannah. If the water is high, you can float back down the creek to the cabins on inner-tubes. When the water is low, there's still a great little swimming hole a few meters from the cabins. At night, Macoy can take you in the boat to go crocodile-spotting.

The cabins themselves are thatch-roofed, with four individual beds apiece and mosquito nets hanging down. The mattresses are surprisingly thick – the sort you'd find in a good hotel – and the linens fresh and clean. But what makes the cabins lovely is their screen walls, which let in all the sounds and sights around you. Sunsets and sunrises are sublime, accompanied by the songs of countless birds. Meals (US$4) are served in a separate building.

The cabins are about an hour by motorized *cayuco* from Brus Laguna, and transportation is included in the price. Macoy or Dorcas meet you at the airport or pier, and accompany most guests, along with a guide and a cook, for their stay at Yamari. Do not simply make your own way there – not only do few boatmen in town know the way, the cabins are opened only when the Woods (who live in Brus Laguna proper) are expecting guests.

RÍO PATUCA

Honduras' second-longest river stretches 500km from its headwaters in Olancho to the Caribbean Sea. It passes through the pristine Patuca National Park, the Tawahka Asangni Biosphere Reserve, and along the edge of the Reserva de la Biósfera del Río Plátano. Most travelers reach this remote area by plane, to Ahuas or Wampusirpi, though week-long rafting expeditions starting in Olancho are possible – and tempting – too.

AHUAS
pop 1553

Ahuas is the largest town along the Río Patuca, which is not to say it's huge: about 1500 people live here, mostly Miskito. It is a quiet place a few kilometers from the river itself, with wood homes, a few churches and an airstrip. It also has a **hospital** that is run by volunteer doctors from abroad and considered one of the best in the region. Ahuas used to be the main jumping off point for trips into the Tawahka region, but the travelers who make it here – very few indeed – now tend to fly all the way to Wampusirpi, and start upriver from there.

Sleeping & Eating

Hotel Mi Estrella (r US$6) Upstairs rooms here are cheaper, yet nicer, with more air and light. The mattresses are extremely thin, however, and tall travelers may have some overhang. Meals (US$2 to US$3) are served upon request.

Getting There & Away

SAMI (☎ in Brus Laguna 433 8031, in Puerto Lempira 433 6016) is the only airline with services to Ahuas. Virtually all flights come from Brus Laguna (US$30) or Puerto Lempira (US$33). There is no fixed schedule, and as with all SAMI flights you may have to wait a day or two before getting on a plane.

Boats from Barra Patuca stop in Ahuas to load and unload cargo, and either continue upriver to Wampusirpi, or turn around and go back. You may be able to talk your way onto one of those boats, though they have no fixed schedule or prices. Note that the river is a solid hour's walk from the town itself.

WAMPUSIRPI

pop 1509

An appealingly rustic little town, Wampusirpi is of Tawahka origin, but most of its residents are now Miskito. They live simple though somewhat precarious lives, surviving on small plots of rice, beans, bananas, and yucca, supplemented by fish from the Patuca River and whatever small game they can hunt down in the surrounding hills. Wampusirpi proper is a collection of wooden homes on stilts – the river and a nearby lagoon are prone to flooding – while some 23 smaller communities (some just a cluster of homes) are scattered nearby.

Wampusirpi is by no means a tourist town, though townspeople are accustomed to a trickle of foreign missionaries, service workers and travelers. A number of people pass through on their way to Tawahka, further upriver. It's easy to spend a day or more quietly exploring the town, meeting local folks and soaking up the small-town atmosphere.

There are no formal services in Wampusirpi, save a small *centro médico* (health center) on the road between town and the airport. The lagoon is used by children for swimming and by women for laundry. A thick pipe drawing a good flow of cold spring water is used for bathing and for drinking. You may be able to find bottled water at one of the *pulperías* in town – locals drink straight from the pipe – but it's essential travelers in this area carry plenty of water purification tablets or a small bottle of chlorine. See p326, for more info.

February to March is the best and driest time of year to come. During the rainy season, especially June and July, the paths get extremely muddy and the mosquitoes are especially voracious. No matter what time of year, a pair of good boots is a must; if you only brought flip-flops, a pair of rubber boots runs at about US$7 in the small market here, or in any Moskitia town.

Sleeping & Eating

At least three families rent rooms in their homes to travelers and volunteers. None of the houses have signs, but anyone in town would be able to point you in the right direction. All are very basic, with cots and latrine toilets. One guesthouse, known as **La Cabaña** (r US$5), is in the middle of town and has large-ish rooms. The others are near the *puente roto* (broken bridge) at the far end of the main road, near the lagoon. The one on the right as you approach charges US$4 per person, and the hosts can help you arrange transport up- or downriver. Some travelers have reported staying at the **Catholic Mission** (dm US$2), which has dorm-like lodging.

There are no *comedores*, per se, but you should be able to arrange a meal at your guesthouse or another home in town, just by asking around. The Catholic Mission may have a kitchen guests can use, provided you pay for the gas.

Getting There & Away

As usual, **SAMI** (☎ in Brus Laguna 433 8031, in Puerto Lempira 433 6016) has the only air service to Wampusirpi. Flights typically come from

Brus Laguna (US$53) or Puerto Lempira (US$49), usually stopping at Ahuas on the way in or out.

Wampusirpi's grass airstrip is a 15-minute walk outside of town. Trucks meet arriving planes, charging US$0.50 for a ride into town. SAMI has a small office on the road into town where you can buy and confirm tickets.

Boats, mostly carrying cargo, come and go occasionally and you may be able to convince a passing captain (and pay him enough) to give you a ride upriver to Krausirpe in the Tawahka region, or downriver to Ahuas and Barra de Patuca, on the ocean. A more reliable, and more expensive, alternative would be to negotiate with a local boatman for a trip of a certain time and distance, depending on your designs and his availability.

TAWAHKA REGION

Further up the Río Patuca, and deep in the rainforest, are the towns of Krausirpe and Krautara. Both are considered Tawahka communities, though Krausirpe, like Wampusirpi, has a growing Miskito population. Krautara is smaller and more isolated, and remains 100% Tawahka.

Community leaders in Krausirpe have tried to establish eco-tourism programs like the ones in Las Marías and elsewhere in the Moskitia, though with little lasting success. Whether this is due to a lack of infrastructure or experience, the remoteness of the area, or reticence on the part of ordinary Tawahka – or some combination of these factors – is not entirely clear. But as tourism in La Moskitia grows, it stands to reason that the Tawahka region will slowly open to foreign visitors as well.

THE TAWAHKA

Honduras' smallest ethnic group is the Tawahka indigenous people. By most accounts there are only about 1000 Tawahka people in Honduras (another 8000 or so live in Nicaragua). They are also the most isolated of Honduran ethnic groups, living in a handful of communities along the Patuca and Wampú rivers, including Krausirpe (the largest), Krautara, Yapawas, Kamakasna and Parwas. They were the last of Honduras' indigenous groups to be contacted by European explorers, and also the last to be converted to Christianity.

The Tawahka live much as they have for centuries, through fishing and subsistence farming, growing mostly plantains, rice, beans and yucca. European colonizers introduced them to panning for gold, which remains a source of extra income for some. The Tawahka are also adept hunters, using trained dogs – only a quarter of households own a gun of any sort – to capture armadillos, peccaries, and tapirs. But the Tawahka are perhaps best known for their production of enormous dugout canoes. Made from a single mahogany log, the canoes can measure a remarkable 10m long. The Tawahka rarely use their impressive creations, though – most are sold downriver.

The Tawahka language – called *twanka* – is still widely spoken. However, it has been deeply infiltrated with Miskito and subsequently English (since almost a third of Miskito words come from English). More alarming is the illiteracy rate: a study of one typical community found 96% of men, and 100% of the women, could not read. Few children attend school beyond the third grade.

Accustomed to isolation, the Tawahka have seen their ancestral lands severely reduced by the encroachment of mainstream farmers, ranchers and timber harvesters in the Río Patuca area. In 1999 – after much foot dragging – the Honduran government approved the creation of the Reserva de la Biosfera Tawahka Asangni, setting aside 250,000 hectares of traditional Tawahka territory. A victory for the Tawahka people was a victory for the environment as well. The reserve accounts for just 2% of Honduras' landmass, but contains a whopping 90% of its mammal species. It borders three other protected areas – the Reserva de la Biósfera del Río Plátano to the north, the Río Patuca National Park to the south, and the Bosawas National Park in Nicaragua to the east – and together they form a key nexus in the Mesoamerican Biological Corridor, spanning all seven Central American countries.

The Tawahka were for many years referred to as Sumo, a term you still read and hear occasionally. It was the name Miskitos used when describing their upriver neighbors to European explorers. But it was almost certainly pejorative – the Miskito and Tawahka have historically been rivals, and some say the name was Miskito for 'inferior.' True or not, today it is considered very un-PC.

Sights & Activities

By far the best way to see the Tawahka region – and the Moskitia rainforest as a whole – is on a seven- to 10-day rafting expedition down the Río Patuca. That trip, and a similar one down the Río Plátano, are among the most adventurous to be had in Honduras, and unforgettable ways to experience La Moskitia in its full glory. The Patuca trip starts near the town of Catacamas in Olancho and takes you right through the Tawahka Asangni Biosphere Reserve, with stops along the way, including Krausirpe. Omega Tours and La Moskitia Ecoaventuras, both based in La Ceiba, offer recommended trips down the Patuca and Plátano rivers. See p280 for more info.

In Krausirpe, it's possible to arrange **hikes** through the rainforest, which has abundant birds and wildlife (though spotting them, as always, can be tough). Local guides can also take you to nearby **caves** and **petroglyphs**. Lorenzo Macling, a local resident and leader, is a good source of information and assistance.

Sleeping

There is a rural medical center in Krausirpe where travelers can ask to stay the night. There is no fee, but the doctors and staff certainly appreciate small donations. Krautara has no formal accommodations or guesthouses, but you can ask around for a room or a place to camp.

Getting There & Away

Without a doubt, the best way to visit the Tawahka region is on a seven- or 10-day rafting trip down the Río Patuca. The trip takes you right through the Tawahka Asangni Biosphere Reserve, with stops along the way, including in Krausirpe.

If you have the time and money, a rafting trip down the Río Patuca (see above) is hard to beat. If you're already in La Moskitia – those trips start in Olancho – you can visit the region by catching a boat upriver from Barra Patuca, Ahuas or Wampusirpi. There are no fixed prices or schedules – you may have to wait several days in any of those towns before a boat (with room for passengers) passes by. You also can catch a flight on SAMI to Ahuas or Wampusirpi from Puerto Lempira or Brus Laguna, and take a boat from there.

LAGUNA DE CARATASCA

Laguna de Caratasca is by far the largest of La Moskitia's lagoons; if you include the cluster of smaller lagoons around it, the area practically amounts to an inland sea, complete with tides, waves and powerful currents. The lagoon is curiously shallow, however, averaging just 3m deep. Manatees, birds and other wildlife abound, especially in those areas isolated from human encroachment and poaching. Puerto Lempira is the largest town on the lagoon (and in La Moskitia) and there are a handful of other places around the lagoon worth visiting as well.

PUERTO LEMPIRA
pop 5110

Puerto Lempira is situated on the inland side of the Laguna de Caratasca. Connecting with several sub-lagoons, the lagoon is very large but not deep.

It is the largest town in La Moskitia, which is not to say it has, for example, paved roads. (It doesn't.) Still, it has much more of a big-town feel than any other place in the region, with a church, parque central, cars, city blocks, restaurants, Internet access and a bank.

Most travelers come (or leave) by plane, making for the biggest and busiest of the airports in La Moskitia. Some are on their way to or from Nicaragua's back door, via the town of Leimus on the Río Coco. For some, Puerto Lempira is an unavoidable stop in their quest for more and more remote adventures. Others welcome the return, however brief, to the trappings of modernity.

If you stay, there are at least two interesting side trips, doable in a day, but more pleasant as overnight excursions – Mistruk (p299) and Kaukira (p300).

Information

Banco Atlántida (🕑 8am-4:30pm Mon-Fri, 8:30-11:30am Sat) No ATM, but the teller can exchange traveler's checks and issue credit card advances on Visa cards. Often has long lines.

Cyberphone (☎ 419 0024; near Hotel Flores; Internet per min US$1.30; 🕑 8:40am-10:30pm) Calls to USA (per minute US$0.25) and Europe (per minute US$0.30 to US$0.40) too.

LA MOSKITIA

Hondutel Centro Comunitario (☎ 433 6270; to USA per minute US$0.15; ☯ 6:30am-10pm). Calls to other parts of the world start at US$0.50. It's situated a half-block west of park.

Hospital Puerto Lempira (☎ 433 6078, emergency 433 6978; ☯ 24hr) Located 1.5km southwest of town. From the airport, go roughly 10 blocks west until you cross a small concrete bridge. Turn left (south) and continue another 750m. If in doubt, ask any passerby.

Immigration office (☎ 433 6055; ☯ 8am-noon & 2-5pm Mon-Fri) Located on the 2nd floor of a commercial building, a half-block from Calle Principal on the same street as Hotel El Gran Samaritano.

Pharmacy (☯ 24hr) Located inside the hospital.

Dangers & Annoyances

As a port town and La Moskitia's largest town, Puerto Lempira is somewhat edgier than other places in the region, but not overly so. Most problems have something to do with alcohol, or sometimes drugs. Avoiding drugs and drunks altogether is the best way to stay safe.

Sleeping & Eating

Hotel Yu Baiwan (☎ 433 6348; s/d with fan US$16/19, with air-con US$19/24; ☒) Puerto Lempira's best hotel is also its best value, considering that the other hotels in town charge only a few dollars less for significantly inferior rooms. Here you get plenty of space, firm beds, clean linens, cable TV, and friendly service. The original nine rooms are all on the ground floor, while a rather grand curving stairway leads to nine new rooms being built on the 2nd floor. To get here, look for a narrow cement passageway

off Calle Principal, a half-block from the pier.

Hotel El Gran Samaritano (☎ 433 6482; s/tw with fan US$14/16, with air-con US$19/24; ☒) The 2nd-floor lobby of this small hotel is bright and airy, but the rooms are decidedly less so, with just a small window high on the wall to let in sunlight. Rooms are clean and come with cable TV, though, so it's not a bad option if the Yu Baiwan is full or you're really pinching pennies. You'll find it 1½ blocks west of Calle Principal.

Hotel Flores (☎ 433 6421; s/d/tr US$15/21/27; ☒) A half-block from the parque central east of Calle Principal, the Hotel Flores has somehow cultivated a reputation for being the best hotel in town, and is sometimes even full with visiting business people. Barring the existence of a secret luxury wing off-limits to inquiring guidebook writers, however, the hotel's stuffy rooms and vaguely smelly bathrooms don't justify the price or the hype. Service can be a bit gruff to boot.

Restaurante Lakou Payaska (mains US$5-8; ☯ breakfast, lunch & dinner) Miskito for 'lake breezes,' the Lakou Payaska gets plenty of them – and strong – on its 2nd-floor open-air dining area a few steps from the lagoon. Operated by (and opposite) Hotel Yu Baiwan, this is easily the most reliable meal in town, if not the most creative. Chicken, beef, lobster, and conch are served with the standard accompaniments, and sometimes a serving of loud country music. The main restaurant is out the back of the bar-snack joint that faces the street and is decidedly less appealing.

GETTING TO NICARAGUA

Getting to Nicaragua is easier than it used to be, thanks mainly to changes on the Nicaraguan side. From Puerto Lempira, trucks leave once a day for the town of Leimus along the Río Coco (US$11, 7:30am, four to five hours). You can pick up the truck outside its owners' house – three blocks west and two blocks south of the pier – or on parque central, near Banco Atlántida. Look for a large truck with a canvas covering. In Leimus, you pass Honduran immigration on one side of the river, and Nicaraguan immigration on the other. A new road means you can board a bus right there for Puerto Cabezas (five hours).

Before the new highway was built, you had to take a boat or 4WD downriver to Waspán to clear Nicaraguan immigration and catch a bus to Puerto Cabezas. That remains an alternative, if there are no buses from Leimus or the immigration office there is closed.

It costs US$7 to enter Nicaragua, US$3 to enter Honduras; neither is supposed to charge an exit fee, but occasionally officials ask for a nominal one. Trucks return from Leimus to Puerto Lempira twice daily, around 7am and 4pm.

THE MORAVIAN CHURCH

The Moravian Church, a Christian sect formed in present-day Czech Republic during the 1400s, has played an influential role in the Moskitia since its arrival in 1928. At that time, and well into the 1950s, the Honduran government paid little attention to conditions in the remote Moskitia province. Early Moravian missionaries found communities with no clinics, no schools, and no prospects for either. Poverty levels in the Moskitia were then – and remain today – some of the highest in the Americas, but have been significantly alleviated by Moravian efforts and programs.

The church opened the Moskitia's first health clinic in 1946 in Ahuas, and it remains the best medical center in the region. Other clinics followed in Kaukira and Ocotales. Moravian-run schools in Brus Laguna and Ahuas offer kids a chance to study beyond elementary school, a rarity in this part of the country, where children rarely attend school beyond the third grade and illiteracy is sky high. In the process, the Moravians have converted many thousands of Miskitos. The church began with a single congregation in Brus Laguna and today boasts nearly 100 congregations and over 22,000 members.

The Moravian Church in the Moskitia experienced a bitter split in 1999 when one of its ministers undertook a 40-day fast that resulted in spontaneous dancing and speaking in tongues. Believing he'd had a revelation, the minister introduced fasting to members of his congregation, which resulted in harsh disapproval from traditionalists in the church. 'Reformed' and 'traditional' factions formed, and disagreement soon spread to other matters. Most notably, the reformists condemned the use of pre-Christian rites, which had long been accepted in the traditional church. The conflict resulted in an official split in the church, and many communities now have two Moravian congregations.

Getting There & Away

The most reliable plane service to/from Puerto Lempira is on **Aerolineas Sosa** (☎ 433 6432; www.aerolineassosa.com; ✆ 8:30am-5:30pm Mon-Fri, to noon Sat & Sun), which has a large office facing the airstrip, and another in town, located 2½ blocks west of the parque central past the Hondutel office. **SAMI/Air Honduras** and **Atlantic Airlines** (☎ 433 6016; ✆ airport 6am-5pm, ice-cream shop 8am-6pm) share counter-space and a telephone at the airport, or you can buy tickets for either at an ice-cream shop a block and a half from the pier.

Atlantic has flights to Tegucigalpa (US$171) at 8am on Tuesday and Friday, while both Sosa and Atlantic have flights to La Ceiba (US$100) at 8am daily from Monday to Saturday. SAMI serves destinations inside the Moskitia, including Ahuas (US$33), Wampusirpi (US$49), Brus Laguna (US$45), Belén (US$50), and Palacios (US$57). Departure times vary, but you should be able to catch a flight from Puerto Lempira to any of those towns within a day or two. Note that prices and schedules change frequently and unexpectedly – always call ahead.

A taxi into town from the airport is US$2.25, or you could walk it in about 20 minutes.

You can usually rent a bike from one of the repair shops along the main drag – look for handwritten 'Se repara bicicleta' signs, especially near the pier. You'll have to negotiate a price, probably between US$5 and US$8 per day.

A small number of travelers take the overland route between Puerto Lempira and Puerto Cabezas, in Nicaragua. See boxed text, opposite, for details on getting to and from the border.

MISTRUK

A great day-or-two trip from Puerto Lempira is to Mistruk, a tiny Miskito community 18km south of town along the banks of the Laguna de Tansing. About 400 people live there, mainly by agriculture and fishing. The beach is grainy and attractive, shaded by tall, long-armed almond trees, with a long pier to avoid walking in the shallows. The water here is clear and fresh (not salted), a nice change from most of the Moskitia's rivers.

A handful of wooden **bungalows** (r US$16-22), spaced well apart along a pleasant freshwater beach, are popular with visiting tours and service groups. The bungalows have two pretty good beds apiece, private bathroom with flush toilets, wood floors, and high thatched roofs. Sunlight coming through the walls by day means mosquitoes by night – bring a mosquito net or plenty of bug spray. Solar panels charge batteries. There's not much to do here but relax on the beach and strike up conversations with local kids and boatmen.

A bike is by far the best and most pleasant way to get here. The well-maintained dirt road winds through expansive grassland with a thin sprinkling of spindly pine trees; there are no major climbs, just a few mild rollers to keep it interesting. Follow the road past the airport out of Puerto Lempira – anyone can point you in the right direction. At 13km, the road splits, left to Leimus and the Nicaraguan border, right to Mistruk. In another 3km, you'll reach a simple wood gate, which you can easily open or go around, and the town is a short distance further. The bungalows are big enough to store a bike or two inside, which is probably the smart thing to do. Bikes can be rented in Puerto Lempira (see p299). Taxis regularly take locals and visitors to Mistruk, charging US$32 for the round-trip, including time at the beach.

KAUKIRA

Red and blue macaws can sometimes be seen flying around this medium-sized town, tucked away on the northeast side of Laguna de Caratasca. A nice beach is about a 15-minute walk from town, but the town is better known for its bird-watching, wildlife and *pesca deportiva* (sport fishing). Ralston Haylock (☎ community telephone 433 6081) can arrange excursions of just about any kind and length, and maintains a simple lodge for overnight trips. He's a fount of information and lore, and also speaks excellent English.

From Puerto Lempira, *colectivo* boats leave the main pier at around 10am to 11am (US$4, 1½ hours). Getting back the same day can be tricky, however, as the boats 'live' in Kaukira; they leave every morning between 5am and 6am, but if there aren't enough passengers, they may not make an afternoon run. Ask the boat driver in Puerto Lempira – or Ralston by phone – about an afternoon service the day you're thinking of going. You may need to hire an *expreso* boat, which runs around US$55 each way.

Directory

CONTENTS

Accommodations	301
Activities	303
Business Hours	304
Children	304
Climate Charts	304
Courses	305
Customs	305
Dangers & Annoyances	305
Disabled Travelers	306
Embassies & Consulates	306
Festivals & Events	307
Food	308
Gay & Lesbian Travelers	308
Holidays	308
Insurance	308
Internet Access	308
Legal Matters	309
Maps	309
Money	309
Photography & Video	310
Post	310
Shopping	310
Solo Travelers	310
Sustainable Travel	311
Telephone & Fax	311
Time	311
Toilets	312
Tourist Information	312
Visas	312
Volunteering	312
Women Travelers	312
Work	312

ACCOMMODATIONS

Honduras has all levels and sorts of hotels, from luxury resorts to colonial guesthouses to super-cheapies. There are bed-and-breakfasts and hostels, though both are still pretty rare. No matter where you stay, it's almost always a good idea to see a few rooms since the hotel receptionist may have a different opinion about which is the most desirable room in the place. Hotels of all levels sometimes suffer from what could be called Stinky Bathroom Syndrome, which is caused by bad plumbing; covering the shower drain usually helps significantly.

At the low-budget end, hotels tend to have cold-water bathrooms and ceiling fans. Rooms with shared bathrooms are less and less common, though the state of some bathrooms being what they are, you may wish you didn't have to sleep next to it. Cable TV is increasingly standard, even in cheap rooms.

In this book, the budget range goes as high as US$30 per night. Travelers who generally think of themselves as midrangers may be perfectly happy in one of the nicer budget listings. In those, you are likely to have hot water, and can often choose between fans and air-conditioning. Rooms are still modest, but beds are usually newer, the paint fresher and the bathrooms cleaner.

Midrange hotels – US$30 to US$60 – will certainly have hot water and air-conditioning, and may include parking, breakfast or a pool. They tend to be in more secure neighborhoods, which often translates to 'away from downtown'. You may need to take cabs to and from the sights in the center.

Top end hotels are typically high-rise chain hotels, plus a handful of deluxe private resorts on Roatán and outside La Ceiba. These cost over US$60 per night. They have all the amenities you'd expect at a Real InterContinental in any country, including marble bathrooms, air-conditioning, quality beds, bellhop and taxi service, room service, in-room telephones, safety deposit boxes, parking, etc. Wireless Internet access is increasingly available; in some cases executive rooms have in-room access, while guests in standard rooms can get online in the lobby.

B&Bs

True bed-and-breakfast hotels are few and far between in Honduras; you'll see plenty of places with 'Bed & Breakfast' in their name, though just 'Bed' would be more accurate. Ask if morning eats are included before you plunk down your cash. Actual B&Bs are found in places with large expatriate populations, like Roatán, Copán Ruínas and Tegucigalpa.

PRACTICALITIES

- *Honduras Tips* is an essential English/Spanish language tourist magazine with up-to-date information. *Honduras This Week* is Honduras' only English-language weekly newspaper. *El Heraldo, La Tribuna, La Prensa, El Tiempo,* and *El Nuevo Día* are the country's daily newspapers. Occasionally, day-old *New York Times* and *Miami Herald* are sold at top end hotels and English-language bookshops.

- Honduran TV consists largely of programming imported from Mexico and the United States – some English-language programs are dubbed, some subtitled straight from American providers. FM radio plays a mix of ballads, Mexican ranchero music and American rock.

- DVD and VHS systems (NTSC) are commonplace.

- The standard current is 110 volt AC (like the USA and Canada); threeprong outlets, however, are uncommon.

- The metric system is used for everything except gasoline, which is measured in gallons, and laundry, which is weighed in pounds.

- Most cities and large towns have full service laundromats that charge US$2.50 to US$4 per 10lbs. Many hotels also provide laundry service, but often charge per item of clothing, which adds up pretty fast

---

Camping

Camping is not pursued by many Hondurans and as a result, campsites such as those in the USA or Europe are scarce. Camping is allowed, however, in several national parks, including Parque Nacional Montaña de Celaque, Parque Nacional Cerro Azul Meámbar, Parque Nacional Santa Bárbara and Parque Nacional Sierra de Agalta. Running water and latrines are sometimes available, and occasionally even a kitchen.

Camping on the fly – on beaches, in the countryside, in the forest – is typically hassle-free. Just be sure to ask permission at the *alcaldía* (city hall) or at the nearest home – you never know if you're camping on someone's property.

Plan on bringing your own gear; visitor centers rarely have tents or sleeping bags (with the notable exception of the one at Cerro Azul Meámbar). Travelers, however, can occasionally rent gear from guides or establishments that cater to foreign travelers – they can at least help track some down.

Finally, as you would at home, leave any campsite as you found it (or better). Carry out your trash, throw dirt or sand on any leftover ashes, and tidy up the site for the next camper.

Homestays

Staying in a home with a local family – sharing their space and meals – gives travelers a rare insight into everyday Honduran life; depending on the length of stay, and the family, of course, it often becomes a highlight of any trip here.

Homestays typically cost US$9 per person and include a private room, private bathroom and at least one meal. The quality of rooms varies from home to home, but in general, they are modern and clean. In fact, most homestay rooms (and families) must be 'approved' by the local tourism board, city hall or Spanish-language school before they are added to a roster of recommended places.

Places with established homestays include Copán Ruínas, which can be arranged through the Spanish-language schools (p140), Santa Rosa de Copán (p156), La Esperanza (p171), Ojojona (p95) and Isla del Tigre (p105).

Hostels

There are a handful of hostels in Honduras, which are great for saving a few lemps and meeting other travelers. All have dorms, shared bathroom, and at least one common area to relax. There are also hostels with extras and amenities including kitchens, lockers and Internet access. You'll find hostels in Copán Ruínas, San Pedro Sula, Tegucigalpa, La Ceiba, Trujillo and Roatán. Utila doesn't have any true hostels, but has plenty of cheap dorm-style lodging, used especially by backpackers taking open-water diving courses.

Hotels
Most travelers will stay most nights in a hotel. Note that a 'motel' is not the same thing, and is usually used for prostitution and people having affairs (hence the high walls, lack of windows and individual garages).

ACTIVITIES
Honduras has a host of outdoor activities for travelers – from flying high through the forest to dropping to the ocean's floor, from bird-watching in national parks to rafting down a raging Class V river. Whatever it is that interests you, you may be surprised by how much Honduras has to offer.

Canopy Tours
Canopy tours involve donning a special harness and sliding along fixed cables high in the treetops. Honduras' first such tour is along the Río Cangrejal near La Ceiba (p214). It has since been copied by other outfits, one east of La Ceiba and two in Roatán.

Diving & Snorkeling
Honduras' Bay Islands – Roatán, Utila and Guanaja, plus Cayos Cochinos off the North Coast – are famous for their diving, with clear warm water and a magnificent coral reef. You can learn to dive here for less money than just about anywhere in the world, without sacrificing an iota of quality. Dozens of dive shops, especially on Roatán and Utila, offer all levels of courses, from beginner to instructor. Snorkeling gear can be rented or bought, or you can bring your own, for snorkeling right off the shore or on inexpensive tours.

Fishing
Anglers can go trolling, deep-sea fishing or flat fishing on the Bay Islands, especially Roatán where local outfits have experienced guides. La Moskitia is also an excellent place for fishing, especially Brus Laguna, where behemoth 75kg tarpon have been landed.

Hiking & Trekking
Honduras has excellent hiking, especially in the national parks. Most of the best hikes involve climbing one of Honduras' many peaks, so hikers should be well prepared for moderate to challenging outings. Some parks have well-maintained trails and permanent visitors centers, others have little or no infrastructure at all. In the latter case, it is highly recommended that you hire a guide, as it's very easy to get lost (and much harder to be found). Some favorite hiking areas include Parque Nacional Montaña de Celaque (p163), Parque Nacional La Tigra (p91), Parque Nacional Cerro Azul Meámbar (p179), Parque Nacional Sierra de Agalta (p117), and Parque Nacional Montañ de Santa Bárbara (p180) as well as around Copán Ruínas (p141) and the Reserva de la Biósfera del Río Plátano (p290).

Horseback Riding
Horseback riding is a popular activity at Copán Ruínas (p141), though travelers should steer clear of the rides offered by local kids on the street, which are notoriously bad. It's much better to go with one of the listed tour operators instead. Horseback riding is also available in La Ceiba (p215).

Mountain Biking
At least two tour operators in La Ceiba (p214) offer half- and all-day mountain biking trips. It is rare to see independent travelers exploring Honduras by bike, though not for shortage of good dirt roads or places to go. A few highways in Olancho are known for roadside robberies, however, and are best avoided.

River Running & Kayaking
White-water rafting is popular on the Río Cangrejal near La Ceiba; several companies in La Ceiba offer rafting tours on this river. For even more adventure, try one of the week-plus expeditions down the Río Plátano or Río Patuca, starting in Olancho and ending in La Moskitia (p120).

Small-boat tours are a good way to visit a number of national parks and wildlife refuges along the north coast, including Parque Nacional Jeannette Kawas (Punta Sal), Refugio de Vida Silvestre Punta Izopo, Refugio de Vida Silvestre Cuero y Salado and Refugio De Vida Silvestre Laguna De Guaimoreto. A number of the trips in

La Moskitia are also conducted by small boat.

Bird-Watching

Birding is becoming a popular activity in Honduras, where you can spot hundreds of species, including quetzals, toucans, scarlet macaws (Honduras' national bird) as well as brilliant green and green-and-yellow parrots. Many of the national park and wildlife reserves are excellent birding locations, including Parque Nacional Cusuco (p130), Parque Nacional Montaña de Celaque (p163) and Parque Nacional La Tigra (p91).

Lago de Yojoa (p175) is another excellent place for birding – 375 species have been counted there so far.

Migratory birds are present along the North Coast during the northern winter months from November to February. They are easiest to spot in the lagoons and coastal reserves, like Parque Nacional Punta Izopo and Jardín Botánico de Lancetilla, both near Tela. The Lodge at Pico Bonito (p225) outside of La Ceiba has 300 hectares of private forest, with viewing platforms and available guided tours.

BUSINESS HOURS

Businesses are open during the following hours. Any exceptions to these hours are noted in specific listings.

Banks 8:30am to 4:30pm Monday to Friday and 8:30 to 11:30am Saturday

Restaurants 7am to 9pm daily

Shops 9am to 6pm Monday to Saturday and 9am to 1pm or 5pm Sunday

CHILDREN

Like most of Latin America, Honduras is very open and welcoming of children. There's no taboo about bringing children to restaurants or performances, and pregnant women are ushered to the front of the line in banks, government offices, and many private businesses.

Practicalities

Travelers will be hard-pressed to find child-specific amenities like car seats, high chairs and bassinettes, except perhaps in top end hotels and resorts. Hondurans simply do not have the quantity and variety of kid-specific paraphernalia that Americans, at least, are accustomed to. Disposable diapers, wipes, formula and other basics, however, are available in most large supermarkets.

Sights & Activities

The North Coast, Western Honduras and the Bay Islands are the best areas for those traveling with children. Assuming the little ones are up for some outdoor excursions, Tela and La Ceiba have a number of good options, including canopy tours, mangrove tours, short hikes, a butterfly and insect museum in La Ceiba and (as a last resort) the beach in Tela. The north also has a number of forts, including in Omoa and Trujillo, which kids might enjoy too. In the west, the area around Copán Ruínas has a number of activities suitable for children, including a butterfly enclosure, bird park and of course the ruins. And the Bay Islands have a number of kid-friendly resorts, notably Anthony's Key (p257), which has dolphin encounter programs.

CLIMATE CHARTS

The temperature in Honduras does not change dramatically by the season, perhaps 5°C throughout the year. Instead, the temperature is entirely dependant on the elevation. For instance, the mountainous interior ranges from 16°C to 20°C, and is a little warmer in the dry season. Tegucigalpa, at 975m, has a temperate climate, with temperatures between 24°C and 29°C during the day in the dry season (they're a bit cooler in the rainy season). The coastal lowlands on the Pacific and Caribbean sides are warmer and more humid year-round. Their temperatures range from 28°C to 32°C in the dry season; they're about 3°C cooler (and more comfortable) in the rainy season.

In general, the rainy season in Honduras runs from May to November in the interior and from September to January along the north coast and Bay Islands (with a chance of severe storms any time of the year). Heavy rains can cause flooding in the lowlands and mudslides in the mountains, and both can cause serious damage and impede travel. Hurricane season is from August to November; direct hits are uncommon, but are devastating when they do. Travelers should take evacuation orders very seriously.

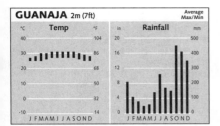

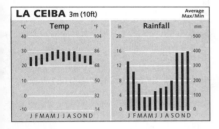

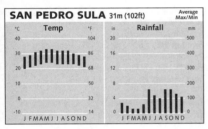

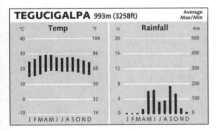

COURSES

Scuba diving courses bring thousands of travelers to Honduras every year because of the world-class dive sites and the bargain basement prices. Besides open-water and advanced open-water certifications, dive shops offer upper-level courses and specialties, including nitrox, divemaster and instructor. While the vast majority of dive shops are on the Bay Islands, there are also fully equipped shops servicing Cayos Cochinos and Omoa.

Spanish courses are becoming increasingly popular. Travelers have the option of studying in Copán Ruínas (p140), Tegucigalpa (p78), La Ceiba (p215) and the Bay Islands (p268).

CUSTOMS

Customs officers are pretty lax; while police and customs officers are entitled to search you at any time, especially in border areas, they rarely do. Even searches at the airport tend to be perfunctory. The exception is if something in your appearance or demeanor suggests to the officer you may be carrying drugs. Beyond drugs, travelers are not allowed to remove any ancient artifact or endangered animal or plant, whether live or a product made from one. It's smart to keep receipts for any item you buy, and especially for one that may be confused for being a restricted product, like an especially good Maya replica. If you're traveling with a pet, you may be asked to provide proof of vaccination and a medical certificate from home.

DANGERS & ANNOYANCES
Hiking Hazards

The greatest hazard while hiking is getting lost – at least two travelers have died in Parque Nacional Montaña de Celaque, evidently after getting off the trail and being unable to find it again. Even in a well-traveled park like Celaque, the trails can be overgrown in places, and secondary paths used by animals and hunters can easily lead hikers astray. Guides are readily available at most hiking areas, and it is strongly recommended you use them.

Although mostly found on the north coast and in La Moskitia, you should be alert for poisonous snakes throughout Honduras; coral snakes, rattlesnakes and barba amarilla (fer-de-lance; otherwise known as the lancehead) are among the most common types seen. Wear long pants and boots and be careful where you step.

Thefts & Muggings

Honduras has a very high crime and violence rate, though the vast majority of travelers experience no problems. Pickpocketing and petty theft are most common, and assault is possible. Take ordinary precautions, like not wearing flashy jewelry, walking around with your camera out or pulling out a wad of cash. Tegucigalpa and San Pedro Sula are the worst places for street crime; the downtown areas of both are fine during the day, but less-so after dark. Consider taking a cab when it gets late. If you are mugged, do not resist.

In general, small towns are much safer than the big cities. Watch yourself on the north coast, especially on the beach: avoid leaving items unattended and do not walk on the beach at night. It seems to be a favorite tactic of thieves to wait in the trees along a deserted stretch of beach, especially after dark, and wait for someone to happen by.

DISABLED TRAVELERS

Disabled travelers will find few facilities designed for their convenience, other than in more expensive hotels and resorts. Wheelchair-bound visitors will find it difficult to get around major cities like Tegucigalpa or San Pedro Sula, because of street congestion and generally poor road or sidewalk surfaces. Even smaller villages are difficult to negotiate, since the road surfaces are either unpaved or made of cobblestones. Toilets for the disabled are virtually nonexistent, other than in four- or five-star hotels.

EMBASSIES & CONSULATES
Honduran Embassies & Consulates
TEGUCIGALPA

Belgium (☎ 232 3954; fax 231 1974; Edif Plaza Bancatlán, 3rd fl, Blvd Miraflores; ☒ 8:30am-2pm Mon-Fri)
Belize (Map p81; ☎ 238 4616; fax 238 4617; Centro Comercial Hotel Honduras Maya, Av República de Chile; ☒ 9am-noon & 2-5pm Mon-Fri)
Canada (☎ 232 4551; fax 239 7767; Edif Financiero Banexpo, Local 3, Blvd San Juan Bosco; ☒ 8am-4:30pm Mon-Thu, 8am-1:30pm Fri)
Costa Rica (☎ 232 1054; Residencial El Triángulo, 1a Calle 3451; ☒ 8:30am-3:30pm Mon-Fri)
Denmark (☎ 236 6482; fax 236 8443; Edif La Paz, Av de los Próceres 206; ☒ 8am-4pm Mon-Fri)
El Salvador (☎ 239 7017; 239 7909; Diagonal Aguán 2952; ☒ 8am-3:30pm Mon-Fri)
Finland (Map pp72-3; ☎ 236 7322; fax 236 6740; Edif Comercial, Av de los Próceres; ☒ 8am-5:45pm Mon-Fri)
France (Map p81; ☎ 236 6800; fax 236 8051; 3a Calle at Av Juan Lindo; ☒ 8am-12:30pm Mon-Fri)
Germany (Map p81; ☎ 232 3161; fax 232 9018; Edif Paysen 3rd fl, Blvd Morazán; ☒ 9am-noon Mon-Fri)

Guatemala (☎ 231 1543; fax 232 1580; Calle Alfonso 13; ☒ 9am-1pm Mon-Fri)
Israel (Map p81; ☎ 232 0776; fax 231 1874; inside CONVERSA Language School; Paseo República de Argentina 257; ☒ 8am-5:30pm)
Italy (Map pp72-3; ☎ 236 6391; fax 236 5659; ambitalia@sigmanet.hn; Av Enrique Tierno Calvan; ☒ 9-11:30am Mon-Thu)
Japan (Map p81; ☎ 236 6828; fax 236 6100; Calzada República de Paraguay btwn 4a & 5a Calles; ☒ 8:30am-noon Mon-Fri)
México (☎ 232 1670; fax 232 4719; Calle Eucalipto; ☒ 9am-12:30pm Mon-Fri)
Netherlands (☎ 239 0525; fax 239 0526; 3a Av 2315; ☒ 9am-noon Mon-Fri)
Nicaragua (Map pp72-3; ☎ 232 4290; fax 231 1412; Bloque M-1, Col Lomas de Tepeyac; ☒ 8am-noon Mon-Fri)
Norway (☎ 236 5665; fax 236 8904; Av Los Próceres; ☒ 8am-5pm Mon-Fri)
Panamá (Map p81; ☎ 239 5508; ephon@hondudata .com; Edif Palmira, 3rd fl, behind Hotel Honduras Maya; ☒ 8am-2pm Mon-Fri)
Spain (Map pp72-3; ☎ 236 6589; fax 236 8682; embesphn@hondutel.hn; Calle Santander 801; ☒ 9am-1pm Mon-Fri)
Sweden (Map pp72-3; ☎ 232 4935; ambassaden .tegucigalpa@sida.se; Centro Comercial El Dorado, 6th fl; Blvd Morazán; ☒ 8am-noon, 1-5pm Mon-Fri)
Switzerland (☎ 236 8052; 6a Av 702, Col Lara; ☒ by appointment)
Taiwan (☎ 239 5837; fax 235 5662; Calle Eucalipto 3750; ☒ 8:30am-4:30pm Mon-Fri)
USA (Map p81; ☎ 236 9320; www.usmission.hn; Av La Paz near 3a Av; ☒ walk-ins 8-11:30am Mon-Fri, telephone service 8am-5pm Mon-Fri)

SAN PEDRO SULA

Belize (☎ 551 6247; fax 551 6460; Edif Industrias Global, highway to Puerto Cortés; ☒ 7-11am Mon)
El Salvador (Map p126; ☎ 557 5591; fax 557 2718; Edif Park Plaza, 11a Av NO btwn Calles 5a & 6a NO; ☒ 8:30am-noon & 1:30-4pm Mon-Fri)
Finland (☎ 553 1642; fax 552 6426; Megaplaza Mall; highway to La Lima; ☒ 8am-5pm Mon-Fri)
France (Map p126; ☎ /fax 553 1178; Alliance Française, 23a Av btwn 4a & 5a Calles SO; ☒ by appointment only)
Germany (Map p128; ☎ 553 1244; fax 553 1868; Edif Banco Sogerin, 1a Calle O btwn 8a & 9a Avs SO; ☒ 9-11am Mon-Fri)
Guatemala (Map p126; ☎ 556 9550; fax 556 9551; 12a Av SO near 24a Calle SO; ☒ 9am-12:30pm & 2-4pm Mon-Fri)
Italy (Map p128; ☎ 552 3672; fax 552 3932; Edif La Constancia, 3rd fl, 5a Av NO near 1a Calle O; ☒ 9am-1pm Mon-Fri)

México (Map p126; ☎ 553 2604; fax 552 3293; 2a Calle at 20a Av SO; ⏱ 8-10am Mon-Fri)
Netherlands (Map p126; ☎ 557 1815; fax 552 9724; Plaza Venecia, 15a Av btwn 7a & 8a Calles; ⏱ by appointment)
Nicaragua (Map p128; ☎ 550 0813; fax 550 8377; Hi-landeras de Sula; 5a Av SO btwn 4a & 5a Calles; ⏱ 10am-3pm Mon-Fri)
Norway (☎ /fax 557 0856; Finca Guaymura, Highway to El Carmen; ⏱ 8am-4pm Mon-Fri)
Panama (Map p126; ☎ 557 4499, ext 3504; fax 557 3838; Edif Banco Ficohsa, Av Circunvalación at 4a Calle NO; ⏱ 9-11am & 1-4pm Mon-Fri)
Spain (Map p128; ☎ 553 2480; fax 557 1680; Edif Agencias Panamericanas, 2 Av NO btwn 3a & 4a Calles NE; ⏱ 1:30-3:30pm Mon-Fri)
Taiwan (Map p126; ☎ 556 8490; fax 556 5802; 24a Av btwn 11a & 12a Av SO; ⏱ 8:30am-5:30pm Mon-Fri)
UK (Map p126; ☎ 550 2337; fax 550 6146; 2a Calle btwn 18a & 19a Avs NO; ⏱ 8am-noon & 1-5pm Mon-Fri, 8am-noon Sat)
USA (Map p128; ☎ 558 1580; www.usmission.hn; Edif Bancatlán, 11th fl, Parque Central; ⏱ 1-4:30pm Mon, Wed & Fri)

Honduran Embassies & Consulates
Belgium (☎ 2/734 0000; fax 2/735 2626; 106-101.2432@compuserve.com; Ave des Gaulois 8, Brussels B-1040)
Belize (☎ 245 889; fax 230 562; No 91 North Front Street, Belize City)
Canada (☎ 613/233 8900; fax 613/232 0193; www .embassyhonduras.ca; 151 Slater St, Suite 805, Ottawa, Ontario K1P 5H3)
Costa Rica (☎ 234 9502; fax 253 2209; emhondcr@sol .racsa.co.cr; Del ITAN, 300 Este, 200 Norte y 100 Este Yoses Sur, San José)
El Salvador (☎ 264 7841; embhond@es.com.sv; 89 Av Nte No 561, Col Escalón, San Salvador)
France (☎ 1/4755 8645; fax 1/4755 8648; 8 Rue Crevaux, 75116 Paris)
Germany (☎ 30/3974 9710; www.embahonduras.de; Cuxhavener Str 14, Berlin, D-10555)
Guatemala (☎ 335 3281; fax 335 2851; embhond@concyt.gob.gt; 12 Calle, 1-25 Zona 10, Edif Geminis 10, Oficina 1211, Guatemala City)
Holland (☎ 70/364 1684; fax 70/364 9134; eholan@honduras.demon.nl; Nassauplein 17, Den Haag, 2585 EB)
Israel (☎ 9957 7686; Calle Zohar Tal No 1, Herzlya Pituach, CP 46741, Tel Aviv)
Italy (☎ 6/320 7236; ambhondu@tin.it; Via Gian Battista de Vico 40, Interno 8, Rome)
Japan (☎ 3/3409 1150; honduras@interlink.or.jp; 38 Kowa Bldg 8F No 802, 12-24 Nishi Azabu 4 Chome, Minato Ku, Tokyo 106)

México (☎ 55/5211 5747; emhon mex@mail.Internet .com.mx; Alfonso Reyes No 220, Colonia Condesa, CP 06140, México DF)
Nicaragua (☎ 278 3043; embhonduras@ideay.net.ni; Del Gimnasio Hércules 1 cuadra al Sur y 1/2 cuadra arriba, Reparto San Juan 312, Managua)
Panama (☎ 225 8200; hondupma@sinfo.net; Calle 31 at Av Justo Arosemena, Panama City)
Spain (☎ 91/579 0251; fax 91/345 0665; www.emba honduras.es; Paseo de la Castellana Nº 164, 2º Derecha, Madrid 28046)
Sweden (☎ 8/731 5084; embahon@ telia.com; Stjärnvägen 2, 7 fl, 181, 34 Lindingo, Stockholm)
Taiwan (☎ 2/8775 5507; fax 2/2875 5726; honduras@ms9.hinet.net; 9F, 9, Lane 62, Tien-Mou West Rd, Taipei)
UK (☎ 020/7486 4880; hondurasuk@lineone.net; 115 Gloucester Place, London W1H 3PJ)
USA (☎ 202 966 7702; fax 202 966 9751; www.hondu rasemb.org; 3007 Tilden Street NW, Suite 4M, Washington DC 20008)

FESTIVALS & EVENTS
Just about every city, town and village in Honduras has a patron saint around which an annual festival or fair is celebrated. There are some big events, however, that attract crowds from far and wide

February
The Feria de la Virgen de Suyapa (p78) is a festival held in honor of the tiny patron saint of Honduras, a 6cm wood statue who is believed to have performed thousands of miracles. Held in the town of Suyapa, on the outskirts of Tegucigalpa, the event kicks off on All-Saints Day (February 3) and continues for a week. Pilgrims from all over Honduras and Central America come to honor the Saint during this period.

March
Comayagua's Semana Santa (p187) is packed with impressive religious processions the week before Easter. The height of the celebration is on Friday morning, when the *Vía Crucis* procession walks over *alfombras*, intricate 'carpets' made of colored sawdust, on the city streets throughout the historical center.

April
April 12 marks the arrival of the Garífunas in Honduras in 1797. Although it is celebrated in many Garífuna communities,

Punta Gorda's festival is among the best attended. It lasts four days and includes a re-enactment of the Garífuna arrival on Roatán, the naming of a Queen, and plenty of music and dancing (p262).

May
La Ceiba's patron-saint festival, La Feria de San Isidro (p216), has morphed into one of the country's largest festivals. Also known as the Gran Carnival Nacional (Great National Carnival), the party culminates on the third Saturday in May, but crowds start arriving mid-week and 'mini-celebrations' in neighborhoods around town start even earlier. Over a quarter of a million people come for parades, street performances, floats and – after night falls – raucous partying at La Ceiba's nightclubs.

June
The Feria Juniana (p130) is San Pedro Sula's patron-saint festival and a party of national proportions. Held the last week of June, the celebration includes live music, street performances, and plenty of food and drink. The height of the party is on June 29, when a huge parade makes its way down Avenida Circunvalación.

July
The Garífuna Festival (p195), the largest of its kind, is held July 9 to 24 (usually) in the town of Baja Mar, east of Puerto Cortes. The party's peak is typically July 16, with an all-night dance competition.

August
Utila's Sun Jam (p272) is held on an uninhabited cay near the western end of the main island. DJs spin music all day and all night for some 1500 people, who cram the islet for an all-day/all-night party. There's lots of food and drink, but buy your tickets in advance to be sure you get a spot.

FOOD
Honduras does not have an especially rich national cuisine, as any long-time traveler here can attest. Seafood figures prominently along the north coast, of course. And while chicken is the mainstay inland, pork and beef, especially *pinchos*, or kabob, are also popular. See the Food & Drink chapter (p62) for more information.

GAY & LESBIAN TRAVELERS
Honduras is very much 'in the closet,' and open displays of affection between gay or lesbian couples are definitely frowned upon. Discreet homosexual behavior was more tolerated before the advent of HIV/AIDS in Honduras around 1985. Since then anti-gay incidents have increased, along with stricter legislation, and gay and lesbians must take extra care anywhere they are uncertain of prevailing attitudes. However, the AIDS crisis has also increased gay advocacy; organizations serving the gay, lesbian and transsexual/transgender communities, include **Grupo Prisma** (☎ 232 8342; prisma@sdnhon.org.hn), **Colectiva Violeta** (☎ 237 6398; alfredo@optinet.hn), and **Comunidad Gay San Pedrana** (☎ 550 6868).

HOLIDAYS
New Year's Day January 1
Day of the Americas April 14
Semana Santa (Holy Week) Thursday, Friday and Saturday before Easter Sunday
Labor Day May 1
Independence Day September 15
Francisco Morazán Day October 3
Día de la Raza (Columbus Day) October 12
Army Day October 21
Christmas Day December 25

INSURANCE
Travel insurance is always something worth considering, though relatively few tourists actually use it. Policies vary widely, but can include compensation for lost, damaged or stolen luggage, for cancelled or delayed trips (a concern mostly for cruise-ship passengers), and even for bad weather. Some include coverage for medical treatment or evacuation, or for car rental. Travel insurance makes the most sense for those spending a significant amount of money in one place, a week at a dive resort for example. Independent travelers may be interested in theft or damage insurance, and a plan with medical care and evacuation may be a good idea if you'll be doing any adventure activities.

INTERNET ACCESS
Virtually every city, town and village travelers are likely to go to has at least one Internet café. Connections tend to be relatively fast, and cost US$0.50 to US$1.10 per hour.

Access on the Bay Islands has improved immensely thanks to satellite connection, but is still the country's most expensive, around US$8 per hour.

LEGAL MATTERS

Police officers in Honduras tend to be friendly, but are not above squeezing tourists for a little extra cash now and then. This usually happens at road stops, where police will often tell you the plain truth: they need money to put gas in the patrol truck. You can politely say that you can't help, or you can hand over a couple of bucks and be on your way. A number of cities have tourist police, who are part of the same police force but are trained to deal with tourists (and wear simple khaki uniforms rather than camo); do not hesitate to contact them (or a regular police officer if that's easier) if you experience or witness a crime.

MAPS

Good maps are hard to find in Honduras. Tourist offices and visitors centers are the best places to get a decent one of Honduras or the region, department or city you happen to be in. Bookstores occasionally carry maps but don't count on it; they're often the same ones that the tourist office gives out for free (and in a bookshop, you're likely to drop US$5 on it).

The Instituto Geográfico Nacional in Tegucigalpa (ITM; p71) publishes high-quality maps of the various departments (states), both political and topographic. They sell a few city and municipal maps as well, though oddly enough, the Tegucigalpa one is unwieldy and expensive.

MONEY

The local currency is the lempira and it's considered to be relatively stable. For exchange rates see the inside front cover of this book. Also, consider checking out www.oanda.com, a website that generates handy currency conversion cheat-sheets, which you can print out and keep in your wallet for easy conversions. For information on prices and the cost of traveling within Honduras, see p21.

ATMs

Cash machines are prevalent throughout the country. ATMs operated by BAC/

Credomatic, Banco Atlántida, and Unibanc are the most reliable, and most likely to accept out-of-country debit cards. Always be alert to your surroundings when withdrawing cash; whenever possible, take out money during the day, and at a machine that's in a lockable cabin (to get in, you typically have to swipe your ATM card at the door) or inside the bank itself. ATMs typically spit out 500-lempira bills, which can be a hassle to break – get in the habit of using big bills at hotels and larger restaurants, and saving the small bills for taxis, small eateries, street stands, etc.

Cash

Banks in larger cities usually exchange US dollars, and occasionally euros; bring your passport and go in the morning. Your hotel may let you pay in US dollars, or exchange them for you.

Credit Cards

Visa and MasterCard are widely accepted, including at major supermarkets, retail stores, hotels and car rental agencies. Expect a 6% to 12% surcharge.

Cash advances on Visa cards are available at most banks, including BAC/Credomatic, Banco Atlántida and Banco de Occidente. BAC/Credomatic can usually process advances on MasterCard too. There's typically no transaction charge on the Honduran end for Visa or MasterCard cash advances, but of course the interest rates tend to be astronomical.

Moneychangers

Freelance moneychangers can be found – in fact, they'll find you – in the airports and in parque central in San Pedro Sula. It's not recommended you use them unless the banks are closed or the line is out the door (which is often the case). There are moneychangers at all border crossings, too; they are equally suspect, but using them is the best way to get rid of Guatemalan *quetzales* or Nicaraguan *córdobas* if you know you won't need them anymore (El Salvador uses the US dollar).

Tipping

A 10% tip is customary for tour guides and restaurant waiters, but not taxi drivers. At hotels, it is nice to tip someone for carrying your bags to your room, and the house-cleaning staff – US$1to US$2 per day is fair; you should pay more at higher-end hotels or for especially good service.

Traveler's Checks

American Express traveler's checks can be changed in all major towns; Banco Atlántida and BAC/Credomatic are the best banks to use. They will need your passport, and may charge a commission. Some banks only change traveler's checks and foreign cash in the morning.

Taxes & Surcharges

There is a hotel tax of 12% to 16% that is added at most larger hotels but often not charged at smaller hotels. In many cases, the tax is charged if you use a credit card, but not if you pay in cash.

PHOTOGRAPHY & VIDEO

The main concern for travelers when it comes to photography and video is downloading pictures from your camera once your memory card is full. Most Internet cafés can download your pictures and burn them onto a CD for a couple of bucks. Definitely bring the USB cable specific to your camera, as most cafés won't have them. If you need an accessory or replacement part, try electronics stores in Tegucigalpa, San Pedro Sula or La Ceiba, especially in the malls.

POST

Post offices in most Honduran towns typically are open Monday to Friday 8am to 5pm (often with a couple of hours off for lunch between noon and 2pm) and on Saturday from 8am to noon. Postcards/letters cost US$0.80/US$1.30 to the US, US$1.30/US$1.80 to Europe and US$1.80/US$2.15 to Australia. Delivery takes 10 to 14 days, longer for Australia. Despite the apparent long delivery times for postal items, Honducor, the Honduran postal service, is considered relatively reliable. In fact, travelers from Nicaragua or Guatemala often hang on to their postcards and mail them from Honduras.

You can theoretically receive mail by general delivery, known in Latin America as *lista de correos,* at any post office; have it directed to you at:

(Name),
Lista de Correos (town and department),
República de Honduras,
Central America.

For more secure delivery, try FedEx, DHL, Express Mail Service (EMS), or Urgent Express; all have offices in Tegucigalpa, San Pedro Sula and other major cities.

SHOPPING

Honduras doesn't have the myriad and varied folk art found in, say, Guatemala or Mexico, but a number of items are worth looking for. Around Copán Ruínas, replicas of Maya marks and glyphs, made of clay or stone, are great souvenirs; Lenca 'negative' pottery – recognizable for its black and white designs – is beautiful and affordable; and baskets from the Santa Bárbara region as well as tree-bark art *(tunu)* from La Moskitia make colorful, lightweight gifts. For a more modern selection, the malls in Tegucigalpa, San Pedro Sula and La Ceiba have stores of all sorts, including designer shoes and clothes. As always, avoid buying items made from black coral or sea turtle shells. They do make for beautiful jewelry, but are protected species and buying such items only supports their destruction. The same goes for animal pelts, and jewelry or artesanía made from exotic bird feathers, like macaws or quetzales (though such items are rare in Honduras).

Bargaining

Bargaining is expected in Honduras, though not to the degree or intensity that is common in Guatemala. Most merchants list their wares with reasonable prices, and have little room to go down and still make a profit. Avoid low-balling merchants too much, or haggling over every penny.

SOLO TRAVELERS

Honduras is a perfectly fine place to travel alone, assuming you take common-sense precautions for safety and security. Solo women should expect to get more stares and comments than they would if they were with a man or even another woman. In cities, solo men (and even twosomes) may get approached more frequently by prostitutes than if they were traveling with a woman.

Honduran hotels are divided in the way rooms are priced – some charge according to the number of beds, others by the number of people; the listings in this book indicate which rate each hotel uses. There are also a few hostels, mostly in popular destinations.

It's relatively easy to meet other travelers in Honduras, especially in destinations like Copán Ruínas and the Bay Islands where bars, hostels, guided excursions and, of course, dive classes serve as mixers. There is also a substantial foreign and expatriate community in many Honduran cities.

SUSTAINABLE TRAVEL

Sustainable travel can be practiced in large gestures and small ones, from choosing to never fly again (because of the huge fuel usage it represents) to picking up a discarded Doritos bag on a forest trail. Most travelers are quite conscientious about minimizing their physical impact: not littering, not disturbing flora and fauna (above water or below it), not buying food or gifts that are made from protected species. In Honduras, especially on the Bay Islands, limit your water use – take short showers! – and try reusing bottles and plastic bags to cut down on trash.

Controlling your 'cultural impact' is a but more tricky. Taking photos is such an integral part of traveling – if you didn't get a photo, were you really there? – but it's vital that travelers exercise restraint in taking pictures, especially of local people, and doubly so if those people happen to be indigenous. Travelers may not realize how intrusive other habits are, like talking loudly or dressing sloppily, especially in a church or government office.

One last tip: even if you don't speak much Spanish, do learn how to use 'Usted' and the formal tense. It goes a long way in showing respect in everyday situations.

TELEPHONE & FAX

Many Internet cafés offer clear, inexpensive phone service using high-speed Internet connections. Calls to the US typically cost US$0.10 per minute, occasionally with rates as low as US$0.05. Expect to pay a bit more to call Europe, per minute US$0.25 to US$0.50.

Hondutel has call centers at its offices throughout the country. Rates to the US are competitive at just US$0.10 per minute. Calls to the rest of the world are higher. Call centers are usually open 7am until around 9pm every day.

Some Hondutel offices and Internet cafés with phone service have fax service. Prices vary widely, but are usually per page, as opposed to per minute. You can receive faxes as well, with a minimal per-page fee. Fax service typically has more limited hours, usually 8am to 4pm Monday to Friday.

Cell Phones

Honduran carriers Aló and Telefónica use GSM 850 and 1900 protocols, which are used by North American carriers Cingular, T-Mobile, Fido and others, but will be incompatible with GSM 900/1800 phones common in Europe, Australia, New Zealand and many Asian countries.

Phone Codes

Honduras' country code is ☎ 504. There are no area codes beyond the country code; when dialing Honduras from abroad simply dial the international access code plus the Honduran country code plus the local number. For domestic long distance calls within Honduras, there is no need to dial the area code.

To reach a domestic long distance operator, dial ☎ 191; for local directory assistance, dial ☎ 192; for directory assistance for government telephone numbers, dial ☎ 193; for an international operator, dial ☎ 197. A direct connection to an operator in the USA is available by dialing ☎ 800 0121 for Sprint, ☎ 800 0122 for MCI WorldCom and ☎ 800 0123 for AT&T.

Phonecards

Hondutel sells 'Telecards' which have a code on the back and can be bought at most Hondutel offices. From any pay phone, simply follow the instructions on the back to make a call.

TIME

Honduras is in one time zone, six hours behind Greenwich Mean Time (Mountain Standard Time in the USA). Honduras adopted daylight savings time in 2006, but many small towns around the country refused to implement it; when getting the time, always ask if it's *'hora nueva'* (new

DIRECTORY

time) or 'hora vieja' (old time). This is especially important for bus schedules.

TOILETS

Public toilets are few and far between in Honduras, so you should take 'rest breaks' at your hotel or at convenient restaurants. Western-style flush toilets are the norm in most places although toilet paper goes in the wastepaper basket, not down the hatch. The exception to the rule is La Moskitia, where running water is rare and latrines are typical.

TOURIST INFORMATION

The national tourist office is the **Instituto Hondureño de Turismo** (IHT; ☎ 220 1600, 800-222 8687; www.letsgohonduras.com) in Tegucigalpa. IHT also maintains a **US office** (☎ 800-460 9608; PO Box 140458, Coral Gables, FL 33114). Around the country, tourist information offices are run by the municipal government and public agencies; these offices are listed in the Information section of each destination.

VISAS

Citizens of the United States, Canada, most European countries, Australia, Canada, Japan and New Zealand normally receive 90-day tourist cards when entering the country. A yellow slip of paper will be stapled or folded into your passport – don't lose it, as you'll have to turn it in when you leave, or get it stamped if you extend your stay.

You can extend your stay once for another 90 days. After that, you'll be required to leave the country for at least three days. To extend your stay, take your passport to any immigration office and ask for a *prórroga* (visa extension); you'll have to fill out a form and pay US$20. Practically every city and town in Honduras has an immigration office *(migración)* where you can do this.

VOLUNTEERING

A number of organizations offer volunteer opportunities in Honduras, on projects in many parts of the country and ranging from building homes to teaching English to involving school children in environmental programs. The website www.travel -to-honduras.com has a long list of groups that run volunteer programs in Honduras, from large operations like Casa Alianza and i-to-i, to smaller ones like the Cofradía Bilingual School and the Utila Iguana Conservation Project.

WOMEN TRAVELERS

Honduras is basically a good country for women travelers. As elsewhere, you'll probably attract less attention if you dress modestly. On the Bay Islands, where lots of beach-going foreigners tend to congregate, standards of modesty in dress are much more relaxed, though topless bathing is most definitely frowned upon.

Cases of rape of foreign tourists have been reported in a few places along the north coast. As peaceful and idyllic as the coast looks – and usually is – be wary of going to isolated stretches of beach alone, and don't walk on the beach at night.

WORK

Most independent travelers who stay in (or come to) Honduras to work do so on the the Bay Islands; dive instructors are almost exclusively foreigners, and many people completing divemaster training raise a little extra cash working as waiters or bartenders in West End, West Bay or Utila. Most do not have work permits and either leave every three to six months to get a new tourist visa or, more likely, pay the islands' head immigration officer a bribe to extend their tourist visas every three months.

Transportation

CONTENTS

Getting There & Away   313
Entering the Country   313
Air   313
Land   315
Sea   316
Getting Around   317
Air   317
Bicycle   317
Boat   317
Bus   317
Car & Motorcycle   318
Hitchhiking   319
Local Transportation   319

THINGS CHANGE

The information in this chapter is particularly vulnerable to change. Check directly with the airline or a travel agent to make sure you understand how a fare (and ticket you may buy) works and be aware of the security requirements for international travel. Shop carefully. The details given in this chapter should be regarded as pointers and are not a substitute for your own careful, up-to-date research.

GETTING THERE & AWAY

ENTERING THE COUNTRY

Entering Honduras, whether by air or land, is a relatively painless process. Arriving by air, you'll be given immigration and customs forms on the plane. After disembarking, you'll pass through immigration first; there's a line for residents and one for foreigners (*extranjeros*). There is no fee to enter, and tourists are typically issued 90-day tourist cards. You will be given a thin slip of paper – don't lose it, you'll need it when you exit the country. After passing through immigration, collect your bags and pass through customs.

As in many Latin American countries, customs inspections are conducted at random. All passengers queue up to press a mechanical button; if the red light comes on you get inspected, if it's green you go through. Of course, customs officers may choose to inspect your bags anyway, so it's worth acting and dressing a bit sharp.

Most people entering by land do so at El Florido, Guatemala near Copán Ruínas. Other busy crossings are Corinto, Guatemala, and El Amatillo or El Poy, El Salvador. A smaller number cross from Nicaragua. The drill is the same at all the crossings: go through the exit procedures for the country you're leaving, then present your passport at the Honduran office or window. There is no fee to enter the country, but some officers charge US$3 simply because they can.

You can extend your tourist visa once for another 90 days for US$20 at almost any immigration office. In fact, the smaller offices tend to be faster and friendlier than the ones in Tegucigalpa or San Pedro Sula.

Passport

All foreign visitors must have a valid passport to enter Honduras. Be sure you have room for both an entry and exit stamp, and that your passport is valid for at least six months beyond your planned travel dates. For special visa requirements, see opposite.

AIR

Frequent direct flights connect Honduras with all the Central American capitals and many destinations in North America, the Caribbean, South America and Europe. Most international flights arrive and depart from the airports at Tegucigalpa and San Pedro Sula; there are also direct flights between the USA and Roatán, coming from Houston, Miami and Atlanta. A charter flight from Milan, Italy also arrives in Roatán once a week.

Airports & Airlines

Honduras has three international airports: San Pedro Sula, Tegucigalpa and Roatán.

HONDURAS TRANSPORTATION

Of the three, San Pedro Sula is the busiest. In addition, La Ceiba has a small domestic airport and there are airstrips in Utila, Guanaja, and throughout La Moskitia.

Aeropuerto Golosón (LCE; ☎ 443 3925) La Ceiba's airport, just west of town.

Aeropuerto Internacional Ramón Villeda Morales (SAP; ☎ 668 8880) San Pedro Sula's airport, located 15km east of town.

Aeropuerto Internacional Toncontín (TGU; ☎ 234 2702) Tegucigalpa's airport, located within the city limits.

Aeropuerto Juan Ramón Galvez (RTB) Roatán's airport, located just east of Coxen Hole.

Domestic and international carriers servicing Honduras include:

Aerolineas Sosa (NSO; Map p81; ☎ in San Pedro Sula 550 6545, in Tegucigalpa 233 5107, in La Ceiba 443 1894, in Roatán 445 1658; www.laceibaonline.net /aerososa/sosaingl.htm)

Air France (AF; Map pp72-3; ☎ in Tegucigalpa 236 0029; www.airfrance.com)

Atlantic Airlines (ZF; Map pp72-3; ☎ in San Pedro Sula 557 8088, in Tegucigalpa 237 8597, in La Ceiba 440 2343, in Roatán 445 1179; www.atlanticairlines.com.ni)

American Airlines (AA; ☎ in Honduras 800 220 1414, in San Pedro Sula 553 3508, in Tegucigalpa 220 7585; www.aa.com)

Continental Airlines (CO; Map p81; ☎ in San Pedro Sula 557 4141, in Tegucigalpa 220 0999, in Roatán 445 0224; www.continental.com)

Copa Airlines (CM; ☎ in Tegucigalpa 235 5610; www .copaair.com)

Delta Air Lines (DL; ☎ 550 1616; www.delta.com)

TACA/Isleña (TA; Map p81; ☎ 516 1061 in San Pedro Sula, in Tegucigalpa 236 8222, in La Ceiba 441 3191, in Roatán 445 1088; www.taca.com)

SAMI (☎ in La Ceiba 442 2565, ☎ in Brus Laguna 433 8031)

Tickets

It goes without saying that, for independent travelers, the Internet has most of the best travel deals. Flying Monday to Thursday is generally cheaper.

Canada

Expedia (☎ in US & Canada 888 397 3342; www .expedia.ca)

Travel Cuts (☎ 800-667-2887; www.travelcuts.com) Student travel specialist.

Travelocity (☎ 877 282 2925, in Ottawa 613 780 1431; www.travelocity.ca)

France
Anyway (☎ 0892 893 892; www.anyway.fr)
Lastminute (☎ 0892 705 000; www.lastminute.fr)
Nouvelles Frontières (☎ 0825 000 747; www.nou velles-frontieres.fr)
OTU Voyages (www.otu.fr) Student and youth travel specialist.
Voyageurs du Monde (☎ 01 40 15 11 15; www.vdm .com)

Germany
Just Travel (☎ 089 747 3330; www.justtravel.de)
Lastminute (☎ 01805 284 366; www.lastminute.de)
STA Travel (☎ 01805 456 422; www.statravel.de) Specializes in travelers under 26.
www.travelocity.de (089 27276 555)

Italy
CTS Viaggi (☎ 06 462 0431; www.cts.it) Student and youth travel specialist.

Netherlands
AirFair (☎ 020 620 5121; www.airfair.nl)

Scandinavia
Kilroy Travels (☎ in Norway 815 59 633; www.kilroy travels.com)

Spain
Barceló Viajes (☎ 902 116 226; www.barceloviajes.com)
Viajes Zeppelin (☎ 902 384 253; www.v-zeppelin.es)

United Kingdom
Discount air travel is big business in London. Advertisements for many travel agencies appear in the travel pages of the weekend broadsheet newspapers as well as *Time Out, Evening Standard,* and the free online magazine **TNT** (www.tntmagazine.com).
Bridge the World (☎ 0870 444 7474; www.b-t-w.co.uk)
Flight Centre (☎ 0870 890 8099; flightcentre.co.uk)

DEPARTURE TAX

Honduras levies a departure tax of US$30 for people flying out of the country, which includes US$5 in immigration and airport fees; it is payable in cash – US dollars or lempiras – after you've checked in but before you pass through security. For departures by land or sea, there is no departure tax.

Flightbookers (☎ 0870 814 4001; www.ebookerscom)
Journey Latin America (☎ 020 8747 3108; www .journeylatinamerica.co.uk)
North-South Travel (☎ 01245 608 291; www.north southtravel.co.uk) Part of the profits are donated to projects in the developing world.
Quest Travel (☎ 0870 442 3542; www.questtravel.com)
STA Travel (☎ 0870 160 0599; www.statravel.co.uk) Specializing in travelers under 26.
Trailfinders (☎ 020 7937 1234; www.trailfinders.co.uk)
Travel Bag (☎ 0870 890 1456; www.travelbag.co.uk)

United States
Discount travel agents in the USA are known as consolidators. San Francisco is the ticket-consolidator capital of the country, although some good deals can be found in Los Angeles, New York and other big cities.
Amex Travel (www.itn.net)
Cheap Tickets (☎ 888 922 8849; www.cheaptickets.com)
Expedia (☎ 800 397 3342; www.expedia.com)
Lowest Fare (☎ 800 678 0998; www.lowestfare.com)
Orbitz (☎ 888 656 4546; www.orbitz.com)
Smarter Travel (☎ 617 886 5555; www.smarterliving .com)
STA Travel (☎ 800 781 4040; www.sta.com) Specializing in travelers under 26.
Travelocity (☎ 888 709 5983; www.travelocity.com)

LAND
Bus
Ordinary buses do not cross the border, which means you have to cross on foot and pick up another bus on the other side. However, several bus lines offer international service, including **Tica Bus** (www.ticabus .com), **King Quality** (www.kingqualityca.com), **Hedman Alas** (www.hedmanalas.com) and **El Rey Express** (www .reyexpress.net). Between them, they offer service from Tegucigalpa and San Pedro Sula to San Salvador, Guatemala City, Antigua (Guatemala), Tapachula (México), Managua (Nicaragua), San José (Costa Rica) and Panama City.

Car & Motorcycle
Most rental car agencies (p318) do not allow you to drive out of Honduras. Avis is the exception, though be sure that this is clear in your contract and that the vehicle remains covered by insurance.

El Salvador
The main crossings into El Salvador are at El Poy (see p157) and El Amatillo (see p102);

TRANSPORTATION

BORDER CROSSINGS

International borders in Central America tend to be busy, dirty and a bit dodgy. You're sure to be harangued by money changers when you arrive; if you need to change money, have it ready in a separate pocket and calculate ahead of time roughly what you expect to receive. Changers make a fair profit simply on mathematical trickery, believe it or not. You probably won't get a great rate, but don't be afraid to negotiate. Watch your bags at all times.

Border officials are notoriously corrupt, though they tend not to bother travelers, preferring bigger fish like truck drivers, importers etc. Crossing the border is supposed to be free, but you may be charged a fee to leave or enter Honduras; assuming it's a small amount – around US$3 – it's best to just pay and move on. If it's a large amount, ask to see the regulation in writing, and say you want a receipt, either of which may discourage the agent from pursuing it.

Always be respectful and dress your best at the border; searches are very rare, but are most likely to occur if you have a disheveled appearance, which might encourage guards to stop and search.

---

there is a third crossing south of Marcala, but because of a longstanding border dispute, there is no Salvadoran immigration post there. There's no one to stop you, either, but entering here is technically illegal and you can be fined if your status is discovered. Some travelers have crossed into El Salvador as far as Perquín, Morazán, and returned to Honduras by the same crossing with no problem. Nevertheless, if you plan to go further or stay longer than a few days, it is best to use one of the official crossings. However, a final agreement between the two countries seemed very much in the works at the time of publication – ask around for the latest.

BUS

From Tegucigalpa, Tica (US$15, 6½ hours) and King Quality (US$28 to US$41, six to seven hours) offer direct service to San Salvador. King Quality has service from San Pedro Sula as well (US$28 to US$41, 6 hours).

Guatemala

To Guatemala, the main crossings are at El Florido (see p145), Agua Caliente (see p145) and Corinto.

BUS

From Tegucigalpa, King Quality has the most convenient service to Guatemala City, with just a two-hour layover in San Salvador (US$53 to US$74 one way, 14 hours). Tica Bus has cheaper service (US$26 one way) but includes an overnight in San Salvador. From San Pedro Sula, you can take **El Rey Express** (www.reyexpress.net) for US$26 (8½

hours), or the much nicer **Hedman Alas** (www .hedmanalas.com) for US$45 to US$59 (eight hours), which has continuing service to Antigua. You can also catch the Hedman Alas bus in La Ceiba, Copán Ruínas or San Pedro Sula's airport.

Nicaragua

There are three Nicaraguan borders crossings in southern Honduras, at Las Manos, La Fraternidad/El Espino and Guasaule (see p102), and a fourth in La Moskitia, at Leimus (see p298).

BUS

All international buses to Managua pass through Tegucigalpa and use the Las Manos crossing via Danlí. Service is offered by Tica (US$20, eight hours) and King Quality (US$25 to US$37, seven to eight hours). In La Moskitia, there are daily buses from Puerto Lempira to Leimus.

SEA

If you arrive or depart from Honduras by sea, be sure to clear your paperwork (visa, entry and exit stamps) immediately with the nearest immigration office.

Belize

FERRY

The only regularly scheduled passenger boat service between Honduras and another country is a small boat operated by **Gulf Cruz** (☎ 984 9544, 982 6985). It runs twice weekly from Puerto Cortés to Dangriga (US$35, two hours) and Belize City (US$55, 3½ hours). See p194 for details.

El Salvador
MOTOR BOAT
There is no regular boat service to El Salvador but it is possible to hire a fisherman in Amapala to take you across the Golfo de Fonseca to La Unión, El Salvador.

GETTING AROUND
AIR
Domestic flights are surprisingly affordable, and flying can be a good way to save some time if your schedule is tight. Of the airlines listed in the previous section, Sosa, Atlantic, Isleña and SAMI offer domestic services.

There are three or more daily flights to Roatán, fewer to Utila and Guanaja; most originate in San Pedro with a stop in La Ceiba.

You can also fly to La Moskitia, and within the region once you get there. All flights go through La Ceiba; when we passed through, Sosa had daily flights to Puerto Lempira (p299) and three flights weekly to Brus Laguna. Atlantic also has daily departures to Puerto Lempira, but is less reliable.

SAMI is a private operation with just one pilot and a couple of tiny planes. Service is semiregular at best – don't plan any tight schedules around SAMI flights. Still, it is a convenient and affordable way to get around the vast Moskitia region; stops include Palacios, Brus Laguna, Ahuas, Wampusirpi and Puerto Lempira.

BICYCLE
Mountain biking around Honduras is not common, which is not to say it wouldn't be a great adventure, although there are plenty of lightly trafficked dirt roads through beautiful terrain. Some of the highways in Olancho are known for roadside robberies – thieves may not know what to think of a cyclist, but better to play it safe and avoid

---

DEPARTURE TAX

There is a US$3 departure tax to fly within Honduras. It is payable in cash after you've checked in but before you pass the security checkpoint.

---

those areas. Try Ruta Lenca and parts of the north coast, instead.

Rental
Bike rental is still uncommon in Honduras. There are rental outfits in Tela (p204), and mountain-biking tours and rentals in La Ceiba (p214). A few hotels also offer bicycles for guest use. Expect to pay US$10 to US$20 per day.

BOAT
Ferry
Two comfortable air-conditioned passenger ferries, the MV *Galaxy II* and the *Utila Princess,* serve Roatán (US$16, one hour; see p243) and Utila (US$22, one hour; see p272) respectively. There is no service between the two islands – you have to go via La Ceiba. There is no scheduled service to or from Guanaja.

Motorboat
In La Moskitia, almost all transportation is along the waterways, including the long ride up to Las Marías (p292) where a number of popular outings begin. You will also take motorized canoes from town to town in La Moskitia, and across one or more of the region's huge lagoons.

BUS
Buses are an easy and cheap way to get around in Honduras. Service usually starts very early in the morning – at 3am or 4am on some routes – but may end by early evening, or even late afternoon. Buses between Tegucigalpa and San Pedro Sula run later. *Microbuses* or *rapiditos* are smaller minivan-type buses that cover some routes, and tend to go faster and leave more frequently than regular buses.

Classes
On major bus routes, you'll often have a choice between taking a *directo* (direct) or *ordinario* (ordinary), also known as *parando* or *servicio a escala.* The *directo* is almost always worth the extra money, even on short trips. *Directos* can be twice as fast as regular buses, which stop frequently to let passengers on and off.

Deluxe buses offer even faster service between Tegucigalpa, San Pedro Sula, Copán Ruínas, La Ceiba and Trujillo, and use modern air-conditioned buses (with service including movies and soft drinks). Fares on *ejecutivo* (executive) or *servicio de lujo* (luxury service) buses are often double those on *directos,* and sometimes more, but can be a worthwhile splurge for long trips.

King Quality and Hedman Alas even have 'super-deluxe' seats on international buses, with almost fully reclining seats and additional food and drink service, all in a special area below the main cabin.

Contrary to common wisdom, chicken buses are targeted for robbery more often than the direct or deluxe lines, mainly because there are more opportunities for ne'er-do-wells to board. You don't have to avoid chicken buses altogether – they're often your only option – but do try using direct and deluxe buses whenever possible.

Costs

Buses are very affordable. *Directo* fares include: US $6 for Tegucigalpa–San Pedro Sula (4½ hours); US$4.80 to US$5.50 for San Pedro Sula–Copán Ruínas (three hours), US$2.50 for La Ceiba–Tela (1½ hours).

Reservations

Reservations aren't usually necessary and are rarely taken, even on *ejecutivo* buses. For travel during Semana Santa (the week preceding Easter), however, you should buy your ticket a day or two in advance, which assures you a spot and saves you the time and hassle of waiting in line in a jam-packed bus terminal.

CAR & MOTORCYCLE
Bring Your Own Vehicle

Bringing your own car into Honduras can be a headache, mostly due to all the fees and paperwork. Arriving at the border you'll be swarmed by *tramitadores,* young men who help you through the morass and are worth the expense. Travelers report widely different experiences and costs – from US$20 to US$150 and from an hour to all day – depending mostly on the number and amount of bribe money it takes. Get to the border early and bring plenty of cash (though try not to pull out a huge wad, of course). As frustrating as the process can be, be patient and never insult a customs officer.

Driver's License

In general, foreign drivers can drive a car using their home driver's license for up to 30 days. Be sure your license is valid and won't expire while you're on the road. As with all important documents, make a copy of your license and stash it in a safe place.

Fuel & Spare Parts

Gas is expensive in Honduras, at least compared to the US. It costs around US$3.50 to US$4 per gallon (about 4L), and is sold in diesel, 'plus' and the higher grade 'premium'. Annoyingly, many gas stations don't offer plus so you're forced to pay extra for premium. Luckily, there are many gas stations in both urban and rural areas.

Finding spare parts is not usually a problem, unless you're driving a very uncommon vehicle. Toyotas are extremely common in Honduras, so you'll have an easier time repairing them than any other brand.

Rental

Rental cars are available in all the major cities and on Roatán. Prices start at around US$30 per day for an economy car and US$50 for midsize cars or larger ones. Remember that renting at the airport typically costs 10% to 15% more than in town simply because of airport taxes. Rental agencies include the following.

Advance Rent A Car (☎ in La Ceiba 441 1105, in San Pedro Sula 552 2295, in Tegucigalpa 235 9531; www.advancerentacar.com)

Arena Rent a Car (☎ in Roatán 445 1882; arenacarrental@yahoo.com)

Avis (☎ in Roatán 445 0122, in San Pedro Sula 553 0888, in Tegucigalpa 239 5712; www.avis.com)

Budget (☎ in Tegucigalpa 235 9528; www.budget.com)

Caribbean Rent a Car (☎ in Roatán 455 6950; www.caribeanroatan.com)

Econo Rent-a-Car (☎ in Tegucigalpa 235 8582; www.econorentacar.net)

Hertz (☎ in San Pedro Sula 668 3156, in Tegucigalpa 238 3772; www.hertz.com)

Molinari Rent A Car (☎ in La Ceiba 443 0055, in San Pedro Sula 553 2639, in Tegucigalpa 237 5335; molinarirentacar@yahoo.com)

National/Alamo (☎ in Tegucigalpa 220 5000 ext 7814; national.hond@multivisionhn.net)

Insurance

Insurance is required on vehicles in Honduras; if you're renting, it will be included in the rate. A few companies – like **Advance Rent a Car** (www.advancerentacar.com), with offices in all the large cities – will allow you to waive the collision damage insurance if you have coverage through your Visa or MasterCard. This can save you US$10 per day or more. If you think you might rent a car in Honduras, take the time before you arrive to familiarize yourself with the terms of your credit card coverage. Be sure to ask if the insurance covers dirt roads and pickup trucks.

Road Conditions

Honduras' main highways are paved and well maintained, and seem to improve every month. (The busy CA-5, which connects San Pedro Sula and Tegucigalpa is being widened and straightened, which makes a big difference.) Away from the highways, road conditions range from excellent to disastrous. The rainy season can make traveling on dirt roads tough, since many develop deep, hungry mudholes. Always ask about road conditions before setting out, especially if you're using a secondary road.

Road Rules

Basic road rules here don't differ much from the US or most European countries. A few things to remember: it is illegal to turn right at a red stoplight, and seat belts are required for the driver and front-seat passenger at all times. Many towns and cities have a confusing system of one-way streets though, which are often unmarked.

There are a number of police checkpoints on the highways, which may look like military stops because Honduran police wear camouflage. If you're not waved down, keep rolling through. If you're stopped, you'll be asked for your driver's license and the vehicle registration card. Be polite and respectful at all times. Very rarely, you'll be asked for money; you are not obligated to give any, and you can usually get away with politely saying you can't. You can also give the officer 50/100 lempira – US$3 to US$5 – and be on your way. Mostly the money is used for gas for the police truck.

HITCHHIKING

Hitchhiking – *tomando un jalón,* or 'taking a hitch' – is never entirely safe in any country in the world, and we don't recommend it. However, it is very common in much of Honduras, especially in rural areas like the Ruta Lenca and along the North Coast. Peace Corps volunteers, for example, do it frequently. Generally you just stand on the side of the road and wave down a pickup truck. You should offer the driver money, though many drivers will not accept it. Usually there are locations where people go to get *un jalón* – ask at your hotel.

LOCAL TRANSPORTATION
Boat

In La Moskitia, boats are the local transport of choice, as there are few roads and fewer bridges. On Roatán, water taxis are the best way to get from West End to West Bay, and around the town of Oakridge. *Lanchas* (motorboats) are also used to ferry passengers to and from Isla El Tigre, in southern Honduras.

Bus

It is highly recommended that travelers do not use city buses, especially in San Pedro Sula and Tegucigalpa. Not only is pickpocketing and petty theft common, but public buses are occasionally targeted by area gangs for what amounts to a 'toll' for passing through certain neighborhoods. With taxi fares so low (and *colectivo* taxi fares even lower) buses just aren't work the risk.

Moto-taxi

Small Thai-style three-wheeled moto-taxis have burst onto the Central American scene, going from unknown to ubiquitous in just a few years. Loud and slightly obnoxious, they are cheaper and more plentiful than taxis, making them a good option when you're lugging bags to or from the bus terminal on a hot day.

Taxi

Taxis don't have meters in Honduras, but in most towns there is a fixed one-ride fare, usually from US$0.50 to US$1 per person. You can expect longer journeys in a major city to cost around US$4. In many cities, *colectivos* (shared taxis) ply a number of prescribed routes, costing around US$0.50 per passenger. In all cases, confirm the price of the ride before you get into the cab. If it seems exorbitant, negotiate or simply wait for another cab.

Health Dr David Goldberg

CONTENTS

Before You Go	**320**
Insurance	320
Recommended Immunizations	320
Medical Checklist	321
Internet Resources	321
Further Reading	321
In Transit	**321**
Deep Vein Thrombosis (DVT)	321
Jet Lag & Motion Sickness	322
In Honduras	**322**
Availability & Cost of Health Care	322
Infectious Diseases	322
Travelers' Diarrhea	325
Environmental Hazards & Treatment	325
Children & Pregnant Women	326

Travelers to Honduras and the Bay Islands need to be concerned chiefly about food-borne diseases, though mosquito-borne infections can also be a problem. Most of these illnesses are not life threatening, but they can certainly have an impact on your trip or even ruin it. Besides getting the proper vaccinations, it's important that you bring along a good insect repellent and exercise great care in what you eat and drink.

BEFORE YOU GO

Since most vaccines don't produce immunity until at least two weeks after they're given, visit a physician four to eight weeks before departure. Ask your doctor for an International Certificate of Vaccination (otherwise known as the yellow booklet), which will list all the vaccinations you've received. This is mandatory for countries that require proof of yellow-fever vaccination upon entry, but it's a good idea to carry it wherever you travel.

Bring medications in their original containers, clearly labeled. A signed, dated letter from your physician describing all medical conditions and medications, including generic names, is also a good idea. If carrying syringes or needles, be sure to have a physician's letter documenting their medical necessity.

INSURANCE

Honduran medical treatment is generally inexpensive for common diseases and minor treatment, but if you suffer a serious medical problem or emergency, it is highly recommended you go to a private hospital or even fly home (if your condition allows it). Unfortunately, public hospitals in Honduras are extremely overcrowded and understaffed. Travel insurance can typically cover the costs. Some US health-insurance policies stay in effect (at least for a limited time) if you travel abroad, but it's worth checking exactly what you'll be covered for in Honduras. For people whose medical insurance or national health systems don't extend to Honduras – which includes most non-Americans – a travel policy is advisable. Check out the insurance section of www.lonelyplanet.com for more information.

You may prefer a policy that pays doctors or hospitals directly rather than one requiring you to pay on the spot and claim later. If you do have to claim later, keep all documentation. Some policies ask you to call collect to a center in your home country, where an immediate assessment of your problem is made. Check that the policy covers ambulances or an emergency flight home. Some policies offer lower and higher medical-expense options; the higher ones are chiefly for countries such as the US, which has extremely high medical costs. There is a wide variety of policies available, so be sure to check the small print.

RECOMMENDED IMMUNIZATIONS

The only required vaccine is the one for yellow fever, and that's only if you're arriving in Honduras from a yellow-fever–infected country in Africa or South America. However, a number of vaccines are recommended: see boxed text p321.

RECOMMENDED VACCINATIONS

Vaccine	Recommended for	Dosage	Side effects
chickenpox	travelers who've never had chickenpox	2 doses 1 month apart	fever; mild case of chickenpox
hepatitis A	all travelers	one dose before trip with booster 6-12 months later	soreness at injection site; headaches; body aches
hepatitis B	long-term travelers in close contact with the local population	3 doses over a 6-month period	soreness at injection site; low-grade fever
measles	travelers born after 1956 who've had only 1 measles vaccination	1 dose	fever; rash; joint pain; allergic reaction
tetanus-diphtheria	all travelers who haven't had booster within 10 years	1 dose lasts 10 years	soreness at injection site
typhoid	all travelers	4 capsules by mouth, 1 taken every other day	abdominal pain; nausea; rash
yellow fever	required for travelers arriving from yellow fever–infected areas in Africa or South America	1 dose lasts 10 years	headaches; body aches; severe reactions are rare

MEDICAL CHECKLIST

- Antibiotics
- Antidiarrheal drugs (eg loperamide)
- Acetaminophen/paracetamol (Tylenol) or aspirin
- Anti-inflammatory drugs (eg ibuprofen)
- Antihistamines (for hay fever and allergic reactions)
- Antibacterial ointment (eg Bactroban) for cuts and abrasions
- Steroid cream or cortisone (for poison ivy and other allergic rashes)
- Bandages, gauze, gauze rolls
- Adhesive or paper tape
- Scissors, safety pins, tweezers
- Thermometer
- Pocket knife
- DEET-containing insect repellent for the skin
- Permethrin-containing insect spray for clothing, tents and bed nets
- Sun block
- Oral rehydration salts
- Iodine tablets or chlorine drops (for water purification)
- Syringes and sterile needles

INTERNET RESOURCES

There is a wealth of travel-health advice on the Internet; www.lonelyplanet .com is a good place to start. The World Health Organization publishes a superb book called *International Travel and Health,* which is revised annually and is available online at no cost at www.who .int/ith. Another website of general interest is www.mdtravelhealth.com, which provides complete travel health recommendations for every country, updated daily, also at no cost.

FURTHER READING

For further information, see *Healthy Travel Central & South America,* also from Lonely Planet. If you're traveling with children, Lonely Planet's *Travel with Children* may be useful. The *ABC of Healthy Travel,* by E Walker et al, and *Medicine for the Outdoors,* by Paul S Auerbach, are other valuable resources.

IN TRANSIT

DEEP VEIN THROMBOSIS (DVT)

Blood clots may form in the legs during plane flights, chiefly because of prolonged immobility. The longer the flight, the greater the risk. Though most blood clots are reabsorbed uneventfully, some may break off and travel through the blood vessels to the lungs, where they could cause life-threatening complications.

The chief symptom of DVT is swelling of or pain in the foot, ankle or calf, usually but not always on one side. When a blood clot travels to the lungs, it may cause chest pain and breathing difficulties. Travelers with

HEALTH

any of these symptoms should immediately seek medical attention.

To prevent the development of DVT on long flights you should walk about the cabin, perform isometric compressions of the leg muscles (ie contract the leg muscles while sitting), drink plenty of fluids, and avoid alcohol and tobacco.

JET LAG & MOTION SICKNESS

Jet lag is common when crossing more than five time zones, resulting in insomnia, fatigue, malaise or nausea. To avoid jet lag try drinking plenty of fluids (nonalcoholic) and eating light meals. Upon arrival, get exposure to natural sunlight and readjust your schedule (for meals, sleep etc) as soon as possible.

Antihistamines such as dimenhydrinate (Dramamine) and meclizine (Antivert, Bonine) are usually the first choice for treating motion sickness; their main side effect is drowsiness. A herbal alternative is ginger, which works like a charm for some people.

IN HONDURAS

AVAILABILITY & COST OF HEALTH CARE

There are a number of first-rate hospitals in Tegucigalpa (Honduras Medical Center; p71) and San Pedro Sula (Hospital Centro Mêdico Betesda; p127) In general, private facilities offer better care than public hospitals, though at greater cost.

Adequate medical care is available in other major cities, but facilities in rural areas may be limited.

Many doctors and hospitals expect payment in cash, regardless of whether you have travel health insurance. If you develop a life-threatening medical problem, you'll probably want to be evacuated to a country with state-of-the-art medical care. Since this may cost tens of thousands of dollars, be sure you have insurance to cover this before you depart. You can find a list of medical evacuation and travel insurance companies on the **US State Department website** (www.travel.state.gov/medical .html).

Honduran pharmacies are identified by a green cross and a 'Farmacia' sign. Most are well supplied and the pharmacists well trained. Some medications requiring a prescription in the US may be dispensed in Honduras without a prescription. To find an after-hours pharmacy, you can look in the local newspaper, ask your hotel concierge, or check the front door of a local pharmacy, which will often post the name of a nearby pharmacy that is open for the night.

INFECTIOUS DISEASES

Cholera

Cholera is an intestinal infection acquired through ingestion of contaminated food or water. The main symptom is profuse, watery diarrhea, which may be so severe that it causes life-threatening dehydration. The key treatment is drinking oral rehydration solution. Antibiotics are also given, usually tetracycline or doxycycline, though quinolone antibiotics such as ciprofloxacin and levofloxacin are also effective.

A handful of cholera outbreaks have been reported in Honduras over the last few years. The vaccine is no longer mandatory, though many health workers still recommend it.

Dengue Fever

Dengue fever is a viral infection found throughout Central America. It is most prevalent during the rainy season, which peaks from September to November on the North Coast. Wet weather is possible year round, however, and outbreaks can occur at any time. Dengue is transmitted by Aedes mosquitoes, which bite preferentially during the day and are usually found close to human habitations, often indoors. They breed primarily in artificial water containers, such as jars, barrels, cans, cisterns, metal drums, plastic containers and discarded tires. As a result, dengue is especially common in densely populated, urban environments.

Dengue usually causes flu-like symptoms including fever, muscle aches, joint pains, headaches, nausea and vomiting, often followed by a rash. The body aches may be quite uncomfortable, but most cases are resolved uneventfully in a few days. Severe cases usually occur in children under 15 who are experiencing their second dengue infection.

There is no specific treatment for dengue fever except to take analgesics such as acetaminophen/paracetamol (Tylenol) and drink plenty of fluids. Severe cases may require hospitalization for intravenous fluids and supportive care. There is no vaccine. The cornerstone of prevention is insect protection measures.

Hepatitis A

Hepatitis A occurs throughout Central America. It's a viral infection of the liver usually acquired by ingestion of contaminated water, food or ice, though it may also be acquired by direct contact with infected persons. The illness occurs worldwide, but the incidence is higher in developing nations. Symptoms may include fever, malaise, jaundice, nausea, vomiting and abdominal pain. Most cases are resolved uneventfully, though hepatitis A occasionally causes severe liver damage. There is no treatment.

The vaccine for hepatitis A is extremely safe and highly effective. If you get a booster six to 12 months later, it lasts for at least 10 years. You really should get it before you go to Honduras or any other developing nation. Because the safety of hepatitis A vaccine has not been established for pregnant women or children under two years, they should instead be given a gammaglobulin injection.

Hepatitis B

Like hepatitis A, hepatitis B is a liver infection that occurs worldwide but is more common in developing nations. Unlike hepatitis A, the disease is usually acquired by sexual contact or by exposure to infected blood, generally through blood transfusions or contaminated needles. The vaccine is recommended only for long-term travelers (on the road more than six months) who expect to live in rural areas or have close physical contact with the local population. Additionally, the vaccine is recommended for anyone who anticipates sexual contact with the local inhabitants or a possible need for medical, dental or other treatments while abroad, especially if a need for transfusions or injections is expected.

Hepatitis B vaccine is safe and highly effective. However, a total of three injections are necessary to establish full immunity.

Several countries added hepatitis B vaccine to the list of routine childhood immunizations in the 1980s, so many young adults are already protected.

Malaria

Malaria occurs in every country in Central America, and is especially prevalent in Honduras' eastern coastal areas. It's transmitted by mosquito bites, which usually occur between dusk and dawn. The main symptom is high spiking fevers, which may be accompanied by chills, sweats, headache, body aches, weakness, vomiting, or diarrhea. Severe cases may involve the central nervous system and lead to seizures, confusion, coma and death.

Taking malaria pills is strongly recommended when visiting lowland rural areas and in the departments of Gracias a Dios, Colón, Olancho, Yoro, Alántida, Cortés and the Bay Islands.

For Honduras, the first-choice malaria pill is chloroquine, taken once weekly in a dosage of 500mg (be sure to check that the amount of ingredient is in each pill, not just the size of the pill itself), starting one to two weeks before arrival and continuing through the trip and for four weeks after departure. Chloroquine is safe, inexpensive and highly effective. Side effects are typically mild and may include nausea, abdominal discomfort, headache, dizziness, blurred vision or itching. Severe reactions are uncommon.

Protecting yourself against mosquito bites (p325) is just as important as taking malaria pills, since no pills are 100% effective.

If you anticipate not having access to medical care while traveling, bring along additional pills for self-treatment, which you should undertake if you develop symptoms that suggest malaria, such as high spiking fevers and can't reach a doctor. One option is to take an anti-malarial (such as chloroquine). If you start self-medication, you should try to see a doctor at the earliest possible opportunity; also see a doctor if you are still developing the disease while taking an anti-malarial – it suggests resistance to the drug.

If you develop a fever after returning home, see a physician, as malaria symptoms may not occur for months.

HEALTH

Typhoid Fever

Typhoid fever is caused by ingestion of food or water contaminated by a type of *Salmonella* known as *Salmonella typhi*. Fever occurs in virtually all cases. Other symptoms may include headache, malaise, muscle aches, dizziness, loss of appetite, nausea and abdominal pain. Either diarrhea or constipation may occur. Possible complications include intestinal perforation, intestinal bleeding, confusion, delirium or (rarely) coma.

Unless you expect to take all your meals in major hotels and restaurants, typhoid vaccine is a good idea. It's usually given orally, but is also available as an injection. Neither vaccine is approved for use in children under two years.

The drug of choice for typhoid fever is usually a quinolone antibiotic such as ciprofloxacin (Cipro) or levofloxacin (Levaquin), which many travelers carry for treatment of travelers' diarrhea. However, if you self-treat for typhoid fever, you may also need to self-treat for malaria, since the symptoms of the two diseases can be indistinguishable.

Yellow Fever

Yellow fever no longer occurs in Central America, but many Central American countries, including Honduras, require yellow-fever vaccine before entry if you're arriving from a country in Africa or South America where yellow fever occurs. If you're not arriving from a country with yellow fever, the vaccine is neither required nor recommended. Yellow-fever vaccine is given only in approved yellow-fever vaccination centers, which provide validated International Certificates of Vaccination ('yellow booklets'). The vaccine should be given at least 10 days before departure and remains effective for approximately 10 years. Reactions to the vaccine are generally mild and may include headaches, muscle aches, low-grade fevers or discomfort at the injection site. Severe, life-threatening reactions have been described but are extremely rare.

Other Infections

Brucellosis: This is an infection occurring in domestic and wild animals that may be transmitted to humans through direct animal contact or by consumption of unpasteurized dairy products from infected animals. Symptoms may include fever, malaise, depression, loss of appetite, headache, muscle aches and back pain. Complications can include arthritis, hepatitis, meningitis and endocarditis (heart valve infection).

Chagas' disease: This is a parasitic infection transmitted by triatomine insects (reduviid bugs), which inhabit crevices in the walls and roofs of substandard housing in South and Central America. In Honduras, most cases occur in lowland and coastal areas. The triatomine insect lays its feces on human skin as it bites, usually at night. A person becomes infected when he or she unknowingly rubs the feces into the bite wound or any other open sore. Chagas' disease is extremely rare in travelers. However, if you sleep in a poorly constructed house, especially one made of mud, adobe or thatch, you should be sure to protect yourself with a bed net and good insecticide.

Gnathostomiasis: This is a parasite acquired by eating raw or undercooked freshwater fish, and in ceviche, a popular lime-marinated fish salad. The chief symptom is intermittent, migratory swellings under the skin, sometimes associated with joint pains, muscle pains or gastrointestinal problems. The symptoms may not begin until many months after exposure.

Histoplasmosis: Caused by a soil-based fungus, this is acquired by inhalation, often when soil has been disrupted. Initial symptoms may include fever, chills, dry cough, chest pain and headache, sometimes leading to pneumonia.

HIV/AIDS: There have been reports from all Central American countries. Be sure to use condoms for all sexual encounters.

Leishmaniasis: This occurs in the mountains and jungles of all Central American countries. The infection is transmitted by sand flies, which are about one-third the size of mosquitoes. Leishmaniasis may be limited to the skin, causing slowly-growing ulcers over exposed parts of the body, or (less commonly) disseminate to the bone marrow, liver and spleen. The disease may be particularly severe in those with HIV. There is no vaccine for leishmaniasis. To protect yourself from sand flies, follow the same precautions as for mosquitoes (opposite), except that netting must be finer mesh (at least 18 holes to the linear inch).

Onchocerciasis (river blindness): This is caused by a roundworm invading the eye, leading to blindness. The infection is transmitted by black flies, which breed along the banks of rapidly flowing rivers and streams.

Typhus: This may be transmitted by lice in scattered pockets of the country.

TRAVELERS' DIARRHEA

To prevent diarrhea, avoid tap water unless it has been boiled, filtered or chemically disinfected (iodine tablets or chlorine drops); only eat fresh fruits or vegetables if cooked or peeled; be wary of dairy products that might contain unpasteurized milk; and be highly selective when eating food from street vendors.

If you develop diarrhea, be sure to drink plenty of fluids, preferably an oral rehydration solution containing lots of salt and sugar. A few loose stools don't require treatment, but if you start having more than four or five stools a day you should start taking an antibiotic (usually a quinolone drug) and an antidiarrheal agent (such as loperamide). If diarrhea is bloody or persists for more than 72 hours or is accompanied by fever, shaking chills or severe abdominal pain you should seek medical attention.

ENVIRONMENTAL HAZARDS & TREATMENT
Animal Bites

Do not attempt to pet, handle or feed any animal, with the exception of domestic animals known to be free of any infectious disease. Most animal injuries are directly related to a person's attempt to touch or feed the animal.

Any bite or scratch by a mammal, including bats, should be promptly and thoroughly cleansed with large amounts of soap and water, followed by application of an antiseptic such as iodine or alcohol. Contact the local health authorities immediately for possible postexposure treatment, whether or not you've been immunized against rabies. It may also be advisable to start an antibiotic, since wounds caused by animal bites and scratches frequently become infected. One of the newer quinolones, such as levofloxacin (Levaquin), which many travelers carry in case of diarrhea, is an appropriate choice.

Mosquito Bites

To prevent mosquito bites, wear long sleeves, long pants, hats and shoes (rather than san-

dals). Bring along insect repellent, preferably one containing DEET, which should be applied to exposed skin and clothing, but not to eyes, mouth, cuts, wounds or irritated skin. Products containing lower concentrations of DEET are as effective, but for shorter periods. In general, adults and children over 12 should use preparations containing 25% to 35% DEET, which usually lasts about six hours. Children between two and 12 years of age should use preparations containing no more than 10% DEET, applied sparingly, which should last about three hours. Neurological toxicity has been reported from DEET, especially in children, but appears to be extremely uncommon and generally related to overuse. Don't use DEET-containing compounds on children under two years.

Insect repellents containing certain botanical products, including oil of eucalyptus and soybean oil, are effective but last only 1½ to two hours. Where there is a high risk of malaria or yellow fever, use DEET-containing repellents. Products based on citronella are not effective.

For additional protection, apply permethrin to clothing, shoes, tents and bed nets. Permethrin treatments are safe and remain effective for at least two weeks, even when items are laundered. Permethrin should not be applied directly to skin.

Don't sleep with the window open unless there is a screen. If sleeping outdoors or in accommodation that allows entry of mosquitoes, use a bed net treated with permethrin, with edges tucked in under the mattress. The mesh size should be less than 1.5mm. Alternatively, use a mosquito coil, which will fill the room with insecticide through the night. Repellent-impregnated wristbands are not effective.

Snake & Scorpion Bites

Venomous snakes in Central America include the bushmaster, fer-de-lance (common lancehead), coral snake and various species of rattlesnakes. The fer-de-lance is the most lethal. It generally does not attack without provocation, but may bite humans who accidentally come too close as its lies camouflaged on the forest floor. The bushmaster is the world's largest pit viper, measuring up to 4m in length. Like all pit vipers, the bushmaster has a heat-sensing pit between the eye and nostril on each side

HEALTH

of its head, which it uses to detect the presence of warm-blooded prey.

In the event of a venomous snake bite, place the victim at rest, keep the bitten area immobilized, and move them immediately to the nearest medical facility. Avoid tourniquets, which are no longer recommended.

Scorpions are a problem in many regions. If stung, you should immediately apply ice or cold packs, immobilize the affected body part and go to the nearest emergency room. To prevent scorpion stings, be sure to inspect and shake out clothing, shoes and sleeping bags before use, and wear gloves and protective clothing when working around piles of wood or leaves.

Sun

To protect yourself from excessive sun exposure, you should stay out of the midday sun, wear sunglasses and a wide-brimmed hat, and apply sunscreen with SPF 15 or higher, providing both UVA and UVB protection. Sunscreen should be generously applied to all exposed parts of the body approximately 30 minutes before sun exposure and be re-applied after swimming or vigorous activity. Drink plenty of fluids and avoid strenuous exercise when the temperature is high.

Tick Bites

To prevent tick bites, follow the same precautions as for mosquitoes; boots, with pants tucked in, are preferable to shoes. Perform a thorough tick check at the end of each day. You'll generally need the assistance of a friend or mirror for a full examination. Remove ticks with tweezers, grasping them firmly by the head. Insect repellents based on botanical products, described above, have not been adequately studied for insects other than mosquitoes and cannot be recommended to prevent tick bites.

Water

Tap water in Honduras is generally not safe to drink. Vigorous boiling for one minute is the most effective means of water purification. At altitudes greater than 2000m, boil for three minutes. You can improve the taste of boiled water somewhat by pouring it back and forth between containers; it re-oxygenates the water.

Another option is to disinfect water with iodine pills. Instructions are usually enclosed and should be carefully followed. Or you can add 2% tincture of iodine to 1L (quart) of water (five drops to clear water, 10 drops to cloudy water) and let stand for 30 minutes. If the water is cold, a longer time may be required. The taste of iodinated water can be improved by adding vitamin C (ascorbic acid). Don't consume iodinated water for more than a few weeks. Pregnant women, those with a history of thyroid disease and those allergic to iodine should not drink iodinated water. Chlorine is also an effective way to purify water, and may be easier to find in Honduras – ask for 'cloro'. Two drops per liter does the trick; there should be a slight swimming-pool smell. Always wait 10 minutes before drinking.

A number of water filters are on the market. Those with smaller pores (reverse osmosis filters) provide the broadest protection, but they are relatively large and are readily plugged by debris. Those with somewhat larger pores (microstrainer filters) are ineffective against viruses, although they remove other organisms. Manufacturers' instructions must be carefully followed.

CHILDREN & PREGNANT WOMEN

In general, it's safe for children and pregnant women to go to Honduras. However, because some of the vaccines listed previously are not approved for use in children, or pregnant women, these travelers should be particularly careful not to drink tap water or consume any questionable food or beverage. Also, when traveling with children, make sure they're up to date on all routine immunizations. It's sometimes appropriate to give children some of their vaccines a little early before visiting a developing nation. You should discuss this with your pediatrician. If pregnant, bear in mind that should a complication such as premature labor develop while abroad, the quality of medical care may not be comparable to that in your home country.

Since yellow-fever vaccine is not recommended for pregnant women or children younger than nine months old, obtain a waiver letter (if you are arriving from a country with yellow fever), preferably written on letterhead stationery and bearing the stamp used by official immunization centers to validate the International Certificate of Vaccination.

Language

CONTENTS

Who Speaks What Where? 327
Spanish **327**
Pronunciation 327
Gender & Plurals 328
Accommodations 328
Conversation & Essentials 329
Directions 329
Emergencies 330
Health 330
Language Difficulties 330
Numbers 330
Shopping & Services 331
Time & Dates 331
Transport 332
Travel with Children 333
Garífuna **333**

Spanish is the official language of Honduras and the main language the traveler will need. Every visitor to the country should attempt to learn some Spanish, the basic elements of which are easily acquired.

WHO SPEAKS WHAT WHERE?

Spanish is spoken throughout mainland Honduras, though it is a second language for some indigenous communities in La Moskitia and in Garífuna areas on the north coast. Miskito (see p333), Garífuna (see p333) and English (in the Bay Islands and along the Caribbean Coast) are also used. While Bay Islanders traditionally speak English, an influx of mainlanders in search of construction jobs has begun to tip the balance toward Spanish, especially on Roatán.

SPANISH

A month-long language course taken before departure can go a long way toward facilitating communication and comfort on the road. Alternatively, language courses (see p305) are also available in Honduras. Even if classes are impractical, you should

make the effort to learn a few basic words and phrases. Don't hesitate to practice your new skills – in general, Hondurans meet attempts to communicate in their languages, however halting, with enthusiasm and appreciation.

For a more comprehensive guide to the Spanish of the region, get a copy of Lonely Planet's *Latin American Spanish Phrasebook*.

PRONUNCIATION

Spanish spelling is phonetically consistent, meaning that there's a clear and consistent relationship between what you see in writing and how it's pronounced. In addition, most Spanish sounds have English equivalents, so English speakers shouldn't have too much trouble being understood.

Vowels

a	as in 'father'
e	as in 'met'
i	as in 'marine'
o	as in 'or' (without the 'r' sound)
u	as in 'rule'; the 'u' is not pronounced after **q** and in the letter combinations **gue** and **gui**, unless it's marked with a diaeresis (eg *argüir*), in which case it's pronounced as English 'w'
y	at the end of a word or when it stands alone, it's pronounced as the Spanish **i** (eg *ley*); between vowels within a word it's as the 'y' in 'yonder'

Consonants

As a rule, Spanish consonants resemble their English counterparts; the exceptions are listed below.

While the consonants **ch**, **ll** and **ñ** are generally considered distinct letters, **ch** and **ll** are now often listed alphabetically under **c** and **l** respectively. The letter **ñ** is still treated as a separate letter and comes after **n** in alphabetical listings.

b	similar to English 'b'; referred to as 'b larga'
c	as in 'celery' before **e** and **i**; otherwise as English 'k'
ch	as in 'church'

d	as in 'dog,' but between vowels and after **l** or **n**, the sound is closer to the 'th' in 'this'	
g	as the 'ch' in the Scottish *loch* before **e** and **i** ('kh' in our guides to pronunciation); elsewhere, as in 'go'	
h	invariably silent. If your name begins with this letter, listen carefully if you're waiting for public officials to call you.	
j	as the 'ch' in the Scottish *loch* (written as 'kh' in our guides to pronunciation)	
ll	as the 'y' in 'yellow'	
ñ	as the 'ni' in 'onion'	
r	as in 'run', but strongly rolled, especially in words with **rr**	
rr	very strongly rolled	
v	similar to English 'b,' but softer; referred to as 'b corta'	
x	usually pronounced as **j** above; as in 'taxi' in other instances. Note that in Mayan words **x** is pronounced like English 'sh'	
z	as the 's' in 'sun'	

Word Stress

In general, words ending in vowels or the letters **n** or **s** have stress on the next-to-last syllable, while those with other endings have stress on the last syllable. Thus *vaca* (cow) and *caballos* (horses) both carry stress on the next-to-last syllable, while *ciudad* (city) and *infeliz* (unhappy) are both stressed on the last syllable.

Written accents will almost always appear in words that don't follow the rules above, eg *sótano* (basement), *América* and *porción* (portion).

GENDER & PLURALS

In Spanish, nouns are either masculine or feminine, and there are rules to help determine gender (there are of course some exceptions). Feminine nouns generally end with **-a** or with the groups **-ción**, **-sión** or **-dad**. Other endings typically signify a masculine noun. Endings for adjectives also change to agree with the gender of the noun they modify (masculine/feminine **-o/-a**). Where both masculine and feminine forms are included in this language guide, they are separated by a slash, with the masculine form first, eg *perdido/a*.

If a noun or adjective ends in a vowel, the plural is formed by adding **s** to the end. If it ends in a consonant, the plural is formed by adding **es** to the end.

ACCOMMODATIONS

I'm looking for ...	*Estoy buscando ...*	e·*stoy* boos·*kan*·do ...
Where is ...?	*¿Dónde hay ...?*	don·de ai ...
a hotel	*un hotel*	oon o·*tel*
a guesthouse	*un hospedaje*	oon os·pe·*da*·khe
a youth hostel	*hostal*	os·*tal*

MAKING A RESERVATION

(for phone or written requests)

To ...	*A ...*
From ...	*De ...*
Date	*Fecha*
I'd like to book ...	*Quisiera reservar ...* (see the list under 'Accommodations' for bed and room options)
in the name of ...	*en nombre de ...*
for the nights of ...	*para las noches del ...*
credit card ...	*tarjeta de crédito ...*
number	*número*
expiry date	*fecha de vencimiento*
Please confirm ...	*Puede confirmar ...*
availability	*la disponibilidad*
price	*el precio*

I'd like a ... room.	*Quisiera una habitación ...*	kee·*sye*·ra oo·na a·bee·ta·*syon* ...
double	*doble*	do·ble
single	*individual*	een·dee·vee·*dwal*
twin	*con dos camas*	kon dos ka·mas

How much is it per ...?	*¿Cuánto cuesta por ...?*	kwan·to kwes·ta por ...
night	*noche*	no·che
person	*persona*	per·*so*·na
week	*semana*	se·*ma*·na

private/shared bathroom	*baño privado/ compartido*	ba·nyo pree·*va*·do/ kom·par·*tee*·do
full board	*pensión completa*	pen·*syon* kom·*ple*·ta
too expensive	*demasiado caro*	de·ma·*sya*·do ka·ro
cheaper	*más económico*	mas e·ko·*no*·mee·ko
discount	*descuento*	des·*kwen*·to

Are there any rooms available?

¿Hay habitaciones libres?	ay a·bee·ta·*syon*·es lee·bres

Does it include breakfast?
¿Incluye el desayuno?   een-*kloo*-ye el de-sa-*yoo*-no
May I see the room?
¿Puedo ver la   pwe-do ver la
habitación?   a-bee-ta-*syon*
I don't like it.
No me gusta.   no me *goos*-ta
It's fine. I'll take it.
Está bien. Lo tomo.   es-*ta* byen lo *to*-mo
I'm leaving now.
Me voy ahora.   me *voy* a-o-ra

CONVERSATION & ESSENTIALS

In their public behavior, Hondurans, like most Central Americans, are very conscious of civilities, sometimes to the point of ceremoniousness. Never approach a stranger for information without extending a greeting, and use only the polite form of address, especially with the police and public officials. Young people may be less likely to expect this, but it's best to stick to the polite form unless you're quite sure you won't offend by using the informal mode. The polite form is used in all cases in this guide; where options are given, the form is indicated by the abbreviations 'pol' and 'inf.'

Saying *por favor* (please) and *gracias* (thank you) are second nature to most Central Americans and a recommended tool in your travel kit. The three most common Spanish greetings are often shortened to simply *buenos* (for *buenos diás*) and *buenas* (for *buenas tardes* and *buenas noches*).

Hello.	Hola.	o-la
Good morning.	Buenos días.	bwe-nos dee-as
Good afternoon.	Buenas tardes.	bwe-nas tar-des
Good evening/ night.	Buenas noches.	bwe-nas no-ches
Goodbye.	Adiós.	a-dyos (rarely used)
Bye/See you soon.	Hasta luego.	as-ta lwe-go
Yes.	Sí.	see
No.	No.	no
Please.	Por favor.	por fa-vor
Thank you.	Gracias.	gra-syas
Many thanks.	Muchas gracias.	moo-chas gra-syas
You're welcome.	De nada.	de na-da
Pardon me.	Perdón.	per-don
Excuse me.	Permiso.	per-mee-so
(used when asking permission)		
Forgive me.	Disculpe.	dees-kool-pe
(used when apologizing)		

How are things?
¿Qué tal?   ke tal
What's your name?
¿Cómo se llama?   ko-mo se ya-ma (pol)
¿Cómo te llamas?   ko-mo te ya-mas (inf)
My name is ...
Me llamo ...   me ya-mo ...
It's a pleasure to meet you.
Mucho gusto.   moo-cho goos-to
The pleasure is mine.
El gusto es mío.   el goos-to es mee-o
Where are you from?
¿De dónde es/eres?   de don-de es/er-es (pol/inf)
I'm from ...
Soy de ...   soy de ...
Where are you staying?
¿Dónde está alojado?   don-de es-ta a-lo-kha-do (pol)
¿Dónde estás alojado?   don-de es-tas a-lo-kha-do (inf)
May I take a photo?
¿Puedo sacar una foto? pwe-do sa-kar oo-na fo-to

SIGNS

Entrada	Entrance
Salida	Exit
Información	Information
Abierto	Open
Cerrado	Closed
Prohibido	Prohibited
Policía/Policía Turística	Police Station
Servicios/Baños	Toilets
Hombres/Caballeros	Men
Mujeres/Damas	Women

DIRECTIONS

How do I get to ...?
¿Cómo puedo llegar   ko-mo pwe-do ye-gar
a ...?   a ...
Is it far?
¿Está lejos?   es-ta le-khos
Go straight ahead.
Siga/Vaya derecho.   see-ga/va-ya de-re-cho
Turn left.
Volteé a la izquierda. vol-te-e a la ees-kyer-da
Turn right.
Volteé a la derecha.   vol-te-e a la de-re-cha
I'm lost.
Estoy perdido/a.   es-toy per-dee-do/a
Can you show me (on the map)?
¿Me lo podría indicar   me lo po-dree-a een-dee-kar
(en el mapa)?   (en el ma-pa)

north	norte	nor-te
south	sur	soor

EMERGENCIES

Help!	¡Socorro!	so·ko·ro
Fire!	¡Incendio!	een·sen·dyo
I've been robbed.	Me robaron.	me ro·ba·ron
Go away!	¡Déjeme!	de·khe·me
Get lost!	¡Váyase!	va·ya·se

Call ...!	¡Llame a ...!	ya·me a
an ambulance	una ambulancia	oo·na am·boo·lan·sya
a doctor	un médico	oon me·dee·ko
the police	la policía	la po·lee·see·a

It's an emergency.
Es una emergencia.   es oo·na e·mer·khen·sya
Could you help me, please?
¿Me puede ayudar,   me pwe·de a·yoo·dar
por favor?   por fa·vor
I'm lost.
Estoy perdido/a.   es·toy per·dee·do/a
Where are the toilets?
¿Dónde están los baños?   don·de es·tan los ba·nyos

east	este/oriente	es·te/o·ryen·te
west	oeste/occidente	o·es·te/ok·see·den·te
here	aquí	a·kee
there	allí	a·yee
avenue	avenida	a·ve·nee·da
block	cuadra	kwa·dra
street	calle/paseo	ka·lye/pa·se·o

HEALTH

I'm sick.
Estoy enfermo/a.   es·toy en·fer·mo/a
I need a doctor.
Necesito un médico.   ne·se·see·to oon me·dee·ko
Where's the hospital?
¿Dónde está el hospital?   don·de es·ta el os·pee·tal
I'm pregnant.
Estoy embarazada.   es·toy em·ba·ra·sa·da
I've been vaccinated.
Estoy vacunado/a.   es·toy va·koo·na·do/a

I'm allergic ... to ...	Soy alérgico/a ... a/al ...	soy a·ler·khee·ko/a ... a ...
to antibiotics	a los antibióticos	a los an·tee·byo·tee·kos
to nuts	a las nueces	a las·nwe·ses
to peanuts	a las maníes	a los·ma·nee·es
to penicillin	a la penicilina	a la pe·nee·see·lee·na

I'm ...	Soy ...	soy ...
asthmatic	asmático/a	as·ma·tee·ko/a
diabetic	diabético/a	dya·be·tee·ko/a
epileptic	epiléptico/a	e·pee·lep·tee·ko/a

I have ...	Tengo ...	ten·go ...
a cough	tos	tos
diarrhea	diarrea	dya·re·a
a headache	un dolor de cabeza	oon do·lor de ka·be·sa
nausea	náusea	now·se·a

LANGUAGE DIFFICULTIES
Do you speak (English)?
¿Habla/Hablas (inglés)?   a·bla/a·blas (een·gles) (pol/inf)
Does anyone here speak English?
¿Hay alguien que hable   ai al·gyen ke a·ble
inglés?   een·gles
I (don't) understand.
Yo (no) entiendo.   yo (no) en·tyen·do
How do you say ...?
¿Cómo se dice ...?   ko·mo se dee·se ...
What does ... mean?
¿Qué quiere decir ...?   ke kye·re de·seer ...

Could you please ...?	¿Puede ..., por favor?	pwe·de ... por fa·vor
repeat that	repetirlo	re·pe·teer·lo
speak more slowly	hablar más despacio	a·blar mas des·pa·syo
write it down	escribirlo	es·kree·beer·lo

NUMBERS

1	uno	oo·no
2	dos	dos
3	tres	tres
4	cuatro	kwa·tro
5	cinco	seen·ko
6	seis	says
7	siete	sye·te
8	ocho	o·cho
9	nueve	nwe·ve
10	diez	dyes
11	once	on·se
12	doce	do·se
13	trece	tre·se
14	catorce	ka·tor·se
15	quince	keen·se
16	dieciséis	dye·see·says
17	diecisiete	dye·see·sye·te
18	dieciocho	dye·see·o·cho
19	diecinueve	dye·see·nwe·ve
20	veinte	vayn·te
21	veintiuno	vayn·tee·oo·no

30	treinta	trayn·ta
31	treinta y uno	trayn·ta ee oo·no
40	cuarenta	kwa·ren·ta
50	cincuenta	seen·kwen·ta
60	sesenta	se·sen·ta
70	setenta	se·ten·ta
80	ochenta	o·chen·ta
90	noventa	no·ven·ta
100	cien	syen
101	ciento uno	syen·to oo·no
200	doscientos	do·syen·tos
1000	mil	meel
5000	cinco mil	seen·ko meel
10,000	diez mil	dyes meel
50,000	cincuenta mil	seen·kwen·ta meel

SHOPPING & SERVICES

I'd like to buy ...
Quisiera comprar ...   kee·sye·ra kom·prar ...
I'm just looking.
Sólo estoy mirando.   so·lo es·toy mee·ran·do
May I look at it?
¿Puedo mirarlo/la?   pwe·do mee·rar·lo/la
How much is it?
¿Cuánto cuesta?   kwan·to kwes·ta
That's too expensive for me.
Es demasiado caro   es de·ma·sya·do ka·ro
para mí.   pa·ra mee
Could you lower the price?
¿Podría bajar un poco   po·dree·a ba·khar oon po·ko
el precio?   el pre·syo
I don't like it.
No me gusta.   no me goos·ta
I'll take it.
Lo llevo.   lo ye·vo

Do you accept ...?   ¿Aceptan ...?   a·sep·tan ...
American dollars   dólares americanos   do·la·res a·me·ree·ka·nos
credit cards   tarjetas de crédito   tar·khe·tas de kre·dee·to
traveler's checks   cheques de viajero   che·kes de vya·khe·ro

less   menos   me·nos
more   más   mas
large   grande   gran·de
small   pequeño/a   pe·ke·nyo/a

I'm looking for (the) ...   Estoy buscando ...   es·toy boos·kan·do
ATM   el cajero automático   el ka·khe·ro ow·to·ma·tee·ko
bank   el banco   el ban·ko

bookstore	la librería	la lee·bre·ree·a
embassy	la embajada	la em·ba·kha·da
exchange house	la casa de cambio	la ka·sa de kam·byo
general store	la tienda	la tyen·da
laundry	la lavandería	la la·van·de·ree·a
market	el mercado	el mer·ka·do
pharmacy/ chemist	la farmacia/ la droguería	la far·ma·sya/ la dro·ge·ree·a
post office	el correo	el ko·re·o
supermarket	el supermercado	el soo·per·mer·ka·do
tourist office	la oficina de turismo	la o·fee·see·na de too·rees·mo

What time does it open/close?
¿A qué hora abre/   a ke o·ra a·bre/
cierra?   sye·ra
I want to change some money/traveler's checks.
Quiero cambiar dinero/   kye·ro kam·byar dee·ne·ro/
cheques de viajero.   che·kes de vya·khe·ro
What is the exchange rate?
¿Cuál es el tipo de   kwal es el tee·po de
cambio?   kam·byo
How many quetzals per dollar?
¿Cuántos lempiras   kwan·tos lem·pee·ras
por dólar?   por do·lar
I want to call ...
Quiero llamar a ...   kye·ro lya·mar a ...

airmail	correo aéreo	ko·re·o a·e·re·o
letter	carta	kar·ta
registered mail	certificado	ser·tee·fee·ka·do
stamps	estampillas	es·tam·pee·lyas

TIME & DATES

What time is it?	¿Qué hora es?	ke o·ra es
It's one o'clock.	Es la una.	es la oo·na
It's four o'clock.	Son las cuatro.	son las kwa·tro
midnight	medianoche	me·dya·no·che
noon	mediodía	me·dyo·dee·a
half past two	dos y media	dos ee me·dya
now	ahora	a·o·ra
today	hoy	oy
tonight	esta noche	es·ta no·che
tomorrow	mañana	ma·nya·na
yesterday	ayer	a·yer
Monday	lunes	loo·nes
Tuesday	martes	mar·tes
Wednesday	miércoles	myer·ko·les
Thursday	jueves	khwe·ves
Friday	viernes	vyer·nes

| Saturday | sábado | sa·ba·do |
| Sunday | domingo | do·meen·go |

January	enero	e·ne·ro
February	febrero	fe·bre·ro
March	marzo	mar·so
April	abril	a·breel
May	mayo	ma·yo
June	junio	khoo·nyo
July	julio	khoo·lyo
August	agosto	a·gos·to
September	septiembre	sep·tyem·bre
October	octubre	ok·too·bre
November	noviembre	no·vyem·bre
December	diciembre	dee·syem·bre

TRANSPORT
Public Transport

What time does	¿A qué hora ...	a ke o·ra ...
... leave/arrive?	sale/llega?	sa·le/ye·ga
the bus	el autobus	el ow·to·boos
the plane	el avión	el a·vyon
the ship	el barco/buque	el bar·ko/boo·ke

airport	el aeropuerto	el a·e·ro·pwer·to
bus station	la estación de autobuses	la es·ta·syon de ow·to·boo·ses
bus stop	la parada de autobuses	la pa·ra·da de ow·to·boo·ses
luggage check room	guardería/ equipaje	gwar·de·ree·a/ e·kee·pa·khe
ticket office	la boletería	la bo·le·te·ree·a

I'd like a ticket to ...
Quiero un boleto a ... kye·ro oon bo·le·to a ...
What's the fare to ...?
¿Cuánto cuesta hasta ...? kwan·to kwes·ta a·sta ...

student's	de estudiante	de es·too·dyan·te
1st class	primera clase	pree·me·ra kla·se
2nd class	segunda clase	se·goon·da kla·se
single/one-way	ida	ee·da
return/round trip	ida y vuelta	ee·da ee vwel·ta
taxi	taxi	tak·see

Private Transport

I'd like to hire a/an ...	Quisiera alquilar ...	kee·sye·ra al·kee·lar ...
bicycle	una bicicleta	oo·na bee·see·kle·ta
car	un auto/ un coche	oon ow·to/ oon ko·che
4WD	un cuatro por cuatro	oon kwa·tro por kwa·tro
motorbike	una moto	oo·na mo·to

ROAD SIGNS

Acceso	Entrance
Estacionamiento	Parking
Ceda el Paso	Give way
Despacio	Slow
Dirección Única	One-way
Mantenga Su Derecha	Keep to the Right
No Adelantar/ No Rebase	No Passing
Peaje	Toll
Peligro	Danger
No Estacionar	No Parking
Prohibido el Paso	No Entry
Pare/Stop	Stop
Salida de Autopista	Exit Freeway

pickup (truck)	pickup	pee·kop
truck	camión	ka·myon
to hitchhike	pedir jalón	pe·deer ja·lon

Is this the road to ...?
¿Se va a ... por esta carretera? se va a ... por es·ta ka·re·te·ra
Where's a petrol station?
¿Dónde hay una gasolinera? don·de ai oo·na ga·so·lee·ne·ra
Please fill it up.
Lleno, por favor. ye·no por fa·vor
I'd like (10) gallons'
Quiero (diez) galones. kye·ro (dyes) ga·lo·nes

| diesel | diesel | dee·sel |
| petrol (gas) | gasolina | ga·so·lee·na |

(How long) Can I park here?
¿(Por cuánto tiempo) Puedo estacionar aquí? (por kwan·to tyem·po) pwe·do es·ta·syo·nar a·kee
Where do I pay?
¿Dónde se paga? don·de se pa·ga
I need a mechanic.
Necesito un mecánico. ne·se·see·to oon me·ka·nee·ko
The car has broken down (in ...).
El carro se ha averiado (en ...). el ka·ro se a a·ve·rya·do (en ...)
The motorbike won't start.
No arranca la moto. no a·ran·ka la mo·to
I have a flat tyre.
Tengo un pinchazo. ten·go oon peen·cha·so
I've run out of petrol.
Me quedé sin gasolina. me ke·de seen ga·so·lee·na
I've had an accident.
Tuve un accidente. too·ve oon ak·see·den·te

HANDY MISKITO PHRASES

With more than 150,000 native speakers scattered along one of the Caribbean's most beautiful and untouched stretches of coastline, Miskito isn't a bad language to know for the visitor to Honduras. Here are a few phrases to get you started.

Hello/Goodbye.	*Naksa/Aisabi.*
Yes/No.	*Ow/Apia.*
Please/Thank you.	*Plees/Dingki pali.*
How are you?	*Nakisma?*
good/fine	*pain*
bad/lousy	*saura*
friend	*pana*
Does anyone here speak Spanish?	*Nu apo ya Ispel aisee sapa?*
How much is it?	*Naki preis?*
My name is (Jane).	*Yan nini (Jane).*
What's your name?	*An maninam dia?*
Could you tell me where a hotel is?	*Man ailwis hotel ansara barsa?*
Excuse me, but could you help me?	*Escyus, man sipsma ilpeimonaya?*
I'm a vegetarian.	*Yan wal wina kalila pias.*
I feel sick.	*Yan siknes.*
I'm allergic to mangos/peanuts.	*Yan siknes brisna mango/mani.*
Where is the bus station?	*Ansarasa buskaba takaskisa?*
What time does the bus/boat leave?	*Man nu apo dia teim bustaki/duritaki sapa?*
How do I get to Bonanza?	*Napkei sipsna gwaiya Bonanza?*
Is it far/near?	*Nawina lihurasa/lamarasa?*
May I cross your property?	*Sipsna man prizcamku nueewaiya?*
Are there landmines?	*Danomite barsakei?*
Where can I change dollars?	*Ansara dalas sismonaya sipsna?*
Can I smoke here?	*Yan cigaret diaya sipsna?*
Do you have a bathroom?	*Baño brisma?*

TRAVEL WITH CHILDREN

I need ...	*Necesito ...*	ne·se·*see*·to ...
Do you have ...?	*¿Hay ...?*	ai ...
a car baby seat	*un asiento de seguridad para bebés*	oon a·*syen*·to de se·goo·ree·*da* pa·ra be·*bes*

a child-minding service	*un servicio de cuidado de niños*	oon ser·*vee*·syo de kwee·*da*·do de nee·nyos
a children's menu	*una carta infantil*	oona *kar*·ta een·fan·*teel*
a creche	*una guardería*	oo·na gwar·de·*ree*·a
(disposable) diapers/nappies	*pañales (de usar y tirar)*	pa·*nya*·les de oo·sar ee tee·*rar*
an (English-speaking) babysitter	*una niñera (de habla inglesa)*	oo·na nee·*nye*·ra (de *a*·bla een·*gle*·sa)
formula (milk)	*leche en polvo*	le·che en *pol*·vo
a highchair	*una trona*	oo·na *tro*·na
a potty	*una pelela*	oo·na pe·*le*·la
a stroller	*un cochecito*	oon ko·che·*see*·to

Do you mind if I breast-feed here?
¿Le molesta que dé de pecho aquí?	le mo·*les*·ta ke de de pe·cho a·*kee*

Are children allowed?
¿Se admiten niños?	se ad·*mee*·ten *nee*·nyos

GARÍFUNA

Until 1993 the Garífuna language had no standardized written form. The publication of the *People's Garífuna Dictionary* (National Garífuna Council of Belize, 1993) was a part of an ongoing effort to preserve a language that has been slowly dying, as it is not generally taught in schools, and most Garinagu use Kriol (the local creole) or English as their first language.

It's not necessary to learn Garífuna – every Garífuna speaker will almost certainly have a better command of English than non-Garífuna will ever have of Garífuna – but we've included some handy phrases to use as ice-breakers or just to make a big impression on the locals.

The language itself is a mixture of Arawak, Yoruba, Swahili, Bantu, Spanish, English and French. For more information, look for the books *Garífuna History, Language and Culture of Belize, Central America and the Caribbean* (Cayetano, 1993) and the bilingual (English/Garífuna) *Marcella Our Legacy* (Lewis, 1994).

Pronunciation

Consonants are pronounced as they are in English (**g** is always as in 'go'), and vowels are similar to those in Spanish (see Pronunciation on p327). Stress is usually placed on the first syllable of two-syllable words and the second syllable in longer words.

Greetings & Conversation

Hello.	*Mabuiga.*
Good morning.	*Buiti binafi.*
Good afternoon.	*Buiti amidi.*
Good evening.	*Buiti raba weyu.*
Good night.	*Buiti gunyon.*
How are you?	*Ida biangi?*
I'm well.	*Magadietina.*
How about you?	*Angi buguya?*
Have a good day.	*Buidi lamuga buweyuri.*
Thank you.	*Seremein, nian bun.*
Thank you very much.	*Owembu seremein na bun.*
What's your name?	*Ka biri?*
My name is ...	*... niribei.*
Where do you come from?	*Halia giendibu sa?*
I come from ...	*... giendina.*

I was born in America.	*Meriga naguruwa.*
Where are you going?	*Halion badibu?*
I'm going to ...	*Neibuga ...*
I want to learn Garífuna.	*Buseintina nafureinderu Garífuna.*
Teach me a little Garífuna.	*Arufudahaba murusu Garífuna nu.*
What's this called in Garífuna?	*Ka liri le lidan Garífuna.*
This is ... in Garífuna.	*... le lidan Garífuna.*
I don't understand.	*Uwati gufaranda nanibu.*
Tell me again.	*Arienga ya bei nu.*
Do you like it?	*Hiseinti bun?*
I like it.	*Hisienti nun.*
I don't like it.	*Misienti.*
It's nice.	*Semeti.*
It's not nice.	*Mesemeti.*
It's good.	*Buiti.*
It's bad.	*Wuribati.*

Glossary

Here are some useful words you may come across during your time in Honduras. For definitions of food and drink terms, see p66.

aguardiente – a clear, potent liquor made from sugarcane; can also be referred to as *caña*
alcaldía – city hall
alfombras – colorful and intricate carpets made of sawdust and seeds
artesanías – handicrafts
Av – abbreviation for *avenida* (avenue)

bahía – bay
balneario – public swimming area
barrio – district, neighborhood

cabaña – cabin or bungalow (also called *cabina*)
calle – street
calzada – causeway
carretera – highway
catedral – cathedral
catracho – slang for Honduran
cayo – cay; small island of sand or coral fragments
cayuco – dugout canoe
centro de llamadas – public calling center
cerro – hill
cerveza – beer
ceviche – seafood marinated in lime juice, garlic and seasonings
Chac – Maya rain god, his likeness is on many ruins
chicha – liquor made from fermented pineapple peels
churrasco – Argentinean-style beef
cine – movie theater
ciudad – city
colectivo – taxi or minibus that picks up and drops off passengers along its route
comedor – a basic and cheap eatery, usually with a limited menu
completo – complete, fully booked
conquistador – any of the Spanish explorer-conquerors of Latin America
Contras – counter-revolutionary military groups fighting against the Sandinista government in Nicaragua throughout the 1980s
costa – coast
criollo – Creole; born in Latin America of Spanish parentage; on the Caribbean coast it refers to someone of mixed African and European descent (see also *mestizo* and *ladino*)

cuadra – city block
cueva – cave

edificio – building
entrada – entrance
expreso – express bus

feria – a fair or festival
finca – farm, plantation, ranch
fuerte – fort

Garífuna – descendants of West African slaves and Carib Indians, brought to the Caribbean coast of Central America in the late 18th century from the island of St Vincent; also referred to as Black Caribs
golfo – gulf
gringo/a – mildly pejorative term used in Latin America to describe male/female foreigners, particularly those from North America; often applied to any visitor of European heritage
guancasco – an annual ceremony that confirms peace and friendship between neighboring communities

hacienda – agricultural estate, plantation
hospedaje – guesthouse

iglesia – church
invierno – winter; the rainy season, which extends roughly from May through November
isla – island

junco – type of basket weaving

ladino – a person of mixed Indian and European parentage, often used to describe *mestizos* who speak Spanish; see also *mestizo* and *criollo*
lago – lake
laguna – lagoon or lake
lancha – boat, usually a small motorboat
lempira – Honduras' national currency
licuado – fresh fruit drink, blended with milk or water
lista de correos – poste restante (general delivery) mail

mar – sea
mercado – market
mestizo – person of mixed ancestry (usually Spanish and Indian; see also *criollo* and *ladino*)
metate – flat stone on which corn is ground
migración – immigration; office of an immigration department

mirador – lookout point
muelle – pier
museo – museum

Navidad – Christmas
NGO – nongovernmental organization

ordinario – slow bus

PADI – Professional Association of Diving Instructors
palapa – thatched, palm-leaf-roofed shelter with open sides
pan de coco – coconut bread
parque – park; also used to describe a plaza
parque central – the center of many cities and towns in Honduras
parque nacional – national park
pasteles – pastries stuffed with meat and veggies
pesca deportiva – sport fishing
pila – laundry station
pipante – flat-bottomed boat made from a single tree trunk
plato del día – plate (or meal) of the day
plato típico – a mixed plate of various foods typical for breakfast, lunch or dinner
platos fuertes – main dishes
playa – beach
puente – bridge
puerta – gate; door

puerto – port; harbor
pulpería – corner store, mini-mart
punta – point; traditional Garífuna dance involving much hip movement
pupusa – typical Honduran cornmeal mass stuffed with cheese or refried beans (or a mixture of both)

quetzal – Guatemala's national currency, named for the tropical bird

río – river

sacaguía – head guide
santos – saints
Semana Santa – Holy Week, the week preceding Easter
sendero – path or trail
sierra – mountain range; a saw
stela, stelae – standing stone monument(s) of the ancient Maya, usually carved
supermercado – supermarket, from a corner store to a large, US-style supermarket

típica – basic Honduran fare

verano – summer; Honduras' dry season, roughly from December to May

yaba ding ding – island term for pre-Colombian artifacts

Behind the Scenes

THIS BOOK

This 1st edition of *Honduras & the Bay Islands* was coordinated and written by Gary Chandler and Liza Prado. Dr David Goldberg wrote the Health chapter. The 'Rise and Fall of the Maya' boxed text was adapted from a much longer essay by Dr Allen J Christenson. Matthew Firestone wrote the boxed text on 'Putting Down the Guide'. Paige Penland contributed to the 'William Walker' boxed text. This guidebook was commissioned in Lonely Planet's Oakland office and produced by the following:

Commissioning Editor Greg Benchwick
Coordinating Editor Cahal McGroarty
Coordinating Cartographer Owen Eszeki
Coordinating Layout Designer Katie Thuy Bui
Managing Editor Imogen Bannister
Managing Cartographer Alison Lyall
Assisting Editors Michelle Bennett, Carolyn Boicos, Adrienne Costanzo, Nadine Davidoff, Chris Girdler, Victoria Harrison, Helen Koehne
Assisting Cartographers Daniel Fennessy, Kusnandar
Assisting Layout Designers Jacqueline McLeod, Wibowo Rusli
Cover Designer Marika Kozak
Project Managers Eoin Dunlevy, Kate McLeod
Language Content Coordinator Quentin Frayne

Thanks to David Burnett, Amy Carroll, Sin Choo, Sally Darmody, Bruce Evans, Mark Germanchis, Martin Heng, Julie Sheridan, Naomi Stephens, Celia Wood

THANKS

We have many, many people to thank for their help in the research and writing of this book.

Thank you, first, to everyone at Lonely Planet who had a hand in this project, especially our commissioning editor Greg Benchwick, and Alison Lyall, Eoin Dunlevy, Cahal McGroarty, Carolyn Boicos, Owen Eszeki and all the fabulous folks in Melbourne.

In Honduras, very special thanks go to Matt Humke of Rare Conservation for his amazing generosity and assistance; Kimberly Marks and Daniel Spatz of Utila Water Sports for the same; and to Lise Fogh and Soeren Borch, whose enormous help and hospitality came by a chance meeting in a crowded Ceibeño restaurant.

We received a tremendous amount of help from current and former Peace Corps volunteers, whose ready answers to our endless questions made this book immeasurably better. Thanks to Jeremy Anhalt, Anne & Mike Becker, Luke Bowman, Alexandra Chewning, Qalim Cromer, Karen Drachler (and neighbor Juan José Mesa), Kevin & Kathy Donoher, Julia Funes, Tom Hinds, Anthony Ives, Zachary Job, Lacy Kilgraine, Keri Krefetz, Katie Long, Heatherjean MacNeil, Suzanne Mills, Nick Mucha, Claire Pestak, Daniel Proctor, Anna Richter, Martin Rivera, Manny Sanchez, Barbara Seymour, Caroline Sherony, Sidney Slover, Tara Smarsh, Jim Stefon & Colleen Hennessey, Bonnie Tappan, Leo Tkach, Max Wilson & Lynette Acosta, David Wrathall and Casey Young.

Thank you too, to friends, travelers and volunteers along the way, particularly Josh Deutsch,

THE LONELY PLANET STORY

The story begins with a classic travel adventure: Tony and Maureen Wheeler's 1972 journey across Europe and Asia to Australia. There was no useful information about the overland trail then, so Tony and Maureen published the first Lonely Planet guidebook to meet a growing need.

From a kitchen table, Lonely Planet has grown to become the largest independent travel publisher in the world, with offices in Melbourne (Australia), Oakland (USA) and London (UK). Today Lonely Planet guidebooks cover the globe. There is an ever-growing list of books and information in a variety of media. Some things haven't changed. The main aim is still to make it possible for adventurous travelers to get out there – to explore and better understand the world.

At Lonely Planet we believe travelers can make a positive contribution to the countries they visit – if they respect their host communities and spend their money wisely. Every year 5% of company profit is donated to charities around the world.

338

Michael Irvine, Prepare-To-Get-Wet Wendy, and especially Chris Lyke, for their on-the-road insight and assistance.

A number of people from organizations and businesses in Honduras were also very generous with their time and expertise. Thank you to Elmor Wood of Rare Conservation, Juan Carlos Molina & Angela Bendeck of Hostal Tamarindo, Andrew & Audrey from Reef Gliders, Will Welbourn of Coconut Tree Divers, Kenya Mejía of REDHES, Patrick Ahern of Oxfam International, and his daughter Ana Luisa Ahern, our SPS nightlife guru.

Back home, we're grateful to have Rukaiyah in our lives and just a mile away, to Marisa for the supreme airport pickup, Joey and Sue for pre-deadline provisions, Beatriz and Rich for the post-deadline champagne, Kevin & Cindi for the Christmas scuba fund, Brian for his afternoon commute, Kelly & Dan for watching the car, Kaitlyn & TJ for train-station balloons, our brothers and sisters for knowing when to call, and our parents always for their unfailing love and support.

SEND US YOUR FEEDBACK

We love to hear from travelers – your comments keep us on our toes and help make our books better. Our well-traveled team reads every word on what you loved or loathed about this book. Although we cannot reply individually to postal submissions, we always guarantee that your feedback goes straight to the appropriate authors, in time for the next edition. Each person who sends us information is thanked in the next edition – and the most useful submissions are rewarded with a free book.

To send us your updates – and find out about Lonely Planet events, newsletters and travel news – visit our award-winning website: **www.lonelyplanet.com/contact**.

Note: We may edit, reproduce and incorporate your comments in Lonely Planet products such as guidebooks, websites and digital products, so let us know if you don't want your comments reproduced or your name acknowledged. For a copy of our privacy policy visit www.lonelyplanet.com/privacy.

Index

A

accommodations 301-3
activities 76-7, 303-4, *see also*
    individual activities
adventure travel 58
    caving 115, 119, 180
    hiking 58-9, 303
    La Picucha 118-19
    mountain biking 59, 214-15, 303
    rafting 59-60, 120, 192, 214,
        303-4, **12**
aguardiente 63
Ahuas 294-5
AIDS 45, 127, 193
air travel
    to/from Honduras 313-15
    within Honduras 317
Amapala 104-6
animals 52, 120, **11**, *see also*
    individual animals
    books 53
animal bites 325-6
archaeological sites
    Copán archaeological site 146-54,
        147, 6
    Los Sapos 145-6
    Parque Eco-Arqueológico de los
        Naranjos 175-6
    Sitio Archeológico El Puente 138
Arellano, Colonel López 36
artesanía 48, **15**
    shopping 86-7, 91, 94-5, 165,
        310
arts 48-50
ATMs 309

B

Baja Mar 195-6
banana industry 36, 42, 210, 235
    internet resources 34
bargaining 23, 310
baseball 44
Basílica de Suyapa 75
bathrooms 312
Bay Islands 236-7, **238**
    history 33

000 Map pages
000 Photograph pages

beaches
    Guanaja 275
    La Ceiba 214
    Palmetto Bay 260-1
    Puerto Cortés 193
    Tela 200
    Tornabé 206
    Utila Town 265
    West Bay 237, 254
beer 63
Belén 285-6
Belén Gualcho 168
bicycle travel, *see* cycling
birds 51, 52, **10**
bird-watching 91, 120, 122, 146,
    304
    Jardín Botánico Lancetilla 204
    Kaukira 300
    Lago de Yojoa 175
    Parque Eco-Arqueológico de los
        Naranjos 176
    Parque Nacional Jeannette Kawas
        (Punta Sal) 205
    Refugio de Vida Silvestre Laguna
        de Guaimoreto 234
boat travel
    to/from Honduras 316-17
    within Honduras 317
Bonacca, *see* Guanaja Town
books
    animals 53
    biographies 34
    diving 60
    food 62, 64
    health 321
    history 32, 36
    literature 40
    Theroux, Paul 235
    travel literature 22-4, 57, 60
border crossings 316
    El Salvador 102, 157, 174
    Guatemala 158
    Nicaragua 102, 298
Brick Bay 260
British influence 33
Brus Laguna 292-4
    fishing 61
bus travel 22
    to/from Honduras 315
    within Honduras 317-18, 319

business hours 304
butterflies 146, 246, 284-5, **10**

C

Callejas Romero, Rafael Leonardo
    38-40
Camp Bay 262-3
camping 61, 302
Cannon Island 293
canoeing 214, 277, *see also*
    kayaking
canopy tours 58, 214, 303
car travel
    driver's license 318
    insurance 318-19
    rental 318
    road rules 319
    to/from Honduras 315
    within Honduras 318-19
Carambola Botanical Gardens 257
Carías Andino, General Tiburcio 35-6
Carnaval del Aniversario de La Ceiba
    216
Catacamas 114-17
Catedral de la Inmaculada Concepción
    187
Catholicism 42, 47
caving 115, 119, 180
Cayos Cochinos 192, 227-8
Cedeño 103
Cedros 109-10
ceiba trees 53-6, 210
cell phones 42, 311
Central America & Dominican Republic
    Free Trade Agreement 30, 39-40,
    42-3, 104
Chachauate 23, **9**
child abuse 86
children, travel with 77-8, 304
    Casa K'inich 140
    food 64-5
    Gumbalimba Park 255
    handy phrases 333
    health 326
    itineraries 29
    Museo Para La Infancia El Pequeño
        Sula 129
cholera 322
Choluteca 100-2
Chortí, *see* Maya-Chortí

churches & cathedrals
  Basílica de Suyapa 75
  Catedral de la Inmaculada
    Concepción 187
  Iglesia de San Francisco 76
  Iglesia de Suyapa 75-6
  Iglesia Los Dolores 76, 8
  itineraries 28
  Las Mercedes church 160, 8
  San Manuel colonial church
    166-7
  San Pedro Sula cathedral 129
  Tegucigalpa cathedral 76
cigar making 68, 98, 155
  Noche de Fumadores 156
climate 21, 304-5
clubbing 85-6
cockfighting 44
Cocobila 286-7
coffee 63
Columbus, Christopher 31, 229, 239,
  273, 278
Comayagua 124, 185-9, **186**
comedores 63
conservation 61, 311
  coral 254, 13
consulates 306-7
Contras 37, 279
Copán archaeological site 146-54,
  147, 6
  sights 151-4
  tours 154
Copán Ruínas 36, 124, 138-45,
  139
  accommodations 141-2
  drinking 143-4
  emergency 139
  entertainment 143-4
  festivals 141
  food 142-3
  medical services 140
  shopping 144
  sights 140
  tourist information 140
  tours 141
  travel to/from 144-5
  travel within 145
coral 254, 13
costs 21-22
courses 305
  Spanish language 78, 140, 155,
    215, 231, 268
  yoga 140
Coxen Hole 258-9
credit cards 309

crime 30, 121, 128-9, 193, 200, 305-6
  gangs 39, 40
  Tegucigalpa 74
crocodiles 290
Cuevas de Susmay 107
Cuevas de Talgua 115
  skulls of Talgua 117
culture 30, 39, 41-50, 14
  British influence 33
  languages 46
  local lore 75, 155, 209, 258, 279
  sustainable travel 311
customs regulations 305
cycling 317, see also mountain biking

D
dance 49, 262
dangers & annoyances 305-6
  Bay Islands 240
  La Moskitia 280
  Las Marías 290
  north coast 193
  Parque Nacional La Tigra 92
  Parque Nacional Montaña de
    Celaque 163
  Parque Nacional Sierra de Agalta
    118
  Puerto Lempira 298
  San Pedro Sula 128-9
  Tegucigalpa 74
  Tela 200
Danlí 97-100
day trips 130
deep vein thrombosis 321-2
deforestation 56-7
del Valle, José Cecilio 100
dengue fever 322-3
diarrhea 325
disabled travelers 306
diseases 322-5
dive shops
  Roatán 247-8
  Utila Town 266-7
diving 60, 192, 237, 240-2, 303, 11,
  13, see also snorkeling
  books 60
  Cayos Cochinos 228
  costs 22
  Guanaja 274
  internet resources 59
  itineraries 29
  Omoa 197
  Roatán 247
  Utila 267
  West Bay 254-5

drinks 62-3
  glossary 67
driver's license 318
DVDs 302

E
East Harbour, see Utila Town
economy 30, 41, 42-3, 47, 104
  Central America & Dominican
    Republic Free Trade Agreement
    30, 39-40, 42-3, 104
ecotourism 58, 61
El Corpus 102-3
El Paraíso 99
El Paraíso department 95-9
El Pino 225
El Puente 138
electricity 302
embassies 306-7
emergency services 70
environmental issues 56-7, see also
  conservation
  illegal logging 30
Erandique 170
ethnicity 44, 46
  Garífuna 33, 43, 45-6, 207, 15,
    16
  ladinos 44
  Lenca 43, 44, 161
  Maya-Chortí 43, 44, 153
  Miskito 33, 43, 45, 283, 15
  Pech 43, 44-5, 210
  Tawahka 44-5, 279, 296
  Tolupanes 43, 45, 112

F
fax services 311
festivals 23, 307-8
  Carnaval del Aniversario de La
    Ceiba 216
  Feria de Café 174
  Feria de Copán Ruínas 141
  Feria de la Virgin de Suyapa 78
  Feria de San Isidro 216
  Feria de Santa Fe 233
  Feria Juniana 130, 308
  Festival de Mangos 96
  Festival del Amor y Amistad 216
  Festival Nacional de Maíz 98
  Festival Navideño 216
  Garífuna Festival 192, 195, 308,
    16
  La Feria de los Llanos 156
  La Feria de San Isidro 308
  Noche de Fumadores 156

INDEX

festivals *continued*
  Punta Gorda Festival 262, 307-8
  Semana Santa 78, 124, 156, 187, 200, 215, 307
  Sun Jam 272, 308
film 42, 46, 49
fishing, *see* sport fishing
Flores Facusse, Carlos Roberto 39
food 62, 64-5, 308
  books 62, 64
  customs 65
  glossary 66-7
  internet resources 62
  language 65-7
Fortaleza de San Fernando de Omoa 196-7
Fortaleza de Santa Bárbara de Trujillo 230, **8**
French Harbour 259-60

G
Galería Nacional de Arte 74
Gamero de Medina, Lucila 48
Garífuna 42, 45-6, 207, 239, 280, **14, 15, 16**
  artesanía 48
  Baja Mar 195
  books 64
  Chachauate 23, **9**
  dance 49, 50
  food 62
  Guadalupe 234
  history 33
  internet resources 43
  language 333-4
  Plaplaya 287-8
  Punta Gorda 262
  Sambo Creek 226
  San Antonio 234
  Santa Fe 233-4
  tours 224
  Travesía 23
Garífuna Festival 192, 195, 308, **16**
gay travelers 45, 134, 308
geography 30, 51, 106
geology 51, 58
golf 215-16
government 47
  Zelaya, Manuel 30, 39
Gracias 23, 124, 159-63, **160**
Guadalupe 234

Gualaco 119-20
Guanaja 237, 273-6, **273**, **12**

H
handicrafts, *see* artesanía
health 63, 320-6
  books 321
  internet resources 321
Hepatitis A 323
Hepatitis B 323
hiking 58-9, 303
  Belén Gualcho 168
  El Corpus 102-3
  El Pino 225
  Isla del Tigre 111
  La Campa 165
  La Ceiba 214
  Marcala 173
  Monumento Natural El Boquerón 114
  Parque Nacional Cerro Azul Meámbar 179-80
  Parque Nacional La Muralla 121-2
  Parque Nacional La Tigra 92-3
  Parque Nacional Montaña de Celaque 161, 163-4
  Parque Nacional Montaña de Comayagua 189
  Parque Nacional Montaña de Santa Bárbara 181
  Parque Nacional Sierra de Agalta 117-19
  Rais Ta 284
  Río Cangrejal 226
  safety 305
  San Juan 169
  San Manuel de Colohete 167
  Utila Town 266
  West End 246-7
history 31-40
  banana industry 34-5
  books 32, 36
  British influence 33
  Contras 37, 279
  Federal Republic of Central America 33
  independence from Spain 33-4
  internet resources 31, 37
  labor movement 37
  Maya period 148-9
  pirates 196, 229
  slavery 32, 33
  soccer war 35
  Spanish rule 31-2
  US military 37

hitchhiking 319
HIV/AIDS 45, 127, 193
horseback riding 165, 215, 261, 286, 303
Hurricane Mitch 38, 57

I
Iglesia de San Francisco 76
Iglesia de Suyapa 75-6
Iglesia Los Dolores 76, **8**
iguanas 53, 260, 265, **4**
immigration 30, 313, *see also* visas
independence from Spain 33-4
infections, *see* diseases
insect bites, *see* animal bites
insurance 308
  health 320
Internet access 70-1, 308-9
Internet resources 24, 41
  banana industry 34
  diving 59
  ecotourism 61
  food 62
  Garífuna 43
  health 321
  history 31, 37
  human rights 39
Iriona 282-3
Isla del Tigre 104-6
itineraries 20, 24, **20**
  around the country 25, **25**
  children, travel with 29, **29**
  colonial towns & cathedrals 28, **28**
  diving & snorkeling 29, **29**
  La Moskitia 27, **27**
  national parks & reserves 26, **26**

J
jaguars 52
Jardín Botánico Lancetilla 54, 204
Jewel Cay 23
Juticalpa 112-13

K
Kaukira 300
Kawas, Jeannette 205
kayaking 59-60, 214, 277, 303-4, *see also* canoeing
  Utila Town 266
  West End 246

L
La Campa 165-6
La Cascada de Los Jutes 115

000 Map pages
000 Photograph pages

La Ceiba 210-22, **211, 213**
  accommodations 216-17, 219
  activities 213-15
  drinking 220-1
  emergency services 210
  entertainment 220-1
  festivals 215-16
  food 218-20
  medical services 212
  rafting 59-60
  sights 212-13
  tourist offices 212
  tours 213, 215
  travel to/from 221-2
  travel within 222
La Ensenada 208-9
La Entrada 137-8
La Esperanza 170-2
La Feria de los Llanos 156
La Feria de San Isidro 308
La Moskitia 277-300, **278**
  itineraries 27
  travel to/from 281-2
  travel within 282
La Paz 190-1
La Picucha 107, 118-19
La Pintada 145-6
La Ruta Lenca 154-75
La Unión 121
ladinos 44, 280
Lago de Yojoa 124, 175-9, **176**
  fishing 61
Laguna de Caratasca 297-300
languages 65-7, 327-34
  Spanish courses 78, 140, 155, 215,
    231, 268
Las Marías 23, 289-92
laundry 302
legal matters 309
Lempira 32
Lenca 43, 44, 161, 172
  Lempira 32
lesbian travelers 45, 134, 308
literature 24, 48-9, 50
local transportation 319
logging 30, see also deforestation
Los Sapos 145-6

M
macaws 51, 10
Maduro, Ricardo 40
magazines 46
mahogany 56
malaria 323
manatees 52

mangroves 53, 57, 223, 7
maps 309
Marcala 173-5
Maya 31, 148, see also Maya-Chortí
  Copán archaeological site 146-54, 6
  Los Sapos 145-6
  Sitio Archeológico El Puente 138
Maya-Chortí 43, 44, 153
measures, see weights & measures
medical services 71, 322
Melgar Castro, General Juan Alberto 36
Mexican Empire 33
Miami 23, 206-8
Miskito 33, 43, 45, 277, 279, 283,
  289-90, 15
  artesanía 48
  Belén 285-6
  language 333
  Las Marías 23
  Rais Ta 23
Mistruk 299-300
money 21-2, 309-10, see also inside
  front cover
moneychangers 309
monkeys 52, 68, 104, 205
Monumento Natural El Boquerón 107,
  113-14
Moravian Church 299
Morazán, General Fransisco 33
motorcycle travel
  driver's license 318
  to/from Honduras 315
  within Honduras 318-19
mountain biking 59, 214-15, 303
museums
  Museo Colonial de Arte Religioso
    187
  Museo de Arqueología e Historia
    de San Pedro Sula 129
  Museo Histórico de la República 75
  Museo Nacional de Historia y
    Antropología Villa Roy 74
  Museo para la Identidad Nacional 75
  Museo Regional de Arqueología 187
  Museum of Butterflies & Insects 212
  Roatán Museum 257
music 49-50

N
national parks & reserves 26, 54,
  222-4, **55**
  Carambola Botanical Gardens 257
  Jardín Botánico Lancetilla 54, 204
  Parque Nacional Capiro-Calentura
    234

Parque Nacional Cerro Azul
  Meámbar 179-80
Parque Nacional Cusuco 54
Parque Nacional Jeannette Kawas
  (Punta Sal) 54, 192, 204-6
Parque Nacional La Muralla 121-2
Parque Nacional La Tigra 54, 68,
  91-4
Parque Nacional Marino Cayos
  Cochinos 54
Parque Nacional Montaña de
  Celaque 54, 163-4
Parque Nacional Montaña de
  Comayagua 189
Parque Nacional Montaña de Santa
  Bárbara 180-1
Parque Nacional Montaña de
  Yoro 111
Parque Nacional Montecristo-El
  Trifinio 159
Parque Nacional Pico Bonito 54,
  224-6, 12
Parque Nacional Pico Pijol 111
Parque Nacional Sierra de Agalta
  107, 117-19
Monumento Natural El Boquerón
  107, 113-14
Refugio de Vida Silvestre Cuero y
  Salado 54, 192, 222-4, 7
Refugio de Vida Silvestre Laguna
  de Guaimoreto 54, 234-5
Refugio de Vida Silvestre Ojochal
  68, 104-6
Refugio de Vida Silvestre Punta
  Izopo 54, 206
Reserva Biológica Misoco 109
Reserva Biológico El Chile 109
Reserva de la Biósfera del Río
  Plátano 54, 56, 277, 288-92,
  289, 15
Reserva de la Biosfera Tawahka
  Asangni 54
Reserva Marina Turtle Harbour 54
Sandy Bay & West End Marine Park
  54, 246
nature reserves, see national parks
  & reserves
newspapers 46
Nueva Ocotepeque 158-9

O
Oak Ridge 261-2
Ojojona 94-5
Olancho 112-23
Omoa 196-8

opening hours, *see inside front cover*
orchids 53, 56, 91, 226, 246

P
painting 49
Palacios 283-4
Palmetto Bay 260-1
Parque Eco-Arqueológico de los
  Naranjos 175-6
Parque Nacional Capiro-Calentura 234
Parque Nacional Cerro Azul Meámbar
  179-80
Parque Nacional Cusuco 54
Parque Nacional Jeannette Kawas
  (Punta Sal) 192, 204-6
Parque Nacional La Muralla 121-2
Parque Nacional La Tigra 54, 68, 91-4
Parque Nacional Marino Cayos
  Cochinos 54
Parque Nacional Montaña de Celaque
  54, 124, 161, 163-4
Parque Nacional Montaña de
  Comayagua 189
Parque Nacional Montaña de Santa
  Bárbara 180-1
Parque Nacional Montaña de Yoro 111
Parque Nacional Montecristo-El
  Trifinio 159
Parque Nacional Pico Bonito 54,
  224-6, 12
Parque Nacional Pico Pijol 111
Parque Nacional Sierra de Agalta 107,
  117-19
passports 313, *see also* visas
Paya Bay 262-3
Paz García, General Policarpo 36
Pech 43, 44-5, 210, 279, 289-90
petroglyphs 97
phonecards 311
photography 310
Pico Dama 277
Pigeon Cay 23
pine trees 53, 56
pirates 33, 196, 229
planning 21-4, *see also* itineraries
  vacations 308
plants 53-6, *see also individual plants*
Plaplaya 287-88
plato típico 62
population 30, 41, 43, *see also*
  ethnicity

000 Map pages
000 Photograph pages

postal services 310
protected areas, *see* national parks
  & reserves
Protestantism 47
Puerto Cortés 193-5
Puerto Lempira 297-9
Pulhapanzak falls 177, 7
Punta Gorda 262
Punta Gorda Festival 262, 307-8

R
radio 47, 302
rafting 59-60, 120, 192, 214, 303-4, 12
  Tawahka region 297
Rain of Fish 107, 110
Rais Ta 23, 277, 284-5
Refugio de Vida Silvestre Cuero y
  Salado 54, 192, 222-4, 7
Refugio de Vida Silvestre Laguna de
  Guaimoreto 54, 234-5
Refugio de Vida Silvestre Ojochal
  68, 104-6
Refugio de Vida Silvestre Punta Izopo
  54, 206
religion 42, 47, 299
  Catholicism 42, 47
  Moravian church 299
  Protestantism 47
Reserva Biológica Misoco 109
Reserva Biológico El Chile 109
Reserva de la Biósfera del Río Plátano
  54, 56, 277, 288-92, **289**, 15
Reserva de la Biosfera Tawahka
  Asangni 54
Reserva Marina Turtle Harbour 54
reserves, *see* national parks &
  reserves
restaurants 63
Río Cangrejal 225-6
Río Plátano 294-7, 7
Roatán 237, 242, 243-63, **242-3**, 9,
  11, 13
  day trips 263
  travel to/from 243
  travel within 243-4
Roatán Museum 257
ruins, *see* archaeological sites
Ruta Lenca, *see* La Ruta Lenca

S
safety 305-6
Sambo Creek 226-7
San Antonio 234
San Juan 168-70
San Manuel de Colohete 166-7

San Marcos de Caiquín 166
San Marcos de Colón 23, 103-4
San Pedro Sula 125-37, **126**, **128**
  accommodations 130-2
  clubbing 134
  day trips 130
  drinking 133-4
  emergency services 127
  entertainment 134
  festivals 130
  food 132-3
  Internet access 127
  medical services 127
  safety 128-9
  shopping 134-5
  sights 129-30
  travel to/from 135-6
  travel within 136-7
San Pedro Sula cathedral 129
San Sebastián 167-8
Sandy Bay 256-8
Sandy Bay & West End Marine Park
  54, 246
Santa Bárbara 182-3
Santa Fe 233-4
Santa Lucía 23, 68, 89-90
Santa Rosa de Aguán 235
Santa Rosa de Copán 154-8
Savá 235-6
sea turtles 52, 277, 287-8
Semana Santa 78, 124, 156, 187, 200,
  215, 307
  food 65
shopping 23, 310
  artsenía 86-7, 91, 94-5, 165, 310
Siguatepeque 183-5, **184**
skulls of Talgua 117
slavery 32, 33
snorkeling 60, 192, 237, 303, 13, *see
  also* diving
  Guanaja 274
  itineraries 29
  Trujillo 230
  Utila Town 266
  West End 246
soccer 43-44
  Estadio Nacional Tiburcio Carías
    Andino 86
  soccer war 35
solo travelers 310-1
Spanish rule 31-2
spelunking, *see* caving
sports 43-4
  Bay Islands International Triathlon
    255

sport fishing 61, 248, 303
Sun Jam 272, 308
sustainable travel 311
Swan Islands 276

T
Tawahka 44-5, 279, 296
Tawahka region 296-7
taxes 310, 315, 317
Tegucigalpa 70-89, **72-3**, **79**, **81**
    accommodations 78-83
    children, travel with 77-8
    day trips 77
    drinking 85
    entertainment 85-6
    festivals 78
    food 83-5
    safety 74
    shopping 86-7
    sights 74-6
    travel to/from 87
    travel within 87-9
    walking tour 77, **77**
Tegucigalpa cathedral 76
Tela 198-204, **199**
telephone services 42, 311, *see also inside front cover*
Tenampua 190-1
theft 305-6
Theroux, Paul 235
time 311-2
típico 62
tipping 309-10
toilets 312
Tolupanes 43, 45, 112
Tornabé 206
tourist information 71, 312

tours 141, 155
    canopy tours 214, 261
    La Moskitia 280-1
    Reserva de la Biósfera del Río Plátano 290, 291, **289**, 15
    Tela 200
    walking tours 77, **77**
    West End 248
traveler's checks 310
Travesía 23, 195-6
trekking, *see* hiking
Trinidad 181-2
Triunfo de la Cruz 209
Trujillo 229-33, **229**
TV 302
typhoid 324

U
Unesco 56, 146-8, 207
Utila 237, 263-73, 13
Utila Cays 272-3
Utila Town 263-9

V
vacations 308
vaccinations 320-1
Valle de Ángeles 90-1
Valle de Azacualpa 172-3
Valle de Copán 137-54
vegetarian travelers 64
    food 67
video systems 302, 310
visas 312, *see also* passports
volunteering 312

W
Walker, William 34, 231
Wampusirpi 295-6

waterfalls
    Cascada de Barro 97
    Cascada El Bejuco 226
    Cascada La Fortuna 97
    Cascada Río Grande 173
    Cascada Zacate 225
    Cataratas de Santa María de Gualcho 168
    El Chorrón 121
    La Cascada de Los Jutes 115
    La Cascada de Río Negro 230-1
    La Chorrera 119
    Los Golondrinas waterfall 90-1
    Pulhapanzak falls 177, 7
    Yamaranguila 172
weather 21, 304-5
weights & measures 302
West Bay 254-6
West End 244-54, **245**
whale sharks 52, 237, 239, 265-6, 11
white-water rafting, *see* rafting
women in Honduras 47
women travelers 310, 312
women's health 326
work 312

Y
Yamaranguila 172
Yarumela 189-90
yellow fever 324
yoga 140
Yoro 110-2
Yuscarán 23, 96

Z
Zelaya, Manuel 30

INDEX

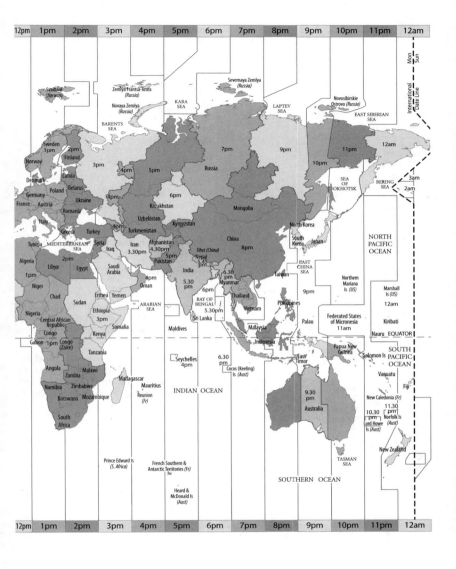

12pm | 1pm | 2pm | 3pm | 4pm | 5pm | 6pm | 7pm | 8pm | 9pm | 10pm | 11pm | 12am

Mon
Sun

International Date Line

Svalbard (Norway)

Zemlya Frantsa-Iosifa (Russia)

Severnaya Zemlya (Russia)

Novosibirskie Ostrova (Russia)

Novaya Zemlya (Russia)

KARA SEA

LAPTEV SEA

EAST SIBERIAN SEA

BARENTS SEA

7pm

9pm

11pm

12am

Sweden 1pm

Norway

2pm

Finland

3pm

10pm

SEA OF OKHOTSK

3am

BERING SEA

2am

Denmark

Latvia

Belarus

4pm

5pm

Russia

Germany

Poland

France   Austria

Ukraine

4pm

6pm

Romania

Kazakhstan

Mongolia

NORTH PACIFIC OCEAN

Italy

Greece   Turkey

4pm

Uzbekistan

Kyrgyzstan

North Korea

Tunisia   MEDITERRANEAN SEA

Syria

4pm

Turkmenistan

Afghanistan 4.30pm

China

8pm

South Korea

Japan

Algeria

Libya

2pm

Iraq

Iran 3.30pm

Pakistan 5pm

Tibet (China)

Nepal 5.45 pm

EAST CHINA SEA

Egypt

Saudi Arabia

India 5.30 pm

6.30 pm Myanmar

Taiwan

Northern Mariana Is (US)

Marshall Is (US)

Niger

Chad

Eritrea   Yemen

4pm

Oman

6pm

Thailand

5.30pm

Philippines

9pm

12am

Nigeria

Sudan

ARABIAN SEA

BAY OF BENGAL

Vietnam

Kiribati

Central African Republic

Ethiopia

3pm

Sri Lanka

Malaysia

Palau

Federated States of Micronesia 11am

Congo

Kenya

Maldives

Indonesia

Nauru   EQUATOR

Gabon 1pm

Congo (Zaire)

Tanzania

East Timor

Papua New Guinea

Solomon Is

SOUTH PACIFIC OCEAN

Angola

Malawi

Seychelles

6.30 pm

Vanuatu

Fiji

Zambia

Madagascar

4pm

Cocos (Keeling) Is (Aust)

New Caledonia (Fr)

Namibia

Zimbabwe

Mauritius

11.30 pm

Botswana

Mozambique

Reunion (Fr)

INDIAN OCEAN

9.30 pm

Australia

10.30 pm

Norfolk Is (Aust)

South Africa

Lord Howe Is (Aust)

New Zealand

Prince Edward Is (S. Africa)

French Southern & Antarctic Territories (Fr)

TASMAN SEA

SOUTHERN OCEAN

Heard & McDonald Is (Aust)

12pm | 1pm | 2pm | 3pm | 4pm | 5pm | 6pm | 7pm | 8pm | 9pm | 10pm | 11pm | 12am

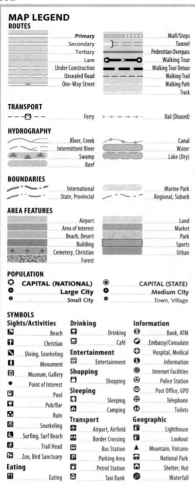

MAP LEGEND

ROUTES

Primary	Mall/Steps
Secondary	Tunnel
Tertiary	Pedestrian Overpass
Lane	Walking Tour
Under Construction	Walking Tour Detour
Unsealed Road	Walking Trail
One-Way Street	Walking Path
	Track

TRANSPORT

Ferry	Rail (Disused)

HYDROGRAPHY

River, Creek	Canal
Intermittent River	Water
Swamp	Lake (Dry)
Reef	

BOUNDARIES

International	Marine Park
State, Provincial	Regional, Suburb

AREA FEATURES

Airport	Land
Area of Interest	Market
Beach, Desert	Park
Building	Sports
Cemetery, Christian	Urban
Forest	

POPULATION

✪ **CAPITAL (NATIONAL)**	◉ CAPITAL (STATE)
● **Large City**	● Medium City
● Small City	○ Town, Village

SYMBOLS

Sights/Activities	Drinking	Information
Beach	Drinking	Bank, ATM
Christian	Café	Embassy/Consulate
Diving, Snorkeling	**Entertainment**	Hospital, Medical
Monument	Entertainment	Information
Museum, Gallery	**Shopping**	Internet Facilities
Point of Interest	Shopping	Police Station
Pool	**Sleeping**	Post Office, GPO
Pub/Bar	Sleeping	Telephone
Ruin	Camping	Toilets
Snorkeling	**Transport**	**Geographic**
Surfing, Surf Beach	Airport, Airfield	Lighthouse
Trail Head	Border Crossing	Lookout
Zoo, Bird Sanctuary	Bus Station	Mountain, Volcano
Eating	Parking Area	National Park
Eating	Petrol Station	Shelter, Hut
	Taxi Rank	Waterfall

LONELY PLANET OFFICES

Australia
Head Office
Locked Bag 1, Footscray, Victoria 3011
☎ 03 8379 8000, fax 03 8379 8111
talk2us@lonelyplanet.com.au

USA
150 Linden St, Oakland, CA 94607
☎ 510 893 8555, toll free 800 275 8555
fax 510 893 8572
info@lonelyplanet.com

UK
72–82 Rosebery Ave,
Clerkenwell, London EC1R 4RW
☎ 020 7841 9000, fax 020 7841 9001
go@lonelyplanet.co.uk

Published by Lonely Planet Publications Pty Ltd
ABN 36 005 607 983